1940 *Public Administration Review*

The first scholarly journal in the field.

1943 Abraham Maslow

His "needs hierarchy" provides a framework for gaining employees' commitment.

1946 Dwight Waldo

Contrary to Wilson (1887), Waldo argued that all theories of public administration are theories of politics. Waldo's *The Administrative State* examines the scholarly public administration literature in terms of the great issues in political philosophy.

1947 Herbert A. Simon

Believed that the traditional study of administration was too preoccupied with unsubstantiated principles of action, which he called "proverbs." In *Administrative Behavior*, he looks at decision making scientifically and finds "bounded rationality." To find out what that is, see page xxx.

Robert A. Dahl

Argues that no science of public administration is possible unless the place of normative values is made clear, the nature of humanity in the arena of public administration is better understood, and a body of comparative studies, from which it may be possible to discover principles that transcend national boundaries, is developed.

1949 Norton E. Long

In an influential *Public Administration Review* article, Long argued that "the lifeblood of administration is power."

Ohio State Leadership Studies

Researchers surveyed leaders to study hundreds of dimensions of leadership behavior. They identified two major dimensions of leadership: sensitivity to subordinates and orientation to goal achievement.

1952 Samuel P. Huntington

Put forward a theory of bureaucratic capture: industries regulated or licensed come, over time, to heavily influence or even control the regulating agencies.

1957 Douglas M. McGregor

Emphasized social psychology and research on human relations in achieving a better fit between the personality of a mature adult and the requirements of a modern organization.

1959 Frederick Herzberg

Developed a popular theory of motivation based on job satisfiers and dissatisfiers. See pages 367–368.

Charles A. Lindblom

In his influential essay "The Science of Muddling Through," Lindblom attacked the rational model of decision making in government. In reality, the model did not work; decision makers depend heavily on small, incremental decisions.

1960 Richard Neustadt

In *Presidential Power*, Neustadt suggested that a chief executive's most important source of power is not formal but is rather the power to persuade—the power to get someone to do something because that person thinks it is in his or her best interest.

1961 Aaron Wildavsky

In the article "The Political Implications of Budgetary Reform," Wildavsky developed the concept of budgetary incrementalism and its political nature that led to his landmark work, *The Politics of the Budgetary Process* (1964).

MANAGING
THE PUBLIC SECTOR

NINTH EDITION

Grover Starling

UNIVERSITY OF HOUSTON–CLEAR LAKE

WADSWORTH
CENGAGE Learning™

Australia • Brazil • Japan • Korea • Mexico • Singapore • Spain • United Kingdom • United States

WADSWORTH
CENGAGE Learning™

Managing the Public Sector
Grover Starling

Executive Editor: Carolyn Merrill

Acquiring Sponsoring Editor: Edwin Hill

Publisher: Suzanne Jeans

Editor in Chief: PJ Boardman

Development Editor: Kate MacLean

Editorial Assistant: Matt DiGangi

Senior Marketing Manager: Amy Whitaker

Marketing Coordinator: Josh Hendrick

Marketing Communications Manager: Heather Baxley

Senior Content Project Manager: Josh Allen

Art Director: Linda Helcher

Print Buyer: Paula Vang

Senior Rights Acquisition Account Manager, Text: Katie Huha
Senior Rights Acquisition Account Manager, Images: Jennifer Meyer Dare

Production Service: KnowledgeWorks Global Limited

For product information and technology assistance, contact us at
Cengage Learning Customer & Sales Support, 1-800-354-9706

For permission to use material from this text or product, submit all requests online at **www.cengage.com/permissions**.
Further permissions questions can be emailed to
permissionrequest@cengage.com.

Library of Congress Control Number: 2009940354

Student Edition:

ISBN-13: 978-0-495-83319-2

ISBN-10: 0-495-83319-3

Wadsworth
20 Channel Center Street
Boston, MA 02210
USA

Cengage Learning is a leading provider of customized learning solutions with office locations around the globe, including Singapore, the United Kingdom, Australia, Mexico, Brazil and Japan. Locate your local office at **international.cengage.com/region**

Cengage Learning products are represented in Canada by Nelson Education, Ltd.

For your course and learning solutions, visit **www.cengage.com**.

Purchase any of our products at your local college store or at our preferred online store **www.cengagebrain.com**.

Printed in the United States of America
1 2 3 4 5 6 7 13 12 11 10 09

Contents

Box List

Preface

My goal in this, the ninth edition of *Managing the Public Sector*, remains the same as it was in the first: to create a better kind of public administration text. Once again, I have tried to write a book that maintains a tight, integrated flow between chapters, is comprehensive and up to date, and makes important concepts accessible and interesting.

Integrated Progression of Topics

Content integration in *Managing the Public Sector* has been achieved by structuring topics so that each chapter logically builds on the materials covered in the previous chapters. Throughout the book, the relationship of new material to topics discussed in earlier chapters is pointed out to the students to reinforce their understanding of how the material comprises an integrated whole.

Chapter 1, "The Nature of Public Administration," provides an overview of the key issues to be addressed and explains the plan of the book. See Figure 1.2, "The Process of Public Administration," on page 15 for an overall view of the interconnection of the text's topics. Part One, "Political Management," consists of Chapters 2 through 4 and investigates the political and legal environments of public administration. The purpose of Part One is to describe and explain the political actors and institutions external to a government agency that help determine the success of failure of that agency in accomplishing its mission. Part Two, "Program Management," consists of Chapters 5 through 9 and shifts focus from the environment to the agency. From here the book examines the strategies and structures that agencies adopt to operate effectively and efficiently in their environments. Part Three, "Resources Management," consists of Chapters 10 through 12 and narrows the focus further to investigate government systems designed for managing human, fiscal, and information resources.

What's New in the Ninth Edition?

The success of the first eight editions of *Managing the Public Sector* was based in part on the incorporation of leading-edge research into the text, the use of up-to-date examples and statistics to illustrate trends and government strategy, and the discussion of current events within an appropriate conceptual framework. The ninth edition continues this tradition.

As part of the revision process, substantial changes have been made to every chapter in the book. Some material has been updated to incorporate the most recently available data. New examples, cases, and boxes have been added, and older examples have either been updated to reflect new developments or deleted for greater concision. New sections have been inserted wherever appropriate to reflect recent academic work, legal or legislative decisions, or important current events. Among the major updates and additions in the chapters are the following:

- Chapter 1 opens with a new case: "What Do We Do Now?" The title comes from the 1972 movie, *The Candidate,* about the politically disillusioned son of a former California governor who is persuaded to launch a long-shot candidacy for the Senate. Unexpectedly, the son (played by Robert Redford) wins. In the movie's famous closing scene, he confronts his campaign manager with the question, "What do we do now?" The line has come to symbolize the idea that politicians must not only get elected, but also *govern*—the central concern of this book. Chapter 1 also contains a new section on the scope and size of the nonprofit sector and closes with an extensively revised and updated case on the ever-fascinating FBI.
- Chapter 2 begins with a new case about Michelle Rhee, a Korean American whom Washington, DC, Mayor Adrian Fenty appointed chancellor of that city's schools in 2007. The case raises some basic questions. Can politics be divorced from reform, and if not, how then might a political strategy support a reform strategy?
- To explore intergovernmental relations, Chapter 3 opens with a new case, "Supermayor," about the merger of Louisville, Kentucky, with surrounding Jefferson County. Users of the last edition of *Managing the Public Sector* will be acquainted with the closing case, "The Katrina Breakdown." Not surprisingly, the worst natural disaster in U.S. history continues to generate many scholarly articles. A new section in this case analyzes three recent ones that offer different interpretations of what went wrong, what went right, and what needs to be done. Each provides a fertile basis for class discussion.
- Chapter 4 opens with a new case, "The Food and Drug Administration," that allows students to explore a host of ethical dilemmas facing civil servants in this vitally important federal agency. The closing case, "Doing the Right Thing," is also new—and as fresh as today's headlines. What position should newly appointed CIA

director Leon Panetta take regarding an investigation of his agency's alleged torture under the previous administration? Often the biggest ethical challenge in government is not to do the right thing, but to determine what the "right thing" is.

- Chapter 5 contains a new section on what government can learn from the private sector about productivity improvement. The new closing case, "A Strategy Is Born," focuses on General David Petraeus and other key players who effected a change in U.S. strategy in Iraq in 2006–2007.

- Chapter 6 opens with a new case, "Deciding How to Decide," that describes the procedures the Obama administration set up for making decisions about economic policy. As users of earlier editions know, the closing case, "Wild Horses," was designed to allow students to apply some of the analytical techniques presented in the chapter to a nettlesome problem facing the Bureau of Land Management. In this completely revised version of the case, the scope has widened to include issues of environmental politics and policy.

- Chapter 7 contains new material on charismatic leaders, with a particular focus on Robert J. Oppenheimer, the brilliant head of the Los Alamos project where hundreds of scientists worked in the desert outside of Santa Fe, New Mexico, to develop the first atomic bomb. Also, the discussion of how the public sector is using matrix organizations has been expanded. One more major addition to Chapter 7 should be noted. In an age of globalization, books on American public administration cannot afford to ignore valuable lessons from around the world. Therefore, for an excellent example of aligning organizational structure with mission, we turn to Aravind Eye Hospital in India for the chapter's closing case.

- "Unless objectives are converted into action, they are not objectives; they are dreams." Thus, Peter Drucker tersely reminds us of the importance of execution— of implementation. To illustrate Drucker's powerful point, the new opening case of Chapter 9 shows how the New York Police Department established its own mini-CIA. The section on deciding who will implement a government program has been expanded to include the latest permutations and combinations of cooperation among the public sector, the private sector, and the nonprofit sector.

- Few Supreme Court cases have roiled public opinion and public administration in recent years as much as the New Haven firefighters' case (*Ricci v. DeStefano*), decided June 25, 2009. Chapter 10 opens with this case because it provides a good basis for discussing (a) the future of affirmative action in human resources management and (b) the best methods for selecting people to leadership positions. Another major addition to the chapter merits mention. Introductions to public administration usually have much to say about recruiting, training, classifying, compensating, and promoting employees, but precious little about *retaining the best and brightest*. New material in Chapter 10 explains how cutting-edge public organizations are addressing this issue.

- The opening case of Chapter 11, "Find Me the Money," was virtually mandated by the worst recession in 60 years, since state and local officials had never dealt with a recession as precipitous and rapid as the one that began in late 2007. Not only did they have to make painful spending cuts, but they also had to consider as never before the revenue side of the ledger. Chapter 11 also addresses *earmarks* in a fresh way. This hot topic has been much discussed by politicians and journalists—how expensive, how unfair, how many, and so forth—but seldom do these discussions involve the *administrative implications* of earmarks. New material in Chapter 11 fills this gap. The closing case, "Dangerous Stratagems," is also new.

- Chapter 12 has been drastically reorganized to make the students' journey as smooth as possible through one of the most important and most neglected topics in contemporary public administration—information management. Let me briefly elaborate. No public administrator would turn the selection and development of his or her employees over to the human resources director, nor would any agency head accept without any negotiation next year's funding allocation from the budget director. So why should a public administrator let chief information officers (CIOs) manage their information? Information management concerns every manager—just as much as personnel and budgetary issues.

- Both the content and organization of chapter 12 are new. Take the opening case, "Making It Happen." The U.S. government has not done badly on "e-government 1.0"—that is, providing its citizens with information—but making the rest happen will be a lot harder. To help appreciate the challenge, this case focuses on Vivek Kundra, who goes, in 2009, from being Washington, DC's, chief technology officer to the federal government's first CIO. The chapter also contains new material on security management and a major new section on "The Future of E-Government," which discusses both rosy scenarios and pessimistic scenarios. The closing case on knowledge management in the U.S. Army has been expanded to cover two new initiatives—one involving the software behind Wikipedia, and the other showing the advantages of building a knowledge management system bottom-up rather than top-down (as is often the case).

This ninth edition retains the innovative features of the eighth and earlier editions. Numerous international examples draw parallels between public administration as it is practiced in the United States and abroad. Throughout, students are put in immediate touch with the real world of public organizations by introducing them not just to abstract ideas but to men and women working in the public sector. Another key feature of the book is the use of diagrams that illustrate how important concepts fit together. This edition also makes extensive use of photographs, cartoons, and maps accompanied by detailed captions that explain how the visual materials relate to chapter topics. These photos and illustrations convey the vividness, immediacy, and concreteness of management in today's public sector.

Pedagogical Features

Pedagogical features intended to help students learn and retain the material in *Managing the Public Sector* include the following: First are chapter introductory sections that feature a clear statement of chapter objectives and provide an overview of what is to come. Second are boldfaced key terms that highlight the key concepts students should learn in each chapter. Third are "Key Points" sections at the end of each chapter, providing a trenchant summary of main points that students should retain—all twelve "Key Points" sections have been rewritten and expanded for this edition.

Fourth, you will also find at the end of each chapter a set of problems and application. Let me briefly explain their role. The philosopher and mathematician, Alfred North Whitehead, once said, "A merely well-informed man is the most useless bore on God's earth." He added, "Above all things, we must beware of what I will call 'inert ideas'—that is to say, ideas that are merely received into the mind without being utilized, or tested, or thrown into fresh combinations." To battle the pestilence of inert ideas, this new edition retains end-of-chapter "Problem and Applications" sections as well as one case placed at the end of each chapter that are intended to elicit critical, analytical thinking from the reader. These cases and problems provide opportunities for students to apply concepts to real events and to sharpen their diagnostic skills. Each of the "Problems and Applications" sections has been thoroughly updated to reflect new chapter content.

Ancillaries

Instructors who adopt the ninth edition of Managing the Public Sector will be able to use an array of resources contained in the E-Bank Instructor's Manual/Test Bank written to accompany the text. The IM/TB includes teaching notes for the cases at the end of each chapter, suggested answers to the "Problems and Applications" sections, teaching strategies, and an extensive array of test questions.

A set of PowerPoint slides highlighting chapter topics is available for use in classroom lectures.

Acknowledgments

The reactions, insights, suggestions, and efforts of many people have been instrumental in the success of past editions. I would first like to express special thanks to the following people, whose useful comments helped guide the revision of this and past editions: Ann Altmeyer, State University of New York at Brockport; Emmanuel N. Amad, University of Mississippi; David N. Ammons, North Texas State University; Mel Arslaner, Drake University; Curtis R. Berry, Shippensburg University of Pennsylvania; Margaret C. Bowen, Florida State University; Rufus Browning, San Francisco State University; Julie Bundt, University of Northern Iowa; David S. Calihan, Longwood College; Roslyn K. Chavda, University of New Hampshire; William P. Collins, Samford University; David R. Connelly, Western Illinois University; Wilkie A. Denley, South Carolina State University; Darrell J. Downs, Winona State University; Larry Elowitz, Georgia College; Kim Fox, Shippensburg University of Pennsylvania; Brian R. Fry, University of South Carolina; James A. Gazell, San Diego State University; Betty Hecker, Boise State University; Michael King, Pennsylvania State University; Robert W. Kweit, University of North Dakota; Eugene B. McGregor Jr., Indiana University; Perry Moore, Wright State University; Samuel C. Patterson, Harvard University; James Penning, Calvin College; Faith Prather, State University of New York at Brockport; James R. Purdy, University of Central Florida; Ruth A. Ross, California State University, Long Beach; Michelle A. Saint-Germain, California State University, Long Beach; Vidu Soni, Central Michigan University; Jennifer Symonds, University of Alabama; Carol Waters, Texas A&M International; and Dean L. Yarwood, University of Missouri, Columbia

Second, thank you to all the people at Wadsworth who have worked with me on this project. So many parties have been involved this cycle, it's hard to single out individuals. It was a tremendous team.

Finally, two people deserve special acknowledgment. One is my wife, Yolanda, an everlasting source of encouragement. The other is my former professor and mentor, the late Emmette S. Redford, a man from whom I learned much more than public administration.

Grover Starling

1 The Nature of Public Administration

AP Photo/The White House, Eric Draper

WHAT DO WE DO NOW?

After a 21-month campaign, Barak Obama was elected president of the United States on November 4, 2008. Now he and his team would have to govern. As Adlai Stevenson put it when he accepted the Democratic presidential nomination in 1952, "Even more important than winning the election is governing the nation. That is the test of a political party—the acid, final test. When the tumult and the shouting die, when the bands are gone and the lights are dimmed, there is the stark reality of responsibility." Following his election Obama had 77 days to lay the foundation for his administration. Then, on the afternoon of Inauguration Day, January 20, 2009, his people would have to start answering the phones in the White House. Could he bring the same talent for management to the transition that he brought to his political campaign?

Members of Obama's transition team were heavily influenced by two previous transitions—Bill Clinton's in 1992 and Ronald Reagan's in 1980. They were determined to avoid the mistakes of the Clinton team, which was slow off the mark. Instead, they wanted to follow the Reagan model and hit the ground running.

Essentially, presidents-elect face three tasks during the transition period. The first task is to prioritize policy goals—what to start with on the first day and what to make long-term objectives. The second task is to decide how to decide, that is, to organize the decision-making process in the White House, balancing efficiency and creativity. One design is a circle of advisers with the president at the center, forming a kind of "spokes in the wheel" system. This arrangement is closely associated with President Franklin Roosevelt. Another design, the pyramid, is principally identified with President Dwight Eisenhower, who knew how to make a hierarchical system, with a chief of staff at the top, work for him. Yet another design is a pyramid with a flat rather than sharply pointed top, thus providing the president's chief of staff some company at the top and allowing ideas and information to flow to the president more freely from the people at the bottom.

The third task facing the president-elect is to appoint a staff. Presidents get to appoint only 3,000 of the federal government's two million civilian employees, but some of those appointments are critical. Following the Reagan model, the Obama team wanted to complete White House staff appointments by Thanksgiving and Cabinet appointments by Christmas.

The 2008–2009 presidential transition was, arguably, the most difficult since Abraham Lincoln entered office. Although no civil war confronted Obama, he did inherit staggering economic problems. Franklin Roosevelt also faced great economic challenges, but as Paul C. Light points out, the nation was not at war, the federal government was much smaller, and the transition was six weeks longer. In the final analysis, Obama's success would depend on two things: maintaining political support to get things done and having laid a solid management foundation during the transition.

What mistakes can a president make in setting policy goals? What are the strengths and weaknesses of the three ways of designing a decision process in the White House? What should the criteria be for making appointments to the White House staff and Cabinet? What initial instructions should a president give his or her appointees? If you were an appointee, how would you prepare for that first obligatory meeting with the president in the Oval Office?

SOURCES: Thomas H. Stanton, "Improving the Managerial Capacity of the Federal Government: A Public Administration Agenda for the Next President," *Public Administration Review* (November/December 2008): 1027–36; Shailagh Murray and Carol D. Leonning, *Washington Post* (December 3, 2008); *The Economist* (November 15, 2008); Michael D. Watkins, "Obama's First 90 Days," *Harvard Business Review* (June 2009), 34–35; Paul C. Light, "Analysis," *Washington Post* (November 5, 2008); Stephen Hess, *What Do We Do Now? A Workbook for the President-Elect* (Washington, DC: Brookings, 2008).

Traditionally, public administration is thought of as the accomplishing side of government. It is supposed to comprise all the activities involved in carrying out the policies of elected officials and some activities associated with the development of those policies. Public administration is, as the Stevenson quotation suggests, all that comes after the last campaign promise and the election night cheer: the means and ends of government.

Public administration today is perhaps the most important field in the discipline of political science. The reason is that people in the United States—and indeed most people around the world—want less government but more governance; and in the final analysis, **Governance** is just another way of saying **public administration.** What then is governance? It is *the exercise of authority by government or, more precisely, the system and method by which that authority is exercised.* If there is any difference between these two terms, it is this: *governance* is a slightly broader term than *public administration*. Governance views the traditional concerns of public administration, which this chapter introduces, in a broader context.

Thus, when we look at a government agency (the Environmental Protection Agency [EPA], for example) providing goods and services (clean air, for example) to citizens, the concept of governance suggests that we should be concerned with more than that agency's organizational structure, policy mandates, finances, and operating procedures. Equally important is the multilayered network of other agencies, private companies, and nonprofit organizations required to deliver clean air; the norms, values, and rules that allow that network to work; and the political processes that gave birth to the agency's mandates—and that may change those mandates someday.[1]

In this book, we will also define public administration broadly as *the process by which resources are marshaled and then used to cope with the problems facing a political community.* The aim of this chapter is to make this definition clear, as well as to show why narrow definitions will not do.

The first few sections introduce you to public administration by looking at who public administrators are, where they work, and what they do. Finally, the chapter wraps things up by discussing why public administration is important and how the field of study has evolved since the late 1700s.

Who Are Public Administrators?

New York City's transportation commissioner Iris Weinshall was doing paperwork at 8:46 A.M. at her desk when she heard the noise.[2] The first low-flying jet had hit the World Trade Center. She ran to the other side of the floor, saw the fire, and called her deputies to make sure they would help clear traffic from the area to give firefighters easier access. Then the second plane hit. She realized this was more than a local traffic problem.

Quickly, she took out a street map of Manhattan and counted the blocks from the north tower to Stuyvesant High, where her daughter, Jessica, was a senior. The distance was roughly four blocks. The transportation commissioner then tried to calculate the height of the World Trade Center tower, the length of an average city block, and therefore, whether the tower would hit the school if it should fall. She wanted to go find Jesse but couldn't: She was in charge of many people and had responsibilities.

Weinshall deployed her entire staff to fan out in yellow emergency vests and divert all traffic out of lower Manhattan. Amazingly, one staffer spotted Jessica with her classmates running down the street. He scooped her up and brought her to Weinshall's office.

When the second tower collapsed, her office lost all power and phone service. So she and her staff, with Jessica in tow, began moving uptown in a caravan to a hastily formed Transportation Department command center. She worked there until about 11:00 P.M., when she got her driver to take her home so she could change her soot-laden clothes before attending a midnight emergency meeting with the mayor. As the driver began to go over a bridge—which, like all bridges, had been closed to the public—a police sergeant leaned in and said scuba teams had not yet been able to check the bridge's base for bombs. Weinshall thanked him and told her driver to "gun it." They raced over at 100 miles per hour, she recalls, "as if we were trying to get a good running start in case it blew up."

Moving ahead 15 days, we find Weinshall attending the mayor's morning meeting in a tiny room on Pier 92 at a table covered with plates of bacon and sausage. One of the issues on the agenda that morning concerned the flow of traffic in lower Manhattan. For a number of reasons, traffic had become a nightmare. First, the Holland Tunnel was entirely closed to regular traffic to expedite the movement of heavy equipment into and out of ground zero. Second, extra security caused bottlenecking at the other entrances into Manhattan. And third, the train to the World Trade Center had been destroyed. Traffic was so badly snarled that emergency vehicles were having difficulty getting around.

What to do? Given the circumstances, Weinshall argued for prohibiting cars with only one occupant from entering Manhattan in the mornings. Despite the attacks on the World Trade Center, the mayor's staff was ready for a spirited debate.[3]

> DEPUTY MAYOR TONY COLES: I'm skeptical of HOV [high occupancy vehicle] rules. There're other ways to discourage traffic, such as promoting the trains and subways.
>
> COUNSEL LARRY LEVY: Forbidding any cars says, "You can't come."
>
> POLICE COMMISSIONER BERNIE KERIK: The restrictions send a mixed message. We're telling everybody they gotta come back to the city, get back to normalcy. Then, on the other hand, don't come back unless you have more than one person in the car.
>
> DEPUTY MAYOR FOR OPERATIONS JOE LHOTTA: You've got to live in an outer borough to understand this. Your thinking is upside down here. Traffic's backed up to Suffolk County. The state troopers are literally getting under the cars with mirrors— it's taking 30 seconds per car. Iris gave me the exact number today. Between 6:00 A.M. and noon, 65 percent of the cars have one driver.
>
> DEPUTY MAYOR FOR ECONOMIC DEVELOPMENT JOHN DYSON (turning to Lhotta): You're going to strangle the economy of the city if you do restrictions!

LHOTTA: But subway use is down. We're actually seeing an increase in the number of cars.

DYSON: Think about why. People remember Tokyo and sarin gas in the subways. You have to deal with what's going on in people's heads.

COLES: Barring cars is really regressive. We should do incentives and other things, but it sends the wrong signal if we prevent anyone from entering.

MAYOR GIULIANI: We've done such good work getting out the get-back-to-normal message over the last two weeks that we've almost fooled ourselves into not remembering that we are in an emergency. . . . There's going to be anticipation as the president prepares to fight in Afghanistan. And then there's going to come a time when we actually strike. Both of those are points at which there could easily be attacks directed at the bridges and tunnels. That would be easier to handle with fewer cars.

CHAIRMAN OF THE PLANNING COMMISSION JOE ROSE: There are other mechanisms available, like raising the cost of entering during "peak" hours and discounting the other times.

LHOTTA: There are alternative ways into the city, too. Let's get the ferry system going better, and we might actually make the waterways an unintended third-party beneficiary.

GIULIANI: There's no perfect solution. If you don't do the restrictions, it's a traffic disaster and no one wants to come into the city. If you do the restrictions, you discourage certain people from coming, and you may still have a traffic disaster. Let's reassess this after we get the morning report from Iris. But for now, I'm in favor of trying her idea out for a week and seeing how it works. I don't think it's so awful to remind people we're in an emergency—we are.

New York City's difficulties might seem exceptional, but Iris Weinshall and Rudy Giuliani are not the only public administrators who have to deal with uncertainty and crisis on an almost daily basis. Managers in all public organizations are continually dealing with uncertainty and unexpected events, whether it be something as small as the loss of a key employee or something as large and dramatic as a terrorist attack, a hurricane, or an earthquake.

Stereotypes of who public administrators are—and what they do—usually prove wrong. "Do they," Charles T. Goodsell asks, "wear green eyeshades? Do they sit at desks all day and shuffle papers? . . . Do they order people around and enforce rules to the letter? Are they empire builders? Do they sabotage policies they don't like?" Here's his answer:

As to the specific question of whether they wear green eyeshades, the answer is no. They wear instead the sunglasses of hurricane pilots, the helmets of firefighters, the Smokey-the-Bear felts of state troopers, the magnification glasses of neurosurgeons, the sealed hoods of toxic-substance investigators, and [the] baseball caps of ordinary citizens.

Moreover, most bureaucrats don't sit at a desk all day. If they do, they are working at computer terminals rather than shuffling papers. And, if you call them at their desk, they may be elsewhere in the office conferring with fellow employees—or out of the building talking to community leaders. A bureaucrat's principal workplace may not even be a desk at all. It may be a noisy classroom, a quiet museum, a ward of a veterans' hospital, the home of a family suspected of child abuse, a border crossing with Mexico, a reconstruction site in Iraq, or an interstate highway crowded with drivers doing 85.[4]

According to the *Statistical Abstract of the United States 2009,* the United States has roughly 21.7 million civilian government employees of all types at all levels. Let's bring that number to life by introducing some more real people.[5]

- The first weeks of 2004 were trying times for *Orlando Figueroa,* director of NASA's Mars Exploration Program. After a six-month journey from Earth and only 18 days on the surface of the red planet, the remotely operated, six-wheeled rover wasn't talking to its earthbound controllers. After two days of hard work and just hours before a second rover arrived, engineers eventually discovered a problem in the first rover's software and got the golf-cart-sized machine running again. Within a week, says Figueroa, "My two babies were healthy, taking their first steps, and interacting."
- *Barbara Turner,* deputy assistant administrator, U.S. Agency for International Development, began her work with the agency in Egypt in the early 1980s helping implement a new approach to fighting childhood disease. She then moved on to the former Soviet Union, educating the citizenry about free markets and property ownership. More recently, she helped promote the Global Development Alliance, which matches $500 million in AIDS funds with $2.5 billion in private sector resources.
- *Alan Estevez,* assistant deputy undersecretary of defense, helps military logisticians know the precise location and condition of everything they buy. The technical term for this is "supply chain integration," but the bottom line is this: Estevez makes sure every military service member has exactly the right equipment at the right time—no more and no less.
- *Teri Takai,* Michigan's chief information officer, consolidated executive branch technical departments into a centralized organization and launched planning initiatives that saved state taxpayers $100 million.
- As Chief Judge of the Hennepin County District Court in Minneapolis, *Kevin Burke* instituted a program of videotaping judges. People with business before the court are interviewed five minutes after their cases are finished and asked whether they are satisfied with their treatment. When they are not, Burke offers the judge instruction on job improvement.
- In the early 1990s, *Kenneth Kizer,* former director of the California Department of Health Services, was selected to run the Veterans Health Administration's sprawling health-care system. For years, this system was criticized by veterans groups and government investigators for providing inferior care, and Oliver Stone attacked the

system in *Born on the Fourth of July* for indifferent care. But in the past decade, the system has undergone a dramatic transformation and now outperforms Medicare and most private plans. Now computers measure everything at Veteran's Administration (VA) sites with an aim toward improving care. Kizer brought about this seismic shift not only through high-tech breakthroughs but also through a fundamental change in the VA culture. The new culture emphasizes patient safety and a work ethic that stresses constant examination and reexamination of the processes and procedures that go into caregiving.

No doubt you have your own thoughts about these vignettes, but let me offer one observation. These men and women exemplify the proposition that public administration is grounded in a strong desire to serve the public and solve its problems. Although government must still ensure that the drinking water is safe, the homeless have shelter, Social Security checks arrive on time, everyone's civil rights are protected, and third graders learn to read, many of today's challenges are more complex than those of previous decades. Besides combating the AIDS pandemic and planning for a host of other potential epidemics, government must also clean up toxic waste, ensure air travel safety, deter insider trading, stop terrorism (remember—terrorists have to be successful only once, while the U.S. Department of Homeland Security has to get it right every time), hold down escalating health-care costs, promote market competitiveness, fight drug abuse, and support cutting-edge technologies such as the Human Genome Project (an effort to obtain a complete, detailed picture of the genetic material found in every human cell).

Making a difference as a public administrator today and tomorrow requires integrating solid, tried-and-true management skills with new approaches that emphasize the human touch, enhanced flexibility, and political savvy. Successful government programs don't just happen—they are managed to be that way.

Where Do Public Administrators Work?

The short answer is "in government." But we need to be more exact. Thus far, we have been speaking loosely about "government" and "the nonprofit sector" without really defining either term. However, if we are to know where public administrators work, then we must be clear about what government refers to and how government differs from the nonprofit and private sectors. We begin by looking at the building blocks of government: departments, agencies, commissions, and government corporations. Then, we do the same for the nonprofit sector and differentiate that sector from government. Next, we contrast the public sector and the private sector ("business"). Lastly, we consider the independence of these three sectors.

The Public Sector: Government

The Building Blocks of Government   Two factors complicate the organization of government in the United States: its three branches (executive, legislative, and judicial) and the three levels (federal, state, and local). Because the configuration of state and local governments is roughly similar to that of the national government, we focus here on just the latter. See Figure 1.1.

The most familiar form of organization in national government are the 14 executive departments, such as the Department of Defense and the Department of Health and Human Services. Each is headed by a secretary who is a member of the president's cabinet and directly responsible to him. Departments vary in the extent to which their constituent agencies respond to central direction. Indeed, some individual agencies may have more political influence than does the department as a whole. For example, the Federal Bureau of Investigation (FBI), which is part of the Department of Justice, can often operate as if it were independent. (See Case 1.1.)

In addition to the executive departments and their agencies, numerous **independent executive agencies** operate independently of executive departments and generally report directly to the president. For example, the EPA and the Small Business Administration exist as independent agencies to underscore their importance. Yet another form of organization is the **independent regulatory commission.** The Federal Trade Commission, the Federal Energy Regulatory Commission, and other commissions differ from independent executive agencies in that they do not perform executive functions but rather act independently to regulate certain segments of the economy. Once the president has appointed the members of a commission, the application and formulation of regulations are largely beyond his control.

The characteristics of **government corporations** were spelled out in President Truman's 1948 budget message. Although they were never made into law, those characteristics have been referred to by public administration experts. According to Truman, a corporate form of organization is appropriate for the administration of government programs that

- Are predominantly of a business nature
- Produce revenue and are potentially self-sustaining
- Involve a large number of business-type transactions with the public
- Require a greater flexibility than the customary type of congressional funding ordinarily permits

Among the better-known examples of government corporations are the Federal Deposit Insurance Corporation, which provides bank deposit insurance, and the Tennessee Valley Authority (TVA), which produces and markets electrical power.

The Size of Government   There are 2.7 million federal civilian employees, but given the fact that President Barack Obama's Fiscal Year 2010 sets the stage for an expansion of the federal work force, one might say 2.7 million underestimates the size of the federal government. Actually, 2.7 million plus any Obama increment is still way off the mark. Here's why: A 2006 study estimates that the "hidden" federal workforce of contractors and grantees accounts for 10.5 million jobs. [6] So, if we add active duty military (2.8 million) and postal service (772,000) jobs and that 10.5 million to the 2.7 million, the real size of the federal government is at least 16.8 million. Now, if we add to the total the 19 million working

Figure 1.1   Comparison of Governmental, Nonprofit, and Private Entities

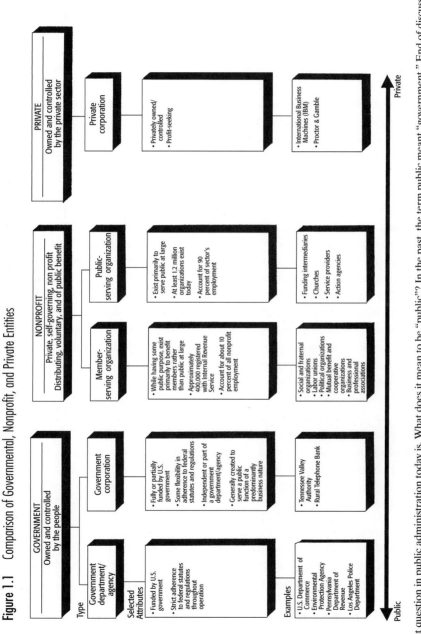

An important question in public administration today is, What does it mean to be "public"? In the past, the term public meant "government." End of discussion. Today scholars understand public administration to include government plus all those organizations and institutions that contract with, or somehow cooperate with, government to do government work. But now that distinction is increasingly fuzzy. Institutions on the right, while profit-making, can serve the public. Conversely, nonprofits can, at times, generate "revenue streams" that look to some like profits. "Nonprofit" hospitals are a case in point.

for state and local government, we can say the size of the government workforce is 35.8 million, or over one-fifth of the whole U.S. labor force. This figure understates, of course, because it does not include those working for state and local governments on contracts and grants. The functions performed by these men and women range from air traffic control to zookeeping.

The Public Sector: Nonprofits

What Is a Nonprofit Organization?   **Nonprofit organizations** such as those shown in Figure 1.1 are set up for charitable purposes, and their Internal Revenue Service (IRS) classification confers special tax-exempt status. Nonprofits are chartered by each state, which may also grant exemption from property, sales, use, and income taxes. Therefore, nonprofits may generate profits (or "surplus"), but they may not distribute them. All the assets of a non-profit must be dedicated to its exempt purposes.

There are other critical distinctions between for-profit and nonprofit organizations. A nonprofit has no owner, there are no private shareholders, and the organization is governed by a board of directors or trustees who may not receive any individual benefit—direct or indirect—from the organization. These boards involve themselves in long-range planning and general policy. Lastly, all nonprofits have mission statements (see Chapter 5), and the IRS forbids such organizations from engaging in activities unrelated to their charitable mission.

But these traits do not take us to the essence of nonprofit organizations. In *The State of Nonprofits in America,* Lester M. Salamon argues than nonprofits are "value guardians." They embody, and therefore help to nurture and sustain, a crucial national value emphasizing individual initiative in the public good. They thus give institutional expression to two seemingly contradictory principles that are both important parts of American national character: the principle of *individualism*—the notion that people should have the freedom to act on matters that concern them—and the principle of *solidarity*—the notion that people have responsibilities not only to themselves but also to their fellow human beings and to the communities of which they are part. By fusing these two principles, nonprofit organizations reinforce both, establishing an arena of action through which individuals can take the initiative not simply to promote their own well-being but to advance the well-being of others as well.[7]

The Basic Division of Nonprofits   As indicated in Figure 1.1, the nonprofit sector comprises two categories of organization: member-serving organizations and public-serving organizations. **Member-serving organizations**, while having some public purpose, exist primarily to provide a benefit to the organization's members rather than to the public at large. They include social clubs, business and professional associations (e.g., chambers of commerce, the American Bankers Association, local bar associations, and labor unions), mutual benefit and cooperative organizations (e.g., farmers cooperatives and benevolent life insurance associations), and political organizations (e.g., political parties and political action committees).

⌐The second category of nonprofit organizations, **public-serving organizations**, exist mainly to serve the public at large rather than the organization's membership. When you see the term **nongovernmental organization**, it usually refers to this type of nonprofit. Public-serving organizations fulfill their function in a variety of ways—providing health and education services, sponsoring cultural or religious activities, advocating for certain causes, aiding the poor, and financing other nonprofits, to name a few. ⌐

The distinction between member-serving and public-serving nonprofit organizations is far from perfect, of course. The former produce some public benefits, and the latter often deliver benefits to their members. The one goal most public-serving agencies do have in common—certainly to a much greater degree than member-serving agencies—is that of *changing people.* Peter F. Drucker, a noted management theorist, calls them "human-change institutions." He writes, "The product of the hospital is a cured patient. The product of a church is a changed life. The product of the Salvation Army—the one organization that reaches the poorest of the poor regardless of race or religion—is a derelict becomes a citizen. The product of the Girl Scouts is a mature young woman who has values, skills, and respect for herself."[8]

Measuring the Size of the Nonprofit   Nonprofit organizations are almost 1.6 million in number and contribute 8% of the gross domestic product. Over the past 25 years, the 2.5% annual average growth rate for employment in the nonprofit sector outpaced that of for-profit business (1.8%) and government (1.6%). Nonprofit employees —12.5 million strong— now constitute 9.5% of the total American workforce. In other words, one in every 12 Americans works for a nonprofit. Although these figures shed light on the size and scope of the sector, a complete picture cannot be obtained without considering two critical components of the sector—volunteerism and charitable giving. In 2005, 29% of Americans volunteered through a formal organization, and individuals, corporations, and foundations gave $260 billion in charitable contributions to nonprofits.[9]

These dry figures hide the rich variety of issues with which nonprofit organizations deal. Just consider a few: For hunger relief, there is America's Second Harvest and Share Our Strength; for youth leadership, City Year and YouthBuild USA; for the environment, the Environment Defense; for science education, Exploratorium; for housing, Habitat for Humanity; for education reform, Teach for America. (Michelle Rhee, the first chancellor of Washington, DC schools and the subject of the opening case in Chapter 2, is a product of Teach for America.)

The Private Sector

Despite the size of the nonprofit sector, it has in recent years faced pressure from the private, or for-profit, sector. How can that be? The simple answer is that private companies are increasingly entering into social services, the traditional domain of the nonprofit sector.

Perhaps the first shock wave felt in the nonprofit community came on September 15, 1996, when the front page of *The New York Times* announced that Lockheed Martin,

a defense corporation, and Anderson Consulting were each preparing to bid for the management of $563 million in welfare operations in Texas. Nonprofits are no longer considered automatically entitled—or even best qualified—to provide social services in the United States. In addition to Lockheed Martin, other for-profits are doing work in the social services:[10]

- America Work, a job placement specialist, has contracts in several locales, including New York City.
- Children's Comprehensive Services, one of the largest and fastest-growing for-profits, provides services in the at-risk youth market.
- Maximum, a management and information systems consultant to hundreds of federal, state, and local human service agencies, operates welfare-to-work programs in 18 jurisdictions.
- Youth Services International, founded by Jiffy Lube entrepreneur W. James Hindman, runs programs for adjudicated youth.

Although all three sectors—private companies, nonprofit organizations, and government—might be engaged in delivering social services, it does not follow that private management and public management are the same. Indeed, they differ in four respects: structures, incentives, settings, and purposes.

Different Structures   One fundamental difference between business administration and public administration is that *responsibility in public administration is blurred.* In other words, government does not give complete authority for government policy to any one individual or institution. Let us hope that the Pod People from the far side of the Great Nebula in Andromeda do not land in Washington, asking to be taken to our leader. It would be embarrassing.

As a consequence of the blurred authority, heads of federal agencies, unlike their counterparts in industry, cannot set the level of their agencies' budgets. Rather, budgets must be submitted to department heads, who submit them in turn to the Office of Management and Budget, which submits them in turn to the president, who in turn submits them to Congress. Then things really get complicated.

Needless to say, the time lag in the process makes quick responses to new problems and opportunities—not to mention long-range planning—difficult. Unlike their industrial counterparts, agency heads lack full power to hire and fire (among other things). Finally, any planning that public administrators engage in must be shared with legislative bodies, city councils, or governing boards.

Different Incentives   Another fundamental difference may be one that you have experienced personally. Because public-sector organizations receive a significant amount of financial support from sources other than their clients, the *incentive is to satisfy those who provide resources.* In fact, some agencies even view additional clients not as an opportunity but as an additional strain on resources. In contrast, the very survival of a private-sector business hinges on its ability to get and retain customers. And that is why the attendants at

McDonald's are more polite to you than the better-educated, better-paid bureaucrats at your state's department of motor vehicles.

Different Settings   Public administration could almost be described as business administration in a fishbowl. The press and the public feel that they have a right to know everything that goes on in a public agency, and the Freedom of Information Act ensures that they can find out if they want. To quote a businessman-turned-bureaucrat: "My biggest surprise here is how government is ruled by leakage. Employees use the press and Congress to accomplish their goals instead of meeting the issue head-on in an honest fashion. I know that if I make a decision against someone, that person will be on the phone to Congress and the press within an hour."[11] In the next chapter, you will see the many external forces that play on the public administrator.

Another way in which the settings differ involves *turnover.* In the federal government, a completely new top management team is possible every four years. Between elections, assistant secretaries average less than two years in the job—not much longer than the time required to find the cafeteria. In contrast, private-sector business managers tend to stay with a firm longer and thereby provide continuity.

Different Purposes   Both public and private organizations use resources (inputs) to produce goods and services (outputs). In a public-sector organization, however, outputs are hard to quantify. The Constitution is just not much help: Congress is to provide "for the common defense and general welfare"; the president is to recommend "such Measures as he shall judge necessary and expedient."

Without a single, broad measure of performance, such as profit, it becomes difficult for governments to delegate important decisions to lower-level managers to the same extent that a business firm can. Moreover, the absence of this measure of performance makes comparison between alternative investments difficult. For example, should the cancer-detection program or the school lunch program be funded with the extra $10 million? How many main battle tanks equal one guided-missile frigate? To save whales, should we prohibit Eskimos from slaughtering them, even though their entire culture is built around the whale? If the national speed limit were reduced to 20 miles per hour, the carnage on U.S. highways would be virtually eliminated. Are 30,000 lives worth millions of hours of additional travel time? At this point, the student of public administration is inclined to wonder, "Where is the bottom line around here?" Do not be too discouraged, however. As we shall see in later chapters, there *are* performance measures in the public sector—we just have to look a little longer and harder for them.

In sum, business managers seek profitability while public administrators are more concerned with the commonweal—that is, the common or public good. Putting it differently, a private firm is organized for the well-being of its employees and stockholders, whereas a public agency is supposed to serve the interests of people outside itself. This outside public focus helps to explain why the individuals who run organizations such as those listed in Figure 1.1 can be categorized as essentially public administrators.

Compare + contrast public vs private sector

The Interdependence of the Three Sectors

Thus far, we have tried to clarify public administrators' work in government by emphasizing the differences between the sectors—especially between the public and private sectors. But, by way of conclusion, it is equally important to note the independence of the three sectors. While the public sector is dependent on business for resources (especially revenue and the performance of some activities through contracts), the reverse is equally true. Consider this example: Despite its recent financial problems, California remains the richest state in the union. That is not merely because of its factories, thriving crops, and private affluence. Little of that would have been possible had it not been for government action. Despite its great natural advantages, California has relied for decades on public investment perhaps more than any other state. If government had not spent billions on irrigation, crops would not have grown. If it had not built up the great intellectual resource of the University of California, agribusiness, Silicon Valley, and other high-tech industries would not have flourished. In short, the public sector performs many functions that are of critical importance to the health of the private sector.

Conversely, the other two sectors perform functions that are of critical importance to the mission of government agencies. As we will see repeatedly in later chapters, the public sector tries to achieve public goals by providing various incentives to both the private sector and nonprofit sector to undertake certain tasks. One of the simplest and most direct ways in which government can provide these incentives has already been noted—contracts.

Sometimes the cooperation involves all three sectors simultaneously. Just consider the twin threats of bioterrorism and new virulent diseases such as severe acute respiratory syndrome (SARS). These threats have underscored the continuing need for innovative therapeutics. Yet biotechnology companies remain reluctant to fund basic research, preferring to concentrate on later-stage drug development. So, bioterrorism and untreatable infectious diseases have led to new relationships among government (which provides new funding), independent laboratories, academia, and industry. "Successful partnering," says Andrew S. Fauci at the National Institutes of Health, "is one way of keeping up with these infectious microbes, to fill the gap between research in medicine. Nothing is more true than the need for a successful biotech industry to partner with government and academic institutions. *There is no one group that can do it alone.*"[12]

How Do Public Administrators Manage?

We have just seen how public management differs from private management with respect to structures, incentives, settings, and purposes. In this section, we will see some important similarities with respect to what managers in both sectors do. This will not be easy: Just as no two organizations in Figure 1.1 are alike, no two managerial jobs are quite the same. But researchers have developed, after many years of study, some specific categorization

Figure 1.2   The Process of Public Administration

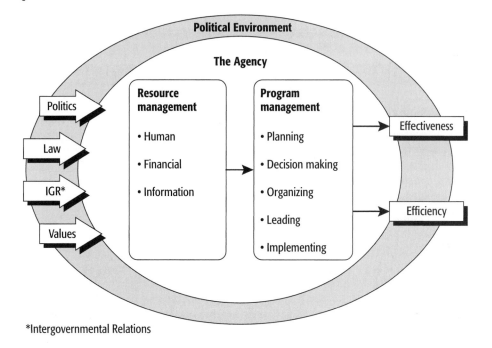

*Intergovernmental Relations

schemes to describe what managers do. In this section, we will look at what public managers do in terms of skills and roles.

Management Skills

A public manager's job is complex and, as we will see throughout this book, requires a range of skills. Although some management theorists propose a long list of skills, the necessary skills for managing any public sector organization can be summarized in three categories: political management, program management, and resource management. Figure 1.2 provides an overview of these skills and shows how this book connects them.

Political Management   Late in the afternoon on October 17, 1989, a large earthquake struck northern California, destroying or severely damaging several sections of freeway. Eighteen months later only the San Francisco Bay Bridge had been completely repaired. How can we explain this delay? Certainly, repairing damaged highway structures is no great engineering feat. The delay is best explained in political terms: No one demonstrated an ability to mobilize sufficient political support and resources to take action. Meanwhile, the continued closure of the Oakland section of the freeway was costing some $23 million per year in extra fuel and transportation costs (stemming from, for example, increased traffic delays).

Transportation costs and fuel are one thing; life and death, another. Surely, when lives are at risk, people find the political will to act. But anyone who has read Randy Shilts's *The Band Played On: Politics, People, and the AIDS Epidemic* knows otherwise. In July 1981, epidemiological evidence led many members of the medical community to conclude that the so-called gay cancer was in fact a contagious disease, spread by both sexual contact and blood transfusions. Nine months later, Don Francis at the Centers for Disease Control and Prevention (CDC) wanted to put blood banks on the alert. By late 1984, even though public health officials agreed AIDS could be spread by transfusions, a widespread screening of blood had not begun. Shilts writes: "An estimated 12,000 Americans were infected from transfusions largely administered after the CDC had futilely begged the blood industry for action to prevent spread of the disease. 'How many people have to die?' Francis had asked the blood bankers in early 1983. The answer was now clear: thousands would."[13]

How can one explain this? Again, the answer is to be found in the absence of effective political management or, more accurately, a mismatch in the political skills of those at the CDC and the blood banks. Blood banks and associated organizations such as the Red Cross had, Shilts writes, "years of experience in working with the media. They had experience, too, in working the corridors of power in Washington, particularly the government health establishment. . . . [T]he blood bank industry cultivated allies, was shrewd in its use of language to make the risks appear negligible, and mustered all its resources to solve and delay policies that might harm the industry." Meanwhile, the scientists and epidemiologists at the CDC "felt that truth would triumph, if the data were presented forcefully. But they were not at first influential enough to gain the upper hand in the struggle to change policies on AIDS."[14]

As these two examples suggest, public administrators must have a knowledge of political institutions and processes. Unfortunately, political knowledge alone is not enough; good administrators must also have *political skills*—to analyze and interpret political, social, and economic trends; to evaluate the consequences of administrative actions; and to persuade and bargain and thereby further their organization's objectives. Society suffers a great loss when otherwise talented people are so politically inept that they can contribute only a small fraction of their talents. For good reason, Chapter 2 addresses the politics of administration.

Chapter 2 also serves as a gateway to the other three chapters of Part One by previewing the most important forces in the political environment of a public administrator. Two of these forces, as it turns out, are too important to be adequately discussed in a single chapter. One of these forces is intergovernmental relations—that is, the relationship between Washington, DC and the 50 state governments as well as the thousands of relationships between other jurisdictions (state-state, state-local, local-local). The importance of these relationships cannot be overemphasized. As one experienced public administrator notes: "Even after 200 years, we still have not worked out clearly who does what among the three levels of government—federal, state, and local. The result is usually confusion and duplication of effort on overlapping problems. Often the aims of the manager at one level of government must be filled at a another level. . . . Yet, because what one level of government intends is not necessarily what another level wants to do or is capable of doing, the end product is not always what was intended. As the adage goes, 'Many a slip occurs between cup and lip.' "[15] For example, in 1996 national welfare reform authorized states to establish their own welfare programs using federal funds. The law forced state officials to change their focus from determination of eligibility and issuance of checks to employment and jobs. Unless welfare case managers at the local level made this change, the federal law had no chance of success.

The other major force in the political environment is the public—or, more precisely, the values and expectations of society about governance. Given the public administrator's mandate to manage change in the pursuit of society's values, it should not be surprising that ethics, which is the study of values, is the focus of Chapter 4. There we will confront a number of tough questions. How do public administrators handle conflicts between their personal values and public policy? When is a public administrator acting responsibly? Irresponsibly? How can we best foster ethical behavior in public administration? And, perhaps the toughest question of all, does virtue itself need limits?

Program Management   Besides being good political managers, public administrators should be good program managers. To understand what a program is, we need to first understand the nature of public policy. Public policies are choices that governments make in response to some issue such as crime, national security, economic growth, income maintenance, education, health care, energy, or the environment. For example, the Clean Air Act of 1978 and the Federal Water Pollution Control Act Amendments of 1972 provide the foundation of American environmental policy. Similar to policies, programs differ only with respect to specialty and focus. For instance, welfare policy is a broad, general concept composed of the following major programs:

- Old Age, Survivors, and Disability Insurance: payments to retired or disabled people and to surviving members of their families.
- Medicare: payments by federal government for part of the cost of hospital care for retired or disabled people covered by Social Security; paid for by payroll tax on employers and employees.
- Unemployment insurance: weekly payments to workers who have been laid off and cannot find work; states determine benefits and requirements.
- Temporary Assistance for Needy Families (TANF): payments to needy families with children.
- Supplemental Security Income (SSI): cash payments to aged, blind, or disabled people whose income is below a certain amount.
- Supplemental Nutrition Assistance Program (known as Food Stamps until 2008): vouchers given to people whose income is below a certain level in order for them to buy groceries.
- Medicaid: payment of medical expenses of persons receiving TANF and SSI.
- Public housing assistance.

Of course, someone has to manage these programs. Checks must be sent (on time) to retirees each month, payroll taxes must be collected for the Medicare trust fund, those receiving temporary assistance must be helped to find (and hold) jobs, those receiving

Supplemental Nutrition Assistance, and Medicaid must be certified as eligible, and so forth. The public administrators skilled at program management ensure that these and many other tasks are done in an efficient and effective manner.

Efficiency refers to getting the most output from the least amount of input. Because public administrators deal with scarce inputs (such as people, money, and equipment), they are concerned with the efficient use of those resources. From this perspective, efficiency is often referred to as "doing things right"—that is, not wasting public resources. But people expect more than efficiency. Governance is also concerned with being effective—that is, taking actions that actually solve, or at least alleviate, community problems. (*Community* can refer to any group—from a neighborhood to a village to a city to a region to a country to even a "global community.") **Effectiveness** is often described as "doing the right thing"— that is, engaging in activities that will help a government agency reach its goals. In sum, governance concerns not only meeting goals (effectiveness) but also doing so as efficiently as possible. In successful program management, high effectiveness and high efficiency typically go hand in hand. Conversely, poor program management most often stems from both inefficiency and ineffectiveness—or from effectiveness achieved through inefficiency ("throwing money at a problem").

Effective *and* efficient program management requires a thorough grasp of the five traditional management functions: planning, decision making, organizing, leading, and implementing. These functions are the focus of Part Two. Let's take a quick look at each. **Planning** defines where the organization wants to go in the future and how it is going to get there. Chapter 5 demonstrates how public administrators define goals for future agency performance and decide on the tasks and the use of resources needed to attain them. The chapter also shows how a lack of planning—or poor planning—can hurt an agency's performance.

Closely related to planning is the process of identifying problems and opportunities, generating alternatives, and selecting an alternative. This process is called **decision making,** the subject of Chapter 6. A knack for solving tricky problems is one of the hallmarks of a good administrator.

Organizing typically follows planning and decision making and, accordingly, is the subject of Chapter 7. Organization reflects how an agency tries to attain the objectives of its programs; it involves the assignment of tasks ("These are the things we must do") and the grouping of such tasks into various organizational units (for example, departments, divisions, bureaus, branches, offices, and so on).

The fourth basic management function, described in Chapter 8, is to provide **leadership** for employees in the organization. Leading is the use of influence to motivate civil servants to achieve program objectives. It involves communicating those objectives to employees throughout the agency and developing in them a commitment to perform at a high level. One of the more exciting aspects of studying public administration is viewing the way in which the great public executives have performed this function. The chapters ahead provide ample opportunity to do just that. We will see how these men and women made "ungovernable" cities governable once again, made fragile and besieged new agencies viable, revitalized demoralized organizations, and created bold new ways of attacking some of society's oldest problems.

The last basic management function is **implementing**. Absolutely critical to the success of a program are the monitoring and adjusting of the agency employees' activities to ensure that the program remains on track toward its objectives. Program implementation is the focus of Chapter 9.

Resource Management   Success in conceiving and implementing public policy is predicated on the administrator's skill at resource management; indeed, this chapter opened by defining public administration as "the process by which *resources* are marshaled." It is therefore fitting that Part Three (Chapters 10–12) closes the book by discussing this important subject.

Chapter 10 is concerned with the management of *human* resources. Economists speak of some industries as being capital intensive, meaning that they require heavy investments in plant and equipment. Because public administration is so *people* intensive—about four-fifths of a police department budget goes to salaries, for example—superior performance is ultimately based on people in an organization. The right plans, structures, and procedures play an important role, but the capabilities that lead to program success come from people—their skills, discipline, motivation, and intelligence. Leading and developing these people is the heart of successful high-performance administration; people make it happen.

Chapter 11 concerns the formulation and implementation of budgets in government. An adequate flow of money forms the sinews of public administration. Because few of a government agency's activities are voluntary, little happens unless it is paid for. How public administrators obtain fiscal resources (taxes) from their environment is also discussed.

Chapter 12 concerns the management of information. Some argue that in the twenty-first century, it is *the* most important resource. Suffice it to say, relative to human and fiscal resources, the importance of information has increased rapidly in the past two decades—and there is little reason to think this trend will abate in either the public or private sector.

Management Roles

Having looked at the skills needed by public administrators, let's now consider their roles. The term **management roles** refers to specific categories of managerial behavior. Just as each of us is expected to exhibit and play different roles, such as student, sibling, employee, or volunteer, managers too are expected to play different roles. Henry Mintzberg, a prominent management researcher, developed a categorization scheme for defining what managers do in terms of 10 different but highly interrelated roles. Follow-up research has tested the validity of his role categories among different types of organizations and at different levels within a given organization.[16] The evidence generally supports the idea that managers—whether public, private, or nonprofit—perform similar roles.

Mintzberg groups his 10 management roles into three categories: those primarily concerned with interpersonal relations (figurehead, leader, and liaison); those concerned with the transfer of information (monitor, disseminator, and spokesperson); and finally, those concerned with decision making (entrepreneur, disturbance handler, resource allocator, and negotiator) (see Table 1.1). Before we take a closer look at these roles, some

Q's 2

Table 1.1   Ten Manager Roles

Category	Activity
Monitor	Seek and receive information, scan periodicals and reports, maintain personal contacts.
Disseminator	Forward information to other organization members, send memos and reports, make phone calls.
Spokesperson	Transmit information to outsiders through speeches, reports, memos.
Figurehead	Perform ceremonial and symbolic duties.
Leader	Direct and motivate subordinates; train, counsel, and communicate with subordinates.
Liaison	Maintain information links both inside and outside organizations via e-mail, phone calls, readings.
Entrepreneur	Initiate improvement projects, identify new ideas, delegate idea responsibility to others.
Disturbance handler	Take corrective action during disputes or crises, resolve conflicts among subordinates, adapt to crises.
Resource allocator	Decide how to use organization's resource; schedule, budget, set priorities.
Negotiator	Represent department during negotiation with outside parties.

SOURCE: Adapted from Henry Mintzberg, *The Nature of Managerial Work* (New York: Harper & Row, 1973), 92–93.

qualifications are in order. As Mintzberg himself has recently pointed out, this list of roles does not provide an integrated description of managing. Further, "when managers manage, the distinctions between their roles were at the margins. In other words, it may be easy to separate these roles conceptually, but that does not mean they can always be distinguished behaviorally.[17]

Interpersonal Roles   These roles, which arise directly from the manager's formal authority, involve relationships with organizational members and other constituents. The **figurehead role** involves the handling of ceremonial and symbolic activities for the department or organization. It would be wrong to think that this role is played only by kings, queens, and plenipotentiaries. When managers greet visitors, present awards, or sign documents, they are fulfilling this role. Although some of this might seem perfunctory, the figurehead role can sometimes be one of the most powerful roles a manager plays. Significantly, former New York City mayor Rudy Giuliani devotes an entire chapter in his book *Leadership* to the subject of funerals and weddings.

> Until the World Trade Center attacks made it impossible, I attended the funeral of everyone who died in the line of duty in New York City. Being there not only showed people how important their loved one was, but had a reverberating effect,

Los Angeles Mayor Antonio Villaraigosa, like former New York City Mayor Rudy Guiliani, takes the figurehead role seriously.

underlining the importance of the survivors as well. It's a lesson I learned from my father, who defined himself by helping people when they needed him most. He used to take me with him to wakes and funerals when I was a little boy, and I sensed how much it meant to our neighbors and friends that he made the effort. My father drilled the message into me with his trademark tenacity: weddings are discretionary, funerals are mandatory.[18]

Antonio Villaraigosa in Los Angeles is another mayor who grasps the importance of the figurehead role.

He seems to be everywhere at once: handing out toys to kids in Watts; speaking at a B'nai B'rith luncheon on the Westside; huddling with business executives downtown; appearing on Spanish- and English-language television stations; presiding over announcements of economic development projects large and small; presenting Section 8 housing vouchers to poor families; traveling to police and fire stations to meet with their officers; showing up at community parades and neighborhood tree-decorating parties in even the most far-flung corners of his immense city.[19]

The **leader role**, in Mintzberg's system, is essentially one of influencing or directing others. It is the set of responsibilities people typically associate with a manager's job, because the organization gives the manager formal authority over the work of other people. To the extent that managers are able to translate this authority into actual influence, they are exercising what would be called leadership behavior. The leader role involves, among other things, motivating and encouraging employees and reconciling their individual needs with the goals of the organization.

Besides motivating and encouraging employees and reconciling their individual needs with the goals of the organization, the leader role also involves such direct activities as hiring and training staff. Elias Zerhouni, director of the National Institutes of Health (2002–2008), recalls that when he became chair of his department at the Johns Hopkins School of Medicine, he received this advice from his predecessor: "Look, nobody is going to look at whether or not you're under budget or whether or not the trains are arriving on time in your department. They're going to look at the quality of who you recruit."[20]

What does it take to be a leader? Dr. Zerhouni, who was born in Algeria and came to the United States in 1975, gave this answer in an interview after his first year as director of the Institutes:

> I think there are three things. First you have to have a big heart. Because if you don't have a big heart you will never be able to lead. And a big heart means several things to me. You have to have a passion. You have to believe in some things that are your core values.
>
> The second is you have to have a spine, which means stand up for what you think and take the risks that you think are important. And third and least important is brains. People often think that a high intelligence is a prerequisite. I don't believe so. I think a big heart and a strong spine are more important than high intelligence.[21]

Excessive attention to the role of leading has probably been matched by an underappreciation of the **liaison role**, in which managers link their organizations to individuals outside the vertical chain of command. That this role is often overlooked is quite remarkable because research shows managers spend as much time with peers and other people outside their organizations as they do with their own workers and bosses. One need not look far to find public administrators playing this role:

> In Norfolk, Virginia, city manager Regina Williams assembled a small group of peers from nearby jurisdictions. The topic of the meeting was a new pistol range for Norfolk's police department. Since she knew other departments in her area also needed new ranges, Williams proposed a regional range. According to *Governing* magazine, which selected her as one of the Public Officials of the Year in 2003, "In her first four years as Norfolk's city manager, Williams's most fundamental goal has been to connect city government to the widest possible range of constituencies—neighborhoods, educational institutions, civic organizations and business interest alike—in the name of policies and projects at work for the whole city, and even the Tidewater region."[22]

Information Roles   Given their wide range of personal relations, managers emerge as the nerve center of the organizational unit. In his classic study of presidential power, Richard Neustadt reports that although Franklin Roosevelt may not have known about everything going on in Washington, he likely knew more than any of his subordinates:

> The essence of Roosevelt's technique for information gathering was competition. "He would call you in," one of his aides once told me, "and he'd ask you to get the story on some complicated business, and you'd come back after a couple of days of hard labor and present the juicy morsel you'd uncovered under a stone somewhere, and then you'd find out he knew all about it, along with something else you didn't know. Where he got this information from he wouldn't mention, usually, but after he had done this to you once or twice you got damn careful about your information."[23]

Or consider what happened when Winston Churchill became First Lord of the Admiralty (at age 36). He engaged in a whirlwind of information gathering:

> With the Admiralty's yacht, the *Enchantress,* as his home and office, he mastered every detail of navy tactics and capabilities. He appeared to be everywhere at once, inquiring, badgering, learning. He was interested in everything from gunnery to the morale of his soldiers. He was fascinated with airplanes and immediately understood their utility for warfare. He spent hundreds of hours learning how to fly. He crawled into the cramped quarters of gun turrets and learned how they work. It became his practice to solicit information and opinions from junior officers and ordinary seamen, often ignoring or arguing with their superiors. The respect he showed them, and the increases in pay he won for them, made him a favorite in the ranks.[24]

Unfortunately, not all American presidents and secretaries of defense have had Churchill's curiosity.

As the Roosevelt and Churchill examples suggest, the **monitor role** pertains to scanning the environment for information, interrogating peers and subordinates, and analyzing not only formal reports but also gossip, hearsay, and speculation. Few are more keenly aware of the importance of this role than Sally K. Ride, the first American woman in space. In the aftermath of the space shuttle *Columbia* disaster in February 2003, Ride was asked about the head of its mission management team, Linda Ham. Some of Ham's engineers wanted Ham to ask the Pentagon to take spy satellite pictures of the shuttle so they could better assess the effects of foam from the external fuel tank hitting the wings. Because Ham could not track down who was urging that, she dropped the matter. Ride did not think that good enough. She explains:

> One of the responsibilities of a NASA manager is to be inquisitive to a fault. You have to ask and ask and ask. If you think there's any hint of a problem, you have to get to the bottom of it. In my mind, the question was not, Who is asking this question? What the managers needed to be asking is, What are the potential consequences of this foam hit? And tell me *now*.

There wasn't any of that quality that Mission Control is almost famous for, which is grabbing onto the pants legs of a problem and not letting go until it understands what the problem is and what the implications are. And that didn't happen in this case. The managers, the Mission Management Team and Mission Evaluation Room, did not grab onto this problem and insist on an answer. It was really quite the opposite. They assumed they knew the answer. They assumed the foam was not going to be a problem. And they were insisting that people disprove the preconception they had.[25]

Managers monitor in different way. Because Villaraigosa is determined to reform city operations, he holds monthly meetings with the 44 general managers—some of whom used to go for years without meeting the mayor—to make sure they're following his directions. In contrast, Obama decided not to hold numerous meetings, thinking they might chew up too much presidential time. According to his press secretary, Robert Gibbs, Obama's style is to drop by an aide's office—a restless man, he roams the White House corridors—or stop an aide in a hallway and ask, "How are you coming on that thing we were talking about?" Gibbs says, "The worst thing is not to have an answer." Asked what happens then, Gibbs replied, "He gets his disappointed parent look, and you better go find an answer."[26]

A manager not only receives information but also sends it. The **disseminator role** involves passing some privileged information—information received from outsiders or subordinates—directly to others who need it. A consummate player of this role is Denise Johnson, a deputy branch chief at the CDC. At the heart of an international effort to eliminate polio from the world, Johnson is, according to her colleagues, the glue that holds the operation together. Many days she is at her office in Atlanta at sunrise taking calls from the World Health Organization, UNICEF, and CDC employees abroad. "I think everyone, both overseas staff as well as staff in Atlanta, feels they can call on Denise any time of day or night, and have her devote 110 percent of her efforts on their problem," says an activity director of CDC's polio eradication team.[27]

So far we have seen the managers in two information roles: gathering information from outside the organization (the monitor role) and relaying it to others within an organization, project, or network (disseminating role). The third informational role is, as you might guess, sending information to outsiders—which often means the public. In the *spokesperson role,* managers transmit to outsiders information on an organization's plans, actions, and results. The head of CDC offers a splendid example of a public administrator fulfilling this role.

Once the CDC had a reputation for responding slowly to public crises. "Everything could wait until Monday" seemed to be the attitude. That ceased in 2002 when Julie Gerberding became the first woman to direct the agency. In less than a year, she held 17 television press conferences and made several appearances before Congress. She became the most visible CDC director in history, advising the public how to cope with major disease threats such as West Nile virus, smallpox, and SARS.

Decisional Roles   Information is only a means to an end—namely, decision making. Here again we see managers playing a central role, for only they have the formal authority to commit the organizational unit to a new course of action. Managers must make choices. Decisional roles pertain to those events about which a public administrator must make a choice.

The **entrepreneur role** involves the initiation of change. Based on an analysis of innovative managers from a diverse group of more than 30 successful public programs and agencies over the past two decades, Martin A. Levin and Mary Bryna Sanger conclude that what distinguishes public-sector entrepreneurs most is "their willingness to scan broader environments for approaches that suit their objectives: they are not captives of sectoral conventions or institutional traditions." More specifically, Levin and Sanger identify four characteristics of these bureaucratic entrepreneurs. First, finding themselves in agencies with weak or diffuse mandates, entrepreneurial managers carve out new and personal missions for their organizations in response. Second, they are opportunistic, taking advantage of available resources and windows of opportunity (which is to say, they are masters of good timing). Third, they "are willing to take risks, often ignoring and consciously underestimating the bureaucratic and political obstacles." Fourth, eschewing the careful, methodical approach indicative of many public-sector executives, they have a bias toward action— taking immediate action, moving quickly, and measuring the results.[28]

One of the best-known innovators in government in recent years has been William Bratton, now police chief in Los Angeles. During his tenure as commissioner of the NYPD in the late 1990s, he is remembered for putting two big ideas into practice: (1) Compstat meetings, which not only analyze crimes and share tactics and information but help hold precinct captains accountable for reducing crime in their neighborhoods; and (2) "broken windows" or "quality of life" policing—that is, the notion that going after low-level crime and signs of civil disorder has indirect benefits such as helping to identify criminals and reducing public fear. Both practices can now be found in police departments around the country.

More and more, managers in the nonprofit sector are also playing entrepreneurial roles, although this fact has been widely overlooked. David Burnstein, author of *How to Change the World: Social Entrepreneurs and the Power of New Ideas,* writes, "The past decade has produced vastly more social entrepreneurs than terrorists, but you would never know with following the news."[29] Unlike, say, Mother Teresa's Missionaries of Charity, these groups are led by men and women who are neither idealistic dreamers nor do-gooders; rather, they are entrepreneurs in the truest sense of the word. They are adept at marshaling resources behind an idea, creating organizations that operate both effectively and efficiently, and applying sound management tools to the task at hand. They demand from employees not compassion but results.

A case in point in Bangladesh is Muhammad Yunus (pronounced Iunus) and the bank he founded, Grameen Bank, which created a new category of banking by granting millions of small loans to people with no collateral. The bank even runs a project called Struggling Members Program that services 55,000 beggars. Under Yunus, Grameen Bank has spread the idea of microcredit throughout the developing world.

Muhammad Yunus, one of the world's leading social entrepreneurs, founded a bank that lends half a billion dollars to five million of the world's poorest people. The Nobel committee said it awarded him the 2006 Nobel Peace Prize for his "efforts to create economic and social benefits from below." Above he shares that moment of joy with his daughter.

While entrepreneurs voluntarily initiate change, managers in the role of **disturbance handler** find themselves responding to events largely beyond their control—strikes, budget deficits, disasters (natural and human-made), scandals, and so on. Sometimes these pressures are generated by conflicts between the manager's departments or subordinates. A classic example follows:

> General Dwight D. Eisenhower, Supreme Commander of the Allied Expeditionary Force between 1943 and 1945, had to spend valuable time mediating disputes between Britain's Field Marshal Montgomery and U.S. General Patton. No doubt he would rather have spent the time fighting Germans instead of assuaging these two rather large egos. But part of what made Eisenhower a great commander was his ability to handle disturbances and maintain cooperation between British, American, and other forces in the great battle for the European continent.

Another decisional role is that of **resource allocator**. Most importantly perhaps, managers must decide how to allocate their own time. But they must also allocate people (who works on what project), equipment (who gets what), and money (who gets how much). Consider how top officials at the Pentagon and the FBI must decide how to allocate funds:

- While the money sought for the F-22 fighter represented only a fraction of the Pentagon's total annual budget, the fight over the jet in 2009 was emblematic of Defense

Secretary Robert Gates' broader effort to rebalance the priorities of the U.S. military toward counterinsurgency and away from conventional warfare. Gates adamantly opposed buying more of the highly sophisticated fighters, which he said have little relevance in today's conflicts in Iraq and Afghanistan.

- The FBI categorizes its investigations into different programs, such as domestic terrorism, organized crime/drugs, violent crime, white collar crime, civil rights, and so forth. FBI managers in charge of each program submit requests for resources on an annual basis to the Finance Division. The Finance Division then reviews each request to ensure it supports the FBI's strategic plan and incorporates the requests into the budget submitted to the Attorney General. After approval by the Attorney General, the budget must be approved by the Office of Management and Budget and the Justice Management Division. Congress then discusses the budget request with the FBI director, amending or supplementing the budget as it sees fit. Next, the FBI Resources Management and Allocation Office sets funding levels for each program. The Resources Management and Allocation Office RMA and the FBI manager in charge of the program work together to allocate the program staffing level across headquarters and the FBI's 56 offices. Finally, this allocation is submitted to the director for approval. (For more about the FBI, see the Closing Case. For more about the federal budget process, see Chapter 11.)

Governor Jennifer Granholm in Michigan shows us how leaders often combine roles. A $4 billion budget deficit greeted her when she took office in 2003. So, she went to the people of Michigan for guidance on how to allocate scarce resources. Granholm held 15 town meetings throughout the state, listening to (monitoring) citizens' views about where they would spend the first state dollar and where they would make the first cut. Using electronic voting devices, the citizens told her what services to keep and what to cut. The priorities were clear: protect K–12 education and health care for seniors, pregnant women, children, and the disabled. Those priorities were reflected in the budget Granholm sent to the legislature and eventually signed into law.[30]

The **negotiator role** involves formal negotiations and bargaining to attain outcomes favorable to the mission of the manager's organization. For example, the manager meets and informally negotiates with others—a supplier about a late delivery, a company about an environmental standard, a union about worker grievances, business and citizens groups about the design of a new central library, or community and ethnic groups about the route of a parade. Chapter 3 discusses negotiations in the context of intergovernmental relations.

Why Public Administration at All?

Only an anarchist would deny the need for national defense and a system of justice. Or, to couch it in the prose of economist Adam Smith, government has "the duty of protecting the society from violence and invasion of other independent societies" and "the duty of protecting, as far as possible, every member of the society from the injustice or oppression of every other member of it."

Of course, the range of activities in which public administrators engage goes far beyond soldiering, judging, and policing. How can these other activities be justified? Before tackling that question, let us be clear on one fundamental point. For producing goods and services in abundance, no economic arrangement beats a free market. But society expects more from its economic system than raw output; it also wants equity and efficiency. That fact explains, in a nutshell, the "other activities" of government.

Although Smith believed that, in a free market, the impulse of self-interest would contribute to the public welfare, he was capable of appreciating that the private sector (that is, businesses) might, at times, oppose the public interest. In another famous passage, he wrote, "People of the same trade seldom meet together, even for merriment and diversion, but the conversation ends in a conspiracy against the public." For example, businesspeople might agree to form a monopoly or restrict competition. In such an instance, some would say that the market has "failed" and some of its vaunted efficiency has vanished. Under such circumstances, it may be socially desirable for government to act.

Efficiency is not, however, the only contributor to social welfare. Even where markets are efficient—producing a cornucopia of goods and services—the distribution of those goods, services, and rewards among the members of society may be deemed inequitable. What exactly constitutes an inequitable distribution? For our purposes, theoretical arguments can be set aside, and it can be asserted that a democratic society determines equitable distribution—speaking, of course, through its elected officials.[31]

In sum, then, the justification for government action is twofold: first, to promote efficiency in situations in which the market is said to have failed; and second, to foster a more desirable distribution of goods, services, and rewards among the members of society. The discussion that follows focuses mainly on the first justification for government action. It offers two possible reasons for market failure: externalities and public goods.[32]

One of the more frequently cited market failures involves "spillover," or external, costs of private action. Any time one's actions create costs for another without the other's permission, there is an **externality**. The person taking the action pays private costs but passes the rest on to others. Say it costs $1 million a year to operate a poultry-processing plant and annual revenues are $1.2 million. The plant is therefore generating $200,000 a year in profit. *But is the market really working properly here?* If the plant owner dumps animal waste into the river, he or she has certainly passed on some costs to people who swim and fish in that river. In such situations, governments will act to provide businesses with either negative or positive incentives to literally "clean up their act."

One of the more popular arguments for government action is that a free market fails to provide enough **public goods**. Examples of public goods include public health programs, education, research and development, and police protection. All these goods have at least one thing in common: It is difficult to exclude people who do not pay for the goods from enjoying the benefits they provide. Everyone benefits from living in a community with an effective public health program, an educated population, good roads, advanced technology, and clean air. To be sure, a free market can provide many of these things: Private physicians can treat a communicable disease for a fee, private schools can educate children if parents pay the tuition, corporations can fund some research, citizens can hire security guards to protect lives and property, and so forth. *But the crucial point is that a market will tend to undersupply these public goods.*

The reason is that private firms find it difficult to make a profit selling public goods. Because people obtain the benefits of public goods regardless of whether they pay for them, they have little incentive to pay. "The public good producer can be expected to have the same luck in collecting from beneficiaries as a baker would if he flew over a city, tossing out loaves of bread, and then went door to door to ask for payment from all those who picked up the loaves he dropped."[33] In such situations, governments will either provide the public good itself or encourage others (through subsidies, for example) to provide it.

When Did Public Administration Emerge as a Field of Study?

Public administration has been around for a long time. The man who conceived, designed, and built the Great Pyramid of Cheops in 2680 B.C. was a public administrator—so, too, was Joseph, the cool courtier who advised (correctly) the Pharaoh to plan for a seven-year famine. But public administration as a specific field of study was hardly considered in the United States until 1887, when a young political scientist named Woodrow Wilson wrote his famous essay "The Study of Administration." Nearly four decades would pass, however, before the first text appeared in the United States: Leonard White's *An Introduction to the Study of Administration*. In other words, even though public administration was invented thousands of years ago, it was not studied systematically in the United States until the 1920s. Equally curious is that the study of public administration did not take root in the United States until long after it had in Europe.

What arrested the development of American public administration? To find out, we will travel back to the Constitutional Convention of 1787. From there we will see how the field evolved. Essentially, the story can be told in terms of three perspectives, or schools of thought, about what the main concerns of the field should be. For convenience and to convey a sense of history, each school is identified with one of the following presidents: James Madison, Woodrow Wilson, and Franklin Roosevelt. Although these perspectives emerged at different times and offer strikingly different perspectives on our subject, all three are essential to understanding the theory and practice of American public administration today.

The Madisonian Perspective

Generally speaking, the Founders' approach to public administration was Madisonian. Like James Madison (1751–1836), most of the Founders were concerned about too much governmental power—especially executive power. Law, they believed, was the best way to limit that power. They were not alone. Most Americans then, as today, had an innate fear that administrative units capable of swift, decisive action would usually act unjustly. It follows, then, that law—not people—should be supreme. This notion runs like a steel thread from 1787 right up until the present. This continuity is illustrated in Figure 1.3 and the following historical survey.

Figure 1.3   Perspectives on American Public Administration over Time

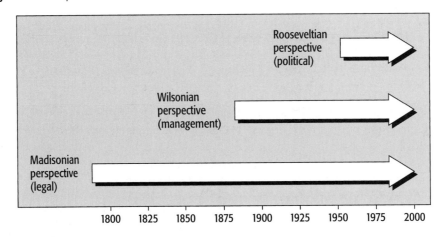

1787: In *Federalist No. 51,* Madison writes: "In framing a government which is to be administered by men, over men, the great difficulty lies in this: you must first enable the government to control the governed: and in the next place oblige it to control its self."

1803: In his opinion in *Marbury v. Madison,* Chief Justice John Marshall indicates that the Constitution is a "supreme paramount law, unchanged by ordinary means." It is "emphatically the province and duty of the judicial department" to say what that fundamental law means.

1835: French politician and writer Alexis de Tocqueville observes with wonderment the absence in America of even the most basic level of public administration.

> The public administration is, so to speak, oral and traditional. No one cares for what occurred before his time: no methodical system is pursued, no archives are formed, and no documents are brought together when it would be very easy to do so.[34]

1844: In his essay "Politics," Ralph Waldo Emerson writes: "The less government we have the better."

1882: In *United States v. Lee,* the U.S. Supreme Court warns that, "No man is so high that he is above a law. No officer of a law may set that law at defiance with impunity. All the offices of government, from highest to lowest, are creatures of the law, and are bound to obey it."

1926: In his dissent in *Myers v. United States,* Justice Louis Brandeis writes: "The doctrine of the separation of powers was adopted by convention in 1787, not to promote efficiency but to preclude the exercise of arbitrary power. The purpose was not to avoid friction but, by means of the inevitable friction incident to the distribution of government powers among these three departments, to save the people from autocracy."

1983: In *Immigration and Naturalization Service v. Jagdish Rai Chadha,* Chief Justice Warren Burger writes:

> It is crystal clear from the records of the Constitutional Convention, contemporaneous writings and debates, that the framers rank other values higher than efficiency. . . . There is no support in the Constitution . . . for the proposition that the cumbersomeness and delays often encountered in complying with explicit constitutional standards may be avoided.

September 2001: The American Civil Liberties Union and some of the most conservative Republicans in the House of Representatives form an alliance to oppose legislation proposed by the U.S. Attorney General that would ease restrictions on wiretaps and other investigatory tools to more efficiently fight terrorists.

Government and oppression, government and waste, government and cumbersome folly: These are as synonymous in the average American's mind today as they were in 1787 and are indicative of the Madisonian perspective on public administration. Thus, the Founders in Philadelphia strove to make administrative actions slow, cautious, and easily checked. They believed, in the words of Madison, that they were "so contriving the interior structure of the government as that its several constituent parts may, by their mutual relations, be the means of keeping each other in their proper places." Yet, in fact, they were contriving a perilously weak administrative state. Time and demands of modernity (the rise of big business, rapid changes in technology, and so on) and the repeated mortal dangers of an increasingly interconnected world would force many to rethink the direction of public administration. A second school of thought about American public administration was about to emerge.

The Wilsonian Perspective

In 1887, Woodrow Wilson, then a professor of political economy, wrote an essay that may serve as the symbolic beginning of American public administration. He began by noting the curious fact that although the study of politics had begun some 2,200 years earlier, it was not until the nineteenth century that administration—"the most obvious part of government"—began to demand attention: "Public administration is government in action, and one might very naturally expect to find that government in action had arrested the attention and provoked the scrutiny of writers of politics very early in the history of systematic thought." But such was not the case; rather, Madisonians had focused on the constitution of government, the nature of the state, the essence of sovereignty, monarchy versus democracy, and other lofty, abstract principles. In Wilson's view, the size and complexity of modern society had grown to a point at which a "science of administration" was essential. The time had come, he argued, to make the execution of government policy more businesslike. "The field of administration is a field of business. It is removed from the hurry and strife of politics."

Slowly, others began to gravitate toward Wilson's perspective on administration. For example, Frank Goodnow, often called the "father of American administration," and William F. Willoughby, another pioneer in the field, also had little trouble dividing government into two functions: political decision and administrative execution. In *Politics and Administration* (1900), Goodnow argued that government is composed of two distinct functions, which were identified in the title of the book. Politics has to do with policies or expressions of the state's will, while administration has to do with the execution of those policies. The implication was that administration was not only different from politics but somehow better. In 1927, Willoughby published the second textbook in the field: *Principles of Public Administration*. The title tells all: certain scientific principles existed, and once they were discovered, administrators would be experts in their work if only they applied those principles.

This view of public administration was influenced by two individuals whose primary interest lay not in government but in industry. One was Henri Fayol, who spent his entire career with one French mining company. The other was an American, Frederick Taylor, who dropped out of an elite boy's school, abandoned plans to attend Harvard, and apprenticed himself at a steam-pump maker in Philadelphia. It is probably more than coincidence that President Wilson's life overlapped with these two men. Consider this: Wilson and Taylor were both born in 1856, and Wilson would die in 1924—just one year before Fayol.

To understand the Wilsonian perspective, we need to know more about Fayol and Taylor, two remarkable and underestimated management philosophers.

Henri Fayol: Administration as a Process

When Fayol began his career, the large French firm for which he worked was in poor financial health; in 1918, when he retired as its managing director, it was prospering. Fayol's success is often attributed to his treating administration as a process, when the prevailing practice was to place administration under the control of specialists. To manage a mine, for example, one studied mining engineering; indeed, that had been Fayol's background. To manage an army, one studied military strategy. Fayol argued to the contrary: Good administration—whatever the setting—was a process consisting of certain common conditions. He then proceeded to name 14 principles of management— fundamental rules of management that could be taught in schools and applied in all organizations. Here are eight of Fayol's principles:[35]

1. *Division of work.* Specialization increases output by making employees more efficient.
2. *Authority.* Managers must be able to give orders. Authority gives them this right. Along with authority, however, goes responsibility.
3. *Unity of command.* Every employee should receive orders from only one superior.
4. *Unity of direction.* The organization should have a single plan of action to guide managers and workers.
5. *Scalar chain.* A chain of authority exists from the highest organizational authority to the lowest ranks.
6. *Order.* People and materials should be in the right place at the right time.
7. *Initiative.* Employees who are allowed to originate and carry out plans will exert high levels of effort.

8. *Esprit de corps.* Promoting team spirit will build harmony and unity within the organization.

What Madison would have thought of this idea—namely, that running a government is like running a mining company—we can only guess. But we do know that Fayol's ideas have had considerable influence in the United States. Called "the founding father of the administrative school," Fayol was the first to look at the organization from the top down, to identify management as a process, to break that process down into logical subdivisions, and to lay out a series of principles to make best use of people—thereby establishing a syllabus for management education.

Another pioneer of American public administration, Luther H. Gulick (1892–1992), derived the classic management acronym POSDCORB directly from Fayol to remind us that managers should plan, organize, staff, direct, coordinate, report, and budget. Although modern scholars have expressed reservations about the inclusiveness of the POSDCORB concept—surely there's more to management than that—it continues to influence government-sponsored training programs.

Frederick Wilson Taylor: The One Best Way

Taylor was born in 1856 into a wealthy Philadelphia family in which gentlemen didn't work and a proper education included several years of traveling in Europe. But, at age 18, Taylor made a decision that would change the practice of work forever: He dropped out of Exeter and, as noted earlier, went to work for a Philadelphia steam-pump maker.

How did Taylor change the world of work? "Taylorism" turned craft work into assembly work—a forerunner of automation in the machine age. To his critics, assembly work turned workers into robots, replaced judgment with the time clock and stopwatch, and stripped workers of their dignity. Or did it? Peter F. Drucker writes:

Few thinkers in history have had greater impact than Taylor. And few have been so willfully misunderstood and so assiduously misquoted. . . . In part, Taylor is ignored because contempt for work still lingers, above all among intellectuals. Surely shoveling sand—the subject of Taylor's most famous analysis [see Figure 1.4]—is not something an "educated person" would appreciate, let alone consider important. In much larger part, however, Taylor's reputation has suffered precisely because he applied knowledge to the study of work.[36]

Significantly, Taylor also argued that workers rather than owners should get the largest share of the application of his "scientific management" techniques and that work should be studied in consultation with the workers.

At the time Taylor wrote, the most powerful and respected unions were in the government-owned arsenals and shipyards, which provided virtually all peacetime U.S. defense production. Membership in these unions was largely restricted to sons or relatives of members.

They required an apprenticeship of five to seven years but had no systematic training or work study. The unions allowed nothing to be written down. . . . Union members were sworn to secrecy and forbidden to discuss their work with nonmembers.

Figure 1.4   Frederick Taylor's "Optimum Shovel Load," a Significant Discovery at a Time When Workers Still Moved Mountains of Coal, Coke, and Other Materials by Hand

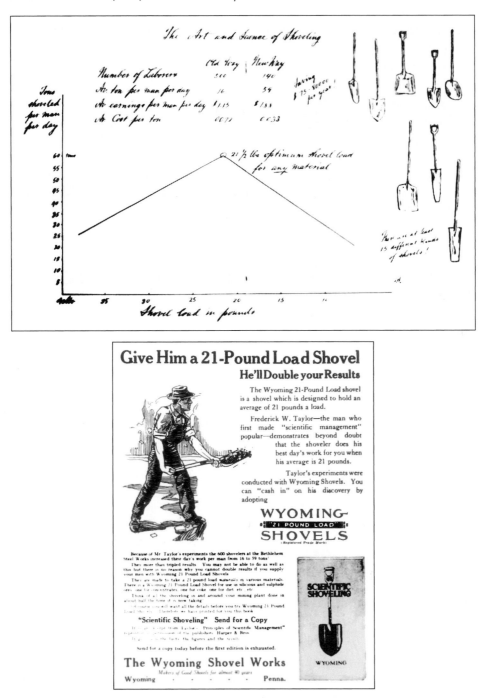

Source: Frederick W. Taylor Collection, Stevens Institute of Technology, Castle Point, Hoboken, NJ.

Taylor's assertion that work could be studied, analyzed, and divided into a series of simple repetitive motions, each of which had to be done in its one right way, in its own best time, and with its own right tools, was indeed a frontal attack on such encrusted guild practices. And so the unions vilified him. They even succeeded in persuading Congress to ban Taylor's "task study" method in government arsenals and shipyards, a ban that remained in force until after World War II.[37]

The concept of efficiency in the sense of productivity—that is, greater output from the same resources—was unknown at the time Fayol and Taylor wrote. Contrary to what Chief Justice Burger implied in the *Chadha* decision previously quoted, the framers did not think of efficiency in government that way. Efficiency meant to them what it had meant to Chaucer—"producing immediate effect."

It was, of course, the industrial revolution that changed the meaning of efficiency. As technologists experimented with different engine designs, an overriding concern was: How can we increase the ratio of output to input? That ratio came to be known as efficiency. Between 1780 and 1880, machine productivity increased severalfold, but the productivity of workers themselves in 1887 (when Wilson wrote his essay) was much as it had been in ancient Greece or Renaissance Florence. In retrospect, the reason for this relative stagnation in worker productivity is not hard to see. Unlike technology, *work itself had not been studied systematically.* Until Fayol and Taylor, no one had thought to apply knowledge to work. But once Fayol's principles and Taylor's techniques were applied in the early 1900s, productivity increased severalfold in all the advanced economies. This explosion in economic growth was too loud for public administration to ignore.

As we will see in later chapters, the views of Fayol and Taylor have been criticized for weakness of analysis and assessment, for internal contradictions, and for an overreliance on top-down bureaucracy and an underappreciation of worker motivation. But these criticisms do not alter the fact that the managerial perspective that Wilson advocated in 1887, and Fayol and Taylor helped make into a reality, is essential to understanding public administration. Indeed, the managerial perspective was institutionalized in 1939 with the founding of the American Society for Public Administration. "We are," its Web site today proclaims, "advocates for greater effectiveness in government—agents of good will and professionalism—publishers of democratic journalism at its very best—purveyors of progressive theory and practice and providers of global citizenship. We believe that by embracing new ideas—and addressing key public service issues—promoting change at both the local and international levels, we can enhance the quality of lives worldwide." For more information about the American Society for Public Administration and what it has to offer those working in the public sector, go to www.aspanet.org.

The Rooseveltian Perspective

After World War II, neither the Wilsonian perspective nor the Madisonian perspective—nor even a combination of the two—seemed adequate to grasp new administrative realities. And, once again, a young political scientist would step forward to write an essay that would crystallize what many sensed was missing from the study of public administration.

In 1947, Robert Dahl at Yale pointed out a major problem with the Wilsonian perspective: It presumed a sharp dichotomy between politics and administration.

Dahl was not alone in his criticism of this dichotomy. The preceding year, Fritz Morstein-Marx's *The Elements of Public Administration* (1946) pointed out that administrators were involved in policy formation, the use of discretionary power, and the general political process. The following year, Dwight Waldo also helped to focus the debate: "The disagreement is not generally with politics-administration itself; only with the spirit of rigid separatism. In some measure, this is an advance into realism. In some measure, it flows from a feeling of strength and security, a feeling that the processes and the study of administration have matured, that they no longer need be isolated from the germs of politics. Administration can even think about invading the field of politics, the field of policy determination."[38]

Besides Dahl, Morstein-Marx, and Waldo, four other prominent voices were heard in the attack on the **politics-administration dichotomy**: David E. Lilienthal (1944), Paul Appleby (1945), Philip Selznick (1949), and Norton Long (1949).

- Based on his experiences as head of the TVA in the 1930s, Lilienthal concluded that the planning process of government was a blatantly political enterprise and that, in a democratic society, *planning should be political.* To see why, one need look no further than the Aral Sea ("The Blue Sea"). In their quest for increased cotton production, Soviet planners created the greatest single irrigation disaster in the twentieth century. By damming the two rivers that fed the world's fourth largest lake, they transformed it into a saltpan the size of Ireland. Needless to say, the planners did not poll local residents on the project beforehand.

- Appleby firmly rejected the Wilsonian school's insistence that government be run as a business. "In broad terms the governmental function and attitude had at least three complementary aspects that go to differentiate government from all other institutions and activities: breath of scope, impact, and consideration; public accountability; political character."[39]

- After examining the process that Lilienthal used in the 1930s to gain support for TVA projects, Selznick coined the term **co-optation**. The term refers to the political strategy of an organization to bring in and subsume outside elements into its planning process to prevent those elements from being a threat to the organization and its mission. As a general rule, critics tend to be more vociferous when they are on the outside looking in than when they are enmeshed in the process.

- Long stressed the significance of prestige and appearance and the need to sometimes sacrifice subordinates to this end. Legal authority and money are not enough to get the job done. More is needed—namely, "a critical evaluation of the whole range of complex and shifting forces on whose support . . . the power to act depends." Long continues:

  > It is clear that the American system of politics does not generate enough power at any focal point of leadership to provide the conditions for an even partially successful divorce of politics from administration. Subordinates cannot depend on the formal chain of command to deliver enough political

power to permit them to do their jobs. Accordingly, they must supplement the resources available through the hierarchy with those they can muster on their own or accept the consequences in frustration. . . . Administrative rationality demands that objectives be determined and sights set in conformity *with a realistic appraisal of power position and potential.*[40]

Thus, by the end of the 1940s, a third perspective on public administration had been established. We call it Rooseveltian for two reasons. First, many of its advocates had been in the Roosevelt administration. Indeed, one of the reasons why these writings were so well received was that many academics had served in the New Deal and World War II. When Dahl described the futility of separating politics and administration, they knew exactly what he meant.

Second, few, if any, presidents were as adroit as Roosevelt at using political means to attain administrative ends. In a 2004 biography, Conrad Black argues that Roosevelt's objectives were almost always benign, "but his techniques, while bloodless, were not always much less ruthless, devious, and cynical than Hitler's or Stalin's." Roosevelt "was a less admirable character, perhaps . . . than his admirers have traditionally believed. But in applying his ruthlessness and often amoral political genius to almost wholly desirable ends, he was a greater statesman than even his greatest supporters have appreciated."[41] Black gives Roosevelt credit for saving Western civilization—although that credit must be shared with Churchill and Russian soldiers. He also gives Roosevelt credit for reinventing the American state and, in the process, restoring the confidence of Americans in their government "as an active promoter of an equitable society." All this was made possible, Black contends, by Roosevelt's unmatched mastery of the American political system: electoral, congressional, and—although his methods were sometimes infuriatingly secretive—administrative.

Black is not the first biographer to note Roosevelt's mastery of blending politics with administration. In 1954, James MacGregor Burns made the following observation:

> He was to show a keen appreciation throughout his later career of the principle that politics is the art of the possible. He profited from Uncle Ted's [Theodore Roosevelt's] warning that being good was not enough—a man must be shrewd and he must be courageous. He had learned at first hand the wisdom of Machiavelli's advice to princes that they must act at times with great valor and at times with great prudence—that they must be something of a lion and something of a fox.[42]

The message for contemporary public administration is clear. It is not enough to have legal authority and ample financial resources and to know something of POSDCORB and the latest management fads. No. To be successful in the public sector, men and women must also possess political skills.

Concluding Observations

Some might disagree with the foregoing selection of perspectives. This is not a bad thing, for the development of a field of study can be charted in many ways. Moreover, each perspective contains numerous themes and variations. For example, within the broad

Wilsonian perspective, one finds not only Taylor's scientific management but also other major management theories such as organizational behavior and the New Public Management, with its emphasis on public servants taking the initiative to improve government performance (more about these theories later). Obviously, there is more than one way to slice and dice the evolution of public administration in the United States.

Nor should Figure 1.3 suggest that the evolution is over. New major perspectives such as globalization might emerge.[43] Indeed, the number of transnational challenges the United States and other nation-states face today suggests that public administrators will increasingly need to think globally while continuing to act locally. Among those challenges are better financial integration; environmental pollution and natural resource depletion; climate change and overfishing; AIDS and of the pandemics; global crime manifested in the trafficking of drugs, arms, and people; and illicit dual-use technology (that is, industrial technology that can also be used to develop weapons of mass destruction). Suffice to say, no nation—no matter how competent its public administrators—can tackle these problems alone.

Concepts for Review

co-optation	management roles
decision making	member-serving organization
effectiveness	nongovernmental organization
efficiency	nonprofit organization
externality	organizing
governance	planning
government corporation	politics-administration dichotomy
implementing	public administration
independent executive agency	public goods
independent regulatory commission	public-serving organization
leading	

Key Points

This chapter sets the scene for the rest of the book. We have defined *public administration* and a closely related term, *governance*. We have seen who public administrators are both in concrete terms (such as Iris Weinshall) and in general terms (classifying them by organizational level). We have looked at where public administrators work and considered how they manage. We have discussed certain deficiencies in the private sector that make public administration necessary. Finally, we have reviewed the development of public administration in the United States since the presidency of George Washington. The following major points were made in this chapter:

1. Traditionally, public administration is thought of as the accomplishing side of government. It is supposed to encompass all the activities involved in carrying out the policies

of elected officials and some activities associated with the development of those policies. Broadly defined, public administration is the process by which resources are marshaled and then used to cope with the problems facing a political community. In the final analysis, governance is just another way of saying public administration. Governance is the exercise of authority by government or, more precisely, the system and method by which that authority is exercised. If there is any difference between the two terms, it is this: Governance is a slightly broader term than public administration.

2. What public administrators try to achieve depends on the efficiency and responsiveness of nonprofit organizations. How the nonprofit sector performs is becoming an important aspect of public administration.

3. Steps that an effective entrepreneur—public or private—should take include listening to the customer, identifying the assets, deciding what business one is in, empowering employees, and creating value.

4. One way of classifying public administrators is by organizational level: elected officials such as presidents, governors, and mayors; political appointees; and career civil servants.

5. The most familiar form of organization in national government are the 15 executive departments. In addition to the executive departments and their agencies, numerous independent executive agencies operate apart from the executive departments and generally report directly to the president. Yet another form of organization is the independent regulatory commission. Finally, government corporations are appropriate for the administration of government programs that (a) are predominantly of a business nature, (b) produce revenue and are potentially self-sustaining, (c) involve a large number of business-type transactions with the public, and (d) require a greater flexibility than the customary type of congressional funding ordinarily permits.

6. A nonprofit organization is set up for charitable purposes, and its IRS classification confers on it special tax-exempt status. Nonprofits are chartered by each state and may generate profits (or "surplus"), but these profits may not be distributed. All the assets of nonprofits must be dedicated to their exempt purposes.

7. Two categories of organizations comprise the nonprofit sector: member-serving organizations and public-serving organizations. The latter exist mainly to serve the public at large rather than the organization's membership. The term nongovernmental organization usually refers to this type of nonprofit.

8. Although all three sectors—government, nonprofit, and private—might be engaged in delivering social services, it does not follow that private management and public management are the same. Indeed, they differ in four respects: structures, incentives, settings, and purposes.

9. The necessary skills for managing any public-sector organization can be summarized in three categories: public management, program management, and resource management.

10. The public administrator's skill at program management ensures that the agency's activities are conducted in an efficient and effective manner. Efficiency refers to getting the most output from the least amount of input. Thus, efficiency is often referred to as "doing things right"—that is, not wasting public resources. Effectiveness is often described as "doing the right thing"—that is, engaging in activities that actually help

an agency reach its goals. Effective and efficient program management requires a thorough grasp of the five traditional management functions: planning, decision making, organizing, leading, and implementing.

11. Mintzberg groups his 10 management roles into those primarily concerned with interpersonal relations (figurehead, leader, and liaison); those concerned with the transfer of information (monitor, disseminator, and spokesperson); and finally, those concerned with decision making (entrepreneur, disturbance handler, resource allocator, and negotiator).

12. Although Adam Smith believed that, in a free market, the impulse of self-interest would bring about the public welfare, he also appreciated that the private sector (that is, business) might, at times, oppose the public interest. One of the more frequently cited market failures involves "spillover," or external costs of private actions. An external cost (an "externality") occurs when one's actions create costs for another without the other's permission. Another popular argument for government action is that a free market fails to provide enough public goods. Examples of public goods include public health programs, education, research and development, and police protection. It is difficult to exclude people who do not pay for public goods from enjoying the benefit they receive. For that reason, markets will tend to undersupply these public goods.

13. Generally speaking, the Founders' approach to public administration was Madisonian. Like James Madison (1751–1836), most of them were concerned about too much government power, especially executive power. Law, they believed, was the best way to limit that power.

14. In 1887, Woodrow Wilson wrote an essay that serves as the symbolic beginning of American public administration. In Wilson's view, the size and complexity of modern society had grown to a point at which a "science of administration" was essential. The time had come, he argued, to make the execution of government policy more businesslike. "The field of administration is a field of business. It is removed from the hurry and strife of politics."

15. After World War II, neither the Wilsonian perspective nor the Madisonian perspective nor even a combination of the two seemed adequate to grasp new administrative realities. A major problem with the Wilsonian perspective was that it assumed a sharp dichotomy between politics and administration.

Problems and Applications

1. Which of the problems that face city and county managers today do you think will improve, and which do you think will worsen, between now and 2020? Explain why.

2. Which of the 10 management roles does Iris Weinshall illustrate?

3. What potential problems do you see arising when the private sector delivers a social service? What are the advantages of this approach to service delivery?

4. What similarities do you see among the management functions of planning, organizing, leading, and controlling? Do you think these functions are related—that is, is a manager who performs well in one function likely to perform well in others?

5. Can you think of other examples of successful partnering between the public sector and the other two sectors that have recently been in the news?

6. A college professor told her students, "The purpose of a public administration course is to teach students about public administration, not to teach them to be managers." Do you agree or disagree with this statement? Discuss.

7. What changes in management skills and roles might occur as one is promoted up the administrative hierarchy? How can managers acquire the new skills?

Favorite Bookmarks

www.gpo.gov It should come as no surprise that one of the biggest document-producing organizations in the world is the U.S. government. Each year the U.S. government produces countless documents, each with its own audience and significance. It is the job of the U.S. Government Printing Office (GPO) to publish these documents and make sure they are archived. Because of the sheer volume of documents the GPO handles, the GPO has effectively cataloged them. This site is aptly named "Keeping America Informed." Click on "Access to Government Information Products."

www.census.gov The job of the U.S. Census Bureau is to gather demographic and economic statistics about the United States. This information is made public, and much of it is available on the Census Bureau's Web site. This site is a fascinating place to browse because there are so many interesting statistics (seriously). See also www.fedstats.gov.

www.fedworld.gov FedWorld is a service supported by the National Technical Information Service, an agency of the U.S. Department of Commerce. Its purpose is to act as a central access point to help you find and obtain the information you want.

www.governing.com This site complements the printed publication *Governing,* a magazine primarily about public administration in states and localities, and extends the discussion beyond its pages.

www.oecd.org/puma In addition to public-sector statistics, this site of the Paris-based Organization for Economic and Cultural Development offers information on engaging citizens, ethics and corruption, human resources management, regulatory reform, and strategic policymaking—all from an international perspective.

www.pfdf.org The Peter F. Drucker Foundation for Nonprofit Management, based in New York City, encourages effective management by recognizing accomplishments by community organizations across the land. Its work is concrete and practical.

www.nonprofits.org More than one million nonprofit organizations are included in a database maintained by the Internet Nonprofit Center. This site includes links to the Web sites of many nonprofit organizations.

Notes

1. Laurence E. Lynn, Jr., Carolyn J. Heinrich, and C. J. Hill. "The Empirical Study of Governance." Paper presented at the Workshop on Models and Methods, University of Arizona, Tucson, 1999.

See also Carolyn J. Heinrich and Laurence E. Lynn, Jr. (eds.), *Governance and Performance: New Perspectives* (Washington, DC: Georgetown University Press, 2000).

2. Profile of Iris Weinshall based primarily on Steven Brill, *After: The Rebuilding and Defending of America in the September 12 Era* (New York: Simon & Schuster, 2003), 8–10, 138–40.

3. Adapted from Rudolph W. Giuliani, *Leadership* (New York: Hyperion, 2002), 146–49.

4. Charlese T. Goodsell, *The Case for Bureaucracy: A Public Administration Polemic* (Washington, DC: CQ Press, 2004), 84.

5. The first three vignettes are based on Beth Dickey, "2005 Service to America Medals," *Government Executive* (October 1, 2005); the next two, on "Public Officals of the Year," *Governing* (November 2005); and the last on "Transformation of the US Veterans Health Administrative," *US News and World Report* (July 8, 2005).

6. Congressional Research Service, *The Federal Workforce: Characteristics and Trends*, RL 34685 (September 30, 2008).

7. Lester M. Salamon (ed.), *The State of Nonprofit America* (Washington, DC: Brookings, 2002), 11.

8. Peter F. Drucker, *The New Realities* (New York: Harper & Row, 1989), 198–99;

9. Leslie R. Crutchfield and Heather McLeod Grant, *Forces for Good: The Six Practices of High-Impact Nonprofits* (San Francisco: Wiley, 2008), 2, 4, 20–21.

10. William P. Ryan, "The New Landscape for Nonprofits," *Harvard Business Review* (January–February 1999).

11. W. Michael Blumenthal, quoted in *Fortune* (January 29, 1979).

12. Quoted in Lawrence M. Fisher, "The New Architecture of Biomedical Research," *Strategy and Business* (Winter 2004): 60.

13. Randy Shilts, *And the Band Played On: Politics, People, and the AIDS Epidemic* (New York: St. Martin's Press, 1987), 579.

14. Jeffrey Pfeffer, *Managing with Power: Politics and Influence in Organizations* (Boston: Harvard Business School Press, 1992), 6.

15. Gordon Chase, *Bromides for Public Managers,* Case N16-84-586 (Cambridge, MA: Kennedy School of Government, 1984).

16. Henry Mintzberg, *The Nature of Managerial Work* (New York: Harper & Row, 1973). For follow-up research, see A. W. Lau and C. M. Pavett, "The Nature of Managerial Work: A Comparison of Public and Private Sector Managers," *Group and Organization Studies* (December 1980): 453–66; M. W. McCall, Jr. and C. A. Segrist, *In Pursuit of the Manager's Job: Building on Minztberg,* Technical Report No. 14 (Greensboro, NC: Center for Creative Leadership, 1980); C. M. Pavett and A. W. Lau, "Managerial Work: The Influence of Hierarchical Level and Functional Specialty," *Academy of Management Journal* (March 1983); 170–77; A. I. Kraut et al., "The Role of the Manager: What's Really Important in Different Management Jobs," *Academy of Management Executive* (November 1989): 286–93; and M. J. Martinko and W. L. Gardner, "Structured Observation of Managerial Work: A Replication and Synthesis," *Journal of Management Studies* (May 1990): 330–57. For descriptions of how public administrators combine Mintzberg's roles, see Mark H. Moore, *Creating Public Value: Strategic Management in Government* (Cambridge, MA: Harvard Unviersity Press, 1995) and Barry Bozeman and Jeffrey P. Straussman, *Public Management Strategies: Guidelines for Managerial Effectiveness* (San Francisco: Jossey-Bass, 1991).

17. Henry Mintzberg, *Managing* (San Francisco: Berrett-Koehler, 2009), p. 91.

18. Giuliani, op. cit., 256.

19. Bob Gurwitt, "Mayor in the Middle," *Governing* (February 2007): 30.

20. Quoted in *The New York Times* (July 12, 2003).

21. Ibid.

22. *Governing* (November 2003): 26.

23. Richard D. Neustadt, *Presidential Power and the Modern Presidents* (New York: Free Press), 153–54.

24. John McCain, "Extraordinary Foresight Made Winston Churchill Great," *Daily Telegraph* (March 20, 2008).

25. *The New York Times* (August 26, 2003).

26. Elizabeth Drew, "The Thirty Days of Barack Obama," *New York Review* (March 26, 2009): 10.

27. Quoted in special section "Stories of Service," *Atlantic* (January–February 2003).

28. Martin A. Levin and Mary Bryna Sanger, *Making Government Work* (San Francisco: Jossey-Bass, 1994), 151, 167. Two more recent books on entrepreneurship and public administration come to similar conclusions. See John D. Donahue (ed.), *Making Washington Work: Tales of Innovation in the Federal Government* (Washington, DC: Brookings, 1999) and Richard N. Haass, *The Bureaucratic Entrepreneur: How to Be Effective in Any Unruly Organization* (Washington, DC: Brookings, 1999).

29. David Burnstein, *How to Change the World: Social Entrepreneurs and the Power of New Ideas* (New York: Oxford, 2004), 281.

30. *Governing* (January 2006).

31. For two outstanding modern contributions to this theoretical debate, see John A. Rawls, *A Theory of Justice* (Cambridge, MA: Harvard University Press, 1971) and Robert Nozick, *Anarchy, State, and Utopia* (New York: Basic Books, 1974).

32. A standard economics text would offer at least three other instances of market failure: asymmetric information, imperfect competition, and transaction costs.

33. Richard McKenzie and Gordon Tullock, *Modern Political Economy* (New York: McGraw-Hill, 1978), 342.

34. Alexis de Tocqueville, *Democracy in America,* trans. Harvey C. Mansfield (Chicago: University of Chicago Press, 2000), p. 75.

35. The principles have been reproduced widely. For further reading on Fayol, see Edward Brech, *The Principles and Practice of Management* (London: Longman, 1975); Stuart Crainer, *Financial Times Handbook of Management* (Upper Saddle River, NJ: Prentice Hall, 2001); and Derek S. Pugh and David J. Hickson, *Great Writers on Organization* (Thousand Oaks, CA: Sage, 1989).

36. Peter F. Drucker, "The Rise of the Knowledge Society," *Wilson Quarterly* (Spring 1993): 61.

37. Ibid.

38. Dwight Waldo, *Administrative State* (New York: Ronald Press, 1948).

39. Paul Appleby, *Big Democracy* (New York: Knopf, 1945).

40. Norton E. Long, "Power and Administration," *Public Administration Review* (Autumn 1949): 257–64.

41. Conrad Black, *Franklin Delano Roosevelt: Champion of Freedom* (London: Weidenfeld & Nicolson, 2004).

42. James MacGregor Burns, *Roosevelt: The Lion and the Fox* (New York: Harcourt, 1956).

43. See, for example, Joseph S. Nye and John D. Donahue (eds.), *Governance in a Globalizing World* (Cambridge, MA: Brookings, 2000), 1–38.

CASE 1.1 FEDERAL BUREAU OF INVESTIGATION

Although the Federal Bureau of Investigation (FBI) resides in the U.S. Department of Justice and its director reports to the U.S. Attorney General, it perceives itself less as a bureaucracy within a cabinet department and more as a quasi-independent agency linked directly to the highest levels of government. Whatever the case, the FBI has fascinated the American people more than any other civilian agency—at least, that is, if Hollywood is any indicator. The cinematic record is familiar. James Cagney joins the FBI in *"G" Men* (1935) when a pal is killed by gangsters. FBI trainee Jodie Foster attempts to get through to a psychotic criminal in *Silence of the Lambs* (1991). Ambitious FBI agent Ryan Phillippe is given the thankless assignment of earning the trust of an agency veteran who has been selling secrets to the Russians in *Breach* (2007). More recently, *Public Enemies* (2009) centers on two dramatic antagonists, bank robber John Dillinger (played by Johnny Depp) and FBI agent Melvin Purvis (Christian Bale). Under the mentorship of the FBI's young director, J. Edgar Hoover (Billy Crudup), Purvis led the hunt for America's most wanted.

Besides pursuing its mission of solving and preventing crimes, the FBI also serves as a key member of the federal intelligence community. That community consists of 15 or 16 "main" intelligence agencies, such as the Central Intelligence Agency (CIA) and the National Security Agency (NSA), plus dozens of other agencies, subagencies, and subordinate units responsible for intelligence and security. The nominal leader of this unwieldy community is the Director of National Intelligence or the "intelligence czar." How well the FBI reconciles its two core functions-—criminal investigation and national security—-offers a fascinating intellectual challenge to the field of public administration.

History

J. Edgar Hoover's Legacy (1924–72)

The FBI originated from a force of special agents that President Theodore Roosevelt's attorney general created in 1908. That force was named the Bureau of Investigation (BOI). When the BOI became the FBI in 1935, J. Edgar Hoover, then director of the BOI, became the FBI's first director. He would hold that position until 1972. This tenure is quite remarkable given that he had become director of the BOI in 1924.

When Hoover became director of the BOI, he began a restructuring to impose discipline and accountability. Where there had been four divisions with ill-defined responsibilities, he created six, each with a different function. Hoover insisted promotion be based on merit alone. To check on compliance with the organization's rules and procedures, he established an Inspection Division. He standardized the work of the bureau—for example, every agent would use the same set of forms. In contrast to the corrupt standards of the previous director, Hoover told his agents to avoid even the appearance of improper conduct. Two ideas were constantly drummed into agents: fear of failure and pride in membership in an elite organization.

Hoover followed these changes with a series of farsighted moves to employ technology and other advanced crime-solving techniques, including creating a national registry of fingerprints, opening a crime lab in 1932, and establishing the FBI's National Police Academy in 1935. In 1967, he established the National Crime Information Center, a computerized data bank of criminal records, names of fugitives, and listings of stolen vehicles, guns, securities, and other property that could be identified by serial number and checked by law enforcement agencies. This center would be one of his last innovations.

During Hoover's tenure, the FBI developed a subculture that operated outside the realm of strict legality: wiretapping, breaking and entering, and engaging in other dubious actions to gather intelligence. Hoover also kept extensive files containing damaging personal information about prominent American politicians and did not hesitate to use this information as leverage to achieve his political and legislative hands. Although subsequent directors curtailed much of these clandestine activities, Congress has continued to keep the FBI on what one senator calls a "long leash" because of fear of retaliation. Who knows what could be in those files?

Louis Freeh (1993–2001)

Fast-forward to the late 1980s, when illegal drug offenses became a priority for the FBI. For example, the "Pizza Connection" case uncovered an elaborate scheme by Mafia figures to distribute drugs and launder money through pizzerias. The lead prosecutor on the case, Louis Freeh, received widespread acclaim and eventually became the FBI's director—the fourth director since Hoover (there were several acting directors who served only briefly).

When terrorists bombed the World Trade Center in New York in 1993, Freeh considered it a "wake-up call." He created a counterterrorism division and arranged for job rotation among senior FBI and CIA counterterrorism officials. The FBI's 1998 five-year plan declared national security, including counterterrorism, a top priority. But, by 2000, the FBI had only about 24 percent of its agents assigned to counterterrorism and counterintelligence—and most of these were working on counterintelligence. Meanwhile, about 28 percent of its agents worked on white collar crime, another 25 percent on organized crime and drugs, and 23 percent on violent crime.

Robert Mueller (2001–present)

One week before 9/11, President George W. Bush nominated Robert Mueller to become the sixth director of the FBI. After only a few months

on the job, Mueller restructured the bureau and began elevating the people he had come to trust. His emphasis was on technology and analysis. Specific actions included:

- Appointing a chief technology officer who reports directly to the director
- Creating an Office of Strategic Planning so that the FBI could anticipate and plan for new threats rather than just respond to them as they arose
- Establishing a new Security Division to try to prevent another Robert Hanssen case (Hanssen had sold documents to the Soviets.)
- Adding an Office of Law Enforcement Coordination to improve liaison with state and local officials
- Ordering a training program for analysis and data mining (As Mueller put it, "The work of the FBI is information.")

But directors must be able to react as well as act. In May 2002, Colleen M. Rowley, the Minneapolis Field Office's legal counsel, wrote Mueller a 13-page, single-spaced letter complaining that headquarters had repeatedly stymied requests from agents in her office who were seeking a search warrant to examine the contents of Zacarias Moussaoui's computer in the weeks before September 11. Further, in the summer of 2001, when agents in the Minneapolis Bureau approached the CIA for help in evaluating whether the suspect was a terrorist, they were reprimanded by FBI headquarters. Clinton Justice Department officials said that reaction demonstrated the difficulties the two agencies have long had in working together. The Bush Justice Department had a different interpretation: the Clinton Justice Department had built up a wall between intelligence and criminal investigations, and this wall had "a debilitating impact" on the ability of counterterrorism investigators to share information with their counterparts in criminal investigations.

Mueller also had to handle the "Phoenix memo." In the month before Rowley's testimony, stories had begun coming out about a memo by Kenneth J. William, an agent from Phoenix, written in July 2001 urging a broad survey of American aviation schools based on his concern that Middle Eastern men, possibly connected to

Osama bin Laden, were training at a flight school in Arizona. Officials at headquarters rejected his proposal. Mueller said that the plan was deferred for lack of resources, but other officials point to another reason: the worry that such an effort might be criticized in Congress as racial profiling.

In response to the problems highlighted by the Rowley letter and the Phoenix memo, Mueller instructed field offices to start terrorism investigations on their own, without having to obtain approval from headquarters. Further, to strengthen the FBI's institutional knowledge, Mueller established "flying squads" of agents from headquarters who would coordinate terrorism investigations. Mueller assigned 25 CIA analysts to help develop the FBI's analysis system, and he assigned another 50 CIA officers to each of the FBI's terrorism task forces.

Lines of Business

Today the FBI is a bit like a large services company that operates several major "lines of business." The list below recapitulates some businesses already mentioned and introduces a few new ones, for a grand total of 10 lines of business for the FBI.

1. **Intelligence:** Establishing an enterprise-wide intelligence capability that optimally positions the FBI to meet current and emerging national security and criminal threats.
2. **Counterterrorism:** Protecting the United States from terrorist attack. Terrorism is the most significant national security threat the United States faces. The FBI counterterrorism goal is specific—it must prevent, disrupt, and defeat terrorist operations before attacks occur.
3. **Counterintelligence:** protecting the United States against foreign intelligence operations and espionage. The foreign intelligence threat within the United States is more complex than it has ever been: It comes not only from traditional foreign intelligence services but also from nontraditional, nonstate actors who operate from decentralized organizations.
4. **Cyber:** protecting the United States against cyber-based attacks and high-technology crimes. The cyber threat confronting the United States is rapidly increasing as the number of actors with

the tools and abilities to use computers against the United States or its interests is rising.

5. **Public corruption:** reducing the level of public corruption that harms the United States. Public corruption poses the greatest single threat to the credibility of government institutions at all levels. Some of these cases grab public attention, such as when, at about 6:00 A.M. on December 9, 2008, an FBI agent called on Illinois Governor Rod Blagojevich at his home on the Chicago north side to say he was about to be arrested. Other corruption cases are less visible but no less insidious. Corruption by those controlling the nation's ports of entry and handling the issuance of visas and other identity documents opens the country's borders to potential terrorists and other criminal actors. The serious increase in cases of law enforcement officers forming or supporting drug-trafficking enterprises threatens the safety and security of American streets.
6. **Civil rights:** preventing the violation of federal civil rights as guaranteed by the U.S. Constitution. Federal criminal civil rights statutes protect individuals from hate crimes that interfere with protected activities such as voting, use of public accommodations, and access to housing.
7. **Transnational/national criminal enterprises:** reducing the effect transnational and national criminal enterprises have on the United States. The geopolitical and technological changes of the past decade have allowed these enterprises to flourish globally, and their effect on the United States is expected to increase.
8. **White-collar crime:** reducing the level of significant white-collar crime. By 2008, *The New York Times* reported, the FBI was struggling to find enough agents and resources to investigate criminal wrongdoing (such as mortgage fraud) tied to the U.S. economic crisis. The Bureau had significantly reduced its criminal investigation workforce to expand its national security role after the 9/11 attacks, shifting more than 1800 agents—or nearly one-third of all agents—in criminal programs to terrorism and intelligence duties.
9. **Significant violent crime:** reducing the level of significant violent crime. This type of crime continues to plague American cities, although

violent crime rates have generally decreased since the mid-1990s.

10. **Partnerships:** increasing support to federal, state, county, municipal, and international partners. An important part of the FBI's mission is to provide leadership in criminal justice services to its partners. This mission has never been more important than today, with globalization and convergence of crime and terrorism.

Organizational Structure

To succeed in these 10 lines of business, the Bureau has organized and reorganized itself in a variety of ways. But one feature has remained constant, namely, its division between headquarters (with about 10,000 personnel) and the field (with about 18,000). Let's briefly examine these two components, beginning with the larger and what some would describe as the Bureau's heart and soul—the individual special agents in the field.

The Bureau's investigations are conducted through 56 field offices. Perhaps the best job in the FBI is the Bureau's version of "district manager": the special agent in charge (SAC) of one of the field offices. Almost all SACs (pronounced es-ay-seez) come up through the criminal investigation division rather than through counterintelligence. What makes SACs' jobs attractive is considerable prestige in their locale, together with some autonomy from headquarters in Washington. To be sure, headquarters sets priorities, sorting out commands that have accumulated over the years from its "Board of Directors"—the White House and the several congressional committees having authority over the FBI. Within this framework, SACs have some freedom to choose which problems to attack in their districts.

Besides the 56 field offices, the FBI also has 45 offices located outside the United States. Known as Legal Attaché Offices or "Legats," these units support investigations and operations around the world.

Headquarters provides a range of central services. In its most recent organizational permutation, headquarters consists of five branches, each headed by an executive assistant director:

- National Security
- Criminal, Cyber, Response, and Services
- Human Resources
- Science and Technology (The FBI's highly regarded technical lab is located here.)
- Information and Technology (The FBI's not-so-highly regarded information technology is located here.)

Two Core Functions

As noted in the case introduction, the FBI pursues two broad missions: national security and criminal investigation. Significantly, these two missions are organizationally represented in the first two branches listed above. How do these functions differ? National security requires, as William J. Vizzard explains,

> great patience as information is sifted to find the proverbial needle in the haystack. In fact, many intelligence cases may result only in information that is passed on to other agencies for action. Because the threshold for an initiating investigation is lower than in criminal cases, even direct investigations of suspected terrorists or associates may result not in arrest and prosecution, but in cutting off funds, barring admission to the country, or revoking resident alien status. In these cases, guilt or innocence may remain unclear even to those most informed about the investigation. In addition, agents may be required to refrain from even talking about the cases for years after they are closed.

In contrast, the standard of success for criminal investigations is prosecution, leading to important consequences. For example, Freeh, in the "Pizza Connection" case cited above, secured 18 convictions, paving his way to a big promotion.

Criminal investigations and national security are functions that share many skills, but the organizational cultures may be so different that they might require separate organizational structures. Some think the United States should have an arrangement like the British, where the primary domestic intelligence service, M15, operates separately from Scotland Yard, the country's primary national law enforcement body.

Case Questions

1. Which skills—political management, program management, or resource management—do you think would be most important to the FBI director?
2. Discuss the relevance of the Madisonian, Wilsonian, and Rooseveltian perspectives in this case. Which do you find most useful in understanding the situation facing the director and the agency?
3. Should the FBI have responsibility for both criminal investigations and domestic intelligence?
4. The foundation of strategic planning is long-term forecasting. What do you consider to be the FBI's global "drivers"—that is, broad factors that can directly or indirectly cause changes in the future threat environment? What effect could they have on how the FBI operates? What "shocks" do you think would have the highest impact on the FBI? What events or trends do you think have the highest and lowest probability of occurring?
5. Check out the FBI Web site (www.fbi.gov). How would working for the FBI differ from working for a business?

Case References

Williams, J. Vizzard, "The FBI, Hundred-Year Retrospective," *Public Administration Review* (November/December 2008): 1079–1086; Eric Lichtblau et al., "FBI Struggling to Handle Wave of Finance Cases," *The New York Times* (October 19, 2008); National Academy of Public Administration, *Transforming the FBI: Progress and Challenges* (Washington, DC: National Academy of Public Administration, 2005); Rhodri Jeffreys-Jones, *The FBI: A History* (New Haven, CT: Yale University Press, 2007); Louis J. Freeh, *My FBI* (New York: St. Martin's, 2005); Ronald Kessler, *The Bureau: The Secret History of the FBI* (New York: St. Martin's, 2003); Gerald Posner, *Why America Slept: The Failure to Prevent 9/11* (New York: Random House, 2003); Eric Schmitt, "F.B.I. Agents' Role Is Transformed by Terror Fight," *The New York Times* (August 19, 2009).

PART ONE

Political
Management

The Political-Legal Environment of Administration

Jeffrey MacMillan Photography

CHANCELLOR MICHELLE RHEE

Washington, D.C. Mayor Adrian Fenty is less interested in politics as usual than in the politics of results. Soon after becoming mayor in January 2007, he focused his energy on improving the city 's schools, which are among the worst-performing in the United States. In 2007, Washington ranked last among 11 urban school systems in math and second to last in reading on the National Assessment of Educational Progress report. The failures are particularly acute for poor students and members of minority groups. A black child from a low-income family in Washington enters kindergarten at the same level as a comparable child in New York City but is two years behind by the fourth grade. Not surprisingly, the system has lost students: The current estimate of the student body, 46,000, is less than half of the 1960 total.

The problems of Washington's schools are not limited to the classroom, however. Although the district's $1 billion budget gave the system the third highest per-pupil spending in the country, much of the money went to a bloated bureaucracy that relied on disorganized paper files, kept paying ex-employees while missing paychecks to current teachers, let new textbooks and equipment languish in warehouses, and lacked even a firm enrollment count.

Given these problems, Fenty figured his first step toward improving schools had better be bold. It was. In July 2007, he hired Michelle Rhee as the first chancellor of the District of Columbia Public Schools. Just 38 years old, she would be the first Korean-American chancellor in a city that is mostly black. More to the point, she was a controversial figure in public education because she was not a product of the traditional educational establishment and embraced nontraditional reform mechanisms such as charter schools, vouchers, and the No Child Left Behind Act. In a profile in *The Atlantic*, Clay Risen described her as

> an obsessive worker, the type normally found in consulting firms and medical schools, up at 6 A.M. and often awake until after midnight. She rarely works from notes, usually shows up at meetings without handlers, speaking with the rapid cadence of a high school debater and peppering her sentences with words like *crappy* and *awesome*. On paper and in public, Rhee comes across as passionate and talented, armed with a casual, biting wit.

When Fenty first approached Rhee about the job, she had been reluctant to accept, for she saw herself as a "change agent" and considered Washington a graveyard for careers like hers. The school board was too powerful and too dominated by unions and special interests to give much of a chance to someone intent on closing schools and renegotiating contracts. But she changed her mind after the mayor explained what his second step would be. He would take over control of the city schools from the powerful school board—as New York City's mayor Michael Bloomberg did in 2002—and then provide whatever political cover Rhee needed to completely overhaul the schools. Fenty successfully effected that takeover in July 2008.

Step three was to begin making changes, and Rhee moved with alacrity, firing 98 central office employees, 24 principals, 22 assistant principals, 250 teachers, and 500 teaching aides. She also announced plans to close 23 underused schools and set about restructuring 26 other schools (together, about a third of the system).

These moves were not without a basis. Education reformers like Rhee are influenced by research suggesting that great teachers are far more important to student learning than class size, school resources, or anything else. One study suggests that if black children could get teachers from the profession's most effective quartile for four years in a row, the achievement gap would disappear. As a result, Rhee proposed that teachers surrender some job protections in exchange for the chance to earn more money—up to more than double the average salary for an American public school teacher. But teachers worry that their performance is difficult to measure, that they will be judged by incompetent principals, and that promised bonuses may later dry up. Negotiations proved difficult.

Rhee's critics view her educational theories as having been developed by insensitive nonprofit organizations to be tested on poor, powerless minorities (the "guinea pigs"); her closing and consolidating of schools as leading to administrative and security problems (especially when students from rival neighborhoods are thrust together); and her staff reductions as being excessive. But mostly, her critics charge that her reforms have run roughshod over *their* community.

For example, they point to what happened at the school Rhee's two daughters attend when she began to hear from other parents that the school's principal, Martha Guzman, was unresponsive to various faculty and parent concerns. Although Guzman was popular with many Hispanic parents ("a role model") and had met most academic benchmarks, the chancellor sent her a letter in May 2008 stating her contract would not be renewed and giving no reason. Guzman accepted her termination, but dozens of Hispanic parents didn't and made accusations of racism and classism.

Complaints about the chancellor have also been heard in city council. As one member told her, "Whether or not you and the mayor want to take it out of the political arena, you cannot, because education all over America has political implications. Parents are also voters."

Rhee disagreed: "I think part of the problem of how the district has been run in the past is bad decisions have been made for political reasons and based on what was going to placate and satisfy adults instead of what was in the best interest of children."

Evaluate Rhee as a change agent. What advice would you give her for the short term, and for the long term?

SOURCES: Clay Risen, "The Lightning Rod," *The Atlantic* (November 2008); Nicholas D. Kristuf, "Education's Ground Zero," *The New York Times* (March 22, 2009); Amanda Ripley, "Rhee Tackles Classroom Change," *Time* (November 26, 2008).

Administrators today cannot ignore the political environment of their agencies. In the first place, administrators are involved in both the formulation and implementation of public policy, and because policy decisions so profoundly influence who gets what, this involvement in policy inevitably involves administrators in politics. The first part of this chapter examines the role public administrators and their agencies play in this process.

The formulation and implementation of public policy does not take place in a vacuum. Just recall Figure 1.2. Rather, this chapter argues that these processes unfold in a kind of political force field. In the second section of the chapter, we consider the main constituents of this field, with particular emphasis on the courts.

Merely recognizing and understanding this political-legal environment is not enough, however. If public administrators are going to be effective, they need political competency. Norton Long put the point forcefully: "The lifeblood of administration is power. Its attainment, maintenance, increase, dissipation, and loss are subjects the practitioners can ill afford to neglect."[1] The last two sections consider the implications of this provocative statement.

Public Administration and the Policymaking Process

Most students will recall the neat textbook diagrams in Government 101 outlining how a bill becomes a law, that very logical process by which legislative bodies make public policy. As defined in Chapter 1, a **public policy** is a purposeful course of action followed by government in dealing with a problem. More concretely, it refers to laws—such as the Clean Air Act of 1990—that are broad in scope and significant in impact. In the process of creating policy, students were told, the chief executive is the chief legislator, because most major policies—roughly 80 percent over the past two decades—originate in that office. Further, students learned that members of Congress submit bills, which must pass through committee, be discussed on the floor and in the other chamber, and (prior to a presidential signature) be discussed further in a conference committee. Things were so simple.

The foregoing interpretation of the **policymaking process** is not so much wrong as it is misleading. In the first place, administrators frequently participate in the process. Chief executives rarely make decisions about issues and solutions that have not bubbled up from the echelon of planners just above the career administrators and just below the political appointees of the cabinet and subcabinet.

In the second place, administrative decisions may, in effect, produce policy. For example, the choice of new weapon systems, new state highway routes, new solar energy programs, or the level of price support for agricultural commodities are all likely to be influenced greatly by administrators. In sum, administrative agencies are influential in *both the formulation and implementation of public policy.* This fact is quite important. And at least one political scientist suggested a redefinition of public administration in terms of policymaking: "Public administration is that organized and purposeful interaction of society which, within law, systematically formulates and applies policies of government agencies."[2] Without necessarily subscribing to this definition, we might at least take a closer look at what the formulation and implementation of policy involve. Before taking that close-up, however, it might be useful to take a broader view of the policymaking process—because it certainly consists of more than formulation and implementation.

The Policymaking Process: A Brief Overview

The model of policymaking process that appears in Figure 2.1 divides the process into seven stages. In actual practice, the stages cannot always be so neatly separated. Note also the two-way arrows between each stage. This configuration should suggest that the process is iterative—which is to say, stages can repeat themselves.

During the first stage, problem identification, interest groups and individuals—often referred to as "policy entrepreneurs"—identify certain conditions in society as problematic. Poverty had always existed in the United States, but not until Michael Harrington's *The Other America* appeared in 1963 were certain economic conditions recognized as policy problems. Pesticides such as DDT were viewed as wonders of modern chemistry until Rachel Carson's *Silent Spring* appeared in 1962. The point of these two examples is this: Problems do not come with labels; someone must identify them.

Just because a handful of people have identified a problem does not mean that a public policy will be forthcoming. The problem must be placed on the government's policy agenda, and this requires media attention to the problem and public sentiment that "something ought to be done." When both attention and sentiment reach a sufficiently high level, we can say the issue is on the agenda of the policymakers in government. Getting on the agenda is not as easy as it sounds because (1) there are always scores of issues clamoring for the attention of policymakers and (2) there is room for only a few issues on the agenda.

Figure 2.1   Stages in the Policymaking Process

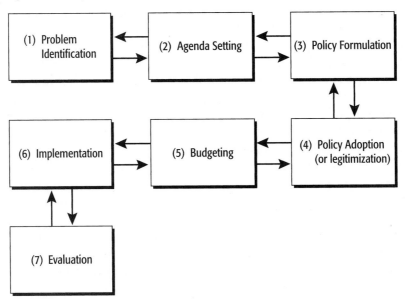

In the next stage, policymakers begin to address the question, What should be done? This means elected officials and administrative agencies—where much of the expertise is located—begin to develop a systematic strategy or a plan of action to solve or at least attenuate the problem. Political scientists call this stage policy formulation.

Most of the action during the fourth and fifth stages occurs in the legislature. The policy that has been formulated must now be approved. This process can be especially contentious. Nonetheless, because the people's representatives are able to debate the merits of a policy proposal and approve it by majority vote, the policy gains legitimacy. Because the policy has legitimacy, even its opponents are likely to support it. That's the way the game is played.

In the language of the legislative process, we say that the policy has been authorized. Now we come to the fifth stage: appropriation. In other words, once the policy has been adopted, the legislature must provide funds to accomplish its objective.

With a budget now in place, the locus of the action returns to the administrative agency or agencies charged with the task of implementing the policy.

The seventh and final stage of the policymaking process is evaluation. The core question here is, How well are the goals of the policy being met? Depending on the answer to that question, several things can happen, ranging from a tweaking of program elements to the outright termination of the policy.

Now that you've seen the big picture, let's take a closer look at the formulation and implementation stages and the role public administration plays in each.

Formulation of Policy

[handwritten: This all has to do with formulatio and how we create processes.]

Although the main movers and shakers in formulating public policies in the executive branch are the political appointees in departments and bureaus, career civil servants themselves provide a productive source of new ideas. In some instances, an administrative agency may conceive of its function largely as accommodating the needs of some interest group, which is representing its specialized clientele (farmers, truckers, bankers, and so on). Thus, the policy proposal is really designed to further those interests.

Such is not always the case. The National Aeronautics and Space Administration (NASA) alone proposed going to the moon. "Operating pretty much in a political vacuum in terms of policy guidance, and basing their choice on what constituted a rational technical program of manned space flight development, NASA planners chose a lunar-landing objective fully two years before President Kennedy announced his choice of the lunar landing as a national goal." Moreover, without the Kennedy decision in 1961, NASA no doubt would have continued pressing for a lunar landing.[3]

Agencies also become involved in policy formulation when they recommend to the legislature amendments to existing laws. A large part—perhaps the major portion—of modern legislation is proposed by administrative agencies. This should not be surprising. Agencies are closest to the action and therefore are more likely to see imperfection and incompleteness in the laws. Indeed, legislatures *expect* that those who deal continuously with problems will suggest improvements.

But bureaucracy probably *stops* far more policy than it formulates. Is this a bad thing? One close observer of Washington thinks not:

> As an entity, the bureaucracy is no better equipped to manufacture grand designs for government programs than carpenters, electricians, and plumbers are to be architects. But if an architect attempted to build a house, the results might well be disastrous. . . . Effective functioning of the governmental machine requires a high degree of stability, uniformity, and awareness of the impact of new policies, regulations, and procedures on the affected public.[4]

Implementation of Policy

Chapter 9 examines the implementation process from a management perspective, but here the perspective is political. More specifically, we want to see how administrative decisions made during the implementation process can, over the long run, shape a policy.

During implementation, administrators find themselves engaged in the following four activities: program operations, rulemaking, investigation, and adjudication. The last three of these activities make up what is known as the **administrative process**. Administrative process involves the administration of laws by administrative agencies, in contrast to **judicial process**, which involves the administration of laws by the courts. Most of what follows will be about administrative process.

Program Operations   Much of an agency's day-to-day **program operations** are not directly concerned with rulemaking, adjudication, or law enforcement. The agency simply administers a program, which means it distributes certain benefits and services, makes loans, provides insurance, constructs dams, puts out fires in a national park, improves the educational opportunities available to educationally disadvantaged children of low-income families, and so forth. But the kinds of decisions an agency makes in administering the programs for which it has been given responsibility can, over time, help determine policy. And the more general the language in the statute, the more this is true. Indeed, some legislative grants of authority to administrators are very broad—for example, the delegation of authority to agencies to make "reasonable" policies for the protection of public health or to eliminate "unfair" trade practices. (What is reasonable? Unfair?)

Rulemaking   Administrative **rulemaking** is the establishment of **prospective rules**—that is, agency statements of general applicability and future effect that concern the rights of private parties. These guidelines have the force and effect of law.

Under the requirements of the federal **Administrative Procedures Act (APA)** of 1946, general notice of proposed rulemaking must be published in the *Federal Register,* as shown in Figure 2.2. The *Register,* published five days a week, also contains the latest presidential orders and rules adopted by agencies and a great variety of official notices. Items range from the results of mileage tests on model autos to a notice that the Mississippi conservation director was granted a federal permit to "capture and transport alligators" in that state and move them "to more advantageous locations."

Figure 2.2   Parallel Codification of Legislation and Regulation

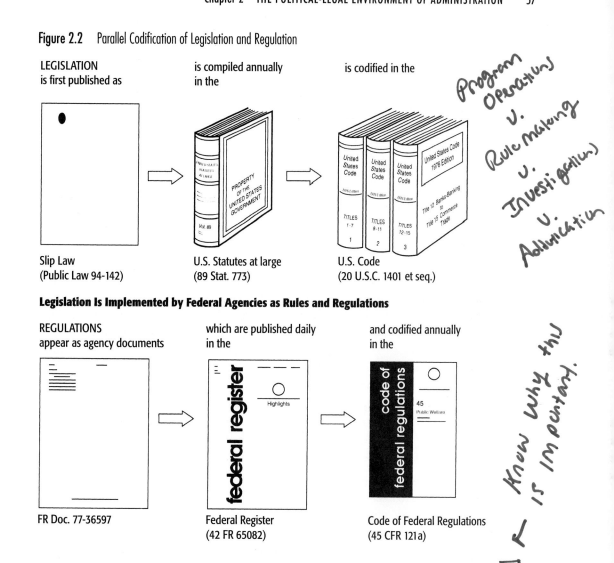

Handwritten notes (right margin): Program Operations v. Rule making v. Investigations v. Adjudication

Handwritten notes (right margin, lower): Know why this is important.

LEGISLATION
is first published as

is compiled annually
in the

is codified in the

Slip Law
(Public Law 94-142)

U.S. Statutes at large
(89 Stat. 773)

U.S. Code
(20 U.S.C. 1401 et seq.)

Legislation Is Implemented by Federal Agencies as Rules and Regulations

REGULATIONS
appear as agency documents

which are published daily
in the

and codified annually
in the

FR Doc. 77-36597

Federal Register
(42 FR 65082)

Code of Federal Regulations
(45 CFR 121a)

Administrative agencies also establish **interpretive rules**. These rules are not legally binding on the public but simply indicate how an agency plans to interpret and enforce its statutory authority. For example, the Equal Employment Opportunity Commission periodically issues interpretive rules, usually referred to as enforcement guidelines, indicating how it plans to interpret and apply a provision of a certain statute, such as the Americans with Disabilities Act. When making interpretive rules, an agency need not follow the requirements of the APA.

The most commonly used rulemaking procedure is called **notice-and-comment rulemaking**. This procedure involves three basic steps: (1) notice of the proposed rulemaking, (2) a comment period, and (3) the final rule.

1. *Notice of the proposed rulemaking.* As noted, when a federal agency decides to create a new rule, the agency publishes a notice of the proposed rulemaking proceedings in

the *Federal Register*. The notice states where and when the proceedings will be held, the agency's legal authority for making the rule (usually its enabling legislation), and the terms or subject matter of the proposed rule.

2. *Comment period*. Following publication of the notice of the proposed rulemaking proceedings, the agency must allow ample time for persons to comment in writing on the proposed rule. This comment period gives interested parties the opportunity to express their views on the proposed rule in an effort to influence agency policy. The comments may be in writing or, if a hearing is held, may be given orally. A typical hearing might involve an Environmental Protection Agency (EPA) official discussing proposals to curtail hydrocarbon emission in a city. The proposals might range from controversial (for example, gasoline rationing and limiting car travel) to mundane (for example, establishing carpools and installing vapor-recovery systems at service stations). In any event, the agency comes up with the final proposals.

The agency need not respond to all comments, but it must respond to any significant comments that bear directly on the proposed rule. The agency responds by either modifying its final rule or explaining, in a statement accompanying the final rule, why it did not make the proposed changes. In some circumstances, particularly when the procedure being used in a specific instance is less formal, an agency may accept comments after the comment period is closed. The agency should summarize these private, "off-the-record" comments in the record for possible review.

3. *The final rule*. After the agency reviews the comments, it drafts the final rule and publishes it in the *Federal Register*. As shown in Figure 2.2, the final rule is later compiled with the rules and regulations of other federal administrative agencies in the *Code of Federal Regulations*. Final rules have binding legal effect—unless the courts overturn them.

Rulemaking is a continual national activity for more than 100 agencies. Collectively, the volume of rules is to a substantial extent its policy. Rulemaking involves modifying existing policies as well as adopting new ones: the Department of Agriculture describes the labeling requirements for pesticides one day; the Food and Drug Administration (FDA) prescribes safe levels of pesticide residues on plants the next; and an agency in the Department of the Interior sets a different standard of pesticide toxicity for fish and fowl on another.

Investigations   Administrative agencies conduct investigations of the entities that they regulate. One type of agency investigation occurs during the rulemaking process to obtain information about a certain individual, firm, or industry. The purpose of such an investigation is to ensure that the rule issued is based on a consideration of relevant factors rather than being arbitrary and capricious. After final rules are issued, agencies conduct investigations to monitor compliance with those rules. A typical agency investigation of this kind might begin when a citizen reports a possible violation. (See Cartoon.)

Many agencies gather information through on-site inspections. Sometimes, inspecting an office, a factory, or some other business facility is the only way to obtain the evidence needed to prove a regulatory violation. Administrative inspections and tests cover a wide range of activities, including safety inspections of underground coal mines, safety tests of

commercial equipment and automobiles, and environmental monitoring of factory emissions. An agency may also ask a firm or individual to submit certain documents or records to the agency for examination.

Normally, business firms comply with agency requests to inspect facilities or business records because it is in any firm's interest to maintain a good relationship with regulatory bodies. In some instances, however, such as when a firm thinks an agency request is unreasonable and may be detrimental to the firm's interest, the firm may refuse to comply with the request. In such situations, an agency may resort to the use of a subpoena or a search warrant.

Adjudication   After conducting an investigation of a suspected rule violation, an agency may begin to take administrative action against an individual or organization. Most administrative actions are resolved through negotiated settlements at their initial stages, without the need for formal adjudication. Depending on the agency, negotiations may take the form of a simple conversation or a series of informal conferences. Whatever form the negotiations take, their purpose is to rectify the problem to the agency's satisfaction and eliminate the need for additional proceedings.

If a settlement cannot be reached, the agency may issue a formal complaint against the suspected violator. For example, if the EPA finds a factory polluting groundwater in violation of federal pollution laws, the agency will issue a complaint against the violator in a effort to bring the plant into compliance with federal regulations. The factory charged in the complaint may respond by filing an answer to the EPA's allegations. If the factory and the EPA cannot agree on a settlement, the case is heard in a trial-like setting before an administrative law judge (ALJ).

The ALJ presides over the hearing and has the power to administer oaths, take testimony, rule on questions of evidence, and make determinations of fact. Although the ALJ formally works for the agency prosecuting the case, the law requires the ALJ to be an unbiased adjudicator (judge).

Certain safeguards prevent bias on the part of the ALJ and promote fairness in the proceedings. For example, the APA requires that the ALJ be separate from an agency's investigative and prosecutorial staff. The APA also prohibits ex parte (private) communications between the ALJ and any party to an agency proceeding, such as the EPA or the factory. Finally, provisions of the APA protect the ALJ from agency disciplinary actions unless the agency can show good cause for such an action.

Hearing procedures vary from agency to agency. Administrative agencies generally exercise substantial discretion over the type of hearing procedure that will be used. Frequently, disputes are resolved through informal adjudication proceedings. For example, the parties, their counsel, and the ALJ may simply meet at a table in a conference room for the dispute-settlement proceedings.

In contrast, a formal adjudicatory hearing resembles a trial in many respects. Prior to the hearing, the parties are permitted to undertake extensive discovery (involving depositions and requests for documents or other information). During the hearing, the parties may give testimony, present other evidence, and cross-examine adverse witnesses. A significant difference between a trial and an administrative agency hearing, though, is that normally much more information, including hearsay (secondhand information), can be introduced as evidence during an administrative hearing.

Following a hearing, the ALJ renders an initial order, or decision, on the case. Either party can appeal the ALJ's decision to the board or commission that governs the agency. If a party is dissatisfied with the commission's decision, it can appeal the decision to a federal court of appeals. If no party appeals the case, the ALJ's decision becomes the final order of the agency. The ALJ's decision also becomes final if a party appeals and the commission and the court decline to review the case. If a party appeals the case and the case is reviewed, the final order comes from the commission's decision or (if that decision is appealed to a federal appellate court) that of the court.

To summarize, as administrative agencies implement policy, conflicts can arise between agencies and citizens. **Adjudication** is a quasi-judicial process conducted by the agency to ensure—as guaranteed in the Constitution—that no person can be deprived of "life, liberty, or property without due process of law." The APA spells out the procedures that make those memorable words realities and the safeguards that protect individuals from "arbitrary and capricious" actions by a government agency. When a "person," a term that includes corporations, is charged by an agency with wrongful conduct and is subject to sanctions, the person must have an opportunity for a hearing before that body. Implicit in these proceedings is the right of the defendant to a fair and impartial hearing.

A Simple Descriptive Model of the Administrative Process

Having looked at each of the three key activities of the administrative process—rulemaking, investigation, and adjudication—it might be useful to bring them together a simple descriptive model.[5] Figure 2.3 outlines the relationships among the various actors and institutions in the administrative justice system. Each agency differs somewhat in its method of dealing with administrative law problems, but this general description provides a kind of road map.

The road begins in the lower right-hand corner of the figure, where single-shot and repeat players place demands on the system. Who are these players? *Single-shot players* are generally individuals who rarely deal with government agencies. Examples include those who apply for benefits from the Department of Veterans Affairs or the Social Security Administration. They are not usually represented by legal counsel, are generally under pressure to get a response quickly, and may know very little about the agencies and programs with which they are dealing.

Figure 2.3   A Simple Model of the Administrative Process

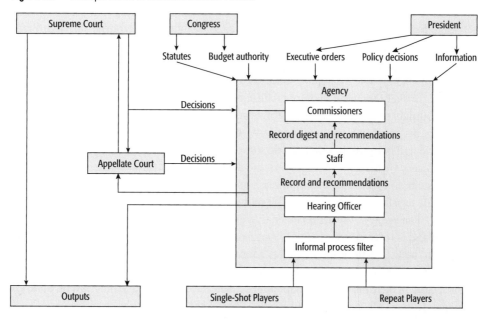

SOURCE: *From Cooper, Public Law and Public Administration, 4E*, p. 15. (c) 2007 Wadsworth, a part of Cengage Learning, Inc. Reproduced by permission. HYPERLINK "http://www.cengage.com/permission" www.cengage.com/permission.

Repeat players, on the other hand, are typically organizations such as drug companies and manufacturing firms that have more or less continuous, long-term relationships with particular agencies. They generally have counsel to represent them and substantial financial and technical resources to deploy. Consequently, they operate with greater flexibility when dealing with agencies.

As mentioned, single-shot and repeat players place demands on the system. The demands of the former may be nothing more than a telephone call to the Department of Veterans Affairs requesting information on the procedure to apply for educational benefits. Repeat players frequently seek different kinds of information. Whatever the demand, it is usually passed through an *informal process filter,* in which an attempt is made to resolve problems short of formal legal actions.

Now let's see what happens when the "players" and the government agency can't reach a settlement. A common first step in cases requiring a more formal process is consideration of the matter by a hearing officer, or an ALJ. The ALJ develops a record containing pertinent documents, written submissions, and in some cases transcripts of oral testimony; decides questions of fact; and makes preliminary conclusions as to the disposition of the matter under consideration. If an appeal is needed, it will usually be an administrative appeal in which the record will be examined by other officers within the agency. In rule-making proceedings, the record developed by the ALJ moves up to agency heads for a final decision on whether and in what form to issue a regulation. Given the number and complexity of the decisions that department heads or commissions are called on to make, the work of agency staff members in aiding the decision makers is crucial.

Some form of review of agency decisions can be sought in the courts, although there are significant limits on the scope and nature of judicial review (more about these limits later). If a case presents important legal questions, there may be appeals within the judicial system leading to a possible—although extremely rare—hearing in the U.S. Supreme Court. More likely, the road to outputs will run from either the commissioners or a hearing officer. Outputs can take a variety of forms such as opinions on claims, licenses, services, rules, benefits, sanctions, recommendations, routes, and rates. Whatever the outcome, this much is clear: There will be winners and losers.

As shown in Figure 2.3, both Congress and the president also influence the administrative justice system. Congress creates, empowers, funds, and conducts oversight of the agencies, as do the state legislatures at that level. The statutes are vital because they define and limit the authority of an agency. Any action taken that exceeds the statutory authority is by definition unlawful and is referred to as an *ultra vires* (pronounced UL-tra VI-res) action. After all, nothing in the U.S. Constitution requires administrative agencies to have or grants agencies any authority. Most are created by statutes under the Article I, Section 8, Powers of Congress. (This section of the Constitution—sometimes called the elastic clause—makes it possible for Congress to enact all "necessary and proper" laws to carry out its responsibilities.)

The executive branch, aside from its general policymaking and management functions, provides specific policy directives to agencies. For example, the rules governing classification of government documents stem from an **executive order** issued by presidents from Franklin D. Roosevelt to George W. Bush. President Clinton used executive orders to provide financial guarantees in the Mexican peso crisis, to seek to block the replacement of

"Isn't it about time we issued some new guidelines for something?"

Comment: The relaxed, nonchalant world depicted here seems inconsistent with the busyness portrayed in Figure 2.2. Which do you think comes closest to capturing the realities of the public administrator's world?

striking workers, and to implement many of the aspects of his administration's "reinventing government" initiative (discussed in Chapter 7).

Public Administration and the Force Field of Politics

As noted above, the model presented in Figure 2.1 drastically simplifies reality in several ways. But one of the biggest simplifications was not noted: The model fails to show that the process unfolds in a highly charged **political force field**.

Figure 2.4   Graphic Representation of Political Field Surrounding a Single Public Administrator

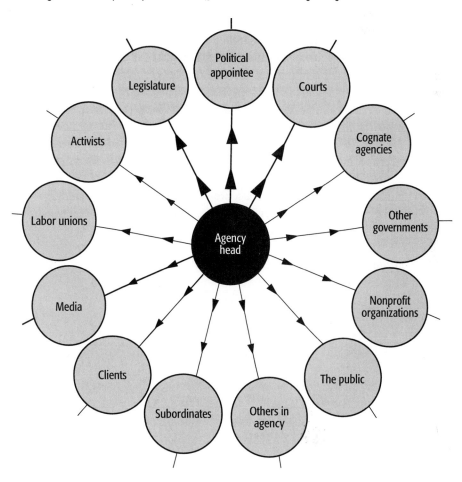

The straight lines radiating in all directions from the public administrator agency head indicate the lines of force that constitute the daily political environment. Although the lines do not quite extend on to infinity, they are likely to extend well beyond any specific individual or group appearing in the surrounding circles. For example, beyond the political appointee may be a chief executive or a board of directors; beyond the legislators, the voters; beyond a district court, the Supreme Court; beyond subordinates, still other subordinates (because everybody in a public agency may feel that he or she has a legitimate piece of the action and must be involved); beyond a client, an interest group or trade association; and so on.

The field concept conveniently lends itself to graphic representation. Consider a single, isolated administrator (Figure 2.4). What is the political field surrounding him or her? If arrows are drawn from the administrator through certain individuals and institutions, the resulting porcupine quills provide a two-dimensional picture of the political field. We may attach arrowheads to the radiating lines to indicate the various directions of "pull" being exerted on the administrator.

The lines constructed in this way are called, as in physics, lines of force. They provide a picture of the administrator's political field; the thickness and number of arrows illustrate the strength of a particular field.

Well, who are the players in the administrator's political force field? Although they obviously vary from agency to agency, we can sketch a general picture of the field. For a federal agency, the "big three" players are clear enough: the political appointee, the legislature, and the courts. Before taking a closer look at this trio, let's take at least a cursory look at the other entities in Figure 2.4.

At the bottom of the figure, you will note *subordinates* and *others in agency.* Many regard politics in organizational life with suspicion. Office politics—that netherworld of innuendo, dissembling, manipulation, and gamesmanship—have tainted the positive aspects of having political skills. Yet the difference between someone who can get an idea off the ground and accepted within his or her agency and someone who can't isn't a question of who has the better idea. It is a question of who has political competency (more about that later).

Moving clockwise, we next come to *clients.* Top administrators are quite sensitive to the dominant interest groups, or **clients**, they represent. Nowhere is this more evident than with the federal regulatory agencies. As one Justice Department deputy assistant attorney general put it: There are "incredible love affairs going on between the regulators and the regulated." As a result, critics say, agencies often condone or even champion monopolistic practices and rubber-stamp higher prices for everything from natural gas to telephone calls. Regulators, on the other hand, say that they are not unduly influenced and that they cannot be insulated from the regulated if they do their jobs right. Every agency has its own constituency that helps it do battle (especially around budget time). The Department of Defense has contractors, the EPA has the Sierra Club, the Foreign Aid Agency has the League of Women Voters, the Labor Department has unions, the Federal Communications Commission has broadcasters, the Department of Housing and Urban Development has the National League of Cities, and so on.

Then there's the news *media.* In his analysis of the press's impact on federal policy-making, Martin Linsky concluded that the better relations policymakers maintain with the media, the more successful they will be in doing their jobs. In short, skill in handling the media means success in governing.[6] Linsky supports his conclusions with extensive polling data from individuals who served as assistant secretaries or above in the administrations of five consecutive U.S. presidents up to and including Reagan. Most of the officials considered time spent with the press as a resource that enhanced job performance rather than as an unwelcome drain on their time. Ninety-seven percent agreed that the press affected federal policy, with the majority stating that the effect is significant. Three out of four of the assistant secretaries reported that they had tried to get media coverage for their agency and its activities, and nearly all had used the media to obtain information about their policy area. Close to half of the officials had spent five hours or more a week dealing with press matters.

Although the membership of *labour unions* has dropped to 8.5 percent in the private U.S. workforce, the share of government workers in unions has held steady at around 38 percent. As we will see in Chapter 10, the political influence of union members in government varies considerably by jurisdiction and profession. In urban industrial states and large urban areas, public unions play major policymaking roles; in less industrialized regions, the involvement is less. Today there are three prominent and powerful public service unions and numerous lesser ones that speak for many—although certainly not all—public employees: the American Federation of State, County and Municipal Employees; the American Federation of Government Employees; and the American Federation of Teachers.

No organization is safe from the wrath of *activist groups*. Besides demonstrations, another popular tactic for activist groups is the boycott. The past two decades have witnessed boycotts over such issues as abortion, gay rights, animal rights, workers' rights, and race. A high-profile, politically motivated boycott can cost a state or a city millions in convention and tourism business. But the most common tactic is the easiest: the lawsuit. Typically the process begins when an advocacy group such as the American Civil Liberties Union, or Legal Aid files a suit on behalf of an aggrieved individual or group, claiming that their civil rights have been violated under federal or state statute. At that point, the government agency generally has two options. The first is to settle with the plaintiff by entering into a consent decree that outlines the specific actions the government will take to fix the problem. The other option, to take the case to trial, is riskier.

Before turning to the big three programs in the public administrator's environment (legislatures, political appointees, and courts), four more entities need mention: cognate agencies, other governments or jurisdictions, nonprofit organizations, and the public.

For every government agency or organization, there exists one or more units that are somehow kindred or related to it. For example, police departments and fire departments may be separate organizations in a city, but they are connected (both are first responders in emergencies) and have an affinity (members of both organizations wear uniforms and have ranks). In considering how government goes about attacking problems—say pollution, regional economic development, and workforce development—the term *cognate agencies* seems a handy way of indicating that seldom will only one agency be involved. Cognate agencies also compete for specific programs: the Bureau of Reclamation versus the Army Corps of Engineers, the Federal Reserve Board versus the Treasury Department, the Air Force versus the Navy, the Soil Conservation Service versus the Agricultural Extension Service, and so on. In the new era of genetic engineering, the National Institutes of Health (NIH), the EPA, the Department of Agriculture, the FDA, and assorted elements of the White House all jockey for position.

Is all this jurisdictional and mission overlap, which breeds so much interagency conflict, bad? The problems are clear enough. Agencies become rigid and uncompromising. The results, at best, can be wasted time and money—at worst, policy stalemate in the face of critical problems. But we must be careful here because more might be involved than economy and efficiency. Do not this duplication and overlap provide greater access to and representation of different views and interests? Might not the duplication of mission management and information gathering by cognate agencies provide backups and correcting forces for errors and bad judgments? Did the United States really become more secure in 2002 after the creation of the Department of Homeland Security? Did the United States really become better at connecting the dots in 2004 after all intelligence activities became subsumed under a director of national intelligence[7]

Agency heads must deal not only with other agencies but also with **other governments**—indeed, if we count counties, municipalities, and townships, there are nearly 40,000 governments in the United States! The importance of these other governments in the political force field cannot be overemphasized. As we will see in Chapter 3, apart from a few programs, such as the Social Security system, the federal government is not a direct provider of domestic public services. Instead, the majority of national domestic programs are implemented through a complex arrangement among federal, state, and local governments. This approach to public services delivery reflects the fact that the United States is a federal system in which responsibilities are both divided and shared among separate levels of government, each possessing a base of legal and fiscal authority. And that makes conditions ripe for political conflict.

The role of ***nonprofit organizations*** in governance was discussed in Chapter 1. For instance, in the aftermath of Hurricane Katrina in 2005, the two most important nonprofit organizations with which federal, state, and local governments had to coordinate were the Salvation Army and the Red Cross. In some of the poorest parts of Mississippi and much of the Gulf Coast, the Salvation Army drew praise for its swift arrival. To some of the desperate residents, the Red Cross, by letting bureaucratic hurdles slow down aid in the disaster area, suffered by comparison.[8]

One last "medium-sized" player needs mention. Elusive, ever-changing, and sometimes the biggest player of all is *the public*. Lincoln put it simply: "Public opinion in this country is everything." Public administration and, in a larger sense, all government rests on public opinion. Administrators who can inform or influence public opinion can influence the accomplishment of goals just as much. How does one do that? **Public relations** is the management function that assesses public attitudes, identifies the policies of an organization with the public interest, and then executes a program of action to earn public understanding and acceptance. Chapter 12 discusses how agency heads can use public relations to inform and constructively influence the people.

The Political Appointee Connection

Presidential appointees head every department and agency in the federal government and work closely with the senior executives of those departments and agencies. As career professionals, the latter continue in their jobs regardless of who is in the White House. Together these two types of executives—political and career—constitute the leadership of the federal bureaucracy. All told, there are 10,000 executives: 3,000 political and 7,000 career. Of the 3,000 political appointees, roughly 600 are subject to Senate confirmation, while the rest are appointed solely by the president. (Governors have much more limited powers of appointment.)

The number of appointees has grown dramatically over the past three decades as the federal government has "thickened" with more layers of leadership and more leaders at each layer. This thickening contributes to a weakening of accountability between the top and bottom of government. Presidents and their political appointees may be unable to see the bottom of government, and that can increase the freedom of public administrators to enforce or not enforce the public policies as they see fit.[9]

Although many political appointees are eminently qualified for their positions, some are not. After Michael Brown's "resignation" as head of the Federal Emergency Management Agency (FEMA) just days after Hurricane Katrina hit Louisiana and Mississippi in 2005, newspapers reported that Brown's previous position had been head of the International Arabian Horse Association. A study by David E. Lewis at Princeton University suggests that the case of Michael Brown represents just one extreme example of the problem of unqualified outsiders heading government agencies. Using the Bush administration's Program Assessment Rating Tool, which grades federal programs on a scale of 1 to 100, Lewis found that agencies headed by career civil servants scored five or six points higher on average than those run by political appointees. He notes that although political appointees tend to have more education and more varied management experience than agency heads, longtime civil servants have experience within the agencies they head and tend to remain in their posts longer than political appointees. In addition, political appointees are likely to have other appointees rather than experienced civil servants as their key advisers. Brown's FEMA, the study notes, had a particularly "appointee-laden" management structure.[10]

The Nature of the Tension   For a number of reasons, tension exists between the executives appointed by elected officials and the government employees they are supposed to lead. First, agencies form alliances with legislative subcommittees and outside interest groups; this enables, and indeed encourages, them to pursue independent policy courses. These alliances are discussed later in the chapter. Second, if the president or his appointees can be at cross-purposes with agencies over the *ends* of policy, so too can they be over the *means*. For example, in attempting to attain policy goals, presidents are often driven to economize and to reorganize—two activities that invariably upset some agency interests. Third, agencies have a tendency to become resistant to change because of strong ties to traditional policies and the professional orientation of careerists. Finally, the average tenure of political appointees is only 18 months.

Not surprisingly, presidents wanting to be effective have increasingly circumvented large bureaucracies either by using their own staff or by setting up new agencies. President John F. Kennedy understood well the difficulty of converting a tradition-ridden bureaucracy into a mechanism for providing information and making decisions. Nevertheless, it was a constant puzzle to him why the State Department remained so formless and impenetrable. He would say, "Damn it, Bundy [one of Kennedy's advisers] and I get more done in one day in the White House than they do in six months in the State Department." Giving the State Department an instruction, he remarked, is like dropping it in the dead-letter box.[11]

Yet the president and his appointees do not stand helpless. In addition to his formidable command over the public attention and his power to appoint key administrators, the president has the **Office of Management and Budget (OMB)**. The largest of the executive office components, the OMB has two main functions: the first is preparation of the budget, a process examined in detail in Chapter 11; the second is **legislative clearance**. Before an agency can submit new legislation to Congress, that legislation must be cleared by the OMB to ensure that it is consistent with the goals and policies of the administration.

In recent years, the OMB has begun to take on a third function: the coordination and evaluation of executive branch programs. Chapter 9 is devoted to a few of the management techniques executives at all levels of government use to gain better control over the bureaucracy.

Surviving in the Political Force Field: Managing the Political Boss   The theme of this chapter is that there is more to public administration than handling an agency's internal affairs. Those who might be effective at handling internal operations may become quite uncomfortable when faced with the variety of external factors portrayed in Figure 2.3. Fortunately, there are strategies for coping with some of the more important of these factors. For instance, more than any other individual, the political executive is critical to the success of a public administrator. His or her support will be vital to attaining the agency's goals and missions. Here, then, are seven approaches for gaining the backing of the political executive—or any boss for that matter:

1. Seek information about the boss's goals, problems, and pressures. Be alert for opportunities to question the boss and others around him or her to test your assumptions. Do this continually because priorities and concerns change.
2. Make sure the boss understands what can be expected from you and what you and your people are concentrating on. Recognize how much your boss is dependent on you.
3. Get the boss personally involved in those programs that are near and dear to his or her heart.
4. Adjust your working style in response to the boss's preferred methods of operating. For example, some bosses like to get information in report form so they can read and study it; others work better with information and reports presented in person so they can ask questions.
5. Keep the boss informed. Send regular reports. Let the chief know of potential problems—few like unpleasant surprises.
6. Work to establish a business "friendship" in addition to an effective boss–subordinate relationship. Establish channels of communication other than through work. If the boss likes you, he or she will be more likely to trust you and see you as a member of the team. In any event, never criticize the boss in public. Take the heat and share the credit.
7. Get along with the boss's staff. If they are competent, they can be useful allies. Even if they are not, they control access to the boss and probably have a good sense of his or her views. Pick your fights with the staff carefully.

The Legislative Connection

"To understand the organization of the executive branch," writes a distinguished scholar of American government, "one must first understand the organization and culture of the Congress and the high degree of congressional involvement in administrative decisions."[12] One important means by which Congress exercises formal authority over agencies is by setting policy, a process already discussed in this chapter. To the extent that congressional power is fragmented, the programs administered by a federal agency are fragmented. Thus, the chaotic character of social programs can often be traced to congressional sources—specifically, the conflicts between congressional authorization and the appropriations committees, the desire of legislators to author their own pet bills regardless of the narrow structure of the categories found in each, the tendency to legislate redundant programs to remain popular with constituents, and the practice of latching onto faddish ideas that seem popular with the public at the expense of more essential programs that are not in vogue.[13]

Legislation with a Pervasive Influence Some congressional policies have a pervasive influence on the operations of agencies. The **Freedom of Information Act (FOIA)** of 1966, sunset laws, and sunshine laws are prime examples. The FOIA gives any person the right to request information from agencies and to file action in federal court if the request is denied.

Pioneered by Colorado, **sunset laws** provide that an agency is automatically abolished, or self-destructs, after a period of years (perhaps seven or ten) unless the legislature passes a law extending its existence. Many states already have such laws, but to date sunset legislation has only been proposed at the federal level.

Another reform, **sunshine laws**, requires that formal government business meetings be open to the public. The federal government's Sunshine Act of 1977 requires all independent regulatory commissions to give advance notice of their meetings. The Sunshine Act was passed to put an end to the infamous smoke-filled room and to give the public "the fullest practicable information regarding the decision-making process of the federal government." Sunlight, as Supreme Court Justice Benjamin Cardozo (1870–1938) once said, is the best disinfectant. The act requires 50 or so federal commissions, boards, corporations, and authorities to "conduct their meetings in the open rather than behind closed doors."

Although the movement to increase the availability of information between government and its constituents has provided better insight into the rationale behind agency decisions, it also has had unintended consequences, especially for collegial decision making. Some agencies have gone to considerable lengths to avoid real debate in these open public meetings. For example, there is an increasing tendency to arrive at decisions by carefully writing out positions on issues. Commissioners also use their special assistants to relay information; hold closed meetings as trial runs for formal, open meetings; and delegate decision making to staffs.[14] Unfortunately, passage of the Sunshine Act actually has meant less robust discussion and debate. After all, who wants to appear uncertain (by expressing tentative or not fully informed views) or unprincipled (by playing the devil's advocate) in a room full of reporters?

Oversight and Appropriations / There was very little about Wednesday, June 21, 2000, that pleased Secretary of Energy Bill Richardson. His appearance before the Senate Armed Services Committee that morning quickly turned into a *grilling*. Legislators were incredulous when Los Alamos and Energy Department officials, testifying along with Richardson, said that no rules prevented certain laboratory employees from signing out highly classified hard drives or from walking out with them.

Richardson, a Democrat, was assailed by legislators of both parties. While Republicans renewed their calls for his resignation, one of the most senior Democratic senators said the energy secretary had shown contempt for Congress by failing to appear at a Senate hearing the previous week to explain the disappearance of the hard drives. What Richardson no doubt thought was a grilling was to Senator Robert C. Byrd and other committee members merely the exercise of congressional **oversight**. At its best, oversight involves continuing, systematic supervision by Congress of the performance of the executive branch—how well government programs are working and how honestly, efficiently, or faithfully the laws are being administered. By and large, though, oversight has been infrequent and slipshod. The reasons are political: There is just more political mileage in running errands for constituents and more satisfaction in passing new laws. Tough oversight, on the other hand, can make enemies among congressional colleagues or powerful interest groups.

Still, some members of Congress practice oversight with a vengeance. Former Senator William Proxmire was perhaps the best-known watchdog of the bureaucracy. Among his targets of waste have been the supersonic transport plane, federal limousines, and National Science Foundation grants. Each month he gave his own Golden Fleece Award for what he felt was the greatest waste of the taxpayer's money. One award went to the National Institute of Mental Health for funding a study of why bowlers, hockey fans, and pedestrians smile. Another went to the Commerce Department's Economic Development Administration, which had provided Bedford, Indiana, a $200,000 grant to build a limestone model of Egypt's Pyramid of Cheops. Although some of his awards were, no doubt, deserved, others showed an ignorance of science. Studying the sexual habits of the Australian toad might bring congressional guffaws, but medical researchers knew that genetic research, the frogs, and birth defects in humans were all related.

Legislative oversight is strengthened by the **Government Accountability Office (GAO)**, an operating staff arm of Congress created in 1921 and originally designed to audit government expenditures. For that reason, it was originally called the General *Accounting* Office. Since 1950 the GAO has been moving into what might be called management audits. These audits are policy oriented, seeking to determine the bases for agency decisions and actions. (See Chapter 11 for a fuller discussion of the GAO.)

Critics of legislative oversight contend that it often leads to micromanagement, which can be expensive. The Agriculture Department cannot even study whether potential savings might result from the consolidation of Forest Service regional offices. The secretary of defense cannot even close a small facility in a state in which both senators say defense spending should be cut. The Veterans Administration needs congressional approval for any personnel action affecting three or more people.[15]

Briefing Suggestions [handwritten]

The other means by which Congress, or any other U.S. legislative body, exercises control over executive agencies is the appropriations process. Harold Seidman summarizes what the words "power of the purse" can mean to a public administrator:

> As allies, the executive agencies and legislative committees make common cause against the "third house of Congress": the appropriations committees. Lords of the executive establishment generally enjoy the cozy atmosphere of legislative committee hearings, where they are received with courtesy and the deference due their office. But they shun, wherever possible, meetings with appropriations subcommittees, whose chairmen on occasion may accord them about the same amount of deference as a hardboiled district attorney shows to a prisoner in the dock.
>
> Actions by the appropriations committees may override presidential directives or nullify laws enacted by the Congress itself. The appropriations "rider" is frequently employed for this purpose. Provisions attached to the appropriations acts reversed administration regulations and policies on school busing and abortion. Riders have also controlled such administrative details as proposed reductions in the time required for Marine Corps basic training, the consolidation of training programs for Navy helicopter pilots, and exemptions from environmental impact statements.[16]

Surviving in the Political Force Field: Influencing Legislators Administrators have the opportunity to exercise influence over congressional committees, state legislative committees, and city councils. Presenting testimony is one such opportunity. Here are some suggestions to make testimony more effective:

- *Tailor the text, delivery, and style of your testimony to fit your own personality.* It should be simple, crisp, sharp, conversational, and natural. The end result should be like a conversation between you and someone you like very much.
- *Be prepared.* You shouldn't testify unless you have fully prepared for every possibility. You should know your material so well that you can make it come alive.
- *Concentrate on your audience.* They are the reason you are testifying. It is important to realize exactly who is listening to you. You have five audiences at most hearings: members of the body holding the hearing, the press, committee staff, other interested persons, and those waiting to testify. The committee members and the press are the most important—and many of them aren't knowledgeable about your field. It is vital to remember that fact, so do not get technical.
- *Come prepared with two texts—one detailed, one abbreviated.* Often the committee's chairperson will interrupt the witness after a few sentences: "Because our time is limited, please summarize your remarks."
- *Get advice* on your remarks from others who are experts.
- *Persuade.* Everyone in your audience falls into one of three ideological categories: those who are on your side, those who oppose your views, and those who haven't made up their minds. The best strategy is to talk to those who haven't decided. It's unlikely that you'll change strongly held views.
- *Remember: Testifying is not merely reading words; it's communicating ideas.*[17]

Administrators also influence legislators in one-on-one settings. Assuming the administrator is seeking favorable treatment of a certain program, what factors will determine a legislator's vote on it? The first factor is a legislator's judgments about the merits of the program. The second is the political angle. What will the vote mean in terms of getting reelected? What will it mean in terms of maintaining influence in the legislative body? Will it cause the legislator to lose support for some other program? The third factor is a procedural one. Members do not want to violate the "rules of the game" in their legislative body. Legislators feel, for example, that they should defer, as much as possible, to the recommendations of a committee that has worked intensively to develop those recommendations. Finally, the demands of loyalty and friendship will affect a legislator's vote.

The Judicial Connection

To analyze the complex relations between courts and administrative agencies, it is useful to think in terms of three broad areas of concern. First is *administrative responsibility*—that is, the rulings of courts help ensure that the actions taken by public administrators are responsive, fair, and honest. Another important area in which courts influence administrative agencies involves *public employees,* for the Supreme Court has placed important limitations on the flexibility of managers to supervise their employees and operate their organizations. The third area of interest to anyone trying to understand the complex relationships between courts and agencies is *administrative law*—that is, the body of law that defines the power, limits, and procedures of administrative agencies. Because administrative responsibility and human resource management are the focus of Chapters 4 and 10, it will be more efficient to deal with the court influence in these areas later rather than now. Here the focus is on administrative law.

In reviewing an administrative agency's decision, a court considers the following types of issues:

1. Whether the agency has exceeded its authority under its enabling legislation
2. Whether the agency has properly interpreted laws applicable to the agency action under review
3. Whether the agency has violated any constitutional provisions
4. Whether the agency has acted in accordance with the procedural requirements of the law
5. Whether the agency's actions were arbitrary, capricious, or an abuse of discretion
6. Whether any conclusions drawn by the agency are not supported by substantial evidence

Unfortunately, these general questions fail to convey the reality of the court's role in public administration. So let's consider the following specific administrative actions, which all have one thing in common—*courts found them illegal:*[18]

- Seeking to budget more rationally and to reduce fraud and error, Connecticut and Pennsylvania established a one-year residency requirement as part of their eligibility standards for receiving welfare benefits.

- In Texas, a constable fired an employee who, after hearing of an attempted assassination of President Ronald Reagan, remarked, "Shoot, if they go for him again, I hope they get him."
- Over a period of years, a small Mississippi town concentrated its economic development and new infrastructure on its business district and an adjacent neighborhood.
- In Delaware, a patrol officer, for no particular reason other than the fact that it was part of his job, made a routine stop of a car to check the driver's license and registration.
- In a city in Georgia, several patrol officers were dismissed for removing the American flags from their uniforms as part of a public protest against racism on the police force.
- In Cleveland, a school district security guard was removed for failing to report that he had once been convicted of a felony.
- Well into the 1970s, Chicago and surrounding Cook County continued to practice the historic art of firing members of the opposition party from public service.
- On the federal level, Congress delegated its legislative authority to an executive branch agency and subsequently attempted to control its use through a legislative veto.
- The Gramm-Rudman-Hollings Budget Deficit Reduction Act of 1985 vested budget-cutting authority in the comptroller-general, who headed the General Accounting Office (now the Governmental Accountability Office).

How can public administrators reduce their chances of being on the wrong side of the law? Is there any hope, short of living with a lawyer (out of the question) or enrolling in law school (almost as bad)? Of course there is.

Preventing Litigation   Here are four time-tested ways to avoid the expense, delay, and hassle of litigation:[19]

1. *Paper the file.* When there is no written agreement or confirming letter, you need to focus on what lawyers call "papering the file." This process involves the preparation of "file documents"—handwritten notes or dictated memos that you write and save in your file, just in case you need them to prove a point later. Think of these notes and memos as the instant replays of oral agreements, promises, and other significant administrative communications. Like football fans who rely on the videotape to see what "really" happened, judges and juries, years after an event, turn to the notes and memos that were prepared as it was unfolding. Remember: If you can't prove it, it doesn't exist. Every minute of every working day, administrators should force themselves to think: How am I going to prove this later on, just in case?

2. *Use procedures to help you act lawfully.* More precisely, rigid, mechanistic, and up-to-date forms and procedures help you and your employees say and do the right thing without always having to think it through, look it up, or call legal affairs. You don't always have to know the intricacies and rationales of law. Many times, all you need to know is what you're supposed to do—the reason doesn't matter. Just do it.

3. *Get the legal office involved even before you have a problem.* For your agency's counsel to do you as much good as possible, his or her role must extend beyond the obvious tasks of designing your forms and advising you on problems. Avoiding litigation means minimizing the hidden problems that catch you by surprise—the ones you never knew you had, until it's too late. That is where the legal office can make a difference.

4. *Educate your employees.* What public executives know about the law must trickle down through their organizations. A lot of organizations forget that. Top management who deal with lawyers are the ones who get educated, but the "street-level bureaucrats" don't get the kind of understanding that could help them recognize a trouble spot or think their way around a potential problem in the field, where it counts. They don't learn the danger signals; they don't develop a feel for what they ought to document. Legally, they remain unrealistic optimists and not healthy pessimists.

Administrative Law: The Essentials   Another way to avoid the dangers of knowing too little and the confusion of knowing too much is to approach law on a strict "need to know" basis. The need to know method works particularly well in the law, which follows a kind of 90-10 rule: 10 percent of the law covers about 90 percent of the problems, and within that 10 percent is an enormous amount of practical, preventive, immediately applicable information. It is much more important to know some things than others, and once you cover what's most important, you quickly reach a point of diminishing return.

Think of the eight concepts listed below as a brief outline of that crucial 10 percent you need to know.

Key Concepts in Administrative Law

1. judicial deference	5. judicial review
2. delegation	6. legislative veto
3. types of rule	7. ex parte communications
4. due process	8. negotiated rulemaking

---

1. *Judicial deference.* Just how much **judicial deference** will judges show to administrative decisions? The Supreme Court laid down a standard for approaching this question in *Chevron U.S.A., Inc. v. NRDC* (1984). The case involved a challenge to the EPA's "bubble" policy, a plan designed to reduce the cost to manufacturers of installing pollution controls. The legality of the plan turned on whether the agency could define the Clean Air Act term "stationary source" to refer to an entire manufacturing plant rather than an individual device within the plant. The court upheld the plan, prescribing two steps that a reviewing court should conduct when reviewing an agency's construction of a statute. The first step was to determine whether Congress has already addressed the precise question at issue. If so, the court would have to "give effect to the unambiguously expressed intent of Congress." However, if the statute were to prove "silent or ambiguous with respect to the specific issue," the second step was

to determine whether the agency's answer was "permissible"—or, as the Court phrased it, a "reasonable interpretation." In other words, to whatever extent the statute remains ambiguous, the reviewing court should presume that Congress has delegated to the agency the task of filling in gaps in some reasonable way.

Let's consider an important recent application of the Chevron case: *FDA v. Brown and Williamson Tobacco Corp.* (2000):

- The FDA asserted it had jurisdiction to regulate tobacco products because nicotine is a "drug" and cigarettes are "drug delivery devices." Applying *Chevron's* step one, the court held that the FDA had no authority to regulate tobacco. Among the arguments the court accepted were that the FDA is required to ban unsafe drugs, but tobacco products can never be safe. Thus, if nicotine were a drug, the FDA would be required to ban tobacco products. Yet Congress clearly did not contemplate that tobacco products would be banned entirely, given numerous statutes (such as cigarette labeling laws) that contemplate the sale of tobacco products. Moreover, the court was guided by its own common sense—it was simply unimaginable that Congress had implicitly given to the FDA such an extraordinary power as the power to ban tobacco products.

2. *Delegation.* The Constitution (Article I, Section I) provides that all legislative authority rests with Congress and makes no mention of agency rulemaking. Nevertheless, since the founding of the nation, the Supreme Court has permitted the **delegation** of legislative authority to executive officers—with one notable exception. In the 1930s, the Great Depression led Congress to delegate authority to the executive branch on a scale never before seen. For the first and only time in U.S. history, the Supreme Court in 1935 struck down two delegations. *Panama Refining Co. v. Ryan* challenged the National Industrial Recovery Act of 1933, which allowed the president to prohibit transportation of certain oil products in interstate commerce. The other case, *Schechter Poultry Co. v. United States,* challenged the National Industrial Recovery Act, which allowed the president to approve "codes of fair competition" for the poultry industry. Because of their subject matter, these cases are often referred to as the "hot oil" and "sick chicken" cases.

Since 1935, the Supreme Court has not struck down any delegations of legislative power. A delegation of legislative authority is constitutional if Congress establishes the national fundamental legislative policy and leaves only the "gap filling" to the agency. For example, the Clean Air Act instructs the EPA to adopt ambient air quality standards "which in the judgment of the Administrator . . . and allowing for an adequate margin of safety, are requisite to protect public health." The law obviously gives the EPA little guidance on where to set the standards for, say, emissions of particulate matter from diesel engines. But, as the Supreme Court sees it, the statute does provide a sufficiently intelligible principle. That principle arises from the word "requisite," meaning not higher or lower than necessary to protect the public health with an adequate margin of safety.[20]

In sum, the court affords Congress wide latitude in delegating its authority as long as it provides sufficient standards or establishes an intelligible principle to guide the delegatee in its exercise of authority. However, when individual liberties are involved—as opposed to property interest—delegation must be more precise.

3. *Legislative rules and nonlegislative rules.* Before defining these two terms, a little recent history is in order. One of the most important developments in administrative law during the past generation has been the growing reliance of agencies on rulemaking—rather than case-by-case adjudication—as a means of formulating policy. Much can be said in favor of this trend. First, rulemaking can resolve a multiplicity of issues in a single proceeding. Clear general rules produce rapid and uniform compliance among the affected firms and individuals. In contrast, the scope of an adjudication precedent may be harder to define, because its reach usually depends on the facts of a particular case.

Second, rulemaking can provide individuals with important protection. When a public administrator has the authority to make discretionary decisions under a broad statutory standard—case-by-case decision making—fairness may be compromised. But when the same administrator uses rulemaking, the regulated persons must be provided with more precise notice of what conduct will be allowed. Further, rules are fair because they apply across the board; no individual or firm is singled out for special treatment. Third, rule-making proceedings require notification of all affected parties of impending changes in regulatory policy and thus gives them an opportunity to be heard before the agency's position crystallizes. Fourth, because rules are prospective rather than retrospective, they are less likely to disappoint affected parties. And fifth, the rulemaking process is designed to gather broad public support, thus improving the quality and increasing the legitimacy of the rule.

Despite these advantages of rules over adjudication, from an agency's perspective, writing a general rule often causes more difficulties than deciding a particular case. As we saw earlier, the APA imposes certain administrative "chores" on the agency. Specifically it requires agencies to publish a notice of proposed rulemaking in the *Federal Register,* cite legal authority, consider input, write the rule up, publish the rule, and so on.

In addition to these administrative burdens, rulemaking can generate political problems, because general rules are more likely to inspire concerted opposition from those who will be adversely affected by them. An adjudicative case isolates one respondent—generally selected because of questionable actions—for possible sanctions, but a general rule can mobilize an entire industry in the political action. Given these and administrative burdens as well as political realities, administrators may be tempted to regulate through the back door—either intentionally or inadvertently. How do they do this? This is where legislative rules and nonlegislative rules come in. Actually, the APA establishes *three* different types of rules: legislative rules (sometimes referred to as substantive rules), interpretive rules, and policy statements.

If the rule is made pursuant to a legislative delegation of rulemaking power, it is referred to as a **legislative rule** and, if it is within the scope of delegated power, it is *as binding as a statute.* Interpretive rules and policy statements are **nonlegislative rules**. An **interpretive rule** differs from a legislative rule in that it is intended not to alter the legal rights of anyone but to state the agency's view of what existing law already requires. **Policy statements** set forth the manner in which the agency intends to exercise discretion.

Now we can answer the question posed previously. How do agencies regulate through the back door? Section 553 of the APA exempts interpretive rules and policy statements from its requirements for notification, hearings, and so on. As you might expect, more than a few lawsuits have been filed charging that what an agency purported to be a mere interpretive rule or policy statement is, in fact, a legislative rule—carrying the full force and effect of law rooted in a grant of quasi-legislative power by Congress.[21]

4. *Due process.* Besides the agency's growing reliance on rulemaking, another important development in administrative law in recent years has been a growing concern for the cost and burdens associated with the use of **due process**.

What is due process? The Fifth and Fourteenth Amendments to the U.S. Constitution guarantee individuals the right of due process of law, which is often referred to simply as "due process." The Fifth Amendment states, "No person shall be . . . deprived of life, liberty, or property, without due process of law." The Fourteenth Amendment applies the same principle to the states. These two due process clauses provide that government must act fairly, according to established legal procedures, with regard to a person's rights to life, liberty, and property.

Well, how much process is due? In *Goldberg v. Kelly* (1970), due process meant that people cannot have their welfare benefits terminated without first affording them a full evidentiary hearing. The court observed that welfare entitlements are more like "property" than a "gratuity." But, six years later, in *Matthews v. Eldridge,* the Supreme Court significantly shifted away from expanded due process protection. Litigants now encounter demands from judges that they clearly identify a specific legal right they claim within a narrower interpretation of liberty and property than before. Further, they must demonstrate that more or different adjudication procedures are needed to remedy defects in the fact-finding process the agency used. For example, did the Social Security Administration really need to set up a hearing for Eldridge and his lawyer before they cut off his disability benefits when they already had his medical records in hand? Justice Powell gives the court's answer:

> Financial cost alone is not a controlling weight in determining whether due process requires a particular procedural safeguard prior to some administrative decision. But the Government's interest, and hence that of the public, in conserving scarce fiscal and administrative resources is a factor that must be weighed. At some point the benefit of an additional safeguard to the individual affected by the administrative action and to society in terms of increased assurance that the action is just, may be outweighed by the cost. Significantly, the cost of protecting those whom the preliminary administrative process has identified as likely to be found undeserving may in the end come out of the pockets of the deserving since resources available for any particular program of social welfare are not unlimited. We conclude that an evidentiary hearing is not required prior to the termination of disability benefits and that the present administrative procedures fully comport with due process.

5. *Judicial review.* The power of courts to examine the actions and decisions of all three branches of government to determine whether they are in accord with the federal Constitution is known as **judicial review**. Both federal and state courts exercise the power of judicial review,

with the United States Supreme Court being the final judgment of what is constitutional in the federal system. Although the constitution is silent on the subject, in 1803 the Supreme Court established the precedent of judicial review by declaring a law of Congress unconstitutional for the first time in the case of *Marbury v. Madison.*

But for a person to bring a court challenge to an administrative decision, he or she must have **standing** to seek judicial review. The standing doctrine requires that the person bringing a lawsuit have a personal interest in the case. The constitutional source of the standing doctrine is Article III, Section 2, which limits the federal judicial power to "cases" and "controversies." The American judicial process is an adversary system that depends on the litigants to gather and present the information needed for a sound decision.

Another barrier to judicial review is **ripeness**. Ripeness is concerned with maturity— that is, whether a case is sufficiently mature to be heard by a court. For example, in *Abbott Labs v. Gardner* (1967), an FDA rule required that drug companies place certain information on their labels. Lawyers for Abbott argued that this requirement exceeded FDA powers, whereas the FDA argued that the case was not ripe for review because the rule had not been enforced yet. The Supreme Court held that the case was ripe because the plaintiff would suffer significant harm if the rule were enforced.

Despite the twin barriers to judicial review—standing and ripeness—many cases do make it to the courthouse. Then we confront the most critical issue in determining the relationship between the courts and administrative agencies: *the extent of the court's power to substitute its judgment for that of the agency.* The issue is referred to as the "scope," or "standard," of judicial review. Among the many standards of review, the two most commonly applied are the substantial evidence standard and the arbitrary and capricious standard. The substantial evidence standard means "such relevant evidence as a reasonable mind might accept is adequate to support a conclusion."[22] Thus, the substantial evidence standard does not permit a court to substitute its judgment for that of the agency. Even if the court disagrees with the agency's finding, it must affirm those findings if they are reasonable. Further, a reviewing court must look at the "whole record"—that is, both sides of the record. It is insufficient to merely look at the evidence that supports the agency's conclusion.

Now let's turn to the **arbitrary and capricious standard** of judicial review. Under the APA, the court shall "hold unlawful and set aside agency action, findings, and conclusions found to be . . . arbitrary, capricious, and an abuse of discretion or otherwise not in accordance with law." (All three terms—arbitrary, capricious, and abuse of discretion—mean the same thing.)

In the leading case on this question, *Citizens to Preserve Overtone Park v. Vole* (1971), the Supreme Court stated that judges who are called on to review an exercise of discretion must engage in a "substantial inquiry." Although the agency's decision is entitled to a "presumption of regularity," that presumption must not prevent a probing, in-depth review." First, the court must determine whether the discretionary action falls within the area of discretion delegated to the agency by the legislature. Second, the court must determine whether the decision was based on a consideration of all the relevant factors. This means that the agency must consider *all the relevant factors* and not consider irrelevant factors. Even if the agency exercised discretion within statutory bounds and considered all the right factors, the court could reverse if the agency's decision was unreasonable—that is, if the agency made a "clear error of judgment." Finally, the court must consider whether the agency *followed all appropriate procedures* when it exercised discretion. If the discretionary action was part of the rulemaking process, for example, the court should ascertain whether the requirements for rulemaking were observed.

Here is an example of the application of the arbitrary and capricious standard:

- In 1977, the National Highway Traffic Safety Administration adopted a rule requiring all new cars produced after September 1982 to use air bags or automatic seat belts. This rule was upheld by the courts. In 1981, however, the National Highway Safety Administration rescinded the rule because it found that passive restraints could be easily detached and there was no reason to expect seat belt usage to increase sufficiently to justify the cost of the new equipment. The Supreme Court held that revocation of the rule was arbitrary and capricious.[23]

6. *Legislative veto.* Because the Constitution permits the president to veto, or reject, legislation passed by Congress, Congress has tried to create its own legislative veto. During the 1970s, Congress considerably expanded its use of the legislative veto over many executive agency regulations. For example, in the case of *Immigration and Naturalization Service v. Chadha* (1983), the House of Representatives had overruled the attorney general's decision to suspend an order to deport an individual. In this case, the Supreme Court ruled that a one-house legislative veto was an unconstitutional violation of the separation of powers. In cases in which people's legal rights are at stake, the Court declared, both houses of Congress must enact legislation or pass a joint resolution to be signed by the president. In short, the legislative veto violated the integrity of the constitutional process.

7. *Ex parte communication.* If a formal agency adjudication is to be fair like a trial, then participants must be able to know what evidence may be used against them and to contest it through cross-examination and rebuttal evidence. These rights can easily be nullified if the decision makers are free to consider facts outside the record, without notifying the participants or giving them an opportunity to respond. Therefore, the APA prohibits any "interested person outside the agency" from making, or knowingly causing, "any ex parte communication relevant to the merits of the proceeding" to any decision-making official. It also imposes a similar restraint on the agency decision makers. (*Ex parte* means "from one party only.")

To some observers, the extensive involvement of White House officials in rulemaking proceedings makes it easy for even the most careful person to engage in ex parte communication. In particular, private meetings between the Office of Information and Regulatory Affairs—which scrutinizes proposed rules for cost-effectiveness and consistency with presidential policy—and officials at rulemaking agencies risk subverting the essential fairness and openness of the administrative process.

When an improper ex parte communication does take place, the APA requires that it be placed on the public record. Ultimately, the decision whether to impose a sanction is a matter of judicial discretion. Here is a famous example involving an interest group:

- *Professional Air Traffic Controllers v. FLRA* (1982) arose out of a Federal Labor Relations Authority (FLRA) proceeding to decertify a union of air traffic controllers that had led its members in an illegal strike against the government. The evidence showed that a prominent labor leader had met privately with a member of the FLRA, urging him not to revoke the union's certification. Although the court was convinced that this communication was illegal, it did not overturn the FLRA's order because the discussion of the union's situation had been brief, the labor leader had made no threats or promises, and the conversation had not affected the outcome of the case.[24]

8. *Negotiated rulemaking.* **"Neg reg"** is another mechanism—albeit a legal one—through which interest groups can influence administrative policymaking. The federal Negotiated Rulemaking Act of 1990 supplements the APA's provisions for informal rulemaking. Here is how it works:

Traditionally, when an agency publishes proposed regulations, it allows a period for public comment. The "comment" often becomes a pitched battle in which the spokespersons for all sides duke it out, which sometimes leads to litigation, usually to delay. Negotiated rulemaking brings together representatives of all those affected by the draft regulations *before* they are issued. Using a facilitator, the parties strive to negotiate a consensus on the regulations. They are able to listen to each other and look for creative solutions to their differences because the process takes place outside the glare of public scrutiny. It's less formal, more educational, and far more effective than relying solely on insurmountable walls.[25]

Having discussed at some length the political force field surrounding a public administrator, we will now consider how he or she might cope with it.

How Political Strategies Complement Management Strategies

Who has not heard this campaign message: "Put government back into the hands of a person who knows the meaning of a dollar, who has met a payroll, and who understands business methods"? Unfortunately, in governing a large city, many business methods cannot be readily translated into political reality. Consider a couple of practical examples:

- Center City operates a number of recreation programs in school playgrounds and parks. Some programs have many participants, others few. Good management would say to close those programs that have relatively few participants, but this would mean some neighborhoods would have no programs for those who would use the facilities. Recreation centers must be reasonably close to everyone, so all of them stay open.
- Center City needs a new, modern airport suitable for the needs of the twenty-first century. Federal officials and airlines agree that the best location would be in another state, just across the river from Center City. Jobs would be created, the area's economy given a boost, and the city's tax base improved. But Center City interests—union and business—want the contracts and jobs that would flow from the new airport. Even though Center City does not have a site or funds for the land, those interests would block the building of the airport out of state. Would a good manager

turn down an investment opportunity because one group of workers or subcontractors received the benefits rather than another? Not one who wanted to survive. Yet political reality forces other government leaders to oppose the out-of-state site.

The point here is not that people from the private sector are ill suited for the public sector, but rather that their business acumen needs to be combined with political savvy. Put another way, good management requires good politics.

To attain policy objectives, public administrators need political strategies to complement their management strategies. The reason is not hard to see. As the two examples above suggest, public executives must engage people over which they have no direct authority. Business executives accustomed to issuing orders for instant execution by deferential underlings might not be adept in this milieu. You cannot run a government this way—at least in a democracy. Legislators, city councils, and voters insist on knowing the reason the public executive is taking a certain action. Democratic government operates not by command and obedience but by persuasion, compromise, and consent. Although these qualities may be desirable in business, they are not always essential to success in the public sector. Here, success demands the ability to pull people together for meaningful purposes despite the thousands of forces that push them apart; otherwise, public institutions risk sinking slowly into a mediocrity characterized by bureaucratic infighting, parochial politics, and vicious power struggles.

As Figure 2.5 illustrates, the management and political strategies of a public administrator are interrelated. An agency's activities in pursuing program objectives can generate

Figure 2.5   The Interaction of Management Strategy and Political Strategy

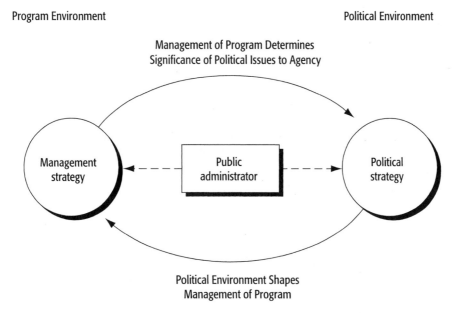

Program Environment   Political Environment

Management of Program Determines
Significance of Political Issues to Agency

Management strategy → Public administrator → Political strategy

Political Environment Shapes
Management of Program

political issues and stimulate action that affects the political environment. Consider a government regulator who makes decisions about transferring wealth between members of two interest groups (in effect, business and consumers). The bureaucrat affects interest groups through the costs and benefits generated by regulatory enforcement. Interest group members then decide to "vote" for or against the regulator in the next election, based on the regulator's decisions. Reading the election returns, legislators influence the bureau through budgets, oversight, and legislation.

Or reconsider the opening case of Michelle Rhee, who had just been picked by the mayor to lead a transformation that would send shockwaves through Washington, DC's entrenched and bloated school district. Undertaking such a politically sensitive mission requires a well-thought-out political strategy, although the case presents no evidence that Rhee had one. Although every political strategy needs to be tailored to specific circumstances, here are some general issues she might have wanted to address:

- What measure can I take to generate the right kind of publicity at the appropriate time?
- Where are the sources of potential conflict? How might they be neutralized?
- How can I avoid alienating school board and city council members?
- What kind of lieutenants do I *not* want? (Answer: Those with a tin ear for politics.)
- How do I handle critics—even those who may be guardians of special interests? (Answer: With persuasion, patience, and negotiating skills.)
- Who should I put in the information loop?
- How fast should I move, and which things should I do first?
- How can I leverage the political clout of the mayor?

Whatever Rhee's passion for educational issues and knack for developing policies, unless she thinks through these kinds of issues—unless she develops a *political* strategy—her management strategy is apt to fail.

Political Competency

To recap, the administrator is placed squarely in the policymaking process. Further, day-to-day events force administrators to operate in a field crisscrossed by political forces generated by overhead authority (Congress and the president), client groups, cognate agencies, other levels of government, and the media. The greater the number of these forces, the more time and energy a public administrator tends to spend on power-oriented behavior.

What follows is neither an essay on realpolitik nor revelations on the political art—the former would be improper, the latter presumptuous. This concluding section only attempts to introduce a few basic political concepts pertinent to good administration. And by *good administration,* it is simply meant administration that can mobilize support for its programs and, in short, get things done. "There is no more forlorn spectacle in the administrative world than an agency and a program possessed of statutory life, armed with executive orders, sustained in the courts, yet stricken with paralysis and deprived of power. An object of contempt to its enemies and of despair to its friends."[26]

What are these concepts so pertinent to good administration? Recall for a moment the Center City airport example. If the mayor had decided to attempt to get the airport built in another state, then what basic *political* considerations would have been involved? First, she probably would have wanted to assess her strength—or, to put it in the political vernacular, her clout—to see if she should even try. Assuming she did have sufficient political strength, she then would probably have asked herself: Does my objective really merit such an expenditure of political capital?

It is important to be clear on the meaning of this third question. If it is financially possible, say, for Larry to buy a Lamborghini, it does not necessarily follow that he should. Where else could Larry have invested his limited capital? How much would he have left for future contingencies?

Assume, however, that the mayor of Center City is in a better position than Larry. Therefore, she decides that she has the political capital *and* that the price (in terms of allies lost, favors asked, and so on) is not too high. Now she must consider the specific strategies and tactics she must use to attain her objective. *In sum, the administrator must think through four political questions concerning resources, costs, stakeholders, and strategies.*

Resources

Essentially, the administrator's political resources appear in one of three forms: external support, professionalism, and individual power. The prudent administrator assesses each before attempting any major political act.

External Support   One of the more enduring sources of bureaucratic power is the phenomenon of **subsystem politics**, or **iron triangles**. Agencies ally themselves with congressional committees and interest groups. Examples are legion: agriculture committees, the American Farm Bureau Federation, and agencies within the Department of Agriculture; subcommittees on Indian affairs, the Association on American Indian Affairs, and the Bureau of Indian Affairs; the House Agriculture Committee, the sugar industry, and the Sugar Division of the Department of Agriculture; and so forth. The most immediate consequence of the alliance is that agencies are able to take less seriously supervision by superiors in the executive branch.

Hugh Heclo points out that the system of iron triangles is now overlaid by an amorphous system of **issues networks**.[27] There is more widespread participation in bureaucratic policymaking, and many participants have technical policy expertise and are drawn to issues because of intellectual or emotional commitments rather than material interest. So—different models for different policies. Certainly, if one wants to understand the politics of health care, Heclo's model offers a much richer picture of reality than the cozy iron triangle does.

In assessing their *own* strength, administrators must at the same time assess the strength of their *support.* But considering size alone is not enough; also important are the dispersion and unity of the constituency. For example, the secretary of the interior's strength increased with the establishment of the Bureau of Outdoor Recreation, which broadened the department's base from just the western states to the urban Northeast. For similar reasons, state university systems try to establish satellite campuses in as many state senatorial districts as possible. Regarding the importance of unity, one need only compare the influence of the large, loosely knit consumer movement with the relatively small, tightly knit National Rifle Association.

Professionalism   The second source of agency power is **professionalism**. *Profession* can be defined as a reasonably clear-cut occupational field that ordinarily requires higher education—at least the attainment of a bachelor's degree—and offers a lifetime career to its members.[28] As society becomes more specialized and dominated by technological concerns, one can surely expect to see more people in jobs fitting this description in government agencies. Consequences of this trend are twofold.

Professionals in an agency are obviously in an excellent position to mobilize the support of relevant external professional organizations. Actually, the arrangement is reciprocal, for each profession tends to stake its territory within the appropriate government agency—as, for example, the medical profession does in the FDA.

Another consequence of professionalism is that within the agency, professionals tend to form a kind of elite with substantial control over operations. At least three elements form the base of this power, which can override political control from the top:

- Full-time attention to a problem
- Specialization that develops expertise by breaking the function, issue, or problem into subparts
- Monopolization of information

Bases of Individual Power   Thus far, we have examined the administrator's political resources in terms of interest groups and professional elites. We now consider the political resources that individual administrators themselves can generate.

If leadership is the process by which one person successfully influences another, then power is the means by which he or she does it. Over the years, students of human behavior have identified eight important **bases of individual power**:

1. *Coercive power* derives from a leader's ability to threaten punishment and deliver penalties. Its strength depends on two factors. First is the magnitude of punishment, real or imagined, that the leader controls. Second is the other party's *estimate* of the probability that the leader will, in fact, mete out punishment (e.g., undesirable work assignments, reprimands, dismissal) if necessary.
2. *Connection power* derives from a leader's personal ties with important persons inside or outside an organization. The ability of assistants to influence the chief executive is governed by the "rule of propinquity": In general, those who are present when a decision is made wield more power than those who are away. Aides thus can be

classified in terms of their proximity to the chief executive. According to Robert Caro, one of the key elements of Lyndon Johnson's political genius was his ability to build connections with powerful people:

> He was very deliberate about it. After he was elected to the Senate—before he was even sworn in—he sought out Bobby Baker, a 21-year-old cloakroom clerk, because he had heard that Baker knew "where the bodies were buried." And what did he want to ask Baker? Not what the Senate rules were but who had the power. Bobby Baker told Johnson that there was only one man in the Senate who had the power— Richard Russell. That was perhaps the most important piece of information that Lyndon Johnson acquired during his first year in office. And what was Johnson's first act in the Senate? It wasn't to rise on the floor and speak. It wasn't to sponsor legislation. It was to get close to Richard Russell.[29]

Other elements of Johnson's political genius, according to Caro, are worth noting: "utter realism, his ability to look facts—even very unpleasant facts—in the face," "his ability to find common ground," and his ability "to read people." For more on the Johnson method, see page 90.

3. *Expert power* derives from a leader's reputation for special knowledge, expertise, or skill in a given area. Lobbyists who maintain their credibility with members of the legislature find this kind of power far more effective than the preceding two. Consider how Louis Freeh (see Chapter 1, Case 10.1) used expert power when he joined the FBI immediately after law school. He started off in the Manhattan field office, where he made himself indispensable by becoming the only agent in the place who fully understood the intricate workings of the new Racketeer Influenced and Corrupt Organizations Act, which still provides the bureau with its main tools for building antiracketeering cases against organized crime. Usually new agents go out and check bank records or do surveillance under the auspices of other agents. But Freeh was sitting back planning the next move against some organized crime group, coordinating all the information, doing the job it normally took 10 years to get.

4. *Dependence power* derives from people's perception that they are dependent on the leader either for help or for protection. Leaders create dependence through finding and acquiring resources (e.g., authority to make certain decisions, access to important people) that others need for their jobs. Consider, for example, Stephen E. Reynolds, who for 34 years held the prosaic title of New Mexico state engineer. But as water boss in a desert state, Reynolds ranked among the most powerful public officials in the Rocky Mountain region. He controlled who got water—and where and how they could use it—in a land where rainfall averages 15 inches a year.

5. *Obligation power* derives from leaders' efforts to do favors for people who, they expect, will feel an obligation to return those favors and from leaders' efforts to develop true friendships with those on whom they depend.

6. *Legitimate power* derives from the formal position held by the leader. In recent years, textbooks on the president of the United States have tended to emphasize a theory

of presidential power based on persuasion. But it could also be argued that the ability to persuade affects power at the margins; it does not determine its use or set its limits. Perhaps the key to understanding presidential power "is to concentrate on the constitutional authority that the president asserts unilaterally through various rules of constitutional construction and interpretation in order to resolve crises or important issues facing the nation."[30] Although persuasion is an important tool, it has limits. To make it work requires time and people who listen; but both are sometimes absent.

7. *Referent power* derives from the identification of others with the leader. This identification can be established if the leader is greatly liked, admired, or respected. "Managers develop power based on others' idealized views of them in a number of ways. They try to look and behave in ways that others respect. They go out of their way to be visible to their employees and to give speeches about their organizational goals, values, and ideas."[31] When Martin Luther King Jr. gave his famous "I Have a Dream" speech, he was fostering the listener's subconscious identification with his dream.

8. *Reward power* derives from the leader's ability to make followers believe that compliance with the leader's wishes will lead to pay, promotion, recognition, or other rewards. Here is a particularly dramatic application of reward power combined with referent power: Early in 1944, General George Patton asked his troops how they would answer when their grandchildren asked them what they did in the war. He then went on to suggest that they could either say they shoveled manure in the States—or that they rode through Europe with Patton's Third Army.

According to John Kotter, managers who successfully exercise power tend to share a number of characteristics. They are sensitive to what others consider legitimate uses of power and to the "obligation of power." Consequently, they know when, where, and with whom to use the various types of power. And they do not rely on any one type of power.

They use all their resources to develop still more power. In effect, they invest in power. For example: "By asking a person to do him two important favors, a manager might be able to finish his construction program one day ahead of schedule. That request may cost him most of the obligation-based power he has over that person, but, in return, he may significantly increase his perceived expertise as a manager of construction projects in the eyes of everyone in his organization."[32] That is, when the leader has more power, the follower need not have less. Studies by Likert and Tannenbaum indicate that organizations with a greater amount of power at all levels are likely to be more effective and their members more satisfied.[33]

Costs

Virtually every important administrative action has an indirect cost. Pulitzer Prize–winning journalist David Halberstam describes the following incident from the Kennedy years:

> In 1962 [Secretary of Defense] McNamara came charging into the White House ready to save millions on the budget by closing certain naval bases. All the statistics

were there. Close this base, save this many dollars. Close that one and save that much more. All obsolete. All fat. Each base figured to the fraction of the penny. Kennedy interrupted him and said, "Bob, you're going to close the Brooklyn Navy Yard, with twenty-six thousand people, and they're going to be out of work and go across the street and draw unemployment, and you better figure that into the cost. That's going to cost us something and they're going to be awfully mad at me, and we better figure that in too."[34]

It was Paul H. Appleby who remarked that there are four questions every administrator should always ask before making an important decision: Who is going to be glad? How glad? Who is going to be mad? How mad?

Because actions have political costs, administrators can go into debt. If they use top-level support, it is quite likely that higher officials will later demand bureau backing for other administration programs or demand influence in bureau policy in return. Presidents, too, sometimes go into the red. As Richard Neustadt[35] suggests, when Truman dismissed General MacArthur during the Korean War he "exhausted his credit"; as a consequence, he was unable to make his case with Congress, the court, or the public in a steel strike that came the next year.

Stakeholders

The various forces in the political environment of a government agency as depicted in Figure 2.4 are fairly generic in the sense that most, if not all, would apply to any public sector organization. But some individuals, groups, and organizations are specific to certain types of organizations and certain types of decisions. It is useful to think of these players as **stakeholders** because they have a stake in the decisions and actions of the government agency. One decision will activate one set of stakeholders, while another decision by the same agency will activate a quite different set. It all depends on how the stakeholders' perceived interests are being affected or, in less measured language, whose ox is being gored.

Let's see what stakeholder analysis might look like for the administrator of a large urban hospital. First, one should identify all the stakeholders. This step is not as easy as it sounds. Often administrators are surprised to learn only *after* they launched a program who the major opponents are. Figure 2.6 shows not only who these parties might be but also how they are related. As we will see in a moment, these relationships are important when one begins to build a coalition in support of a particular program or project.

Once the stakeholders and their relationships have been identified, one needs to ask two critical questions. First, what are the positions of each stakeholder on the various issues of importance to the hospital? Table 2.1 provides a stakeholder issues matrix for a hypothetical hospital. Second, how much power does each stakeholder have? Many stakeholders in Figure 2.6 may support what you want to do, but if only one or two powerful ones oppose it, you might need to modify your plans—or even abandon them altogether.

Figure 2.6   Stakeholder Map of a Large U.S. Hospital

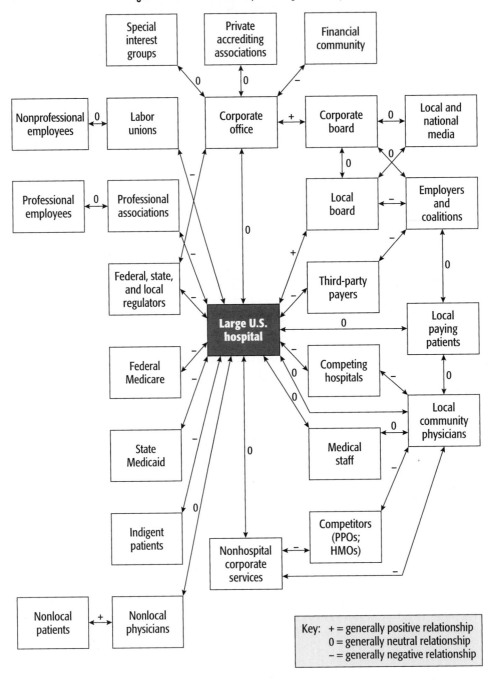

SOURCE: *Used with permission from Hospital and Health Services Administration* 34:4, 541. Chicago:
Health Administration Press 1989.

Table 2.1 Stakeholder Issues Matrix for a Hypothetical Hospital*							
	Issues						
Stakeholder	New Services	Truth in Advertising	Patient Death Rates	Price Policy	Clinical Quality	Services Quality	Financial Return
Medical staff	2	4	2	4	1	3	5
Patients	2	1	1	3	1	1	5
Hospital management	1	4	2	2	3	2	1
Professional staff	2	2	2	4	2	3	4
Board of trustees	2	3	2	3	2	3	2
Federal government	5	2	1	1	2	4	4
Corporate office	2	4	3	3	3	4	1
Nonprofessional staff	4	5	4	5	3	3	4
Third-party payers	4	4	3	1	2	3	2
Elected public officials	2	2	2	2	3	2	3
Local business/industry	2	1	2	1	2	3	2
Media	4	2	1	3	3	3	3
Competitors	1	1	3	2	3	2	5

*Issues were rated on a scale from 1 to 5: 1 = critically important to stakeholder, 3 = somewhat important to stakeholder, 5 = not at all important to stakeholder.
SOURCE: *Used with permission from Hospital and Health Services Administration* 34:4, 541. Chicago: Health Administration Press 1989.

Obviously, determining how much power each stakeholder has requires making sub-jective judgments. Nonetheless, our earlier discussion of resources and costs can provide useful guidance.

Strategies

Top administrators can draw from a wide range of strategies to deal with the agency's political environment. And all administrators may safely assume that, voluntarily or otherwise, they will become involved in these strategies. To ignore them is to ignore a very big part of day-to-day administration. For the purposes of this discussion, the strategies will be classified rather broadly as (1) cooperation, (2) competition, and (3) conflict.

Cooperation   **Cooperation** is based on the idea that two groups can share compatible goals without one having to completely give in to the other. All parties can be winners, although some more than others. In the language of game theory, a cooperative strategy means that parties are engaged in a **variable-sum game** in which both parties win.

Cooperative strategies come in many varieties. One is **persuasion**, the essence of which is described by Neustadt as follows: to induce someone to believe that what you want of them is what their own appraisal of their own responsibilities requires them to do in their own self-interest.[36] Or as one aide to President Eisenhower put it: "The people . . . [in Congress] don't do what they might like to do, they do what they think they have to do in their own interest as they see it." But the undisputed master of persuasion was Lyndon Johnson (see box: "The Johnson 'Treatment'").

The Johnson "Treatment"

In *Master of the Senate*, Robert A. Caro describes how then Senate Majority Leader Lyndon Johnson used his powers of persuasion to pass the Civil Rights Act of 1957:

> He used his stories, and he used his jokes, he used his promises, used his threats, backing senators up against walls or trapping them in their chairs, wrapping an arm around their shoulders and thrusting a finger in their chests, grasping lapels, watching their hands, watching their eyes, listening to what they said, or to what they didn't say: "The greatest salesman one on one who ever lived"— trying to make his biggest sale. Never had he tried harder.

SOURCE: Robert A. Caro, *Master of the Senate* (New York: Vintage Books, 2002), 959–960.

George Tames/The New York Times/Redux Pictures

Another variety of cooperation is **bargaining**—that is, the negotiation of an agreement for the exchange of goods, services, or other resources. Universities bargain the name of a hall in return for the donor's contribution. The attorney general's antitrust division signs consent decrees with firms that promise not to pursue actions further without first admitting guilt. And, as we will see in the next chapter, the federal, state, and local levels of government must bargain to make a federal system work.

To add precision to the analysis, a distinction must be drawn between two bargaining techniques. **Compromise**, the first, usually results from bargaining over a single, isolated issue when the outcome is one of more or less. Examples include such matters as hiring and promotion requirements in government employment, amounts of public housing for inner-city areas, trade-offs between environmental and energy needs, and types of learning programs for the unemployed. Los Angeles Mayor Antonio Villaraigosa (see Chapter 1) compromises on small issues to pursue larger goals such as redeveloping downtown, long a shadow of its more robust counterparts in other cities. When the owner of downtown's premier existing hotel held up a new convention center hotel project by threatening to sue to stop the city from subsidizing it, the mayor settled the matter by agreeing that the owner could convert one-third of the hotel's rooms to lucrative condos in exchange for dropping his challenge. Then, when hotel workers complained that the move would cost them jobs, he agreed to promote the unionization of other downtown hotels.

Although American democracy was founded on compromise—the Founders offered less populous states two senators each to draw them into the Union—it can lead to ludicrous solutions. In 1961, the director of defense research and engineering had to negotiate between the Air Force and the Navy on the requirements for a fighter to be used by both. The Navy argued for a wingspan of 56 feet; the Air Force, 90 feet. The solution? Seventy-three feet, of course.

With the second bargaining technique, **logrolling**, more than one issue is involved. Logrolling involves reciprocity of support for different items of interest to each bargainer. For example, a governor's task force on welfare, in return for the support of a powerful adviser to the governor, might be willing to let that adviser's office develop some other plan that would properly belong with the task force. Or when a top administrator from the Department of Labor concedes something to a representative of the U.S. Treasury, he often can expect a concession at some later date. Charles Lindblom puts it well: "He has stored up a stock of goodwill on which he can later draw."[37]

In addition to persuasion and bargaining, **coalition** is considered a type of cooperation. Coalition is a combination of two or more organizations for a specific purpose. A good example is Project Mohole, which sought to develop new technology that would allow an anchored drilling ship to penetrate the Earth's mantle.[38] The original group of sponsoring scientists was concerned with maximizing the scientific returns from the drilling. The contractor understandably sought to confine the project as nearly as possible to a straightforward engineering task. Meanwhile, the president's Office of Science and Technology was concerned with the international ramifications and prestige of the success or failure of the project. The National Academy leadership was concerned with preserving the prestige of science, free from controversy. Finally, the National Science Foundation sought to sustain the impetus of an important project in the earth sciences but, at the same time, to support orderly progress in all other fields of science it was sponsoring. Similarly, today NASA, the Air Force, and contractors form a coalition backing the space shuttle program.

What is known about the art of coalition building? Good administrators have learned that clarity—sometimes, but not always—is essential; in other words, if a coalition is to form around a proposal, then that proposal must be as unambiguous as possible. The NIH provides an example of how ambiguity gets eliminated. In 1955, the NIH's National Microbiological Institute was renamed the National Institute of Allergy and Infectious Diseases. No longer would it be handicapped because "no one died of microbiology."[39]

Coalition builders have also learned the advantage of associating their agency's proposal with the goals of other agencies and political authorities. Advocates of the nuclear plane in 1953 were successful in linking that proposal in an unmistakable way to a high-priority defense need. Similarly, President Johnson increased the coalition backing the Elementary and Secondary Education Act of 1965 by linking the proposal of federal aid to public schools to his antipoverty program. And as was suggested in Chapter 1, the International Space Station became virtually impervious to "attack" when it became a multinational enterprise and a key player in U.S.–Russian relations in the post–Cold War world.

Competition   In the past few pages, the discussion has involved the various forms that a cooperative strategy might take. The second classification of strategy is **competition**. Competition may be defined as a struggle between two or more parties with a third party mediating. Often, in competitive situations, the winnings of one competitor are equaled by the losses of the other. A simple example is when a project is transferred from one agency to another. Game theorists call this kind of competitive situation a **zero-sum game**. In other words, if you add all the wins and losses in a transaction, the sum is always equal to zero, because any wins for one party must cover the losses of the other. Another name for the outcome of this situation is "win–lose." In the next chapter, we will see how skillful negotiators try to avoid these situations and seek "win–win" outcomes in which the sum of wins and losses is positive. Thus, everyone leaves the negotiation better off than when he or she entered it.

What can an administrator do in a zero-sum situation? Although the alternatives are, no doubt, many, consider two examples—seizing the initiative and co-opting the opposition. In the early 1960s, it became apparent to the Air Force and the Navy that the defense secretary was going to choose a single plane, with certain modifications, to be built for both services. The plane would be a modification of either the Air Force's TFX or the Navy's F-4. Under these conditions, the Air Force immediately and successfully launched a campaign emphasizing the flexibility of its plane; at the same time, it glossed over how well the TFX would suit its special needs.[40]

Administrators sometimes co-opt their adversaries. As noted in Chapter 1, **co-optation** deliberately seeks participation as a means of gaining public agreement to agency programs. In his study of the Tennessee Valley Authority, Selznick tells how potential opposition from the community and regional groups was brought into the Authority's decision-making process.[41] Awarding lucrative government contracts can provide an enormously flexible way for an agency to co-opt legislators. Similarly, certain federal agencies seek to co-opt the scientific community by appointing scientists to advisory boards and giving research grants.

Conflict Although cooperation and competition are essentially peaceful and governed by formal rules and informal normative constraints, **conflict** involves situations in which actors pursue goals that are fundamentally incompatible. Consider the case of John Kennedy and U.S. Steel. On Tuesday, April 10, 1962, President Kennedy was surprised to note that his appointment calendar included a 5:45 P.M. appointment with U.S. Steel chairman Roger Blough. The purpose of Blough's visit was to hand the president a press release announcing a $6-a-ton price increase. The president was stunned. He felt his whole fight against inflation was being reduced to tatters. Above all, he felt duped. The man seated on the sofa next to his rocking chair had personally, knowingly, accepted his help in securing from workers a contract that *would not* lead to an increase in prices. Although being challenged in an area in which he had few weapons, the president would not accept this fait accompli without a fight. His main strategy was to divide and conquer; more specifically, he focused his efforts on the Inland Steel Company of Chicago in order to obtain an agreement that it would not follow U.S. Steel's lead. He also followed other courses of action. In brief, he convinced Senator Kefauver and the Justice Department to begin investigating steel activities, used a press conference to sway public opinion, and made implied threats to cancel certain defense contracts.

Within 72 hours, Blough capitulated before the onslaught. This episode showed the ability of the chief executive "to mobilize and concentrate every talent and tool he possessed and could borrow to prevent a serious blow to his program, his prestige, and his office."[42]

Conflict, of course, occurs at less lofty levels and does not always end in a government victory. Journalist Tom Wolfe paints a vivid picture of how ghetto youth and militants can intimidate the bureaucrats at city hall and in the local Office of Economic Opportunity. Wolfe calls the practice "mau-mauing." One constituent named Chaser, Wolfe relates, almost gave classes in mau-mauing:

> Then Chaser would say, "Now when we get there, I want you to come down front and stare at the man and don't say nothing. You just glare. No matter what he says. He'll try to get you to agree with him. He'll say, 'Ain't that right?' and 'You know what I mean?' and he wants you to say yes or nod your head . . . see . . . it's part of his psychological jiveass. But you don't say nothing. You just glare . . . see. . . . Then some of the other brothers will get up on that stage behind him, like there's no more room or like they just gathering around. Then you brothers up there behind him, you start letting him have it. . . . He starts thinking 'Oh God! Those bad cats are in front of me, they all around me, they behind me. I'm surrounded.' That shakes 'em up."[43]

Timing and forbearance are also important. In the steel price dispute, Kennedy realized that he had to act swiftly before a parade of companies, rushing to imitate U.S. Steel, began to increase prices. But one must also know when to stop pressing the attack—how to avoid overkill. Benjamin Disraeli recognized this factor when he said, "Next to knowing when to seize an advantage, the most important thing in life is to know when to forego an advantage."

Conflictive situations, however, do not require backroom politics. They can be managed with forthrightness and even a certain dignity. Indeed, even in the ultimate conflict—war—men and women still have this option. The following letter from Winston Churchill to the Japanese ambassador illustrates this point:

> Sir,
>
> On the evening of December 7th His Majesty's Government in the United Kingdom learned that Japanese forces without previous warning either in the form of a declaration of war or of an ultimatum with a conditional declaration of war had attempted a landing on the coast of Malaya and bombed Singapore and Hong Kong.
>
> In view of these wanton acts of unprovoked aggression committed in flagrant violation of International Law and particularly of Article I of the Third Hague Convention relative to the opening of hostilities, to which both Japan and the United Kingdom are parties, His Majesty's Ambassador at Tokyo has been instructed to inform the Imperial Japanese Government in the name of his Majesty's Government in the United Kingdom that a state of war exists between our two countries.
>
> I have the honour to be, with high consideration,
>
> Sir,
> Your obedient servant,
> Winston S. Churchill

As Churchill noted: "Some people did not like this ceremonial style. But after all when you have to kill a man it costs nothing to be polite."[44]

Concepts for Review

administrative process

Administrative Procedures Act (APA)

adjudication

arbitrary and capricious standard

bargaining

bases of individual power

client

coalition

cognate agencies

competition

compromise

conflict

cooperation

delegation

due process

executive order

Federal Register

Freedom of Information Act (FOIA)

Government Accountability Office (GAO)

interpretive rule

iron triangles	policy statement
issues networks	political force field
judicial deference	professionalism
judicial process	program operations
judicial review	prospective rules
legislative clearance	public relations
legislative rule	ripeness
logrolling	rulemaking
"neg reg"	stakeholders
nonlegislative rule	standing
notice-and-comment rulemaking	substantial evidence standard
Office of Management and Budget (OMB)	subsystem politics
oversight	sunset laws
persuasion	sunshine laws
policy	variable-sum game
policymaking process	zero-sum game

Key Points

This chapter reviewed how political forces in the public administrator's environment limit what government can do—even when trying to be efficient and effective. Yet, when properly managed, the untoward effect of these forces can be mitigated, eliminated, or even turned to the public administrator's advantage. In this chapter, the following points have been made:

1. The management strategy an agency follows in implementing a program is related to its political strategy. The management of a program determines the significance of political issues to an agency. Conversely, the political environment shapes the management of a program.

2. Public administrators frequently participate in the policymaking process. Chief executives rarely make decisions about issues that have not bubbled up from the echelons of planners just above the career administrators and just below the political appointees of the cabinet and subcabinet.

3. During implementation, administrators find themselves engaged in the following four activities: program operations, rulemaking, investigation, and adjudication. The last three activities compose the administrative process, which involves the administration of laws by administrative agencies, in contrast to the judicial process, which involves the administration of laws by the courts.

4. Administrative rulemaking is the establishment of prospective rules—that is, agency statements of general applicability and future effect that concern the rights of private parties. These guidelines have the force and effect of law.

5. Under the requirements of the federal APA of 1946, general notice of proposed rulemaking must be published in the *Federal Register.*

6. Administrative agencies also establish interpretive rules. These rules are not legally binding on the public but simply indicate how an agency plans to interpret and enforce its statutory authority.

7. The most commonly used rulemaking procedure is called notice-and-comment rulemaking. This procedure involves three basic steps: (1) notice of the proposed rule, (2) a comment period, and (3) the final rule.

8. After conducting an investigation of a suspected rule violation, an agency may begin to take administrative action against an individual or organization. Most administrative actions are resolved through negotiated settlement at their initial stages, without the need for formal adjudication. If a settlement cannot be reached, the agency may issue a formal complaint against the suspected violator. An ALJ presides over the hearing and has the power to administer oaths, take testimony, rule on questions of evidence, and make determinations of fact. Adjudication is a quasi-judicial process conducted by the agency to ensure—as guaranteed in the Constitution—that no person can be deprived of "life, liberty, or property without due process of law."

9. Securing compliance from bureaucratic agencies is not easy for legislators. Agencies can implement policies that differ considerably from what legislators had in mind, and corrective devices such as budgetary sanctions, hearings, and so on cannot reinstate the enacted policy.

10. Some congressional policies have a pervasive influence on the operations of agencies. The FOIA of 1966, sunset laws, and sunshine laws are prime examples.

11. Oversight involves continuing, systematic supervision of the performance of the executive branch by Congress—how well government programs are working and how honestly, efficiently, or faithfully the laws are being administered. By and large, though, oversight has been infrequent and slipshod. Legislative oversight is strengthened by the GAO. The other means by which Congress—or any other U.S. legislative body—exercises control over executive agencies is the appropriations process.

12. For a number of reasons, there is tension between the executives appointed by elected officials and the government employees whom they are supposed to lead. First, agencies form alliances with legislative subcommittees and outside interest groups. Second, if the president and his appointees can be at cross-purposes with agencies over the ends of policy, so too can they be over the means. Third, agencies have a tendency to become resistant to change because of strong ties to traditional policies and the professional orientation of careerists. Finally, the average tenure of political appointees is only about 18 months.

13. The president and his appointees are not powerless vis-à-vis the bureaucracy. In addition to his formidable command over the public attention and his power to appoint administrators, the president oversees the OMB. The largest of the executive office components, the OMB has two main functions: budget preparation and legislative clearance. Legislative clearance refers to the fact that before an agency can submit new legislation to Congress, the legislation must be cleared by the OMB to ensure that it is consistent with the goals and policies of the administration.

14. To analyze the complex relations between courts and administrative agencies, it is useful to think in terms of three broad areas of concern: (1) administrative responsibility—that is, the rulings of courts help ensure that the actions taken by public administrators are responsive, fair, and honest; (2) influence on public personnel management, for the Supreme Court has placed important limitations on the flexibility of managers to supervise their employees and operate their organizations; and (3) administrative law—that is, the body of law that defines the power, limits, and procedures of administrative agencies.

15. In reviewing an administrative agency's decision, a court considers the following types of issues: (1) whether the agency has exceeded its authority under its enabling legislation; (2) whether the agency has properly interpreted laws applicable to the agency action under review; (3) whether the agency has violated any constitutional provisions; (4) whether the agency has acted in accordance with procedural requirements of the laws; (5) whether the agency's actions were arbitrary, capricious, or an abuse of discretion; and (6) whether any conclusions drawn by the agency are not supported by substantial evidence.

16. Besides Congress, political appointees, and courts, other important political forces in the public administrator's environment are clients, cognate agencies, the media, activist groups, and the public in general ("the people").

17. The administrator's political resources appear in one of three forms: external support, professionalism, and individual bases of power. The prudent administrator assesses each before taking any political action. One of the more enduring sources of bureaucratic power is the phenomenon of subsystem politics, or iron triangles. Agencies ally themselves with congressional committees and interest groups. Professionals in an agency are obviously in an excellent position to mobilize the support of relevant external professional organizations.

18. If leadership is a process by which one person successfully influences another, then power is the means by which he or she does it. Over the years, students of human behavior have identified eight important bases of individual power: coercive power, connection power, expert power, dependence power, obligation power, legitimate power, referent power, and reward power.

19. The various forces in the political environment of a government agency as depicted in Figure 2.4 are fairly generic in the sense that most, if not all, would apply to any public sector organization. But some individuals, groups, and organizations are specific to certain types of organizations and certain types of decisions. It is, therefore, useful to think of these players as stakeholders because they have a stake in the decisions and actions of the agency. Once the stakeholders and their relationships have been identified, one needs to ask two critical questions: What are their positions on the various issues of importance to the agency? And how much power does each stakeholder have?

20. Top administrators can draw from a wide range of strategies to deal with an agency's political environment. These strategies can be classified rather broadly as cooperation, competition, and conflict.

Problems and Applications

1. Typically, one of the distinguishing characteristics of public managers is how dependent they all are on actions of a variety of other people to perform their jobs. Unlike physicians, mathematicians, and baseball pitchers, whose performance depends more directly on their own talents and efforts, public managers can be dependent in varying degrees on all the players we saw in Figures 2.1 and 2.4. Because these dependent relations are an inherent part of the public manager's job, building political advantage becomes an important part of that job.

   Kathleen Kelly Reardon, professor of management at the University of Southern California, argues that being politically savvy doesn't mean being unethical or devious. Rather, it involves listening to and relating to others and making choices that advance everyone's goals. In *It's All about Politics* (New York: Doubleday, 2005), she suggests several ways to build political advantage. For each of these strategies, address the following three questions: What does this statement mean to me? How much do I agree (or disagree) with the statement? What examples drawn either from written accounts of famous leaders or from my own personal experience illustrate the statement? Here are some of her statements:

   - Political intuition is not clairvoyance but rather acute attentiveness to what others say and how they act.
   - Developing empathy for the benefit of political advantage starts with an interest in other people, what they have to say, and how they think and feel.
   - Because they devote the necessary time to study and practice, experienced politicians are rarely blindsided by the unexpected. They have asked themselves in advance what they might say should a delicate discussion go awry.
   - Of all the skills important to the development of political intelligence, the ability to see things as others see them is paramount.
   - The most effective politicians convey a strong interest in what other people are saying to them. They don't impose their views on others so much as manage their interactions so that others will feel they contributed considerably to the development of those views.
   - Each of us is at least 75 percent responsible for the way we are treated, because we have the choice to influence what others think and say about us and the obligation to learn how.
   - Becoming a skilled interpreter of meanings at a number of levels is hard work. Yet that is exactly what it takes to move up from bench warmer to star.
   - You don't need to become a "duck," you just need to be able to communicate with one.
   - If you're going to be labeled, you might as well have some input into what the label will be. Your reputation should not be manufactured solely by others but rather crafted with your own skilled assistance.
   - An ability to learn from others, to listen to their stories and discover how technical knowledge merges with practical and evaluative knowledge, is indispensable to gaining political power.

- The less personal the veiled threat, the better. To use a dental analogy, you don't want to hit a nerve when you only intended to fill a tooth.
- Politically courageous people know one very important fact of life: that achieving the goal is often not as important as the way it's achieved. They realize that there's truth in the adage that winning a battle is not always the way to win a war.
- Without a political compass, it's a lot easier to slip into political ways of acting and being that go against what you truly believe in.
- One thing to remember about business: any question that seems too personal probably is.

2. Some top administrators hold the view that they should *welcome* congressional oversight in areas in which committees or members have legitimate concern. Why do you think a public administrator might hold this view?

3. "Vote trading and arm twisting are effective when the issue is not that big, when it isn't a glaring national issue. But it doesn't work when you've got the full focus of national attention on it." Do you agree or disagree? Support your answer with recent examples.

4. Redraw Figure 2.4 with a hospital administrator in the center. What do you think the figure would look like with the chief executive of a multinational corporation at its center? The president of Princeton University? The director of the international environmentalist group Greenpeace? Be specific.

5. What kinds of power do even "powerless" people have? (Remember Chaser and his "mau-mau" tactics.)

6. Early in her tenure, the president of a major American university was criticized for refusing to compromise and for failing to understand the political dimension of her job. Her response was crisp: "I am not a politician. And I resist political measures of this job in this institution. In this job, the test of success is substance, not form, not posturing. I want to represent a different point of view: objectivity, principle as distinct from politics. I am resistant to a lot of the style and trappings people have come to associate with leadership of any sort in this society." What kind of problems do you foresee for her? Be as specific as possible.

7. The following inventory provides an opportunity to assess your own political skills. Read the following statements and circle the number that best describes your level of agreement. For each item, a 1 indicates weak agreement, and a 5 indicates that you strongly agree.

I study how power is established and used where I work.	1 2 3 4 5
I take steps to establish my credibility with others rather than assuming that my work will do it for me.	1 2 3 4 5
I try to establish myself as the one to go to in terms of specific types of knowledge.	1 2 3 4 5

I am skilled in making people feel good about working for or with me.	1 2 3 4 5
I use words and ways to convey a sense of confidence in power.	1 2 3 4 5
I avoid flaunting power.	1 2 3 4 5
I choose my battles wisely.	1 2 3 4 5

Favorite Bookmarks

www.house.gov   The House of Representatives' library is one of the better government-supported resources on the Web. The site contains the full text of pending legislation and congressional testimony.

www.c-span.org   You can watch the U.S. government at work from the comfort of your desktop. C-SPAN is a public-oriented cable TV channel, owned by the U.S. cable television industry. Its goal is to allow Americans to watch the proceedings in the House of Representatives, the Senate, and other public forums. (The name C-SPAN stands for Cable-Satellite Public Affairs Network.)

www.apsanet.org   The American Political Science Association is the major professional society for people who study politics, government, and public policies in the United States and around the world.

Notes

1. Norton Long, "Power and Administration," *Public Administration Review* (Autumn 1949): 257.
2. William W. Boyer, *Bureaucracy on Trial: Policy Making by Government Agencies* (Indianapolis, IN: Bobbs-Merrill, 1964).
3. William H. Lambright, *Governing Science and Technology* (New York: Oxford University Press, 1976).
4. Harold Seidman, *Politics, Position, and Power: The Dynamics of Federal Organization* (New York: Oxford, 1998), 76.
5. This discussion draws heavily on Philip J. Cooper, *Public Law and Public Administration* (Itasca, IL: F.E. Peacock Press, 2000), 14–18.
6. Martin Linsky, *Impact: How the Press Affects Federal Policy Making* (New York: Norton, 1986).
7. Clark Kent Ervin, Former Inspector General of the Department of Homeland Security, thinks the answer to the last question is no. See *Open Target: When America Is Vulnerable to Attack* (New York: Macmillan, 2006).
8. See Chad Therune, "Along Battered Gulf, Katrina Aid Stirs Unintended Rivalry," *Wall Street Journal* (September 29, 2005).
9. See Paul Light, *Thickening Government: Federal Hierarchy and Diffusion of Accountability* (Washington, DC: Brookings, 1995).
10. David E. Lewis, "Political Appointees, Bureau Chiefs, and Federal Management Performance," Woodrow Wilson School of Public Affairs and International Affairs Policy Brief (October 2003).
11. Arthur M. Schlesinger, *A Thousand Days* (Boston: Houghton Mifflin, 1965), 406.
12. Seidman, op. cit., 28.
13. Eliot Richardson, "The Maze of Social Programs," *Washington Post* (January 21, 1973).
14. *Wall Street Journal* (September 25, 1986).

15. James O. Wilson, *Bureaucracy* (New York: Basic Books, 1989), 241–44.
16. Seidman, op. cit., 38.
17. Arch Lustberg, *Testifying with Impact* (Washington, DC: Chamber of Commerce, 1983).
18. David H. Rosenbloom and James D. Carroll, *Toward Constitutional Competence: A Casebook for Public Administrators* (Englewood Cliffs, NJ: Prentice Hall, 1990).
19. Michael G. Trachtman, *What Every Executive Better Know about the Law* (New York: Simon & Schuster, 1987).
20. Daniel Hall, *Administrative Law: Bureaucracy in a Democracy* (Upper Saddle River, NJ: Prentice Hall, 2001), 99.
21. For example, in *Morton v. Ruiz* (1974), the court reversed a decision of the BIA denying benefits to Indians under a federal assistance program. The BIA's Indian Affairs Manual denied assistance to claimants who lived off the reservation, and the secretary of interior argued that the residential restriction was an interpretation of the Synder Act by the agency. But the court held that, although this decision might be a reasonable response to limitations in the program's funding, it could not be implemented through ad hoc decisions; the BIA had to issue valid legislative rules, which would be published in the *Federal Register*, before it could cut off the claimants' eligibility in this fashion. In addition to interpretative rules, the other kind of actions exempted in the APA from regular rulemaking procedures are policy statements. In *McLouth Steel Products Corp. v. Thomas* (1988), the D.C. Circuit Court agreed with the company's complaint that the EPA's use of a computer model constituted a substantive (legislative) rule and therefore should have been made by the formal rulemaking process. The computer model helped the EPA determine which companies were to be the target of regulation under the Resource Conservation and Recovery Act.
22. *Consolidated Edison Co. v. NLRB,* 305 V.S. 197, 229 (1938).
23. *Motor Vehicle Manufacturers Association v. State Farm Mutual Insurance Co.* (1983).
24. Ernest Gellhorn and Ronald M. Levin, *Administrative Law and Process* (St. Paul, MN: West, 1997), 268.
25. Russel M. Linden, *Seamless Government* (San Francisco: Jossey-Bass, 1994), 264–65.
26. Pete Correll, CEO of Georgia Pacific and chairman of the Atlanta Committee for Progress, quoted in *U.S. News and World Report* (October 31, 2005): 80.
27. Hugh M. Heclo, "Issue Networks and Executive Establishment," in Anthony King, ed., *The New American Political System* (Washington, DC: American Enterprise Institute, 1978).
28. Frederick Mosher, *Democracy and the Public Service* (New York: Oxford, 1968), 106.
29. "Lessons in Power: A Conversation with Historian Robert A. Caro," *Harvard Business Review* (April 2006): 47–52.
30. R. M. Pious, *The American Presidency* (New York: Basic Books, 1979).
31. John P. Kotter, "Power, Dependence and Effective Management," *Harvard Business Review* (July–August 1977): 131.
32. Ibid., 136.
33. R. Likert, *New Patterns of Management* (New York: McGraw-Hill; 1961); S. Tannenbaum, ed., *Control in Organizations* (New York: McGraw-Hill, 1968).
34. David Halberstam, *The Best and the Brightest* (Greenwich, CT: Fawcett Crest Books, 1969).
35. Richard D. Neustadt, *Presidential Power and the Modern Presidents: The Politics of Leadership from Roosevelt to Reagan* (New York: Free Press, 1990), 31.
36. Ibid., 46.
37. Charles E. Lindblom, *The Policy Making Process* (Englewood Cliffs, NJ: Prentice Hall, 1968), 96.
38. David S. Greenberg, *The Politics of Pure Science* (New York: New American Library, 1967), Ch. 9.
39. Seidman, op. cit., 24.
40. R. F. Coulam, "The Importance of the Beginning: Defense Doctrine and the Development of the F-111 Fighter-Bomber," *Public Policy* (Winter 1975).
41. Phillip Selznick, *TVA and the Grassroots* (New York: Harper & Row, 1949).
42. Theodore C. Sorenson, *Kennedy* (New York: Harper & Row, 1965), 516.
43. Tom Wolfe, *Radical Chic and Mau-Mauing the Flak Catchers* (New York: Farrar, Straus, and Giroux, 1970), 22–23.
44. Winston S. Churchill, *Memoirs* (Boston: Houghton Mifflin, 1959), 508.

CASE 2.1
THE PRINCE

....

Great political thinkers often write about specific historical situations and yet succeed in making recommendations that apply to times other than their own. Niccolo Machiavelli must be numbered among such thinkers. His book, The Prince, first published in 1532, five years after his death, marks him as one of the most controversial, enduring, and realistic political theorists of the modern world. Nobody else has dealt with the political requirements of leadership with such brutal clarity as Machiavelli. His thoughts about the proper use of power have always fascinated the greatest thinkers.

A member of the impoverished branch of a distinguished family, Machiavelli entered public service in the Florentine republic and rose rapidly in importance. "It was a great job," Michael A. Ledeen writes in Machiavelli on Modern Leadership, "a cross between today's White House Chief of Staff and ambassador-at-large, with additional military responsibilities thrown in for good measure. Until the downfall of the republic in 1512, Machiavelli not only participated in high-level policy discussions, but also traveled throughout Europe, carrying messages to popes and kings, negotiating treaties and other arrangements, organizing and training the militia, and commanding them in battle."[1] These experiences may have provided him with something like an outsider's view of Italian politics. Machiavelli moved in circles high enough to observe the highest fliers at very close quarters, and he was already shrewdly weighing their actions and characters in his diplomatic reports to these masters in Florence. What follows are selections from four of the 26 chapters that compose this classic.

* * *

Chapter XV
Things for Which Men, and Especially Princes, Are Praised or Blamed

It remains now to see what ought to be the rules of conduct for a prince towards subject and friends. Many have written on this point. But, it being my intention to write a thing which shall be useful to him who understands it, it appears to me more appropriate to follow up the real truth of the matter than the imagination of it; for many have pictured republics and principalities which in fact have never been known or seen, because how one lives is so far distant from how one ought to live, that he who neglects what is done for what ought to be done, sooner effects his ruin than his preservation; for a man who wishes to act entirely up to his professions of virtue soon meets with what destroys him among so much that is evil.

Hence it is necessary for a prince wishing to maintain his power to know how not to be good, and to make use of this knowledge or not according to necessity. Therefore, putting on one side imaginary things concerning a prince, and discussing those which are real, I say that all men when they are spoken of, and chiefly princes for being more highly placed, are remarkable for some of those qualities which bring them either blame or praise. Thus it is that one is reputed liberal, another miserly, one is reputed generous, one rapacious; one cruel, one compassionate; one faithless, another faithful; one effeminate and cowardly, another bold and brave; one affable, another haughty; one lascivious, another chaste; one sincere, another cunning; one hard, another easy; one grave, another frivolous; one religious, another unbelieving, and the like. I know that every one will confess that it would be most praiseworthy

....

1   Michael A. Ledeen, *Machiavelli on Modern Leadership* (New York: St. Martin's Press, 2000), xi.

in a prince to exhibit all the above qualities that are considered good; but because they can neither be entirely possessed nor observed, for human conditions do not permit it, it is necessary for him to be sufficiently prudent that he may know how to avoid the reproach of those vices which would lose him his state; and also to keep himself, if it be possible, from those which would not lose him; but this not being possible, he may with less hesitation abandon himself to them. And again, he need not make himself uneasy at incurring a bad reputation for those vices without which the state can only be saved with difficulty, for if everything is considered carefully, it will be found that something which looks like virtue, if followed, would be his ruin; while something else, which looks like vice, yet followed brings him security and prosperity.

Chapter XVII
Cruelty and Clemency, and Whether It Is Better to Be Loved Than Feared

Coming now to the other qualities mentioned above, I say that every prince ought to desire to be considered merciful and not cruel. Nevertheless he ought to take care not to misuse this mercy. Cesare Borgia was considered cruel; notwithstanding, his cruelty reconciled the Romagna, unified it, and restored it to peace and loyalty. And if this be rightly considered, he will be seen to have been much more merciful than the Florentine people, who, to avoid a reputation for cruelty, permitted Pistoia to be destroyed. Therefore a prince, so long as he keeps his subjects united and loyal, ought not to mind the reproach of cruelty; because with a few examples of cruelty he will be more merciful than those who, through too much mercy, allow disorders to arise, from which follow murders or robberies; for these usually harm the whole people, whilst those executions which originate with a prince offend the individual only.

Nevertheless he ought to be slow to believe and to act, nor should he himself show fear, but proceed in a temperate manner with prudence and humanity, so that too much confidence may not make him incautious and too much distrust render him intolerable.

Upon this a question arises: whether it be better to be loved than feared or feared than loved? It may be answered that one should wish to be both, but, because it is difficult to unite them in one person, it is much safer to be feared than loved, when, of the two, either must be lacking. Because this is to be asserted in general of men, that they are ungrateful, fickle, false, cowardly, covetous, and as long as you succeed they are yours entirely; they will offer you their blood, property, life, and children, as is said above, when the need is far distant; but when it approaches they turn against you. And that prince who, relying entirely on their promises, has neglected other precautions, is ruined; because friendships that are obtained by payments, and not by greatness or nobility of mind, may indeed be earned, but they are not secured, and in time of need cannot be relied upon. And men have less scruple in offending one who is beloved than one who is feared, for love is preserved by the link of obligation which, owing to baseness of men, is broken at every opportunity for their advantage; but fear preserves you by a dread of punishment which never fails.

Nevertheless a prince ought to inspire fear in such a way that, if he does not win love, he avoids hatred; because he can endure very well being feared whilst he is not hated, which will always be as long as he abstains from the property of his citizens and subjects and from their women. But when it is necessary for him to proceed against the life of someone, he must do it on proper justification and for manifest cause, but above all things he must keep his hands off the property of others, because men more quickly forget the death of their father than the loss of their patrimony. [A patrimony is an estate from one's father or ancestors.] Besides, pretexts for taking away the property are never wanting; for he who has once begun to live by robbery will always find pretexts for seizing what belongs to others; but reasons for taking life, on the contrary, are more difficult to find and sooner lapse. But when a prince is with his army, and has under control a multitude of soldiers, then it is quite necessary for him to disregard the reputation of cruelty, for without it he would never hold his army united or disposed to its duties.

Among the wonderful deeds of Hannibal this one is enumerated: that having led an enormous army, composed of many various races of men, to fight in foreign lands, no dissensions arose either among them or against the prince, whether in his bad or in his good fortune. This arose from nothing else than his inhuman cruelty, which, with his boundless valour, made him revered and terrible in the sight of his soldiers, but without that cruelty, his other virtues were not sufficient to produce this effect. And short-sighted writers admire his deeds from one point of view and from another condemn the principal cause of them. That it is true his other virtues would not have been sufficient for him may be proved by the case of Scipio, that most excellent man, not only of his own times but within the memory of man, against whom, nevertheless, his army rebelled in Spain; this arose from nothing but his too great forbearance, which gave his soldiers more license than is consistent with military discipline.

Returning to the question of being feared or loved, I come to the conclusion that, men loving according to their own will and fearing according to the will of the prince, a wise prince should establish himself on that which is in his own control and not in that of others; he must endeavour only to avoid hatred, as is noted.

Chapter XVIII
The Way in Which Princes Should Keep Faith

Everyone admits how praiseworthy it is in a prince to keep faith, and to live with integrity and not with craft. Nevertheless our experience has been that those princes who have done great things have held good faith of little account, and have known how to circumvent the intellect of men by craft, and in the end have overcome those who have relied on their word.

There are two ways of striving for mastery, the one by the law, the other by force; the first method is proper to men, the second to beasts; but because the first is frequently not sufficient, it is necessary to have recourse to the second. Therefore it is necessary for a prince to understand how to avail himself of the beast and the man. This has been figuratively taught to princes by ancient writers, who describe how Achilles and many other princes of old were given to the Centaur Chiron to nurse, who brought them up in his discipline; which means solely that, as they had for a teacher one who was half beast and half man, so it is necessary for a prince to know how to make use of both natures, and that one without the other is not durable.

A prince, therefore, being compelled knowingly to adopt the beast, ought to choose the fox and the lion; because the lion cannot defend himself against snares and the fox cannot defend himself against wolves. Therefore, it is necessary to be a fox to discover the snares and a lion to terrify the wolves. Those who rely simply on the lion do not understand what they are about. Therefore a wise lord cannot, nor ought he to, keep his word when such observance may be to his disadvantage, and when the reasons that caused him to pledge it exist no longer. If men were entirely good this precept would not hold, but because they are bad, and will not keep faith with you, you are not bound to observe it with them. A prince never lacks legitimate reasons to break his promise. Of this endless modern examples could be given, showing how many treaties and engagements have been made void and of no effect through the faithlessness of princes; and he who has known best how to employ the fox has succeeded best.

But it is necessary to know well how to disguise this characteristic, and to be a great pretender and dissembler; and men are so simple that he who seeks to deceive will always find someone who will allow himself to be deceived.

Therefore it is unnecessary for a prince to have all the good qualities I have enumerated, but it is very necessary to appear to have them. And I shall dare to say this also, that to have them and always to observe them is injurious, and that to appear to have them is useful; to appear merciful, faithful, humane, religious, upright, and to be so, but with a mind so framed that should you require not to be so, you may be able and know how to change to the opposite.

And you have to understand this, that a prince, especially a new one cannot observe all those things for which men are esteemed, being often forced, in order to maintain the state, to act contrary to his promise, friendship, humanity, and religion. Therefore it is necessary for him to have a mind ready to turn itself accordingly as the winds and variations of fortune force it, yet, as I have said above, not to diverge from the good if he can avoid doing so, but, if compelled, then to know how to set about it.

Chapter XXV
What Fortune Can Effect in Human Affairs and How to Withstand Her

It is not unknown to me how many men have had, and still have, the opinion that the affairs of the world are in such wise governed by fortune and by God that men with their wisdom cannot direct them and that no one can even help them; and because of this they would have us believe that it is not necessary to labour much in affairs, but to let chance govern them. Sometimes pondering over this, I am in some degree inclined to their opinion. Nevertheless, not to extinguish our free will, I hold it to be true that Fortune is the arbiter of one-half of our actions, but that she still leaves us to direct the other half, or perhaps a little less.

I compare her to one of those raging rivers, which when in flood overflows the plains, sweeping away trees and buildings, bearing away the soil from place to place; everything flies before it, all yield to its violence, without being able in any way to withstand it; and yet, though its nature be such, it does not follow therefore that men, when the weather becomes fair, shall not make provision, both with defences and barriers, in such a manner that, rising again, the waters may pass away by canal, and their force be neither so unrestrained nor so dangerous. So it happens with fortune, who shows her power where there is no organized strength to resist her, and thither she turns her forces where she knows that barriers and defences have not been raised to constrain her.

I say that a prince may be seen happy today and ruined tomorrow without having shown any change of disposition of character. This, I believe, arises firstly from causes that have already been discussed at length, namely, that the prince who relies entirely on fortune is lost when it changes. I believe also that he will be successful who directs his actions according to the spirit of the times, and that he whose actions do not accord with the times will not be successful. Because men are seen, in affairs that lead to the end which every man has before him, namely, glory and riches, to get there by various methods; one with caution, another with impetuousness; one by violence, another by guile; one by patience, another by its opposite; and each one succeeds in reaching the goal by a different method. One can also see of two cautious men the one attain his end, the other fail; and similarly, two men by different observances are equally successful, the one being cautious, the other impetuous; all this arises from nothing else than whether or not they conform in their methods to the spirit of the times. This follows from what I have said, that two men working differently bring about the same effect, and of two

working similarly, one attains his object and the other does not.

Changes in prosperity also issue from this, for if, to one who governs himself with caution and patience, times and affairs converge in such a way that his administration is successful, his fortune is made; but if times and conditions change, he is ruined if he does not change his course of action. But a man is not often found sufficiently circumspect to know how to accommodate himself to the change, both because he cannot deviate from what nature inclines him to do, and also because, having always prospered by acting in one way, he cannot be persuaded that it is well to leave it; and, therefore, the cautious man, when it is time to turn adventurous, does not know how to do it, fortune would not have changed.

I conclude, therefore that, fortune being changeful and mankind steadfast in their ways, so long as the two are in agreement men are successful, but unsuccessful when they fall out. For my part I consider that it is better to be adventurous than cautious, because fortune is a woman, and if you wish to keep her under it is necessary to beat and ill-use her; and it is seen that she allows herself to be mastered by the adventurous rather than by those who go to work more coldly. Fortune is, therefore, always, woman-like, a lover of young men, because they are less cautious, more violent, and with more audacity command her.

Case Questions

1. What are the principal ideas advanced by Machiavelli? Can you give modern examples using not only public executives but also figures from business, the military, sports, religion, and so on?

2. Do you agree or disagree with Machiavelli?

3. Discuss the following statement: "Human nature doesn't change, above all at the top, where questions of success and survival are paramount and there is little time for the niceties. The serious study of the past provides the raw material for wise decisions today and tomorrow. We are prone to make the same kinds of mistakes our predecessors made, and we must emulate the acts of past heroes."

Source: Adapted from www.gutenberg.net/etext98/tprnc11.txt. Some text has been deleted or paraphrased.

Intergovernmental Relations

Lisa F. Young / © 2009, used under license of Shutterstock.com

SUPERMAYOR

Aaccording to an ancient Greek poet, the fox knows many things, but the hedgehog knows one great thing. If the poet is right, then Jerry Abramson is a hedgehog. First elected mayor of Louisville, Kentucky in 1985 and then reelected twice, Abramson knew his city must learn to work with other jurisdictions in its area if it was to prosper. Between 1960 and 2000, Louisville's population dropped from 391,000 to 256,000, its factories drastically reduced their workforce, and its middle-class whites drifted to suburbs and beyond. A Brookings report did not paint a pretty picture:

> Louisville and the surrounding Jefferson County had split into politically separate and routinely hostile enclaves—an increasingly poor, black, and highly taxed core city; a cluster of relatively affluent eastern suburbs, with scores of small cities more akin to homeowners' associations than municipalities; and a large swath of unincorporated, blue-collar neighborhoods to the south and southwest characterized

by meager public services, inadequate roads, dysfunctional drainage, and deep resentments. All were further separated from their metropolitan neighbors to the north by the Ohio River, the Kentucky-Indiana [s]tate line that follows it, and a long history of mutual disdain. And in every other direction, they were surrounded by small rural Kentucky counties averse to change.

So, in 2003, Louisville merged with surrounding Jefferson County—thanks in large measure to the efforts of Abramson and Jefferson County Judge/Executive Harvey Sloane. Abramson easily won the top job in the new "Louisville Metro," acquiring a domain six times bigger than the city of Louisville and containing twice as many people as the city had in 1985. He became responsible, reports *The Economist*, "not just for urban areas, from the old rubber plants to the newly hip Butchertown, but suburban subdivisions and farms." Within the new consolidated city–county government, Abramson led efforts to:

★ Create a "City of Parks," a public-and-private partnership to add 4,000 acres of suburban parkland

★ Improve public safety, adding police officers and launching a new communications network for emergency responders

★ Revitalize downtown with projects such as a new riverfront arena, an entertainment district expansion, a Museum Plaza tower, the Muhammad Ali Center, new hotels, and more

★ Keep Louisville's economy strong by attracting and creating new jobs, with initiatives in the life sciences area

★ Transform a public housing project into a mixed-income neighborhood

★ Improve public health by establishing a new community-wide Emergency Medical Service and launching a Healthy Hometown Movement with community partners to cut high rates of obesity, diabetes, heart disease, and cancer

★ Reduce the size of government by 10 percent while improving the delivery of basic services

Outside of Metro Louisville, Abramson's influence grew, extending northward across the Ohio River into southern Indiana, with which Metro Louisville shares an economic future. Indeed, Greater Louisville Inc., the metropolitan chamber of commerce, helped companies like Geek Squad, a computer-service outfit, move beyond the city's borders, based on the philosophy that it's better that a company locate in the next county than in, say, Chicago or Atlanta. Greater Louisville Inc. also addressed a big problem for a city that claims to be a logistics hub, namely, the two aging, congested bridges that link Louisville and Indiana. Greater Louisville Inc. joined with its equivalent in southern Indiana to promote plans for two new bridges and began considering whether, and how, to share revenue from a new industrial park in southern Indiana.

Besides the creation of Metro Louisville and the work of Greater Louisville Inc., there is a third element in the economic development of the area that should be mentioned. The state of Kentucky embraced sweeping educational reforms, including major support for expanded research at the University of Louisville and a "new economy" agenda emphasizing the commercialization of research-generated knowledge.

Why are so many mayors across the country forming alliances with nearby settlements? What factors make these alliances—not to mention consolidation—so hard to achieve?

Chapter 2 argued that public administrators find themselves, for better or worse, in a force field of politics. To drive that point home, the chapter presented a simple model of the political environment in which the head of an agency must operate (see Figure 2.4). In that model, the agency is surrounded by legislative bodies, political bosses, courts, cognate agencies, other governments, clients, nonprofit organizations, the media, subordinates, and labor unions.

This chapter takes a close look at just one set of relationships in that force field of politics: the relationships between an agency and other jurisdictions. And what a set of relationships this is! First, there are the relationships between scores of federal agencies and 50 state governments. Then, there are the relationships between state capitals and their local governments. How many local governments do you think there are in the United States? Here are the latest figures from the *Statistical Abstract of the United States 2009*:

Counties	3,033
Municipalities	19,492
Townships and towns	16,519
Total	39,044

This means that state capitals must, on average, manage relationships with 781 local governments (39,044 divided by 50).

But the universe of intergovernmental relations (IGR) does not end there. In addition to counties, municipalities, and townships and towns, there are 13,051 school districts and 37,381 special districts. The latter are authorized by state or local law to provide only one or a limited number of designated services—such as water and/or sewage services, natural resource management, fire control, public housing, library and educational services, and/or health care. Special districts or authorities are the fastest-growing form of local government, with almost triple the number since 1952. Meanwhile, the other forms of local government remain about the same, and because of consolidation, the number of school districts has declined to one-fifth of what it was in 1952.

The importance of IGR to program management cannot be overemphasized. Apart from a few programs, such as the administration of the Social Security system, the federal government is not a direct provider of domestic public services. Instead, the majority

Sources: Edward Bennett and Carolyn Gatz, *Louisville, Kentucky: A Restoring Prosperity Case Study* (Washington, DC: Brookings, 2008); www.louisville.gov/mayor/biography; "The Rise of the Super-Mayor," *The Economist* (March 8, 2008); Carolyn Gatz, "Job Sprawl Could Weaken Louisville," *Courier-Journal* (May 17, 2009); Conor Dougherty, "Localities Facing Merger Push," *Wall Street Journal* (March 5, 2009); www.citymayor.com/mayors/louisville-mayor.

of national domestic programs are implemented through a complex arrangement among federal, state, and local governments. This approach to public services delivery reflects the fact that the United States is a federal system in which responsibilities are both divided and shared among separate levels of government, each possessing a base of legal and fiscal authority.

Given the sheer number, importance, and—as we will see in this chapter—complexity of these IGR, it should not be surprising that we are devoting an entire chapter to the subject. The discussion is straightforward. First we will distinguish IGR from federalism. Next we will survey the evolution of this intergovernmental system, putting particular emphasis on the relationship between the national government and the state governments. This historical perspective on federal–state relations is followed by an economic perspective, in which we will consider the economic rationale for the national government's role in the system. Then we will turn to other important relations: state-to-state (interstate), state-to-local, and local-to-local (interlocal) government. Lastly, we will examine the implications of the intergovernmental system for public administration.

Federalism and Intergovernmental Relations Compared

Some might say that IGR is just another term for federalism. But that would not be accurate.

What, then, is **federalism?** In its most formal sense, a federal system (such as that of the United States, Canada, Switzerland, and Germany) stands in contrast to a unitary or centralized system (such as that of France or Great Britain). A federal system divides power between central government and regional governments (states, provinces, cantons, and lands); each government, central or regional, is legally supreme in its own area of jurisdiction. Thus, in the United States the federal government controls external affairs, regulates interstate commerce, and establishes rules for immigration and naturalization. But the Constitution reserves certain powers for the states: control of elections, local governments, and public health, safety, and morals. Although some powers are shared between governments—taxing and spending for the general welfare, defining and punishing crimes, and so forth—the traditional or **"layer cake" model of federalism** assumes that functions appropriate to each level can be defined with reasonable precision and should be kept independent. This view holds that the three levels of government—national, state, and local—are almost totally separate, like a cake baked in three layers, which are placed one on the other with icing in between.

Morton M. Grodzins and Daniel J. Elazar reject this model of the federal system, preferring instead a **marble cake model of federalism.**[1] According to Grodzins and Elazar, separation of functions is both impractical and undesirable when governments operate in the same area, serve the same clients, and seek comparable goals. This view holds that the cooperative relations among the various levels of government result in an intermingling of activities like a cake made of light and dark batter mixed to give a streaked, marblelike appearance.

Models should simplify the world, but layer cakes and marble cakes take this simplification a little too far. We need a more accurate picture of how governments operate together in the same program area. That is, what are the *relationships* among administrators in the federal system? We also need to recognize that many more governments are involved than the concept of federalism implies.

A major deficiency of federalism as a descriptive model is that it tends to recognize mainly national–state and interstate relations but to ignore national–local, state–local, national–state–local, and interlocal relations. In contrast, **intergovernmental relations** "includes as proper objects of study all the permutations and combinations of relations among the units of government in the American system."[2]

Federal–State Relations: A Historical Perspective

Talk about the evolution of the intergovernmental system may offend bureaucrats in Washington, a city where a feeling of national dominance and self-importance always seems to be in vogue. It may bore the life out of many journalists, who tend to be preoccupied with what is current rather than long-range historical changes in the relationship among national, state, and local governments and agencies. Nevertheless, the relationship of states to the federal government is the cardinal question of the U.S. constitutional system. "It cannot be settled," Woodrow Wilson once wrote, "by the opinion of any one generation, because it is a question of growth, and every new successive stage of our political and economic development gives it a new aspect, makes it a new question." Wilson could not have been more right. As we shall see in this section, IGR have changed greatly since the early nineteenth century. These changes are closely linked to the overall growth of government in American society. As public administration has come to play a larger and larger role in our lives, the links among the different levels of the federal system have become both tighter and more complex.

Dual Federalism (1789–1933)

The idea of dual federalism is simple: The functions and responsibilities of the federal and state governments are separate and distinct. For example, in the first half of the nineteenth century, when emerging economic interests sought subsidies or tax breaks, they were likely to go to their state government. But when those interests wanted protection from competition by cheap imports, they had to go to the national government.

Roughly speaking, it can be said that this era lasted until the New Deal years of the 1930s, despite the fact that cooperation between national and state governments on matters such as railroad construction and banking existed both before and during Franklin Roosevelt's administration. But not until the New Deal did the idea really take hold that the national government and the states were complementary parts of a single governmental mechanism for coping with problems.

Cooperative Federalism (1933–1960)

The Great Depression of the 1930s led to several new and important changes in IGR. The Social Security Act of 1935, for example, included national grants for state and local unemployment and welfare programs, and the Housing Act of 1937 was the first instance of national involvement in local public housing. The Tennessee Valley Authority, created in 1933, was charged with developing the Tennessee River and its tributaries to promote their use for electricity, irrigation, flood control, and navigation.

During the era of **cooperative federalism,** IGR became more centralized in Washington, and the role of federal dollars became more important. Without question, the national government had given money to states since its creation; in fact, the first such **grants-in-aid** were used to pay the debts the states had incurred during the American Revolution. Since the early 1800s, however, the tendency had been for the national government to give money for specific purposes. Such **categorical grants**—as they are also called—require that funds be spent for particular programs in particular ways (in other words, "with strings attached").

Creative Federalism (1960–1968)

If the great growth in national aid to state and local government began with Franklin Roosevelt's New Deal in 1933, then it is fair to say that the most explosive period of such growth occurred during Lyndon Johnson's Great Society (1963–1968). The number of grant programs grew at an astounding pace—from about 50 in 1961 to some 420 by the time Johnson left office. These programs included both legislative landmarks—Medicaid, the Elementary and Secondary Education Act, and the Model Cities program—and smaller initiatives tailored to the interests of narrower constituencies. Federal aid to states and localities in this period almost doubled—from $7.9 billion in fiscal year 1962 to $13 billion in fiscal year 1966. Johnson called his program "creative" federalism. Scholars disagree as to the inventive merit, the insight, and the imagination that went into the design of some of these programs, but none dispute Johnson's creation of many new categorical grant programs.

Creative federalism constitutes a turning point in the development of the intergovernmental system for several reasons:

- The federal government became a far more significant presence in the daily lives of state and local administrators and in the delivery of government services to citizens, raising practical and philosophical questions. Did the individual programs created in Washington work as intended when implemented in dozens, hundreds, or thousands of state and local sites?
- The intergovernmental system became more difficult to manage. Federal administrators now had to manage a larger number of separate and increasingly complex programs, work with many more governmental units, and oversee the expenditure of increasing amounts of money.
- Because governors, mayors, and other state and municipal officials had a growing financial stake in intergovernmental aid, creative federalism developed a strong constituency that was prepared, when necessary, to lobby for the programs. This lobbying

activity was carried out either individually or collectively, through scores of organizations. For links to over 140 of these organizations, go to www.governing.com/govlinks. Five of the largest and most influential of these organizations are listed below:

1. National League of Cities (NLC)
   www.nlc.org
2. United States Conference of Mayors (USCM)
   www.usmayors.org/uscm
3. National Conference of State Legislatures (NCSL)
   www.ncsl.org
4. National Association of Counties (NACo)
   www.naco.org
5. National Governors Association (NGA)
   www.nga.org

- Governors and mayors complained about categorical grants because their purposes were often defined so narrowly that it was impossible for a state to adapt federal grants to local needs. A mayor seeking federal money to build parks might discover that the city could get money only if it launched an urban renewal program that entailed bulldozing several city blocks.
- Because grants frequently went directly to agencies that ran federal programs, governors and mayors found they had less power.

New Federalism (1968–1980)

Richard M. Nixon, who won the presidency in 1968, recognized the five political realities listed above and created his new policy for IGR accordingly. He would call it the "new federalism." To effect the policy of **new federalism,** Nixon proposed **revenue sharing**, in which states and localities would receive funds with virtually no restrictions on how they might be used. He also proposed the consolidation of existing categorical programs into broad-purpose **block grants** in a particular policy area, such as education, with relatively few restrictions on their use. (The idea of block grants actually had begun in the mid-1960s, when such a grant was created in the health field.)

Thus far, we have noted two types of grants, and before going further, let's be clear on how each works.

1. **Categorical grants** appropriate funds for special purposes such as Food Stamps (now the Supplemental Nutrition Assistance Program) for the poor and the construction of transportation and sanitation systems. Such grants usually require the state or locality to put up money to "match" some part of the federal grant. Categorical grants may be made in one of two ways: by formula or by individual application. **Formula grants** are available across the board to all who are eligible in a category, such as the blind. In contrast to formula grants, **application** or **project grants** are made only for specific purposes and require a complex application procedure. Examples are grants by the National Science Foundation to universities and research institutes to support the work of scientists or grants to states and localities to support training and development pro-

grams. Although there are hundreds of grant programs, about two dozen, including Medicaid, account for more than half of total spending for categorical grants.

2. **Block grants** are broad grants to states for prescribed activities with few strings attached. States have considerable flexibility in deciding how to spend block grants. Examples include the Housing and Community Development Block Grant (created in 1974) to provide funds to states and localities for general development purposes and Temporary Assistance to Needy Families (created in 1996) to provide funds to states to design and implement their own welfare programs.

In sum, Nixon's revenue sharing and block grants were part of a strategy to give more policymaking discretion and responsibility to the subnational governments by diminishing Washington's policy control. At the same time, the Nixon administration increased the fiscal resources of state and local governments to "do things."

The New New Federalism (1980–1993)

The inauguration of President Ronald Reagan in 1981 signaled the arrival at the national level of a chief executive committed to reducing the size and scope of government and creating an intergovernmental system that gave much greater prominence to states and localities. In particular, Reagan wanted to return to a more dual form of federalism by stepping back from the cooperative federalism that had developed over the previous 50 years. He also wanted to devolve certain federal responsibilities to the subnational level. Although the president experienced moderate success in these efforts, governors and local officials found that their jobs had become considerably more difficult for two reasons—money and unfunded mandates. During the 1980s, the era of **"new new federalism,"** there was less of the former and more of the latter.

Changing national priorities, tax cuts, and mounting deficits drove federal policymakers to cut funds going to states and localities. The numbers speak for themselves: In 1980, federal grants to states accounted for almost 40 percent of state and local government expenditure; by 1985, they had dropped to 30 percent and would continue dropping until they bottomed out in 1990 at 25 percent.

Another way to look at what was happening in the 1980s is to consider federal grants to states as a percentage of total federal spending. In 1980, grants to states constituted 15.5 percent of total federal spending—by 1990 they were only 10.8 percent. However, during George H. W. Bush's administration, federal funding would rise to about 31 percent and remain at that level during the administrations of both Bill Clinton and George W. Bush.

Compounding the money problem was the problem of **unfunded mandates.** Most of these requirements dealt with health, safety, and education. For example, Aurora, Colorado had to cut thousands of street curbs to make them wheelchair compatible—and in compliance with the Americans with Disabilities Act. Bids on curb repairs averaged about $1,500 apiece—and Aurora, not Washington, had to find the money to pay for these repairs. Although Reagan had pledged to give states and localities more flexibility and authority, that pledge was undercut by an avalanche of such mandates imposed by Washington. Indeed, more than a quarter of all statutes in which the federal government preempts state and local laws—setting its own standards and telling the states to enforce them—were enacted in the Reagan years.

Federal courts also created unfunded mandates for the states, issuing orders in areas such as prison construction and management. These court orders often required states to spend funds to meet standards imposed by the judge.

Devolution? (1993–2008)

Like Reagan, Bill Clinton came to office wary of Washington and committed to cooperating with state governments. As a former governor, he especially wanted to reform federal–state relations. Except in the area of civil rights, he claimed to support state activism. During the period from 1994 through the end of his administration, Clinton and congressional Republicans supported policies that delegated or devolved power to the states.

In government, the term **devolution** (from the Latin *devolutus,* rolling down) refers to the transfer of power or authority from a central government to a state or local government. The idea suggests that solutions to national problems in health, welfare, crime, and the like can emerge from the experiences of various states—the "laboratories of democracy." For example, in recent years, states have embraced a rich variety of education reforms: merit pay for teachers, teacher certification through testing, minimum competency standards for high school graduation, and the so-called no-pass, no-play rules for student extracurricular eligibility. In contrast, the federal Elementary and Secondary Education Act and its progeny set up rigid rules, spent billions of dollars on programs to upgrade the education of children of low-income parents, and generally failed in their purpose. *no child left behind*

An often-cited example of the devolution during the Clinton years is the 1996 welfare reform legislation that replaced the basic welfare program with a program called Personal Responsibility and Work Opportunity Reconciliation Act. Its name captures two themes of the law—(1) individuals should take more responsibility for themselves, and (2) work, not welfare, is the goal of public assistance. The burden of administering the new program was shifted entirely to states. The federal government now gives block grants of money to the states and generally requires that the states match these funds. The law has significant ramifications for federal–state relations. This evolution of power in the area of welfare is seen as a testing ground for the future. If the states are creative and successful in enacting welfare reform, other federal programs and powers may be handed down to the states.

Clinton and Congress also addressed the vexatious issue of unfunded mandates. In 1995, Congress passed and Clinton signed a law that requires both chambers to take a separate, majority vote in order to pass a bill that would impose unfunded mandates of more than $50 million on state and local governments. All antidiscrimination legislation—and most legislation requiring state and local governments to take various actions in exchange for continued federal funding (such as grants for transportation)—are, however, exempt from this procedure. The problem with the Unfunded Mandates Reform Act is that it allows federal agencies themselves to determine whether the proposed rules are "economically significant." In the first three years of the act, no more than three federal actions triggered its provisions.

Like Clinton, George W. Bush came to the presidency from the governorship of a southern state. Unlike Clinton, who advocated targeting specific areas for decentralization, Bush advocated, in principle, the return of power to the states—what might be called a state-centered federalism. Clinton favored delegating rule implementation to state agencies, but he insisted on the right of federal agencies to set national standards, such as those for clean air and water as well as consumer and worker safety. In contrast, Bush, within months of taking office, issued a new order making it harder for federal officials to overrule state decisions.

But the Bush administration sent mixed signals on state-centered federalism. For example:

- Although an advocate for devolution in domestic policymaking, especially regulatory policy, Bush believed in greatly strengthening the office of the president and the national armed forces.
- His support for expanding the role of the states in making and implementing welfare reform was countered by his intervention in public education to impose mandatory national testing on local systems.
- He disagreed with the majority of governors who wanted to regulate the distribution of electric power in their states. Bush argued that state regulation was inefficient.
- He disagreed with the majority of mayors who wanted more funding for homeland security.

Obama and States and Cities (2009–)

What can states and cities expect from the administration of Barack Obama and, just as important, a new Congress? A lot, because the Obama administration bought the idea that

AP Photo/Alex Brandon, File

one of the most effective ways to stabilize the economy is through massive aid to states and localities. The Recovery Act of 2009 is estimated to cost about $787 billion over several years, of which about 280 billion will be administered by states and localities. About 90 percent of the estimated $49 billion is to be provided to states and localities in fiscal year 2009 for health, transportation, and education programs. Within these categories, the three largest programs are increased Medicaid assistance grants, funds for highway infrastructure investment, and the State Fiscal Stabilization Fund, which provides aid to states to plug holes in their budgets.[3]

Beyond the economic stimulus package is the sense that the Obama administration will modify or reverse policies many states disfavored. It's unlikely that the No Child Left Behind education law will survive in its present form. Environment and energy policies will probably change even more. For example, states, which have fought with Washington for years over carbon dioxide emissions, will probably find their adversary becoming their leader.

Possibly the biggest change will come not in the relationship between the national government and the states, but rather between the national government and the cities. For the past 40 years, "urban policy" in the United States largely meant dealing with the problems of the poor. But Obama and his chief urban adviser, Valerie Jarrett, want federal urban policy to evolve into something more: a means of helping cities and their regions become institutions of American economic growth. As Obama told a group of mayors in June 2008, "We also need to stop seeing our cities as the problem and start seeing them as the solution. Because strong cities are the building blocks of strong regions, and strong regions are essential for a strong America." Jarrett has made the same point. "We're going to change things. We understand that it is the cities that are the economic engines of our country."[4] Significantly, Obama created a White House office devoted to formulating and promoting urban policy.

These changes should not surprise us, since Obama is the first big-city president the United States has had for nearly a century. To be sure, other modern presidents have lived in cities at various times in their lives, but before Obama, none had been rooted in a major city. Obama grew up in Honolulu, went to college in Los Angeles and Manhattan, and has spent virtually his entire working life in Chicago.

Alan Greenblatt explains the significance of Obama's urban orientation:

> Obama has fundamentally accepted the argument of mayors and other local officials that metropolitan areas are the primary economic drivers in the country and deserve to be treated as assets rather than problems. It's not just that many central cities have experienced downtown revival and an uptick in population over the past decade. It's that metro areas are punching well above their weight in contributing to the nation's economic activity, even during the economic downturn.[5]

In other words, urban policy is not just about poverty. Rather, it is about making the economic investment in core cities and their suburbs to keep the United States economically competitive in an increasingly knowledge-driven global economy.

Most state and local leaders will probably welcome what appears to be a new sense of collaboration rather than confrontation with the national government. But it might be a good idea not to assume too much. When it comes to IGR, the only safe assumption is that nothing will go quite the way either side expects.

Looking Ahead

Is the beginning of the twenty-first century really a time of devolution in the federal system? This view is derived from the passage of welfare reform in 1996 (discussed above) and a series of Supreme Court decisions that have sought to strengthen states (discussed below). The view is simplistic, however. Change is occurring—as it always has in American federalism—but it is going in contrary directions—centralizing and decentralizing at the same time. To sort out what is happening, we will examine two spheres of activity: constitutional interpretations by the Supreme Court and the everyday work of government as manifest in policies and programs.

The Supreme Court   Although recent decisions have not had the sweep of the historic *McCulloch* and *Gibbons* decisions (see box: "The Supreme Court and Federal–State Relations"), they have had a considerable effect incrementally on IGR. We might examine those decisions in four areas: (1) commerce clause, (2) Tenth Amendment, (3) Eleventh Amendment, and (4) eminent domain.

The Commerce Clause   Article I, Section 8 of the Constitution states that the federal government has the power to regulate commerce among the states. In a widely publicized 1995 case, *United States v. Lopez,* the Supreme Court held that Congress had exceeded its constitutional authority under the commerce clause when it passed the Gun-Free School Zones Act in 1990. The Court stated that the act, which banned the possession of guns within 1000 feet of any school, was unconstitutional because it attempted to regulate an area that had "nothing to do with commerce, or any sort of economic enterprise." This marked the first time in six years that the Supreme Court had placed a limit on the national government's authority under the commerce clause.

In 2000, in *United States v. Morrison,* the Court held that Congress had overreached its authority under the commerce clause when it passed the Violence Against Women Act of 1994. The Court invalidated a key section of the act that provided a federal remedy for gender-motivated violence, such as rape. Chief Justice Rehnquist said that "the Constitution requires a distinction between what is truly national and what is truly local." (The states can, of course, pass such laws, and many have.)

Just when some thought they were witnessing a clear trend toward the centralization, in 2005, the Supreme Court ruled, 6-3, that the commerce clause gave Congress the power to outlaw the local, noncommercial production and use of marijuana for medical purposes, which had been legalized in California and a number of other states. The case, *Gonzalez v. Raich,* had begun as an attempt to block enforcement of federal antidrug laws against medicinal marijuana use in California.

The Tenth Amendment   The Tenth Amendment states that powers not delegated to the national government by the Constitution, nor prohibited by it, are reserved to the states.

The Supreme Court and Federal–State Relations
The Early Years

The Founders defined federalism, but the Supreme Court fine-tuned it. No case was more important to establishing the supremacy of the national voice in governance than *McCulloch v. Maryland* (1819). To raise a little money, the state of Maryland decided to place a tax on a branch of the Bank of the United States. When the tax collector called on James McCulloch, cashier of the Baltimore branch, McCulloch refused to pay. The national courts faced two questions: (1) Because creating banks was never listed as an enumerated power of Congress, was its creation of the Bank of the United States thereby unconstitutional? and (2) Does a state have the power to tax the national government?

Chief Justice Marshall recognized that the power to create banks was not one of the powers specifically delegated to the federal government by the Constitution, but he interpreted the "necessary and proper" clause of Article I broadly so that it enhanced those powers that were specifically delegated and enumerated by the Constitution. By means of this interpretation, Marshall found the creation of the Bank to be a necessary and proper exercise of congressional power. He also held that the state of Maryland lacked the power to tax the national bank. In Marshall's opinion, the power to tax included the power to destroy, and he held the state law providing this power to be unconstitutional and void under Article VI of the Constitution.

The *McCulloch* decision has been used to support a broad construction of the Constitution that enables the federal government to apply the supreme law flexibility to meet the new problems of changing times. In this case, Marshall made a memorable statement, which is often quoted to support a broad interpretation of the national government's constitutional powers: "This . . . is . . . a Constitution we are expounding, intended to endure for ages to come, and consequently, to be adapted to the various crises of human affairs."

The Marshall Court strengthened its argument five years later in *Gibbons v. Ogden*. This case involved a steamboat operator, Aaron Ogden, who had a New York license to operate the only ferry on the interstate waters between New York and New Jersey. A competitor named Thomas Gibbons sued, arguing that only Congress could regulate interstate waters.

The Marshall Court agreed unanimously. The Constitution had specifically granted Congress the power to regulate commerce, but there was much more room for interpretation in this broad grant. Marshall interpreted "commerce" broadly, and he further held that commerce power was complete in itself, with no limitations other than those specifically found in the Constitution.

The *Gibbons* case paved the way for later federal regulation on all transportation, communication, buying and selling, and manufacturing. In the twentieth century, for example, the court has ruled that the commerce clause permits Congress to fine a farmer for producing a small amount of wheat for his own use in violation of the quota set by the Department of Agriculture. Suffice it to say, little economic activity remains outside the regulatory power of Congress today.

In *New York v. United States* (1992), the Supreme Court held that requirements imposed on the state of New York under a federal act regulating low-level radioactive waste were inconsistent with the Tenth Amendment. According to the Court, the act's "take title" provision, which required states to accept ownership of waste or regulate waste according to Congress' instructions, exceeded the enumerated powers of Congress. Although Congress can regulate the handling of such waste, it may not order state governments as its agents in attempting to enforce a program of federal regulation.

In 1997, the Court revisited the Tenth Amendment issue. In *Printz v. United States*, the Court struck down the provisions of the federal Brady Handgun Violence Prevention Act of 1993 that required state employees to check the backgrounds of prospective handgun purchasers. The federal government, the Court said, "may neither issue directives requiring the states to address particular problems, nor command the States' officers . . . to administer or enforce a federal regulatory program." The Court held that the provisions violated "the very principle of separate state sovereignty," which was "one of the Constitution's structural protections of liberty."

The Eleventh Amendment   The Eleventh Amendment, which protects states from lawsuits by citizens of other states or foreign governments, has also helped advance state power. As interpreted by the Court, that amendment precludes lawsuits against state governments even for violations of rights established by federal law—unless the states consent to be sued. For example, in *Alden v. Maine* (1999), the Court held that Maine state employees could not sue the state for violating the overtime pay requirements of a federal act. According to the Court, state immunity from such lawsuits "is a fundamental aspect of sovereignty." Similarly, in *Kimel v. Florida Board of Regents* (2000), the Court held that the Eleventh Amendment precluded employees of a state university from suing the state to enforce a federal statute prohibiting age-based discrimination. Although private-sector employees are protected under this federal law, state employees are not.

In 2002, the Court further expanded the states' sovereign immunity from private lawsuits. Writing for the majority, Justice Clarence Thomas declared in *Federal Maritime Commission v. South Carolina Ports Authority* that dual sovereignty "is a defining feature of our nation's constitutional blueprint." States, he continued, "did not consent to become mere appendages of the federal government" when they ratified the Constitution.

Because the majority of pro-state sovereignty decisions have been decided by a tenuous five-to-four margin, the president's authority to nominate justices will be one of the decisive factors—perhaps *the* decisive factor—in determining the future trajectory of federal–state relations.

Eminent Domain   In 2005, the Court greatly expanded the power of local governments in relation to the property rights of private citizens. In *Kelo v. New London*, the Court ruled, five to four, that local governments may seize people's homes and businesses—even against their will—for private economic development. Roughly 70 percent of Americans own their own homes, a statistic that helps explain why the ruling was widely reviled. The New London, Connecticut residents who challenged the loss of their property had conceded that the city government could properly take private property for a clear public use such as roads or schools under the well-established power of **eminent domain.** But, they argued, government should *not* be able to take private property for projects such as shopping malls and hotel complexes to generate local tax revenue.

At first blush, the *Kelo* decision appears to be a clear win for cities. Homeowners could be forced now to sell not just to a city but to private developers who want to build a project that would expand the city's tax base. The court clearly indicated that localities have a legitimate role in planning and that economic development—and particularly, improving blighted areas—cannot be halted simply because some property owner objects. But the courts do not make decisions in a political vacuum. According to the Institute for Justice, since *Kelo*, 43 states have amended their laws to protect private property more vigilantly. Federal legislation curtailing eminent domain was introduced but did not pass.[6]

Policies and Programs   Those who see devolution point to welfare reform in 1996 as "proof." But those who see the federal system as centralizing have their own "proof": the No Child Left Behind Act of 2001 that imposes new rules on a 200-year-old state and local education responsibility. Those who see the balance of power shifting to Washington also remind us that Congress continues to refuse to pay for programs in special education and homeland security that it insisted on enacting. Further, the jointly administered State-Federal Medicaid program has brought some states to the brink of insolvency.

In the view of some federalism experts, the American federal system has evolved into one in which Congress simply seizes control of any state issue it wishes to grab. Paul Posner, for example, cites a dramatic increase in the number of state laws that Congress has voted to preempt in recent years, especially in the fields of health, environment, transportation, and public safety. According to Posner, before 1970, there were rarely as many as 40 of these preemptions in a decade. Since then, the number appears to have roughly tripled.[7]

Yet one could argue that the reason the number of preemptions has risen is that *states have become more active.* When Congress failed to pass meaningful health-care legislation in the 1990s—much less solve the riddle of how to provide health insurance for the 46 million Americans who lack it—many states acted. For example, the Massachusetts legislature passed a bill in 2006 that would make health insurance compulsory. Just as everyone who drives a car must insure it, so everyone with a body must insure that, too. The same pattern of states taking charge of the agenda, while Washington remains too politically polarized to act, can be seen with such disparate policy issues as utility regulation, stem cell research, abortion, immigration, minimum wage, and mercury emissions.[8]

One of the more powerful arguments against the centralization thesis has been the crucial activism of attorneys general. With regard to these state officials, Alan Ehrenhalt writes, "In the years since their first important victory—the multibillion-dollar legal settlement reached by more than 40 states with the major tobacco companies—attorneys general have been active on almost every conceivable legal front: suing utilities to limit carbon dioxide emissions; filing legal actions against mutual funds and insurance companies; taking pharmaceutical companies to court with accusations of illegal marketing of prescription drugs."[9]

Federal—State Relations: An Economic Perspective

Thus far, we have been looking at federal–state relations in historical terms. But historians, political scientists, and constitutional lawyers are not the only ones who have something valuable to say about the nature of these relations. In this section, we will hear from the economists in the *Economic Report of the President, 1996*:

> Some might make the case that the federal government should do nothing other than national defense. After all, states and localities are better able to tailor their programs to meet the different needs and preferences of their residents, and competition among the states may enhance efficiency and innovation, just as it does in the private sector. But this view ignores the benefits of [f]ederal action in a number of areas. The enumeration of powers given to the federal government under the Constitution suggests that even in the early infancy of the Republic, [the Founders] recognized the advantages of federal involvement across a broad range of endeavors. The economic strength of the United States rests in part on [its] vast national market, fostered not only by the free flow of commerce without artificial trade barriers, but also by national standards and a national transportation and communications system.
>
> Economists have sought to identify some general principles that would elucidate a "rational" division of responsibilities between levels of government. At least four categories of arguments justifying federal action can be identified.

The Need For Uniformity

Although diversity among state government programs is often desirable, in some cases the benefits of uniform government action across the states tip the scale toward federal involvement. Uniformity of standards and regulations may improve efficiency. For example, uniform rules for interstate commerce preserve one of America's strengths: our large national market. Conflicting state regulations could fragment this market and impede producers' ability to take advantage of economies of scale. Likewise, uniformity in minimum safety net benefits would guarantee that all needy Americans, regardless of where they live, enjoy at least a certain level of well-being, and would avoid distorting and inefficient movements of households in response to differences in benefits.

Direct Spillovers

Actions taken or not taken by states sometimes affect residents of other states. Residents of a state might be willing to tolerate pollution of their ground water, but the contaminated water could seep across state boundaries and harm residents of other states. States may also engage in activities that unintentionally benefit the residents of other states. For example, one state's successful innovation in its schools can lead the way for other states to reform their education systems, and states' efforts to prevent communicable diseases can benefit the health of nonresidents. Similarly, when states invest more in education, and incomes rise as a consequence, they confer a positive benefit on all taxpayers: The federal government reaps some of the rewards of the higher incomes in the form of higher federal tax revenues. When the policies of one state affect the residents of others, for good or for ill, states may lack the right incentives to provide an appropriate level of public services, because the effects of policies on nonresidents may not factor strongly in their decision making.

The Effects of Policy-Induced Mobility

The freedom of people and firms to move at will from state to state promotes competition among state governments. Although this competition can enhance the efficiency of government, it can also make it difficult for states to pursue certain worthwhile policies. For example, the fear of welfare-induced migration may cause states to reduce welfare benefits to a level below what they would otherwise provide. Similarly, state competition for jobs may limit the generosity of unemployment insurance programs.

Inequality of Resources

States that are poorer than the average, or that are experiencing temporary downturns, are able to raise less revenue, yet have to spend more than other states to provide services for the needy. Clearly, only the federal government can transfer resources among the states. Not only does such redistribution help poorer states, but financial assistance from the federal government that increases during economic downturns can also help to stabilize regional economies. This assistance can be given through a number of channels: direct transfers of cash or in-kind benefits to lower-income individuals, grants to lower-income states or localities, matching grants to state or local programs for the needy, or direct provision of public services in poor communities. The role of the federal government in transferring resources to states and localities is more complicated, both in theory and in practice, than is often recognized.

These rationales for a federal role are not mutually exclusive, and sometimes it is their interaction that makes a strong case for a federal role in policy. For example, national safety standards, when desirable, might evolve on their own, were it not for spillovers. States could simply agree to a set of voluntary standards, and each state would weigh the benefits and costs of complying. In doing so, however, it would ignore the costs it might impose on others. A state might adopt more lax safety regulation for its cars, but then when its cars cross over into another state, the other state bears part of the costs. Federal action is therefore needed to ensure uniform national standards that avoid these spillover effects. [10]

Other Important Relationships in the Intergovernmental System

The first three sections of this chapter have focused primarily on relationships between the federal government and the 50 states. But IGR also comprise state–state (interstate) relations, state–local relations, and local–local (interlocal) relations. To these important relations we now turn.

State–State Relations

Some aspects of interstate relations are governed by constitutional rule, while other aspects are the result of practical needs.

Constitutional Aspects   Three clauses in the Constitution are especially relevant to interstate relations. First, the **full faith and credit clause** (Article IV, Section 1) requires state courts to enforce the civil judgments of the courts of other states and accept their public records and acts as valid. It does not require states to enforce the criminal laws of other states; in most cases, for one state to enforce the criminal laws of another would raise constitutional issues. The clause applies especially to enforcement of judicial settlements and court awards.

The full faith and credit clause became part of the national debate on May 17, 2004, when Massachusetts became the first state to allow same-sex couples to get married. Although much has been written about how other states should treat these marriages, the real legal conundrum concerns how they treat the breakup of a same-sex marriage. Because states are not prohibited by federal law from recognizing same-sex marriages performed in other states, they should be able to grant same-sex divorces. Even the 39 states that oppose gay marriage may have an interest in doing so, because they would be ending something they view as a problem in the first place. If they refuse to do so, they would be making same-sex marriage even more binding than those between heterosexuals.[11]

Article IV, Section 1 of the Constitution also asserts that when individuals charged with crimes have fled from one state to another, the state to which they have fled is to deliver them to the proper officials upon the demand of the executive authority of the state from which they fled. This process is called **extradition.**

Second, under Article IV, Section 2, states must extend to citizens of other states the privileges and immunities granted to their own citizens, including the protection of the laws, the right to engage in peaceful occupations, access to the courts, and freedom from discriminatory taxes. Because of this clause, states may not impose unreasonable residency requirements—that is, withholding rights of American citizens who have recently moved to the state and thereby have become citizens of that state.

Third, Article 1, Section 10 permits states to enter into **interstate compacts,** or agreements (with the consent of Congress). The Crime Compact of 1934, which allows parole officers to cooperate across state lines with a minimum of red tape, is now subscribed to by all states. States lacking adequate facilities make compacts with other states to help them with problems that might arise, such as with professional education, welfare, tuberculosis, and mental illness.

As state officials have had to cope with problems involving transportation, energy, pollution, water resources, and fishing rights across state boundaries, the number of compacts has risen accordingly. Whereas there were only 24 compacts before 1900, today more than 170 exist.

The Port Authority of New York and New Jersey is one of the more notable and larger interstate agencies established by an interstate compact. Created in 1921 to develop and operate the harbor facilities in the area, the authority now also constructs and operates bridges, tunnels, terminal facilities, and airports.

Practical Aspects   States collaborate—must collaborate—on many issues. For example, few highways end abruptly at a state's border, so states must coordinate road construction. Likewise, few mosquitoes end their flight paths at a border, so states must coordinate insect control.

Sometimes states cooperate not because they *must* but because it can save money. For example:

> Hawaii chose to piggyback on Arizona's system for medical patients, instead of building its own. The system Arizona runs for both itself and Hawaii is a huge and complex Prepaid Medical Management Information System for managed care. Arizona operates Hawaii's system from its (Arizona's) Department of Administration mainframe with the same staff that manages its own. Not all of Hawaii's state requirements are the same as Arizona's, but Arizona enhanced its system so that it could support Hawaii's requirements. All the information on doctors and hospitals and the services delivered to patients in Hawaii are run through Arizona's system, and the data resides there.[12]

One important way the states collaborate is by adopting uniform laws. A notable example of this is the Uniform Commercial Code (UCC), which was created in 1952 through the joint efforts of the National Conference of Commissioners on Uniform State Laws and the American Law Institute. All 50 states have adopted the UCC. The UCC facilitates commerce among the states by providing a uniform, yet flexible, set of rules governing commercial transactions. The UCC assures businesspersons that their contracts, if entered into validly, normally will be enforced.

Another means of interstate collaboration is the establishment of regional commissions. With the backing of the federal government, various states have formed the following regional commissions: the Appalachian Regional Commission, the Northern Great Plains Regional Commission, and the Delta Regional Authority.

One type of cooperative action, the first of its kind in the nation, came after the George W. Bush administration decided not to regulate the greenhouse gases that contribute to global warming. In 2005, officials in nine northeastern states agreed to freeze power plant emissions at the current levels and then reduce them by 10 percent by 2020. Although any reduction achieved in the region would be significant, environmentalists believe that the real importance of the cooperative effort is the example it sets for other states.

One final means of collaboration between states should be mentioned: *bartering*. Some barter systems might have made sense at any time because they allow states to cut the size of government, split their cost, and share services. But the urgent political will to barter was absent until the 2008–2009 recession, which forced states to share. Consider, for example, how Minnesota and Wisconsin have teamed up:

> Minnesota was looking for a bargain on the tiniest walleye fish, known as frylings, that the state stocks in some of its lakes. Wisconsin needed more of the longer fingerlings for its fishing lakes. So the neighbors have decided to share a fish— Wisconsin's frylings for Minnesota's fingerlings—along with hundreds of other items: bullets for the police, menus for prisoners, trucks for bridge inspections, and sign language interpreters.[13]

State–Local Relations

As the federal government became a less dependable source of financial assistance to local government, expectations about the role of states in domestic policy shifted. That states moved to replace some lost federal grant funds to local governments contributed to a widespread sense among observers of the intergovernmental system that states were "on the move." In 2000, local governments received $327 billion in revenue from state governments, while $292 billion came from Washington.

Cash is not the only connection between states and localities. Although we associate police forces, firefighting companies, and public health and zoning agencies with the very essence of local government, it is important to note that all those functions and agencies operate under state laws. The state legislature and courts allow cities to adapt state laws to local needs, but cities remain under state authority. This principle was confirmed in 1868 in a famous ruling known as **Dillon's rule.** Judge John F. Dillon of Iowa ruled that *state legislatures were supreme over cities.* Legislatures could, in his words, "sweep from existence" all cities—and the latter could not do a thing to prevent it.

Of course, state governments did not sweep cities from existence. Quite the contrary. They gave them more power and autonomy. The most important means of giving cities independence was **home rule.** Essentially, home rule is *the power vested in local units of government—mostly cities—to carry on their affairs with a minimum of external legislative or administrative control.* Home rule implies that local units have the power to write and adopt a charter, to change the charter, and to adopt ordinances and make administrative decisions that have the force of law. State home rule laws vary, but all permit a measure of freedom for cities. Most home rule provisions are incorporated in state constitutions. These provisions guarantee that state legislatures will not pass legislation concerning the local affairs, property, and government of cities except by laws of statewide application. In other words, no city can be subjected to special legislation imposed on that city alone by the state legislature.

Although some states have departments to coordinate state and local affairs, administrative relations between the city and the state generally are conducted on a functional basis. Thus, the state department of education supervises the activities of local school districts, and the state department of health, the activities of local health departments.

State bureaucracies have several techniques of supervision. First, they can simply require reports from local communities. Reports warn the state agency when trouble spots (for example, excessive debts) begin to appear. Second, state agencies can, as the federal government does for them, furnish advice and information. Third, with larger budgets and more specialized equipment and personnel, the state can provide technical aid. Finally, if all else fails, the state can use its coercive power. For example, it can grant or withhold permits for certain things (for example, to dump raw sewage into a stream under prescribed conditions); issue orders (for example, to prescribe the standards for water-supply purification); withhold grants-in-aid; require prior permission from a state agency for an action; and appoint or remove certain local officials.

State bureaucracies clamor for relief from unfunded mandates, but many of them do unto their localities what Washington does unto them. After spending more than a decade

Figure 3.1   Forms of City Governments

A. The mayor-council form of city government organization

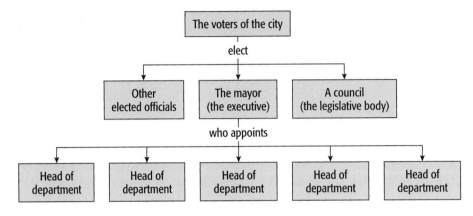

B. The council-manager form of city government organization

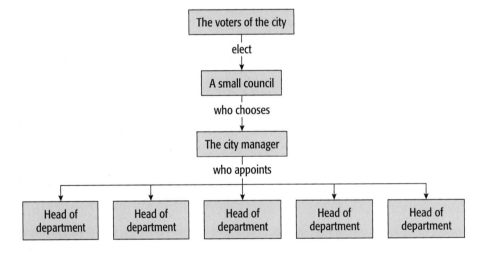

deliberating the propriety of federal mandates imposed on states, politicians and administrators have begun to focus on the tension between states and their localities. South Carolina has in effect 695 administrative and legislative mandates—some dating from 1842. The cumulative effect of such mandates to a town is burdensome, if not devastating.

Local–Local Relations

Cities   Although there are some variations, most municipalities have one of two basic types of institutional arrangements: a mayor-council form of government or a council-manager form. The **mayor-council form** reproduces at the municipal level the standard institutions of American government with a separately elected legislature (the city council) and chief executive (the mayor). See Figure 3.1(A). The council typically has five to nine members, except in very large cities, such as Chicago, where the council has 50 members.

The **council-manager form** is unique in American government. See Figure 3.1(B). It is the closest thing the United States has to a parliamentary system. In the council-manager form, as in a parliamentary system, there is no independent executive. Instead, the legislature (city council) appoints the chief of the executive branch, the city manager. Unlike in the parliamentary system, however, the city manager is not a political leader. Instead, the city manager is a professional trained in city management and is supposed to administer city services in an expert, nonpartisan way. It is useful to think of these forms as being at the ends of a continuum (as shown below), and city residents as being able to adapt extensive variations along that continuum (as indicated by points A, B, and C).

If we ask ourselves what it is we admire about a successful corporation, it's not hard to see why city residents might want to be on the right end of the continuum. First, successful corporations are efficient: They get their work done with a minimum of wasted effort and resources. Second, top management is accountable. Ideally, chief executive officers are held firmly responsible for their performance and results. Although a city can't become a corporation, it can hire a professional manager or chief administrative officer to replace wasteful political patronage with nonpartisan administration. The downside of this arrangement is that the city loses the benefits of having highly visible political leadership. Now it lacks any public figure with the power and influence to make tough decisions and get them accepted.

So some cities might want to be on the left end of the continuum. Residents in these cities can choose a strong mayor and get the leader they seek. The downside of this move is that it can bring an element of management cronyism and politically tainted policy decisions. Thus, cities at either end of the continuum will have incentive to adapt at least a few of the features of the alternative form of government—in other words, move to positions A, B, or C.

What might a move from a pure council-manager form of government to, say, point C involve? Whereas the council used to select the mayor, now the people directly elect him or her. Whereas the mayor did not have veto power, now he or she may have it. Whereas the people used to elect council members at-large—in other words, in citywide elections—now they can choose some members by district. The upshot of this change is to make the member more beholden to the political and economic interest of particular neighborhoods rather than the best interest of the entire city.

And what might a move from a pure mayor-council form of government to, say, point A look like? Whereas voters elected most council by district, now voters may elect some at large. Whereas the city had no chief administrative officer, now it may. Whereas council had a staff, now it may not. Whereas the mayor served as the chief administrative officer, now he or she may hire and fire one without consent of counsel.

For empirical support of this analysis of how and why cities might adapt their structures, we turn to a recent study by H. George Frederickson and his colleagues. I cannot present here a thorough discussion of their findings but will outline some relevant points:

1. In 1900, virtually all U.S. cities employed the mayor-council form of government.
2. "For much of the 20th century, council-manager city government was thought to be the new idea, the reform model. As we approach the 100th anniversary of council-manager government, it is no longer a new idea. . . . Council-manager government was designed to solve corruption, inefficiency, and management problems, and it did. Now . . . most reform cities with council-manager structures have turned their attention to economic development, political responsiveness, political leadership and accountability, and equity."
3. For the first half of the 20th century, the mayor-council and council-manager forms of government were relatively good descriptions of distinctly different structures. Beginning in the 1950s, cities using both structures began a steady process of structural adaptation. "But these cities continue to be legally categorized as mayor-council or council-manager structures, categories that often mask actual structural details."
4. As early as the late 1920s, some council-manager cities began moving to point C.
5. "Beginning in the 1950s, the most prominent features of council-manager government, such as a professional executive and a merit civil service, were widely adopted in mayor-council cities. At the same time, the most prominent features of mayor-council government, such as a directly elected mayor and some or all members of the city council elected by districts, were being widely adopted in council-manager form government."
6. In summary, over the past 50 years, more and more mayor-council cities have adopted many of the key features of council-manager cities to increase their administrative efficiency. Meanwhile, more and more council-manager cities have adopted many of the key features of mayor-council cities to increase their political responsiveness. "Fewer cities now are either distinctly mayor-council or council-manager form, and most cities are structurally less distinct, constituting a newly merged or hybrid model of local government."[14] Point B represents that hybrid model.

Counties and Special Districts   The difference between a county and a municipality is that a county may not be created at the behest of its inhabitants. The state sets up counties on its own initiative to serve as political extensions of the state government. Counties are sometimes called "invisible governments." The media tend to ignore them—and many citizens are not even aware of the functions counties provide. (County governments' responsibilities include zoning, building regulations, health, hospitals, parks, recreation, highways, public safety, justice, and record keeping. Counties also run airports, bridges, water systems, and sewage systems.) Size—even enormous size—is no guarantee of public attention. Los Angeles County's 10 million people make it the nation's most populous local jurisdiction. It has more people than all but eight states, and it boasts a land area bigger than Delaware and Rhode Island combined. Yet even local residents frequently become confused over just who is a county supervisor and who is on the Los Angeles City Council. The supervisors, among the most powerful public officials in America, still manage to operate in anonymity most of the time.

Although the media and most of the electorate have continued to ignore counties, the fact is that they are becoming more important players in American government with each passing year. As the state and federal governments have pulled back on funding in areas such as health care, aid to the poor, and criminal justice, it is counties—much more than states and cities—that are generally obligated to fill the gap.

Towns—not to be confused with the word "town" when used as a synonym for city—are a unique governmental creation. In Maine, Massachusetts, New Hampshire, Vermont, and Connecticut, the unit called the town combines the roles of city and county in one governing unit. A New England town typically consists of one or more urban settlements and the surrounding rural areas. Consequently, counties have little importance in New England.

Townships operate somewhat like counties. Where they exist—there may be several dozen within a county—they perform the same functions that the county would otherwise perform. Indiana, Illinois, Kansas, Michigan, Minnesota, New Jersey, New York, Ohio, Pennsylvania, and Wisconsin all have numerous townships.

Special districts are usually run by commissioners who may be elected or may be appointed by elected officials in other governmental units. Among the largest special districts in the United States are the following: Port Authority of New York and New Jersey, Salt River Project District (Arizona), Washington Public Power Supply System, Washington [D.C.] Metropolitan Area Rapid Transit Authority, Chicago Transit Authority, Massachusetts Bay Transportation Authority, Southern California Rapid Transit, Southeastern Pennsylvania Transit Authority, and Southern California Metropolitan Water District. One important feature of special districts is that they cut across geographic and governmental boundaries. Sometimes special districts even cut across state lines. For example, a metropolitan transit district may provide bus service to dozens of municipalities and several counties.

Fragmentation, Cooperation, and Competition   The following story took place several decades ago—and it's all true. After hearing about the impressive governmental reforms Frederick Gardiner had effected in Toronto, a group of Pittsburgh civic leaders invited him to a dinner in their city. Naturally, they asked how he had managed to accomplish so much. One reform, Gardiner said, made it all possible: consolidation of many small and inefficient municipal governments into a single, all-encompassing metropolitan regime. As he spoke, guests at tables in the front row began to notice small missiles flying over their heads and toward Gardiner. The assembled mayors, council members, and police chiefs of Allegheny County were throwing dinner rolls at Gardiner for advocating consolidation![15]

It is not difficult to figure out why they were upset. Pittsburgh and surrounding Allegheny County are home to possibly the most unwieldy and inefficient patchwork of local governments in America. The 1.3 million county residents live in 130 different municipalities, the vast majority of them with fewer than 10,000 residents. Yet each tiny government has its own mayor and council as well as its own struggle to maintain police forces, public utilities, street maintenance, and a host of other services. Today most urban experts would agree with the ill-fated Gardiner from Toronto: Any big city needs to join forces with the suburbs around it in order to survive.

Although the situation in Allegheny County may be extreme, fragmentation of local government is not a problem unique to this county. Each governing body in thousands of cities and towns tends to look at problems from its narrow perspective. As a result, local bodies fail to cooperate with one another and plan effectively for the region's future needs.

Traditionally, regional cooperation on specific policy areas—for example, transportation and water and sewage—has been undertaken through the use of the special districts discussed above. But there are limits to the number of districts that can be established efficiently and the level of coordination these districts can achieve. What then can be done to coordinate a variety of public services in a metropolitan area? For starters, local governments can enter into interlocal service arrangements or agreements to determine/deliver services to their citizens. Essentially, there are three types of such arrangements.[16]

1. *Intergovernmental service agreements:* One jurisdiction pays another to deliver certain services to its residents. Most favored services delivered through intergovernmental service agreements are prisons and programs for the elderly and public health.
2. *Joint service agreements:* Two or more governments agree to the joint planning, financing, and delivering of certain services to the residents of all participating jurisdictions. Libraries and public safety communication are popular areas.
3. *Intergovernmental service transfers:* A jurisdiction permanently transfers one of its responsibilities to another government, private corporation, or nonprofit agency. Favored areas of transfer are public works and utilities, health, and welfare.

In many areas of the country, a **council of governments** (frequently referred to as a COG) exists wherein officials from various localities meet to discuss mutual problems and plan joint, cooperative action. These cooperative arrangements facilitate a regional approach to growth, transportation, pollution, and other problems that affect a region as a whole. These COGs are often formally very weak, being underfunded, poorly staffed, and lacking in any real legislative or taxing power. However, a few areas have developed superlocals, institutional arrangements that act almost as general-purpose governments for an entire region. Seattle, Miami, and Minneapolis-St. Paul all have a metropolitan council that serves such a function. For example, the Minneapolis-St. Paul Metropolitan Council operates the region's bus service, provides sewer and water services, operates a regional housing and development authority, and funds and plans regional parks and trails—all activities that cut across traditional local government's physical and policy area boundaries.

Unfortunately, such examples of institutions for regional coordination are the exception rather than the rule. For the most part, Americans have shown little interest in promoting regional cooperation to correct the inequalities and coordination problems that result from metropolitan fragmentation. Generally speaking, the United States lacks the strong tradition of regional planning evident in Europe. Consider how British planners prevented the overgrowth of London: They encircled the city with a "green belt"—a designated area in which the countryside would be preserved and no new development permitted. The growth of the region's population was absorbed in planned "new towns" that were built some distance from the central city. The result was a mixture of city and countryside in a metropolitan area and the avoidance of American-style urban sprawl.[17]

Global trends might also have a decisive effect on complacent American urban areas such as Pittsburgh. Neal Peirce argues that the actions of "citi-states," or great metropolitan regions, whether they be Singapore or Seattle, are increasingly driving the global economy.[18] Accordingly, each regional economy must define its own profitable niche, and its localities and leaders must work collaboratively toward that end. That work will involve regional systems of governance, regional transportation and environmental planning, fiscal equity between big cities and their suburbs, and, according to Peirce, preparation for a multicultural future.

It will also involve rethinking the notion of what a city is. For official purposes, such as allocating federal funds, OMB has produced a formal definition of metropolitan areas. They are referred to as **metropolitan statistical areas (MSAs)** and defined as a county or group of counties that contains at least one city of 50,000 or more. The contiguous counties are included in an MSA if they are all metropolitan in character and are socially and economically integrated with the central city. The Pittsburgh MSA, for example, consists of Allegheny County, Armstrong County, Beaver County, Butler County, Fayette County, Washington County, and Westmoreland County.

Robert Lang and Dawn Dhavale at Virginia Tech advocate that the federal government use an even broader overlay than the MSA to capture regional economic and social realities. They identify ten *megalopolises* in the United States that function in the same ways as giant cities. Many features define and create a megalopolitan area. The flow of goods, services, and people—where the branch offices of a company are, where associated businesses and industries locate or emerge—plays an important part. But the principal piece of infrastructure is the interstate highway. For example, one megalopolis, which stretches from Kansas City down through Oklahoma City, Dallas, Austin, and San Antonio, is knitted together by I-35. Similarly, I-85 and I-81 pull together the Charlotte, Atlanta, and Raleigh megalopolis. The second largest of the ten megalopolises is the Midwest, stretching from Pittsburgh to Chicago. See Figure 3.2.

Lang and Dhavale would argue, along with Peirce, that megalopolises are the new competitive units in the global economy. Robert Yaro, president of the Regional Planning Association in New York City, says: "We've used up the capacity in our existing infrastructure systems, and we need to build more in a focused, thought-out way. Our competitors in Europe and Japan are doing this already."[19]

Managerial Implications

Besides the political skills noted in the previous chapter and the program management skills discussed in Part Two, what else does it take to be effective at managing IGR? This section suggests two additional tools: agency theory and negotiating. Although we will be discussing them chiefly in the context of IGR, it should be kept in mind that these tools have very broad application in public administration.

Principal–Agent Theory

Economists have developed an analytical framework well suited to the task of managing in an interorganizational setting: the **principal–agent model.** Essentially, the model expresses analytically any relationship in which one party, the principal, considers entering

Figure 3.2   Megalopolises and Interstates

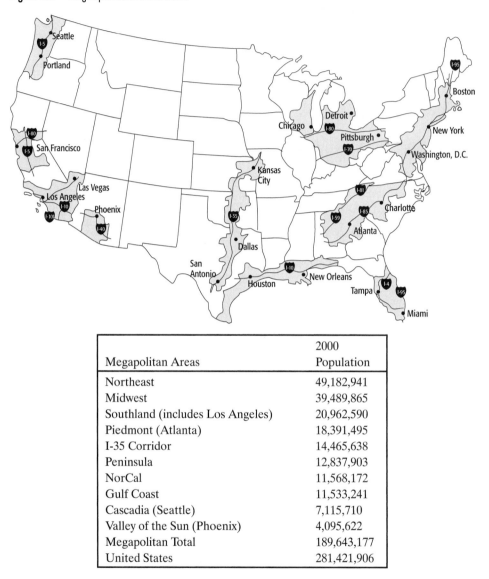

Megapolitan Areas	2000 Population
Northeast	49,182,941
Midwest	39,489,865
Southland (includes Los Angeles)	20,962,590
Piedmont (Atlanta)	18,391,495
I-35 Corridor	14,465,638
Peninsula	12,837,903
NorCal	11,568,172
Gulf Coast	11,533,241
Cascadia (Seattle)	7,115,710
Valley of the Sun (Phoenix)	4,095,622
Megapolitan Total	189,643,177
United States	281,421,906

Source: Robert E. Lang and Dawn Dhavale, *Beyond Megalopolis: Exploring America's New "Megapolitan" Geography*, Metropolitan Institute Census Report Series (July 2005), 14 and 15.

into a contractual agreement with another, the agent, in the expectation that the agent will subsequently choose actions that produce outcomes desired by the principal. The employer (the principal) seeks to purchase the skills of an employee (the agent) to perform the organization's task. The government agency (the principal) hires another organization (the agent) to help in the attainment of the principal's goals. Other examples of agency relationships include doctor–patient, broker–investor, lawyer–client, politician–citizen, and politician–administrator. Obviously, principals seek agents for various reasons. They may lack the requisite knowledge or the legal certification that the agent has, or they may find the task too large or complex to perform alone.

Adverse Selection and Moral Hazard   Regardless of the reason for relying on an agent, the principal faces two problems:

- *Adverse selection.* Consider an example in which a government bureau seeks bidders for a project requiring independent, creative work. Although the bureau would like to attract highly qualified and motivated companies, its top administrators cannot know any given company's true intellectual resources or work habits. So they must proceed on the basis of rough indicators, such as educational credentials and previous work experience, thus declaring the government's willingness to pay a certain price for companies that are nominally qualified according to these indicators. "The price is, in effect, a statistical average, reflecting both the estimated implications of the indicator for productivity and the estimated variation in productivity across all [companies that] qualify."[20] In other words, the company's true worth may be substantially above (or below) the price offered. If the company is, in fact, highly qualified, it will tend to find that the government's proxy-based price is too low; if the company is, however, severely lacking in qualifications but still meets the proxy requirement, it will tend to find the price attractive indeed. The highly qualified type of agent is, however, likely to look elsewhere for "better" jobs with proxy categories that are either more finely measured or are simply "pitched" at a higher level. Thus, the **adverse selection theory** contends that principals tend to hire lower-quality agents than desired.

- *Moral hazard.* Once the contract has been signed, the bureau faces another problem: The actual behavior of the company is not entirely observable. Because the principal cannot know for sure to what extent the agent is productive, it must again rely on proxies: quality of reports, timeliness, diligence, and so forth. As a result, the agent has an incentive to redirect its efforts toward the proxy measures rather than abstract goals implicit in the contract. For example, a city (the principal) hires a company (the agent) to treat people with drug addiction. Although the real goal of the program may be to turn hard-core drug addicts into drug-free, solid citizens, the proxy measure of performance is "people treated per month." Therefore, the agent has an incentive to sign up as many people as possible (some of whom may be only recreational users) and process them through the program as rapidly as possible. Further, the agent has an incentive to substitute leisure or shirking behavior for productive effort, because the agent knows that inadequate performance may not be detected. After all, the city has numerous contracts at a variety of locations and cannot possibly have an employee at each site all the time monitoring the work. This problem is an example of **moral hazard,** which is the form of postcontractual opportunism that arises because actions that have efficiency consequences are not freely observable. So the person taking these actions may choose to pursue his or her private interest at the other's expense. In short, the term *moral hazard* refers to *any behavior under a contract that is inefficient.* Interestingly, the term originated in the insurance industry, where it referred to the tendency of people with insurance to change their behavior in a way that leads to larger claims against the insurance company. For example, being insured may make people lax about taking precautions to avoid or minimize losses.

Principles of Agency Theory   How, then, can the principal design an incentive structure that will induce the agent to pursue the principal's objectives? The answer is "bound up with the development of monitoring systems as well as mechanisms for inducing the agent to reveal as much of his privately held information as possible."[21] Several concepts have emerged in the literature regarding the principal–agent relationship to explain why different relationships entail different levels of monitoring and types of incentives, and why this monitoring and incentive structure exists. Some concepts are self-evident but have implications that are frequently overlooked:[22]

1. There tends to be less monitoring, or monitoring of poorer quality, when monitoring is expensive.
2. Administrative difficulties are the most severe when the interests or values of the principal and agent diverge substantially, and information monitoring is costly. See example below.

Some concepts are less obvious, or counterintuitive, but no less important:

3. Ideally the agent's information *and* action should both be monitored. However, in a range of real-world situations, much more limited monitoring—say of an indicator of output—can be successful.
4. A large stock of value, such as reputation or assets subject to suit, that could be lost because of bad behavior is a strong incentive for good behavior.
5. Long-term relationships, among other benefits, develop the stocks of value needed for "enforcement" and make limited monitoring more effective.
6. The benefits of a reduction in agency costs or an increase in agency output will be shared between principal and agent in most situations. For example, if a contractor hired by a state to deliver some service discovers a cheaper way to do so, the savings will be shared with the state. Therefore, the principal (the state) and the agent (the contractor) have a common interest in defining a monitoring-and-incentive structure that produces outcomes as close as possible to ones that would be produced if information monitoring were costless.

An Example   Bureaucratic institutions in the United States have evolved in large numbers and remarkable variety, making the search for generalization difficult. Kettl has suggested a way to use agency theory to better understand how administrative practice varies.[23]

Agency behavior varies with respect to two factors: information costs and goal congruency. Consider the Federal Aviation Administration's (FAA's) air traffic controllers. Because they work with willing clients (pilots) who have a keen interest in avoiding traffic, **goal congruency**, or the amount that both parties strive in common toward a goal, is

Figure 3.3   Variance of Programs by Information and Goal

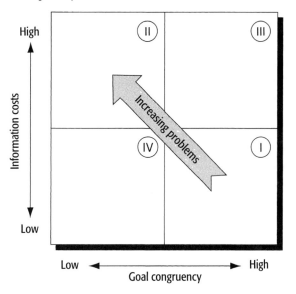

Source: Adapted from Donald F. Kettl, "The Perils—and Prospects—of Public Administration," *Public Administration Review* (July–August 1990): 416.

very high. Because radar and computers observe precisely what is happening in the skies, **information costs** to controllers are low. Such programs belong in quadrant I of Figure 3.3. Generally speaking, programs with high goal congruency exhibit fewer problems than most. Perhaps for that reason, governments often administer them directly.

But not all FAA programs reside happily in quadrant I. Air safety regulation is a case in point. FAA employees who regulate and inspect the airline industry to ensure the safe maintenance and operation of airline fleets find this job markedly different from that of air traffic controllers with respect to both factors, goal congruency and information costs. With so many planes and so few inspectors, regulators can only randomly and indirectly try to determine whether companies are complying with the FAA's myriad regulations. Because airlines are constantly seeking to minimize expense and downtime in one of the country's most competitive industries, goal congruency between company and government is relatively low. Most regulatory programs appear in quadrant II.

Figure 3.3 also offers insight into the difficulty of managing grants and contracts. The information costs associated with these activities are high. How does government know for sure that the contractor is qualified—much less best qualified—for the job? How does government get good feedback about the contractor's day-to-day operations while keeping information costs low? Goal congruency is seldom as neat and automatic a fit as in the air-traffic control programs, but high goal congruency can be achieved through negotiated agreements. Accordingly, grants and contracts can be placed in quadrant III.

Programs such as Medicare and welfare, which involve payments by a government to individuals who provide no goods or services in return, appear in quadrant IV. Transfer programs such as these account for 36 percent of federal expenditures.

Information costs are relatively low with such programs. "In the U.S. Department of Health and Human Services (HHS), officials know how much money is being spent on different medical services through the Medicare program because they know to whom they are writing checks and in which categories. Beyond the mailing of checks by HHS and cashing those checks by recipients, there needs to be little coordination."[24] Not so with goal congruency. Administrators of transfer programs must be concerned with whether recipients spend their money according to the government's goals.

How does the principal–agent conceptual framework apply to federalism? Arguably, the states are the principal because they hold political legitimacy and have delegated authority to the national government. The states ratified the Constitution—a document that begins, "We the people of the United *States* . . . do ordain and establish this Constitution." But the federal government can be the principal. For example, federal welfare law shifts authority back to the states that act as its agents.[25]

Negotiating

Like agency theory, negotiating is a valuable tool for public administrators trying to cope with the demands of IGR. Just consider the case of a federal official who is responsible for increasing the fire safety of nursing homes in Massachusetts:

> A state agency has jurisdiction over the fire inspections he is seeking. To get the inspection carried out, his actions must reach across organizational and jurisdictional lines. The traditional direct management tools and systems are inaccessible to him. He has little or nothing to do with the state agencies; their budget processes; or rewards, punishments, and other aspects of their employees' career paths. In short, if he seeks their "agreement" to carry out these inspections, his ability to manipulate [the consequences of not agreeing] is extremely limited. But the federal official's political and organizational superiors hold him accountable for achieving results. Should there be a disaster in such a federally funded nursing home, he would be held responsible by members of the legislature, the victims, the general public, elements of the media, and quite conceivably, the courts.[26]

Like agency theory, negotiating has relevance outside the context of IGR. Recall that Chapter 1 identified *negotiator* as one of the 10 basic roles all managers must play. For instance, they may have to negotiate for resources from their boss, work out differences with associates, or resolve conflicts among subordinates. By using negotiation, public executives save time and money. Parties are better satisfied with dispute resolution processes over which they have control, and negotiated settlements are implemented at higher rates. As a general proposition, negotiating an acceptable settlement is preferable to enduring protracted litigation or waging war. (See cartoon.)

What then is **negotiation?** It is a process in which two or more parties, who have different preferences, must make joint decisions and come to an agreement. Many people view negotiation not as a process but as an event—haggling or trading offers at the bargaining table. But to be an effective negotiator, that view must change. Essentially, the negotiating process consists of three activities: preparing, probing, and proposing.

"We're going to try to negotiate first."

Preparing The most important aspect of negotiating occurs before negotiators ever meet. Most people clearly realize that preparation is important, yet they don't prepare in an effective fashion. Faulty preparation is not due to lack of motivation; rather, it has its roots in negotiators' failure to know the right questions to ask. Among the more important questions to address during the preparation stage are the following:

1. *What are the precedents?* As one experienced negotiator explains, if you don't know what has happened in similar situations in the past, "you can't quote or cite, as well as learn from, those events that have already happened, thereby giving legitimacy and credence to your position. Knowing how similar transactions turned out in the past may also guide you in structuring this one. But don't focus on a single precedent, such as one that supports your position. Be familiar with precedent(s) the other side might use."[27]

2. *What are the issues and alternatives?* Leigh L. Thompson, at the Kellogg Graduate School of Management, writes:

   Many negotiators make the mistake of identifying only a single issue to be negotiated in a situation. Usually, this is money (for example, in the sale of a house, the selling price may seem like the central issue of negotiation; similarly, in a job negotiation, salary may emerge as the key issue). It is a grave mistake to focus on a single issue in a negotiation because, in reality, there are more issues at stake in most negotiation situations. By identifying other issues, negotiators can add value to negotiations. For example, in the purchase of a car, the payment terms, cash up-front, loan agreement, or warranty could all be negotiable issues. Negotiators should take time to brainstorm how a single-issue negotiation may be fractionated into multiple issues. Unbundling negotiations into several issues goes against rationality because people have a tendency to simplify situations into single issues. However, negotiators should try to make single-issue negotiations more complex by adding in issues.

Once the negotiator has identified the issues to be negotiated, it is a good idea to identify several alternative courses of action within each issue. In a negotiation for a new car, for example, loan payment terms might be broken down into percentage paid up-front or percentage of interest or a loan agreement might involve how many months or years the option is available to the purchaser. By identifying issues and alternatives, negotiators create a type of matrix, organized such that the identified issues in the negotiation are located along the columns and the alternatives are located along the rows.[28]

3. *What are the interests?* Among the many valuable suggestions Roger Fisher and William Ury of the Harvard Negotiation Project make in *Getting to Yes* is to "focus on interests, not positions."[29] If you are locked into a position, you might overlook other ways to achieve what you want. An example was the Camp David Treaty between Israel and Egypt in 1978. The two sides were at an impasse for a long time over where to draw the boundary line between the two countries. Israel wanted to keep part of the Sinai Peninsula, while Egypt wanted all of it back. Resolution became possible only when they looked at each other's underlying interests. Israel was concerned about security: It wanted no Egyptian tanks on its border. Egypt was concerned about sovereignty: The Sinai had been part of Egypt from the time of the Pharaohs. The parties agreed on a plan that gave all of the Sinai back to Egypt while demilitarizing large parts of it.

4. *What are the deadlines—for me and for them?* Knowing your own realistic deadline in advance will tell you how much leeway you have before you take an entrenched position. Similarly, understanding the other side's deadline may give you an edge or allow you to forgo a point in order to gain elsewhere. Deadlines are pressure points. Herb Cohen, a practicing negotiator, writes:

If there is no perception of a deadline there's little inducement for taking action, much less for accommodation and compromise.

Unfailingly, all of us know that legislative bodies from Parliament to Congress enact most of their bills and appropriations just prior to recess.

Where a manager or secretary is asked to complete a report at his or her leisure, when will it get done? Even the most conscientious person will put it off to work on matters that have a more immediate due date.

Still not convinced? Ask your child to clean his or her room when they have time. Just see when it gets done.[30]

5. *What are the strengths and weaknesses of the participants?* Ronald M. Shapiro, a negotiator in the sports industry, thinks that virtually all negotiators overestimate their own weaknesses and the other side's strengths. He recommends trying to take an honest inventory of each side's real strong points and vulnerabilities. "Ask yourself," he writes, "if your vulnerabilities appear as weaknesses to the other side or if you are more sensitive to them. The same applies to strengths. Give yourself credit for your pluses. Assess the other side's strengths analytically, not emotionally. The real strength you have is knowing your strengths and weaknesses."[31]

6. *What is your BATNA?* A negotiator needs to determine his or her best alternative to a negotiating agreement. Doing so is so important that Fisher and Ury made it into an acronym: BATNA (Best Alternative to a Negotiated Agreement). A BATNA determines the point at which you are prepared to walk away from the negotiation table. In practice, this means that you should be willing to accept any set of terms that is superior to your BATNA and reject outcomes that are worse than your BATNA. Surprisingly, negotiators often fail on both counts.

A BATNA is not something to strive for—rather, it is something that harsh reality and external factors sometimes force you to accept. A common problem is that negotiators are reluctant to recognize their real BATNAs; they fall prey to wishful thinking and unrealistic optimism. The best means of preparation is to continually try to improve your BATNA. Max H. Bazerman and Margaret A. Neale at Northwestern University suggest a strategy for doing this: Follow the "falling in love" rule, which applies to most negotiation situations.

To see how the rule applies, consider the following situation. A friend finds a house listed at $249,000, makes an offer of $222,000, and receives a counteroffer of $237,000. The friend wants your advice on what to do. But this is a no-win situation for you. If your advice leads to a higher price than the friend had hoped, he or she is unimpressed with your expertise. If your advice leads to losing the house to another buyer, the friend might be angry with you. So what advice can you give your friend? Here is the answer Bazerman and Neale give:

We say that he or she has already violated the most important rule of buying houses (or making any other important exchange, with the possible exception of mate selection): "Fall in love with three, not with one." To make a well-informed decision, a buyer must first think about what would happen if he or she did not buy the house. How attractive is the next best option? To the extent that the buyer loves only this house and has to have it, any bargaining position is weakened.

Falling in love with one house (or car, or company) prevents you from thinking clearly and rationally about your best alternative and compromises your competitive edge in the negotiation. If you have an alternative, you are better able to risk losing the first house by waiting for the other party to make a concession. An alternative strengthens your position.[32]

7. *What is the other party's BATNA?* Lisa Bingham provides this illustration:

> Is the other party a small supplier whose primary contracts are with your agency? If the supplier desires a continuing relationship with the agency, its BATNA is not going to be as desirable as negotiating. However, if the other party is a member of a major regulated industry and has substantial financial resources, it may conclude that its BATNA (for example, to delay implementation of a new environmental or safety technology through protracted litigation) is more desirable than negotiating to comply now. Collect as much information as you can on the cost of compliance, the cost of litigation, and the resources of the party you are dealing with. Also, determine whether you can worsen the party's BATNA through punitive sanctions or criminal prosecution of responsible executives. Sometimes a party's BATNA is so undesirable that it really has no choice but to negotiate. For example, a felon caught red-handed can either face prosecution or plea-bargain and turn state's evidence. If the felon's BATNA is a long prison sentence, bargaining may be the only reasonable choice.[33]

Probing   Skilled negotiators are better listeners, ask more questions, focus their arguments more directly, are less defensive, and have learned to avoid words or phrases that can irritate the person with whom they are negotiating (such as "generous offer," "fair price," or "reasonable arrangement"). In other words, they are better at creating the open and trusting climate that is necessary for reaching a win–win settlement.

"Ask questions," Shapiro tells us, "and an amazing thing happens: you get answers." He continues: "Most people don't ask questions. They seem to think it's a sign of weakness, as if they should already know everything. And they are reluctant to go to the key source of information about the other side, *which is the other side.*" Shapiro recommends asking the other side direct questions, such as: What do you really want? Why have you taken this position? What are your short-term goals? What are your long-range plans? He also recommends asking questions that seem unrelated to the negotiation issues, such as: Where do you live? Where did you go to school? What do you do when you're not working? Answers to these questions provide clues as to how the other side thinks, acts, and feels.[34]

One further point about the probing phase to negotiation: Address problems, not personalities. Concentrate on the negotiation issues, not on the personal characteristics of the individual with whom you are negotiating. When negotiations get tough, avoid the tendency to attack this person. Remember, it is the person's ideas or positions that you disagree with—not him or her personally. Fisher and Ury sum up the idea neatly: Separate the people from the problem.

Proposing   Experts differ on whether one should make the first offer or encourage the other side to make it. In any event, initial offers—whoever makes them—are usually only points of departure. Initial proposals tend to be extreme and idealistic and should be treated as such. When you finally do propose, remember that the quality of your proposal is only as good as the quality of your preparation and probing. For example, if you considered interests broadly and looked for new options that might bring advantages to both sides—in other words, you generated many options—then the chance of a better agreement increases.

This brings us to the fundamental dilemma in the proposing stage of the negotiation. Is the process a win–win situation in which all participants can walk away from the table better off, although not necessarily to the same degree that they were when they first sat down? Or is this process analogous to slicing a pie—the bigger my piece is, the smaller your piece must be? David A. Lax and James K. Sebenius at Harvard described this dilemma not as a choice between a win–win game and win–lose game (as we have here) but as a choice between "creating value" and "claiming value."

> Value creators tend to believe that, above all, successful negotiators must be inventive and cooperative enough to devise an agreement that yields considerable gain to each party, relative to no-agreement possibilities. Some speak about the need for replacing the win–lose image of negotiation with win–win negotiation. In addition to information sharing and honest communication, the drive to create value can require ingenuity and may benefit from a variety of techniques and attitudes. The parties can treat the negotiation as solving a joint problem; they can organize brainstorming sessions to invent creative solutions to their problems.
>
> Value claimers, on the other hand, tend to see this drive for joint gain as naive and weak-minded. For them negotiation is hard, tough bargaining. The object of negotiation is to convince the other guy that he wants what you have to offer much more than you want what he has; moreover, you have all the time in the world, while he is up against pressing deadlines. To "win" at negotiating—and thus make the other fellow "lose"—one must start high, concede slowly, exaggerate the value of concessions, minimize the benefits of the other's concessions, conceal information, argue forcibly on behalf of principles that imply favorable settlements, make commitments to accept only highly favorable agreements, and be willing to outwait the other fellow.[35]

To better see the difference between these two orientations toward negotiations, we need only think of a process most Americans know well: the purchase of a new car. As we go through this example, keep in mind that the lesson applies to anything public administrators might purchase for their organizations. Let's look first at the claiming value, or win–lose, approach:

> The dealer starts with some fanciful "sticker price," and the buyer starts somewhere lower, depending on the quality of his or her research. The parties then take turns taking positions that move incrementally toward each other's stance. This negotiation style assumes a fixed pie (in this case, the parties are negotiating over how much the dealer will profit from the sale). One party's concession is the other party's gain. Each party's BATNA is to walk away from the deal. The buyer can go to a different dealer; the seller can sell to a different buyer.[36]

Now let's consider what the negotiations might look like if the same parties took the creating value, or win–win, approach:

They would discuss issues such as the dealer's cost, the salesperson's interest in meeting a particular monthly quota or commission target, the buyer's ability to pay, the fact that there is a profit in light of the time of the year or the demand for the particular model, and a variety of other objective criteria that relate to the parties' respective interests in sealing the deal. The parties would focus on interests, not positions. They would try to identify ways to enlarge the pie. Will the customer refer friends? Will the customer be purchasing another car anytime soon? (Agencies can provide a continuing source of business for many vendors.) How will the customer's experience affect the dealer's reputation in the community? Can the customer provide the dealer with some free advertising?[37]

Thus, there are two dramatically different approaches to the question of negotiations. But do public administrators choose between them? They might ask how much opportunity exists for achieving a win–win outcome. If everyone will be much better off with an agreement than without one, it makes sense to emphasize creating value. If the administrator will have to work with the same people again in the future—which is very often the case in the public sector—it would be very dangerous to use value-claiming tactics that leave anger and mistrust in their wake. Administrators who have a reputation for being manipulative and self-interested will have a hard time building the networks and coalitions that are requisites for effectiveness.

In his influential *The Evolution of Behavior,* Robert Axelrod suggests that when negotiators must work together over time, they adopt a strategy of "conditional openness." This strategy tells the negotiators to start with open and collaborative behavior and to maintain this approach if the other party does too. If the other party becomes adversarial, however, the negotiator should respond in kind and remain adversarial until the opponent makes a collaborative move. Axelrod's strategy is, in effect, a friendly and forgiving version of the old rule "Do unto others as they do unto you." In Axelrod's experimental research, this conditional openness strategy worked better than even the most cold-blooded adversarial strategies.[38]

When public administrators choose a negotiating strategy, there is, of course, another consideration: What is the ethical thing to do? Negotiators often deliberately misrepresent their positions, even though few actions are more universally condemned than lying. This leads to a profoundly difficult question for the public administrator as negotiator: What actions are ethical and just? The next chapter examines that question in some depth.

Concepts for Review

adverse selection theory	council of government (COG)
application or project grant	creative federalism
block grants	devolution
categorical grant	Dillon's rule
cooperative federalism	dual federalism
council-manager form	extradition

federalism

formula grant

full faith and credit clause

goal congruency

grant-in-aid

home rule

eminent domain

information costs

intergovernmental relations (IGR)

interstate compacts

layer cake model of federalism

marble cake model of federalism

mayor-council form

metropolitan statistical area (MSA)

moral hazard

negotiation

new federalism

new new federalism

principal-agent model

revenue sharing

unfunded mandates

Key Points

This chapter focused on the thousands of relationships that exist among a bewildering number of jurisdictions that make up the U.S. federal system. We explained how that system evolved, what its economic implications are, and how public administrators can still make things happen within it. Although some say this is a time of decentralization in the federal system, the view presented here is more complicated: Change is going on simultaneously in contrary directions—centralizing and decentralizing. The chapter made the following points:

1. The U.S. federal system stands in contrast to the unitary or centralized systems such as those of France or Great Britain. The federal system divides power between central government and regional governments; each government, central or regional, is legally supreme in its own area of jurisdiction.

2. Although some powers are shared between governments—taxing and spending for the general welfare, defining and punishing crimes, and so forth—the traditional layer cake model of federalism assumes that functions appropriate at each level can be defined with reasonable precision and should be independent. Some scholars reject this model of the federal system, preferring a marble cake model, which holds that the cooperative relationships among the various levels of government result in an intermingling of activities.

3. A major deficiency of federalism as a descriptive model is that it tends to recognize mainly national–state and interstate relations but to ignore national–local, state–local, national–state–local, and interlocal relations. In contrast, IGR include as proper objects of study all the permutations and combinations of relationships among the units of government in the American system.

4. The history of federal–state relations in the United States can be divided into six eras: dual federalism (1789–1933), cooperative federalism (1933–1960), creative federalism (1960–1968), new federalism (1968–1980), new new federalism (1980–1993), and devolution (1993–present).

5. Because governors, mayors, and other state and municipal officials had a growing financial stake in intergovernmental aid, creative federalism developed a strong constituency that was prepared, when necessary, to lobby for the programs.

6. Categorical grants may be made by formula or by individual application. Formula grants are available across the board to all who are eligible in a category, such as the blind. Application or project grants are made for specific purposes and require a complex application procedure. In contrast to categorical grants, block grants are broad grants to states for prescribed activities with few strings attached.

7. The federal government giveth and taketh away. Unfunded mandates are regulations that impose burdens on state and local governments—without appropriating enough money to cover costs.

8. In 1980, federal grants to states accounted for almost 40 percent of state and local government expenditure. By 1990, they had dropped to 25 percent. During George H. W. Bush's administration, federal funding would rise again to about 31 percent and remain at that level during the administrations of Clinton and Bush the Younger.

9. In government, devolution refers to the transfer of power or authority from a central government to a state or local government. An often-cited example of devolution is the 1996 welfare reform legislation that replaced the basic welfare program with a program called the Personal Responsibility and Work Opportunity Reconciliation Act. The burden of administering the new program was shifted entirely to states. The federal government now gives block grants to the states and generally requires that the states match these funds. This devolution of power in the area of welfare is seen as a testing ground for the future.

10. Besides launching bold initiatives like creative federalism, new federalism, new new federalism, and devolution, presidents can influence the future of IGR in three other ways: regional offices, Internet commerce, and Supreme Court appointments.

11. Since the 1990s, the Supreme Court has been (1) reining in the national government's power under the commerce clause, (2) increasing state power under the Tenth Amendment, and (3) giving new life to the Eleventh Amendment.

12. Economists have sought to identify principles that would elucidate a rational division of responsibilities among levels of government. At least four categories of arguments justifying federal action can be identified: the need for uniformity, direct spillovers, the effects of policy-induced mobility, and inequality of resources.

13. Three clauses in the Constitution are especially relevant to interstate relations: Article I, Section 1, which requires state courts to enforce the civil judgments of the courts of other states and accept their public records and acts as valid; Article IV, Section 2, which requires states to extend to citizens of other states the privileges granted to their own citizens; and Article I, Section 10, which permits states to enter into interstate compacts.

14. The state legislature and courts allow cities to adapt state laws to local needs, but cities remain under state authority. This principle is known as Dillon's rule. The most important means of giving cities independence is home rule. Essentially, home rule is

the power vested in local units of government—mostly cities—to carry on their affairs with a minimum of external legislative or administrative control.

15. Although there are some variations, most municipalities have one of two basic types of institutional arrangements: a mayor-council form of government or a council-manager form.

16. A state sets up counties on its own initiative to serve as political extensions of state government. The responsibilities of county governments include zoning, building regulation, health, hospitals, parks, recreation, highways, public safety, justice, and record keeping.

17. Towns are a unique governmental creation. In Maine, Massachusetts, New Hampshire, Vermont, and Connecticut, towns combine the roles of city and county in one governing unit. Townships operate somewhat like counties. Where they exist—there may be several dozen within a county—they perform the same functions that the county would otherwise perform. Special districts are usually run by commissioners who may be elected or may be appointed by elected officials and other governmental units.

18. Economists have developed an analytical framework well suited to the task of analyzing IGR: the principal–agent model. Essentially, the model expresses analytically any relationship in which one party, the principal, considers entering into a contractual agreement with another, the agent, in the expectation that the agent will subsequently choose actions that produce outcomes desired by the principal. Regardless of the reason for relying on an agent, the principal faces two problems: adverse selection and moral hazard.

19. Negotiation is a process in which two or more parties, who have different preferences, must make joint decisions and come to an agreement. Essentially, the negotiating process consists of three activities: preparing, probing, and proposing.

20. Among the more important questions to address during the preparation stage are the following: What are the precedents? What are the issues and alternatives? What are the interests? What are the deadlines—for me and for them? What are the strengths and weaknesses of the participants? What is my BATNA? What is the other party's BATNA?

21. This is the fundamental dilemma in the proposing stage of the negotiation: Is the process a win–win situation—in which all participants can walk away from the table better off, although not necessarily to the same degree that they were when they first sat down? Or is the process analogous to slicing a pie—the bigger my piece is, the smaller your piece must be?

Problems and Applications

1. Some of the major social and economic innovations in the United States have begun with small-scale experiments on the state level. For example, Wyoming permitted women's suffrage 50 years before the Nineteenth Amendment was ratified. Can you think of other examples? What current state experiments might one day be taken up by the federal government?

2. How do you think business executives view centralizing power in Washington rather than decentralizing it via the 50 states?

3. A respected faculty member of a major university came up with a potentially valuable invention working in the basement laboratory of her home on weekends. With visions of altering the course of industry, she approached the dean for free laboratory space at the university so that she could perfect her breakthrough. But the dean bluntly informed her that university policy clearly states that any invention developed by a faculty member while at the university is owned by the university. She does not, however, want to sign over the invention. How might she negotiate with the dean?

4. The fragmentation and redundancies of the U.S. federal system are expensive in terms of coordination and personnel costs. Would you favor or oppose greater consolidation? Why or why not?

5. "American federalism was born in ambiguity, it institutionalizes ambiguity in its form of government, and changes in it tend to be ambiguous too." Discuss.

Favorite Bookmarks

lcweb.loc.gov/Global/state/stategov The Library of Congress was established as a legislative library for the U.S. Congress. Today the Library of Congress has grown to encompass many information-related activities, including a topical index of state government Web pages. It also provides a useful index for state and local government information.

www.icma.org The International City Management Association is a professional organization for appointed chief executives of cities, counties, towns, and other local governments. Its primary goals include strengthening the quality of urban government through professional management and developing new concepts and approaches to management through information services.

www.nlc.org
www.btg.com/uscm
www.ncsl.org
www.naco.org
www.nga.org

These are the Web sites of the five largest lobbies for state and local government: National League of Cities, United States Conference of Mayors, National Conference of State Legislatures, National Association of Counties, and National Governors Association. These organizations do more than advocate for state and local government interests: They foster intergovernmental cooperation and provide technical assistance and information sharing.

www.kellogg.nwu.edu/research/des_res/
www.PON.harvard.edu

A wide range of case, simulation, gaming, role-playing, and exercise material in the areas of negotiation and dispute resolution is available from the Kellogg School of Management at Northwestern University and from Harvard Law School. The first of the two negotiation materials collections is that of the Dispute Resolution Center of Northwestern University, whose offices are located within the Kellogg School of Management, but the collection is sponsored by faculty from the Schools of Law, Management, and Arts and Sciences, with affiliations with other schools in the Chicago area. The second is the Program on Negotiation at Harvard Law School.

Notes

1. Morton M. Grodzins and Daniel J. Elazar, *The American System* (Chicago: Rand McNally, 1966).
2. Dwight Wright, *Understanding Intergovernmental Relations* (Monterey, CA: Brooks/Cole, 1982).
3. *Recovery Act: As Initial Implementation Unfolds in States and Localities, Continued Attention to Accountability Issues Is Essential,* GAO-09-63IT, April 23, 2009.
4. Quoted in Alan Greenblatt "Obama and the Cities," *Governing* (April 2 2009): 24.
5. Ibid.
6. See Jeff Benedict, *Little Pink Houses: A True Story of Defiance and Courage* (New York: Grand Central, 2008).
7. Alan Ehrenhalt, "States' Not-so-Dire Straits," *Governing* (March 2005): 6.
8. See Deborah Solomon, "State Leaders Take Charge of Agenda amid Washington Gridlock," *Wall Street Journal* (February 25, 2006).
9. Ehrenhalt, op. cit.: 8.
10. This section is taken from *Economic Report of the President, 1996* (Washington, DC: U.S. Government Printing Office, 1996), 110–113.
11. *Economist* (April 3, 2004): 34.
12. *Governing* (August 2001): 44.
13. Monica Davey, "Trading Fish and Ammunition, States Team Up to Save Money," *The New York Times* (May 23, 2009).
14. H. George Frederickson, Gary Alan Johnson, and Curtis Wood, "The Changing Structure of American Cities: A Study of the Diffusion of Innovation," *Public Administration Review* (May/June 2004): 322–23.
15. Alan Ehrenhalt, "Cooperate or Die," *Governing* (September 1995).
16. Nicholas Henry, *Public Administration and Public Affairs* (Upper Saddle River, NJ: Prentice Hall, 2001), 384.
17. Peter Hall, *Urban and Regional Planning* (London: Routledge, 2002).
18. Neal R. Peirce, *Citistates: How Urban America Can Compete in a Competitive World.* (Arlington, VA: Seven Locks Press, 1992).
19. *Governing* (August 2005): 68.
20. Terry M. Moe, "The New Economics of Organizations," *American Journal of Political Science,* 20 (1984): 754.
21. Ibid., 756.
22. John W. Pralt and Richard J. Zeckhauser, *Principals and Agents: The Structure of Business* (Boston: Harvard Business School Press, 1985), 5–6.
23. Donald F. Kettl, "The Perils—and Prospects—of Public Administration," *Public Administration Review* (July–August 1990).
24. Ibid., 415.
25. John Chubb analyzes U.S. federalism in principal–agent terms explicitly and only treats the federal government as the principal vis-à-vis the states. See "The Political Economy of Federalism," *American Political Science Review* 79 (1985): 994.
26. David A. Lax and James K. Sebenius, *The Manager as Negotiator* (New York: Free Press, 1986), 315.
27. Ronald M. Shapiro and Mark A. Jankowski, *The Power of Nice* (New York: Wiley, 2001), 98.

28. Leigh Thompson, *The Mind and Heart of the Negotiator* (Upper Saddle River, NJ: Prentice Hall, 2001), 15.

29. Roger Fisher and William Ury, *Getting to Yes* (New York: Penguin, 1983), 11.

30. Herb Cohen, *Negotiate This!* (New York: Time Warner, 2003), 176.

31. Shapiro and Jankowski, op. cit., 99.

32. Max H. Bazerman and Margaret A. Neale, *Negotiating Rationally* (New York: Simon & Schuster, 1992), 69.

33. Lisa B. Bingham, "Negotiating for the Public Good" in James L. Perry, ed., *Handbook of Public Administration* (San Francisco: Jossey-Bass, 1996), 652.

34. Shapiro and Jankowski, op. cit., 68.

35. Bazerman and Neale, op. cit., 30–32.

36. Bingham, op. cit., 654.

37. Ibid.

38. Robert Axelrod, *Evolution of Cooperation* (New York: Basic Books, 1984).

CASE 3.1
THE KATRINA
BREAKDOWN

Catastrophe struck the Gulf Coast on August 29, 2005, when the eye of Hurricane Katrina made landfall near Buras, Louisiana, packing high storm surges and sustained winds of over 140 mph. The Category 4 hurricane would move slowly inland, carving a path of destruction across low-lying regions of southern Louisiana, Mississippi, and Alabama. See map.

Experts had long warned of the flood danger faced by New Orleans, much of which lies below sea level in a bowl bordered by levees that hold back Lake Pontchartrain to the north and the Mississippi River to the south and west. In fact, in the summer of 2004, hundreds of regional and federal officials had met in Baton Rouge for an elaborate simulation exercise. The fictional "Hurricane Pam" left the city under 10 feet of water. The report from the simulation warned that transportation would be a major problem.

The simulation proved disconcertingly accurate. Katrina caused breaches in the levees, leaving about 80 percent of New Orleans under water and knocking out electrical, water, sewage, transportation, and communication systems. Katrina also flattened much of Gulfport and Biloxi, Mississippi, flooded Mobile, Alabama, and leveled or inundated small cities and towns across an area the size of Great Britain. Up to 100,000 people were stranded in New Orleans for days in squalid and dangerous conditions awaiting relief and evacuation.

Katrina was the deadliest hurricane to hit the United States in more than 75 years. The confirmed death toll exceeded 1200, with more than 80 percent of the fatalities in Louisiana, predominantly in the New Orleans area. It was among the costliest natural disasters in U.S. his-

tory. Nearly three-fourths of all the homes in New Orleans, the fifty-ninth largest city in the United States, were damaged or destroyed.

Poor coordination between local, state, and federal officials raises important questions not only about U.S. disaster preparedness but also about federalism. The following five government officials, in particular, were criticized for their response to the distaster: New Orleans Mayor C. Ray Nagin, Louisiana Governor Kathleen Blanco, Federal Emergency Management Agency (FEMA) Director Michael Brown, Department of Homeland Security Secretary Michael Chertoff, and President George W. Bush. Before considering those criticisms, we need to review the facts of the case.

Timeline

Saturday, August 27, 2005

5:00 A.M.: Hurricane Katrina is in the Gulf of Mexico 435 miles southeast of the Mississippi River Delta, gathering strength and moving forward at just 7 mph.

10:00 A.M.: FEMA Director Michael Brown appears on CNN to encourage residents of southeastern Louisiana to leave as soon as possible for safety inland.

5:00 P.M.: Governor Kathleen Blanco and Mayor C. Ray Nagin appear in a press conference to warn residents of the storm. Nagin declares a state of emergency in New Orleans.

7:25–8:00 P.M.: Max Mayfield, director of the National Hurricane Center, calls officials in Alabama, Louisiana, and Mississippi to warn them of the severity of the coming storm.

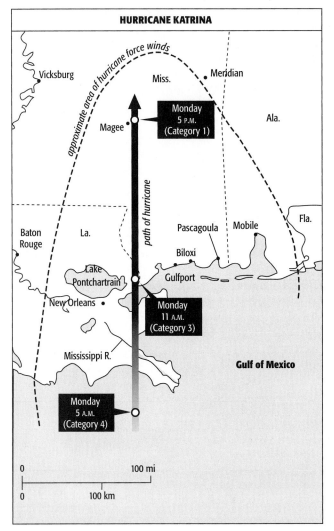

HURRICANE KATRINA

approximate area of hurricane force winds

Vicksburg

Miss.   • Meridian

Magee •   Monday
5 P.M.
(Category 1)

Ala.

path of hurricane

Baton
Rouge   La.   Pascagoula   Mobile   Fla.

Biloxi

Lake
Pontchartrain   Gulfport

New Orleans •   Monday
11 A.M.
(Category 3)

Mississippi R.   **Gulf of Mexico**

Monday
5 A.M.
(Category 4)

| 0 | | 100 mi |
| 0 | | 100 km |

Source: National Hurricane Center

Sunday, August 28, 2005

7:00 A.M.: Gulf Coast residents awaken to the news that Katrina is a Category 5 hurricane, with winds blowing steadily at 160 mph. The eye is 250 miles away, moving now at 12 mph.

9:25 A.M.: President George W. Bush calls Blanco, advising that she and Nagin order a mandatory evacuation.

9:30 A.M.: With the storm due to come ashore in about 15 hours, Nagin orders a mandatory evacuation of New Orleans.

4:15 P.M.: Mayfield conducts an electronic briefing for Bush, Brown, and Chertoff and warns them of the danger of destruction and flooding in the wake of Katrina. Brown also tries to prepare federal leaders for the magnitude of the coming disaster: "We're going to need everything that we can possibly muster, not only in this state and in the region, but the nation, to respond to this event."

10:30 P.M.: The last people seeking refuge in the Superdome in New Orleans are searched and allowed in. Between 8000 and 9000 citizens are in the stands and about 600 are in a temporary medical facility. About 550 National Guard troops provide security.

Monday, August 29, 2005

6:10 A.M.: The eye of Katrina makes its landfall near Buras, Louisiana.

6:30 A.M.: Buras is obliterated.

7:50 A.M.: A massive storm surge causes immediate flooding in St. Bernard Parish and eastern neighborhoods of New Orleans. Water levels in most areas are 10 to 15 feet.

10:30 A.M.: Bush declares emergency disasters in Louisiana, Mississippi, and Alabama.

11:00 A.M.: Brown issues a memo ordering 1000 FEMA employees to the Gulf Coast and gives them two days to arrive.

8:00 P.M.: Blanco speaks with Bush to impress upon him the destruction caused by Katrina: "Mr. President, we need your help. We need everything you've got."

9:27 P.M.: FEMA officials give Chertoff's chief of staff a first-hand description of the levee breaks and the extensive flooding in New Orleans.

9:30 P.M.: Bush goes to bed without taking any action on the Katrina disaster or Blanco's request for assistance.

Tuesday, August 30, 2005

7:00 A.M.: In San Diego, staff tells Bush of the severity of the crisis along the Gulf Coast and advises him to end his six-week vacation early. He agrees.

9:00 A.M.: Chertoff flies to Atlanta, where he will attend a conference on avian flu.

10:00 A.M.: The breach in the 17th Street Canal has grown to about 200 feet. Looting is reported all over New Orleans.

10:53 A.M.: Nagin declares a mandatory evacuation for the city and orders police to forcibly take residents away, if necessary.

7:00 P.M.: Chertoff designates the Katrina destruction an "incident of national significance."

Wednesday, August 31, 2005

10:00 A.M.: Blanco makes a joint announcement with FEMA that plans have been laid to evacuate residents remaining in New Orleans to the Astrodome in Houston. Air Force One flies low over the Gulf Coast so Bush can see the damage. Lt. General Russell Honore is placed in charge of Joint Task Force Katrina, the Pentagon's command center for disaster response.

12:15 P.M.: Bush political adviser Karl Rove advises Blanco that Bush wants to federalize the evacuation of New Orleans.

2:20 P.M.: Blanco telephones Bush, informing him that federalization of evacuation and the Louisiana National Guard will not be necessary.

3:00 P.M.: Bush convenes a task force at the White House for an hour to discuss ways to improve the response.

4:11 P.M.: Bush addresses the nation in his first speech devoted to Hurricane Katrina.

7:00 P.M.: Martial law is declared in New Orleans. Nagin orders police to stop rescue efforts and focus entirely on controlling the looting, which has become rampant.

Thursday, September 1, 2005

7:00 A.M.: In a radio interview, Chertoff calls the reports of thousands of people stranded in and around the Convention Center in New Orleans "rumors," and states, "Actually, I have not heard a report of thousands of people in the Convention Center who don't have food and water."

Friday, September 2, 2005

6:20 A.M.: The head of emergency operations for New Orleans expresses his frustration: "This is a national disgrace. FEMA has been here three days, yet there is no command and control. We can send massive amounts of aid to tsunami victims, but we can't bail out the city of New Orleans."

10:35 A.M.: At the start of a tour of the Gulf Coast, Bush praises Brown: "Brownie, you're doing a heck of a job."

4:00 P.M.: Bush meets with Blanco, Nagin, and others aboard Air Force One. An agitated Nagin demands that the president and the governor work out a chain of command for the deployment of military personnel. After that, the president would privately raise a sensitive question with the governor: Would she relinquish control of local law enforcement and the 13,000 National Guard troops from 29 states that fall under her command?

11:20 P.M.: Bush Chief of Staff Andrew Card sends Blanco a fax indicating that she need only sign an attached letter requesting that the federal government assume control of the rescue and recovery in Louisiana, including oversight of the National Guard troops.

Saturday, September 3, 2005

7:56 A.M.: Blanco faxes a letter to Card refusing the federal government's attempt to assume control.

8:00 A.M.: Bush announces the deployment of 7000 active-duty troops that would arrive in the Gulf Coast over the next three days.

9:30 A.M.: Brown announces that millions of army rations and water bottles are now in the disaster area.

12:00 NOON: Buses arrives at the Convention Center to take people to safety and comfort elsewhere.

Issues

The events between August 27 and September 3 can be viewed productively from several standpoints: disaster management (based on the Katrina experience, how well would the United States handle another major terrorist attack?), organization theory (should FEMA have remained an independent agency?), and leadership (what would a Giuliani or an Eisenhower or a Johnson have done?). But here we want to consider these events in terms of intergovernmental relations. For that limited purpose, the following issues seem particularly relevant.

Did Nagin Have a Plan? Despite all appearances to the contrary, the city of New Orleans had a plan. In 2000, city officials and various consultants prepared a 14-page booklet "City of New Orleans Comprehensive Emergency Management Plan." It offered a series of clear-cut guidelines that seemed to be ignored by Nagin, a former executive with Cox Communications who was elected in 2002. After suggesting that "evacuation zones" based on probable storm flooding should be used as the basis of mass evacuation, the plan advised that such zones "will be developed pending further study." They never were. The city of New Orleans followed virtually

no aspect of its own plan in the disaster caused by Hurricane Katrina and failed to implement most federal guidelines. Douglas Brinkley writes:

> Apparently unimpressed by the emergency management plan, even though it was posted on the City Hall Web site . . . Nagin behaved in a hesitant, perplexing fashion. The plan was the collective wisdom of an entire generation of New Orleans political thinking, going back as far as those who had grappled with Hurricane Betsy in 1965. The plan instructed that when a serious hurricane approached, the city should evacuate 72 hours prior to the storm to give "approximately 100,000 citizens of New Orleans [who] do not have the means of personal transportation" enough time to leave. Mayor Nagin also ignored FEMA guidelines, which urged City Hall to "coordinate the use of school buses and drivers to support evacuation efforts."

Before any disaster, the first responsibility of local responders is to evacuate hospitals, nursing homes, and special needs populations. Aside from some informal plans to rely on churches and neighborhoods to get people out, the city had not developed any solution to that challenge in time for Katrina.

Where Did the Federal Money Go? In 2003, the federal government gave New Orleans a $7 million grant for a communications system that would connect all the region's first responders. Soon after the hurricane struck, the radios used by police, firefighters, and the mayor drained their batteries. Then their satellite phones would not recharge. And, of course, landline and cell phones went out. For two days the mayor and his emergency team were cut off from the outside world.

That did not need to happen. For example, emergency officials across Florida are linked by a system of satellite phones, and lines of authority between local and state officials are sharp. And in Texas, ham operators share a place at the table in the emergency bunker in Austin along with the high-tech communication experts.

The bigger question is, Why were federal funds that might have been used to strengthen the levees around New Orleans diverted to widening ship channels? Brinkley writes:

> Over the years, improvements were made [in the 17th Street Canal], patches introduced and the need for repairs noted and sometimes neglected. Incredibly, no one was in charge: no one was fully responsible for overseeing just who was doing what to the levees. Various entities had a hand in the fortunes of the system—and fortunes are all that the levee system meant to a great many of the greedy scoundrels involved through the years. . . . For example, in the months just before Katrina, while a $427,000 repair to a crucial floodgate languished in inexcusable bureaucratic delay, [the board of directors of the Orleans Levee District] went ahead with happier pursuits, building parks, overseeing docks that it had constructed, and investing in on-water gambling . . .

"We Need Everything You've Got" That is what Blanco, who became governor in 2003, told Bush the day the storm hit. The question of whether she requested federal government assistance as effectively or as forcefully as the catastrophe demanded still haunts her. And yet, with the exception of Nagin, no one was in a better position than her to know precisely what was needed and how soon. Not until Thursday did she come up with specifics: 40,000 troops (a number she says she "pulled out of the air"); urban search-and-rescue teams; buses; amphibious personnel carriers; mobile morgues; trailers of water, ice, and food; base camps; staging areas; housing; and communication systems. State officials concede, according to *Time*, that Blanco had unrealistic expectations of precisely what the federal government could do. "She thought it would be more omniscient and more omnipresent and more powerful than it turned out to be."

Getting Through to the President Wednesday morning Blanco tried to telephone the president to tell him that the expected federal resources still had not arrived. In response to the call, the White House did not make the president available. After attending some official ceremonies, she returned to her office and tried to reach the president again. After a short delay, her call was transferred to the White House Office of Intergovernmental Affairs. During the course of the morning, Blanco did receive calls from presidential surrogates, including one from Chief of Staff Andrew Card, who was on vacation in Maine. According to Blanco, Card didn't exactly promise help; rather, he affirmed that he believed he could help her.

Brown's Method of Operation Bush appointed Brown head of FEMA in 2003. At the time, he was staff attorney and second in command. He had been brought into the agency by his longtime friend Joseph Allbaugh, then agency head. Before joining FEMA, Brown had been the head of the International Arabian Horse Association.

Now, three years into the new job, his agency was being inundated by requests from thousands of organizations, jurisdictions, and individuals—requests for medical equipment, chlorine bleach, cleaning supplies, generators, body bags, inoculations, tents, boats, and the like. During this period, Brown's focus was on the "recovery," which was to be executed as carefully and precisely as possible. Otherwise, so he thought, FEMA risked lawsuits, distributional problems, and sundry other worries. *Time* reports that foreign nations, responding to urgent calls from Washington, readied rescue supplies, then "were told to stand by for days until FEMA could figure out what to do with them." Florida airboaters complained that they had an armada ready for rescue work but FEMA wouldn't let them into New Orleans. Brown defended his agency's measured steps saying aid "was to be coordinated in such a way that it's used most effectively."

Brown's Boss At 7:00 P.M. Monday, Brown received an urgent telephone call from his FEMA representative in New Orleans. The call had a sobering effect on Brown; for the first time, he fully understood the gravity of the situation. Convinced that Blanco was "dysfunctional," Brown called his boss, Chertoff, pleading for help. It was the first time Brown and Chertoff had spoken together that day.

Eight months earlier, Bush had appointed U.S. Court of Appeals Judge Chertoff to head the nation's second-largest cabinet agency, the sprawling Department of Homeland Security. As the head of the criminal division in the Justice Department in 2001, Chertoff had helped formulate the government's response to the 9/11 terror attacks. Now, as Homeland Secretary, Chertoff was in charge of all major disasters—whether from international terrorism, natural causes, or infrastructure collapse. Until Chertoff designated it "an incident of national significance" and appointed someone (presumably the FEMA director in the case of hurricanes) as the "principal federal official," relief would be halting at best. Without that designation, Brown could not legally take charge, giving orders to local and state officials and overseeing deployment of National Guard and other U.S. military personnel. Unfortunately for the people in New Orleans, Brown could not convince Chertoff that things were going as badly as Brown (and the media) were suggesting. Brown tried to maneuver around Chertoff, to appeal directly to the president, but it was hard to get through to the White House.

A Government Accountability Office report noted that the delay in Chertoff's response was critical: "The DHS secretary designated Hurricane Katrina as an incident of national significance on August 30—the day after a final landfall. However, he did not designate the storm as a catastrophic event, which would have triggered additional provisions of the National Response Plan (NRP) calling for a more proactive response. . . . In the absence of a timely and decisive action and clear leadership responsibility and accountability, there were multiple chains of command, a myriad of approaches and processes for requesting and providing assistance, and confusion."

A DVD for GWB Early Friday morning, the president boarded Air Force One for the flight to Mobile, Alabama, as his first stop on his inspection of the disaster area. Because White House staffers were uncertain that he actually understood what was going on—had "situational awareness," as they say in the military—they had prepared a compilation of news coverage recorded onto a DVD for him to watch during the three-hour flight.

"I Don't Know Whose Problem It Is" In a radio interview the day before Bush's flight to the disaster area, Nagin had said, "I don't know whose problem it is. I don't know whether it's the governor's problem. I don't know whether it's the president's problem, but somebody needs to get their ass on a plane and sit down, the two of them, and figure this out right now."

Later the next day that's pretty much what happened. Bush met with Blanco and Nagin aboard Air Force One on the tarmac of the New Orleans Airport. Nagin said, "Mr. President, Madame Governor, you to need to get together on the same page, because of the lack of coordination, people are dying in my city."

Three Perspectives on Katrina and Federalism

Not surprisingly, the worst natural disaster in U.S. history generated many scholarly articles. This section briefly summarizes three recent ones that offer different interpretations of what went wrong, what went right, and what needs to be done. Each provides a basis for class discussion.

(1) Stephen M. Griffin, professor of constitutional law at Tulane, argues in "Stop Federalism before It Kills Again" that the national government might need to become more directive in numerous areas. Although much attention has been focused on the response and recovery that followed Katrina's landfall, Griffin explores the role of federalism prior to Katrina. Why would the federal government fund levee construction then turn different parts of the project over to four different local sponsors who worked at cross-purposes? Why would it help fund the purchase of communication technology and not require that states and local governments develop interoperable communications? The general answer is that, according to Griffin, federalism is as much a commitment to localism as it is to states' rights. As Chertoff has stated on several occasions, disasters are typically to be managed at the "lowest possible, geographic, organizational, and jurisdictional levels." To the contrary, Griffin thinks the failure to respond to Katrina exposed one of the few real structural weaknesses in the U.S. Constitution: a lack of a mechanism to coordinate the work of local, state, and national governments.

Interestingly, federal responses to natural disasters—events nearly by definition beyond the capacity of state and local governments—is a relatively recent phenomenon. In fact, it took many decades of repeated disasters such as the vast flooding unleashed by the Mississippi River in 1927 to convince national officials that the federal government had a role to play in alleviating the effects of natural disasters. For much of U.S. history, victims of natural disasters were on their own. "The federal system as it exists today," Griffin writes, "is our system, not that of the founding generation. We—generations still alive—created it and we continue to change it. The best example during the Bush administration was the No Child Left Behind Act, legislation that involved an unprecedented intrusion into a subject, education, that everyone used to argue should be left to the states."

(2) Martha Derthick, professor emeritus at the University of Virginia, argues that the "governmental response to Katrina was not the unalloyed failure that is often portrayed. The response was a mixture of success and failure. Successes occurred when a foundation had been laid for intergovernmental cooperation, as with the largely successful pre-landfall evacuation of Greater New Orleans, the multistate mobilization of the National Guard, and the search and rescue operations of the U.S. Coast Guard and the Louisiana Department of Wildlife and Fisheries." The failures include New Orleans' failure to limit its growth, its lack of flood protection plans, and the influence of politics on flood protection there.

Above all, Derthick argues, "do no harm to the first responders. Dependency on them is inescapable. Indeed, they could become the country's only functioning and legitimate governments in case of a successful terrorist attack on Washington, D.C. Continue to think of federalism in the traditional way, as a source of strength through cooperation."

(3) Marc Landy at Boston College calls Katrina a "mega-disaster" and argues that such events put federalism to an especially difficult test because they require speed, efficiency, decisiveness, and effective coordination. Faced with such events, the big advantage of federalism, he maintains, is its greater flexibility, responsiveness, and capacity to mobilize mutual aid. "It presumably benefits from the unique virtues that each level of government and that the citizen himself or herself possess. These virtues compensate for its inherent complexity and redundancy. The example of personal responsibility and neighborly concern is a superior substitute for government intervention."

Clearly, Landy conceptualizes federalism as being composed of four dimensions: three levels of government and the civic realm. With regard to the latter, it's worth recalling that Alexis de Tocqueville recognized in the early nineteenth century that "government can't match the energy and resourcefulness of citizen cooperating informally or through voluntary associations."

Landy finds the direst examples of civic failure in the city of New Orleans, and an especially edifying example of its success in Mississippi. Landy does not sugarcoat the former:

> The impression given by the media was that those who did not get out of New Orleans could not, either because they had no car or were disabled. This impression stuck even though the visuals accompanying those media reports showed streets crowded with abandoned cars. A congressional report confirmed that the pictures were more reliable than the words. It stated that more than 250,000 cars remained in the city during the storm and the cars were found parked in the driveways of many of the dead. The report chastised the governor of Louisiana, and the mayor of New Orleans for being slow to issue mandatory evacuation orders, and those individuals "share the blame" for incomplete evacuation. Resorting to the verb "share" shows just how reluctant the report writers were to concede that not all bad things that happen are the fault of the government. Those car owners who fail to evacuate in the face of mandatory evacuation orders that, however tardy, still left them plenty of time to leave, do not *share* in the blame, they *are* to blame. If indeed a major, or perhaps even the major, cause of death from Katrina was a failure to obey a mandatory evacuation order, this puts the whole Katrina problem in a different light. It shifts the blame from errors made by the various levels of government to the actions of the populace itself.

Case Questions

1. Which of the three perspectives do you find most persuasive? Least persuasive? Support your answer.

2. Much of the debate over the response to Hurricane Katrina centers on the question of the division of responsibility among different levels of government—local, state, and federal. If the federal government played a more aggressive role—say, taking command of all response

efforts and placing them in the hands of the regular army—would that violate tenets of federalism, specific provisions of the Constitution, and specific statutes (such as the Posse Comitatus Act of 1878, which limits military participation in law enforcement)? What other legal options are there besides giving the federal government a more powerful role?

3. Setting aside the philosophical and legal issues this case raises, what are the management or efficiency arguments for and against a more centralized response to large national disasters like Hurricane Katrina? Why would we not want to have a federal fire department? If the federal government tells the states and cities they will receive no assistance in the event of a disaster, what do you think will happen?

4. To what extent was the Katrina breakdown due to federalism, and to what extent was it due to the players in the story?

Case References

Marc Landy, "Mega-Disasters and Federalism," *Public Administration Review* (December 2008): S186–S198; Stephen M. Griffin, "Stop Federalism Before It Kills Again," *St. John's Journal of Legal Commentary* (Spring 2007); Martha Derthick, "Where Federalism Didn't Fail," *Public Administration Review* (December 2007: 36–47; Douglas Brinkley, *The Big Deluge: Katrina, New Orleans, and the Mississippi Gulf Coast* (New York: HarperCollins, 2006); U.S. Government Accountability Office, *Preliminary Observations Regarding Preparedness and Response to Hurricanes Katrina and Rita* (Washington, DC: GPO, February 1, 2006); Christopher Swope and Zach Patton, "In Disaster's Wake," *Governing* (November 2005); "Four Places Where the System Broke Down," *Time* (September 19, 2005); "How Bush Blew It," *Newsweek* (September 19, 2005); David Brown, "Live by the Rules, Die by the Rules," *Washington Post National Edition* (October 9, 2005); Spencer S. Hsu, "Chertoff, After the Storm," *Washington Post National Edition* (November 21, 2005); *The Wall Street Journal* (September 1, 2005 and September 6, 2005); *The New York Times* (September 2, 2005); *The Economist* (September 3, 2005).

4 Administrative Responsibility and Ethics

Kevin Irby Photography

THE FDA TASK FORCE

The Food and Drug Administration (FDA) is one of the nation's oldest and most respected consumer protection agencies. Stated simply, the FDA's mission is to promote and protect the public health by helping safe and effective products reach the market in a timely way and monitoring products for continued safety after they are in use.

The FDA is expected to regulate annually $1.5 trillion in food, drugs, vaccines, medical devices, blood and tissues, radiation-emitting machines, animal feeds and drugs, cell phones, dietary supplements, biotechnology and gene therapy—and, post 9/11, to uncover any food-borne terrorist plot. Yet the agency's annual funding, $2 billion, is only about what Fairfax County, Virginia, pays for its public schools. And despite mounting concerns about the safety of Chinese-made drugs, the agency had only enough field inspectors in 2008 to check a mere 13 of the 714 Chinese factories that produce medicines for U.S. consumers.

Industry dollars now pay for more than half of the FDA's drug-review budget; in five years, that proportion is expected to jump to 70 percent. Called *user fees*, this

$400 million a year is designed to speed decisions on applications for new drugs and save taxpayers money. But some critics maintain that they undermine public confidence in the FDA's independence and impose time pressures that could end up costing lives.

Assume you have been appointed to a task force to review "Guidelines on Good Clinical Practice in FDA-Related Clinical Trials." To test the efficacy of promising new drugs, current regulations require that pharmaceutical companies conduct trials with two groups of people. The first group, the *treatment group*, consists of at least 300 people with the condition the drug is designed to alleviate—for example, high blood pressure. The second group, the *control group,* consists of another 300 people as similar to the first group as possible with respect to age, sex, vital signs, and of course the condition. The first group receives the new drug, while the second group receives a placebo. At the end of a one-year trial, the progress of each group is measured. If there is a significant statistical difference in the progress of the first group over that of the second group—and no serious side effects occur—the drug is approved.

During one task force meeting a respected colleague makes the following remarks: "Look, I'm all for the scientific method. But how can we in good conscience literally assign some people to death? I thought we were supposed to be helping people— not killing them."

Somewhat puzzled, you ask your colleague to clarify.

"O.K.," he continues, "Suppose the wizards at some company come up with a potent new drug that lowers cholesterol. Preliminary research on animals suggests that the drug is not only safe but much more effective than other available drugs. Now suppose we have this 70-year-old woman. Let's call her Lucy. Her cholesterol level puts her at risk of a heart attack. And Lucy is taking care of her husband with cancer. But in this trial she only has a 50–50 chance of getting the drug. It seems that there's got to be a better way to run clinical trials and promote health."

One of the great challenges in public administration is ensuring that the actions of government agencies like the FDA are consistent with the wishes of citizens. Presumably, legislators and chief executives—elected and reelected by the people—ensure that consistency. Yet, given the complexity of twenty-first-century government, it seems impossible to avoid delegating large amounts of power to unelected civil servants to use at their discretion. In a famous 1940 essay, Carl J. Friedrich argued that the public administrators' own concern for the public interest was often the only assurance that administrative actions were responsive to the electorate's wishes. Herman Finer disagreed: To maintain responsiveness, public administrators should be subject to strict and rigid control by the legislature. "The political and administrative history of all ages has," he wrote, "demonstrated without the shadow of a doubt that sooner or later there is an abuse of power when external punitive controls are lacking." Who's position—Friedrich's or Finer's—do you find more persuasive?

How would you respond to the objections of the "respected colleague" about the use of control groups? In formulating your answer, what principles are you applying? What other ethical issues might the FDA face? Would you apply those same principles in the same way to these issues that you did with the control group issue? If you can't think of any other ethical dilemmas, try this one. Even though at least 60 percent of Americans disapprove of cloned food, the FDA in 2006 ruled that milk and meat from cloned animals should be allowed on grocery store shelves.

Source: Philip J. Hilts, *Protecting America's Health: The FDA, Business, and One Hundred Years of Regulation* (New York: Alfred E. Knopf, 2003).

Chapter 3 examined how interorganizational (intergovernmental) relations complicate even further the already complicated core function of political management. In that chapter, the concerns were fairly concrete—block grants, unfunded mandates, counties, and so forth. This chapter considers several matters more abstract in nature but also affecting political management. One such matter is the value system of the society in which the administrator works.

Values are simply things or relationships that people would like to have or to enjoy. Obviously, one cannot—and fortunately need not—consider the entire complex of values held by American society. Only those values that are relevant to administration are of concern here. What might these be? Most Americans would agree that government should be responsive, flexible, fair, accountable, honest, and competent. In this chapter, the word *responsibility* is used as a collective term for values such as these, for qualities people would like to see in their government.

The discussion is in three closely related parts. First, the chapter explores how values relate to public administration and what the ideal of responsibility stands for in the literature of public administration. To speak of an ideal implies existence not in the actual world but in the mind; it suggests a perfection exceeding what is possible in reality. So it is with the ideal of **administrative responsibility**. It is something to strive toward.

But certain pitfalls lay along the way. James Madison and the Founders understood this problem well. Given human nature, administrative responsibility simply cannot be assumed. Writing in *Federalist Paper No. 51,* Madison justified the need to protect and foster it:

> If men were angels, no government would be necessary. If angels were to govern men neither external controls nor internal controls on government would be necessary. In framing a government which is to be administered by men over men, the greatest difficulty lies in this: you must first enable the government to control the governed; and in the next place oblige it to control itself. A dependence on the people is, no doubt, the primary control on the government; but experience has taught mankind the necessity of auxiliary precautions.

Going on the assumption that angels still do not govern, the second section reviews the various "auxiliary precautions"—both formal and informal—that have been suggested to make sure that public administration does not fall too short of the ideal of administrative responsibility. One of these methods, ethical analysis, is the special focus of the last section.

Although the concerns of this chapter may be relatively abstract in comparison with other topics found in the book, they are no less important. Quite the contrary: When graduates of public policy and administration schools rated skills they consider most important to success, maintaining ethical standards came in a solid first. See Table 4.1.

Recent empirical research by Stephen Maynard-Moody and Michael Musheno offers additional evidence on the important and often underappreciated role ethics plays in day-to-day public administration. They find that the behaviors of street-level bureaucrats—police officers, teachers, and vocational rehabilitation counselors—are influenced not by organizational rules but rather *by their moral judgments*. The two researchers find that "moral judgments about citizen-clients infuse all aspects of street-level decision-making."[1]

Number 2

Table 4.1   Skills Considered Very Important for Success, by Current Job

one sentence on each one

| | Percent* | | | | |
| | Government | | | Private Sector | Nonprofit Sector |
Skill	Federal	State	Local		
Maintaining ethical standards	**81**	**75**	**84**	**81**	**89**
Leading others	70	62	75	75	76
Managing conflict	52	54	67	64	66
Managing information and communication technology	57	54	67	64	66
Influencing policymakers	56	54	55	57	54
Managing innovation and change	52	53	55	57	57
Doing policy analysis	64	69	61	41	55
Budgeting and public finance	56	54	64	45	46
Managing a diverse workforce	50	39	43	40	42
Analyzing and influencing public opinion	36	34	35	35	42
Raising money and generating extra revenue	17	21	19	34	51
Managing media relations	25	23	29	27	31
Writing regulations and legislation	37	35	23	22	22

*n = 117 for federal, 167 for state, and 109 for local government; n = 275 for the private sector; n = 166 for the nonprofit sector.

Source: Paul C. Light, *The New Public Service* (Washington, DC: Brookings, 1999), 110.

The Ideal of Administrative Responsibility

Although neither exhaustive nor definitive, the following six subsections cover most of the values implied when the term *administrative responsibility* is used. These values are responsiveness, fairness, flexibility, honesty, accountability, and competence. Because each one is essential, it might be useful to think of these values as forming a chain.

Responsiveness

The term **responsiveness** refers to the prompt acquiescence by an organization to the popular demands for policy change. Responsiveness can also mean that government does more than merely react to popular demand. In some cases, it can mean that government takes the initiative in the proposal of solutions for problems and even in the definition of problems.

Degrees of Responsiveness   In the private sector, it is relatively easy to determine what people want: Marketplace activity—where they spend their money—shows what people value. In the public sector, where agencies are usually funded by tax dollars appropriated by legislatures, this kind of feedback is much harder to come by. A responsive government must therefore invent processes to determine preferences.

Survey data can be an important management tool. For example, a city could use surveys to measure attitudes about crime among residents in various police districts. If one district shows a decline in the fear of violence but a rise in concern about public nuisances, the district commander will emphasize more enforcement against crack houses and loitering.

Other ways of asking for ideas and feedback range from "town meetings" to highly structured and videotaped *focus groups*—a technique commonly used in consumer marketing and political campaign research. The key to their success is an effective moderator who is an able interviewer and facilitator of group processes. The aim is to explore how people react to proposals and gather information to develop questionnaires for more formal research methods. It is better to learn such things before going into the field with a full-blown survey or program test.

Government agencies have long used this strategy to solicit information and participation. The Forest Service, the Army Corps of Engineers, and the Environmental Protection Agency (EPA) regularly conduct public meetings and hearings to get information and reactions to various projects and program proposals. The Chicago Welfare Council stages "listen-ins" for black community leaders to get guidance and reactions for program planning. One of the lessons learned from their experiences is that community input must be sought early and often to keep agencies responsive to citizens' interests.

As a successful business executive, Michael Bloomberg was obsessed about being responsive to his customers. Therefore, one month after being sworn in as mayor of New York City (see photo), he proposed a 311 line that would allow citizens to report everything from noise pollution to downed power lines. More important, it would give the mayor better access to his constituents' concerns. In its first four years of operation, the 311 line received nearly 50 million calls (New Yorkers aren't shy about complaining). *Business Week* gives an example:

> Heather Schwartz, a 30-year-old graduate student, is a regular user of the 311 line and says she became a big fan last year when she called about graffiti in a northern Manhattan subway station. Within days the walls were painted over. Each time the graffiti artists returned, the city would paint over their handiwork. Finally, the

Mayor Bloomberg made City Hall "see-though." All meeting rooms had glass windows, so one could look inside. His desk and those of his staff were located in a big room without walls to facilitate better and fast communication.

vandals gave up. Now Schwartz calls 311 for everything from elevator inspections to trash in the streets. I am thrilled with it," she says. "It professionalized the city."[2]

To design a full-fledged customer-driven program, it is convenient to refer to the components of such a program in terms of the **four P's of marketing**—product, price, promotion, and placement. The following sections discuss a few of the public-sector decisions associated with each component.

Product The crucial point about a consumer's attitude toward any goods or services is that it is an evaluation of a variety of features. For example, whether a high school student decides to attend a particular college depends on several features: cost, distance from home, number of friends enrolled, and so forth. Of course, the student will weigh (or value) each of these features differently and hold opinions about the probability that the college does in fact offer each of these features.

Similarly, the attitude of a citizen toward mass transit is an evaluation of several features. We might even express this evaluation in a formula:

Overall attitude =
    (strength of belief that transit system is *fast*) × (importance of speed) +
    (strength of belief that system is *safe*) × (importance of safety) +
    (strength of belief that system is *clean*) × (importance of cleanliness) +
    (strength of belief that system is *economical*) × (importance of economy)

How can such models help college presidents, directors of city transportation authorities, or hospital administrators (who find that physicians are always recommending somebody else's hospital to their patients)? They tell the administrator what is affecting consumers' attitudes most about their "product." For example, the college administrator may be placing too much emphasis on a winning football team when national rankings do not influence applicants—which is what the administrator thought.

Price   What should NASA charge private companies to carry payloads aboard the space shuttle? What should a power company charge for electricity? A highway commission for tolls? Among the pricing strategies a public-sector organization might follow are *no-fare price* (for example, get people to ride buses rather than drive automobiles), *profit maximization price* (for example, sell tickets to a charity ball), *cost-plus price* (for example, open gift shop at museum), *variable price* (for example, charge more for electricity during peak periods), *discriminatory price* (for example, charge higher tuition to out-of-state students), and *cost-recovery price* (for example, recover a "reasonable" part of a toll road's costs). In 1996 the State University of New York began using off-peak pricing at some of its campuses. Tuition is lower for students who take courses at night, on weekends, or during the summer, and for those who attend classes at sites with vacant seats.

Promotion   To promote a service, the agency must communicate with the consumer. As with pricing policies, several strategies are available. Advertising probably comes to mind first, although its effectiveness is widely overestimated. Nevertheless, the federal government is one of the nation's top 20 advertisers, with outlays rivaling those of such business giants as Coca-Cola and Procter & Gamble.

Market segmentation can help. For example, a small private university in Minnesota might develop three brochures for prospective students rather than one. For inquiries from the West, one brochure might emphasize the winter sports; for inquiries from the East, the teaching excellence; and for inquiries from within Minnesota, the opportunity to go to a national, rather than regional, university. (For more on market segmentation, see page 168.)

In Texas, one year after the Department of Highways and Public Transportation launched its "Don't Mess with Texas" antilitter campaign, litter was down 29 percent on state roads, compared with 10 percent in other states with such programs. The key to Texas's success was research showing that 70 percent of deliberate littering could be attributed to people under 25, most of them male. Therefore, the television commercials were aimed directly at the young men who dispose of burger wrappers and beer bottles the easy way—out the window.

Placement   Within cost constraints, a public-sector organization should try to make consumer access to the product or service as easy as possible. Hospitals and medical societies can use cable television or prerecorded radio messages to provide useful information to customers. Blood banks can be set up in neighborhood stations to get donations. Subsidized meals can be distributed to disadvantaged and elderly people by having volunteers drive their own cars. Universities can set up branch campuses, provide courses on commuter trains, or use satellite communication to more remote locations.

Fairness

To ensure that citizens have a chance to present their cases and be heard fairly, agencies follow the principle of **due process.** The concept of due process is stated for the federal courts in the Fifth Amendment and for the state courts in the Fourteenth. It assumes that no citizen should "be deprived of life, liberty, or property without due process of law." In short, it is an assurance that the government will be administered by laws, not by the arbitrary will of people who condemn without a public hearing.

Although the concept of due process originally applied to criminal law, it was later extended to administration. As we saw in Chapter 2, the Administrative Procedures Act of 1946 serves as a major limitation on administrative discretion. Agencies must deal with matters over which they have jurisdiction, must give fair hearings to all persons affected by their rulings, must give notice of such hearings well in advance of the hearing dates, and must allow any interested persons to appear. Their officers must be impartial, with no personal interest in the questions about which they decide. Moreover, their decisions must be based on substantial evidence. In the orders they issue, specific findings of the law and fact must be set forth. The persons affected by such orders must be permitted counsel and given an opportunity to appeal. This is due process in the *procedural* sense of the term.

But fairness concerns *results* as well as procedures. Today, in an effort to protect the rights and property of individual parties and to check abuses of administrative discretion, courts are more inclined to question the logic of the agency's decision. For example, did the National Highway Traffic Safety Administration present adequate justification for repealing a rule requiring the installation of passive-restraining seat belts on all new cars?

Flexibility

In James Jones's novel *From Here to Eternity,* American soldiers are under surprise attack by Japanese planes at Pearl Harbor. The hero, Sergeant Warden, rushes to the arsenal for weapons only to find the door barred by another sergeant loudly proclaiming (over the din of exploding Japanese bombs) that he cannot pass out live ammunition without a written request signed by an officer. The phenomenon of bureaucratic inflexibility is no fiction. We have all faced—and been frustrated by—instances of administrative inflexibility. Buried in almost any daily newspaper can be found an example or two of how some person was made to suffer while a bureaucrat was making sure all the *i*'s were dotted and all the *t*'s were crossed.

In his best-selling book *The Death of Common Sense,* [3] Philip K. Howard argues that regulation has become disconnected from the people who must enforce and live with it. The problem has its roots, he argues, in the noble but misguided principle that "reason" can be achieved through uniform rules that anticipate every conceivable circumstance. Howard argues convincingly that these rules—which are at the heart of modern agencies such as the Occupational Safety and Health Administration (OSHA) and the EPA—have had the perverse effect of eliminating common sense from the equation.

Take the Glen-Gery brick factory in Pennsylvania. Instead of examining the real hazards of this workplace, OSHA applies a set of uniform rules, requires the factory to fill out hundreds of forms, and insists on enforcing the letter of the law. The factory has been cited for having railings 40 inches high rather than the required 42 inches. With all that wasted energy, OSHA cannot focus on what really might put workers in danger. "It is as if OSHA's goal, the safety of workers, is obscured from view by all the rules intended to advance it," Howard writes. "What we need is a system focused on goals and results, not rules and process."

Clearly, in the formulation and implementation of policy, administrators should not ignore individual groups, local concerns, or situational differences relevant to the attainment of policy goals. This imperative applies with particular force in the United States, which has a federal system of government (as discussed in Chapter 3).

To say that the United States is a large and diverse nation surely must be one of the hoariest platitudes around. Yet federal administrators cannot ignore it. When a federal agency suggests legislation, it must be sensitive to the regional biases in Congress. If the legislation passes, the agency then must be sensitive, when it administers the policy, to the different claimants within state boundaries. A survey conducted a few years ago by the Gallup organization captures some of this regional diversity (see Figure 4.1). Such regional diversity helps explain why uniform economic and social programs stamped out in Washington, like so many license plates, can sometimes produce gross misallocation of resources.

Flexibility is a value to be sought at the local level as well as at the federal and state levels. For example, a police chief might strongly advocate neighborhood policing but think that it could work only if the approach was *customized for each neighborhood.*

But flexibility—or customization—can be pursued only so far. Treating everyone individually is usually too expensive and impractical for most situations. On the other hand, treating all citizens or clients the same way may achieve economies of scale but ignores social diversity and probably means that what is offered never meets anyone's needs very well. The three figures below attempt to illustrate some of the difficulty involved.

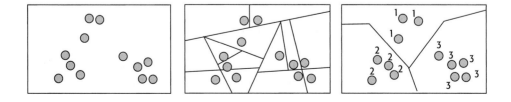

The figure on the left shows a hypothetical "market" (or jurisdiction) consisting of 12 persons who share some need in common; no segmentation is required. The middle figure shows the opposite case: Here the organization has decided to see each of the 12 members of this market as being different. But few organizations find it worthwhile to study every individual member and then customize service to each member's need. Instead, organizations generally search for broad groupings that can be approached as segments. The organization then can choose to deal with all these segments or concentrate on one or a few of them. In the figure on the right, the organization has taken this approach and has used income class as the basis for **market segmentation.**

How might a nonprofit organization whose mission is to help the homeless segment its "market"? Clearly, identifying the major segments in its marketplace would enable the nonprofit to better match supply and demand and identify customer service requirements. Here is how the Weingart Center, a not-for-profit welfare agency in Los Angeles, tackled the problem.

One segment consisted of the "have-nots"—working Americans temporarily derailed by economic downturn or family crisis. They needed relatively little support to provide for themselves and their families. The center's strategy for this group was to "give them an immediate remedy to keep them from becoming so emotionally or economically disabled that they fall into the 'can-nots' category." The "can-nots" consisted of those disabled by mental illness, drug or alcohol addiction, poor health, or inadequate education. The center's short-term strategy for this group was to link them to existing benefits and programs so that they could lead relatively self-sufficient lives with minimal supervision. The aim was to prevent them from becoming completely dysfunctional.

Last were the highly visible "will-nots." Distraught and incapacitated from years of mental illness and living on the street, they were amenable to only limited assistance. As the center's director explained, "While we should not turn our backs on this group, our time and resources should first be invested in services for the two segments of the homeless population that still have the ability and desire to help themselves."[4]

Of course, many variables could have been used other than income or the Weingart Center's tripartite division. The most important fall into three major classes: geographic (by region, county size, climate, and so on), demographic (by age, sex, race, and so on), and psychographic (usage rate, benefits sought, lifestyle, and so on). When governments ignore these kinds of complexities in the formulation and implementation of policy, they tend to fail the standard of flexibility and thereby become less responsive.

Honesty

Why Honesty Matters   The answer is simple: Honesty breeds trust and the more trust there is in a society, the better that society functions. "One of the most important lessons we can learn from examination of economic life," Francis Fukuyama writes, "is that a nation's well-being, as well as its ability to compete, is conditioned by a single, pervasive cultural characteristic: the level of trust inherent in the society."[5] Why is this so?

Figure 4.1   American Political and Personal Attitudes

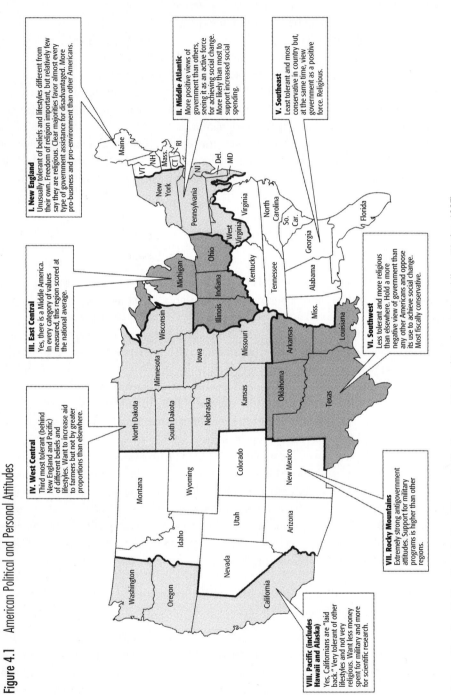

I. New England
Unusually tolerant of beliefs and lifestyles different from their own. Freedom of religion important, but relatively few say they are religious. Clear majorities favor almost every type of government assistance for disadvantaged. More pro-business and pro-environment than other Americans.

II. Middle Atlantic
More positive views of government than others, seeing it as an active force for achieving social change. More likely than most to support increased social spending.

V. Southeast
Least tolerant and most conservative in country but, at the same time, view government as a positive force. Religious.

III. East Central
Yes, there is a Middle America. In every category of values measured, this region scored at the national average.

IV. West Central
Third most tolerant (behind New England and Pacific) of different beliefs and lifestyles. Want to increase aid to farmers but not by greater proportions than elsewhere.

VI. Southwest
Less tolerant and more religious than elsewhere. Hold a more negative view of government than any other Americans and oppose its use to achieve social change. Most fiscally conservative.

VII. Rocky Mountains
Extremely strong antigovernment attitudes. Support for military programs is higher than other regions.

VIII. Pacific (includes Hawaii and Alaska)
Yes, Californians are "laid back." Very tolerant of other lifestyles and not very religious. Want less money spent for military and more for scientific research.

SOURCE: Based on Gallup Organization, *The People, the Press, and Politics* (Reading, MA: Addison-Wesley, 1987).

If people who have to work together in an enterprise trust one another because they are all operating according to a common set of ethical norms, doing business costs less. Such a society will be better able to innovate organizationally, since the high degree of trust will permit a wide variety of social relationships to emerge. Hence highly sociable Americans pioneered the development of the modern corporation in the late nineteenth and early twentieth centuries, just as the Japanese have explored the possibilities of network organizations in the twentieth.

By contrast, people who do not trust one another will end up cooperating only under a system of formal rules and regulations, which have to be negotiated, agreed to, litigated, and enforced, sometimes by coercive means. This legal apparatus, serving as a substitute for trust, entails what economists call "transaction costs." Widespread distrust in a society, in other words, imposes a kind of tax on all forms of economic activity, a tax that high-trust societies do not have to pay.[6]

In *Lying: Moral Choice in Public and Private Life,* Sissela Bok makes the same point with an analogy: "Trust is a social good to be provided just as much as the air we breathe or the water we drink. When it is damaged, the community as a whole suffers; and when it is destroyed, societies falter and collapse."[7]

Government in particular requires trust because many government activities require significant cooperation from many parties.

Why Public Officials Deceive

One reason is to try to hide poor performance. The word to stress in that sentence is "try" because such attempts almost invariably fail, sooner or later.

Another reason public officials deceive is arrogance. "The powerful tell lies," Bok writes, "believing that they have greater than ordinary understanding of what is at stake; very often, they regard their dupes as having inadequate judgment, or as likely to respond in the wrong way to truthful information."[8]

A third reason for mendacity was famously given by Jack Nicholson, as Col. Nathan Jessup, in the film *A Few Good Men:* "You can't handle the truth! Son, we live in a world that has walls, and those walls have to be guarded by men with guns. Who's going to do it? You?" Bok explains the thinking here as follows:

At times, those who govern also regard particular circumstances as too uncomfortable, too painful, for most people to be able to cope with rationally. They may believe, for instance, that their country must prepare for long-term challenges of great importance, such as a war, an epidemic, or a belt-tightening in the face of future shortages. Yet they may fear that citizens will be able to respond only to short-range dangers. Deception at such times may seem to the government leaders as the only means of attaining the necessary results.[9]

Note that the last two reasons for deceiving differ from the first. The first was to hide poor performance and, in that sense, it stems from a feeling of incompetence. In contrast, the last two are, purportedly, in the public interest—and, in that sense, stem from a feeling of superiority. The line of reasoning here is this: "If only the common people were as smart, as far-sighted, and as courageous as I, they would agree with me. But because they are none of these things, they must be deceived for their own good."

The problem with this type of thinking is twofold. First, it presents a slippery slope. Public officials who start using this rationale for issues of great moment might, over time, start applying them to virtually all issues. Lying becomes habitual, a standard operating procedure.

Second, believing that the people must be deceived for their own good might turn out on closer inspection to be, in Bok's words, "private gain masquerading as being in the public interest." She gives the example of President Lyndon B. Johnson portraying himself during the 1964 election as the candidate of peace, while his opponent was an irresponsible war hawk. Yet the Johnson administration had plans in place to escalate the war as soon as the election was over—and it did. Johnson's rationale was that there just wasn't enough time before the election to explain to the American people why escalation was necessary. Bok suggests the real rationale was simply that Johnson didn't want to do anything that would jeopardize his election:

> Johnson thus denied the electorate any chance to give or to refuse consent to the escalation of the war in Vietnam. . . . Deception of this kind strikes at the very essence of democratic government. It allows those in power to override or nullify the right vested in the people to cast an informed vote in critical elections. Deceiving the people for the sake of the people is a self-contradictory notion in a democracy, unless it can be shown that there has been genuine consent to deceive."[10]

Finally, how about matters that involve the private lives of public figures? Might not a certain amount of deception be justified in such cases? Bok makes an important distinction between withholding certain information and lying. "Information about their marriages, their children, their opinions about others—information about their personal plans and about their motives for personal decisions—all are theirs to keep private if they wish to do so. Refusing to give information under the circumstances is justifiable—but the right to withhold information is not the right to lie about it. Lying under such circumstances bodes ill for conduct in other matters."[11]

What Should Be Done?   No doubt there are occasions when deception is called for. Few historians or ethicists would argue that General Dwight D. Eisenhower should have been more forthcoming to reporters on the time and place of the Normandy invasion. Or, say a government is planning to devalue its currency. If the news leaks out to some before it can be announced to all, unfair profits for speculators might result. Or, a city might want to institute a policy of using unmarked police cars to discourage speeding by drivers.

Bok recommends in such cases that these forms of deception be debated and authorized in advance by the elected officials of the public. That's what she means by a *consent to deceive*. "Only those deceptive practices which can be openly debated and consented to in advance are justifiable in a democracy."[12]

What is to be done when one is caught in an apparent deception? The lesson should have been learned by all—once and for all—after Watergate. President Richard Nixon did not directly order the break-in and bugging of the Democratic Party's national headquarters on June 17, 1972, but he created the atmosphere that encouraged his reelection campaigners to take such action: the relentless secrecy, the propensity for back-channel operations, the obsessive concern about press and political criticism. When the story of the break-in broke, he should have done *everything in his power to get the whole truth and nothing but the truth out as fast as possible.* That is the great lesson of Watergate. To be sure, it would have been messy and unpleasant for Nixon in the short run—but his presidency would have likely lived on. Instead, he involved himself in the cover-up that followed the arrest at the Watergate Hotel and, in so doing, wrote out his political death warrant. But political leaders continue to forget how destructive stonewalling is. Again and again.

Corruption [Honesty involves, of course, more than telling the truth. If a Detroit social worker steals funds from a scholarship program intended for needy inner-city youth, that is dishonest. If a New Jersey state police officer forces drivers to give him a hundred dollars in bogus tolling fees, that is dishonest. Both actions are, in fact, examples of **malfeasance.** But malfeasance is more than stealing. It is the performance by public officials of deeds that they are forbidden to perform by constitutional or statutory law, or by commonly accepted moral standards. If the police break and enter without a search warrant, that, too, is malfeasance.]

Malfeasance should be distinguished from misfeasance and nonfeasance. (The stem word *feasance* means the doing of an act, as of a duty.) **Misfeasance** is the improper performance of lawful duties. It involves administrative activity that is within the lawful mission of an agency but that violates constitutional standards or the public interest. If two Border Patrol agents, Ignacio Ramos and Jose Alonso Compean, shoot a drug smuggler evading arrest and then pick up the shells and fail to report the incident, that is misfeasance. According to the U.S. attorney prosecuting them, "The U.S. Supreme Court has ruled it is a violation of someone's 10th Amendment rights to shoot them in the back while fleeing if you don't know who they are and you don't know they have a weapon." The smuggler, who escaped back to Mexico, was not a U.S. citizen.

In October 2006, Ramos and Compean received 11- and 12-year prison sentences, respectively. Many observers were puzzled by the sentence because another pair of border agents the same month received less time (six years) for their part in an immigrant smuggling ring that illegally moved thousands of people from Mexico to the United States. In contrast, Ramos and Compean were pursuing a smuggler driving a van filled with 800 lbs. of marijuana and carrying what was, they thought, a gun. Because crooked Border Patrol agents faced less time for running criminal operations (malfeasance) than Ramos and Compean did for their stopping criminal operations (misfeasance), Republicans and Democrats in both the House and Senate promised to hold hearings after the November 2006 election. On January 19, 2009, President George W. Bush commuted their sentences.

Nonfeasance is the failure of a public official to perform required duties. If the Federal Aviation Administration had a report saying that a particular aircraft was unsafe but took no action, that is nonfeasance.

Accountability

A good synonym for the term **accountability** is *answerability.* An organization must be answerable to someone or something outside itself. When things go wrong, someone must be held responsible. Unfortunately, a frequently heard charge is that government is faceless and that, consequently, affixing blame is difficult.

Immediately after British troops retook the Falkland Islands from Argentina on June 14, 1982, British foreign secretary Lord Carrington resigned his position in Margaret Thatcher's Conservative government. He did so because of the failure of British diplomacy to prevent, and of British intelligence services to anticipate, the Argentine invasion that cost the nation lives, territory, and international embarrassment. Although the recapture of the Falklands proved in time to be a political plus for the Thatcher government (and for British morale), Lord Carrington's action was judged appropriate and was not reversed.

Carrington's action provides an interesting contrast to what happened after the October 23, 1983, bombing of the Marine barracks at the Beirut airport in Lebanon. Although the bombing was a severe setback to American interests in the region, no one resigned, no one was disciplined, and no one was fired. President Reagan said no one should have been because "I accepted responsibility." Nor was anyone disciplined in October 2000 when terrorists in a small boat carrying explosives were allowed to approach a U.S. warship refueling in the Yemeni port of Aden. That explosion killed 17 American sailors. Unlike the September 11 attacks, anticipating and preventing these two attacks required neither a great leap of imagination nor extraordinary security measures.

By late 2004, most informed observers agreed that postwar planning for Iraq was seriously flawed, yet no one was held accountable.[13] Indeed, when the chief architect of the war, Donald Rumsfeld, resigned in November 2006, the administration's vice president called him perhaps "the greatest secretary of defense ever." Two years later, when the U.S. financial system was collapsing, no members of Congress or group of public executives went on television and said they were the ones who allowed Freddie and Fannie (Federal Home Loan Mortgage Corp. and Federal National Mortgage Association) unlimited reign over mortgage securities.

Fortunately, Americans need not go to Britain to find accountability in government. Consider what happened when, in 2008, a Marine jet crashed nose down in a San Diego neighborhood killing four members of a Korean immigrant family. Why was the disabled plane over land? The Marines launched an investigation of themselves. When the results were announced, the assistant wing commander said the crash was "clearly avoidable," the result of "a chain of wrong decisions." Twelve Marines were disciplined; four senior officers, including the squadron commander, were removed from duty. Their military careers were, essentially, over. The pilot was grounded while a board reviewed his future. Residents told reporters that they were taken aback by the report. "Marines aren't trying to hide from it or duck it. They took it on the chin," said one neighbor. See photo for another recent example of taking responsibility rather than engaging in damage control.

Competence

Now meet Fred. He is attuned to the ever-changing demands of his agency's clients; he treats clients not as numbers but as individuals; he knows the law and obeys it; he takes full responsibility for all his actions and keeps the agency head fully informed; his reputation for integrity and candor extends well beyond the agency.

But, alas, Fred is no paragon of administrative responsibility. His administrative actions are hasty rather than prudent, and they display little concern for consequences. He adheres strictly to an 8-hour, 480-minute day. He never volunteers or demonstrates any initiative. Furthermore, Fred uses his resources poorly—he is always over budget and consistently fails to hit the performance objectives for his administrative unit. His "satisfactory"

This photo shows Air Force One soaring over the Statue of Liberty in May 2009, a flight which cost taxpayers $328,835 and incited panic among scores of New Yorkers who, understandably, have an aversion to low-flying, unannounced airliners. The director of the White House Military Office, who approved the flight, was forced to resign.

performance rating satisfies him, although given the tendency for such ratings to be inflated, it shouldn't. He looks forward to retirement. In short, his **competence** is in question. The public does not want to be served by knaves, nor does it want incompetents. Clearly then, administrative responsibility is a multifaceted concept.

Not only is the concept multifaceted, it may also be riddled with contradictions. Efforts to enhance fairness, honesty, and accountability in public administration may be at odds with the ideals of responsiveness, flexibility, and competence. And the contradictions have probably never been more acute than today.

As Americans have increasingly demanded high performance from the public sector, a new model of public administration has emerged in certain quarters, to replace the more traditional model. Sandford Borins at the University of Toronto describes this **new public management** as a "normative reconceptualization of public administration consisting of several interrelated components." He contends that "this new paradigm is not reducible to a few sentences, let alone a slogan." Nevertheless, he suggests, it contains five key ideas:

1. Government should provide high-quality services that citizens value.
2. The autonomy of public managers, particularly from central agency controls, should be increased.
3. Organizations and individuals should be evaluated and rewarded on the basis of how well they meet demanding performance targets.
4. Managers must be assured that the human and technological resources they need to perform well will be available to them; and
5. Public sector managers must appreciate the value of competition and maintain an open-minded attitude about which services belong to the private, rather than public, sector.[14]

And there's the rub. Borins's five key ideas for improving performance of the public sector make the realization of fairness, trust, and accountability more problematic than ever. See box: "The New Public Management and the Moore Paradox."

External and Internal Controls

Various measures can and have been taken to ensure responsiveness, fairness, flexibility, honesty, accountability, and competence. Figure 4.2 can help distinguish and analyze these measures.

This framework divides the measures into four main categories: formal-external, formal-internal, informal-external, and informal-internal. The distinction between formal and informal, though not always easy to draw, is roughly this: Formal relationships are explicitly provided for in the Constitution; informal ones are not. **External controls** are those that reside outside the executive branch; **internal controls,** within.

Because three controls—namely, the media, the legisture, and interest groups—were discussed in Chapter 2, this section will concentrate on the remaining nine.

The New Public Management and the Moore Paradox

The new public managers employ a style that may further undermine public trust. To improve performance, public managers need flexibility, deregulation, and empowerment. To produce results in today's complex policy environment, public managers need particularly high levels of dedication, energy, even audacity. The prototype of the new public manager is not merely entrepreneurial. He or she is often brash and aggressive—taking conspicuous chances, publicly accepting responsibility for both successes and failures, and thumbing a nose at detractors or those who warn of the necessity of caution.

"Public *management* is different from public administration," emphasizes Donald Savoie, one of the critics of the new public management. "Unlike the traditional public administration language that conjures up images of rules, regulations and lethargic decision-making processes, the very word 'management' implies a decisiveness, a dynamic mindset and a bias for action." Yet we citizens are not sure that we trust such governmental entrepreneurs.

All this creates what Mark Moore describes as an "interesting paradox": "On one hand, because personal leadership and responsibility seem to be key to successful innovations, they should be valued. On the other hand, the arrogance and flashy style that often accompany personal leadership often attract hostility and suspicion in the public sector." To be a successful innovator in both business and government, an executive needs a "willingness to take the initiative and accept responsibility while remaining modest about his or her contributions and generous in crediting others." Yet, Moore continues, "executives in the public sector must err

even more on the side of modesty" lest they "trigger close press scrutiny and antipathy." This creates the Moore Paradox: "The public expects a style of management in the public sector that would be ineffective if managers actually engaged in it."

Public managers who exercise little initiative produce few results and thus undermine the public's confidence in government. Public managers who are leaders may produce results but through their style still undermine the public's trust. "The entrepreneurial model," writes James Stever of the University of Cincinnati, "can never legitimate public sector administration in the eye of a skeptical public. The public may envy, even admire the entrepreneur, but the actions of the entrepreneur are illegitimate in that the entrepreneur cannot be expected to function as guardian of the broader public interest."

Three entrepreneurs illustrate the Moore Paradox particularly well: Admiral Hyman Rickover, who advocated nuclear sea power; J. Edgar Hoover, who built the FBI into an efficient crime detection agency; and Robert Moses, who served as New York City Parks Commissioner from 1934 to 1960. All three created major public agencies and achieved significant results—results of which others could not even dream. To do so, reports Lewis, all three achieved "degrees of autonomy and flexibility which are popularly believed to be impossible in government bureaucracies." They employed "buffering and autonomy-seeking strategies," observes Lewis, and managed to make such "behavior appear reasonable, sensible and even occasionally patriotic." Indeed, Lewis concludes that two steps in becoming a public entrepreneur are "the creation of an a political shield" and a continuing "struggle for autonomy." Yet Rickover, Hoover, and Moses

(Continued)

did all of this in a way that we now think of as decidedly undemocratic.

How do we Americans want to resolve the Moore Paradox? Do we want public managers to be entrepreneurs who actively exercise and protect their discretion and in the process create high-performance organizations that produce results? Or do we want public managers to assiduously obey all of the rules and regulations even if this ensures that they accomplish little?

SOURCE: Robert D. Behn, *Rethinking Democratic Accountability* (Washington, DC: Brookings, 2001), 99–100. Text has been slightly edited.

Judiciary

The Administrative Process Revisited   Chapter 2 presented in some detail a model of the administrative process. Because the process in general and judicial review in particular are designed to prevent irresponsible behavior by government agencies, it might be useful to briefly review that process.

Various parties—Aunt Beth, Engulf & Devour Corporation, and others—make demands on the agency that must first pass through an *informal* screening process. The purpose of this step, which comes before any formal hearing, is to resolve a problem in as economical and flexible a manner as possible. A problem here may involve nothing more than answering a telephone call. ("Where is my Social Security check?" "What do you mean I underpaid my taxes by $735?") Or it may involve much larger issues. ("May we merge with General Electric?" "Does our prospectus for a security system look okay?") Even these more complex issues can often be negotiated and resolved congenially.

For the *formal* hearing provisions of the **Administrative Procedures Act** to come into play, an agency's authorizing statute must require it. If the statute is vague on this point,

Figure 4.2   A Framework for Analyzing Controls on Government Organizations

	External	Internal
Formal	• Judiciary • Ombudsman • Legislature*	• Agency head/inspector general • Whistle-blower statutes
Informal	• Citizen participation • Interest group representation* • Media*	• Professional codes • Representative bureaucracy • Public interest • Ethical analysis

*Discussed in Chapter 2.

the courts will look to the legislative history (that is, what members of Congress had in mind) and, of course, ensure that constitutional due process governs. Sometimes the courts favor administrative discretion; other times they favor the benefits of fairness. It all depends.

In cases requiring a more formal process, an administrative law judge generally reviews the evidence and makes preliminary conclusions as to the disposition of the issue. If an appeal is needed, it will usually be an administrative appeal in which the record is examined by other agency officials. Eventually, a final decision is reached. The decision may concern claims and benefits, licenses, rules, rates, routes, or sanctions (for noncompliance). These, in effect, are the output of the administrative agency, and they can have a considerable effect on the involved parties.

After administrative procedures have been exhausted, some form of review of agency decisions can be sought in the courts. If a case presents important legal questions, there may be appeals leading to the Supreme Court. The court may set aside any agency action that entails abuse of discretion, excess of statutory or constitutional authority, improper proceedings, or an action unwarranted by the facts. However, the administrative process is not the only path to the courtroom for agencies and managers: There is also the law of liability.

Accountability Through Liability   This type of control differs from the type we examined earlier when studying judicial review. Those remedies are limited to reversing, modifying, and compelling agency action and do not cover the payment of monetary damages by government.

Let's begin by considering damage action against the government. Persons who are harmed by administrative action often seek to recover damages from the government to compensate them for their injuries. Such efforts always require a statutory basis, for otherwise they might flounder on the ancient doctrine of **sovereign immunity**—that is, the principle that the government may not be sued without its consent. The federal government has always possessed sovereign immunity; the Eleventh Amendment to the Constitution grants similar sovereign immunity to the states. (Local governments, however, lack protection from most court proceedings.) Justice Holmes explained the doctrine as follows: "A sovereign is exempt from suit, not because of any formal conception or obsolete theory, but on the logical and practical ground that there can be no legal right as against the authority that makes the law on which the right depends."

One public policy that does allow government to be sued is the Federal Tort and Claims Act (FTCA) of 1946. The FTCA allows redress for tort claims. (The word *tort* is borrowed from the French, meaning "wrong." In law, more precisely, a tort is a violation of a duty imposed by civil law. When someone breaks one of those duties and injures another, it is a tort.) The FTCA generally renders the government liable in tort for any negligent or wrongful act in the same manner as a private individual under like circumstances. Prior to the passage of the FTCA, when citizens were injured as a result of a government's negligence, they simply could not sue the government to recover damages. To preserve much of the sovereign immunity doctrine, FTCA lists a number of exceptions to tort liability. Another way FTCA preserves sovereign immunity is to prohibit lawsuits when the responsible officials were exercising a "discretionary function," regardless of whether they abused their discretion. The intention here is to prevent the use of torts as judicial "second-guessing" of legislative and administrative decisions grounded in policy. See photo.

When a litigant seeks to recover damages from the pocket of an individual public administrator, sovereign immunity is not an obstacle because that doctrine applies to government units. But a related doctrine, **official immunity**, may be. The long-standing rule has been that a federal employee is absolutely immune from common-law tort liability for any act performed within "the outer perimeter" of his or her line of duty.[15] The rationale for this rule is that officials should feel free to make decisions according to their concept of the public interest without the threat that they might have to bear monetary loss if a member of the public is injured in the process.

Except for those officials who have absolute immunity because of their position—the president, presidential aides, judges, prosecutors, and administrative law judges—government officials do not have absolute immunity from liability for damages. They can be sued for actions that violate statutory limits on their authority or that violate constitutional limits of their authority. For example, federal prison officials may be liable under the Eighth

Because the government failed to exercise reasonable care, two ships loaded with ammonium nitrate exploded offshore in Texas City, Texas, on April 16, 1947. Fire ripped through the town and local refinery. However, in *Dalehite v. U.S.* (1953), the Supreme Court found the government not liable because its officials were exercising a "discretionary function."

Amendment for inflicting cruel and unusual punishment on a prisoner. The test is, as the courts stated it in *Harlow v. Fitzgerald* (1982), whether the defendant violated "clearly established statutory or constitutional rights of which a reasonable person would have known." Partly because of the stringency of the *Harlow* test, successful constitutional tort actions against federal officers have been extremely rare and will probably so remain.

The Importance of Judicial Control   Arguably, the most rapidly expanding control over administration in recent years has been in the courts. But it has also been extended to prison administration (size of cells and number of prisoners per cell), education policy (routes for school buses and content of curriculum), and technical areas such as automobile safety standards and resource management. For example, the Supreme Court has ruled that the Federal Communications Commission cannot require cable television operators to allow free access to a portion of their broadcast facilities and that the Securities and Exchange Commission cannot control private pension plans.

But the court's power is not limited to federal agencies. Sovereign states and independent school districts are also affected. In the state of Alabama, a U.S. district judge, in effect, helped run the state. He supervised the operations of prisons, mental hospitals, the highway patrol, and other state institutions. In the Boston school district, another federal judge helped run things down to such micro issues as whether a particular school's auditorium needed roofing.

Notwithstanding such examples, the roles of the judiciary in public administration should be put in perspective. First, a court's responsibility is always after the fact; that is to say, all that courts can do is alleviate or punish wrongs that have already occurred. A second point is that the Supreme Court and its individual members tend to support federal agencies more frequently than they oppose them. In other words, research suggests that the outlook is not altogether promising for individuals who choose to control agency action in court.

Third, and perhaps most fundamental, do courts really need to decide whether an agency has "failed to consider all relevant factors" or has "abused its discretion" in writing a regulation on how to label peanut butter? Expert opinion is divided on this controversial question, but let us consider the case for the negative. Some argue that a more useful division of labor might be for the peoples' representatives to monitor these matters, while courts concentrate on checking on bureaucrats who are accountable in no other way. Assuming agencies are under *political* control, judges can concentrate on their original job of protecting the Bill of Rights. They can let others worry about the hydrogenated vegetable oil in Skippy peanut butter.

Ombudsman

Suppose the Department of Motor Vehicles mistakenly puts your brother's picture on your driver's license and your picture on his. When you explain the problem to the clerk, the reply is, "Hey, sorry 'bout that. But why don't you just leave it—keep it in the family." "I don't want his face," you declare firmly. The clerk just giggles and continues on his way.

What can be done about similar errors and insensitivity that we all experience from time to time when dealing with big government departments? One answer is to appoint an ombudsman, just as all the Scandinavian countries and much of the British Commonwealth have done, including all but one of the provinces of Canada. In the United States, Alaska, Arizona, Hawaii, Iowa, and Nebraska use ombudsman at the state level, and several cities also employ them. At the federal level, the Internal Revenue Service, the EPA, and the Department of Commerce use ombudsman in some programs. An **ombudsman** is a person, appointed by government, who has the power to interview those who handled a matter in dispute and examine their records, then make a recommendation and use "reasoned persuasion" to achieve a remedy.

In the course of interviewing more than 30 ombudsmen in the United States and abroad for his book on the subject, Sam Zagoria found that most of the time, the ombudsman's findings were accepted in whole or at least in part.[16] A typical ombudsman will find that in half or more of the cases presented, the citizen complaints will be unjustified and the ombudsman can be helpful in clearing a harassed public servant of unwarranted charges. At a minimum, the constituent is offered a readily available office to help her protect her rights, and even when the complaint is not sustained, the constituent has a second opinion to help her accept an unhappy result.

Whistle-Blower Statutes

Ralph Nader originated the term **whistle-blower** to characterize employees who disclosed illegal, immoral, or illegitimate practices by their employers. The most famous whistle-blower during the Nixon administration was Ernest Fitzgerald, a civilian employee of the Department of Defense, who claimed that a transport plane being built for the Air Force had cost vastly more than the sum Congress had appropriated for it and was, moreover, a bad plane.

Perhaps the most famous government whistle-blower in the past few years has been Colleen Rowley, the Federal Bureau of Investigation (FBI) agent whose impassioned protest letter to Director Robert Mueller created a storm of criticism of the bureau's management. (See Case 1.1 in Chapter 1.) In 2002, *Time* selected her, along with two corporate whistle-blowers, as Persons of the Year. (The other two people were Sharon Watkins, the Enron vice president who wrote a letter to Chairman Kenneth Lay warning him that the company's methods of accounting were improper, and Cynthia Cooper, who informed the board of WorldCom that the company had covered up $3.8 billion in losses through its own dubious accounting methods.)

A lawyer in the FBI's Minneapolis office, Rowley criticized her beloved bureau in a secret 13-page memo. According to *Time,* Rowley viewed her memo as "not a reprimand but an act of redemption. It was not about speaking truth to power, because people like Rowley don't see much difference between the two. Truth is power."[17]

What was Rowley's truth? Among other concerns was that the FBI's bureaucracy discouraged innovation, drowned investigators in paperwork, and punished agents who sought to cut through the many layers of gatekeepers at FBI headquarters. But her main concern was that headquarters had ignored calls from her office to take seriously the case of

Zacarias Moussaoui, a French-Moroccan who spoke poor English and had signed up at a local flight school, keen to fly a 747.

It took her 16 straight hours to complete the memo. Knowing it was explosive enough for her to need some protection, she tacked on two sentences of self-preservation at the last minute, asking for federal whistle-blower protection. At the time, she did not know exactly what it was—nor that the legislation offered FBI employees a weak shield. The next day, in Washington, she dropped the memo off with a receptionist for Mueller and two members of the Senate Committee on Intelligence. Two days later, back in Minneapolis, her phone rang: It was CNN. Rowley was now, as *Time* put it, "the public's conscience." Two weeks later she was called back to Washington to testify in open court.

Congress first provided statutory protection for whistle-blowers in the Civil Service Reform Act of 1978, which is discussed in detail in Chapter 10. Among other things, the act was designed to encourage disclosures of fraud, waste, or abuse by providing protection from reprisal to employees, former employees, or applicants who make such disclosures.

In the years following passage of the act, Congress found that the law had little impact on encouraging federal employees to blow the whistle and did not protect employees from reprisals. As a result, Congress enacted the Whistleblower Protection Act of 1989 to strengthen and improve whistle-blower protection. The act established the Office of Special Counsel (OSC) as an independent agency responsible for protecting federal employees, especially whistle-blowers, from prohibited personnel actions. The OSC is responsible for investigating employee complaints of whistle-blower reprisal and, when reprisal is found, initiating corrective and disciplinary actions. Other changes by the 1989 act include easing the employee's burden of proof that reprisal for whistle-blowing has occurred and allowing employees to file appeals with the Merit Systems Protection Board if they did not obtain relief through the OSC. For more information on the OSC, visit www.osc.gov.

Agency Head

The personal example set by the top administrator in an organization conveys a powerful message to others about what he or she thinks responsible behavior is and is not. Consider the case of the city manager who discovers that an employee on the night shift has programmed the city's computer to cast horoscopes. The city manager has called the director of finance:

> Fiona, I'm assuming you didn't know this was going on and that it started in your department. Frankly, that's a partial cop-out for me and not that flattering for you. However, the computer is the city's, paid for by taxpayers, and these horoscopes cost time and money. It stops now. Suspend the young man for as long as it takes at his daily rate until he pays back what it cost us for the time it took for the horoscope program. Then, figure out how much it cost the city for each and every one of those horoscopes. Send me a list of every one who got one because I am going to send them a bill. Look, . . . I don't even use the office Xerox for personal stuff— it's not right.[18]

Here the city manager demonstrates her unequivocal opposition to unethical practices. Using the city's time and equipment to cast horoscopes is wrong. Period. The city manager's follow-up to her employees corrects the problem and reinforces the expected ethical standard.

In addition to setting a moral climate in an organizational unit, the administrator can take a number of concrete steps, such as the following, to ensure proper behavior:

- Recruit those whose backgrounds have been carefully checked.
- Establish training programs on proper conduct.
- Review on a regular basis the actions of subordinates.
- Investigate promptly and vigorously allegations of wrongdoing in the organization.

To help in the last task, some administrators are able to rely on in-house investigators known as **inspectors general (IGs).** Congress created an IG corps for the federal government in 1978. Most of the IGs' work involves routine audits of government programs to ferret out billions of dollars' worth of waste and abuse. Because the IGs send their findings to Congress, which is often more supportive of them than are the agency heads, IGs have produced some friction in the executive branch. This approach could also be adapted to a municipal police department or any unit in which corruption is a problem.

Citizen Participation

When William F. Buckley Jr. wrote that he would rather entrust his governance to the first hundred people listed in the Cambridge telephone directory than to the faculty of Harvard University, he was simply stating the basic philosophy behind including the citizenry in the public decision-making process. Other observers maintain that citizens, as customers of government, are naturally more responsive to public needs than are government officials. It might even be put forth as a tentative proposition that the poorest moral performances and the least accountability by government are generally associated with conditions in which few citizens have any influence. For these reasons, among others, it is not surprising to see government at all levels trying to facilitate the participation of citizens in the administrative process.

The most common forms that *institutionalized citizen participation* assume are the citizen committee as an advisory group, the citizen group as a governing group in a specific policy area, and the idea of neighborhood government, in which citizens have direct responsibility in a number of policy areas.

Advisory groups, as discussed here, refer to the more than 1200 boards, commissions, and committees found in federal executive departments and their regional or district subdivisions and in units of local government. These advisory committees involve more than 20,000 people and cover nearly every imaginable topic—from the president's Council on Energy Research and Development to the Agriculture Department's committee on hog cholera eradication. Local governments create advisory committees on subjects ranging from community planning and police reform to mass transit and air pollution.

Professional Codes

The use of **professional codes** can be traced back at least to the Hippocratic Oath, which has guided the practice of medicine for more than 2000 years. Next to physicians, lawyers probably have the most stringent set of professional codes to be found. (Interestingly, with few exceptions, the Watergate culprits were lawyers.)

A couple of reasons might be suggested to explain why professional codes have such limited usefulness. First, the scope of activities of an administrator seldom limits itself to one profession; inevitably, questions arise that are outside the code's purview. Similarly, the administrator often finds his or her code in conflict with other loyalties (such as a particular client or geographic region, political leader, social class, or union).

A second reason for the limitations of professional codes derives from the wording of these guidelines. If too general, they are useless as a guide to action. If specific enough to serve as a guide to action, they might be so numerous, so detailed, as to be unworkable on a day-to-day basis. The following four principles, taken from the 12 that appear in the Code of Conduct of the American Society of Public Administration, will give an idea of what is meant by "too general":

- Exercise whatever discretionary authority we have under law to promote the public interest.
- Demonstrate the highest standards of personal integrity, truthfulness, honesty, and fortitude in all our public activities in order to inspire public confidence and trust in public institutions. . . .
- Approach our organization and operational duties with a positive attitude and constructively support open communication, creativity, dedication, and compassion.
- Serve in such a way that we do not realize undue personal gain from the performance of our official duties. . . .

Representative Bureaucracy

A **representative bureaucracy** is, roughly speaking, one that represents its society—that is, the percentage of each group in the government approximates the percentage of that group in the entire population. The theory is that hiring more members of some group enhances the representation of that group's attitudes in the bureaucracy. In other words, representative bureaucracy seeks to control bureaucratic power by representing women and minorities in the civil service. But does such representation lead to active representation of a group's interest in the bureaucracy? Let's consider the case of Jose Martinez, an agent with the U.S. Border Patrol. Three hours into his 10-hour shift one cool California night, he gets a call: A dozen Mexicans have been caught sneaking across the border. Minutes later he is directing them into the back of a covered pickup truck and driving them to the station for processing and then return to Mexico. "Give me a chance, officer," one man pleads in Spanish. Such pleas are common among illegal migrants, but for officers like Martinez, a first-generation American whose father was an illegal, the words carry extra weight.

"They call us traitors," Martinez says. "They say, 'How can you do this to us? We could have been your parents. It could have been you coming over a couple years ago.' " To that, he responds: "It's nothing personal. I'm just doing my job."[19]

Ironically, Hispanics make up 30 percent of the Border Patrol's rank and file, a higher proportion than in any other federal agency. Some people—including illegal migrants themselves and their advocates—had hoped that making the border patrol a more representative bureaucracy would change the patrol's culture and turn it into a more compassionate, more lenient institution. As it turns out, the Hispanic agents have proven to be firm. Indeed, their presence on the force has not reduced the number of complaints of agent abuse of migrants. "The way I see it," Martinez explains, "you carry the badge in one hand, and in the other hand, you carry your heart."

The Martinez anecdote, though memorable, does not necessarily provide an objective answer to the question of whether there are conditions under which minority bureaucrats are less likely to provide active representation. However, recent research by Wilkins and Williams finds that, because of organizational socialization, the presence of black police officers is related to an *increase* in racial profiling.[20]

How then can we explain the weak link between ethnic representation and substantive representation? Anthony Down writes, "Officials . . . have no strong incentives to employ representative values in making decisions. The pressure on them to seek representative goals is much weaker than the pressure of their own personal goals or those of their bureaus. . . . Neither do officials face re-election, thus having to account for or justify their policies. This lack of any enforcement mechanism further reduces the probability that officials will behave in [a] representative way."[21] Other explanations might be offered: Officials may lack authority to do very much; formal organizational sanction and peer group pressure may reduce gestures of sympathy by public servants from certain ethnic groups (one "gets ahead by going along"); and uncertainty may exist regarding just what the "proper ethnic perspective" is.[22]

Public Interest

Given the limitations involved in professional codes and representative bureaucracy as internal informal approaches to administrative responsibility, some posit the concept of the **public interest** as a guide to making administrative decisions. According to this view, the administrator should make decisions based on the best interests of some collective, overarching community or national good rather than on the narrower interest of a small self-serving group.

To clearly discern the public interest is no easy task. Walter Lippmann, as lucid a thinker as one is likely to encounter on the subject, could give no better answer than this:

> There is no point in toying with any notion of an imaginary plebiscite to discern the public interest. We cannot know what we ourselves will be thinking five years hence much less what infants now in the cradle will be thinking when they go into the polling booth. Yet their interests, as we observe them today, are within the public interest. Living adults share, we must believe, the same public interest. For them, however, the public interest is mixed with, and is often at odds with, their private

and special interests. Put this way, we can say, I suggest, that the public interest may be presumed to be what men would choose if they saw clearly, thought rationally, acted disinterestedly and benevolently.[23]

But even if the public official could see with this clarity, rationality, and objectivity, would it really be enough? How does one distinguish qualitatively between aggregated private interests (for example, public opinion polls) and genuine common concerns? How does one distinguish between the various "publics": the reasonable and long-range one versus the passionate and temporary one?

Nevertheless, many see the concept as a useful frame of reference for action in day-to-day administration and policymaking. The operative question should be: What action comports best with the well-being of the nation, broadly conceived? Indeed, the first principle of the American Society for Public Administration (ASPA) Code of Ethics (1994 revised version) is, "Serve the public, beyond serving oneself. ASPA members are committed to exercise discretionary authority to promote the *public interest.*"

Ethical Analysis

Ethics is the branch of philosophy that is concerned with what is morally good and bad, right and wrong. Traditionally, ethics has undertaken to analyze values. What are values? They are simply the things one considers to be important—the criteria one uses—when making moral decisions. In terms of human conduct, there are two types of values: *goal values*, which concern where one wants to go; and *conduct values,* which concern how one gets there.[24] How would you rank the values in the following two lists? Which values are most important to you? Least important?

Goal Values

- A comfortable life (a prosperous life)
- An exciting life
- A sense of accomplishment
- A world at peace
- A world of beauty
- Equality
- Security
- Freedom (independence, free choice)
- Happiness (contentedness)
- Pleasure (an enjoyable, leisurely life)
- Self-respect (self-esteem)
- Social recognition (respect, admiration)
- True friendship (close companionship)
- Wisdom
- Ambition (hard-working, aspiring)

Conduct Values

- Broad-minded (open-minded)
- Capable (competent, effective)
- Cheerful (lighthearted, joyful)
- Clean (neat, tidy)
- Courageous
- Magnanimous
- Honest (sincere, truthful)
- Imaginative (daring, creative)
- Self-reliant
- Reflective
- Logical (consistent, rational)
- Loving (affectionate, tender)
- Dutiful
- Polite (courteous, well mannered)
- Responsible (dependable, reliable)
- Self-controlled

Why Study Ethics?

There are several practical reasons for studying ethics. First, such a study can help public administrators arrive at decisions more quickly. When confronted with decisions involving conflicting values, the person who has thought through and clarified his or her own values does not lose time wondering what to do. Such a person can act more swiftly and assuredly.

A second reason is that it leads to greater consistency in decision making. Administrators who are capable of this are seen by subordinates as fair; they avoid the charge of treating employees unequally.

Third, the study of ethics can reveal the value dimensions of a decision that would otherwise seem value-free. For example, consider a fairly straightforward decision involving the U.S. Postal Service's money-order operation. The original question is, How can the service make money orders more profitable? But then a different question might be raised: *Should* they be made more profitable, never mind how? Behind the second question is the recognition that money orders are used primarily by lower-income Americans who do not have checking accounts.

Fourth, the study of ethics can help public administrators make more reflective judgments—ones that can be defended in public. Generally, Americans feel awkward talking about values, as if such talk is something that "real men" do not do. Yet the public and the media continue to clamor for the very qualities that we are reluctant to talk about (honor, enterprise, justice, good faith, mercy, magnanimity, duty, beneficence, and the like). The dangers of flimsy and slipshod arguments arising when one moves from ethical principles to their application in the world of administration are plentiful, and one should be aware of them.

The fifth reason—the most powerful and obvious one—is that grappling with ethical dilemmas is a big part of the public administrator's job—as they say, "it comes with the territory." Here are some common ethical problems with which managers in both the public and private sectors must contend:

1. Drug and alcohol abuse (Should you have a zero tolerance policy?)
2. Employee theft (Does size matter?)
3. Conflicts of interest
4. Fudging, distorting, or concealing information
5. Abuse of expense accounts
6. Misuse of the organization's assets
7. Environmental pollution (Yes, governments pollute too.)
8. Taking credit for the work or ideas of others
9. Receiving excessive gifts and entertainment
10. Giving excessive gifts and entertainment
11. False or misleading statements to the public or one's supervisor
12. Kickbacks
13. Doing "favors" for friends and the politically influential

Here are more examples of the kinds of ethical questions public managers must address:

1. What is the threshold for blowing the whistle on one's agency? What is the trade-off between loyalty to your organization and your perception of the public interest?
2. How should a whistle-blower be handled when it appears the prime motive is pay-back or revenge (say, for not getting a promotion or enough attention)?
3. What do you do if you learn that a 58-year-old employee, who has been a solid performer, lied about his age or education on his résumé?
4. Must all decision making be in the open all the time? How far may one go in discriminating against white or Asian males in order to meet affirmative action goals?
5. Should regulatory agency employees, upon leaving the agency, take jobs within industries that they have been regulating?
6. What kinds of dress standards (ties, Mohawks, shorts, and so on) are appropriate on the job—if any?
7. Should employees ever have to submit to a polygraph? What about people working for the CIA or in a nursing home?
8. When and how do you fire an employee with marginal performance? How does an administrator handle office romances, especially when one or both parties are married to someone else?

Four Approaches to Ethics

In situations such as those just listed, administrators need a more or less orderly way of thinking through the ethical implications of a decision—an approach and a language for assessing alternatives from a moral perspective. Although a rigorous review of the many ways philosophers have sought to organize ethical analysis is beyond the scope of this book, it is possible to briefly sketch four of the more important views: the utilitarian ethic, the obligation to formal principles, the rights ethic, and the ethics of Aristotle.

The Utilitarian Ethic   Jeremy Bentham (1748–1832) thought that all theory, including ethical theory, must be grounded in empirical fact. In the case of human sciences, this fact would have to be the primacy of the pleasure principle—that is, humans are motivated by the desire for pleasure and the aversion to pain. Bentham's innovation was the claim that hedonism does not have to be egoistic; it can be social. That is, one can (and should) be motivated to act in the name of the pleasures of others as well as one's own pleasure. This idea served as the basis for the **utilitarian ethic,** which he developed in the late 1700s. In brief, Bentham asserts that "it is the greatest happiness of the greatest number that is the measure of right and wrong."

Although, with few exceptions, utilitarianism never caught on among business managers, it has attained some degree of popularity among public administrators, who refer to it as the "social benefit function." Note that this approach is not majoritarian because it measures the *intensity* of each individual's support or opposition to an alternative. To see how this works, consider a small community of 20 people who must choose between Plan A and Plan B. Twelve might express a lukewarm support for Plan A, while eight intensely oppose it. Preferences are reversed for Plan B, with 12 mildly opposing it and eight strongly supporting it. To maximize happiness in this small community, the utilitarian ethic would dictate adopting Plan B—even though it didn't garner majority support.

Not without reason, Michael Walzer refers to utilitarianism as *body count morality:*

> When decisions are unavoidable, they must be hard-headed, tough-minded, unsentimental, worked out in terms of the actual or supposed preferences of discrete individuals. The standards must be clear—utiles of pleasure, dollars, lives—qualities that can be turned into quantities, so that the ultimate decision is as indisputable as addition and subtraction and so that there is, once again, no room for moralizing.[25]

Other difficulties are also apparent. From the perspective of innate values the utilitarian approach to personal ethics seems unrealistic; there appears no rational explanation for why an individual should choose an altruistic criterion for making personal decisions. Another difficulty involves issues of equity. For example, how does the utilitarian criterion provide for the interest of future generations?

Perhaps the biggest shortcoming of utilitarianism is the problem of "the greatest bad for the smallest number." In other words, the logic of utilitarianism could lead to decisions in which the rights of a few could be severely curtailed provided that the overall happiness of the community was significantly increased.

Actually, John Stuart Mill (1806–1873), who was raised in strict adherence to Bentham's ideas, had developed certain qualms about those ideas early on. When Jeremy Bentham said that poker is as good as poetry if the pleasure is the same, Mill pointed out that it is better to be a discontented Socrates than a well-fed pig. That might not please the animal-rights people, but it was a devastating criticism nonetheless.

Can utilitarianism be made a little less theoretical so that the general ideas behind it could be incorporated into practical managerial decision making? The answer is yes. One can always write down the pros and cons of the decision in terms of both self and society. Irving L. Janis and Leon Mann take the simple idea one step further and suggest a balance sheet like the following to analyze the ethical dimensions of a course of action[26]:

	Positive Anticipation (+)	*Negative Anticipation (–)*
Gains (+) and losses (–) for self		
Gains (+) and losses (–) for others		
Self-approval (+) or self-disapproval (–)		
Social approval (+) or social disapproval (–)		

In analyzing the gains and losses, the manager can weigh some more heavily than others (+++ or – – –, for example). It is also important to make sure that *all* relevant parties have been identified. When all the entries have been made, the decision maker can then begin to cross out the items in the left and right columns that have equal weight. Eventually, it will be clear whether the positive anticipations outweigh the negative anticipations. Such a table should be prepared for each alternative.

Obligation to Formal Principles   Whereas utilitarians look to the consequences of a decision, Immanuel Kant (1724–1804) and his followers hold that the rightness or wrongness of an action is to be judged by how closely it conforms to some formal principle or principles. Kant found that ultimately all moral decisions should be based on a single principle: Act as if the maxim of your action were to become a general law binding on everyone. Because the principle does not admit to proof but is justified from principles of pure, practical reason, Kant calls his principle the **categorical imperative.** Kant was an absolutist about lying; he could find no justification for any lie whatsoever. In his words, "A lie is an abandonment or, as it were, annihilation of the dignity of man." Principles like Kant's should toll regularly, like cathedral bells, and call us back to the sources of morality. But perhaps Kant was too much of an absolutist—for example, he would have forbade those Christians who sheltered Jews during World War II from turning away the Gestapo at their doors with a lie.

Kant's categorical imperative is not the only formal principle that we can associate with this school of thought. Predating it by nearly 2500 years was the principle of *primum non nocere* ("above all, not knowingly to do harm"), the first responsibility of a professional as spelled out in the Hippocratic Oath. Nor should we overlook the Golden Rule: Do unto others as you would have them do unto you.

In contrast to Kant's categorical imperative, which sets forth a single, uniform principle as the criterion of rightness, other ethical theories that can be associated with this approach put forward *several* rules or principles that should be obeyed: keep one's promises, repay benefits, show consideration of others' feelings, and so forth. A major problem with these theories should be apparent. If fairly limited in number, like the rules embodied in many codes of conduct, they can be replete with contradictions and loopholes.

The Rights Ethic   Rights protect people against abuses and entitle them to important liberties. A strong philosophical movement defining *natural rights,* or rights that can be inferred by reason from the study of human nature, grew during the Enlightenment as a reaction against medieval religious persecutions. Over time, many "natural" rights were given legal status and became legal rights. Basic rights that are today widely accepted and protected in Western nations include the right to life; personal liberties such as expression (free speech), conscience (people should not be forced to do something they consider wrong), religious worship, and privacy; freedom from arbitrary, unjust police actions or unequal application of laws; and political liberties such as voting and lobbying.

Rights imply duties. Because individuals have rights, other people have clear duties to respect them. For example, management should not permit the operation of an unsafe machine because this would deprive employees of the right to a safe workplace. This right is based on the natural right to protection from harm by negligent actions of others. (Of course, common law and the Occupational Safety and Health Act also establish this right.)

In his famous Letter from Birmingham City Jail, written in 1963, Martin Luther King Jr. used the **rights ethic** to explain to his critics why he engaged in nonviolent resistance rather than allowing the battle for integration to continue in the courts.

You express a great deal of anxiety over our willingness to break laws. This is certainly a legitimate concern. Since we so diligently urge people to obey the Supreme Court's decision of 1954 outlawing segregation in the public schools, it is rather strange and paradoxical to find us consciously breaking laws. One may well ask, "How can you advocate breaking some laws and obeying others?" The answer is found in the fact that there are two types of laws: there are *just* and there are *unjust* laws. I would agree with Saint Augustine that "An unjust law is no law at all."

Now what is the difference between the two? How does one determine when a law is just or unjust? A just law is a man-made code that squares with the moral law or the law of God. An unjust law is a code that is out of harmony with the moral law. To put it in the terms of Saint Thomas Aquinas, an unjust law is a human law that is not rooted in eternal and natural law. Any law that uplifts human personality is just. Any law that degrades human personality is unjust. All segregation statutes are unjust because segregation distorts the soul and damages the personality. It gives the segregator a false sense of superiority, and the segregated a false sense of inferiority. To use the words of Martin Buber, the great Jewish philosopher, segregation substitutes an "I-it" relationship for the "I-thou" relationship, and ends up relegating persons to the status of things. So segregation is not only politically, economically and sociologically unsound, but it is morally wrong and sinful.[27]

One problem associated with the rights ethic is that rights are sometimes wrongly expanded into selfish demands or entitlements. Rights are not absolute, and their limits may be hard to define. For example, every person has a right to life, but industry exposes people daily to risk of death by releasing carcinogens into the environment. An absolute right to life would require cessation of much manufacturing activity. Rights, such as the right to life, are commonly abridged for compelling reasons of benefit to the overall public welfare. That is the reason the speed limit between Amarillo, Texas, and El Paso, Texas, is not 20 mph.

The Ethics of Aristotle   Many people, and even a few utilitarians, are content to define the moral life in terms of the basic rules that any decent society requires—no murdering, no stealing, no child abuse, no cannibalism, and so forth. If one is not a scoundrel, what else is there to say?

Aristotle has a different perspective. He is not primarily concerned with analyzing situations so that one can make the right decision. Rather, Aristotle is concerned with the notion of human excellence. The moral life, as understood by Aristotle, concerns more the ordering of one's aspirations and trying, both in one's personal life and professional life, for things that stir the heart and win the admiration of ourselves as human beings. The fundamental philosophical principle in Aristotle is the notion of human excellence as human fulfillment.

What then does the good life for a man or woman turn out to be? He gives it the name *eudemonia*. As so often with ancient Greek, there is a difficulty in translation, but it is roughly: blessedness, happiness, prosperity. It is the state of being well and doing well. It is not pleasure or titillation. We experience it most acutely in moments that modern psychologists might describe as "peak performances." This can be in an athletic competition, a business situation, or any endeavor; the main thing is that everything seems to go perfectly. The result is not just that you won the match or closed the deal, it is also a feeling of exhilaration, of happiness, of fulfillment.

Assuming that one buys into Aristotle's argument that what we all seek is eudemonia, then the question becomes: How do we obtain it? Aristotle says two things of profound importance. First, it is virtually impossible to obtain happiness directly—it is always a dividend. Second, we obtain happiness by practicing these four virtues:

- Courage
- Temperance
- Prudence
- Justice

Let us examine this quartet more closely and then consider how it might be expanded and adapted to the conditions found in modern society.

The Virtues   To understand how Aristotle views courage and temperance, it is necessary to introduce his concept of the **golden mean.** For example, when it comes to facing danger, one can act with excess—that is, show too much fear. This is cowardice. Or one can act deficiently by showing too little fear. This is foolhardiness. Or one can follow the golden mean by showing the right amount of fear. This is true courage.

Aristotle holds courage to be a virtue because it is crucial to the preservation of communities and the very practice of ethics. If a man says that he is concerned about individuals, principles, and ideas but is unwilling to risk harm to himself on behalf of those things, then one must question the authenticity of his professed concern. A person who genuinely cares and does not have the capacity for risking harm has to define himself, both to himself and to others, as a coward.[28]

Like courage, temperance is a virtue best understood in terms of the golden mean. When it comes to enjoying a certain pleasurable activity, one can act with excess. This is gluttony or overindulgence. According to Aristotle, preoccupation with trying to find new nerve endings to stimulate every day will not and cannot bring true happiness; indeed, such a preoccupation has brought more than one man or woman to ruin.

One can also act deficiently by partaking in none of life's pleasures. This is abstinence. Aristotle is not recommending that everyone indulge moderately in *all* of life's pleasures. Rather, he is merely foreshadowing what modern psychology recognizes: Life requires balance (all work and no play makes Jack a dull boy), and too much self-denial can lead to neurosis.

Justice, the third virtue, concerns our relationships with others. It means that we treat them fairly. The best general definition of justice can be attributed to Justinian (483–565): the constant and perpetual will to render to everyone his due.

Aristotle calls courage, temperance, and justice moral virtues and thought they are best acquired through imitation, practice, and habit. His fourth virtue, prudence, is, however both a moral and an intellectual virtue, and it is acquired through a combination of inheritance and education. Again, translation difficulties confront us. We tend to associate prudence with *thrift,* which has the connotation of being cautious and calculating in one's own interest. But for Aristotle it means practical intelligence—that is, knowing how to apply general principles in particular situations. It is the ability to act so that one's adherence to other virtues is exemplified in one's actions. Specifically, practical wisdom is the ability to adapt the universals of morality and politics in particular and concrete situations and knowing exactly when to do what. For example, Aristotle once said that giving away money was easy, but knowing to whom one should give, at what time, and in what manner, this knowledge was the mark of a person who possessed practical wisdom. Hence, it is the keystone of all virtue.

The Rediscovery of Aristotle   Aristotle derived his four virtues from those exhibited by the best and the brightest Athenians living the good life in the age of Pericles (495–429 b.c.). But these virtues will not be the same as those of a medieval man or woman—or today's administrator.

Indeed, the Christian church added to Aristotle's four virtues three of its own: faith, hope, and charity (meaning love)—and thus universalized and humanized a framework designed primarily for the male citizens of Athens. Faith has an obvious theological connotation, but in modern, secular terms we could quite easily render it "commitment." The research literature on the importance of commitment in government and business—especially in new ventures—is substantial. Again, Aristotle was ahead of his time. Hope is a moral virtue that modern research also suggests probably does help sustain the pursuit of the good life—though a professor of psychology would not put it quite that way.[29]

To see what role love might play in an ethical system, we might turn briefly to a non-Western philosopher:

- Confucius was profoundly concerned with one virtue in particular—jen (pronounced "ren"). Imperfectly translated, jen is benevolence or human-heartedness. In his *Analects,* Confucius says: "Human-heartedness consists in loving others" (XII, 22). The man or women who really loves others is the one able to perform his or her duties in society. Confucius is reported in *Analects* as saying that the practice of jen consists in considerations for others: "Desiring to sustain oneself, one sustains others; desiring to develop oneself, one develops others" (VI, 28). There is even a methodology of jen, a way of discovering what people wish or do not wish done to them. Later Confucians would call this method "applying a measuring square"—in other words, using oneself as a standard to regulate one's conduct. The method consists in taking oneself as an analogy and asking oneself what one would like or dislike were one in the position of the other person. "Do not use what you dislike in your superiors in the employment of your inferiors. Do not use what you dislike in your inferiors in the service of your superiors."[30]

Today Aristotle's ethics can be approached three different ways. First is to simply cultivate his four virtues and expect happiness. Second is to adopt the "updated," universalized version that St. Thomas Aquinas and the church fathers put forward during the Middle Ages. Third is to take the shell of his ethics—the methodology, not the exact contents—and build an individualized version. That is what Anthony Robbins, a famous motivational speaker and writer, suggests we do.

Robbins recommends first putting your values in order from the most important to the least important. Robbins's original list appears on the left in Table 4.2. Next, study those values and ask some critical questions: (1) What do my values need to be to create my ultimate destiny, to be the best person I could possibly be, to have the largest impact in my life? (2) What other values would I need to add? (3) What values should I eliminate from my list to achieve my ultimate destiny? The final step is to evaluate each value individually, asking what benefit you get by having this value in this position on your hierarchy. Table 4.2 also shows Robbins's new list.

Ken Winston, a lecturer in ethics at Harvard, takes a similar approach in defining the "moral competency of the practitioner of democratic governance." In particular, he focuses on five "general attributes" of actual people. These attributes are not exactly character traits but rather the qualities that public officials would exhibit in performing their duties. Here are Winston's five virtues:

1. *Fidelity to the public interest.* "Almost every official gets into office via a process that incurs legitimate obligations to specific individuals or limited constituencies. At the same time officials have a duty to enlarge their vision beyond these connections to encompass considerations of the public good. A key requirement of the good practitioner, then, is the ability to reconcile partial with general perspectives."

Table 4.2 The Ethics of Aristotle: A Modern Application	
Anthony Robbins's Original List of Moving Toward Values	Anthony Robbins's New List of Moving Toward Values
Passion	Health/vitality
Love	Love/warmth
Freedom	Intelligence
Contribution	Cheerfulness
Being able	Honesty
Growth	Passion
Achievement/accomplishment	Gratefulness
Happiness	Fun/happiness
Fun	Making a difference
Health	Learning/growing
Creativity	Achieving
	Being the best
	Investing
	Contribution
	Creativity

SOURCE: Anthony Robbins, *Awaken the Giant Within* (New York: Summit Books, 1991), 373 and 377.

2. *The duty of civility.* "The good practitioner . . . has a duty to act in accordance with a *public conscience.* The conscientious democratic official is one whose grounds of decision are beliefs and principles that citizens generally are committed to—or could be, after deliberation and reflection."

3. *Respect for citizens as responsible agents.* "While the practitioner's input is crucial, the process is interacting. Power then consists in the practitioner's capacity to facilitate citizens' capacity for self-direction. The good practitioner is disposed, wherever feasible, toward a *facilitative* rather than directive style of governance, one that enhances citizens' exercise of effective agency."

4. *Proficiency in social architecture.* "I believe the virtue of institutional craftsmanship is an attribute of the good practitioner. . . . The good practitioner has the skill to identify the appropriate form for a given type of problem, guided by the types of relationships that would obtain among citizens if the form were realized. Institutional design is moral legislation. Any specific decision structure leads us to conduct our lives one way rather than another."

5. *Prudence.* Winston is pure Aristotle here: "In the classical sense prudence is the cardinal political virtue: the exercise of practical wisdom in governance."[31]

A Methodology for Ethical Analysis

When managers find themselves in a situation calling for an ethical decision, the danger is that they will first choose a course of action that serves their own interest and *then* search among various ethical systems to find the one that comes closest to justifying that course of action.

Figure 4.3 shows a more appropriate way to approach ethical decision making. In thinking about what you should do in an ethical dilemma, it is useful to consider what matters most to you. What are your core values? (Recall the two lists on page 185.) What would your relevant community consider to be the kind of decision that an individual of integrity would make in the situation?

Another important issue concerns the facts of the situation. How did the situation occur? Are there facts concerning the situation that the administrator should know? Although fact gathering is easier said than done, one should attempt to assemble the facts that are available before proceeding.

Many of us have a knee-jerk response to ethical problems, jumping to a solution without clearly defining the issues at stake and creatively generating alternative solutions. Once the facts have been discerned, moral concerns identified, and alternatives generated, one can begin to analyze each alternative in terms of the four ethical approaches discussed earlier—the utilitarian ethic, the obligation to formal principles, the rights ethic, and the ethics of Aristotle. One should also draw on past experience. In similar situations, what has worked and what has failed? After a decision has been made, some administrators find it useful to develop a logical, systematic explanation for the choice.

The emphasis in these steps has been on rationality. But do not forget intuition. If your gut is bothering you, it might be a signal that something is not right. Perhaps a trusted friend or mentor can help you discover the source of your apprehension. Harlan Cleveland has had

Figure 4.3   Process of Ethical Analysis

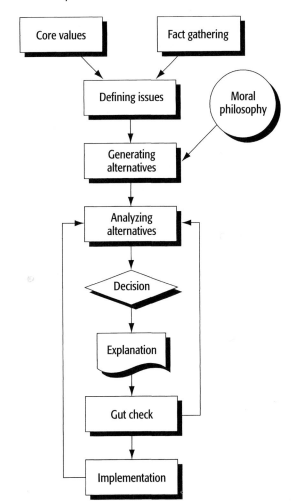

a rich experience as a public executive. The key question that he asks himself before committing to a line of action is not "Will I be criticized?" (After all, operating in the public sector, the answer to that question is frequently yes.) Rather, it is "If this action is held up to public scrutiny, will I still feel that it is what I should have done, and how I should have done it?"[32]

The last stage involves carrying out a decision. Unlike the student of moral philosophy, managers must act on their decisions.

Concluding Observations

"Character," Emerson wrote, "is higher than intellect." What does that mean? Robert Coles, psychiatrist and Harvard professor, thinks he knows. Several years ago a student of his, Marian, was working her way through school by cleaning the rooms of fellow classmates.

Those students had high SAT scores but had, it seemed to her, forgotten the meaning of "please." They were rude, even crude, to her. One young man not so subtly propositioned her. Angry and anxious, Marian came to Coles, saying she was going to quit Harvard and go back to the Midwest. "I've been taking all these philosophy courses," she told Coles, "and we talk about what's true, what's important, what's good. Well, how do you teach people to be good?"[33]

In such situations, books and classroom discussions can help, but ultimately, Coles thinks, we must heed the advice of Henry James: When asked by his nephew what he ought to do in life, James replied, "Three things in human life are important. The first is to be kind. The second is to be kind. And the third is to be kind." To Coles, the key to those words is the exhortation *to be*—the insistence to find the existence that enables one to be kind. How?

By wading in, over and over, with that purpose in mind, with a willingness to sail on, tacking and tacking again, helped by those we aim to help, guided by our moral yearning on behalf of others, on behalf of ourselves with others: a commitment to others that won't avoid squalls and periods of drift, a commitment that will become the heart of the journey itself.[34]

Concepts for Review

accountability	market segmentation
Administrative Procedures Act	misfeasance
administrative responsibility	new public management
categorical imperative	nonfeasance
competence	official immunity
due process	ombudsman
ethics	professional codes
external controls	public interest
flexibility	representative bureaucracy
four P's of marketing	responsiveness
golden mean	rights ethic
inspector general (IG)	sovereign immunity
internal controls	utilitarian ethic
malfeasance	whistle-blower

Key Points

We have looked at the values wrapped up in the idea of administrative responsibility and studied the various "auxiliary precautions" (Madison's term) that had been suggested to ensure its realization in practice. The following points have been made:

1. When graduates of public policy and administration schools rated skills they consider most important to success, maintaining ethical standards came in a solid first.
2. Among the most important values suggested by the concept of administrative responsibility are responsiveness, fairness, flexibility, honesty, accountability, and competence.

3. The term *responsiveness* refers to the prompt acquiescence by an organization to popular demands for policy change. To design a full-fledged customer-driven program, it is convenient to refer to the components of such a program in terms of four P's—product, price, promotion, and placement.

4. To ensure that citizens have a chance to present their cases and be heard fairly, agencies follow the principle of due process. But fairness concerns results as well as procedures. Today, in an effort to protect the rights and property of individual parties and to check abuses of administrative discretion, courts are more inclined to question the logic of the agency's decision.

5. Honesty breeds trust, and the more trust areas in a society, the better that society functions.

6. Public officials deceive for various reasons. One is to hide poor performance and, in that sense, it stems from a feeling of incompetence. But it can also stem from a feeling of superiority. The line of reasoning here runs as follows: "If only the common people were as smart, as farsighted, and as courageous as I, they would agree with me. But, because they are none of these things, *they must be deceived for their own good."* The problem with this line of thinking is twofold. First, it presents a slippery slope. Second, it might turn out, on closer inspection, that this line of thinking is actually private gain masquerading as public interest. Bok recommends in situations that do call for deception that the forms of deception be debated and authorized in advance by the elected public officials.

7. Malfeasance is the performance by public officials of deeds that are forbidden by constitutional or statutory laws or by commonly accepted moral standards. Misfeasance is the improper performance of lawful duties. Nonfeasance is the failure of a public official to perform required duties.

8. The new public management paradigm contains five key ideas: (1) government should provide high-quality service that citizens value; (2) the autonomy of public managers should be increased; (3) organizations and individuals should be evaluated on the basis of how well they meet performance targets; (4) managers must be provided adequate human and technological resources; and (5) public-sector managers must appreciate the value of competition and maintain an open-minded attitude about which services belong to the private rather than the public sector.

9. Various measures ensure administrative responsibility and can be divided into four main categories: formal–external, formal-internal, informal-external, and informal-internal.

10. Persons who are harmed by administrative action often seek compensation. Such efforts always require a statutory basis; otherwise they might flounder on the doctrine of sovereign immunity—that is, the principle that the government may not be sued without its consent. One public policy that does allow government to be sued is the Federal Tort and Claims Act of 1946, which allows redress for tort claims. The word *tort* is borrowed from the French, meaning "wrong." In law, more precisely, a tort is a violation of a duty imposed by civil law.

11. When a litigant seeks to recover damages from the pocket of a public administrator, sovereign immunity is not an obstacle, but a related doctrine, official immunity, may be. The long-standing rule has been that a federal employee is absolutely immune from common law tort liability for any act performed within "the outer perimeter" of his or her line of duty.

12. The utilitarian ethic asserts that it is the greatest happiness of the greatest number that is the measure of right and wrong.

13. Kant found that ultimately all moral decisions should be based on a single principle: Act as if the maxim of your action were to become a general law binding on everyone. Because the principle does not admit to proof—but is justified from principles of pure, practical reason—Kant calls it the categorical imperative.

14. A strong philosophical movement defining natural rights, or rights that can be inferred by reason from the study of human nature, grew during the Enlightenment. Basic rights that are today widely accepted and protected in Western nations include the right to life; personal liberties such as freedom of expression (free speech), conscience (people should not be forced do something they consider wrong), religious worship, and privacy; freedom from arbitrary, unjust police actions and unequal application of laws; and political liberties such as voting and lobbying.

15. Aristotle is not primarily concerned with analyzing situations so that one can make the right decision. Rather, he is concerned with the notion of human excellence as fulfillment.

16. Any process or methodology of ethical analysis will no doubt be highly iterative and personalized. One suggested process of ethical analysis includes consideration of core values, fact gathering, issue definition, generating alternatives, analyzing alternatives, the decision, an explanation of the decision, "gut check," implementation, and feedback.

Problems and Applications

1. Suppose that Derek is a graduating high school senior who has always turned to you for advice. Although he is several years your junior, you have developed a great admiration for this bright young man. Despite the poverty of his family, he has worked hard in school and done quite well. Today Derek has come to you once again for advice. A friend of his, he explains, illegally acquired answers to the college entrance examination, sold them to a few students, and gave him a copy for free. Derek used these answers when he took his exam and now has been accepted for admission by an elite university. Try to imagine this young man sitting across from you. The two of you are alone. As friend and confidant, what do you say to him?

2. Explain how you might use ethical analysis to decide the proper action in each of the 21 incidents listed on page 186–187.

3. Jim Cissell, the court clerk for Hamilton County, whose seat is Cincinnati, decided that it was time to move the county's court records onto the Web. The documents were

already public and electronic; where else to put public electronic documents but the Internet? Discuss.

4. Priscilla Hudson, manager of the main library in Boulder, Colorado, thinks public libraries are society's great equalizer—a place where anyone can go to learn regardless of their economic, social, or political background. She is among a number of librarians in the United States who oppose a provision in the USA PATRIOT Act that gives authorities access to records of what people check out from libraries or buy from bookstores. Discuss.

5. Assume that you are admissions director at the University of South Florida. As part of the college's "marketing strategy," and in an effort to woo students, the president has asked you to make the school appear to be "among the most selective in the nation." How? Simply drop the bottom-scoring 6 percent of students and thereby raise the school's average SAT score about 40 points. How do you respond?

6. The division of corrections in a midwestern state has decided that the state boys' school is grossly inadequate and a dangerous firetrap. The division wishes to build a reformatory in a state forest. Such a location would provide attractive surroundings, isolation from cities, and constructive work for the boys. Unfortunately, conservation groups issue vehement protests and start a public campaign to force the governor and the state corrections board to reverse the decision. Meanwhile, the community in which the present reformatory is located organizes a committee to keep it there. As a public relations director for the division, what are your recommendations?

7. What do you do when an experienced, valued, and otherwise highly reliable employee confesses that she has been dipping into the till? Although the amounts she "borrowed" from petty cash never exceeded $100, she did write false receipts to cover them until she could make repayment.

8. You are on the board of directors of a private voluntary organization that has come to play a crucial operational and advocacy role in the field of international relief and disaster assistance. The founder, John Drake, age 52, transformed the organization from a modest 23-person operation into one of the world's largest and most successful nongovernmental organizations with operations in 44 less-developed countries. He is married, but evidence strongly suggests that, over the years, Drake has had a series of affairs with women both inside and outside the organization. Despite repeated warnings by the board to cease and desist, Drake's photo appeared today in the style section of a national newspaper. An attractive young woman was holding his arm—and it was not his wife. What should the board now do?

9. Most of us would approve of every goal value and every conduct value listed on page 185. The problem is that, in seeking to maximize one value, we must often sacrifice another. Using concrete examples, illustrate the types of trade-offs one might have to make.

10. Discuss the following quote from Thomas Jefferson in terms of the issues raised in this chapter. To what degree do you agree or disagree? "State a moral case to a ploughman and a professor. The former will decide it as well, and often better than the latter; because he has not been led astray by artificial rules."

Favorite Bookmarks

www.usoge.gov   The Office of Government Ethics home page will give you access to data about the services it provides. It should help you understand the executive branch ethics program and its ongoing effort to reach out to federal employees and the general public. Its mission is "not only to prevent and resolve conflicts of interest and to foster high ethical standards for federal employees but also to strengthen the public's confidence that the government's business is conducted with impartiality and integrity."

www.iit.edu/departments/csep   The Library of the Center for the Study of Ethics in the Professions at Illinois Institute of Technology is intended to meet the educational and research needs of people concerned with the study and practice of ethics in the professions. This Web site offers links to other sites focusing on professional ethics.

www.whistleblower.org   In 1977, the nonprofit Government Accountability Project was created to help protect whistle-blowers. Thus, it also provides valuable information about whistle-blowing, government wrongdoing, and official misconduct.

www.jiethics.org   This is the Web site of the Josephson Institute of Ethics. Here you will find some interesting survey data, among other things.

www.depaul.edu/ethics   This site is good for ethics links and other business ethics material.

www.scu.edu/ethics   This site offers an extensive ethics database.

www.publicintegrity.org   The Center for Public Integrity's mission is to provide the American public with the findings of its investigations and analyses of public service, government accountability, and ethics-related issues via books, reports, and newsletters.

www.puaf.umd.edu/IPPP/   Established in 1976 at the University of Maryland and now part of the School of Public Affairs, the Institute for Philosophy and Public Policy was founded to conduct research into the conceptual and normative questions underlying public policy formulation. This research is conducted cooperatively by philosophers, policymakers, analysts, and other experts both in and outside government.

Notes

1. Stephen Maynard-Moody and Michael Musheno, *Cops, Teachers, Counselors: Stories from the Frontlines of Public Service* (Ann Arbor: University Michigan Press, 2003), 93.
2. Tom Lowry, "The CEO Mayor," *Business Week* (June 25, 2007).
3. Philip K. Howard, *The Death of Common Sense* (New York: Random House, 1995).
4. Maxene Johnston, "Non-Traditional Tools Get Results with Traditional Problems." Remarks at the Foundation for American Communication Symposium, Scottsdale, AZ, January 24,1990.
5. Francis Fukuyama, *Trust: The Social Virtues and the Creation of Prosperity* (New York: Free Press, 1995), 7.
6. Ibid., 27–28.
7. Sissela Bok, *Lying: Moral Choice in Public and Private Life* (New York: Vintage Books, 1998), xxx.
8. Ibid., 168.
9. Ibid.
10. Ibid., 172–73.
11. Ibid., 176.

12. Ibid., 181.
13. See Michael G. Gordon and Bernard E. Trainer, *COBRA II: The Inside Story of the Invasion and Occupation of Iraq* (New York: Pantheon Books, 2006).
14. Sandford Borins, *Innovating with Integrity: How Local Heroes Are Transforming American Government* (Washington, DC: Georgetown University Press, 1998), 9.
15. *Barr v. Matteo,* 360 U.S. 564 (1959).
16. Sam Zagoria, *The Ombudsman* (Arlington, VA: Seven Locks Press, 1988).
17. *Time* (December 30, 2002 and January 6, 2003).
18. D. T. Austern et al., *Maintaining Municipal Integrity* (Washington, DC: U.S. Department of Justice, 1978).
19. Quoted in Majorie Valburn, "Border Patrol's Ranks Swell with Hispanics," *The Wall Street Journal* (October 22, 1998).
20. Vicky M. Wilkins and Brian N. Williams, "Black or Blue: Racial Profiling and Representative Bureaucracy," *Public Administration Review* (July/August 2008): 654–64.
21. Anthony Downs, *Inside Bureaucracy* (Boston: Little, Brown, 1967), 233.
22. F. Thompson, "Types of Representative Bureaucracy and Their Linkage" in R. T. Golembienski et al., eds.: *Public Administration* (Chicago: Rand McNally, 1976), 589–90.
23. Walter Lippmann, *The Public Philosophy* (Boston: Little, Brown, 1955), 42.
24. Michael Rokeach, *The Nature of Human Values* (New York: Free Press, 1973).
25. Michael Walzer, "Teaching Morality," *New Republic* (July 10, 1978): 10–12.
26. Irving L. Janis and Leon Mann, *Decision Making* (New York: Free Press, 1977).
27. The full text of the letter can be found in James M. Washington, ed., *The Essential Writings and Speeches of Martin Luther King, Jr.* (San Francisco: HarperCollins, 1986), 289–302.
28. Alasdair MacIntyre, *After Virtue* (South Bend, IN: University of Notre Dame Press, 1981).
29. For a good summary of recent research linking optimism and longevity, see Mary Duenwald, "Power of Positive Thinking Extends, It Seems, to Aging," *The New York Times,* (November 12, 2002).
30. Fung Yu-Lan, *A Short History of Chinese Philosophy* (New York: Macmillan, 1948), 44.
31. Kenneth Winston, "Moral Competence in the Practice of Democratic Governance," in John D. Donahue and Joseph H. Nye Jr., eds., *For the People: Can We Fix the Public Service?* (Washington, DC: Brookings, 2003), 169–87.
32. Harlan Cleveland, "How Do You Get Everybody in on the Act and Still Get Some Action?" *Public Management* (June 1975): 214.
33. Robert Coles, *The Moral Intelligence of Children* (New York: Random House, 1997).
34. Ibid.

CASE 4.1
DOING THE RIGHT THING

Whoever fights monsters should see to it that in the process he does not become a monster.

Frederick Nietzsche

Leon Panetta was a surprise choice to lead the Central Intelligence Agency (CIA), since his reputation rested primarily on his mastery of domestic policy—a mastery acquired as chairman of the House Budget Committee, as President Clinton's budget director, and later as his chief of staff. Although some colleagues say that Panetta can be "principled to the point of rigidity," it was more his reputation for rectitude and integrity than as his grasp of the intricacies of national security issues that got him the CIA job.

In May 2009, Panetta found himself preoccupied not with foreign enemies but with domestic critics, both conservative and liberal. From the right, former Vice President Dick Cheney accused the Barack Obama administration of "making the American people less safe" by banning the enhanced CIA interrogation of terrorism suspects that had been sanctioned by the George W. Bush administration. From the left, human rights activists and some Democratic members of Congress called for the establishment of some sort of inquiry—a special prosecutor, a congressional investigation, a truth commission—to determine whether the Bush administration lawyers who had argued that waterboarding and other harsh interrogation techniques could be employed in the aftermath of 9/11 should be prosecuted. These liberal groups were especially appalled that Panetta had advised Obama against such an inquiry.

As the director of the CIA, Panetta knew this was a sensitive issue for his agency. Critics believe that the agency had lost its moral bearings after 9/11. In 2007, when a confidential Red Cross report became public, no doubt remained that the agency had subjected terror suspects to prolonged physical and psychological cruelty. Officers shackled prisoners for weeks in contorted positions; chained them to the ceiling, wearing only diapers; exploited their phobias; and propelled them headfirst into walls. At least three prisoners died.

There was more bad news for the agency when President Obama released disturbing classified government documents describing how one prisoner was waterboarded 183 times in a month. For more than a century, the United States had prosecuted waterboarding as a serious crime, and a 10-year prison sentence was issued as recently as 1983. Indeed, the memos authorizing interrogators to torment prisoners clashed so glaringly with international and U.S. law that some of them were later withdrawn by lawyers in Bush's own Justice Department. Torture itself is a felony, sometimes even treated as a capital crime. The Convention Against Torture, which America ratified in 1994, requires a government to prosecute all acts of torture; failure to do so is considered a breach of international law.

Although Panetta might oppose an inquiry, that did not mean he took torture lightly. One of his first acts as director was to ask the CIA's inspector general to ensure that there was no one on the payroll who should be prosecuted for torture or related crimes. The inspector general assured him that no officer still at the agency had engaged in any action that went beyond the legal boundaries as they were understood during the Bush years. Panetta's position was therefore consistent with that of President Obama, who had promised immunity from prosecution to any CIA officer who relied on the advice of legal counsel during the Bush years. For the longer term, Panetta was trying to set up a state-of-the-art interrogation unit, staffed by some of the best CIA, FBI, and military officers in the country and drawing on the advice of social scientists, linguists, and other scholars.

Panetta wondered if he had done enough. Should he resist or welcome an investigation of the CIA by the Attorney General that might lead to prosecution? Or should he resist or welcome the creation of an independent "truth commission" that could grant immunity to witnesses? As he pondered the pros and cons of some sort of inquiry, it became increasingly apparent how unappetizing his choices were.

Here are some of the arguments *against* any investigation:

- If Panetta did not argue against investigation, he would not be seen within the agency as someone people want to follow.

- Prosecution would be unfair to CIA officers who thought they were abiding by the law. People shouldn't be punished for doing what they took to be their duty.

- An investigation might look vindictive, as if the Obama administration was trying to go after Cheney and Bush. Such a perception could have a serious political downside, namely, the risk of losing support from independents.

- Prosecution of officials would have a chilling effect on future U.S. government officials. Few would be brave or foolhardy enough to put forward daring proposals that one day could be judged illegal. Putting things down in writing is a useful intellectual exercise and central to good decision making. With the threat of prosecution, serious memos on controversial matters would increasingly become the exception rather than the rule. Bottom line: U.S. national security would be weakened.

- Investigation and prosecution would take time and focus away from what the CIA, the country, and its elected and appointed representatives thought important. Investigations and trials would constitute an enormous distraction at a time when the United States faced a daunting array of international problems.

- Investigation would undoubtedly result in the release of more memos and photos highly unflattering to America's image abroad. Such releases could spark an anti-American backlash among allies and provide a superb recruiting tool for terrorist organizations.

- It is impossible to specify clearly a firm chain of causation. Certainly, a series of actions at the highest levels of government set the conditions for and allowed abuse and torture, but there is no proof that higher policymakers intended severe abuses to occur. And what about top officials who knew about the interrogation program but had no operational control over it? As one former CIA official said, "You can't throw out the entire agency."

Advocates *for* investigation make the following points:

- Failure to investigate leaves the impression that the Obama administration is trying to cover up something.

- The U.S. citizenry needs a full accounting, especially as it relates to the health professionals. Released Justice Department memos contain numerous references to CIA medical personnel participating in coercive interrogation sessions. Were they the designers, the legitimizers, and the implementers—or something else? Their participation is possibly one of the biggest medical ethics scandals in U.S. history.

- The argument that CIA officials thought they were doing their duty because of legal cover provided by the Department of Justice will not stand. Many times courageous individuals objected and walked away from policies that led to abuse and torture. As one FBI assistant director told one special agent who had objected to the enhanced techniques, "We don't do that." That agent was then pulled out of the interrogation by the FBI director Robert Mueller. At the Department of Defense, the *Army Field Manual for Human Intelligence Collector Operations* explicitly prohibits torture or cruel, inhumane, and degrading treatment in specific terms (no waterboarding, for example).

- Some legal scholars think it would be hard not to do something. No criminal charges have ever been brought against any CIA officer involved in the torture program despite the fact that (as noted earlier) three prisoners interrogated by agency personnel died as the result of this treatment. Yet the only Americans who had been prosecuted and sentenced to imprisonment were 10 low-ranking servicepersons—those who took and appeared in the Abu Ghraib photographs.

- Former Vice President Cheney has said the United States must torture, because it's effective. That is, at best, an illogical argument: A crime is not a crime just because it works. After all, terrorism can be quite effective. The argument is not only illogical but also fallacious. According to interrogation experts in the FBI and the U.S. Army, people will say anything to stop their torture.
- The fact that the independent commission would be politically distracting isn't a good argument for resisting it. Jeffrey Rosen writes: "The Bush torture policies are the most serious violation of American values since World War II internment of Japanese-Americans. A closed Senate intelligence committee investigation would be inconsistent with the transparency Obama demanded when he release the memos in the first place. At this point, only a full truth commission-style investigation can allow the Bush lawyers to make clear that they didn't conspire to break the law, while focusing public opprobrium on the real architects and abettors of torture policies: namely, the policymakers .... An independent commission would indeed be politically embarrassing...

but at least it would provide the accountability that the nation deserves."

Case Question

As a man of rectitude and integrity, Panetta wants to do the right thing. Given these arguments for and against further investigation, what do you recommend?

Case References

James P. Pfiffner, "Torture and Public Policy," *Public Integrity* (Fall 2005), 313–329; Richard N. Haass, "The Interrogation Memos and the Law," *The Wall Street Journal,* May 1, 2009; Ali Soufan, " My Tortured Decision," *The New York Times,* April 23, 2009; Philip Gourevitch, "Interrogating Torture," *The New Yorker,* May 11, 2009, 33–34; Mark Danner, "The Red Cross Torture Report: What It Means," *New York Review of Books,* April 30, 2009; Jeffrey Rosen, "Truth or Dare," *New Republic,* May 20, 2009; Jane Mayer, "The Secret History," *The New Yorker,* June 22, 2009.

Program
Management

5 Planning

ROBIN HOOD

It was early in the spring of the second year of his insurrection against the High Sheriff of Nottingham that Robin Hood took a walk in Sherwood Forest. As he walked, he pondered the progress of the campaign, the disposition of his forces, his opposition's moves, and the options that confronted him.

The revolt against the sheriff began as a personal crusade. It erupted out of Robin's own conflict with the sheriff and his administration. Alone, however, Robin could accomplish little. He therefore sought allies, men with personal grievances and a deep sense of justice. Later he took all who came without asking too many questions. Strength, he believed, lay in numbers.

The first year was spent in forging the group into a disciplined band—a group united in enmity against the sheriff, willing to live outside the law as long as it took to accomplish their goals. The band was simply organized. Robin ruled supreme, making all important decisions. Specific tasks were delegated to his lieutenants. Will Scarlett was in charge of intelligence and scouting. His main job was to keep tabs on the movements of the sheriff's men. He also collected information on the travel plans of rich merchants and abbots. Little John kept discipline among the men, and he saw to it that their archery was at the high peak that their profession demanded. Scarlett took care of the finances, paying shares of the take, bribing officials, converting loot to cash, and finding suitable hiding places for surplus gains. Finally, Much the Miller's Son had the difficult task of provisioning the ever-increasing band.

The increasing size of the band was a source of satisfaction for Robin, but also a subject of much concern. The fame of his Merry Men was spreading, and new recruits were pouring in. Yet the number of men was beginning to exceed the food capacity of the forest. Game was becoming scarce, and food had to be transported by cart from outlying villages. The band had always camped together. But now what had been a small gathering had become a major encampment that could be detected miles away. Discipline was also becoming harder to enforce. "Why?" Robin reflected. "I don't know half the men I run into these days."

Although the band was getting larger, their main source of revenue was in decline. Travelers, especially the richer variety, began giving the forest a wide berth. This was costly and inconvenient to them, but it was preferable to having all their goods confiscated by Robin's men. Robin was therefore considering changing his past policy to one of a fixed transit tax.

The idea was strongly resisted by his lieutenants who were proud of the Merry Men's famous motto: "Rob from the rich and give to the poor." The poor and the townspeople, they argued, were their main source of support and information. If they were antagonized by transit taxes, they would abandon the Merry Men to the mercy of the sheriff.

Robin wondered how long they could go on keeping to the ways and methods of their early days. The sheriff was growing stronger. He had the money, the men, and the facilities. In the long run he would wear Robin and his men down. Sooner or later, he would find their weaknesses and methodically destroy them. Robin felt that he must bring the campaign to a conclusion. The question was, How could this be achieved?

Robin knew that the chances of killing or capturing the sheriff were remote. Besides, killing the sheriff might satisfy his personal thirst for revenge but would not change the basic problem. It was also unlikely that the sheriff would be removed from office. He had powerful friends at court. On the other hand, Robin reflected, if the district was in a perpetual state of unrest, and the taxes went uncollected, the sheriff would fall out of favor. But on further thought, Robin reasoned, the sheriff might shrewdly use the unrest to obtain more reinforcements. The outcome depended on the mood of the regent Prince John. The Prince was known as vicious, volatile, and unpredictable. He was obsessed by his unpopularity among the people, who wanted the imprisoned King Richard back. He also lived in constant fear of the barons who were growing daily more hostile to his power. Several of these barons had set out to collect the ransom that would release King Richard the Lionheart from his jail in Austria. Robin had been discreetly asked to join, in return for future amnesty. It was a dangerous proposition. Provincial banditry was one thing, court intrigue another. Prince John was known for his vindictiveness. If the gamble failed he would personally see to it that all involved were crushed.

The sound of the supper horn startled Robin from his thoughts. There was the smell of roasting venison in the air. Nothing had been resolved or settled. Robin headed for camp promising himself that he would give these problems first priority after tomorrow's operation.

What are Robin's key problems? How are they related to each other? How did they emerge? What should Robin do in the short term and in the longer term?

Planning is the keystone of the arch of program management, and government success is often synonymous with planning success. Quite properly, then, Part Two of this book begins with planning.

As will be explained shortly, planning covers a far wider spectrum of meanings than can be encompassed in this chapter. Indeed, many of the things explained in Chapter 2 about policymaking apply to planning, which is interpreted in this chapter quite broadly: reasoning about how an organization will get where it wants to go.

The essence of planning is to see opportunities and threats in the future and to exploit or combat them by decisions made in the present. It is therefore hardly an overstatement to say that planning, as defined here, shapes the whole field of public administration. It determines the limits of government responsibility, the allocation of resources and distribution of costs, the division of labor, and the extent of public controls. Nor is it an overstatement to say that the magnitude of current problems—such as air and water pollution, exploitation of natural resources, and decline in the quality of urban life—is related to our inability to plan effectively.

This chapter describes several important ideas about planning. Special attention is given to goals and plans, for that is where planning starts. Next, several types and models of planning are described. The third section considers several barriers to planning and what public administrators can do to overcome them. The final section explores, in some depth, one particular type of planning, strategic management, and how it is applied in government today.

Overview of Goals and Plans

Some Useful Definitions

Because the thrust of this book is toward the integration—not the fragmentation—of thought, planning will be treated as a general process, recognizable in a great number of human situations. The definition of planning that opened this chapter reflects this more general approach. **Planning** is reasoning about how an organization will get where it wants to go. Its essence is to see opportunities and threats in the future and to exploit or combat them by making decisions in the present.

To really grasp the dynamics of this process, it is of course necessary to understand its components. For example, what is a plan? How does a plan differ from a policy? From a program? For our purposes, a **policy** is a statement of goals and of the relative importance attached to each. A policy comprises one or more plans, and each **plan,** in turn, specifies objectives to be attained. A proposed set of specific actions intended to help implement a plan is called a **program.** Figure 5.1 shows these relationships.

A simple example will perhaps clarify these terse terminological stipulations. Assume that the mayor of a city has among his or her goals an increase in the physical safety of the city's inhabitants and an improvement in housing conditions. The mayor might then announce a policy that these goals, in the order stated, are to have priority over all

Figure 5.1   The Structure of Public Policy: An Idealized View

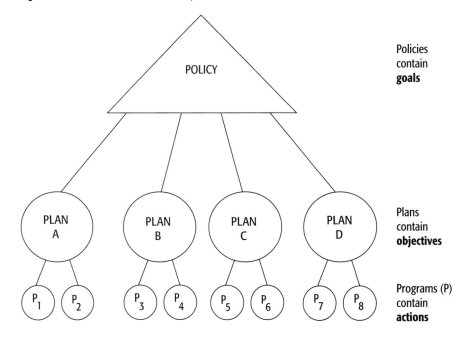

other goals. A plan to implement this policy might specify the objectives of reducing the rate of violent crimes in the city and the death rate from traffic accidents by 25 percent and providing an additional 10,000 housing units. A program would spell out in detail the action to be taken to achieve these objectives, for example, by increasing the police force by 1000 and providing city-backed, long-term loans to construction firms.[1] The crucial difference among the terms *policy, plan,* and *program* is level of generality. As suggested in Chapter 2 and here again in Figure 5.1, the term *policy* should be reserved for statements of intention and direction of a relatively high order.

These terminological stipulations are more than mere academic hairsplitting; they help to make better policy. Let us see why. When *policy* is not clearly differentiated from *tactical and operational matters,* the latter drive out the former. According to journalist David Halberstam, during the Vietnam War the highest level of American policymakers refused to accept the necessity for making decisions at the policy level. They tried to delay such decisions and thus buy a little more time. These policymakers "were above all functional, operational, tactical men, not really intellectuals, and tactical men think in terms of options, while intellectuals less so; intellectuals might think in terms of the sweep of history."[2]

The late Daniel P. Moynihan, who served in the executive branch under three presidents before entering the Senate, argued that one of the more important things about the structure of American government is that too much public policy is defined in terms of *program* rather than true *policy.* The problem with the program approach is that it deals with only a part of the system; policy, on the other hand, seeks to respond to the system in its entirety:

> The idea of policy is not new. We have for long been accustomed to the idea of foreign policy, including defense policy. Since 1946, Congress has mandated an employment and income policy more or less explicitly based on a "general theory" of the endlessly intricate interconnections of such matters. Yet our ways of behavior resist this: only great crises, great dangers, seem to evoke the effort. Or have seemed able to do so in the past. I believe, however, that a learning process of sorts has been going on. Increasingly the idea of systemwide policies commends itself to persons of responsibility in public affairs as an approach both desirable and necessary.[3]

One more term needs clarification: **strategy.** It may be defined as the pattern that integrates an organization's goals, policies, plans, and programs into a cohesive whole. A well-formulated strategy can help public and nonprofit organizations marshall and allocate their resources into a unique and viable posture. That posture should be based on two things: (1) the internal competencies and shortcomings of the organization, and (2) any anticipated changes in the organization's environment.[4]

An organization's strategy explains how its actions will achieve better results for society. Just as no private firm can succeed by being all things to all people, so too must government agencies and nonprofit organizations make critical choices about what they will and will not do. Consider The Nature Conservancy (TNC), one of the largest conservation organizations in the world, and one with a remarkably clear and consistent strategy:

> Since its founding in 1951, TNC has had a clear mission: "To preserve plants and animals and special habitats that represent the diversity of life." The Nature Conservancy fulfills this mission by buying and setting aside land. What it *doesn't* do is engage in advocacy as many other environmental groups do. The money to buy the land comes from individual donors. TNC has specifically targeted those donors for whom protected landscapes are a valuable product. The organization aims its appeal at people who love the outdoors and want to preserve it—and who are looking for groups that are achieving tangible results. They like the fact that TNC uses private-sector techniques to achieve its objectives. TNC protects the environment the old-fashioned way: it buys it. What TNC *doesn't* do, and consciously so, is become dependent on government funding. Thus, The Nature Conservancy neatly positions itself against the alternatives with which it competes for funds as a private organization, financed privately, using free-market techniques.[5]

Where Do Goals Come From?

The answer to that question depends on which of the three sectors we are talking about. If we are talking about a large corporation in the private sector, then the answer will be a board of directors. (In practice, however, it will really depend on how active the board chooses to be. When a board is supine—Enron comes to mind—goal setting tends to become the province of the company's top management.)

In the public sector, goals come from public policy, either passed by legislatures and signed into law by the chief executive or established by important court decisions. For example, although the top administrator in the Environmental Protection Agency (EPA) may have considerable latitude in developing plans and programs, the agency's goals derive from several major statutes:

- Clean Air Act
- Clean Water Act
- Federal Insecticide, Fungicide, and Rodenticide Act
- Safe Drinking Water Act
- Resource Conservation and Recovery Act
- Toxic Substance Control Act
- Comprehensive Environmental Response, Compensation, and Liability Act
    (the Superfund)
- Emergency Planning and Community Right-to-Know Act

If we are talking about the nonprofit sector, the answer is different still. Generally speaking, we can say that goals come from the trustees. The principal areas of responsibility for a nonprofit organization's board of trustees are to determine the organization's mission, set policies for its operation, and, in short, ensure that the organization's charter and laws are being followed. Trustees also set the organization's overall program from year to year and engage in long-range planning to establish its general course for the future. To make the issue of missions and goals in nonprofit organizations as concrete as possible, consider the Girl Scouts of America (GSA):

> The Girl Scouts began by asking: What is our business? Who is our customer? And what does the customer consider of value? In the end, GSA turned down offers from women's activist groups and others who sought scout help in door-to-door fund-raising because it was incompatible with the overriding mission of helping a girl become a good citizen and reach her highest potential. With its mission clearly established, GSA pursued the following goals: (1) Create 300 decentralized, independently run regional councils. (2) Attract and retain the interest of teenage girls. (3) Champion equal access, pushing scouting into minority, low-income areas and publishing bilingual materials. (4) Emphasize young role models, enlisting successful young businesswomen as volunteers. (5) Become activists in education, focusing on such issues as drugs, teenage pregnancy, and child abuse.

Other responsibilities of trustees of nonprofit organizations are worth noting. First is to establish fiscal policy with budgets and financial control. Second is to provide adequate resources for the organization's activities through direct financial contributions and a commitment to fund-raising. Third is to select, evaluate, and, if necessary, terminate the appointment of the chief executive. And fourth is to develop and maintain a communication link with the community.

Important as it is to understand what the duties of trustees include, it is equally important to understand what they do not include. Trustees should not engage in the day-to-day operations of the organization (micromanage), hire staff (other than the chief executive), or make detailed programmatic decisions without consulting staff. In other words, tactical and operational matters are seldom a legitimate concern of trustees; policy and goals are. As we said earlier, distinctions matter.

Planning Types and Models

Once goals have been determined, managers may select a planning approach most appropriate for their situation. Critical to successful planning are flexibility and adaptability to changing environments. Managers have a number of planning approaches from which to choose. Among the most popular are the rational planning model, logical incrementalism, urban and regional planning, contingency planning, and crisis management planning.

The Rational Planning Model

To provide a meaningful and systematic framework for understanding the planning process, the familiar and well-established model known as the **rational planning process** is presented. According to the rational planning model, planners are rational when they undertake the following five interrelated steps:

Step 1: Identify the problem to be solved or the opportunity to be capitalized on.

Step 2: Design alternative solutions or courses of action and forecast the consequences of each.

Step 3: Compare and evaluate the alternatives with each other, and choose the alternative whose probable consequences would be preferable.

Step 4: Develop a plan of action for implementing the alternative selected, including budgets, project schedules, regulatory measures, and the like.

Step 5: Maintain the plan on a current basis through feedback and review.

Although the steps are treated separately and in linear sequence, in actual practice they represent a cyclical process. Evaluation procedures, for example, enter into the process at the outset in the identification of problems and opportunities; they also influence the design of alternative solutions. Likewise, the problem-solving implementation enters into the design stages as constraints that must be taken into account. For this reason, it is probably preferable to think of the model not as a list of steps but as a dynamic and iterative process.

Strengths of the Model   If not followed too rigorously, the rational model can help public administrators avoid several serious mistakes. The first thing the rational model alerts administrators to is the need to translate lofty goals into concrete actions. To speak always of goals is to ensure that nothing will be accomplished.

The second thing rational planning helps guarantee is that priorities will be set and adhered to. Without concentration on priorities, efforts will be diluted over several objectives and squandered in areas where the payoff is low. Congressional investigations, for example, concluded that outside critics were right when they complained that J. Edgar Hoover, former Federal Bureau of Investigation director, had squandered bureau resources on penny-ante cases involving stolen cars and bank robberies. These made for impressive charts at budget hearings but had little real impact on crime.

The third thing the rational model can do is remind the administrator that structure follows strategy—that is, designing an effective organization should occur *after* goals have been set. Not all organizational structures are equally well suited to accomplishing a particular goal.

Fourth and equally important, the rational model alerts the administrator to the ever-present need to analyze, experiment, and evaluate to see what works before launching a program on a grand scale.

Fifth, the rational model highlights the vital and continuing role of feedback in the planning process. Only if the organization continues to learn through feedback can its performance improve and can it know when to abandon programs and activities that are no longer producing positive results.

Sixth, the rational model reminds administrators that they must periodically scan their environments for new threats and opportunities—which is to say, rational-model planning systems force operating administrators to extend their time horizons and see their work in a larger, dynamic framework. Henry Kissinger explains why such a forcing mechanism might be necessary: "The analysis of where one is overwhelms the consideration of where one should be going. Serving the machine becomes a more absorbing occupation than defining the purpose."[6]

Seventh, to the extent that they require rigorous communication about goals, alternatives, and resource allocations, rational models help create a network of information that probably would not otherwise be present in the agency.

Weaknesses of the Model   Against these strengths, however, several weaknesses must be weighed. Let's begin with the fact that the rational model suggests that executives should announce explicit goals. Yet research suggests that effective executives often proceed quite differently. Why? James Bryan Quinn suggests the following reasons:

- Goal announcements centralize and freeze the organization by telling subordinates that certain issues and alternatives are closed.
- Explicitly stated goals provide focal points against which an otherwise fragmented *opposition* can organize. This is what often happens when a town reveals its land-use plan. It also explains why presidents keep their specific budget cuts as fuzzy as possible for as long as possible.
- Once top administrators announce their goals, those goals are difficult to change; the administrators' egos and those of the people in supporting programs become identified with them. To change the goal is to admit to error. Thus, government plunges ahead with obsolete military, energy, and social programs.[7]

A few goals at least should be specific—especially when one wants to create a challenge or signal a major change from the past. But specific goals should be generated with care. Why so much care? Quinn writes, "Effective strategic goals do more than provide a basis for direction setting and maintaining freedom, morale, and timely problem sensing in an enterprise. The benefits of effective goal setting are greatest when people throughout the organization genuinely internalize goals and make them their own."[8]

A second weakness of the rational model is that it is based on a dubious assumption—namely, that the planner can peer clearly and deeply into the future. In reality, a host of unforeseen problems and events can sweep down on the new directions an agency might develop. Although many frustrated Americans might wish for a more specific, cohesive energy policy, logic dictates that massive resource commitments be made as late as possible consistent with the information available. To "go solar" today means that the United States must begin to build a solar industry at least on the scale of the automobile industry. But there are so many social, political, economic, and technological unknowns hiding between here and the year 2020 that logic dictates a more incremental, step-by-step approach.[9]

A third shortcoming of the rational model is that it fails to account for the politics within and outside the organization. In fact, one could argue that some planning decisions are the result of various bargaining games among the political leadership. Although this was not quite the thesis of Chapter 2, it was suggested there that politics and administration cannot be easily separated. It could also be argued that some planning decisions are more the result of regular patterns of behavior than of any rational analysis. Faced with a problem, rather than formulate a new strategy, administrators simply adapt to it some standard operating procedure of their organization.[10]

The fourth and final weakness in the rational model is not easily defined. Crudely put, the rational model discounts the role of subjective and qualitative factors in the policy-planning process. Its step-by-step view of the planning process is hard to reconcile with the experienced observations of flesh-and-blood administrators. Perhaps the following quote by a practicing manager comes close to capturing the realities of planning:

> I start conversations with a number of knowledgeable people. . . . I collect articles and talk to people about how things get done in Washington in this particular field. I collect data from any reasonable source. I begin wide-ranging discussions with people inside and outside the corporation. From these a pattern eventually emerges. It's like fitting together a jigsaw puzzle. At first the vague outline of an approach appears like the sail of a ship in a puzzle. Then suddenly the rest of the puzzle becomes quite clear. You wonder why you didn't see it all along. And once it's crystallized, it's not difficult to explain to others.[11]

Logical Incrementalism

The challenge to students of public administration is, therefore, easy enough to state: How can you build on the strengths of the rational model without including its weaknesses? Quinn—who we saw has his reservations about the rational planning model—suggests a possible solution. It is a synthesis of the rational model and incrementalism.

But before saying any more about Quinn's model, we had better define **incrementalism.** Essentially, incrementalism is an approach to policymaking that is conservative (in the sense of low risk) and practical (in the sense of politically expedient). It recommends that policymakers meet challenges slowly, by taking small—that is, incremental—steps. Recognizing that in policymaking, administrators typically start with an existing body of policies, proponents of incrementalism recommend only minimal departures from the status quo.

The weaknesses of incrementalism—or "muddling through," as some call it—are obvious. It can be slow when conditions require swift action. It can be overly cautious when conditions call for bold departures. Recall Abraham Lincoln's words to Congress in 1862: "The dogmas of the quiet past are inadequate to the stormy present. The occasion is piled high with difficulty, and we must rise with the occasion. As our case is new, so we must think anew and act anew. We must disenthrall ourselves, and then we shall save our country." This is not the language of incrementalism.

In short, policy must be purposeful, politically astute, and active. Yet at the same time it must deal with more uncertainty than the proponents of the rational model will admit. **Logical incrementalism** is an approach to policymaking that builds on the assumption that logic dictates that administrators proceed flexibly and experimentally from broad ideas toward specific commitments, as shown in Figure 5.2.

Spelling out those specific commitments as late as possible narrows the band of uncertainty and allows the administrator to benefit from the best available information. Quinn explains:

> The most effective strategies of major enterprises tend to emerge step by step from an iterative process in which the organization probes the future, experiments, and learns from a series of partial (incremental) commitments rather than through global formulations of total strategies. Good managers are aware of this process, and they consciously intervene in it. They use it to improve the information available for decisions and to build the psychological identification essential to successful strategies. The process is both logical and incremental. Such logical incrementalism is not muddling, as most people understand that word. Properly managed, it is a conscious, purposeful, proactive, executive practice.[12]

According to Quinn, logical incrementalism combines the analysis inherent in the rational planning model with the messy realities of power and uncertainty inherent in any collective effort. Executives cannot merely promulgate a bold new plan and then sit back and watch subordinates carry it out with machinelike precision. They must steadily build pockets of commitment within and outside the organization and establish incentives for participation. They must also demonstrate the flexibility of a battlefield commander. Although every battle has a plan—often a very detailed one—good generals know that as the fight unfolds, unexpected problems and opportunities arise and that they must be prepared to shift resources in response.

Urban and Regional Planning

Although urban planning is not a panacea for all the ills of a city, it is the essential mechanism that a democratic society uses to deal with complex interrelated problems such as suburban sprawl, neighborhood deterioration, visual blight, traffic congestion, air and water pollution,

Figure 5.2 Logical Incremental Planning Model

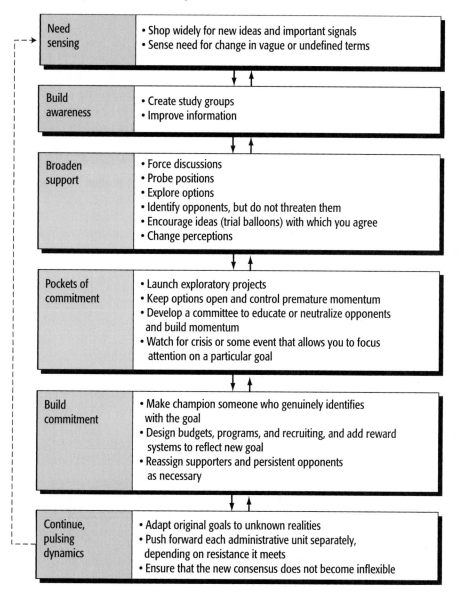

Need sensing	• Shop widely for new ideas and important signals • Sense need for change in vague or undefined terms
Build awareness	• Create study groups • Improve information
Broaden support	• Force discussions • Probe positions • Explore options • Identify opponents, but do not threaten them • Encourage ideas (trial balloons) with which you agree • Change perceptions
Pockets of commitment	• Launch exploratory projects • Keep options open and control premature momentum • Develop a committee to educate or neutralize opponents and build momentum • Watch for crisis or some event that allows you to focus attention on a particular goal
Build commitment	• Make champion someone who genuinely identifies with the goal • Design budgets, programs, and recruiting, and add reward systems to reflect new goal • Reassign supporters and persistent opponents as necessary
Continue, pulsing dynamics	• Adapt original goals to unknown realities • Push forward each administrative unit separately, depending on resistance it meets • Ensure that the new consensus does not become inflexible

When managers produce successful change of any significance in organizations, the process is time-consuming and highly complex—never a 1-2-3 process as suggested by the rational planning model. In the most successful change efforts, people move through several complicated, overlapping stages in which they create a sense of urgency, put together a strong enough team to direct the process, create an appropriate vision, communicate that vision broadly, produce sufficient short-term results to give their efforts credibility and to answer critics, and build momentum and use that momentum to tackle tomorrow's problems.

flooding, despoliation of the environment, an unstable tax base, and economic decline. **Urban planning** is the basic function of city government that deals with these issues in a comprehensive and coordinated manner.

The comprehensive plan, the document resulting from the urban planning process, is the means used to forecast and promote more desirable and efficient growth and patterns of development. The planning process involves all the stakeholders and interest groups—elected officials, business leaders, neighborhood groups, and civic organizations. It results in a shared vision of the city's future—where it is, where it wants to go from here, what kind of city it will be for future generations, and what means it will use to get there. More specifically, the comprehensive plan describes future transportation systems, general land-use patterns, utilities, parks, and public facilities. It also includes strategies for economic development, neighborhood stabilization, environmental protection, preservation of open space, and urban design guidelines for important civic places.

How important is urban planning? Ask Joseph P. Riley Jr., who has been mayor of Charleston, South Carolina, for nearly three decades. Unlike most mayors, who view economic projects largely in terms of dollars, Riley sees each one as a fateful choice for his city's sense of place: Every project, he believes, can add to—or subtract from—the quality of life. Like most mayors, he has no formal training in urban planning, but he thinks it is crucial for mayors and city managers to master a few principles of urban design because so many blueprints come across their desk. That is why Riley established the Mayor's Institute on City Design. Since its establishment in 1985, the Institute has offered two-day seminars in urban design to over 600 mayors.[13] For a two-minute seminar in urban design, see box: "Principles of Urban Design."

Perhaps no issue in urban design generates more attention than urban sprawl. Among those interested in the sprawl issue—besides mayors and city managers—are people worried about the racial and economic polarization generated by uncontrolled growth, environmentalists concerned about the impact on the natural world, and, more recently, local residents stuck in traffic and contemplating the decline in their quality of life. Then there are also those for whom the real problem is just the sheer ugliness of so much sprawl, combined with the loss of the rural landscape. Today, 1000 to 3000 acres of farmland, forest, and other unbuilt-upon land are developed every day.

What should be done? One way to address the problem of sprawl is to adopt some of the ideas of the self-named *new urbanists.* Another, less controversial, way is to think about our evolving world in terms of regions rather than cities—or even in terms of the country as a whole. Let's briefly consider both perspectives.

Today, according to the new urbanists, there is much less reason to separate business and home than there was when smokestack factories made living near one's work undesirable. Now, in suburbs where service professionals are the new industry, office buildings are being built near stores and houses. Indeed, traffic studies show that more Americans are commuting between suburbs than between suburb and city.

Unfortunately, there is little logic to where these suburbs have sprung up. All over the country, one finds office buildings, shopping malls, and housing clusters scattered carelessly along looping roadways near freeway off-ramps. The primary feature of these ubiquitous "centers" is freeway convenience. They create a way of life best seen and understood through the windshield. Thus, the new urbanists have begun to ask how the same basic

Principles of Urban Design

Although the following discussion focuses on planning in one city, Milwaukee, the ideas and principles have broad application.

Cities possess a singular appeal. The proximity of people and activities in cities facilitates efficient use of land and transportation systems and creation of convivial public spaces. Milwaukee must encourage development of housing, commerce, and transportation systems that embrace its urban heritage. The city must recognize its unique assets and build upon its strength as the core of a major metropolitan area.

Coordinated planning and development effectively integrate many elements. Quality housing that enhances a sense of community among neighborhood residents; attractive, customer-friendly commercial streets; green space offering recreational amenities; and a diverse array of transportation options represent only a few of the many elements that, when well designed, contribute to good urban form. Milwaukee must promote urban design practices that emphasize the public qualities of buildings and creation of places with lasting value and civic meaning.

New buildings should be designed in ways that retain the traditional qualities of Milwaukee's architecture. This does not mean that new buildings should nostalgically imitate historical styles. In fact, to do so would be contrary to the creative design traditions that produced Milwaukee's rich architectural legacy. Timeless design principles should be followed that produce architecture that fits with its context and is human scaled. New buildings should be designed to be compatible with neighboring structures, spaces and activities. Visually interesting and human-scaled building facades should prevail over sterile, windowless walls—especially when facing public spaces.

Diversity is the city's unique strength. The rich mix of uses found in Milwaukee's neighborhoods provides convenience, vitality, and individual identity. The transportation network binds the city together. Milwaukee must be organized around a transportation network that offers mobility choice. Needs of pedestrians and automobiles should be balanced to create a legible, walkable, and memorable public realm.

Combining good design with the city's rich architectural heritage will maintain its unique, attractive, "people-friendly" environment and further enhance Milwaukee's residents' quality of life.

The following design principles articulate those unique qualities that characterize Milwaukee's neighborhoods and are meant to promote development and redevelopment that reinforce and preserve these characteristics.

Principle #1:
Neighborhood Compatibility

A cohesive neighborhood environment depends on buildings that complement one another. The size, shape, and location of buildings, as well as the uses contained within them, create "patterns" that define neighborhood character. New development should be compatible with the pattern of its surrounding context.

Development that adheres to this principle will:

A. Relate to the physical character and scale of the neighborhood

B. Enhance linkages to surrounding uses, especially public services and amenities (schools, parks, mass transit)

Principle #2:
Pedestrian-Friendly Design

Cities are for people, and an environment designed to accommodate the pedestrian heightens human experience and sense of place. New development should be designed

(Continued)

to create attractive, comfortable, and safe walking environments.

Development that adheres to this principle will:

A. Locate buildings to define street edges and corners
B. Enliven street frontages to enhance the pedestrian experience
C. Create memorable places for people

Principle #3:
Land Use Diversity

Many Milwaukee neighborhoods are composed of a rich mix of land uses. Such diversity uses land efficiently, provides for neighborhood convenience and contributes to unique urban experiences.

Development that adheres to this principle will:

A. Encourage a compatible mix of uses at the neighborhood scale
B. Identify opportunities for shared uses

Principle #4:
Transportation Diversity

Milwaukee's neighborhoods are connected by a functional circulation network of streets and blocks. This system should be maintained and improved in ways that accommodate various modes of transportation balanced with needs for pedestrians.

Development that adheres to this principle will:

A. Create a balanced circulation system that accommodates mobility choice (pedestrians, automobiles, bicycles, and transit)
B. Enhance public transportation by making it more comfortable and convenient to use

SOURCE: Milwaukee Department of City Development. Retrieved June 17, 2004, from www.mkedcd.org/planning/plg/des.html. Reprinted with permission.

---

components of house, workplace, and store can be configured into small, independent towns. The idea is to foster a sense of community and give towns a higher cultural purpose than the efficient flow of traffic.

According to a group of land-use planners—let us call them the new regionalists—economic progress need not degrade the landscape. They recommend three simple rules for developing the land, or **regional planning.** First and foremost is to develop a *regional point of view.* In the case of New York City, for example, that means considering everything from Times Square to the city's reservoirs lying as much as 110 miles upstate. The reason for this wide-angle perspective is that rampant development of those watersheds could endanger the drinking water of 10 million city dwellers and suburbanites.

Our second rule of regional planning is to *concentrate development* as much as possible. New regionalists encourage more densely built town centers in order to keep at least 50 percent of existing farmland open. That way, change comes about without destroying the spirit of a place. (See drawings.)

The third rule is to make *maximum use of existing sites* to create "urban villages" combining residential, commercial, and office projects. One regional study concluded that the expected residential development needs of the San Francisco Bay Area could be accommodated for the next 20 to 30 years mainly by building on vacant land on the urban fringe, developing downtown areas more densely, and utilizing bypassed land—abandoned commercial waterfront, former rail yards, derelict industrial space.

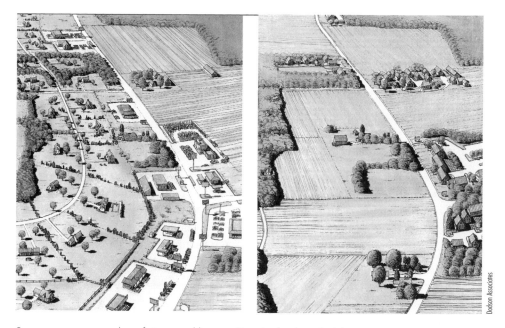

Same area, same number of stores and houses. Creative land use (right) preserves open spaces.

The "new regionalism" appears to be spreading. Ten states—among them Florida, Vermont, Washington, and Maryland—have already adopted growth plans along these lines. In the Connecticut River Valley of Massachusetts, 19 towns and cities have banded together to develop the region coherently.

But this will not be easy. In the first place, although the problems of ecology, traffic, pollution, and even social life are demonstrably all regional, the political jurisdictions do not reflect this reality.

In the second place, if Americans hate anything more than sprawl, it is probably high density—that is, cramming more homes and apartments into high-density pockets for the sake of controlling sprawl elsewhere.

Contingency Plans

We turn from comprehensive, general plans to more focused ones such as **contingency plans** that define an organization's response to specific situations such as emergencies or setbacks. To develop contingency plans, administrators identify uncontrollable factors—such as accidents, economic fluctuations, and technological developments—and then try to decide how to minimize the effects of those factors once they occur. Contingency planning need not be an elaborate process; sometimes it may consist of nothing more than asking "what-if" questions. The virtue of contingency planning is that it compensates for the all-too-human tendency to assume that everything will turn out as planned. Not surprisingly, techniques to scrutinize consequences were weak, if not totally absent, in planning the war in Vietnam:

> In early March 1965, a pessimistic Emmitt John Hughes, a former White House aide under President Eisenhower, went to see McGeorge Bundy [President Kennedy's National Security Adviser]. What, Hughes asked, if the North Vietnamese retaliate by matching the American air escalation with their own ground escalation? Hughes would long remember the answer and the cool smile. "Just suppose it happens," Hughes persisted. Bundy answered, "We can't assume what we don't believe."[14]

Similarly, in the months before the first bombs fell on Baghdad on April 9, 2003, planners in the Bush administration operated on the assumption that after the war, the Iraqi people would realize that they were liberated and be happy that the Americans were there. Therefore, a force to secure the peace could be much smaller than the force to win the war. The first assumption was clearly expressed by Vice President Dick Cheney three days before the war began in an exchange with Tim Russert on *Meet the Press:*

> RUSSERT: If your analysis is not correct, we are not treated as liberators but as conquerors, and the Iraqis began to resist, particularly in Baghdad, do you think the American people are prepared for a long, costly, and bloody battle with significant American casualties?

> CHENEY: Well, I don't think it's likely to unfold that way, Tim, because I really do believe that we will be greeted as liberators. . . . The read we get on the people of Iraq is there is no question but that they want to get rid of Saddam Hussein and they will welcome as liberators the United States when we come to do that.

This anecdote brings to mind an aphorism by the German philosopher Nietzsche: "A very popular error: having the courage of one's convictions; rather it is a matter of having the courage for an *attack* on one's convictions!" Good philosophy, good policy.

An approach called **scenario planning** is also gaining increased importance in today's complex times, although it has been a staple in Pentagon planning for some time. A long-term version of contingency planning, scenario planning involves identifying several alternative future scenarios or "future histories" and then adjusting existing plans to minimize the damage to a program if any of these scenarios should come to pass. Scenarios are really only stories. But they take place in the future and the format is as follows: If A happened tomorrow, then it would be reasonable to assume B the following week. If B occurred, then C would be more likely than before. Given C, then D might be a real possibility, and so on.

One former senior director at the National Security Council explains the power of scenario planning as follows:

> As opposed to the classic strategic method of applying the past to the future—coming up with a single likeliest story about how things will turn out—scenario planning is about applying the future to the present, creating a learning framework for decisions. The idea is not so much to predict the future as to consider the forces

that will push the future along different paths, in order to help leaders recognize new possibilities, assess new threats and make decisions that reach much further into the future.[15]

But can scenario planning work? Ask Shell Oil. In the early 1970s, Royal Dutch/Shell used scenario planning to alert the firm to the possibility that there could be an oil embargo in the Middle East. Accordingly, they began to look for other oil fields. In the mid-1980s, the company again used scenario planning to get top management to think about what Shell should be doing if the Soviet Union were to collapse in the early 1990s.

Crisis Management Planning

A special type of contingency planning is crisis management planning. Before we consider the stages of crisis management, let's first note the various forms of crisis.

Three Forms of Crisis   Being crisis prepared doesn't require organizations to plan for every disaster that could conceivably affect them. That is neither necessary nor possible. But there are ways in which organizations can think broadly about the full range of problems they might encounter and create strategies to lower their own vulnerability. Research by Ian I. Mitroff and Murat C. Alpaslan at the University of Southern California's Center for Crisis Management suggests that organizations ought to distinguish between three general forms of crisis.[16]

The first are *natural accidents,* like fires and earthquakes. For the most part, organizations know how to prepare for these crises and can defend against them reasonably well. For example, ever since the great Chicago fire of 1871, the city of Chicago has emphasized crisis management planning to prepare for fires, floods, chemical spills, or other disasters. The second kind of crisis is what sociologist Charles Perrow calls *normal accidents.* These come in three categories: economic crises (for example, deep recessions), physical crises (for example, accidents and supply shortages), and personnel crises (for example, strikes and exodus of talented employees). The third form of crises are *abnormal accidents*—that is, intentional accidents. These also come in three categories: criminal crises (for example, acts of terrorism), information crises (for example, tampering with records), and reputation crises (for example, rumor mongering). Data suggest that the number of abnormal accidents is on the rise.

Unfortunately, most managers are so conditioned by conventional crisis planning that they don't know how to start imagining unfamiliar dangers without seeming paranoid. One tool Mitroff and Alpaslan use to force top management to think more randomly about crises is a "wheel of crises." They build a wheel, like a spinner on a child's game, and list on it all the familiar crises, grouped in families, that an organization can face. See Figure 5.3. The authors explain how the wheel works:

> Executives take turns spinning the wheel; when the spin stops, they discuss all the normal and abnormal crises of that particular kind they can imagine. We don't exclude any possibility, however bizarre, because each one helps overturn the executive's fundamental belief that they already know what crises the company could face.

Figure 5.3   The Wheel of Crises

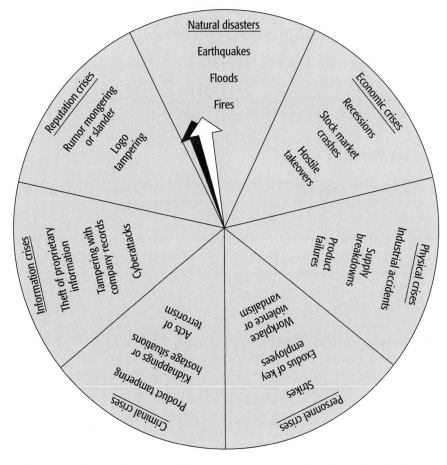

Although organizations face many different crises, research by Mitroff and Alpaslan shows that crises can be grouped into seven families. By including at least one from each of these categories, organizations "can create a crisis portfolio and began to consider vulnerabilities that might otherwise be beyond their imagination."

Source: Adapted from Ian I. Mitroff and Murat C. Alpaslan, "Preparing for Evil," *Harvard Business Review* (April 2003): 114.

In the next stage of this version of Russian roulette, participants cobble together two abnormal crises to create a more improbable combination crisis. That increases the magnitude of the peril and compels executives to accept that abnormal disasters often happen on a very large scale. It also helps them link crises they never thought applied to their company or industry. Chillingly, executives at more than one *Fortune 500* company we worked with back in 2000 combined a car bomb and an aircraft hijacking to come up with the threat of a "flying bomb"—distressingly close to the World Trade Center attack.[17]

The Stages of Crisis Management   There are three essential steps in crisis management: (1) prevention, (2) preparation, and (3) containment.[18]

(1) The prevention stage involves activities managers undertake to try to prevent crises from occurring and to detect warning signs of potential crises. One critical part of the prevention stage is building relationships with key stakeholders such as employees, clients/customers, suppliers, other agencies, other jurisdictions, unions, and the community. Open communication enables the organization and its stakeholders to better understand one another and develop mutual respect. Open communication also helps managers identify problems early so they do not turn into major issues.

(2) The preparation stage of crisis management includes detailed planning to handle a crisis when it occurs. That planning should include the designation of a cross-functional group of people who are designated to take action if a crisis occurs. This crisis management team is closely involved in creating the crisis management plan (CMP). For instance, the U.S. Office of Personnel Management in Washington, DC has nearly 200 people assigned *and trained* to take immediate action in a disaster, including 18 employees assigned to each of 10 floors to handle an evacuation.

The organization should also designate a spokesperson to be the voice of the organization during the crisis. The spokesperson is often the top leader of the organization. After the terrorist attacks on the World Trade Center and the crash of American Airlines flight 587 in a New York neighborhood two months later, Mayor Rudolph Guiliani was the spokesperson for the city of New York. However, organizations typically assign more than one spokesperson so that someone else will be prepared if the top leader is unavailable.

The **crisis management plan** should be a detailed written plan that specifies the steps to be taken by whom in a crisis. The plan should list complete contact information for members of the crisis management team as well as for outside agencies such as emergency personnel, insurance companies, and so forth. It should include plans for ensuring the safety of employees and customers, procedures for backup and recovery of computer systems and protecting proprietary information, details on where people should go if they need to be evacuated, plans for alternative worksites if needed, and guidelines for handling media and other outside communications. Some organizations issue wallet-size cards that inform employees about procedures during and after an evacuation. A key point is that a CMP should be a living document that is regularly reviewed, practiced, and updated as needed.

A major part of the CMP is a communications plan that designates a crisis command center and sets up a complete communications and message system. The command center serves as a place for the crisis management team to meet, gather data and monitor incoming information, and disseminate information to employees, the media, and the public. The plan should designate alternative communication centers in case the main center is disrupted and include plans for every communication method (for example, toll-free call centers and Internet and intranet communications). After a disaster, employees should have multiple ways to communicate with the organization and report their location and status.

Of course, CMPs have to be tailored to specific crises. Consider, for example, a few of the steps federal agencies have taken in planning for a bioterrorist attack: offered training materials to physicians to sharpen their ability to recognize anthrax; used computers to flag odd patterns of illness or medicine use; stockpiled antibiotics; asked health-care workers to volunteer to be vaccinated against smallpox; organized drills to test disaster plans; and provided information on bioterrorism (www.bt.cd.gov).

(3) The containment stage focuses on the organization's response to an actual crisis and any follow-up concerns. Some crises are inevitable no matter how well prepared an organization is. When a crisis hits, a rapid response is crucial. For example, within 24 hours of the outbreak of severe acute respiratory syndrome (SARS), the Centers for Disease Control and Prevention in Atlanta made calls to state health officials and the clinician community. Within 36 hours, the center had issued guidelines on isolating patients to prevent the spread of the disease.

In addition to speed, candor is also vital. As Mitroff and Alpasian put it, "get the awful truth out." During the containment stage, the organization should speak with one voice to minimize the number of conflicting stories. The organization should also strive to get the truth out fast—otherwise, it can create problems for itself during recovery. Consider how the U.S. Postal Service handled (mishandled) the anthrax threat in 2001:

> When letters containing anthrax contaminated the Hart Senate Office Building, congressional staff was tested and immediately given antibiotics. In contrast, the U.S. Postal Service, not wanting to stop mail service, downplayed the danger—even though two of its workers had died. Needless to say, postal workers would not soon forget the slow reaction of top management to protect its employees.

Responding to the emotional as well as physical safety needs of employees is another element of effective crisis management. Trying to downplay the effects of a disaster with facts and figures is a particularly poor way for management to show its employees that it cares about them and understands their concerns.

Similarly, during the containment stage, organizations should also strive to give people a sense of security and belonging. Getting back to regular operations is essential because it helps people believe that things can return to normal. You may recall from Chapter 1 that returning things to normal was a major consideration for Mayor Guiliani and his staff when deciding whether to restrict downtown traffic after 9/11. After an especially devastating crisis, an organization may even provide counseling and other services to help people cope.

Finally, management should *learn* from a crisis and use the crisis itself to strengthen its prevention and preparation capabilities. A crisis provides an opportunity for management to improve employee, public, and stakeholder relationships. By being open and honest, moving quickly, and putting people first, an organization can enhance its reputation as a responsible agency. Not without reason, in the Chinese language there are two characters that, when written together, mean "crisis." But each character, when standing alone, has a separate meaning: the upper character means "danger" and the lower character "opportunity." The Chinese, therefore, view a crisis as a danger that provides an opportunity.

Pitfalls of Public-Sector Planning

Planning is difficult because it deals with complex environments and must look toward an uncertain future. However, public administrators can themselves make certain mistakes that reduce the likelihood that an agency will attain its goals. Public administrators should know these pitfalls of planning—and avoid them. (What follows draws on the works of Mintzberg et al., Bozeman and Straussman, Locke et al., and Chase.)[19]

Expecting Continuance of the Status Quo

Too many managers only spend time coping with the problems they see now. Yet situations change and managers should be just as prepared to cope with different circumstances. Administrators must constantly think aloud about their programs, try to foresee problems before they arise, and instill this same attitude in subordinates. (Recall question 3 in Case 3.1 in Chapter 1.)

They must frequently ask, Is there anything else we should be doing that we are not now doing? But administrators must also recognize that they cannot anticipate everything—some things are bound to go wrong.

Trying to Do Too Much

It is easy to be impressed by the scope of a problem and to want to solve it all at once. Yet an incremental approach, although not as intellectually pleasing as a comprehensive approach, may be more realistic to implement. An administrator can build a comprehensive system as she goes. For example, if she cannot solve all the problems of child health care in a large city, then perhaps she can make progress with a series of categorical programs (for example, lead-poison screening, rat control, immunization, sickle-cell testing).

Public administrators should develop the skill of discerning what is possible and what is impossible, because many of the problems in the public sector are totally intractable. They should not waste valuable time and resources trying to accomplish the impossible. This does not mean they should not tackle tough problems but rather that they should define realistic goals.

Getting Emotionally Involved

When managers get emotionally involved in their plan, they resist changes in it. Planners should see their work as a living thing that can and should be improved upon even after implementation has begun. As a corollary, managers should purposely build into their plans resource buffers and dimensions for flexibility.

Overplanning

Managers should not be too concerned with details. Sometimes it is better to forsake the next increment of effort required to make the plan perfect, because the payoff is not worth it. Be flexible in your plan—change it as you go. Very little is irreversible. Likewise, the implementation plan should be simple and realistic.

Planners have a tendency to want a lot of extras that would be nice if they happened but that are not crucial to achieving the objectives of the program. Therefore, they should identify the factors in a program that, if absent, will cause the program to fail. For example, in setting up a large lead-poison screening program to increase the productivity of testing personnel, a good reporting system would be indispensable. It would be *nice* to have Red Cross mobile vans help in the program, but they would not be critical to getting the program off the ground.

Underplanning

As much as the invasion of Iraq and removal of Saddam Hussein and his army were triumphs of meticulous planning, the mess that Iraq turned into afterward is a failure of planning—or, more accurately, a failure to follow plans that were developed.[20] In the State Department, staffers on the Future of Iraqi Project developed a report that warned, among other things, that "the period immediately after regime change might offer criminals the opportunity to engage in acts of killing, plunder, and looting." But the Department of Defense, which would come to oversee postwar operations, paid little attention to the 13-volume report. None of the senior American officials involved in the State Department's project was taken on board by the Pentagon's planners.

The Office of Reconstruction and Humanitarian Assistance (ORHA) was established in the Defense Department, under General J. Garner, *just eight weeks before the invasion* of Iraq. Because the Pentagon had insisted on throwing out the State Department's work, Garner and his staff had to start more or less from scratch. Thus, ORHA had only two months to figure out what to plan for, plan for it, and then find the people to implement the plan. ORHA drew up plans for housing and feeding Iraqi refugees—of which, it would turn out, there were very few—but gave little thought to other contingencies such as widespread looting. One reason for the looting in Baghdad was that the U.S. war planners had been careful not to attack Iraq's infrastructure; hence, there were many intact buildings to loot.

Individual combat units rehearsed over and over their own roles in the invasion and the contingencies they might face. By contrast, the same units were given virtually no guidance on—much less practice at—postwar operations. Nor was there any guidance on how ORHA's work on humanitarian relief, reconstruction, and civilian administration would integrate with the military command structure on the ground in Iraq.

As the spring of 2003 wore on, the administration continued to insist publicly that nothing was seriously wrong in Iraq. Then in May, President Bush replaced Garner with L. Paul Bremer, who had no postwar reconstruction experience. Bremer's first major act was to announce the complete disbanding of the 400,000-strong Iraqi army. In a country like Iraq, where the average family size is six, firing 400,000 people amounts to leaving 2.4 million people without an income.

How might we explain this underplanning, this reluctance to think through the logical consequences of a decision? Starting at the top, President Bush preferred to make big, bold decisions and leave the details to others. Although boldness goes with greatness, inattention to details can sometimes be fatal. Curiosity should accompany big choices. Curiosity generates questions. A leader must not hesitate to ask questions like, *Why* do you assume that? *How* do you know Iraqis will view American forces as liberators on day two? *What if* this were to happen? *What if* Iraqi soldiers, suddenly finding themselves unemployed, become disgruntled and revengeful? (See photo.)

Underestimating the Importance of Organizational Structure

Some new, large programs fail because no organization is built to support them and to allow for managerial control. This happens to numerous low-income housing programs in which money is distributed to various community groups and contractors before adequate accounting and auditing systems are established. Questions to ask are: How will the program play with the informal organization? Can a coalition be formed within the organization to champion this program? How decentralized (or centralized) should control be? Chapter 7 suggests a number of other pertinent questions that should be addressed during the planning process.

Likka ulmonen/Magnum Photos New York

On October 5, 2003, U.S. troops try to control a demonstration in Baghdad by former Iraqi soldiers. In May 2003, the United States disbanded the Iraqi Army.

Discounting Details

In theory, strategic planners and top administrators are supposed to focus on the big picture and not concern themselves with the details of implementation, that is, carrying out a plan. But detachment can lead planners to plan for things they don't understand. Plans are meant to be guidelines for action—not abstract theories. Consequently, planners need to be familiar with the daily details, the nitty-gritty of their agency's operations if they are to produce plans that work.

If you doubt that details are important to the good execution of the plan, then remember Benjamin Franklin, who thought that such neglect may breed great mischiefs: "For the want of a nail the shoe was lost; for the want of a shoe the horse was lost; and for the want of a horse the rider was lost." If the rider happened to be a general, then a battle might be lost. If the battle happened to be critical, then a war might be lost. Thus, a measly missing nail could mean the loss of a country!

Ignoring Unintended Consequences

Public administration isn't gardening. If you plant radishes, you get radishes. Every time. But if a county wants to, say, reduce traffic congestion, it just builds more roads and then it gets less congestion. Right? Findings on the effect of a major expansion on Interstate 270 outside Washington, DC suggest not. In the 1980s, congestion became especially severe on this roadway. So Montgomery County applied to the Maryland state government for funds to greatly expand the road. The state—using chiefly federal funds—agreed. By 1999, less than eight years after expansion, the highway was again reduced to what one official described as "a rolling parking lot."[21]

Public policy experts have aptly named this and similar phenomena *unintended consequences*. This concept reminds us that a disjunction exists between the intentions or purposes of public administrators and the outcomes of public policy. Public administrators cannot predict with any exactitude what the reaction to their actions will be.

Why is this so? First, outcomes often are the product of bargaining and compromise among many participants with various interests, values, and degrees of influence. Predicting how all these participants will interact and behave is, to say the least, difficult. People have a knack for confounding experts with regard to how they "should" behave. Second, the problems and challenges of the public sector are inherently difficult. The private sector gets the easy jobs (making cornflakes, building houses, etc.); the public sector, the hard ones (eliminating acid rain, global peacekeeping, building a space station, controlling illegal immigration, ending poverty, and so on). A third reason for the disconnect between the aims of policy and the results of policy is that the social sciences possess virtually no laws (in the sense that there are *never* any exceptions to the rule), few substantial generalizations, and no real theories. The fourth reason for the disconnect between intent and outcome is the effect of random events. For example, in 1992 a few minutes of videotape showing a Los Angeles police officer beating an African American man led, in time, to widespread urban rioting that left 52 dead and caused $1 billion in property damage.

What Can Government Learn from the Private Sector?

Since 1996, U.S. private sector productivity (output per hour) has been growing at a rate of 2.5 percent a year. How far behind is government? We can't say for sure because the Bureau of Labor Statistics stopped measuring it in 1996. Analysis by McKinsey & Co. shows that government kept up with the private sector until 1987, when a gap emerged and continued to widen until 1994, and then the data ran out.[22]

The public productivity deficit couldn't come at a worse time. Americans today say they want to limit the cost of government, but they also want more homeland security, better-managed borders, more disaster readiness, extra help in the face of a global economic slowdown, cheaper health care, and better public schools. These demands sit uncomfortably with a huge budget deficit and a natural desire not to pay more taxes. Apparently, Americans want more output but no more input.

Despite numerous attempts at management reforms and an array of opportunities to transfer best practices between private and public sectors, government seems to have missed out on the productivity growth seen in the private sector. Let's briefly review the history. In 1993, President Bill Clinton launched a bold, freewheeling initiative to cut red tape and improve government productivity, putting Vice President Al Gore in charge of an intensive six-month review of the federal government. The project, called the National Performance Review, followed the pattern of a much-publicized Texas initiative in which squads of reformers swept through government agencies to identify targets of waste and opportunities for improvements in management. That same year the Government Performance and Results Act (GPRA) became law. Henceforth, every major federal agency would have to ask itself some basic questions: What is our mission? What are our goals, and how will we achieve them? How can we measure our performance? How will we use that information to make improvements? The GPRA, in short, forced a shift in the focus of federal agencies—away from such traditional concerns as staffing and activity levels and toward the single overriding issue of results. The GPRA required agencies to set goals, measure performance, and report on their accomplishments. It also sought to improve public management through delegation of authority and team building.

Eight years later, President George W. Bush introduced a more structured and targeted reform platform to strengthen agency-level management capacity and boost program performance and results. The Program Assessment Rating Tool (PART) is a 30-question survey that the Office of Management and Budget now requires all federal program managers to complete as a part of each year's budget request. The questions address program purpose, design, planning, and results. PART provides a way to structure debate and frame discussion of how to spend public money and offers a way to hold program managers and government employees accountable. Why was this new tool needed? Since GPRA, many federal agencies have struggled to develop a coherent system for gauging measurable outcomes. Some agencies have resisted the idea. PART proponents see this new assessment tool as moving federal agencies further toward compliance with GPRA. To see how well any federal agency is performing, visit www.expectmore.gov

These two initiatives—GPRA and PART—now serve as models for President Barack Obama, who can cherry-pick the most successful and applicable aspects of each. To help him do that cherry-picking, he appointed the federal government's first "chief performance officer," Jeffrey Zients, who will also serve as deputy of the Office of Management and Budget.

What will Zients' priorities be? If Obama's statements when he made his appointment are any indication, it will be to "scour the budget, line-by-line, eliminating what we don't need, or what doesn't work, and improving the things that do." One way to do this is by improving transparency and reviving government productivity metrics. How much the chief performance officers will use the playbook of high-performance private-sector organizations is an open question.

There is broad agreement among executives, consultants, and scholars on the key characteristics and capabilities of high-performing organizations. They can be summarized in terms of six themes as follows: (1) a clear, well-articulated, and compelling mission; (2) strategic use of stakeholders; (3) analysis of the threats and opportunities in the environment both present and future; (4) clearly defined outcomes; (5) an alignment of activities, core processes, and resources; and (6) an objective assessment of performance.[23]

Even though there is no agreement on what one calls this set of themes or this approach to management, **strategic management** has come to mean a conscious, rational decision process by which organizations formulate goals and then implement and monitor them, making adjustments as the internal and external conditions change. One should not discount the difficulty in applying strategic management—or whatever one calls these ideas—in the public sector. Unlike a private-sector chief operating offer, an agency head must share power with other key players when formulating policy and lacks complete autonomy and control during implementation. But the heart of the problem of applying strategic management is a budget process that often de-prioritizes performance as the driving force of appropriations. Tony Danker and his colleagues at McKinsey write:

> Ideology or policy differences over a particular program continue to dominate budget decisions long after a program is first established; potential public reaction to increasing or reducing a program's budget weighs heavily on a politician's mind; and, above all, benefits accruing to a particular district can often be the most critical driver in budget negotiations. Government managers with whom we spoke said budgeting is about what you can get, rather than what you need. For some programs, getting results has no real impact on getting budget; for others, getting results is necessary, but not sufficient.
>
> So the relationship between the budget and results tends to be weak. This is not necessarily the result of bad behavior—accountability was not designed exclusively as a means to achieve government results, but also to serve other core objectives in the American model of government. From the legislature's point of view, Congress exists to monitor and control the power of the executive branch, acting as guardian of the public's money, and ensure that each state and district's interest are secured. Likewise, in the eyes of the executive branch, a president may face challenges more urgent and specific than widespread improvements in government performance, and agency leaders are ultimately accountable to the president's priorities.[24]

Keeping these limitations in mind, let's now take a closer look at the six themes of strategic management listed above.

Defining the Mission and the Desired Outcomes

The planning process begins when an agency develops a strategic plan. The strategic plan defines the action steps by which the organization intends to attain strategic goals. The strategic plan is the blueprint and defines the organizational activities and resource allocations—in the form of cash, personnel, space, and facilities—required for meeting these targets. Strategic planning tends to be long term and may define organizational action steps up to five years in the future. Since 1997, federal agencies have been required by the GPRA to develop strategic plans covering a period of at least five years and send them to Congress and the Office of Management and Budget (OMB).

Each strategic plan should include a comprehensive **mission statement** based on the agency's statutory requirements (that is, what the legislature by law has authorized it to do), a set of outcome-related strategic goals, and a description of how the agency intends to achieve those goals. The mission statement explains why the agency exists, tells what it does, and describes how it does it. The strategic goals that follow are an outgrowth of this clearly stated mission. The strategic goals explain the purpose of the agency's programs and the results they are intended to achieve. "The experience of hashing out the fundamental purpose of an organization—debating all the different assumptions and views held by its members and agreeing on one basic mission—can be a powerful one. When it is done right, a mission statement can drive an entire organization, from top to bottom. It can help people at all levels decide what they should do and what they should stop doing." Recall the example of TNC cited earlier (p. 211).[25]

In summary, successful government agencies and nonprofits have strong mission-focused strategies. Consequently, they devote a great deal of thought to defining their mission and objectives. A well-defined mission creates an organization that is disciplined, and it helps avoid splintering of effort into unrelated and nonproductive activities. The mission serves as a constant reminder of the need to look outside the organization for measures of services. Finally, focus on a mission can help an organization foster innovation by creating clear criteria against which to evaluate new ideas and by eliminating the reliance on the "way things have always been."

Involving Stakeholders

Successful organizations base their strategic planning, to a large extent, on the interests and expectations of their **stakeholders.** (As defined in Chapter 2, a stakeholder is any group within or outside an organization that has a stake in the organization's performance.) These organizations recognize that stakeholders will have a lot to say in determining whether their programs succeed or fail.

In the federal government, stakeholders' involvement is particularly important because federal agencies face a complex political environment in which legislative mandates are often ambiguous. Thus, the basic questions that must be answered in crafting a mission statement—what is our purpose, what products and services must we deliver to meet that purpose, and how will that be done—will present a significant challenge for many agencies. Although statutory requirements are to be the starting point for agency mission statements, Congress, the executive branch, and other interested parties may all disagree strongly about a given agency's mission and goals. Full agreement among stakeholders on all aspects of an agency's efforts is relatively uncommon because stakeholders' interests can differ often and significantly.

Still, stakeholder involvement is important to help agencies ensure that their efforts and resources are targeted at the highest priorities. Just as important, involving stakeholders in strategic planning efforts can help create a basic understanding among the stakeholders of the competing demands that confront most agencies, the limited resources available to them, and how those demands and resources require careful and continuous balancing. Because of its power to create and fund programs, the involvement of the legislature is indispensable in defining each agency's mission and establishing its goals.

Assessing the Environment

Good managers have understood for a long time that many forces—both inside and outside their organizations—can influence their ability to achieve their goals. But even managers who try to stay alert to those forces often gather their information anecdotally or informally. In contrast, the successful organization monitors its internal and external environments continuously and systematically. Organizations that do this have shown an ability to anticipate future changes and to make adjustments so that potential problems do not become crises. By building environmental assessment into the strategic planning process, these anticipatory organizations are able to stay focused on their long-term goals even as they make changes in the way they intend to achieve them.

Both the external and internal environments are important, and neither can be viewed independently of the other. Assessing the external environment is particularly important, in part because so many external forces that fall beyond an organization's influence can powerfully affect its chances for success. For organizations—both public and private— external forces can include newly emerging economic, social, and technological trends and new statutory, regulatory, and judicial requirements. An organization's internal forces include its culture, its management practices, and its business processes. Today agencies find that monitoring these internal forces is especially important, given the effects of funding reductions and reorganizations.

Defining the Desired Outcomes

There are several barriers to focusing on results in the public sector, where the bottom line is far less apparent than in the private. The barriers most frequently experienced in developing results-oriented program performance measures generally fall into three broad categories: (1) problems in collecting program performance data, (2) the diverse and complex factors that affect agencies' results and the lack of control agencies have over some of those factors, and (3) the long time frames sometimes needed to see the results of agencies' actions.

1. For example, some agencies find themselves in the difficult position of trying to gather data to "prove a negative," such as the number of aircraft accidents that were avoided by the Federal Aviation Administration's efforts to improve airport runways or the number of people who did not get sick because the Food and Drug Administration approved a new drug or kept an unsafe product off the market.
2. For example, one of the EPA's strategic goals is to achieve clean and safe water, which is affected by numerous factors that are outside the EPA's control (for example, natural causes including weather conditions).
3. The latency period between exposure to a hazardous substance, such as asbestos, and a resulting illness can be 20 years or more. Therefore, the results of any action the Occupational Safety and Health Administration takes to reduce exposure to these substances may be equally long in coming.

Despite such barriers, agencies *have* improved results due to their strategic plans. For example, the Veterans Health Administration (VHA) improved services to American veterans by more rigorously assessing the results of the medical care it provides them. In particular, the Veterans Health Administration reported that it used performance information to target the most important improvement opportunities and thereby lowered the mortality rate for cardiac procedures by an average of 13 percent over an eight-year period. Another example involves the Social Security Administration's national toll-free telephone number to handle citizen inquiries. The Administration used customer satisfaction and other performance information to identify and make program changes, including providing additional staff to handle phone calls. As a result, the busy rate decreased and the percentage of calls answered within five minutes increased.[26]

Government agencies do not exist in a vacuum. As agencies develop their mission statements and establish their strategic goals, they should consult with both the legislature and their other stakeholders. Further, agencies need to be alert to the environment in which they operate; in their strategic plans, they should try to identify the external factors that could affect their ability to accomplish what they set out to do.

Aligning Activities, Core Processes, and Resources

Organizations that are truly results oriented—whether public, nonprofit, or for-profit—consistently strive to ensure that their day-to-day activities support their organizational missions and move them closer to accomplishing their strategic goals. In practice, these organizations see the production of a strategic plan—that is, a particular document issued on a particular day—as one of the least important parts of the planning process. This is because they believe strategic planning is not a static or occasional event. It is, instead, a dynamic and inclusive process. If done well, strategic planning is continuous and provides the basis for everything the organization does each day.

In other words, an organization's activities, core processes, and resources must be aligned to support its mission and help achieve its goals. This requires that organizations start by assessing the extent to which their programs and activities contribute to meeting their mission and desired outcomes.

As organizations become more results oriented, they often find it necessary to fundamentally alter old structures and procedures so that they more efficiently produce services to meet customers' needs and stakeholders' interest. This need for change applies in particular to organizational structure, human resources management, budgeting, and information management. For example, the management problems of many agencies may be traced to organizational structures that are obsolete and inadequate to modern demands. (This topic is explored in some depth in Chapter 7.) As agencies become more outcome oriented, they find that outmoded organizational structures must be changed to better meet customer needs and address the interests of stakeholders.

Leading organizations also strive to ensure that their core processes support mission-related outcomes. Such organizations rely increasingly on a well-defined mission to form the foundation for what they do and how they do it on a day-to-day basis. For example, many successful public and private organizations integrate their human resources management activities into their organizational missions, rather than treating them as an isolated support function. This sort of integrated approach may include tying individual performance management, career development programs, and pay and promotion standards to organizational mission, vision, and culture. Human resources management is the focus of Chapter 10.

As agencies align their activities to support mission-related goals, they should also make better linkages between levels of funding and their anticipated results. Then budget officers can focus more on the goals and performance of agencies in making their funding decisions. Budgeting is the focus of Chapter 11.

Information management, the focus of Chapter 12, is another activity that organizations must address when aligning their activities and processes. Modern information management approaches, coupled with new information technology, can make success more or less likely—depending on the way they are handled. Successful organizations pursue strategic information management—that is, comprehensive management of information and information technology to maximize improvements in mission performance. More specifically, strategic information management systems provide agencies the data they need in considering ways to align their processes, reduce costs, improve program effectiveness, and ensure consistent results with a less bureaucratic organization.

Performance Assessment

Essentially, there are two types of program performance assessment: performance measurement and program evaluation. **Performance measurement** is the ongoing monitoring and reporting of program accomplishments, particularly progress toward pre-established goals. Typically, program or agency management conducts it. Performance measurement should address program *outcomes* rather than program activities or outputs. In assessing program outcomes, agency management can't be content to simply measure program activities such as the number of dollars spent per member of a target group—for example, per pupil education expenditure, per capita welfare expenditure, per capita health-care expenditure. These are not really measures of the outcome of a program on the group; rather, they are measures of government activity, of program output. Although many performance measures focus on outputs—for example, plants inspected, criminal arrests, Medicare payments, school enrollments, troop levels—this bean counting may tell us little about the actual achievement in the areas of environmental pollution, crime, health care, education, and national security. Put another way, we cannot be satisfied with measuring how many times a butterfly flaps its wings; we must know how far it has flown.

In performance measurement, we must identify *actual changes in society* that are associated with government actions. What is the ozone level in the air we breathe? How many robberies have been committed (not how many have been reported)? What is the infant mortality rate? Is life expectancy going up? What are the third-grade reading levels? How well do the armed forces fight?

The other form of performance assessment is **program evaluation.** This is an individual, systematic study conducted periodically or on an ad hoc basis to assess how well a program is working. It is often conducted by experts external to the program, either inside or outside the agency, as well as by program managers. A program evaluation typically examines achievement of program objectives in the context of other aspects of program performance. So, a program evaluation would look—as would performance measurement—at the outcome of a program. But unlike a performance measurement, it might also look at other aspects of the program: its side effects, its logic, its efficiency, its consistency with legislative intent, its fairness, and its intervention effect. (For example, is the program causing crime to drop or is it something else, like the economy?)

Having compared and contrasted these two types of program assessment—performance measurement and program evaluation—let's take a closer look at each.

Performance Measurement   The belief that mission and performance are hopelessly at odds in government and nonprofit organizations is widespread because there is no bottom line like profits. This belief is flawed.

> Performance and mission are never in conflict if performance is properly understood and defined. In fact, whether we're talking about a business or a nonprofit organization, performance is impossible without a mission. . . . [For example,] if the mission of a museum is to be cultural custodian for society, then the proper performance measure is the content and value of its holdings. Today most museums have a different mission: cultural advocates. Accordingly, the performance measure must change. It might be to expand the audience (measure: number of visitors) or it might be to build a loyal clientele of genuine patrons (measure: number of museum memberships sold).[27]

Let's now see how local, state, and federal governments measure performance. Effective mayors know how their constituents evaluate. The latter might not understand the sophisticated methods of a social scientist, but they understand the street in front of their house. That is why some mayors have a keen interest in measuring things like the amount of street lighting and the average time to fill a pothole after it has been reported. Performance measures also tell them how much service their constituents are getting for their dollars.

More and more states are creating genuinely useful reports from their performance measurement. And, as with virtually all information, the ease of the Internet has made them widely usable. For example, the Arkansas Department of Human Services and the Arkansas Foundation for Medical Care released a report assessing the quality of care received by the state's 600,000 plus Medicaid recipients. The report compared, or "benchmarked," results from its own primary care physicians with information obtained by the nonprofit National Committee for Quality Assurance, which collects data on performance of managed-care organizations. Progress was tracked, in many instances, for individual counties showing where service improved over a two-year period and where it declined.[28]

Government leaders who want to create useful performance reports have been helped by the Government Accounting Standards Board, which developed 16 criteria for good performance reporting (you can check these out at www.gasb.org).

The federal government spends over $2.4 trillion on 1213 separate programs. Are these programs achieving the desired results? As we saw earlier, President Clinton used GPRA to grapple with that question, and President Bush used PART. Three earlier presidents also had their own tools—and snappy acronyms—to answer that trillion dollar question:

- President Johnson launched his *Planning, Programming, and Budgeting System (PPBS)* in 1966 to "substantially improve our ability to decide among competing proposals for funds and to evaluate actual performance." The system was the first serious effort to link budgets to getting results, and a form of it remains in use at the Pentagon today. (More about PPBS in Chapter 11.)
- President Nixon followed with an effort called *Management by Objectives (MBO)*. This system attempted to identify the goals of federal programs so that it was easier to determine what results were expected of each program and where programs were redundant or ineffective. Nixon said, "By abandoning programs that have failed, we do not close our eyes to problems that exist; we shift resources to more productive use." (More about MBO in Chapter 9.)
- President Carter attempted to introduce a concept known as *zero-based budgeting (ZBB)* in 1977 to force each government program to prove its value each year. "It's not enough to have created a lot of government programs. Now we must make the good programs more effective and improve or weed out those which were wasteful or unnecessary," he told Congress and the American people in his 1979 State of the Union Address. (More about ZBB in Chapter 11.)

Few would dispute the idea behind performance measures: programs should receive taxpayer dollars only when they prove results. Yet making such systems work well can be difficult—and if the wrong measures are picked, the results can be counterproductive. An old saw in management circles is, "What gets measured, gets managed." It follows if one is measuring the wrong things, one must be managing badly. Consider the following examples:[29]

- A hospital uses low mortality rates as its primary goal. *Result:* When elderly patients seem close to death, they are quickly sent to a nursing home. They may die faster that way, but the hospital keeps its mortality rates low.

- A police department uses response time as a performance measure for car theft. *Result:* Deploying police cars to the scene of the crime as quickly as possible only means that the police get to see the grease spot were the car had been. Resources would have been better spent on gathering information by telephone and sending police out in search of the stolen car.

Program Evaluation   In the federal government, there are four types of program evaluation:

1. **Process** (or **implementation**) **evaluation** assesses the extent to which a program is operating as it was intended. It typically assesses program activities' conformance to statutory and regulatory requirements, program design, and professional standards or customer expectations.
2. **Cost–benefit and cost-effectiveness analyses** compare a program's outputs or outcomes with the costs (resources expended) to produce them. When applied to existing programs, they are also considered a form of program evaluation. Cost–benefit analysis aims to identify all relevant costs and benefits, usually expressed in dollar terms. Cost-effectiveness analysis assesses the cost of meeting a single goal or objective and can be used to identify the least costly alternative to meet that goal.
3. **Impact evaluation** looks at whether a program's objectives have been met. The aim here is to quantify what is happening to program participants. How many output units were delivered? Traditionally, when people think about program evaluation, impact evaluations are what they have in mind. Because they involve directly assessing output, they are relatively easy to design.
4. **Outcome evaluation** considers the long-term consequences of a program—assessing its actual effects on a problem. These evaluations are more difficult to design. For example, how does one assess the consequences of a program to eradicate poverty when so many other variables—other social programs, changing economic conditions, technological change, sociocultural change—can influence the long-term status of the problem? Indeed, how does one even measure "poverty"?

Process evaluation is a relatively straightforward exercise and needs no elaboration here. Because cost–benefit analysis is an analytical technique and has other applications besides evaluation, it will be discussed in the next chapter along with other important analytical techniques. That leaves us with two types of program evaluation: impact evaluation and outcome evaluation.

If ever there was a program that deserved impact evaluation, it is Head Start. In the 40 years that it has existed, Head Start has served more than 20 million children at a cost of $40 billion. Growing out of the war on poverty in the mid-1960s, Head Start was created to provide comprehensive health, social, educational, and mental health services to disadvantaged preschool children. The program was, however, built on a philosophy—not a hard-nosed evaluation.[30]

In the decade after Head Start's inception, many studies of the program's impact were conducted. One of the first was done in 1969 for the Office of Economic Opportunity by the Westinghouse Corporation. It found that summer Head Start programs produced no lasting gains in participants' cognitive or affective development and that full-year programs produced only marginal gains by grades one, two, and three.

In 1981, the U.S. Department of Health and Human Services contracted with CSR, Inc. to synthesize the findings of Head Start impact studies. CSR concluded that Head Start participants showed significant immediate gains in cognitive test scores, social-emotional test scores, and health status. Cognitive and social-emotional test scores of former Head Start students, however, did not *remain* superior in the long run to those disadvantaged children who did not attend Head Start.

Whereas impact evaluations assessing the output of Head Start were fairly straight-forward—just test the kids and see if their scores went up—outcome evaluations are a little trickier. To begin, outcome evaluations come in two forms: demonstration projects and field experiments. The philosophy of the **demonstration project** is quite simple: Before an admin-istrator launches a program nationwide—or citywide—he or she tries it in a few selected cities or regions. A good example of evaluation by a demonstration project is the Police Fleet Plan. According to this plan, police are allowed to take their police cars home with them for their private use in off-duty hours—thus putting a lot more police cars on the city streets. A city that had some interest in the possibility of adopting the Police Fleet Plan might try it first in a few precincts before adopting it citywide. The evaluation results were quite positive in the Urban Institute's study of the Indianapolis Police Fleet Plan: Auto thefts went down; and auto accidents went down; and outdoor crime, purse snatching, and robbery went down.

Here is another example of a demonstration project. Why do low-income parents fail to vaccinate their children? Common sense would suggest it is because they cannot afford high vaccine prices. But Bernard Giuyer and associates report that despite Medicaid payments, free vaccine, and available pediatricians, the vaccination rate among low-income Baltimore children remained low because parents would not make appointments to get the shots.[31] Demonstration projects show that parents are more likely to get vaccinations if the department warns that certain government benefits will be terminated if that household's children remain unvaccinated.

With the problems facing public administrators becoming ever more complex, it is a good idea to replace some of the talk and analysis with tests. More specifically, Tom Peters suggests that managers substitute relatively cheap and quick pilots and prototypes—in other words, demonstration projects—for proposals and studies.[32]

The gold standard of outcome evaluations is, however, the randomized, controlled **field experiment.** This means, first, that individuals or groups are selected to be included in a new program entirely by chance and, second, that the program is observed under actual operating conditions ("in the field"). Finally, the results obtained from the participating individuals or groups are compared with results from a similar randomly selected **control group.**

Unlike program impact evaluations, which tend to be retrospective, the demonstra-tion project and field trial may be introduced into public programs either before a major operating program is started or simultaneously with a major operating program. But the principal difference between the field trial and the demonstration project is that in the field trial those responsible for the evaluation exercise have control over input variables (for example, purpose, staffing, clients, length of service, location, size of program, auspices, and management) and carefully measure outputs to determine the extent to which the project reaches its objectives. In short, the conditions are a little closer to those of the laboratory.

Let's consider one example of a field experiment. Can any program reduce teenage pregnancy? Based on a recent field experiment, we can say yes. But, before citing the study, review a little background. Studies of vocational education find no effect on sexual risk taking or pregnancy among teenagers. So far, abstinence-only education—an approach financed and favored by the federal government—has shown no effect on young people's behavior. But one program, created by Dr. Michael Carrera and the Children's Aid Society, has proven successful in a field experiment. The program offers not just traditional sex education, but also tutoring, SAT preparation, job skills, medical and dental care, and sports and creative arts. A three-year evaluation of its 12 sites in poor neighborhoods nationwide found participants had one-third fewer pregnancies than those in the control group.[33]

Concluding Observations

A good planning system should help public executives create an intelligent agenda and build a strong network to implement and evaluate programs. It should encourage them to think strategically, to consider both the long and short terms. It should provide leeway and options, so that as environmental conditions change, public executives can still use the planning system to help them achieve goals. It should not impose a rigid number-crunching requirement on agencies that does nothing but generate paper and distract managers from doing more important things. Quite the contrary: *every minute spent planning should save three or four in execution.*

Concepts for Review

contingency plan

control group

cost–benefit and cost-effectiveness
   analyses

crisis management plan (CMP)

demonstration project

field experiment

impact evaluation

incrementalism

logical incrementalism

mission statement

outcome evaluation

performance measurement

plan

planning

policy

process (or implementation) evaluation

program

program evaluation

rational planning process

regional planning

scenario planning

stakeholders

strategic management

strategy

tax expenditures

transaction costs

urban planning

Key Points

In this chapter we reviewed basic principles of planning and the various ways in which agencies can benefit from applying them, and we looked at the types of planning in which an agency can engage. The following points have been made in this chapter:

1. Planning is the keystone of the arch of program management, and management success is often synonymous with planning success. The essence of planning is to see opportunities and threats in the future and to exploit or combat them by decisions made in the present.

2. A policy is a statement of goals and the relative importance attached to each. A policy comprises one or more plans, and each plan, in turn, specifies objectives to be attained. A proposed set of specific actions intended to help implement a plan is called a program.

3. Once goals have been determined, managers may select a planning approach that is most appropriate for their situation. Critical to successful planning are flexibility and adaptability to changing environments. Managers have a number of planning approaches from which to choose. Among the most popular are the rational planning model, logical incrementalism, vision plans, urban and regional planning, contingency planning, and crisis management planning.

4. Incrementalism is an approach to policymaking that is conservative (in the sense of low risk) and practical (in the sense of politically expedient). It recommends that policymakers meet challenges slowly, by taking small—that is, incremental—steps.

5. Logical incrementalism is an approach to policymaking that builds on the assumption that logic dictates that administrators proceed flexibly and experimentally from broad ideas toward specific commitments.

6. Urban planning is the essential mechanism that a democratic society uses to deal with complex, interrelated problems such as suburban sprawl, neighborhood deterioration, visual blight, traffic congestion, air and water pollution, flooding, despoliation of the environment, an unstable tax base, and economic decline. Urban planning is the basic function of city government that deals with these issues in a comprehensive and coordinated manner.

7. Contingency plans define an organization's response to specific situations such as emergencies and setbacks. To develop contingency plans, administrators identify uncontrollable factors and then try to decide how to minimize the effects of those factors once they occur. A long-term version of contingency planning, scenario planning, involves identifying several alternative future scenarios or "future histories" and then adjusting existing plans to minimize the damage to a program if any of those scenarios should come to pass.

8. There are three essential steps in crisis management: prevention, preparation, and containment.

9. Government in the United States tends to focus more on supplying services than on anticipating problems and preventing them. Government is preoccupied with "rowing" (service delivery) rather than steering. As a result, government suffers from tunnel vision. Blind to the future, bureaucracies lurch from crisis to crisis. In contrast, anticipatory governments do everything possible to build foresight into their planning.

10. Many barriers that interfere with the agency's planning process are self-imposed. If administrators recognize them, they can remove them and facilitate planning. This chapter identified eight barriers: expecting continuance of the status quo, trying to do too much, getting emotionally involved, overplanning, underplanning, underestimating the importance of organizational structure, discounting leadership, and ignoring unintended consequences.

11. Strategic planning includes defining the organization's mission, setting its objectives, and developing strategies to enable it to operate successfully in its environment. The basic components of the strategic management process include not only strategic planning but also the implementation and evaluation phases. Strategic management is the entire set of decisions and actions used to formulate and implement strategies that will provide a good fit between the organization and its environment—and thereby achieve the organization's goals.

12. A program is a governmental action intended to secure objectives whose attainment is by no means certain without human effort. The degree to which the predicted consequences take place is called successful implementation. Implementation might be thought of as the nuts and bolts of the planning process.

13. Different implementation tools have different consequences. These consequences should be explored with respect to their administrative feasibility, effectiveness, efficiency, equity, and political feasibility.

14. Essentially there are two types of program performance assessment: performance measurement and program evaluation. Performance measurement is the ongoing monitoring and reporting of program accomplishments, particularly progress toward pre-established goals. Typically, program or agency management conducts it. Performance measurement should address program outcomes rather than program activities or outputs.

15. Program evaluations are individual, systematic studies conducted periodically or on an ad hoc basis to assess how well a program is working. They are often conducted by experts external to the program, either inside or outside the agency. A program evaluation typically examines achievement of program objectives in the context of other aspects of program performance or in the context in which it occurs.

16. In the federal government there are four types of program evaluation: process or implementation evaluation, cost–benefit and cost-effectiveness analysis, impact evaluation, and outcome evaluation.

Problems and Applications

1. Public officials at all levels of government are frequently criticized for making short-sighted decisions. Elected officials may be accused of looking forward only as far as the next election and of placing narrow, parochial interests above the general welfare. To what extent is such criticism justified? Do you see any solution?

2. Unlike several European countries, the United States does not have a full-fledged national planning body. Nonetheless, a number of institutions, such as the Council of

Economic Advisers, do have important planning functions. What other institutions would you say contribute to planning at the national level?

3. Some argue that forecasts designed to influence public planners are often so exaggerated and simplified that their effect is the very opposite of what their authors desire. Far from alerting planners to important problems, the doomsday forecast may so condition the planners to disaster that the capacity of the human race to survive is undermined. Discuss.

4. Strategic planning, as discussed in this chapter, implies a comprehensive, systematic scanning of the external environment of an organization. With the organization's basic mission in mind, administrators try to identify which parts of the environment are relevant for further study. List two to four questions that a college or university might want to consider under each of the following headings:

a. Economic

b. Demographic

c. Sociocultural

d. Political and regulatory

e. Technological

Favorite Bookmarks

www.csmweb.com   The Center for Strategic Management provides strategic management and consulting services to public and private organizations. The Web site provides useful links to more information on strategic management.

www.npr.gov   The National Performance Review's interactive site includes not only information on strategic management but an actual tool kit to help you do it.

Notes

1. Olaf Helmer, *Report on the Future of the Future* (Middleton, CT: IFF, 1968), 14–16.
2. David Halberstam, *The Best and the Brightest* (Greenwich, CT: Fawcett Books, 1969), 370–71.
3. Daniel P. Moynihan, *Coping: Essays on the Practice of Government* (New York: Random House, 1973), 273.
4. Definition adapted from Henry Mintzberg et al., *The Strategy Process* (Upper Saddle River, NJ: Prentice Hall, 2003), 10.
5. Joan Margretta, *What Management Is* (New York: Free Press, 2002), 91.
6. Henry Kissinger, *White House Years* (Boston: Little, Brown, 1979).
7. James Brian Quinn, *Strategies for Change: Logical Incrementalism* (Homewood, IL: Richard D. Irwin, 1980), 65–96.
8. Ibid., 81.
9. For example, people might begin to practice conservation seriously, which would make massive solar investment less necessary. Or they might decide that acres and acres of solar collectors are an eyesore, which would make tomorrow's solar industry as besieged as today's nuclear industry. Political upheavals overseas might cut off the U.S. supply of raw materials

needed to make photovoltaic cells. Even more likely are technological breakthroughs like fusion energy and hydrogen fuel from water that could make solar energy less attractive economically.

10. Graham T. Allison, *Essence of Decision* (Boston: Little, Brown, 1971).
11. Quinn, op. cit., 35.
12. Ibid., 58.
13. Christopher Swope, "Mastery of the Public Realm," *Governing* (November 2003): 36.
14. Halberstam, op. cit., 640.
15. Philip Bobbitt, "Seeing the Futures," *The New York Times* (December 8, 2003).
16. Ian I. Mitroff and Murat C. Alpaslan, "Preparing for Evil," *Harvard Business Review* (April 2003): 109–15.
17. Ibid., 112.
18. W. Timothy Coombs, *Ongoing Crisis Communication: Planning, Managing, and Responding* (Thousand Oaks, CA: Sage, 1999).
19. Henry Mintzberg et al., *The Strategy Process* (Englewood Cliffs, NJ: Prentice Hall, 2003); Gordon Chase, *Bromides for Public Managers,* Case N16-84-586 (Cambridge, MA: Kennedy School of Government, 1984); Barry Bozeman and J. D. Straussman, *Public Management Strategies* (San Francisco: Jossey-Bass, 1990); Edwin A. Locke et al., "The Determinants of Goal Commitment," *Academy of Management Review,* 13 (1998): 22–39.
20. The following discussion of underplanning is based on James Fallows, "Blind into Baghdad," *Atlantic* (January–February 2004); David Rieff, "Blueprint for a Mess," *The New York Times Magazine* (November 2, 2003); George Packer, "War after the War," *The New Yorker* (November 24, 2003); David Luhnow, "Amid Shortages, New U.S. Agency Tries to Run Iraq," *The Wall Street Journal* (June 5, 2003). For fresh detail on the war's planning and progress, and judicious analysis, see Michael Gordon and Bernard Trainor, *COBRA II: The Inside Story of the Invasion and Occupation of Iraq* (New York: Pantheon, 2006). The authors argue that underplanning turned the occupation of Iraq into a fiasco—a fiasco that proper planning could likely have avoided.
21. Neil R. Peirce, "Building Wider Roads Isn't Always the Best Answer," *Houston Chronicle* (January 24, 1999).
22. Tony Danker et al., *How Can American Government Meet Its Productivity Challenge?* (McKinsey & Co., July 2006).
23. See Government Accountability Office, High Performing Organizations: Metrics, Means, and Mechanisms for Achieving High Performance in the 21st Century Public Management Environment. GAO-04-343SP (February 2004).
24. Danker, op. cit., 14.
25. David Osborne and Ted Gaebler, *Reinventing Government* (Reading, MA: Addison-Wesley, 1992), 130–31.
26. U.S. General Accounting Office, *The Government Performance and Results Act: Government-Wide Implementation Will Be Uneven* (Washington, DC: U.S. Government Printing Office, 1997), 8–9.
27. Magretta, op. cit., 144.
28. Katherine Barrett and Richard Greene, "Plugging in," *Governing* (March 2006): 74.
29. Katherine Barrett and Richard Greene, "The Rise of Cost Accounting," *Governing* (March 2000): 60.
30. For a review of the newer research, see John T. Bruer, *The Myth of the First Three Years: A New Understanding of Early Brain Development and Lifelong Learning* (New York: Free Press, 2000); Alison Gopnik, Andrew N. Meltzoff, and Patricia K. Kuhl, *The Scientist in the Crib: Minds, Brains, and How Children Learn* (New York: Morrow, 1999).
31. Bernard Giuyer et al., "Immunization Coverage and Its Relationship to Preventive Health Care Visits among Inner-city Children in Baltimore," *Pediatrics,* 94, no. 1 (July 1994): 53–58.
32. Tom Peters, *Liberation Management* (New York: Knopf, 1992), 116–70.
33. Tamar Levin, "Program Finds Success in Reducing Teenage Pregnancy," *The New York Times,* (May 30, 2001): A16.

CASE 5.1
A STRATEGY IS
BORN

From the start of the U.S. invasion of Iraq in March 2003, a small group of American officers thought the plan for prosecuting the war was counterproductive and that, with a better plan, the war still might be won. These officers believed that the U.S. military had forgotten the experiences of Vietnam and had been training for something resembling World War II—not counterinsurgency warfare or low-intensity warfare. The generals never expected to fight a guerrilla insurgency in Iraq; and once it began, they concentrated almost entirely on killing and capturing as many insurgents as possible. So, villages were surrounded, doors kicked down, and scores of suspects apprehended. These practices alienated Iraqi civilians and produced new recruits for the insurgency.

By the summer of 2006, Iraq was in a state of anarchy. In Baghdad, 50 people were being kidnapped every day, often by the police. Increasingly, the kidnappers' targets were children, fewer and fewer of whom were being allowed by their parents to venture outside. Once snatched, the victims were typically offered for sale to one of the many kidnapping gangs.

The violence in Iraq was not random but had specific purposes and specific causes. Al Qaeda sought to start a full-scale sectarian war between the Sunnis and Shiites, believing such a war was their only hope of victory. To this end, that terrorist group unleashed suicidal attacks on Shiite civilians, hoping to provoke a backlash and a wider conflict. Indeed, Al Qaeda was increasingly taking over all of Sunni society.

In the first two years of the war, the country's Shiite leadership had held its fire in the face of the Sunni onslaught. Then came the elections in December 2005 that brought to power a Shiite-dominated government. Now, Iraq's new leaders were determined to crush the Sunni insurrection at any cost. Police and paramilitary units were turned loose in the Sunni neighborhoods, where they began massacring military-age men.

In the face of all this, the Americans decided to back away. From the summer of 2004 onward, the objective of the American strategy was less the defeat of the Sunni insurrection than the training and equipping of Iraqis to fight it for them. "As they stand up, we will stand down," President Bush was fond of saying. Iraq security forces had grown in quantity if not in quality and were taking over larger and larger pieces of the war. It was difficult in the summer of 2006 to drive around Baghdad and see any American soldiers. The trouble was that the strategy of Iraqification was manifestly failing, but the Bush administration kept pushing it anyway.

For all of the dramatic developments in Iraq, perhaps the greatest drama was taking place in Washington where very senior officers advocated a different strategy involving increasing U.S. presence and using U.S. forces to secure the population from insurgents rather than keeping them penned in and behind the blast-proof walls. Thomas D. Ricks, senior Pentagon correspondent for the *Washington Post*, chronicles the difficult birth of this "surge" strategy in Iraq and describes the personalities and events that reversed the U.S. strategy. There were three key players in the military establishment who brought about the difficult midcourse correction of U.S. strategy:

- General David Petraeus was the most prominent player. After returning from Iraq, where he had commanded the 101st Airborne Division during the invasion, he was sent to Leavenworth, Kansas, to command the U.S. Army's educational establishment and craft a new counterinsurgency manual. Drafted by a team familiar with the history of such conflicts, the manual prescribed a radical shift for the

U.S. military, away from the traditional focus on capturing and killing the enemy to one of recognizing that *the people are the prize.*

- General Jack Keane, a retired former Army vice chief of staff, was the motivating force. He launched what Ricks calls a "guerrilla campaign" in the defense establishment to get these new ideas accepted at the highest level.

- General Raymond Odierno, assistant to the chairman of the Joint Chiefs of Staff, worked with Keane—largely behind the scenes and often outside the chain of command—trying to sell their model of a workable strategy, even as the war was at its bleakest stage and calls for a pullout were mounting.

Translating ideas into plans is difficult. Surge advocates, for example, faced entrenched interests and inflated egos. Fortunately, Petraeus, Keane, and Odierno would get help from four key actors outside the military. In June 2006 President Bush met with sympathetic war critics at Camp David. Elliott Cohen, Michael Vickers, Fred Kagan, and Robert Kaplan—the first three men, respected national security experts; the last, an influential journalist—were generally supportive of the war but critical of current strategy. They were invited to tell Bush how it might be better run. The meeting didn't sway Bush, but it set in motion a behind-the-scenes effort to change the course of the war. That effort began to take hold after the midterm elections in November, when strong gains by the Democrats led Bush to dismiss Donald Rumsfeld as defense secretary and replace him with Robert Gates

In early December, Cohen, together with Keane and several others, again met with Bush, and this time the professor was determined to be clearer and more emphatic than he had been the previous June, stressing the need for a new strategy, a change in commanders, and more troops.

Meanwhile, General Odierno was doing the same from Baghdad. Taking over as the number two commander in Iraq, he became dissatisfied with the strategy being pursued by the then commanding officer. The chain of command is normally sacrosanct in the military, but Odierno, "making one of the most audacious moves of the entire war," bypassed two levels of command

above him to talk to officials at the White House and aides to the Joint Chiefs of Staff. In doing so, Ricks writes, he "was laying his career on the line."

The efforts of Cohen, Keane, and Odierno paid off in January 2007: Petraeus became the new commander in Iraq with a promise of 30,000 extra troops to support the 126,000 already there. After Petraeus took over, his counterinsurgency field manual became the cornerstone of a strategy. To help carry out the plan, Petraeus assembled a team dominated by military officers who possessed doctorates from top-flight universities as well as combat experience. Also present were many dissidents, skeptics, and outsiders, some of them foreigners. For example, they included David Kilcullen, a freewheeling former Australian Army officer who enjoyed semi-mythical status as Petraeus' counterinsurgency adviser and Emma Sky, a pacifist British expert in Middle East affairs. To her own surprise, Sky became an admirer of the U.S. military. "I love them," she said, adding, "they're better than the country they serve. That's the way I feel about it—America doesn't deserve its military."

Petraeus took as his model for what he was trying to achieve the cowboy painting *The Stampede* by Frederic Remington. Iraq was never going to be a case study in democracy; everything would have to be pretty rough and ready. "Sustainable stability" was the minimalist objective. In Petraeus' words: "We're just trying to get the cattle to Cheyenne."

The surge worked for a number of reasons, one of the biggest being luck. The insurgency had always been a many-headed beast, with no overarching leadership. As the war dragged on, it was the murderous members of Al Qaeda who gained the upper hand. Al Qaeda's gunmen killed everyone—the traditional Sunni tribal leaders, for instance—who did not share their extreme goals.

But then, in late 2006 came the Sunni backlash. In Arabic, it was called the Awakening. Squeezed by Al Qaeda on the one side and the Shiite death squads on the other, the sheiks turned to the Americans to save them. Soon American officers were making deals with sheiks across the Sunni heartland and into western Baghdad. This was possible in large part because Sunni Iraq is still a tribal society. Make a deal with the sheik— promise security, hand him a bag of money—and he can plausibly deliver the rest of his tribe.

Could the surge have worked without the Awakening? Ricks thinks that this question is somewhat irrelevant, because as things played out the two reinforced each other. The surge brought the security that allowed the sheiks to come forward, and the Awakening rapidly took thousands of potential enemies out of the war.

Case Questions

1. Which planning model do you think best represents the events described in this case—the rational planning model (pages 213–15) or logical incrementalism (214–15)?

2. Governmental planning takes many diverse forms. A very partial list of large-scale governmental planning activities would have to include at least the following: planning for the conservation and use of natural resources, city planning, planning for full employment, planning for personal and family security, planning for agriculture, and planning for the improvement of government organization. What lessons do you see in this case that might be relevant to these other planning activities?

3. Ricks concludes that the surge, although successful on the tactical level, faltered on the strategic one. What do you think he means? Does Petraeus' group bear any responsibility?

Case References

Thomas E. Ricks, *The Gamble: General David Petraeus and the American Military Adventure in Iraq, 2006–2008* (New York: Penguin Press, 2009); Kimberly Kagan, *The Surge: A Military History* (New York: Encounter, 2009).

6 Decision Making

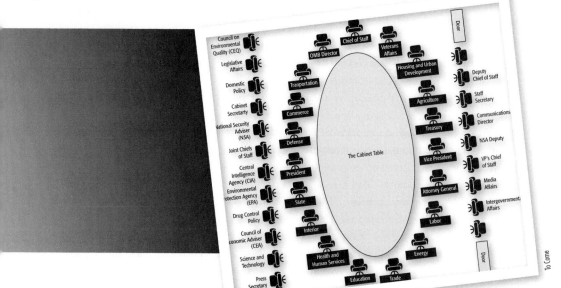

Labels (clockwise from upper left):
Council on Environmental Quality (CEQ), Legislative Affairs, Domestic Policy, Cabinet Secretarty, National Security Adviser (NSA), Joint Chiefs of Staff, Central Intelligence Agency (CIA), Environmental Protection Agency (EPA), Drug Control Policy, Council of Economic Adviser (CEA), Science and Technology, Press Secretary

OMB Director, Chief of Staff, Veterans Affairs, Door

Tranportation, Commerce, Defense, President, State, Interior, Health and Human Services, Education, Trade, Energy, Labor, Attorney General, Vice President, Treasury, Agriculture, Housing and Urban Development

Deputy Chief of Staff, Staff Secretary, Communications Director, NSA Deputy, VP's Chief of Staff, Media Affairs, Intergovernment: Affairs, Door

The Cabinet Table

To Come

DECIDING HOW TO DECIDE

Former Treasury Secretary Paul H. O'Neill told Barack Obama during his 2008 presidential campaign that he needed to set up a rigorous process to solicit ideas on policy, bring all the facts to the president, and come to conclusions in a structured way, with "honest brokers," or neutral mediators, watching the process. Facing big issues, Obama picked big personalities, saying he wanted advisers who would be teammates as well as rivals, long on experience and brainpower, and able to hear all sides of an issue to help him decide. David Axelrod, Obama's senior political strategist, explains: "The president invites debate, but he doesn't tolerate factionalism. And ultimately everybody on the economic team knows that at the end of the day we're going to hold hands and jump together."

The president's choice for director of the National Economic Council was Lawrence H. Summers. President Bill Clinton created the council to be the economic equivalent of the National Security Council—a White House body designed to coordinate advice and action from many other agencies. The National Economic Council was supposed to complement, in particular, the White House Council of Economic Advisers (CEA), which houses academic economists who run numbers and advise the president on technical matters of policy, and the Treasury Department, which typically dominates policymaking, with its offices of tax policy, domestic finance, and international affairs. Summers, the only top economic adviser with a West Wing office, would control the daily economic briefings with the president.

As messy as the decision-making process has sometimes been, insiders say Summers and his colleagues have worked through their differences. Summers has forcefully debated with Christina Romer, chairwoman of the CEA, over how best to make the economic case for changing health-care policy; Treasury Secretary Timothy Geithner over what to do with troubled banks; Peter Orszag, the budget director, over fiscal and health policy issues; and Austan Goolsbee, an economist on the CEA, over whether to rescue Chrysler.

Insiders say Summers's argumentative style has delayed some actions. "The advice I give," he says, "is based on determining the right course of economic action, recognizing all of the political factors." As he sees it, his penchant for debate fits his job as the chief White House economic adviser. "My approach in these things is to be always raising objections and concerns because if you haven't anticipated the objections and concerns, you haven't minimized risk." He adds: "I certainly favored identifying every possibility and presenting every option to the president in response to possible contingencies."

Orszag describes Summers's role this way: "Larry Summers is one of the world's most brilliant economists. He enriches any discussion he participates in, which is particularly valuable given the complexity and importance of the challenges currently facing us."

Geithner describes the role this way: "Larry will come to any issue and say, well, here's all the 16 reasons why there's problems with that proposal. If he's got ideas, particularly if I think they will work, I say to him, 'Well, why don't you make the case against it, Larry, because you're pretty good at making the case against anything.'" But Geithner says that trait makes Summers a good director of the economic council because "he is better than anybody else on the planet at framing the case for and against any particular issue, and reducing something to a set of concrete options." All that said, Geithner also told an interviewer that he was "completely comfortable pushing back at him."

Perhaps no chief executive can assemble a group of really bright people and deal with exceedingly complex problems and not expect to have disagreements. Let's consider two examples:

- Summers, Geithner, and Axelrod disagreed with Goolsbee over whether to bail out Chrysler if a reasonable merger with Fiat could be arranged. Goolsbee argued that rescuing the financial system was one thing, since credit is the economy's life-blood, but the government should not run an automobile company. The arguments became so heated that Summers stormed out of one meeting. Although later he included Goolsbee's objections in a memo to the president, Summers excluded him from the decisive meeting on Chrysler in the Oval Office. During the meeting, when Romer expressed Goolsbee's objections, Obama noticed the author of those objections was not there. So, the president had an aide fetch him in order that he could personally make his case. Although later that evening Obama decided on a course that Summers supported, Goolsbee at least had a chance to give his opinion.

- When Romer released a report stating that health-care reform could make American business more competitive globally, Summers challenged her to support that assertion. He did so again in a well-attended meeting. But Romer cut him off, saying some of his own staff agreed with her and she did not put "schlocky arguments" in her papers. Summers replied he was not making a "schlocky argument." Romer later described the exchange as "good-natured," like an academic seminar.

Wanting to avoid insularity and perhaps further complicating economic decision-making, Obama has also added an Economic Recovery Advisory Board headed by former Federal Reserve chair Paul Volcker. This 15-member panel of outside experts from labor, business, and academe advise the president about his efforts to fix the worst economic crisis in decades. Like Summers, Volcker is a "great cross-examiner, good at drawing in different points of view and pondering them. That can delay decision making, but it means he is less likely to hopscotch from one idea to the next."

The Obama administration has tried to shape a decision-making process so that it will tend to yield more constructive dialogue and debate among team members rather than strong pressures for conformity. In deciding how to decide, executives must address several key questions. Who should be involved in the decision-making process? In what type of environment does the decision take place? What are the "means of dialogue" among the participants? And how will the leader control the process and content of the decision? How well has the Obama administration addressed these questions?

SOURCES: Caren Bohan, "Is Obama Creating an Economic Team of Rivals?" Reuters (February 6, 2009); Jackie Calmes, "President's Economic Circle Keeps Tensions at a Simmer," *The New York Times A1 and All* (June 8, 2009); Jonathan Weissman, "Summers Carves out a Powerful Role," *The Wall Street Journal* p. A6 (February 2, 2009).

Decision making involves *selecting one course of action from various alternatives*. As such, it cannot be divorced from the planning process described in the preceding chapter. Herbert Simon maintains that the "task of 'deciding' pervades the entire administrative organization quite as much as does the task of 'doing'—indeed, it is integrally tied up with the latter."[1]

There are at least four steps in decision making:

1. Identifying the problem (or opportunity)
2. Gathering facts
3. Making the decision
4. Implementing and evaluating the decision

This chapter explores each of these steps.

Identifying the Problem (or Opportunity)

Let's begin by stipulating that administrative problems differ in fundamental ways and that knowing what *type* of problem we are dealing with can help avoid costly mistakes. For instance:

1. Is the problem a pressing one or a dispensable one?
2. Is the "problem" really a symptom masking the underlying problem or a root cause that contributes to actual problems?
3. Is the problem sui generis (one of a kind) or generic (one of a family of quite similar problems)?

The first question to ask about a problem is, When does the problem require a decision? Some problems are pressing and must be decided on immediately. Others are dispensable, and the decision can be deferred, say, until next month. In that case, that is when you make the decision—next month. After all, between now and then, new information, unexpected developments, and—perish the thought—better ideas might surface.

Let us now turn to the second pair of problem types: symptoms and root causes. As suggested in Figure 6.1, many problems that a manager faces are really part of a pattern of problems stemming from one underlying cause. Because this underlying cause is seldom obvious, the tendency is to view the symptoms as the problem and treat them as such. Thus, administrators often find themselves treating symptoms A, B, C, and D rather than the root cause, E.

Effective administrators know that very few problems or events are isolated. Most are manifestations of underlying problems. Therefore, before attempting a quick fix on problems A through D, they try to discover the basic problem, E. Once E is solved, A, B, C, D, and any future problems stemming from E are eliminated. Thus, effective decision makers make few decisions.

Is this not what a good physician does? If the patient complains, on separate visits, of increased thirst, itching, hunger, weight loss, weakness, and nausea, the physician does not simply try to remedy each symptom on an ad hoc basis but, rather, tries to determine the

Figure 6.1   Effective Administrators Make Fewer Decisions Because They Focus on the Root Causes of a Problem (E) — Not the Symptoms (A, B, C, and D)

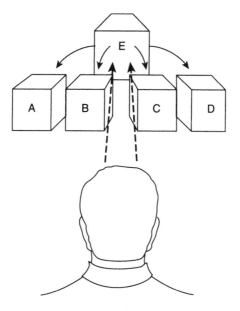

problem that seems to be causing these symptoms. In contrast, too many administrators are forever engaged in quick fixes and cosmetic solutions.

Now let us consider the third pair of problems: sui generis and generic. The former, which takes its name from the Latin for "of its own kind," refers to a problem that constitutes a class alone. Such problems require unique solutions. An agency such as the National Aeronautics and Space Administration (NASA) probably has more than its share of sui generis problems because so much of its work involves new technology. The U.S. military faces two sui generis problems: how to treat openly gay personnel and whether women should be in combat units. And, as we will see in Chapter 12, the information revolution has created a number of such problems throughout the public sector.

But we must be careful. Most problems facing a manager are part of a class—they are generic and occur over and over. An inexperienced detective might treat every case as unique, whereas a more experienced one recognizes that most crimes conform to a pattern. That is why it was disingenuous for the experienced detectives in the O. J. Simpson case to say he was not a suspect from the start. Of the approximately 5000 women murdered every year, about 30 percent are killed by their current or former husband or boyfriend.

By the same token, inexperienced managers tend to treat far too many problems as unique. How do you tell a valuable employee you can't give her a raise? What do you say to an otherwise good performer who has a sexist attitude? How do you control someone who monopolizes the discussion at every meeting? Experienced managers do not have to search far for solutions.

Gathering Facts (ability to solve prob)

Framing a Decision

With the problem accurately defined, the administrator then turns to framing the response. Here, careful attention should be given to what are called the upper and lower limits of the decision.

Upper limits of a decision refer to the ever-present limitations that determine how far the administrator can go. One former presidential aide notes five:[2]

1. The limits of permissibility (Is it legal? Will others accept it?)
2. The limits of available resources
3. The limits of available time
4. The limits of previous commitments
5. The limits of available information

The list is self-explanatory, but the final point merits emphasis simply because administrators rely so much on experience in making decisions. The experienced administrator believes, often without realizing it, that past mistakes and accomplishments are an almost infallible guide in decision-making situations. But this is a fallacy. Administrators must try to visualize the world as a whole and as a total system in which their personal experiences are a very small and inadequate sample. A corrective to the tendency to generalize from personal experience is to use statistical analysis. Modern statistics is based on the concept of probability; it deals with making a judgment regarding the probability of a characteristic occurring in a population (for example, a certain level of income) on the basis of information derived from a small sample of that population.

Lower limits of a decision refer to what, at least, must occur for the problem to be solved. For example, Germany knew at the outbreak of World War I that it could win if and only if two minimum conditions were met: Germany would (condition 1) put up weak resistance against Russia, thus allowing Russia to (condition 2) concentrate forces for a knockout blow to France. But as Russia began to penetrate deeper and deeper into East Prussia, the German general staff decided to pull forces from the Western front. Condition 2, therefore, was not met and the chance for victory was lost.[3]

Chester I. Barnard introduced an idea quite similar to that of lower limits, which he called the **limiting (strategic) factor in decision making.** It is the factor "whose control, in the right form, at the right place and time, will establish a new system of conditions which meets the purpose. Thus, if we wish to increase the yield of grain in a certain field, and we analyze the soil, it may appear that the soil lacks potash; potash may be said to be the strategic (or limiting) factor."[4] If an administrator can discover the strategic factor—can exercise control at the right times and in the right place, right amount, and right form—then the decision becomes not only simpler (for other factors tend to work themselves out) but also more economical.

Here is an example of how the concept of the strategic factor could apply in public administration. Between 1990 and 1994, 155 residents of Boston under the age of 21 were killed by guns. Over a two-year period after Operation Cease-Fire began, not a single juvenile in Boston was killed by a firearm. Operation Cease-Fire started with the realization that a relatively small number of juvenile offenders were both the perpetrators and victims in the cycle of violence. From 1990 to 1994, 75 percent of the teenage homicide victims had criminal records; 60 percent of them were involved in gang activities. Because many actual—as well as potential—victims were well known to the authorities, the strategy was to target resources on youth with prior criminal records.

Schematically, we can think of every possible solution to a problem as being represented by a point shown in the following figure. Solutions in the top section, however, must be ruled out because they violate the upper limits of a decision. Solutions at the bottom must also be ruled out because they fail to satisfy the lower limits of a successful decision. Although this schematic does not directly provide a solution, it does drastically reduce the number of possible solutions an administrator might have to consider.

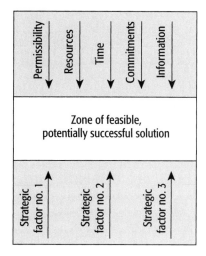

Consulting People

Even kings and queens consult advisers. Queen Elizabeth did not defeat the Spanish in 1588 by reading *Teach Thyself to Thrash Armadas*. No, she consulted underlings. It is also generally a good idea to consult those who will be most affected by the decision, checking your facts with theirs and, above all, *listening* to what they have to say (more about this in Chapter 8).

Effective planning calls for a multiplicity of inputs. To achieve this multiplicity, the planner must studiously avoid becoming the captive of any one group of advisers or experts. To emphasize this point, we might cite one example from the Kennedy administration. Shortly after the Bay of Pigs disaster, a number of members of the Kennedy circle became increasingly uneasy with the decision-making processes of the administration. Arthur Goldberg, the new secretary of labor, finally asked the president why he had not consulted more widely, why he had taken such a narrow spectrum of advice, much of it so predictable. Kennedy said that he meant no offense, that even though Goldberg was a good man, he was in labor, not in foreign policy.

"You're wrong," Goldberg replied. "You're making the mistake of compartmentalizing your cabinet." The secretary then went on to point out—much to the president's surprise—that the two men in the cabinet who should have been consulted were Orville Freeman, the secretary of agriculture, and himself. Freeman had been a Marine, made amphibious landings and knew how tough such landings can be; and Goldberg had been in the Office of Strategic Services (the forerunner of the CIA) during World War II and had run guerilla operations.[5]

A similar mistake occurred early in the Clinton administration. Consider whom President Bill Clinton failed to bring into the decision-making loop when crafting his health-care reform proposal. First was Secretary of Treasury Lloyd Bentsen, who as a senator had written more health-care legislation than anyone in the Clinton administration. Second was Secretary of Health and Human Services Donna Shalala, who had more expertise in her department than anyone else. Then there was Director of the Office of Management and Budget Leon Panetta, another experienced legislator, and his deputy, Alice Rivlin, the former head of the Congressional Budget Office. Also out of the loop on a policy that could have affected one-seventh of the American economy was Laura Tyson at the Council of Economic Advisers. As two distinguished journalists were later to observe: "Issues these people raised inside the administration were the same ones that later undermined the credibility of the Clinton plan on Capitol Hill. But because they lacked those campaign battle scars, their advice was not heeded."[6]

These four decision-making steps—identify the problem, gather the facts, make the decision, and then implement it—provide a timeless, general introduction to the art of decision making. Before turning to modern techniques for improving that process, some historical perspective is useful. Humans have perpetually sought new tools and concepts to help them make decisions. Figure 6.2 presents a small sample of the people, events, and thinking that have contributed to our current understanding of the subject.

Figure 6.2   Decision Making Through History

Fourth Century B.C.

Plato and Aristotle   Unlike Plato, Aristotle seeks truth by examining the actual rather than speculating on the ideal. Indeed, the very first words of his

Politics are "Observation shows us." Raphael illustrates the difference at the center of his *School of Athens*. Plato is gesturing upward to the heavens as if to say to Aristotle that all perceivable things are derived from eternal archetypes, that the great axioms of politics can be deduced as, say, a theorem of geometry. In contrast, Aristotle has his hand outstretched and is looking ahead, not upward.

333 B.C.

Alexander the Great   King Gordius tied his wagon to a temple with a knot so baffling that an oracle said that the man who untied it would become lord of all Asia. This piqued Alexander's interest. He performed the task by drawing his sword and

Aristotle and Plato: detail of School of Athens, 1510–11 (fresco) (detail of 472); Raphael (Raffaello Sanzio of Urbino) (1483–1520) / © Vatican Museums and Galleries, Vatican City, Italy, / ©The Bridgeman Art Library

simply cutting the knot in two. Today "to cut the Gordian knot" means to solve a baffling problem by a single bold, incisive action. Professors are paid to say, "On the one hand. . . ." Leaders are paid to decide. The Marine Corps deals with "decidophobia"—the tendency to continue gathering ever more information and thereby putting off a tough decision—with the *70 percent solution*. If you have 70 percent of the information, have done 70 percent of the analysis, and feel 70 percent confident, then move.

49 B.C.

Julius Caesar   The Rubicon, a river in Italy, marked the boundary between Roman Italy and Gaul, where Julius Caesar governed. When Caesar crossed it, he had invaded the Roman Republic, and there was no going back. Thus, the expression "crossing the Rubicon" became synonymous with taking an irreversible step. Unfortunately, sometimes we think we've taken this "irreversible" step because so much blood and treasure have been sunk into a project. A *sunk cost* should be ignored in decisions about future actions.

Fourteenth Century

William Occam   Occam's razor, the philosophical principle of economy or parsimony, holds that an explanation should contain only those elements absolutely necessary. Bottom line: If you have two or more satisfactory explanations of some phenomenon, then go with the shortest.

Seventeenth Century

Hobson's Choice   An obscure English innkeeper, Hobson, kept some 40 horses on the side to rent. He put his mounts on a strict stall-to-stall rotation basis so that the best horses wouldn't be ruined by overuse. When you rented a horse from Hobson, you rented the horse nearest the stable door—no matter what your preference. Hence, a Hobson's choice is no choice.

René Descartes   Like Francis Bacon (1561–1626), Descartes (1596–1650) derived inspiration from what appeared to be the defects of contemporary decision making: He also perceived the lack of any precisely formed method of inquiry. For Descartes, the aim of any inquiry is certainty, and knowledge could only spring from complete objectivity. He formulated a set of rules that, ideally, compose an infallible method whose application is mechanical and universal. Although this method has worked splendidly in the physical sciences, some contemporary scholars see its application as far more limited in the human sciences. These scholars accuse colleagues who always insist on scientific rigor in studying the subtleties of human interactions as suffering from "physics envy."

Blaise Pascal   Pascal corresponded with the lawyer-mathematician Fermat, and together they worked on problems sent to them by a certain gentleman gambler who was puzzled as to why he lost money by betting on the appearance of certain combinations in the fall of three die. In the course of settling the matter, the two men founded the modern theory of probability. This

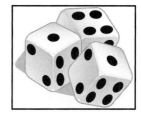

(Continued)

Figure 6.2   *(continued)*

had incalculable importance, for it showed that one could intelligently make decisions under conditions of uncertainty. In 1921, Frank Knight would distinguish *uncertainty* from *risk:* In the former, an outcome's probability is unknowable; in the latter, an outcome's probability can be known and consequently insured against.

Eighteenth Century

Adam Smith   Today Smith's reputation rests on his explanation of how rational self-interest in a free-market economy leads to economic well-being. In the mid-20th century, a group of economists (known as *public choice theorists*) would take the same principle and apply it to people's actions in collective decision making. (See page 311.) Smith also provides the most famous example of the positive unintended consequences of decisions: He maintained that each individual seeking only his own gain "is led by an invisible hand to promote an end which was no part of his intentions," that end being the public interest. "It is not from the benevolence of the butcher, or the baker, that we expect our dinner," Smith wrote, "but from regard to their own self-interest."

© CORBIS

Nineteenth Century

Oliver Wendell Holmes   "The life of the law," Holmes said, "has not been logic, it has been experience." Judges should base decisions not merely on statutes but on the good sense of reasonable members of the community. In this sense, Holmes was in the Aristotelian decision-making camp—not that of Plato or Descartes.

1900

Sigmund Freud   Why does Freud—history's most debunked doctor—still captivate us? His core idea, upon which his reputation must rest, is that causes hidden in the mind often influence our decisions and actions. For example, Freud concluded that Napoleon's rivalry with his brother Joseph was the driving force of his decision making—accounting for his pursuit of Josephine in matrimony and his decision to invade Egypt.

1907

Irving Fisher   Economist Fisher introduced the concept of net present value. When public administrators try to compare the cost and benefits of a project over, say, a 10-year period, they discount future costs and benefits to reflect their present value. See page 271.

1947

Herbert Simon   Rejecting Descartes' notion that decision makers can and should always act perfectly rationally, Simon argues that because of the costs of acquiring information, managers make decisions with only *bounded rationality*—they have limits, or boundaries, on how rational they can be. See page 291. Research conducted by Simon and his colleagues at the Carnegie Institute of Technology contributed greatly to the development of early computer-based decision-support tools. See Chapter 12.

1961

Joseph Heller   In Heller's novel *Catch-22*, American pilots during World War II, forced to fly an excessive number of dangerous missions, could not be relieved of duty unless they were diagnosed as insane. On the other hand, the regulations stipulated that a pilot who refused to fly so that he wouldn't be killed could not be insane because he was thinking too clearly. Today, catch-22 means a decision situation in which there is no way out—an insoluble dilemma, a double bind.

1968

Irving Janis   Irving Janis coined the term "groupthink" for flawed decision making that values consensus over the best result. See page 285.

1972

Michael Cohen, James March, and John Olsen   These three scholars give us a "garbage can model" of organizational decision making. Flowing through organizations are three separate streams: problems, solutions, and choice opportunities (or political climate). Individuals drift in and out of decision-making situations carrying pet problems and solutions with them, looking for windows of opportunity in which they might be aired. Thus, an organization is a kind of garbage can into which participants randomly dump various kinds of problems and solutions. Decisions then are a

function of the mix of garbage (problems, solutions, and political climate). Bottom line: Organizations should search their informational trash bins for solutions thrown out earlier for lack of a problem.

1979

Amos Tversky and Daniel Kahneman   Faced with the uncertainties of real life, do people coolly calculate their self-interest and then rationally reason toward an optimal decision? Not according to these two economists. Often people will use rules of thumb or heuristics to solve problems. See page 294.

2005

Malcolm Gladwell   In *Blink*, Gladwell introduces a range of case studies and experts, including art historians who can tell within seconds that a statue is a fake and a psychologist who can predict whether a couple will get divorced after observing them for only a few minutes. But do your instincts make good decisions? It depends on your education level. The instincts of veteran firefighters have been shaped by years of experience, so when something tells them to stay off that staircase, there's usually a good reason. Less-experienced firefighters perform worse at fire scenes, research suggests, because they lack such subconscious triggers.

© AP/Wide World Photos

SOURCES: Robert Hendrickson, *Word and Phrase Origins* (New York: Checkmark Books, 2000); Michael Useem and Jerry Useem, "Great Escapes: Nine Decision-Making Pitfalls," *Fortune* (June 27, 2005); Leigh Buchanan and Andrew O'Connell, "A Brief History of Decision-Making," *Harvard Business Review* (January 2006); and Isaac Asimov, *A Biographical Encyclopedia of Science and Technology* (New York: Avon books, 1972).

Making the Decision: Five Analytical Techniques

After gathering facts and suggestions, the decision maker should be ready to begin assessing the various alternatives. In this section, we shall consider five *analytical* techniques that can help the administrator in this critical task:

1. Cost–benefit analysis
2. Multiobjective models
3. Decision analysis
4. Systems analysis
5. Nominal group technique

This section emphasizes one particular style of thinking. The analytical method is founded on formal logic; it seeks to break situations down into their component parts and to define problems by isolating them, thus making them more manageable. There are, however, limitations to this way of looking at the world. The last section of this chapter will consider them.

Cost–Benefit Analysis

In an era of scarcity, interest in weighing costs against benefits rises. Today the federal government must do more than assess the benefits of goals such as a cleaner environment, safer products, healthier working conditions, and better mass transit—it must also weigh the costs and other side effects of such action.

The methodology for these kinds of assessments has been around at least since 1936. That was the year that **cost–benefit analysis (CBA)** became a requirement of the Flood Control Act, which established the policy that "the federal government should improve or participate in the improvement of navigable water . . . for flood-control purposes if the benefits to whomsoever they may accrue are in excess of the estimated costs."

Most CBA involves familiarity with certain common elements: the measurement of costs and benefits, the distributional impacts, the discount factor, and the decision rules. The following sections will examine each of these elements.

Measurement of Costs and Benefits   Assume that the U.S. Army Corps of Engineers is about to dig a ditch. To capture all the effects of digging this ditch, the analyst must proceed systematically, breaking down costs and benefits into major categories.

These categories are shown along with examples in Table 6.1. **Real benefits** are the benefits derived by the final consumer of the public project and, as such, represent an addition to the community's total welfare. They must, however, be balanced against the **real costs** of resources withdrawn from other uses in order to provide that public project.

Pecuniary benefits and **pecuniary costs** "come about due to changes in relative prices that occur as the economy adjusts itself to the provision of the public service. As a result, gains accrue to some individuals but are offset by losses that accrue to others. They do not

Table 6.1	Major Categories of Costs and Benefits for Irrigation Project	
Category	Costs	Benefits
Real		
Direct		
Tangible	Costs of pipes	Increased farm output
Intangible	Loss of wilderness	Beautification of area
Indirect		
Tangible	Diversion of water	Reduced soil erosion
Intangible	Destruction of wildlife	Preservation of rural society
Pecuniary		Relative improvement in position of farm equipment industry

SOURCE: R.A. Musgrave and P.B. Musgrave, *Public Finance in Theory and Practice* (New York: McGraw-Hill, 1973), 142. Reprinted by permission of the publisher.

reflect gains to society as a whole."[7] For example, say that earnings of roadside restaurants increase because of a highway project. Such gains do not reflect a net gain to society because they are offset by costs to others (that is, restaurants and grocery stores elsewhere lose business). Or consider building a new stadium. In calculating the *benefits* of building a new stadium, or remodeling an existing one, promoters tend to count pecuniary benefits such as ticket sales and new jobs as pure benefit, when they are not. A ticket sold at the ballpark on a Saturday afternoon is a ticket not sold at the movie theater; in any event, there is that much less money in a citizen's wallet. Similarly, benefits of the job "created" might be canceled by a job taken away from a local industry—after all, a worker cannot be in two places at once. For these reasons, we cannot ignore the pecuniary effects in cost–benefit analysis.

Real benefits and costs can be either direct or indirect. **Direct benefits and costs** are those closely related to the main project objective. **Indirect benefits and costs**—sometimes called **externalities** or **spillovers**—are more like by-products. Admittedly, the line between direct and indirect can be fuzzy, requiring a judgment call by the analyst.

The term **tangible** is applied to benefits and costs that one can measure in dollars; those one cannot—for example, gain in world prestige from space projects—are referred to as **intangible.**

The following items illustrate some of the problems in measuring costs and benefits as well as the techniques involved in measuring them:

- A frequent indirect cost in government programs is *compliance costs*—or, simply, red tape. For example, a new federal law designed to safeguard employee pension rights can cause small firms to terminate their plans because of paperwork requirements.

- It is difficult to measure benefits with rigor. Consider the benefits from air-pollution control. Effective pollution control means less damage to health, vegetation, materials, and property. If estimates of these benefits are called "crude approximations," then what would one call estimates for, say, aesthetic benefits (for example, that the sky is now visible) and human comfort (for example, that one's eyes no longer water)?

- Not all cost–benefit studies reveal benefits exceeding costs. One government study of the benefits and costs of certain pollution-control devices added to autos to comply with federal laws revealed that estimated costs of emission controls exceeded savings from the resulting abatement of pollution caused by auto emissions.

Distributional Impacts of Public Programs In addition to trying to measure costs and benefits, some thought should be given to the distribution of the costs and benefits resulting from a public program. Who actually benefits? What groups? It is sometimes not easy to identify beneficiary groups clearly. What is the distribution of program benefits among beneficiaries? Who should pay the program costs? Who actually does pay the cost of the program? How are program costs distributed among the burdened groups?[8]

Discount Factor Most public projects and programs take place over time, and how the analyst treats this time element is critical.

In order to keep things simple, think of time being divided into years and of future benefits and costs accruing in specific years. Column B of Table 6.2 shows the dollar

Maryland State Highway Administration

In a cost–benefit analysis, measurements are either direct or indirect and either tangible or intangible. A study by two researchers at the University of California–Davis found that 400,000 homes in the United States are close enough to highways to lose value due to noise. That is a *tangible, indirect cost* of building a highway—and provides some justification for building sound barriers. But opaque walls lining highways are unattractive. Transparent sound barriers, as shown here, are aesthetically more pleasing but can cost three times more than a conventional wall. Aesthetics is an *intangible benefit* of transparent sound barriers.

Table 6.2	Hypothetical Cost–Benefit Study (in millions of dollars)				
Year (A)	Benefits* (B)	Costs* (C)	Net Benefits (D)	Discount Factor ($i = 10\%$) (E)	Present Value of Net Benefits (F)
1	$ 0	$ 4	–$4	0.909	$ –3.6
2	0	4	–4	0.826	–3.3
3	1	1	0	0.751	0
4	2	1	1	0.683	0.7
5	3	1	2	0.621	1.2
6	4	1	3	0.564	1.7
7	4	1	3	0.513	1.1
8	4	1	3	0.467	1.4
	Total $18	$14	$4		$ –0.8

*Generally, in cost–benefit computations, only the *direct* costs and benefits are used. The overall study should, however, include a discussion of indirect costs and benefits.

benefits over an interval of eight years. Because two years are required for construction, no benefits accrue until the third year. Column C shows the costs, which are initially high but then level off. Column D simply shows the net benefits (benefits minus costs) for each year.

Is the $1 million net benefit occurring in the fourth year really worth $1 million in present dollars? No, these future proceeds must be adjusted to allow for the fact that future benefits are less valuable than present ones. The reason is that today's $1 million could be invested and certainly return more than that to the investor four years later. Cost must be adjusted in a like manner. We call making these adjustments—that is, reducing future dollars to be comparable to today's dollars—**discounting.**

To find the value of a dollar in any future year, one need only multiply by a discount factor. The formula is

$$\text{Discount factor} = \frac{1}{(1+i)^t}$$

where i is the interest rate and t is the number of years. Using this formula or, more likely, a calculator or a table of discount factors, let's return to the question posed a moment ago: How much is $1 million four years from now worth today? Assuming a modest interest rate of 6 percent, first calculate the discount factor and then multiply the $1 million benefit by it. Thus,

$$\text{Present value} = \frac{1}{(1+0.6)^4} \times \$1,000,000 = 0.792 \times \$1,000,000 = \$792,000$$

Column E in Table 6.2 gives the discount factors for the first eight years of the project but assumes a discount rate of 10 percent. The net benefits in column D are adjusted to reflect present values, which are shown in column F. If column F is totaled, one sees that by the eighth year the project's costs exceed its benefits. Based on this calculation, the project does not appear worth doing. But if the discount rate were changed to 6 percent, the benefits would outweigh the costs—such is the power of a few percentage points in cost–benefit analysis.

One might well ask, Why use a discount rate of 6 percent? It is a good question, because whether one uses 10, 6, or 3 percent makes a difference, as we just saw. One way to decide on a rate is to consider the **opportunity cost** of the use of the funds. Opportunity cost is the value of what certain resources could have produced had they been used in the best alternative way. Presumably, any money used in a project in the public sector will be taken from the private sector by taxation or borrowing. Consequently, the rate of return these resources could earn if they were invested in private-sector projects is the appropriate rate of discount for public-sector projects. For that reason, some suggest that the interest rate for a ten-year treasury note is a fairly good approximation of the opportunity cost, for it is how much the government must pay to lure investment from the private sector. On the day that this is written (November 4, 2009), a ten-year treasury note yields 3.47 percent. Several other issues arise with respect to the selection of a discount rate, but they are beyond the scope of this book.

Decision Rules   If one assumes that benefits do exceed costs, it does not necessarily follow that one should go ahead with a project. What one does depends on the **decision rules for cost–benefit analysis.**

First, one might be faced with a simple project that involves a yes–no decision—that is, the decision is between doing the project and not doing the project. The criterion we wish to use is the net benefit criterion. Define net benefit (NB) as

$$NB = B - C$$

and use the following decision rule: A simple project should be undertaken if and only if its net benefits exceed zero. Thus, in the example in Table 6.2, the net benefit is –$800,000, so the project should not be undertaken. Although this approach might seem obvious, it is an important one since it is frequently used by the Army Corps of Engineers in evaluating whether to approve funds, say, for widening a ship channel.

Second, an administrator might be faced with a choice between two mutually exclusive projects. For example, a department might have the choice of building four different types of bridges but can fund only one. If this is the case, then the general rule is as follows: When choosing one project from a set of mutually exclusive projects, choose the one with the greatest net benefit.

Another criterion, which turns out to be the equivalent of the net benefit criterion mentioned earlier, is the benefit–cost ratio (BCR) criterion. It is defined as

$$BCR = \frac{B}{C}$$

Is the benefit–cost ratio of any use in choosing from among mutually exclusive projects? Unfortunately, the answer is no. In the case of the four bridges, one could be a rather modest footbridge, suitable only for light traffic. Because only a small investment is required, the benefit–cost ratio is likely to be relatively high. But in comparison with a bridge designed for trains and trucks, the net benefits might appear meager indeed.

Third, an administrator might be faced with a case involving nonefficiency objectives. For instance, the distributional consequences of the projects in terms of regional economic development and unemployment might be of central concern; in such cases pecuniary effects become relevant. Thus, larger contractors such as the Defense Department and NASA must be concerned not only with the costs and benefits of a project but also with which state gets the contract, what size the business is that gets the subcontracts, and what kinds of jobs (that is, skill levels) are involved.

Fourth, the administrator might have to select the level at which several projects are to be operated under a budget constraint. In such cases the rule is to push expenditures for each project to the point at which the benefit of the last dollar spent is equal to the last dollar spent on any similar project. (As economists put it, the *marginal* net benefits should be equal.) In other words, if the next million dollars spent on Project Alpha yields $1.2 million in benefits while another million spent on Project Beta yields $1.3 million, then the extra million should go to Beta rather than Alpha.

Cost-Effectiveness Analysis   One technique closely associated with CBA is cost-effectiveness analysis. This technique attempts to answer the question, How much output does one get for a given expenditure? The advantage of **cost-effectiveness analysis** is that output or benefits need not be expressed in dollars.

Let's consider one example of cost-effectiveness analysis. Say that the number of lives saved by expenditures on disease A and disease B are as follows, and that an administrator wanted to determine the preferred mix of disease-control programs:

	Expenditures	Lives Saved (Cumulative)
Disease A	$ 500,000	360
	1,000,000	465
Disease B	$ 500,000	200
	1,000,000	270

"If we only knew the effect of spending $1 million," Robert N. Grosse explains, "we might opt for a program where all our money was spent on controlling disease A. Similarly, if we only knew the effects of programs of half a million dollars, we would probably prefer A, as we'd save 360 rather than only 200 lives. But if we knew the results for expenditures of both half a million and $1 million in each program, we would quickly see that spending half our money in each program was better than putting it all in one, assuming we have $1 million available."[9]

Multiobjective Models

One limitation of CBA is that it accounts for only one objective, usually an aggregate of all accrued benefits in dollar terms. For that reason, the decision maker might want to either replace or supplement it with a newer technique that emphasizes multiple objectives as in a multiobjective model. Formally stated, a **multiobjective model** is a decision-making technique useful in situations in which there are moral goals or when one or two goals cannot be quantified. The model decomposes the solution analysis into three steps: (1) select evaluation criteria, (2) decide on the relative importance of each criterion selected, and (3) assess each alternative in terms of how well it achieves the criteria.

Consider a project typical of the ones that spawned CBA: a waste treatment plant. Assuming four sites are under consideration, experts can be asked to rank order them by five criteria, as follows:

	Ranks of Four Proposed Waste-Treatment Plant Sites				
			Effect of Project on:		
Project	Local Transportation	Land-Use Planning	Neighborhood	Community Economy	Tax Base
A	4	4	3	2	3
B	2	1	1	4	1
C	3	3	4	3	4
D	1	2	2	1	2

Ranks: most positive = 1, least positive = 4.

The experts also can be asked to rank the sites on a scale ranging, say, from −100 (maximum negative effect) to +100 (maximum positive effect). For the first criteria, the results might look like this:

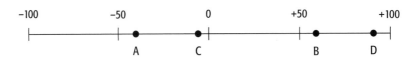

There has been nothing said about the relative importance of each criterion. Therefore, decision makers may and probably should assign relative weights to each of the criteria. To see how this process works, consider a second example. How much weight would you accord each of the following criteria in judging a university faculty member?

Teaching effectiveness	?
Professional accomplishment	?
Community service	?
Compatibility with students and faculty	?
	1.00

Note that the sum of the relative weights must be 1.00.

Assume that one university weighted the criteria this way:

Criteria	Weight Accorded to Criterion	Professor Zarkov— Raw Scores
Teaching effectiveness	0.40	70
Professional accomplishment	0.30	100
Community service	0.15	80
Compatibility with students and faculty	0.15	60

Zarkov's weighted score would be computed thus:

$$70(0.40) + 100(0.30) + 80(0.15) + 60(0.15) = 79$$

The preceding two examples have been highly simplified. In a real application, each criterion would need to be broken down into subfactors, and then weight would need to be assigned to each subfactor. For instance, professional accomplishment in the second example might be broken down into research, consulting, publications, and professional activities.

If the multiple objective model seems tedious and relatively subjective (it is), then the reader is invited to consider other methods of making selections. For instance, what would you say if you were on the *Titanic* and a passenger—let's call him Mr. Abrams—suggested to the captain that precious lifeboat space be assigned alphabetically? Unless your last name was Aadsen, you would probably argue for a multiobjective model.

Decision Trees

This decision-making aid is used for decision situations that occur in sequence; it consists of a pictorial representation of decision alternatives, states of nature, and outcomes of each course of action. The first step in using the technique is to diagram the sequence of decisions and chance events that the decision maker faces.

Consider this situation. A community is threatened with a landslide sometime during the next year before a reforestation program is completed. If a landslide does occur, damage will be only to property because the population can be evacuated. The property damage is estimated to be $3 million. Constructing a wall will cost $200,000. A decision tree for this situation appears in Figure 6.3. You may want to try to figure it out yourself before reading on.

To understand the tree, we begin with the first decision the community faces: Should it build the wall or do nothing? The square, or decision node, at the left indicates that at this point a decision must be made. The two lines forking out from the decision node show two possible choices: build or do nothing. What happens if we follow along the upper branch—in other words, build the wall? We know there is a "toll" to pay, namely, the $200,000 price tag for the wall's construction. Next we come to a circle, or chance node, to indicate that uncertainty must be resolved one way or another. At this chance node, there are two possibilities: a landslide occurs or it does not. Hence, we draw two branches for those possible results and label them accordingly. Moreover, for this decision problem, we know from expert opinion or historical records the probability of the possible outcomes— there is a 20 percent chance that a slide will occur within the next year and an 80 percent chance that it won't. Those numbers are recorded along the appropriate branches. Finally, we recall that the gain from avoiding the damage of a landslide is $3 million. That makes the payoff from the top branch $600,000 ($3 million × 0.2). Because there are neither gains nor losses if no slide occurs, the payoff of the lower branch is zero. Clearly, it makes sense to spend the $200,000. The expected value of the decision to build the wall is $600,000 minus $200,000 construction costs, or $400,000.

Similarly, the two possibilities for the decision not to build, their probabilities, and their payoffs are shown initiating from the lower chance node. The tree thus summarizes all the essential information that is available. Note the order in which events occur: The decision must be made before the decision maker knows what nature will do. Can you see why the decision not to build is tantamount to spending $600,000?

The problem just set forth obviously is drastically simplified. The community might have additional options, including building different kinds of walls (good, better, and best). This would require more decision nodes. Then there is the possibility that a slide

Figure 6.3   A Decision Tree for Controlling Landslides

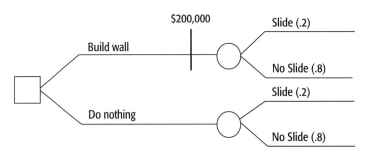

would occur and the wall would—a certain percentage of time—break. To account for that unhappy event, the decision maker would need to add another chance node to the right of the diagram. Or the community might try to secure a long-range weather forecast because landslides are more likely to occur when it rains a lot. This would require another toll gate.

In sum, then, a decision tree is a flow diagram that shows the logical structure of a decision problem. It contains four elements:

1. *Decision nodes,* which indicate all possible courses of action open to the decision maker
2. *Chance nodes,* which show the intervening uncertain advances and all their possible outcomes
3. *Probabilities* for each possible outcome of a chance event
4. *Payoffs,* which summarize the consequences of each possible combination of choice and chance

Systems Analysis

Systems analysis is more a mosaic than a specific analytical technique. And what makes up this mosaic? Bits and pieces from a variety of disciplines—engineering, sociology, biology, philosophy, psychology, economics, and computer science. Very broadly, the **systems analysis** approach forces us to look at problems as systems—that is, assemblies of interdependent components.

Although that may sound commonsensical—even trite—it is often ignored. Consider a classic example:[10] A basic problem in sewage treatment is that, when organic sewage is dumped into a river or lake, it generates an inordinate demand for oxygen. But oxygen is needed as well for the bacteria of decay, which use the oxygen-converting organic matter to break down inorganic products. Consequently, dumping tends to deplete the oxygen supply of surface waters. By killing off the bacteria of decay, dumping brings to a halt the aquatic cycle of self-purification. Enter now the sanitation engineer. Her solution is simply to domesticate the decay bacteria in a treatment plant, artificially supplying them with sufficient oxygen to accommodate the entering organic material. Thus, what is released from the treatment plant is largely inorganic residues. Because these have no oxygen demands, the engineer thinks that she has solved the problem.

Unfortunately, the sanitation engineer did not recognize that she was dealing with a system and that the system includes nature's rivers and streams. The treated sewage is now rich in the inorganic residues of decay—carbon dioxide, nitrate, and phosphate—that support the growth of algae. "Now heavily fertilized, the algae bloom furiously, soon die, releasing organic matter, which generates the oxygen demand that sewage technology had removed."

To better appreciate this approach, the following section will discuss the **four basic steps in systems analysis:** problem formulation, modeling, analysis and optimization, and implementation.

1. *Problem formulation.* Problem formulation is perhaps the most difficult step in analyzing a system, sometimes requiring three-fourths of the total effort. This step includes the detailed description of the task and identification of important variables and their relationships. Consider an investigation into some observed and perceived difficulties in an urban transportation system. In the systems approach, one begins by deciding whether the prime objective is better service, lower cost, less pollution, or something else. One must also decide what data are necessary: passenger miles by mode of transportation; passenger miles by sex, age, race, and income; passenger miles by time and place; and so forth. Finally, one must identify key decision makers in the urban area and their motivations.

2. *Modeling.* The scene changes in this step: One goes from the real world of the problem to the abstract world of the modeler. A model is a simpler representation of the real-world problem; it is supposed to help you. Models can be physical reconstructions of the real thing. The Army Corps of Engineers has built a scale model of part of New Orleans, at one-fiftieth of its actual size, to try to re-create conditions that occurred in Hurricane Katrina and to help figure out why things went so wrong.

Models need not—and sometimes cannot—be scale models of the real thing. What if a 1-km comet crashed into the Atlantic Ocean? To help answer that question, scientists at Sandia National Laboratories programmed a computer, and the computer model showed them the results. As you can see from the photo at the top of page 271, those results were not good. For a live simulation of Castalia, a larger-than-average asteroid, being hit by a house-size rock traveling at 5 km per second, visit www.nasaimages.org. The collision approximates the force of the Hiroshima atomic bomb. Using nuclear weapons has been proposed for breaking up, or at least diverting, asteroids headed toward Earth. Simulations show that such an impact will fracture a solid asteroid.

The modeler's task is probably more artistic than rigorous, more creative than systematic. He must strike a balance between including all relevant aspects of reality and keeping the model simple enough so that it is in line with existing theoretical loads, computation time, and data availability. Ultimately, of course, the test of a model's quality is how effective it is in helping to solve the original problem. Figure 6.4 shows a model for a criminal justice system.

How well might such a model work? Say a politician calls for 100,000 more police officers on the streets. No doubt more arrests will be made. But if there is not a concomitant increase in staff "downstream" in the courts and correctional facilities, the increased number of prisoners will simply clog the system even more—leading to greater delays or, more likely, more criminals being released. Remember: In a system all components are interconnected.

3. *Analysis and optimization.* In this step, an analyst studies the model to find the best strategy for resolving the given problem. Options include computer simulation and sensitivity analysis.

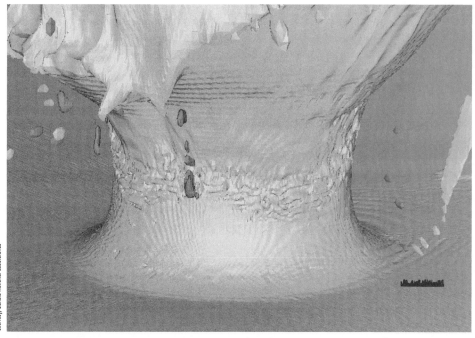

Courtesy, Sandia National Laboratories

What if a 1-km comet crashed into the Atlantic Ocean? To find out, Sandia National Laboratories, a government-owned contractor-operated facility, modeled the event on the teraflops high-performance computer. The image here shows a column of superheated seawater exploding into the atmosphere eight seconds after impact. The skyline of Manhattan, seen lower right, would be overrun by a tidal wave reaching 300 feet high. Debris from the comet and water vapor would traverse the globe, changing the earth's climate and producing a profound effect on agriculture. How far-fetched is this idea? A comet this size collided with Jupiter in 1994.

Simulation models allow users to replicate to a great extent the actual dispatch and patrol operations of most urban police departments. Incidents are generated throughout the city and distributed randomly in time and space according to observed statistical patterns. Each incident has an associated priority number, with the lower numbers designating the more important incidents. For instance, a priority 1 incident would be an officer in trouble, a felony in progress, or a seriously injured person; a priority 4 incident could be an open fire hydrant, a lockout, or a parking violation. As each incident becomes known, an attempt is made to assign (dispatch) a patrol unit to the scene. In attempting this assignment, the computer is programmed to duplicate as closely as possible the decision-making logic of an actual police dispatcher. In certain cases, this assignment cannot be performed because the congestion level of the accumulated incidents is too high; then, the incident report (which might in actuality be a complaint ticket) joins a queue of waiting reports. The queue is depleted as incidents are assigned to available patrol units.

Figure 6.4   Model of Criminal Justice System

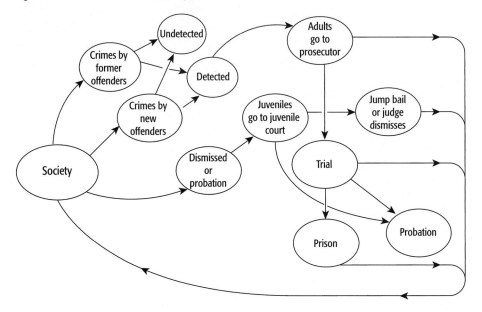

This simulation model is designed to study the patrol-deployment strategy and the dispatch and reassignment policy. The model tabulates several important measures of operational effectiveness. These include statistics on dispatcher queue length, patrol travel times, amount of preventive patrol, workloads of individual patrol units, amount of intersector dispatches, and others.

In sum, simulation provides a tool to assist in answering a wide range of allocation questions. Police administrators should find simulation models valuable for the following purposes:

- They facilitate detailed investigations of operations throughout the city (or part of the city).
- They provide a consistent framework for estimating the value of new technologies.
- They serve as training tools to increase awareness of the system interactions and consequences resulting from everyday policy decisions.
- They suggest new criteria for monitoring and evaluating actual operating systems.

One of the advantages of simulation derives from the **counterintuitive nature of public systems.** To call these systems counterintuitive is to say that they do not react in ways we think they should. The reason intuition provides so little guidance in understanding a system's behavior is that the human brain cannot grasp the totality of relationships among all the variables. Thus, common sense tells us that wider highways reduce congestion, but as urban planners have learned, the reverse is often the case.

Not necessarily requiring the assistance of a computer, **sensitivity analysis** is available in analyzing the model to find the best strategy for solving the original problem. Sensitivity analysis consists of making very small changes in the model to show the extent to which results may be importantly altered because of change in one or a few factors. To see how this might work, re-examine Figure 6.4. Assume that the mayor calls for a large reduction in total operating expenses. Because one does not want to reduce the strength of the police force (the patrol on the line), one looks elsewhere for "fat." Assume, therefore, that the data-input staff in the probation division is reduced. As a result, the input into the computer system of presentence reports of convicted defendants waiting to be sentenced is delayed. Defendants now must spend even more time in jails, and the system's overall operating costs reach a new high.

Try a different tack: Discontinue night courts. But closing these courts adds substantial costs to the police, who will have to house, feed, and guard defendants awaiting court action. Another suggestion might be to reduce the number of judges or prosecutors by 8 percent and the police by 3 percent. What results can be foreseen from such a course of action? Will there be any effects on a city's tax base that might result from cuts in the area of criminal justice?

4. *Implementation.* The systems approach has been discussed in terms of four steps, giving particular emphasis to the first three. The last step, implementation, refers to the procedure by which the results determined from the model are translated as a set of actions to the real world. The four steps, however, seldom occur in perfect sequence; indeed, the systems approach is highly iterative. As such, it might easily move through a sequence of steps such as the following: formulating the problem, selecting objectives, designing alternatives, collecting data, building models, weighting cost against effectiveness, testing for sensitivity, questioning assumptions, reexamining objectives, looking at new alternatives, reformulating the problem, selecting different or modified objectives, and so on.[11]

Group Decision-Making Techniques

Because group decision making is so common in public administration, effective managers must be highly skilled in influencing the group process. This section systematically considers strengths and weaknesses of groups as decision makers, circumstances in which a group decision-making process should be used, and techniques to help groups arrive at better decisions.

Advantages and Disadvantages   Because managers often have a choice between making a decision by themselves and including others, they should understand the advantages and disadvantages of group decision making.

Groups have an advantage over individuals because they bring together a broader perspective for defining the problem and diagnosing the underlying causes and effects.

Most of us tend to develop relatively fixed patterns of thinking, but when people with different styles interact in a group, they can stimulate each other to try new ways of approaching the problem and compensate for the weaknesses in one another's thinking style. (Several of these styles will be identified presently.) Further, groups offer more knowledge and information than individuals can. Indeed, the diversity of experience and thinking styles present in a group can lead to more innovative solutions than an "expert" could produce working alone. Generally speaking, a group decision is easier to implement because more people feel they had a say in it, and they understand the problem (and exactly what needs to be done) more thoroughly.

Among the more important disadvantages of group problem solving is that it is time-consuming and expensive, which is one reason groups should not be used for routine or programmed decisions. Moreover, the dynamics of groups can lead to compromise solutions (which satisfy no one) or the reduction of valuable dissenting opinions. Finally, there is no clear focus for responsibility if things go wrong.

When to Use a Group   The important task for a manager is to determine when a specific group should work on a particular problem. Obviously, group members should possess the required knowledge and analytical skills. Beyond that, the manager must consider the current workload of potential members (are they overloaded?); the members' expectations about involvement (do they think they have a "right" to participate?); and the group's skills at resolving conflict (can group members exchange ideas frankly and openly without becoming emotional?)

Group decision making is generally called for under the following set of circumstances:

- The problem is relatively uncertain or complex and has potential for conflict.
- The problem requires interagency or intergroup cooperation and coordination.
- The problem and its solution have important personal and organizational consequences.
- There are significant but not immediate deadline pressures.
- Widespread acceptance and commitment are critical to successful implementation.[12]

But when does the group have wisdom, and when does it not? James Surowiecki's *The Wisdom of Crowds* is suggestive.[13] He argues that there are several critical preconditions for making the crowd smarter than individuals. First, he says, you need to have *diversity* within the crowd—many different disciplines, perspectives, and areas of expertise must be represented. Second, you have to have *decentralization*, meaning that the crowd has to be dispersed, and people with local and specific knowledge can contribute. Third, you have to have some effective *way of aggregating* all the individual judgments. The Wiki technology is a powerful way to do that. Finally, and most importantly, you must have *independence*. In other words, you can't have individuals being able to sway one another or situations in which pressures for social conformity can affect judgments that you are pooling together. Significantly, Surowiecki's crowds don't look like teams in organizations. Most teams, particularly in organizational settings, violate these four preconditions.

Improving Group Decision Making   A number of techniques are available to help individual managers and groups arrive at better decisions. The **nominal group technique**, for instance, was developed to ensure that every group member has equal input in the process.[14] Because some participants may talk more and dominate group discussions in interactive groups, the nominal group is structured in a series of steps to equalize participation:

1. Working alone, each participant writes ideas on the problem to be discussed. These ideas usually are suggestions for a solution.
2. A round-robin, in which each group member presents ideas to the group, is set up. The ideas are written down on a blackboard for all members to see. No discussion of the ideas occurs until every person's ideas have been presented and written down for general viewing.
3. After all ideas have been presented, there is an open discussion of the ideas for the purpose of clarification only; evaluative comments are not allowed. This part of the discussion tends to be spontaneous and unstructured.
4. After the discussion, a secret ballot is taken in which each group member votes for preferred solutions. It results in a ranking of alternatives in terms of priority.
5. Steps 3 and 4 are repeated as desired to add further clarification to the process.

A second technique is the **devil's advocate.** Here someone is assigned the role of challenging the assumptions and assertions made by the group.[15] The devil's advocate forces the group to rethink its approach to the problem and to avoid reaching premature consensus or making unreasonable assumptions before proceeding with problem solutions. **Dialectal inquiry** is similar to a devil's advocate approach except that groups are assigned to challenge the underlying values and assumptions associated with the problem definition. For example, the State Department might form a couple of groups—say, the Red Team and the Blue Team—to critically examine prevailing assumptions in the department regarding a particular foreign country.

A fourth technique, perhaps the best known, is **brainstorming.** The key idea here is to increase creative thinking and generation of solutions by prohibiting criticism. Groups of five to ten members meet to generate ideas subject to certain rules. Judgment or evaluation of ideas must be withheld until the idea-generation process has been completed. The wilder or more radical the idea, the better. The greater the number of ideas, the greater the likelihood of obtaining a superior idea. Participants should suggest how the ideas of others can be turned into better ideas, or how two or more ideas can be joined into still another idea.

Implementing and Evaluating the Decision

The fourth and final step of the decision-making process involves implementing and evaluating the decision. Although a decision must be implemented before it can be truly evaluated, in this section we will consider evaluation first and then conclude things with some reflections on the difficulties of decision making in the real world.

Program Evaluation

To set down a general procedure for carrying out program evaluation and performance assessment is not easy. Perhaps the best approach to such a formulation is to say that either task follows, ideally, a procedure reminiscent of the classical research experiment. The steps are to (1) define the goals of the program, (2) translate the goals into measurable indicators of goal achievement, (3) collect data on the indicators for those who have been exposed to the program and for those who have not (that is, the control group), and (4) compare the data on program participants and controls in terms of goal criteria.

Define the Goals   There are three points to keep in mind about goals. First, programs are likely to have multiple goals: To evaluate only one is to evaluate partially. A program to reduce air pollution, for example, might be concerned with the reduction of several types of air pollution at several sources. For purposes of evaluation, the sweeping goal of "reduce air pollution" might be broken into components, represented by the following matrix.[16]

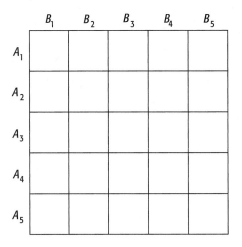

In the matrix the A's represent pollution types (that is, carbon monoxide, sulfur oxides, hydrocarbons, nitrogen oxides, and particles) and the B's, pollution sources (that is, automobiles, industry, electric power plants, space heating, and refuse disposal). Thus, rather than consider air pollution in terms of one composite figure, the evaluator considers it in terms of several separate measures.

Second, many areas of public policy lack standards (or benchmarks) by which a goal can be established. Budweiser may have as its goal for next year to increase sales more than Coors increases its sales. But how does the public decision maker know the proper goals for reduction of poverty and illiteracy in the year ahead?

Third, programs do not only move toward official goals. For example, programs that may increase the supply of workers in a particular occupation (the intended consequence) may result in the exertion of downward pressures on the wages of existing workers in the occupation (the unintended consequence). A good evaluator tries to look at all possible effects of program activity.

Translate Goals into Measurable Indicators   Program goals tend to be ambiguous, hazy. Consider this one for an urban transportation program: "To provide access to community services, facilities, and employment in a safe, quick, comfortable, and convenient manner for all segments of the community without causing harmful side effects." How would one translate those goals into measurable indicators of achievement? Hatry, Winnie, and Fisk suggest the following six criteria along with examples of what might be measured:[17]

1. *Convenience.* By measuring the percentage of residents not within x distance of public transit service and citizen perception of travel convenience.
2. *Time.* By measuring time required to travel between key origin and destination points and duration of delays.
3. *Comfort.* By measuring "bumpiness" of roads and citizen perception of travel comfort.
4. *Safety.* By measuring transportation-related deaths, injuries, and incidents of property damage the number of transportation crime incidents.
5. *Cost.* By measuring cost per trip to users and program costs to city.
6. *Environmental quality.* By measuring noise level along transportation corridors and air pollution attributable to transportation sources.

For another interesting example of how to measure impacts (or long-term effects of society), one could turn to work in the area of social indicators. In a seminal work on the subject, Raymond A. Bauer described social indicators operationally as "statistics, statistical series, and all other forms of evidence that enable us to assess where we stand and are going with respect to our values and goals."[18]

The social indicator movement has developed concurrently with evaluation research. And given the dearth of respectable evaluation studies, some have argued for social indicators as a substitute for experimental evaluations. This substitution would be unfortunate because social indicators cannot tell why a program succeeds or fails. Yet the *why* is often as important as the *how well*.

Collect Data   Data for evaluation research can come from a variety of sources and research techniques. To name but a few: interviews, questionnaires, observations, ratings, institutional records, government statistics, diary records, physical evidence, clinical examinations, financial records, and documents (for example, minutes of board meetings, newspaper accounts of policy actions, and transcripts of trials). Data must be collected not only on those who participated in the program but also on those who did not, the **control group**. Figure 6.5 shows the measurable effect (comprehension scores) of a program involving new foreign language-teaching methods on program participants in comparison with a control group of similar students studying under traditional methods.

Compare Data   The classic design for evaluation is the experimental model, which uses experimental and control groups. Out of the target population, units (for example, people, precincts, or cities) are randomly chosen to be in either the group that receives the program (experimental group) or the control group. Measures are taken of the relevant criterion variable (for example, vocabulary scores) before the program starts and after it ends.

Figure 6.5   Quasi-experimental Analysis for the Effect of Specific Course Work, Including Control Series Design

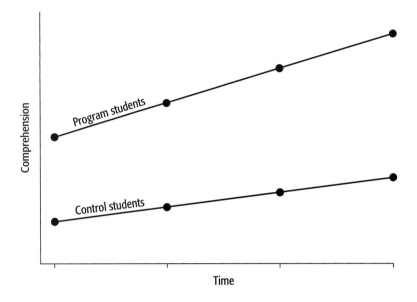

Differences are computed, and the program is deemed a success if the experimental group has improved more than the control group has.[19] Or, in terms of the following model, the program is a success if $(b - a)$ is greater than $(d - c)$.

	Before	After
Experimental	*a*	*b*
Control	*c*	*d*

The model is deceptively simple. How can the evaluator always ensure that nothing else caused the change but the program? For example, suppose a city reports a healthy drop in its crime rate. To attribute that drop solely to the effects of one program would be difficult. During the period of improvement, several major program actions may have occurred—for example, expansion of the police force, buildup of drug-treatment programs, and installation of new street lighting. In addition, social conditions may have changed—for example, the population became older and the unemployment rate dropped (see Figure 6.6).

Regardless of the specific approach taken to evaluation, two final points need to be kept in mind. First, to be useful, evaluation must be viewed as a tool of management. Ideally, evaluators and the administrator cooperate. When the policy decisions about the program design are to be made, the evaluator should (a) ask the manager to specify the objectives of the program and then (b) determine what kind of data would cause the manager to act (that is, make adjustments in the management of the program). Second, because most programs that work well usually produce only relatively small gains in their early stages, evaluation should be built into the new program; its strengths and weaknesses should be examined while it goes forward.

Figure 6.6   Evaluation and Fluctuations of Time Series Data

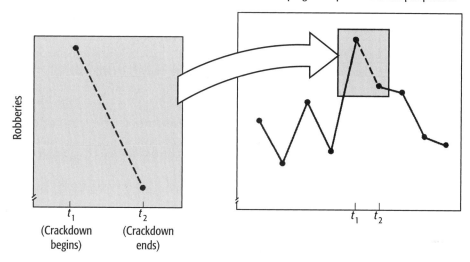

These results look impressive . . .

until the program is put in historical perspective.

Robberies

t_1
(Crackdown
begins)

t_2
(Crackdown
ends)

t_1 t_2

Decision Making in the Real World

The analytical model of decision making presented in this chapter seldom works in practice as it is supposed to in theory. Why not? First, studies show that costs are often misrepresented. Second, there are certain biases in human decision making that seemed to be hardwired into our brains. Third, critics charge that the analytical approach to decision making itself has inherent limitations.

"Strategic Misrepresentation" in Estimating Cost

In 2006, the most ambitious public works project in the United States opened. Boston's Big Dig is an unprecedented effort to route an unsightly highway deep beneath the central city and replace it with a green ribbon of parks. Back in 1985, officials assigned a $2.5 billion price tag to the Big Dig. By the early 1990s, it had risen to $7.5 billion, and before 2000, it had hit the billion-dollar mark. Today, the Big Dig has cost nearly $16 billion. Because it leaks, the amount will surely continue to edge upward.

Although a 600 percent cost escalation is extreme, cost escalation in public works projects in general, and transportation infrastructure projects in particular, are hardly unusual. In fact, they are the norm. Let's first look at some numbers and then try to explain this pattern of underestimating cost. The first statistically significant study of this phenomenon based on a sample of 258 transportation projects found the following:[20]

- Costs are underestimated in almost nine out of ten projects.
- Actual costs are on the average 28 percent higher than estimated costs.
- Cost underestimation exists across 20 nations and five continents; it appears to be a global phenomenon.

Explanations of cost underestimation come in four flavors. First is technical. Was the underestimation the result of "forecasting errors" such as imperfect techniques, inadequate data, honest mistakes, inherent problems in prediction, lack of experience, and the like? The second type of explanation is economic. Do project promoters and forecasters deliberately underestimate cost in order to provide public officials an incentive to cut costs and thereby better serve the public interest? Third is the psychological explanation. Do politicians have a "monument complex" and engineers a need to build stuff? Fourth is political. Are forecasts intentionally biased to serve the interests of project promoters in getting projects started?

The researchers found with statistical significance that the political explanation works best: "The cost estimations used to decide whether such projects should be built are highly and systematically misleading. Underestimation cannot be explained by error and is best explained by strategic misrepresentation, that is, lying."[21]

The policy implications for this consequential and highly expensive field of public administration are clear:

> Those legislators, administrators, bankers, media representatives, and members of the public who value honest numbers should not trust the cost estimates presented by infrastructure promoters and forecasters. Another important implication is that institutional checks and balances—including financial, professional, or even criminal penalties for consistent or foreseeable estimation errors—should be developed to ensure the production of less deceptive cost estimates. The work of designing such checks and balances has begun elsewhere, with a focus on four basic instruments of accountability: (1) increased transparency, (2) the use of performance specifications, (3) explicit formulation of the regulatory regimes that apply to project development and implementation, and (4) the involvement of private risk capital, even in public projects.[22]

Biases in Human Decision Making   Herbert A. Simon, who appears in our timeline in Figure 6.2 presents two important concepts that help us appreciate how people really make decisions: bounded rationality and satisficing. **Bounded rationality** means simply that people have limits, or boundaries, on how rational they can be. **Satisficing** means that decision makers choose the first solution alternative that satisfies minimal decision criteria. Because public administrators lack the time and cognitive ability to process complete information about complex decisions, they must satisfice.

Although administrators can do little to avoid these realities, they can be more aware of certain tendencies in human decision making that lead to mistakes. To make the best decisions, people must understand their own deficiencies. Awareness of the following seven biases can help administrators make better choices:[23]

1. *Failing to seek information.* If, as Simon tells us, our rationality might be bounded, so too might our awareness. That is to say, people often ignore the critical information when making decisions and then wind up asking themselves "How did I miss that?" One

of the most worrisome versions of bounded awareness occurs when decision makers are motivated to favor a particular outcome. For example, Richard Clarke, who was head of the White House antiterrorism unit on September 11, 2001, claims in *Against All Enemies* that when he returned to work on the morning of September 12, Vice President Dick Cheney, Defense Secretary Donald Rumsfeld, and Deputy Secretary of Defense Paul Wolfowitz were discussing the role that Iraq must have played in the attack. We now know that this overly narrow assessment was wrong, but in the months that followed, the Bush administration apparently conducted a motivated search to tie Iraq to 9/11 and terrorism. With such a conformity of effort, information inconsistent with the preferred viewpoint lay outside the bounds of awareness. What then should decision makers do to increase their awareness? They should challenge the absence of this confirming evidence. "Receiving the recommendations without contradictory data is a red flag indicating that your team members are falling prey to bounded awareness. Assign someone to play the role of devil's inquisitor (a person who asks questions, as opposed to a devil's advocate, who argues alternative points of view)."[23] Although decision makers usually seek far too much information, such an "oversearch strategy" should be reserved only for situations in which the costs of an error are extraordinarily high.

2. *Giving too much weight to readily available or recent information.* For example, in 1987 Genentech developed a new blood-clot dissolver, and all the company had to do was obtain Food and Drug Administration (FDA) approval to produce it. Genentech executives were so confident of the FDA's approval that they went ahead and invested heavily in the production and marketing of the drug. After all, research showed that, in a test tube, the drug effectively dissolved blood clots, as required by the FDA. But the FDA also required "other" information not so readily available—namely, clinical data charting the drug's effect on real people. Because those data were not included, the FDA rejected the application, and the company's stock dropped 24 percent (a $1 billion loss on paper). The company's executives had presumed that the information most readily available constituted all the knowledge needed.

3. *Being overconfident.* Because they mistakenly equate confidence with competence, managers are forever giving too much weight to self-assured opinions—either their own or those of their subordinates. They often encourage overconfidence by asking their subordinates to come up with the "right" decision all the time. For example, when a group of people was asked to define quantities about which they had little direct knowledge ("What was the dollar value of Canadian lumber exports in 2003?"), they overestimated their accuracy.

4. *Ignoring the laws of randomness.* Randomness means that the outcome of one event has nothing to do with the outcome of another. Administrators often ignore this principle in making decisions. For example, even though employee performance should be expected to fluctuate each month, an administrator decides that a dip is the beginning of a downward trend and starts an expensive new training program. Trends should not be interpreted from a single, random event. Aristotle said it best: One swallow does not make a summer.

5. *Being reluctant to audit and improve decision making.* Administrators might require very detailed analysis prior to decision making but might also be reluctant to analyze their most important decisions retrospectively. Some organizations do prepare "lessons learned" reports from time to time, but few of the organization's members are likely to read them, much less reflect on them.

6. *Seeing only one dimension of uncertainty.* In experiments, when subjects are asked to evaluate a venture that carries an 80 percent chance of success, they invariably vote to proceed. But if the problem is reframed and they are told the venture has a 20 percent chance of failure, they vote not to proceed. Managers often make a decision after analyzing it from only one or two perspectives.

7. *Escalating commitment to a course of action in which people have made a substantial prior investment.* If people behaved rationally, they would make choices based on marginal cost and benefits of their actions. In other words, What are the incremental benefits and incremental costs of moving forward? They would ignore sunk cost. They would ignore cost that they could never recover, but in fact, people don't ignore sunk cost. In the face of high sunk cost, people become overly committed to certain activities, even if the results have been quite poor. They have a hard time cutting their losses. Worse yet, they throw good money after bad, and the situation continues to escalate. Think of some examples: Smith is at the casino, he's losing money, he promised himself that he would not lose more than $500, but it's very easy to double down and say, "Only one more debt and I'm going to turn this thing around." Sure.

Limitations of Systems Analysis   Let us conclude by considering some specific criticisms of systems analysis—perhaps the quintessential analytical approach.

Systems analysis begins, it will be recalled, with problem definition. Significantly, one of the most distinguished practitioners of the systems approach, Charles Hitch, maintains that the Rand Corporation never undertook a major systems study in which satisfactory objectives could be defined.[24] When attempts were made, objectivity proved elusive. Other researchers have had similar experiences. For example, in a classic systems study on water resources, the goals read as follows: *adequate* pollution control; *reasonable* irrigation development; *proper* erosion control and sediment reduction; *suitable* flood control; *optimum* contribution in alleviating the impact of drought; *full* development of the basin's resources for recreational programs.[25] Where did these goals come from? What do the italicized words mean?

Gathering information is also part of the first step. Writes Ida R. Hoos:

Dear to the hearts of technically oriented analysts is the information-gathering and processing state. In fact, so [agreeable] is the occupation with data that many systems designs, purported to deal with pressing social problems, never progress beyond that point. Displaying the ingestive propensities of a snake, the information system swallows up all the resources allocated to a given project and diverts attention from its larger purpose.[26]

Perhaps the first pitfall to note about modeling is that the analyst structures the problem—that is to say, the analyst inevitably must view the problem through his or her own eyes and determine what the relevant variables are. If one assumes that one wants to wage war against poverty, how does one go about establishing the poverty level? What does one base the calculations on?

The system itself must also be determined. But how inclusive should it be? Clearly, the ill-fated sanitation engineer mentioned on page 269 was not inclusive enough. Conceivably, the criminal justice system depicted in Figure 6.4 is not inclusive enough. (It has no way of indicating the economic effects of crime rate: for example, reduced tax base as residents move away from cities due to increases in crime.) "Systems experts have made a great show of addressing totality but have actually dealt with shreds and patches."[27]

The third step in the systems approach, it will be recalled, is analysis and optimization. Here the analyst runs the risk of becoming locked into attaining the originally stated objectives of the study. This is no paradox, for a good systems study should be **heuristic**—that is, a method to help discover. Obviously, what is waiting to be discovered cannot be known in advance. A famous study of the location of military bases conducted by Albert Wohlstetter and his associates at Rand illustrates this nicely:

> In 1951 the Air Force asked Rand to help select locations for new air bases to be built overseas in the 1956 to 1961 period. Wohlstetter's approach was not to try to answer the straightforward request (Where should the bases go?) but to examine the assumptions inherent in the question itself. After a year and a half of analysis, he and his staff concluded that adding such bases was too risky, because aircraft positioned overseas closer to the Soviet Union were too vulnerable to surprise attack on the ground. They further concluded that overseas bases were more costly, less of a deterrent, and more of a problem for U.S. foreign policy than an alternative. The alternative was to build more bases in the United States and supplement them with small overseas installations for refueling.[28]

A final pitfall in the systems approach is *letting the method supplant the problem.* In other words, some experts tend to begin with the question, What problems are available for my techniques? The proper initial question is, of course, What is the problem?

Such experts are not unlike the drunk the police officer finds late at night under a streetlight. When asked what he is doing, the drunk replies that he is looking for his keys.

"Where did you lose the keys?" the officer asks.

"In the alley."

"Then why are you looking for them here?"

"Because," replies the drunk, "this is where the light is."

In spite of such failures as a description of decision making, systems analysis provides a useful framework for categorizing and diagnosing the nature of the departures of actual decisions from the requirements of rationality. In this sense, it provides a useful benchmark.

Concepts for Review

bounded rationality
brainstorming
control group
cost-benefit analysis (CBA)
cost-effectiveness analysis
counterintuitive nature of public systems
decision analysis
decision making
decision rules for cost–benefit analysis
decision tree
devil's advocate
dialectal inquiry
direct benefits and costs
discounting
externalities (spillovers)
four basic steps in systems analysis
heuristic systems study

indirect benefits and costs
intangible benefits and costs
limiting (strategic) factor in decision making
lower limits of a decision
multiobjective model
nominal group technique
opportunity cost
pecuniary benefits
pecuniary costs
real benefits
real costs
satisficing
sensitivity analysis
simulation
systems analysis
tangible benefits and costs
upper limits of a decision

Key Points

In this chapter, we examined four steps managers should take to make effective decisions. The chapter made the following points:

1. Decision making involves selecting one course of action from various alternatives. As such, it cannot be divorced from the planning process. There are at least four steps in decision making: (1) identifying the problem or opportunity; (2) gathering facts; (3) making the decision; and (4) implementing and evaluating the decision.

2. Effective administrators know that very few problems or events are isolated. Most are manifestations of underlying problems. Therefore, before attempting a quick fix on a series of problems, they try to discover the basic problem.

3. In framing the response to a problem, careful attention should be given to what is called the upper and lower limits of the decision. Upper limits of the decision refer to the ever-present limitations that determine how far the administrator can go. Lower limits of the decision refer to what, at a minimum, must occur for the problem to be solved. Barnard introduced an idea quite similar to that of lower limits that he called the limiting (or strategic) factor in decision making. This is the factor "whose control, in the right form, at the right place and time, will establish a new system of conditions which meets the purpose."

4. In an era of scarcity, interest in weighing costs against benefits rises. The method of choice for these kinds of assessments is cost–benefit analysis (CBA). Most CBA involves familiarity with certain common elements: the measurement of cost and benefits, the distribution impacts, the discount factor, and decision rules.

5. Direct benefits and costs are those closely related to the main project objectives. Indirect benefits and costs, called extra realities or spillovers—are more in the nature of by-products. The term tangible is applied to benefits and costs that one can measure in dollars; those one cannot are referred to as intangible.

6. Opportunity cost is the value of what certain resources could have produced had they been used in the best alternative way.

7. One technique closely associated with cost-benefit analysis is cost-effectiveness analysis. This technique attempts to answer the question, How much output does one get for a given expenditure? The advantage of cost-effectiveness analysis is that output or benefits need not be expressed in dollars.

8. The technique of decision analysis can help us better structure complex problems. In this approach, the decision is not viewed as isolated because today's decisions depend on the ones we will make tomorrow. And the quality of today's decision depends on what may or may not occur tomorrow—and these are chance events we cannot control. In such situations, a payoff matrix or a decision tree can be helpful.

9. The four basic steps in systems analysis are problem formulation, modeling, analysis and optimization, and implementation.

10. Operations research (or management science) and the systems approach share many characteristics, but they are not the same. The scope of the former is narrower. It tends to be concerned with problems that can be represented by mathematical models that can be optimized.

11. Group decision making is generally called for when there are no immediate deadline pressures and the problem is relatively uncertain or complex and has potential for conflict, requires interagency or intergroup cooperation, and its solution has important personal and organizational consequences. Group decision making is also called for when widespread acceptance and commitment are crucial to successful implementation.

12. To make the best decisions, people must understand their own biases. Awareness of the following seven can help administrators make better choices: (1) seeing only one dimension of uncertainty; (2) giving too much weight to readily available or recent information; (3) being overconfident; (4) ignoring the laws of randomness; (5) being reluctant to audit and improve decision making; (6) seeing only one dimension of uncertainty; and (7) escalating commitment to a course of action in which people have made a substantial prior investment.

13. The general procedure for carrying out program evaluation is reminiscent of the classical research experiment. The steps are to (1) define the goals of the program; (2) translate goals into measurable indicators of goal achievement; (3) collect data on the indicators for those who have been exposed to the program and for those who have not; and (4) compare the data on program participants and controls in terms of goal criteria.

Problems and Applications

1. Suppose you were to build a model that would forecast the nationwide demand for nurses 20 years from now. As a start, you must make assumptions about population growth and the effects of new drugs. What else? Do you think the list of variables is endless?

2. As the head of a city housing agency, you must decide whether to submit either plan A or plan B (but not both) to the mayor, who, in turn, must submit it to the city council. You estimate that there is a 90 percent chance that the mayor would accept A but only a 50 percent chance that the council would accept it. The council likes B; indeed, you are certain they would accept it—if, that is, it ever got past the mayor (the odds of that happening are three to one). You prefer A and evaluate its utility at 1.00. In fact, because you think it the most socially desirable, even if the mayor accepts and has it rejected by the council, you would assign a utility of 0.40 to these consequences. Of course, if the rejection came first from your boss, the mayor, the utility would be somewhat less, say 0.20. However, plan B, if accepted by the city council, has a utility of 0.80 to you. But the worst situation is to have it rejected; there would be no utility in such a case. What should you do?

3. Use multiobjective criteria to help you decide among four models of automobiles. Use a form to establish criteria and weight them. The final step in your analysis should be to divide the relevance number by the cost of the automobile; this will give you four benefit-to-cost ratios to compare.

4. The objectives of a city's recreation program are these: "To provide all citizens, to the full extent practicable, with a variety of leisure opportunities that are accessible, safe, physically attractive, and enjoyable. They should contribute to the mental and physical health of the community, to its economic and social well-being, and permit outlets that will help decrease incidents of antisocial behavior, such as crime and delinquency." Establish some measurable evaluation criteria for these objectives.

5. Prepare a paper on recent evaluative research on the U.S. criminal justice system. You may want a narrower topic: "Does punishment cut down on crime?" "Do work-release programs boost a convict's chance of getting a job?" and so on.

6. Give several examples of recent nonincremental decisions made in American government.

7. Gotham City has to dispose of 22,000 tons of refuse daily, an amount increasing by 4 percent a year. Currently, it has eight incinerators that have a usable capacity of 6000 tons a day; residue and nonincinerated refuse must go to sanitary landfills that will be exhausted within five years. Four superincinerators, with a capacity of 20,000 tons a day, have been proposed. Unfortunately, they are quite expensive: $1 billion to build and $50 million a year to operate. Moreover, they would add substantially to hazardous air pollution by emitting thousands of tons of soot particulates a year. Outline and discuss an analytical model that could help the mayor of Gotham City decide what to do. What additional information would you need? What are the upper and lower limits of the decision? Is the decision simply one of whether to build the superincinerators, or are alternatives available?

8. Write a paper comparing the decision-making styles of two or more recent presidents. Which style is most effective? Why?

9. "Experience is not only an expensive basis for decision making but also a dangerous one." Discuss this statement.

10. What are the shortcomings in using "lives saved" as a measure of benefit?

11. Use the concept of opportunity cost to explain why lawyers are more likely than physicians to get involved in politics.

Favorite Bookmarks

www.appam.org   This is the Web site of the Association for Public Policy Analysis and Management. The field of public policy analysis and management that the association supports encompasses decision-making and policymaking theory, quantitative and other methods for analyzing public policies, and their implementation.

www.mapnp.org/library/prsn_prd/decision.htm   This site, assembled by Carter McNamara, Ph.D., includes free, complete, online training programs for decision making in nonprofit as well as for-profit organizations.

www.horizon.unc.edu/courses/papers/anticipatorymanagement.asp   Failure to anticipate change can be fatal. "Anticipatory management" provides tools for better decision making in an age of constant change.

www.thinksmart.com/mission/workout/mindmapping_intro.html   "Mind mapping"—the technique of arranging ideas and their interconnections visually—is a popular brainstorming technique.

http://www.billsgames.com/brain-teasers
http://www.afunzone.come/brainteaserzone.html
http://www.ed.uiuc.edu/courses/satex/sp97/projects/PickYourBrain/BrainTeasers/
Problem solving is part of the decision making process. Just for fun, visit one of these three sites and try to solve some of the brainteasers.

Notes

1. Herbert A. Simon, *Administrative Behavior* (New York: Macmillan, 1957), 1.
2. Theodore C. Sorenson, *Decision Making in the White House* (New York: Columbia University Press, 1963), 22–42.
3. Peter F. Drucker, *The Effective Executive* (New York: Harper & Row, 1966), 132.
4. Chester I. Barnard, *The Functions of the Executive* (Cambridge, MA: Harvard University Press, 1938), 202–5.
5. David Halberstam, *The Best and the Brightest* (Greenwich, CT: Fawcett Crest Books, 1969), 90.
6. Haynes Johnson and David A. Broder, *The System* (Boston: Little, Brown, 1997), 64.
7. Richard A. Musgrave and Peggy B. Musgrave, *Public Finance in Theory and Practice* (New York: McGraw-Hill, 1973), 141.
8. J. T. Bonnen, "The Absence of Knowledge of Distributional Impacts" in Joint Economic Committee, *The Analysis and Evaluation of Public Expenditure* (Washington, DC: U.S. Government Printing Office, 1969), 425–26.
9. R. N. Grosse, "Problem of Resource Allocation in Health" in Joint Economic Committee, *The Analysis and Evaluation of Public Expenditure* (Washington, DC: U.S. Government Printing Office, 1969), 1197.
10. Barry Commoner, *The Closing Circle* (New York: Alfred A. Knopf, 1971), 180.
11. E. S. Quade, *System Analysis Techniques for Planning-Programming-Budgeting* (Santa Monica, CA: Rand, 1966), 10.
12. J. Ware, *Some Aspects of Problem Solving and Conflict Resolution in Management Groups* (Cambridge, MA: Harvard Business School, 1978).
13. James Surowiecki, *The Wisdom of Crowds: Why Many Are Smarter than the Few and How Collective Wisdom Shapes Business, Economics, Societies and Nations* (New York, Anchor, 2004).
14. R. A. Guzzo, *Improving Group Decision Making in Organizations* (New York: Academic Press, 1982), 95–126.
15. D. Schweiger and P. A. Finger, "The Comparative Effectiveness of Dialectical Inquiry and Devil's Advocate," *Strategic Management Journal* (1984): 5.

16. Adapted from T. J. Cook and F. P. Scioli, "A Research Strategy for Analyzing the Impact of Public Policy," *Administrative Science Quarterly* (September 1972).

17. H. P. Hatry, R. E. Winnie, and D. M. Fisk, *Practical Program Evaluation for State and Local Government Officials* (Washington, DC: Urban Institute, 1994), 27.

18. R. A. Bauer, ed., *Social Indicators* (Cambridge, MA: MIT Press, 1966), 1.

19. J. S. Wholey et al., *Handbook of Practical Program Evaluation* (San Francisco: Jossey-Bass, 1994).

20. Bent Flyvbjerg, "Underestimating Cost in Public Works Projects—Error or Lie?," *Journal of the American Planning Association* (Summer 2002): 279–95.

21. Ibid., 279.

22. Ibid., 290.

23. Based on Max H. Bazerman and Dolly Chung, "Decisions Without Borders," *Harvard Business Review* (January 2000), 88–97, and M. H. Bazerman, *Judgment in Managerial Decision Making* (New York: Wiley, 1986).

24. C. J. Hitch, *On the Choice of Objectives in Systems Studies* (Santa Monica, CA: Rand, 1960), 11.

25. R H. McKean, *Efficiency in Government Through Systems Analysis* (New York: Wiley, 1963).

26. I. R. Hoos, "Systems Technique for Managing Society: A Critique," *Public Administration Review* (March–April, 1973): 162–63.

27. Ibid., 161.

28. Quade, op. cit., 125–26.

CASE 6.1
WILD HORSES

© Jeff Vanugo/Corbis

If all you've ever done is gather up horses, and all you have had to think about is only what you've been told to do, well, that's a pretty simple decision-making process. Some people resist having to think more.

Ron Hall, National Wild Horse
and Burro Program

Background

Wild horses have long been a symbol of the independence of the American West, but today, the health of their population depends heavily on government management. At their peak, in the mid-1800s, an estimated two million wild horses roamed America's rangeland. Populations decreased as development reduced habitat for wild horses and native grazers such as bison, and as horses and burros were rounded up to make room for livestock and farming operations. By the early 1900s, most wild horses had disappeared from the Great Plains and those that remained were found primarily in the remote mountains, deserts, and badlands of the West. By 1971, only about 9500 wild horses were thought to live on public rangelands.

Public concerns about abuse and wild horse population declines swelled in the 1950s and 1960s. Subsequently, Congress enacted the **Wild Free-Roaming Horses and Burros Act of 1971** to protect wild horses and burros from abuse and death and to manage them to achieve and maintain a thriving natural ecological balance on the public lands. The 1971 act declared these wild animals to be "living symbols of the historic and pioneer spirit of the West; that they contribute to the diversity of life forms within the Nation and enrich the lives of the American people; and that these horses and burros are fast disappearing from the American scene." Since the passage of the act, wild horse and burro populations have increased, but the way they are managed on public lands has been controversial and wild horse advocates continue to voice concerns about horses being slaughtered.

The 1971 act authorized and directed the Secretary of the Interior, on public lands managed by the Bureau of Land Management (BLM), and the Secretary of Agriculture, on public lands managed by the Forest Service, "to protect and manage wild free-roaming horses and burros as components of public lands." The act also directed the secretaries to manage them *"to achieve and maintain a thriving natural ecological balance on the public lands."* In fiscal year 2007, the program was funded at $36.4 million. Forty-four BLM field units manage approximately 33,100 wild horses and burros on 199 herd management areas (HMA) covering over 34 million acres in ten western states—Arizona, California, Colorado, Idaho, Montana, New Mexico, Nevada, Oregon, Utah, and Wyoming. BLM's Nevada State Office manages about half of the land and animals in the Wild Horse and Burro Program.

In the mid- to late 1970s, population counts indicated that there was a large increase in wild horses and burros and that were contributing to overgrazing of the rangeland. Congress amended the 1971 act in 1978 to protect the range from wild horse overpopulation. The **Public**

Rangelands Improvement Act of 1978 directed the secretaries of the Interior and Agriculture to determine appropriate management levels (AMLs), maintain a current inventory of wild horses and burros, and determine whether and where overpopulation exists. AML has been defined as the "optimum number of wild horses which results in a natural ecological balance and avoids deterioration of the range." The aggregate AML for all herd management areas is approximately 27,200. Because wild horse populations can double every four years and few natural predators remain, managing wild horse and burro populations at AML has become a primary objective of the program. To reach and maintain AML, BLM primarily conducts "gathers" to remove excess animals from the range. In 2001, BLM began implementing its most recent management strategy, to reach AML by increasing removals. Since then, about 10,600 animals have been removed, on average, per year.

Maintaining current and accurate inventories of wild horses and burros is a key component of on-the-range management. If the census numbers are inaccurate, particularly if they underestimate the actual population, BLM runs the risk that adequate forage or water may not be available for the wild horses and burros or for livestock and wildlife in the area.

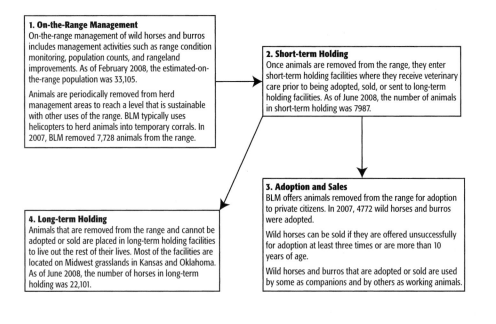

1. On-the-Range Management
On-the-range management of wild horses and burros includes management activities such as range condition monitoring, population counts, and rangeland improvements. As of February 2008, the estimated-on-the-range population was 33,105.

Animals are periodically removed from herd management areas to reach a level that is sustainable with other uses of the range. BLM typically uses helicopters to herd animals into temporary corrals. In 2007, BLM removed 7,728 animals from the range.

2. Short-term Holding
Once animals are removed from the range, they enter short-term holding facilities where they receive veterinary care prior to being adopted, sold, or sent to long-term holding facilities. As of June 2008, the number of animals in short-term holding was 7987.

3. Adoption and Sales
BLM offers animals removed from the range for adoption to private citizens. In 2007, 4772 wild horses and burros were adopted.

Wild horses can be sold if they are offered unsuccessfully for adoption at least three times or are more than 10 years of age.

Wild horses and burros that are adopted or sold are used by some as companions and by others as working animals.

4. Long-term Holding
Animals that are removed from the range and cannot be adopted or sold are placed in long-term holding facilities to live out the rest of their lives. Most of the facilities are located on Midwest grasslands in Kansas and Oklahoma. As of June 2008, the number of horses in long-term holding was 22,101.

After being removed from the range, excess animals are managed in short-term holding facilities, where they are either prepared for adoption or sale, or in long-term holding facilities, where they will live out the remainder of their lives. (See Figure on previous page.) The preferred outcome for healthy animals removed from the range is that they be adopted through BLM's Wild Horse and Burro Program. On average, about 6300 wild horses and burros have been adopted annually since 2001. Under the act, as amended, BLM is required to ensure that adopters can provide humane treatment and care. When adoption demand is not sufficient to absorb all the animals removed, the act directs BLM to either destroy the remaining healthy animals in the most humane and cost-efficient manner possible or, under certain circumstances, sell them "without limitation." BLM has not destroyed any animals since January 1982. To manage for the growing number of unadoptable animals, BLM began opening long-term holding facilities. Unlike the rangelands of the West where the animals normally live, the long-term holding facilities use Midwest grasslands that generally provide the animals with abundant forage and decreased stress. This allows most of the animals to live far longer than they would in the wild. BLM pays the private contractors that operate the long-term holding facilities a fee per horse per day. The sales directive, which was enacted on December 8, 2004, directs BLM to sell excess wild horses and burros without limitation if the animal is more than 10 years of age or has been offered unsuccessfully for adoption at least three times.

Toward Long-Term Sustainability

The number of wild horses and burros removed from the range is far greater than the number adopted or sold, which has resulted in a significant increase in the number of animals in short- and long-term holding and commensurate increases in spending for their care. Since 2001, over 74,000 animals have been removed from the range, while only about 46,400 have been adopted or sold. Thirty-six percent fewer wild horses and burros were adopted in 2007 compared with average adoption rates in the1990s. BLM

officials attribute the steady adoption decline in recent years to the decreasing demand for horses in general and increasing hay and fuel costs associated with their care. As of June 2008, BLM was holding 30,088 animals in short- and long-term holding facilities, far more than in 2001 when it held 9807. From 2001 through June 2008, the average cost per animal increased from $3.00 per day to $5.08 per day. Spending on long-term holding has increased from about $668,000 in 2000 to more than $9.1 million in 2007. In addition, with the long-term holding facilities at full capacity more wild horses are spending a longer time in the more expensive short-term holding facilities.

The long-term sustainabilIty of BLM's Wild Horse and Burro Program depends on the resolution of two significant challenges:

- *If not controlled, off-the-range holding costs will continue to overwhelm the program.* In 2008, BLM anticipates that holding costs will account for about 74 percent of the program's direct costs. As holding costs continue to increase, less funding is available for on-the-range management, which could result in sharp increases in the animal population in the wild. To deal with its long-term holding problem, BLM has primarily sought increased funding to open additional holding facilities. However, funding is not likely to increase in the future, and limited funding is forcing BLM to make the difficult choice among managing the animals on the range to prevent overpopulation, destroying excess unadoptable animals, or selling them without limitation.

- *BLM's options are limited for dealing with unadoptable animals.* The Wild Free-Roaming Horses and Burros Act, as amended, requires that excess animals, for which the adoption demand is not sufficient to absorb all the animals removed from the range, be destroyed in the most humane and cost-efficient manner possible or, under certain circumstances, be sold without limitation. Never less, BLM has still chosen not to destroy or sell excess animals without limitation because of concerns about public and congressional reaction to the large-scale slaughter of thousands of healthy horses.

However, by not destroying or selling them without limitation, BLM is not in compliance with the requirements of the act.

The Horse Lobby View

Defenders of wild mustangs have long portrayed them as the *victims* of ranchers, who prefer cattle on the range, and middlemen, who want to make profit by selling them for horsemeat. Many of these defenders claim that horses have a right to be there. The more extreme groups say, "Let nature take its course. Just leave the horses alone and let them populate naturally."

For groups formed to protect the horses, the specter of euthanasia as a solution remains anathema. "It's not acceptable to the American public," said Virginia Parant, a lawyer who is the director of the American Wild Horse Preservation Campaign. "The mustang," she says, "is part of the American myth. People want to know that they can come to the American West and know that they can see herds of wild horses running. It's part of the imagery." She laughs at the idea of attributing range destruction to horses when cattle greatly outnumber them. Further, Jay F. Kirkpatrick, a scientist who is the director of the Science and Conservation Center in Billings, Montana, contends that BLM has not given sufficient weight to birth control options which could make "serious inroads" on the horse populations.

The Ecological View

Increasingly, environmentalists and scientists have come to see mustangs not as victims but as thousand-pound aliens because they are not native to the region like bison but rather descendents of horses brought to North America by the Spanish. Over time, stray domestic horses belonging to settlers and Native Americans bred with the Spanish mustangs. With hooves and teeth evolved for a different kind of environment, wild horses are especially destructive to the habitats of endangered desert turtles and desert birds in the south and big horn sheep in the north. They damage the waterholes. They damage the grasses, the shrubs, and the bushes, causing negative consequences for all the other plants and animals that live there.

The attitudes of environmentalists toward the horses have changed so much that some are willing to say what was heresy a few years ago: that euthanasia is acceptable if the alternatives are boarding the mustangs for life at taxpayers' expense or leaving them to overpopulate, damage the range and die of hunger or thirst. As one wild horse specialist tells Paula Morin:

> If the wild horse groups can't or won't take them, then I think the proper answer is to implement the law. Personally, I think sale authority would be a good alternative to humane destruction because it would allow us to sell the horses as a last resort. Yes, it would allow those people who buy them to do whatever they want with them, but at least something purposeful happens with the animal. I don't think anybody enjoys the thought of wild horses being euthanized, but it's a fact of life. Hundreds of thousands of domestic horses are put down every year for one reason or another, and so are dogs and cats. Yes, people love horses, and wild horses are special. But they are an animal that must be managed, and if we don't manage them they have problems.

Another sensitive issue besides euthanasia concerns selling wild horses for meat, despite the fact that about 90,000 domestic horses are sold for meat each year. "It is difficult to understand," Ted Williams writes in *Audubon Magazine*,

> why Americans believe that starvation is more humane than culling. In Australia, where there are thought to be as many as 265,000 feral horses and 5 million feral burros, the government shoots them. There, shooting is considered more humane than capture and removal because the animals are not subject to the stresses of the round up, yarding, and long-distance transportation. Moreover, most other nations don't share our taboo against eating horsemeat. It's considered a delicacy in Europe, and in Australia the commercial slaughter of feral horses, burros, and other livestock is a $100 million a year industry.

Could birth control provide an alternative? Herd sizes double every four years, and the BLM is working with a contraceptive that is largely effective for two years in mares. Alan Shepard, who helps run the contraceptive program, says that it showed promise but had limitations. "The ultimate thing is you can't catch them all." Australia also is working on chemical contraception, but an effective agent, practical for field application, may be decades away.

How about the horse lobby's charge that cows do more damage than wild horses? Environmentalists concede that cows do more damage because there are lots more of them, but cattle provide food and livelihoods. When it comes to habitat destruction, what horses lack in numbers they make up for in efficiency. When the grass between the shrubs is gone, a cow is out of luck, but a horse or burro will stomp the plant to death to get that one last blade underneath it. When cows run out of forage, cowboys move them or take them home, but horses and burros are out there all year. Unfenced, they can go anywhere. This means that if horses are left unchecked, they would be the last to survive in the ecosystem, simply because they're more efficient about how much they can eat. But if you let these herds populate "naturally," eventually they would overstock the range and denude it completely — that means it would never grow back.

In the final analysis, a growing number of environmentalists think the horse lobby does not appreciate the importance of maintaining the *whole* ecology and does the horses a disservice when it sets them apart.

Case Questions

1. Which decision-making techniques and concepts described in this chapter are most appropriate to the BLM's situation? Show how you would apply them.
2. What suggestions would you make to help the Bureau improve its handling of the wild horse problem?
3. How would you model this problem?

Case References

U.S. Government Accountability Office, *Bureau of Land Management: Effective Long-Term Options Needed to Manage Unadoptable Wild Horses*, GAO-09-77 (October 2008), 1–10; Deanne Stillman, *Mustang: The Saga of the Wild Horse in the American West* (Boston: Mariner Books, 2009); Jim Robbins, "As Wild Horses Multiply, a Voice for Contraception," *The New York Times* (April 21, 2005/2009); Felicity Barringer, "Mustangs Stir a Debate on Thinning the Herd," *The New York Times* (July 20, 2008); Paula Morin, *Honest Horses: Wild Horses in the Great Basin* (Reno: University of Nevada Press, 2006); Ted Williams, "Horse Sense," *Audubon Magazine* (September-October 2006).

7 Organizing

NASA/JPL

THE LABORATORY

In 1993, the Tucker Company underwent an extensive reorganization that divided the company into three major divisions. These new divisions represented Tucker's three principal product lines.

Mr. Harnett, Tucker's president, explained the basis for the new organization in a memo to the board of directors as follows:

> The diversity of our products requires that we reorganize along our major product lines. Toward this end I have established three new divisions: commercial jet engines, military jet engines, and utility turbines. Each division will be headed by a new vice president who will report directly to me. I believe that this new approach will enhance our performance through the commitment of individual managers. It should also help us to identify unprofitable areas where the special attention of management may be required.

For the most part, each division will be able to operate independently. That is, each will have its own engineering, manufacturing, accounting departments, etc. In some cases, however, it will be necessary for a division to utilize the services of other divisions or departments. This is necessary because the complete servicing with individual divisional staffs would result in unjustifiable additional staffing and facilities.

The old companywide laboratory was one such service department. Functionally, it continued to support all of the major divisions. Administratively, however, the manager of the laboratory reported to the manager of manufacturing in the military jet engine division.

From the time the new organization was initiated until February 1999, when the laboratory manager, Mr. Garfield, retired, there was little evidence of interdepartmental or interdivisional conflict. His replacement, Ms. Hodge, unlike Mr. Garfield, was always eager to gain the attention of management. Many of Hodge's peers perceived her as an empire builder who was interested in her own advancement rather than the company's well-being. After about six months in the new position, Hodge became involved in several interdepartmental conflicts over work that was being conducted in her laboratory.

Historically, the engineering departments had used the laboratory as a testing facility to determine the properties of materials selected by the design engineers. Hodge felt that the laboratory should be more involved in the selection of these materials and in the design of experiments and subsequent evaluations of the experimental data. Hodge discussed this with Mr. Franklin of the engineering department of the utility turbine division. Franklin offered to consult with Hodge but stated that the final responsibility for the selection of materials was charged to his department.

In the months that followed, Hodge and Franklin had several disagreements over the implementation of the results. Franklin told Hodge that, because of her position at the testing lab, she was unable to appreciate the detailed design considerations that affected the final decision on materials selection. Hodge claimed that Franklin lacked the materials expertise that she, as a metallurgist, had.

Franklin also noted that the handling of his requests, which had been prompt under Garfield's management, was taking longer and longer under Hodge's management. Hodge explained that military jet engine divisional problems had to be assigned first priority because of the administrative reporting structure. She also said that if she were more involved in Franklin's problems, she could perhaps appreciate when a true sense of urgency existed and could revise priorities.

The tension between Franklin and Hodge reached a peak when one of Franklin's critical projects failed to receive the scheduling that he considered necessary. Franklin phoned Hodge to discuss the need for a schedule change. Hodge suggested that they have a meeting to review the need for the work. Franklin then told Hodge that this was not a matter of her concern and that her function was merely to perform the tests as requested. He further stated that he was not satisfied with the low-priority rating that his division's work received. Hodge reminded Franklin that when Hodge had suggested a means for resolving this problem, Franklin was not receptive. At this point, Franklin lost his temper and hung up on Hodge.

Can you draw a simple organizational chart showing Tucker Company's three divisions, including the location of the laboratory? Why would the laboratory be located in the military jet engine division? Do you think the conflict between Hodge and Franklin is based on personalities or on the way in which the organization is structured? Sketch out a new organizational chart showing how you would restructure Tucker Company so that the laboratory would provide equal services to all divisions. What advantages and disadvantages do you see in the new structure compared with the previous one?

Source: Theodore T. Herbert, *Organizational Behavior: Readings and Cases,* 2nd ed. (Englewood Cliffs, NJ: Prentice-Hall, 1981), 385–87.

Planning and decision making, the subjects of the two preceding chapters, cannot be separated from **organizing**. If people are to work together effectively in managing a program, they need to know the parts they are to play in the total endeavor and how their roles relate to one another. To design and maintain these systems of roles is basically the managerial function of organization. This definition is a good one. Although many management theorists give loose and woolly definitions, this chapter will simply try to look at organization as the practicing manager does. Organizing thus becomes the grouping of activities necessary to attain a program's objectives.

The first section introduces you to a few important organizational concepts upon which the rest of the chapter will build. The second looks at five generic organizational designs. The third section considers how managers can design organizations. The reason for organizational design is clear: As organizations grow, they add new departments, functions, and hierarchical levels; a major problem is how to tie the whole organization together. In the last section, we address macro concerns about organizations: Why might an entire government want to reorganize itself? What does it mean to "reinvent government"?

Fundamentals of Organizing

Few topics in public administration have undergone as much change in the past few years as that of organizing and organizational structure. Traditional approaches to organizing work are questioned and re-evaluated as managers search out structural designs that will best support and facilitate employees doing the organization's work—designs that are efficient but also flexible enough for success in today's dynamic environment. Recall from Chapter 1 that organizing is *the process of creating an organizational structure.* That important process:

- Divides work into specific jobs and departments
- Assigns tasks and responsibilities associated with individual jobs
- Coordinates diverse organizational tasks
- Clusters jobs into units
- Establishes relationships among individuals, groups, and departments
- Establishes formal lines of authority
- Allocates and deploys organizational resources

The challenge for public managers is to design an organizational structure that allows employees to accomplish the agency's mission—not to "just throw everything together." See cartoon.

Just what is an organizational structure? An organizational structure is the formal framework by which job tasks are divided, grouped, and coordinated. When managers develop or change an organization's structure, they are engaged in organizational design, a process that involves decisions about four key elements: division of labor (specialization), hierarchy (scalar principle), span of control, and line and staff.

Charles Barsotti/Cartoonbank.com

"Wentworth, could I take another look at that reorganization plan?"

"And so you just threw everything together? Mathews, a posse is something you have to organize."

Comment: If people are to work together efficiently, they need to know what part they are to play in the total endeavor and how their roles relate to one another. To design and maintain these systems of roles is basically the managerial function of organization.

Division of Labor

Without a doubt, the cornerstone of the four principles is the division of labor into specialized tasks. But how does the administrator do it? The administrator should begin by determining the necessary activities for the accomplishment of overall organizational objectives, then divide these activities on a logical basis into departments that perform the specialized functions. In this way, the organizational structure itself becomes the primary means for achieving the technical and economic advantages of specialization and division of labor. The procedure is hardly as simple as it sounds, however, for there are at least four ways by which the administrator can divide and place in separate departments the functions of the organization: objective, geography, process, and client.

The most common, of course, is by *objective.* For example, the U.S. Department of Health and Human Services organizes along health and welfare lines; similarly, the National Aeronautics and Space Administration (NASA) subdivides into the Office of Manned Space Flight and the Office of Space Science and Applications. Such divisions according to use or objective can present problems, however. For example, the interrelationship among components often turns out to be much more complicated than it would appear at first. Increasingly, the interfaces become blurred as technology progresses. In nuclear power plants, for instance, one finds no neat dividing lines among the functions of fueling, heating, and power generation.

Another criterion the manager might use in making these structural decisions is *geography.* In other words, administrative authority is distributed not by function but by area. In the national government, the Department of State, the Tennessee Valley Authority and, to a lesser degree, the Department of the Interior have followed this criterion. In other departments and agencies, division by geography appears in modified form. For example, the secretary of the Department of Health and Human Services also has regional representatives who try to shepherd into one flock the regional commissioner of Social Security, the regional public health services offices, and others.

Division of labor might also be based on either *process* or *client.* Process-type departments have at their roots a particular technology, a particular type of equipment, or both. Technology, as used here, refers not only to hardware technology (such as welding in a transportation-maintenance work center) but also to software technology (such as accounting or operations research). Obvious examples of client-based agencies include the Bureau of Indian Affairs and the Department of Veterans Affairs.

Litterer notes at least three drawbacks to the division of labor by function.[1] First, a high degree of specialization may tend to make the occupants of the subunits more concerned with their specialty than with the organization's goals. Second, because of their interest in their own specialty, employees may find it difficult to communicate with other organizational members. Coordination suffers, eventhough its need has increased because of specialization. Third, "in many instances people who have risen through several levels of the organization within a functional specialty have advanced within a unique professional environment and, consequently, may be poorly equipped eventually to assume overall organization responsibilities."[2] Hence, an agency may have difficulty finding chief administrators within its own ranks.

Sayles and Chandler offer a fourth criticism of specialization. It conflicts with the interdisciplinary efforts required—almost by definition—in large mission- or problem-oriented programs:

> The biologist is asked to conceive of the impact of a hard vacuum on genetics and to work with aerospace engineers on joint endeavors. The project manager is asked to move for six months to a distant location to be closer to a critical development team and to shift both his organizational identity and his family's home every several years. Specialists are asked to give up their specialties in favor of joining multidisciplinary teams and to learn from those whom they would normally ignore or consider beneath their dignity.[3]

Hierarchy

The second principle of administrative management is **hierarchy**. It is based on the **scalar principle,** which states that authority and responsibility should flow in a direct line vertically

From Adam Smith's Wealth of Nations (1776)

Adam Smith began his classic study of economics, *Wealth of Nations* (1776), with a discussion of specialization in pin making. Eight men, each performing a simple task, could turn out far more pins than eight men each performing all required series of task.

from the highest level of the organization to the lowest level. This flow is commonly referred to as the **chain of command.** In such an arrangement, a cardinal sin—at least in the view of a bypassed supervisor—is to fail to go through the proper channels in trying to get a message to the top.

We cannot discuss the chain of command without discussing three other concepts: authority, responsibility, and unity of command. *Authority* refers to rights inherent in a managerial position to tell people what to do and to expect them to do it. To facilitate decision making and coordination, an organization's managers are part of the chain of command and are granted a certain degree of authority to meet their responsibilities. As managers coordinate and integrate employees' work, those employees assume an obligation to perform any assigned duties. This obligation or expectation to perform is known as *responsibility.* Finally, the **unity of command** principle—one of Fayol's 14 principles of management, noted in Chapter 1—helps preserve the concept of a continuous line of authority. It states that a person should report to only one manager. Without unity of command, conflicting demands and priorities from multiple bosses can create problems. One shudders to think what Fayol would have thought of the unity of command in the Bush White House. See Figure 7.1.

One of America's foremost sociologists, Robert K. Merton, in a marvelous, although involved, analysis of bureaucracy, traces people's difficulties with bureaucracies to, among other things, hierarchy.[4] His analysis begins with a demand for control made by the top administrators: More specifically, they are concerned with increasing the reliability of behavior within the organization. Therefore, standard operating procedures (SOPs) are instituted, and control consists largely in checking to ensure that those procedures are followed.

Three consequences of this type of control usually follow—none of which is good. First, the amount of personalized relationships is reduced. The full human resources of bureaucracy are not used due to mistrust, fear of reprisals, and so on. Second, participants internalize the rules of the organization; in fact, rules originally devised to achieve organizational goals assume a positive value *independent* of the goals. Third, the categories used in decision making become restricted to a relatively small number. For example, when a specific problem arises, the bureaucrat tends to say that this problem is essentially a certain type of problem. And because the type has been encountered before, one knows exactly

Figure 7.1 Bush White House (March 2006): A Lack of Unity of Command

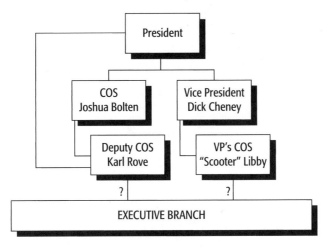

In March 2006, Joshua Bolten became White House chief of staff (COS) with Karl Rove as his deputy. The position is like a chief operating officer (COO) in a corporation, coordinating and executing the chief executive officer's strategy as well as advising him or her on policy. Presumably, Rove, as deputy, would report to Bolten, who is higher in the hierarchy. Not so. Rove reported directly to the president—and other Cabinet-level officials were subordinate to him. Further complicating things was a powerful vice president who shared many of Bolten's chief of staff duties. The lack of clarity in organizational structure only worsened in January 2007 when Cheney claimed that the vice president is not really part of the executive branch, since the only constitutional responsibilities of the office were to preside over the Senate and vote to break ties. One final organizational puzzle: Who was responsible for the actions of "Scooter" Libby? Can the president affect what the vice president's chief of staff does?

how to handle it. Never mind nuances. In this way, an increase in the use of SOPs decreases the search for alternatives.

These three consequences combine to make the behavior of an organization's members highly predictable. This is a nice way of saying that the result is an increase in the *rigidity of behavior* of participants. One of the major costs of rigid behavior is increased difficulty dealing satisfactorily with clients of the organization. Yet client satisfaction is, or should be, a near-universal organizational goal. Another cost of such rigidity in behavior is borne by the organization's own employees in terms of less opportunity for personal growth and development of a mature personality.

Span of Control

Closely related to the principles of division of labor and hierarchy is **span of control.** This principle concerns the number of subordinates a superior can effectively supervise. Traditional theory advocates a narrow span to enable the executive to provide adequate integration of all the activities of subordinates. Most federal agencies, apparently mindful of the span of control principle, have kept their principal subordinates to less than 20. But a president without a chief of staff could have more than 200 individuals, commissions, departments, agencies, and other groups reporting directly to him or her.

All things being equal, the wider or larger the span, the more efficient the organization will be. A simple example can show you why. Assume that we have an organization with approximately 4100 employees. If this organization has a span of control at every level of eight—in other words, every manager supervises eight employees—then you will have a relatively "flat" organization with only five levels. It would look like this:

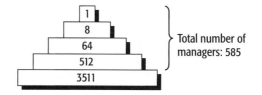

Now assume that over time the span begins to narrow to four. Our old organization is no longer quite so flat:

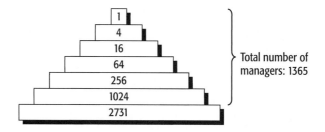

What really matters in determining the span of control is not how many people report to a manager but how many people *who have to work with each other* report to a manager. For example, the secretary of energy, who has reporting to her a number of top administrators, each concerned with a major function, should indeed keep the number of direct subordinates to a fairly low number—between 8 and 12 is probably the limit. Why? Because these subordinates must work closely with each other. Consider how the secretary attempts to exploit solar energy as a potential solution to the energy squeeze. Solar research is assigned to the Office of Research; solar technology to the Office of the Assistant Secretary for Technology; and implementation to the Office of the Assistant Secretary for Conservation and Solar Applications. The Solar Energy Institute conducts and funds activities in all facets of solar energy. Clearly, the heads of these units have to work closely and frequently with each other. Accordingly, a small span of control is called for because the problems of coordination are greater than those of, say, a police sergeant, who supervises several patrols. Each patrol is discrete and relatively autonomous because there is usually little need for interaction among them; hence, a broader span of control is possible.

A second shortcoming of span of control should be apparent from Figure 2.4 on page 63. The span of control concept assumes that a manager's main relationship is downward, to subordinates, but that direction, as illustrated in the figure, is only part of the picture. The upward relationship to overhead authority is at least as important as the downward relationship to subordinates. Likewise, lateral relations with cognate agencies and interest groups are also important. What is needed, then, is to replace the concept of span of control with a more relevant concept: the span of managerial relationships. The span of control, in short, is a terribly limited concept in public-sector management.

Which of the two figures on page 302 best represents the federal government? Paul C. Light, of the University of Minnesota, would probably say the bottom figure. He argues persuasively that *bloat* in government is everywhere, and that bloat at the top may be the real reason government seems to function so poorly at times.[5] The evidence is hard to dispute. Light's analysis shows that the number of senior executives and presidential appointees increased nearly 430 percent between 1960 and 1992, up from 451 to 2393.

And with that increase has come a proliferation of layers: Whereas in 1960 there were 17 tiers from top to bottom in any given agency, now there are 32. Compare that with the Federal Express courier who picks up your package: just six levels of management separate her from FedEx's chairman at headquarters in Memphis.

With additional tiers has come a baffling array of finely calibrated titles: deputy under-secretaries, assistant deputy undersecretaries, and deputy assistant secretaries—the list goes numbingly on. Two years ago, the Department of Energy created a new title that sounds like self-parody: principal associate deputy undersecretary.

This outbreak of modifiers has, if anything, made it harder for government to do its job. It takes longer for 32 managers to sign off on a document than 17 and, naturally, informa-tion gets distorted as it passes through additional hands. The true cost of this thickening, Light writes, appears to be the diffusion of accountability that comes with the proliferation of decision points.

Perhaps, but the easiest cost to see is increased salaries. If the average manager made $60,000 a year, the flatter organization on page 302 would save nearly $470 million a year in managerial salaries alone. Although the wider span is far more efficient in terms of cost, at some point very wide spans can reduce effectiveness. That is, when the span becomes too wide, employee performance suffers because managers no longer have the time to provide necessary leadership and support.

Line and Staff

The simplest way to understand this principle is probably by a military analogy. Soldiers with weapons stand in the front lines (the line), carrying out a military organization's essential functions; meanwhile, usually somewhere behind the front lines stands (or sits) the staff to investigate, to research, and to advise the commanding officer. Only through the commanding officer can the staff influence line decisions. (What are the staff positions in Figure 7.2?)

As any organization—military or otherwise—becomes more complex, managers begin to need advice. Staffs aid managers in many ways. As Anthony Downs points out, a large staff can function as "a control mechanism 'external' to a line hierarchy, promote changes in opposition to the line's inertia, and act as a scapegoat deflecting hostility from its boss."[6] Top executives can use staffs to help bring change to organizations. The innovative capacity of a staff appears to result from the technical orientation of its members, who tend to be younger and better educated than line managers; and it results from the incentive structure of the staff, which helps the top administrator improve the line's performance.

The importance of understanding the **line-staff concept**—that is, the division between those agencies and individuals engaged mainly in implementing programs and those

Figure 7.2   Line and Functional Authority

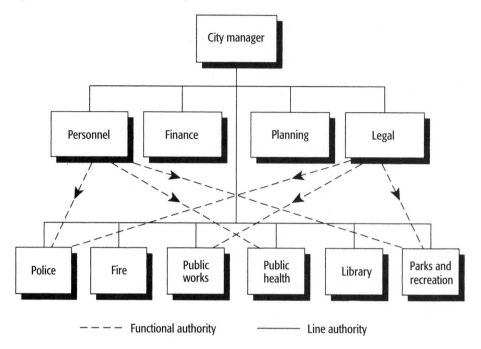

concerned chiefly with providing advice and assistance to top management—cannot be overemphasized. Superior and subordinate alike must know whether they are acting in a staff or line capacity. Lack of clarity on this point often causes friction. **Line authority** means that people in management positions have formal authority to direct and control immediate subordinates. **Staff authority** is narrower and includes the right to advise, recommend, and counsel in the staff areas of expertise. Staff authority is a communication relationship; staff specialists advise managers in technical areas. For example, the financial department of a city would have staff authority to coordinate with line departments about which accounting forms to use to facilitate equipment purchases and standardize payroll services.

Why do staff functions seem inexorably to grow? C. Northcote Parkinson, who has a knack for conveying serious thoughts in the form of a joke, provides the most famous answer.[7] He notes that the number of ships and men in the British Navy decreased by 68 percent and 32 percent between 1914 and 1928. Meanwhile, the number of officials in the admiralty *increased* 78 percent. He also notes, for the same period, that the number of dockworkers increased only 10 percent, whereas the number of dockyard officials and clerks increased 40 percent. More recently, Parkinson detected the same problem at work in sunny California. The Transbay Bridge between San Francisco and Oakland originally had a staff of 12 to keep it repainted. Over the years, the staff grew to 77, even though, in the meantime, they acquired labor-saving machinery.

Parkinson attributes this kind of growth not to increased work but to the dynamics of staff operations. To begin with, officials tend to multiply subordinates. Thus, if a civil servant—call him A—thinks he is overworked, he will have B and C appointed under him. This act increases his importance and precludes any colleague from taking over some of his work. In time, Parkinson suggests, B will find himself overworked; when A allows him subordinates D and E, he must likewise allow C the same numbers; hence, F and G. (One might wonder why *two* subordinates are necessary in each case. One subordinate would result in a division of work with the original supervisor and, to that extent, the subordinate might assume almost equal status.)

Seven Officials are now doing what one did before. How can this be? Parkinson offers another "proposition": Officials make work for each other. For example, an incoming document arrives or comes to D, who decides it really falls within the province of E. A draft reply to E is then prepared and placed before B, who amends it drastically before consulting C, who asks F to deal with it. But F goes on leave at this point, handing the file over to G, who drafts an amendment that is signed by C and returned to B, who revises his draft accordingly and lays the new version before A.

Now, what does A do? This person is beset by many problems created by the new subordinates (for example, promotions, leaves, domestic problems, raises, transfers, and office affairs). A could, of course, simply sign it unread. Parkinson thinks not:

> A is a conscientious man beset as he is with problems created by his colleagues for themselves and for him—created by the mere fact of these officials' existence—he is not the man to shirk his duty. He reads through the draft with care, deletes the fussy paragraphs by B and G, and restores things back to the form preferred in the first instance by the able (if quarrelsome) E. He corrects the English—none of these young [people] can write grammatically—and finally produces the same reply he would have written if officials B and G had never been born. Far more people have taken longer to produce the same result. No one has been idle. All have done their best.[8]

Parkinson's story cannot be dismissed as mere whimsy. As a real-life example of the same situation, here is a list of actual titles of employees in the District of Columbia School District before the arrival of Chancellor Michelle Rhee (see the opening case in Chapter 2): community coordinator and community organizer; attendance aide, attendance officer, and attendance counselor; assistant for research and assessment and assistant for research and planning; employee counseling assistant, employee counseling specialist, employee development specialist, employee relations assistant, and employee relations specialist; not to mention interagency liaison and (clearly overworked) position classification specialist.

Nor is higher education exempt from Parkinson's Law. Over the past two decades, colleges and universities have doubled their full-time support staff, while enrollment increased only 40%, according to analysis by the Center for College Affordability and Productivity, a nonprofit research center. During the same period, the staff of full-time instructors rose only 50%.[9]

In recent years, several American economists have attempted a more rigorous examination of why bureaucracy continues to grow and grow. These scholars start from the assumption that politicians and bureaucrats behave like consumers and business executives. That assumption allows scholars to apply conventional economic analysis to the behavior and decisions of actors in the public sector. Accordingly, this field of economics is called **public choice.**

Among the most famous contributors to the field are Anthony Downs, William Niskanen, and Gordon Tullock.[10] According to Downs, the central problem is that government bureaucracy is not subject to disciplines as those that operate in the private sector are. In the public sector, there is little competition and consumer choice to constrain the self-interest of bureaucrats. Because growth is in the self-interest of the bureaucrat (among other things, growth improves chances for promotion), bureaucracies grow far in excess of what the public wants or efficiency justifies. Public bureaucracies, these economists argue, are like private-sector monopolies—except that they seek bigger budgets rather than bigger profits.

Of course personal aggrandizement is not the only reason for the decline in the "tooth-to-tail" ratio—that is, the ratio of line to staff. First, and most obvious, is the highly reactive and interactive nature of managerial work. Second, new regulations and mandates imposed from the outside can mean more paperwork, and that in turn means more staff. New federal legislation concerning the disabled, bilingual education, and other matters has certainly contributed to the growth of overhead in public schools. Similarly, new complex technology has led in many cases to larger staffs. Increasingly, administrators have to rely on the judgment of physicists, microbiologists, software engineers, systems designers, operations researchers, and the like in making their decisions.

Common Organizational Designs

Leader–Follower Organization

The most natural of human relationships is that between leader and followers. The relationship, however, is not as simple as it might appear at first blush.

The leader's authority, for instance, can seldom be satisfied with obedience based merely on the grounds of common sense or respect. Rather, as the German sociologist, economist, and political scientist Max Weber (1864–1920) has noted, authority seeks to arouse something else (love, fear, even awe) in the followers. This line of inquiry led Weber to conclude that there are three types of legitimate authority: legal, traditional, and charismatic. **Legal authority** we associate with constitutional governments; **traditional authority**, with kings and parents. But it is **charismatic authority** that is most relevant to the leader–follower cluster. *Charisma* is a Greek word meaning "gift from God." The Greeks saw people with charisma as divinely inspired and capable of incredible accomplishments. Weber viewed charisma as a special bond between leaders and followers, noting that the qualities of charismatic leaders enable them to strongly influence followers. Weber also noted that charismatic leaders tend to emerge in times of crisis and that the radical solutions they propose enhance the admiration that followers feel for them. Indeed, charismatic leaders tend to have incredible influence over their followers, who may be inspired by their leaders and become fanatically devoted to them. From this perspective, charismatic leaders often seem larger than life.

Charismatic leaders have strong, confident, dynamic personalities that attract followers and enable the leaders to create strong bonds with their followers. Followers trust charismatic leaders, are loyal to them, and are inspired to work toward the accomplishment of the leader's vision. Therefore, we can define charismatic leadership as the behavioral tendencies and personal characteristics of leaders that create an exceptionally strong relationship between themselves and their followers.

Does charismatic leadership work? Studies indicate that it often does. In general, the followers of charismatic leaders are more committed and satisfied, are better performers, are more likely to trust their leaders, and simply work harder.[11] The charismatic leadership of the eminent physicist J. Robert Oppenheimer at Los Alamos during World War II certainly worked. There, on a barren mesa 35 miles outside Santa Fe, in 20 remarkable, feverish months, the first atomic bomb was designed and built—a success that made Oppenheimer America's most famous scientist. The following three excerpts from Jennet Conant's biography of Oppenheimer give us a glimpse of this special type of leader–follower relationship:[12]

- Los Alamos' pay scale was a particularly sore subject, because the distinguished university scientists on the project were being paid less than technicians and construction crews. Oppenheimer agreed to hear their grievances. After a group of about 20 explained their "beef," Oppenheimer smiled and said, "Well, there's a difference. You know why you're here, and what you're doing, and they don't." Then he turned and walked out. At times like that Oppenheimer radiated power. With his grave, almost priestly manner, he could electrify a crowd, or with one masterful gesture silence opposition. On the rare occasions he lost patience, his usual warmth would be displaced by the infamous "blue glare," an icy stare leveled at those who crossed him.

- In one way or another, everyone became caught up in the Oppenheimer charisma. He established the tone, and it followed that they would do what needed to be done and know how to invent what did not yet exist. "Oppenheimer stretched me," recalled Bob Wilson. "His style, the poetic vision of what we were doing, of life, of a relationship to people, inflamed me. In his presence, I became more intelligent, more vocal, more intense, more prescient, more poetic myself."

- He inspired love, loyalty, hard work, and dedication. He seemed to expect no less, and he reciprocated with his warmth and solicitude, and by living up to his own high standards and never dictating what should be done. "He brought out the best in all of us," said Hans Bethe... "Los Alamos might have succeeded without him, but certainly only with much greater strain, less enthusiasm, and less speed. As it was, it was an unforgettable experience for all the members of the laboratory. There were other wartime laboratories ... but I have never observed in any of these other groups

Bethmann / Corbis

Under the charismatic leadership of Robert J. Oppenheimer, a group of scientists worked. 20 feverish months at a top-secret military facility at Los Alamos, New Mexico, to build the first atomic bomb—a success that made Oppenheimer America's most famous scientist. See chart on p. 315.

quite the spirit of belonging together, quite the urge to reminisce about the days of the laboratory, quite the feeling that this was really a great time of their lives."

Bureaucracy

Most of us have a general idea of what a **bureaucracy** is, and, so far, this text has admittedly taken the liberty of using the term without providing a formal definition. Once again, the surest guide is Max Weber, who in the early part of the twentieth century spelled out in considerable detail the features of the bureaucratic structure.[13] In simplified terms, those features are (1) division of labor based on functional specialization, (2) well-defined hierarchy of authority, (3) system of rules covering the rights and duties of employment, (4) system of procedures for dealing with work situations, (5) impersonality of interpersonal relations, and (6) promotion and selection based on technical competence.

That bureaucratic model is not a description of reality but an *ideal type*—that is, what organizations to varying degrees approximate. Some organizations are more bureaucratic than others, but none is a perfect example of bureaucracy.

The first two of these traits—division of labor and hierarchy—were discussed at some length earlier. Since the remaining four characteristics primarily concern personnel, we will discuss them in Chapter 10.

Because bureaucracy is sometimes used as a derogatory term, allow me two cheers for it. First, with regard to its division of labor and hierarchy, one would be hard pressed to imagine how any group of people could accomplish a moderately complex job without some specialization ("Jones, you concentrate on task X; Smith, you do Y; and López, you do Z") and without someone in charge and responsible. Think about it. If X is an especially arduous or unpleasant task—yet vital to completion of the project—it might not get done unless Jones, who happens to be pretty good at it, is assigned to it. And, if there's no chain of command, then no one is in charge. Yes, the buck needs to stop somewhere.

My second cheer for bureaucracy concerns its other features. Would you really like to work at a place where the whims of your boss determined your rights and duties and where no system of procedures for dealing with work situations existed? In such an organization, there would be no institutional learning: Everyone would have to figure out the job for himself or herself (which would mean a lot of wheels would be reinvented). And pity the poor clients: They can never be sure how they would be treated on any given day. Finally, your boss would be free to hire relatives and promote friends—regardless of technical competence.

We can't quite give bureaucracy three cheers, however, because it does have serious weaknesses. Perhaps the greatest weakness of bureaucracy is its low capability for innovation. Bureaucracy is a performance structure, not a problem-solving structure. It is designed to carry out standard programs, not to invent new ones. Sophisticated innovation requires a very different structural configuration, one that fuses experts drawn from different disciplines into smoothly functioning ad hoc groups.

A related weakness, one that becomes especially acute in an information age, is that the bureaucratic structure impedes the spread of knowledge. Ideas and commands move up and down between headquarters and the units, leading to the creation of vertical "silos" with very little communication between them.

In the remainder of this section we will see how other organizational structures attempt to overcome these weaknesses.

Matrix Approach

The third common organizational design gets its name from the fact that a number of project (team) managers exert planning, scheduling, and cost control over people who have been assigned to their projects, whereas other managers exert more traditional line control (for example, technical direction, training, and compensation) over the same people. Thus, two administrators share responsibility for the same subordinate. The subordinate, in turn, must please two supervisors.

A simple matrix arrangement is shown in Figure 7.3. The five vertical arrows indicate the vertical chain of command for *functions;* the four horizontal arrows show the lateral chain of command for *projects.* The numbers in the boxes indicate the number of assigned personnel.

Figure 7.3   Matrix Organization

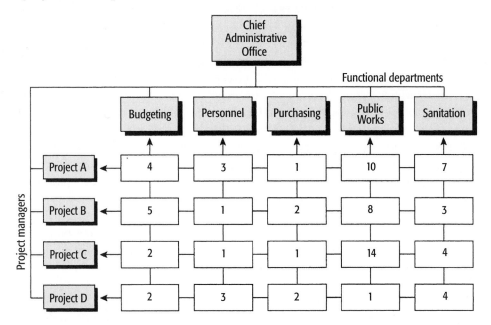

Thus, 22 employees are at work on project C, while 33 employees are assigned to the public works function. The program manager is essentially a "contractor" who "hires" personnel from the line organization. The project manager is assigned the number of personnel with the essential qualifications from the functional departments for the duration of the project.

A number of government agencies have used matrix formats with some success. Here are two examples:[14]

- The Government Accountability Office has used a matrix to assemble project-specific teams to examine complex and crosscutting issues. Employees from various disciplines bring their specific expertise to the group, and there are no traditional organizational boundaries that would prevent the agency from assigning the right people to solve a problem.

- The Air Traffic Organization (ATO) within the Federal Aviation Administration (FAA) uses a matrix structure to counteract the effects of functional silos. "The ATO's mission is to provide air space services to FAA customers, implement advanced cost and performance tools and techniques, and focus on employee performance and accountability. To address issues in a rapidly changing aviation environment, the FAA needed to create a flexible work environment within the ATO. A matrix model has helped to reduce silos and promote a shared work experience among ATO employees. Decision-making and support are institutionalized across the FAA, which helps break down organizational 'stovepipes' and promote cross polymerization of expertise between service units."

Again, the question arises—when should this particular form of organization be used? Try approaching the answer from the opposite direction. A **matrix organization** should *not* be used when the work performed by an agency is applied to standardized services with high volumes (for example, waste disposal). However, the matrix structure *can* be used effectively when the work performed is for specific, narrowly defined projects (for example, antitrust cases). As specific projects end, they can be deleted from the organization, for the matrix organization is a fluid one. A general rule then would be this: When an organization has a large number of specialists—and coordination is therefore difficult—the matrix approach might be a solution.

Project groups do, however, have their problems. They make it difficult for personnel to develop the expertise that they could gain from working in one functional area. Further, technical personnel who are often shifted back and forth among projects can feel isolated and rootless. Finally, with personnel constantly moving from one project to another, an organization can find it difficult to build up a source of accumulated wisdom, such as is possible in functional departments.

Team Approach

What Is a Team?   Today both public and private organizations are trying to find ways to delegate authority, push responsibility to low levels, and create participative teams that engage the commitment of employees. This approach enables organizations to be more flexible and responsive in an environment characterized by rapid change in information flows and information technology.

It is important to distinguish a team from a mere group of people with a common assignment. Katzenbach and Smith offer this definition:

> A team is a *small number* of people with complementary skills (technical, problem-solving, and interpersonal) who are committed to a *common-purpose performance goal and approach* (that is, how they will *work together*) for which they hold themselves *mutually accountable.*[15]

This definition has four components. First, three or more people are required. If the group is less than three, it is a dyad. A dyad is a partnership, not a team; adding a third person often raises productivity. Teams can be quite large, although most have fewer than 15 people. Research shows that team productivity peaks at around five.[16] Unfortunately, teams tend to be overstaffed, often because managers don't want to leave out anyone. Too large groups, alas, usually backfire. If the manager doesn't break a large group down, members will do it for her: They'll form cliques.

Second, people in a team share a performance goal, whether it be to identify, analyze, and solve work process problems (self-managed teams or quality circles) or to treat wounded troops in Iraq (eight-person forward surgical teams). The goal of the latter might be to save a certain percentage of wounded who will die unless they receive critical care within 24 hours. Instructors often assign students to teams to make presentations, in which case the goal is to receive an acceptable grade.

Third, although a team is a group of people, the two terms are not interchangeable. A manager, an instructor, or coach can put together a group of people and never form a team. The concept implies a sense of shared mission and *mutual accountability*. A group has a designated, strong leader who holds individuals accountable. A team may share or rotate leadership and hold members accountable to each other.

Fourth, the team has a particular way of working together. Organizational theorist Robert W. Keidel uses a sports metaphor to describe the kind of interaction, communication, and chemistry evident in certain organizations today.[17] Baseball exemplifies the first kind of team. Players are *on* the team but, they do not play as a team. When a player is at bat, he is totally alone. Players whose paycheck depends on their batting average do not like to sacrifice bunt—which does nothing for their individual numbers—to get a base runner into scoring position. (And the manager finds that these millionaire players often possess the most clout with the team owner.)

"Baseball teams," then, are any decentralized, individually oriented organizations based on professional autonomy, such as law firms, university faculty, R & D centers, or surgical teams. Anesthesiologists, for example, do not come to the assistance of the surgical nurse or surgeon. Because all players occupy fixed positions and can be trained intensely for performance in that position, the baseball model is ideal to show what happens in organizations built around repetitive tasks with clearly established rules. The only problem is that there is less and less of that kind of work in both the public and private sectors.

Keidel's second type of team is the "football team." It is a centralized, top-down organization; the word of the coach is law. Symphony orchestras and hospital emergency teams are based on this model.

> On this team, too, all players have fixed positions. The tuba players in the orchestra will not take over the parts of the double basses. They stick to their tubas. In the crisis team at the hospital, the respiratory technician will not make an incision in the chest of the patient to massage the heart. But on the teams, the members work as a team. Each coordinates his or her part with the rest of the team.[18]

Unlike the baseball team, the football team has considerable speed and flexibility—if the game plan is clear and the team is well led.

Finally, there are the "basketball teams"—small, group-based, cooperative forms that require speed, flexibility, and innovation through cooperation. Players have preferred, rather than fixed, positions and cover for one another. Examples of these cooperation-based, basketball-type organizations are jazz combos, advertising agencies, management-consulting firms, and the Executive Office of the President. Because the total performance of this kind of team is greater than the sum of the parts—it has synergy—it is the strongest team of all. It is particularly well suited for work in the information revolution. Drucker explains:

> In the baseball-type team, players get their information from the situation. Each receives information appropriate to his or her task, and receives it independently of the information the teammates all receive. In the symphony orchestra or the [football] team, the information comes largely from conductor or coach. They

control the "score." In the [basketball] team, the players get their information largely from each other. This explains why the change in information technology, and the move to what I have called the "information-based organization" has made necessary [changing the team].[19]

Types of Teams Teams can be classified in a number of ways, such as permanent or temporary and functional or cross-functional. They can also be classified by the amount of autonomy they possess. Autonomy is the degree to which workers have the discretion, freedom, and independence to decide how and when to accomplish their jobs. Below we will look at three of the most important types of teams in the public sector.

Cross-functional teams consist of employees from various functional departments who are responsible to meet as a team and resolve mutual problems. Team members typically still report to their functional departments, but they also report to the team, one member of whom may be the leader. Louisville, Kentucky's CityWork engages frontline workers in the process of sharing recommendations with quick-responding managers. CityWork sessions, often initiated from within the departments themselves, begin by convening 8 to 12 city workers and managers, including a Cabinet-level official. Within that group, smaller teams—cutting across organizational and hierarchical boundaries—are formed.

Permanent teams are brought together as a formal department in an organization. Instead of just working together, employees are placed in the same location and report to the same supervisor. Figure 7.4 provides one example of reorganizing into permanent teams in city government. The process of obtaining business licenses is generally a time-consuming (2 days or longer) affair. Citizens wanting to open a business have to have a license, and that requires going through several different departments. In a system based on permanent teams, applicants go to one office, where a small team helps the applicant fill out a one-page form. There is no waiting, no running from building to building, and no photocopying because all the expertise required is there. Result: What used to take two or more days now takes less than half an hour.

Special-purpose or **project teams** are created outside the formal organizational structure to undertake a project of special importance or creativity. Special-purpose teams focus on a specific project and are expected to disband once that specific project is completed. Undoubtedly, the most important special purpose team in U.S. history was the Manhattan Project. (See Figure 7.5.) Here are a couple of more recent examples:

- Not long ago, U.S. Customs Service agents seized a fishing boat returning to Miami from the Bahamas. The "fishermen" seemed unusual: One wore a Pierre Cardin pullover, and the other, a Sassoon jacket. Under a concealed floor the agents found 1000 pounds of marijuana. The agents were part of the South Florida Task Force, a group made up of elements not only from the Customs Service (drawn from cities across the country) but also from the Army, Navy, Air Force, Coast Guard, Federal Bureau of Investigation (FBI), and Drug Enforcement Administration.

- In the wildlands of the Northern Rockies, more than 15,000 people from the Forest Service, the Bureau of Land Management, the National Park Service, the Bureau of Indian Affairs, the Army, and numerous state and local agencies have formed a

Figure 7.4   The Team Structure in City Government

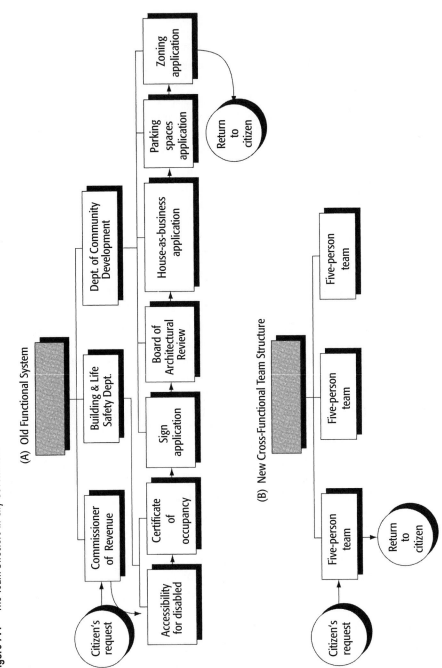

(A) Old Functional System

(B) New Cross-Functional Team Structure

Figure 7.5   Manhattan Project Organizational Chart

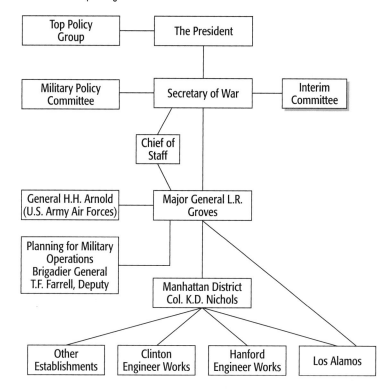

SOURCE: Chart adapted from Leslie R. Grove, *Now It Can Be Told* (Cambridge, MA: De Capo Press, 1983).

special-purpose team to battle fires. In the past, the Forest Service had one person in charge, a fire boss, whose single task was to put out the blaze. Other tasks, such as conducting evacuations, repairing environmental damage, or even protecting homes (instead of trees) from fire, fell haphazardly to other agencies and people. Under the new arrangement, the people in charge are called the incident commanders.[20]

Advantages and Disadvantages   Your high school coach was right: Teamwork matters. In July 2004, the Greek national soccer team won the European championship, led by relatively unknown players. They prevailed over several countries filled with superstars. A month earlier, the Detroit Pistons defeated the heavily favored Los Angeles Lakers in the NBA finals. The Lakers had four players likely to be in the Hall of Fame some day (Shaquille O'Neal, Kobe Bryant, Karl Malone, and Gary Peyton), whereas the Pistons had only one second-team all-NBA player.

Scholarly studies support your coach. Research shows that teams boost productivity and innovation. In the case of heart surgery, teamwork literally can be a matter of life and death. Robert Huckman and Gary Pisano at Harvard analyzed the work of heart surgeons who practice at more than one hospital. They found that the death rates from similar procedures performed by the same surgeons can vary as much as fivefold at different hospitals. Most of the time, patients did better in the hospital where their surgeons performed more operations. Hackman says the results suggest that the surgeon's interactions with anesthesiologists, nurses, and technicians are crucial to the outcome of the surgery. "The argument has always been that if you want to get something done well, you go to the best surgeon," he says. "Our findings suggest that the skills of the team, and of the organization, matter."[21]

Cross-functional teams allow organizations to retain some advantages of a functional structure, such as economies of scale and in-depth training, while gaining the benefits of team relationships. Barriers across departments melt away; team members know each other's problems better and are more willing to compromise (pass the ball off for an easy layup); organizations make decisions quicker when not every decision needs to work its way up to the top of the hierarchy for approval; administrative costs of overhead decline; and finally, morale rises as responsibility expands and jobs are enriched.

One of the most common misperceptions about teams is that, at some point, members become so comfortable and familiar with one another that they start accepting one another's foibles and, as a result, performance drops. The evidence fails to support that premise. Consider crews flying commercial airplanes. The National Transportation Safety Board found that 73% of the incidents in its database occurred on a crew's very first day of flying together, before people had the chance to learn through experience how best to cooperate as a team. Also, a NASA study found that the fatigued crews who had a history of working together made about half as many errors as crews composed of rested pilots who have not flown together before.[22]

But the team approach has its downside. As seen with the matrix organization, employees may experience conflicts and dual loyalties as the cross-functional team places different demands on members than do their department managers. Although teams may decrease costs because less administrative overhead is required, teams can also *increase* costs because of more time spent in meetings and coordinating. Nor should the dangers of overdecentralization be ignored. Public executives, who traditionally have made the decisions and take the blame when things went wrong, may have some justifiable concern when a team moves ahead too far on its own. Team members are less likely to see the big picture and the political ramifications of their decisions. Top management must not shirk its duty to keep the team aligned with the agency's objectives.

Table 7.1 shows the factors that help a manager know when to use a team and when to use a traditional group.

Network

In business, the network structure means that the organization disaggregates major functions into separate units that are brokered by a small headquarters organization. Rather than house various services under one roof, the services are provided by separate organizations working under contract and connected—probably electronically—to the central office. The

Table 7.1 Factors Determining a Manager's Choice of Team Structure	
Factors Favoring Teams	Factors Favoring a Traditional Group
• There is a clear, engaging reason or purpose.	• There isn't a clear, engaging reason or purpose.
• The job can't be done unless people work together.	• The job can be done by people working independently.
• Rewards can be provided for teamwork and team performance.	• Rewards are provided for individual effort and performance.
• Ample resources are available.	• The necessary resources are not available.
• Teams will have clear authority to manage and change how work gets done.	• Management will continue to monitor and influence how work gets done.

SOURCE: Ruth Wageman, "Critical Success Factors for Increasing Superb Self-Managing Teams," *Organizational Dynamics,* 26, no. 1 (1997): 49–61.

network approach is revolutionary because it is difficult to answer the question "Where is the organization?" in traditional terms. For example, an organization may contract for expensive services such as training, transportation, legal, and engineering, so these functions are no longer part of the organization.

In government, **network organization** refers to those instances in which the government chooses to create, through its power to contract and fund, a network of nongovernmental organizations to implement policy. "In government by network the bureaucracy is replaced by a wide variety of institutions, almost all of which have better reputations (and sometimes better performance) than bureaucratic government. In government by network the government stops trying to do anything itself; instead it funds other organizations to do the work the government wants done. An immense variety of organizations are part of government by network. Churches, research labs, nonprofit organizations, and for-profit companies have been called on to perform the work of the government."[23]

This model of government has grown more popular for two reasons. First, the complexity of problems modern society faces makes it difficult for a single organization to address them. Just think of the problems that the Department of Homeland Security and the Centers for Disease Control and Prevention must manage. Or, to make the point more generally, consider Table 7.2. It shows that certain conditions favor a network model of delivery and another set of conditions supports a more traditional hierarchical approach. Suffice it to say the conditions on the left are appearing more and more frequently in the early years of the twenty-first century than those on the right.

One factor favoring a network does not appear in the table, however. As Lawrence O'Toole and Kenneth J. Meier have recently reminded us, "The main benefit of working through networked patterns—from the government's point of view—has been political." A diffuse network of actors allows political authorities to distance themselves from

Table 7.2 Factors Determining Government's Choice of Governance Model	
Factors Favoring a Network Model	Factors Favoring a Hierarchical Model
• Need for flexibility	• Stability preferred
• Need for differentiated response to clients or customers	• Need for uniform, rule-driven response
• Need for diverse skills	• Only a single professional skill needed
• Many potential private players available	• Government predominant provider
• Desired outcome or outputs clear	• Outcome ambiguous
• Private sector fills skill gap	• Government has necessary experience
• Leveraging private assets critical	• Outside capacity not important
• Partners have greater reach or credibility	• Government experienced with citizens in this area
• Multiple services touch same customer	• Service is relatively stand-alone
• Third parties can deliver service or achieve goal at lower cost than government	• In-house delivery more economical
• Rapidly changing technology	• Service not affected by changing technology
• Multiple levels of government provide service	• Single level of government provides service
• Multiple agencies use or need similar functions	• Single agency uses or needs similar functions

SOURCE: Stephen Goldsmith and William D. Eggers, *Governing by Network: The New Shape of the Public Sector* (Washington, D.C.: Brookings, 2004), 51.

controversial issues. O'Toole and Meier argue that individual networks have a "dark side"—namely, "individual network nodes can work to bias the organization's action in ways that benefit the organization's more advanced clients." In other words, the rich and powerful have disproportionate influence over networks.[24]

The second reason for the growing use of networks is the digital revolution (see Chapter 12). Recent advances in computers and telecommunications enable organizations to collaborate in real time with external partners in ways not previously possible. That is not to say governments did not use networks before the digital revolution. One example of government by network, Elaine Ciulla Kamark reminds us, is the much maligned military-industrial complex that began to emerge after World War II.

> During the Cold War, the United States engaged countless corporations, along with their own internal research laboratories, in developing sophisticated weaponry. At the same time, the Soviet Union kept its weapons research within the bureaucracy of the communist state. By 1989, this real-world experiment was over. When the Soviet empire fell, we learned that its technological and military capacity had fallen behind that of the United States. Government by network had won; bureaucratic government had lost.[25]

As the following two examples of networks illustrate, this structure is not limited to large-scale military endeavors, Goldsmith and Eggers give these examples:

- *The Golden Gate National Recreation Area.* This national park relies so heavily on partners to do everything from maintain historic buildings to rehabilitate standard marine mammals that National Park Service employees constitute only 18 percent of its total work force.
- *Arizona Motor Vehicle Department (MVD).* The combination of a growing population and a spending freeze forced the MVD to search for new ways to meet the growing service demand. The result: the MVD's third-party program, an initiative to improve customer service by enlisting third-party providers to administer some of the transactions that previously would have been done exclusively by the MVD staff. Rather than put a service out for bid and award a contract to a single provider, the third-party statute was written to allow any number of third parties to offer services, so long as they were duly qualified and authorized and met compliance standards set by the program. This "many provider" aspect of the program was the cornerstone of the MVD's competitive government approach to doing business.[26]

Managing a network requires a different set of skills than managing a hierarchy. Goldsmith and Eggers note the following skills: big picture thinking, coaching, mediation, negotiation, risk analysis, contract management, strategic thinking, interpersonal communications, project management, and team building. These are not skills American public administration has emphasized over the past 100 years. Not only will future generations of public administrators need to acquire these skills, but they will also need the ability to tackle unconventional problems.

The Process of Organizational Design

Limitations of the Organizational Chart

"Show me the organizational chart," Leon Panetta ordered when he took over in mid-1994 as White House chief of staff. The new boss was dismayed but not exactly surprised when he got his answer. No one had an organizational chart detailing who did what in the Clinton White House. As for access to the Oval Office, Panetta recalls, "As far as I know, anybody who walked down the hall could walk in."[27] Three years later, when Panetta was ready to return to California, the White House had a chart and President Clinton had a second term. Admirers say Panetta could take a large share of credit for both.

Despite the importance of organizational design, most administrators approach it rather informally—one might almost say their approach amounts to little more than drawing boxes on a page. Eventually, a new organizational chart appears, which the administrator can more or less defend.

Organizational charts are by no means useless in designing and understanding organizations. The organizational chart of most agencies shows—indeed is designed to show—at least two things: how work is to be divided into components and who is (supposed to be) whose supervisor. Moreover, it implicitly shows several other things: the nature of the work performed by each component; the grouping of components on a functional, regional, or service basis; and the levels of management in terms of successive layers of superiors and subordinates. Some can show more. (See Figure 7.6.)

Nevertheless, what the chart does not show is often the most interesting part—at least to someone interested in organizational design.[28] In the first place, the chart by itself cannot tell

Figure 7.6   Organizational Chart for the Federal Government, Showing Department Sizes

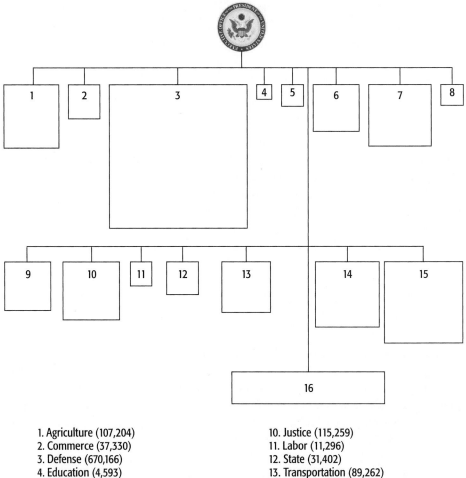

1. Agriculture (107,204)
2. Commerce (37,330)
3. Defense (670,166)
4. Education (4,593)
5. Energy (15,823)
6. Health and Human Services (67,240)
7. Homeland Security (150,350)
8. Housing and Urban Development (10,660)
9. Interior (74,818)
10. Justice (115,259)
11. Labor (11,296)
12. State (31,402)
13. Transportation (89,262)
14. Treasury (134,302)
15. Veterans Affairs (226,171)
16. All independent establishments and government corporations except U.S. Postal Service (183,008)

SOURCE: Based on data in *Statistical Abstract of the United States, 2006* (Washington, DC: U.S. Government Printing Office).

the reader much about the degree of responsibility and authority exercised by positions on the same management level. Two persons on the same management level may have vastly different degrees of authority. In a word, the chart cannot show the degree of decentralization.

Second, attempting to determine line and staff positions from an organizational chart is an arduous academic chore. In some agencies, charting methods are used to attempt to make this distinction. For example, the so-called staff units are charted on one horizontal plane, line units on another. Other agencies use skinny lines to connect staff but robust ones to connect line units. To try to interpret these differences in terms of line-staff responsibilities, authorities, and relationships is as difficult as reading the degree of decentralization from the chart.

Third, some view the linear distance from the chief executive officer as a measure of status or importance; but this interpretation may or may not be correct. It has the same limitations as trying to infer relative importance in an organization by comparing the size of one's office, files, parking lot space, and so forth.

Fourth, although the chart shows some major lines of communication, it does not show all. It is axiomatic that every organization is an intricate network of communication; if it were not, then nothing would get done.

Closely related to the preceding **limitations of the organizational chart** is a fifth. The chart fails to show the **informal organization**—that is, "those aspects of the structure which, while not prescribed by formal authority, supplement or modify the formal structure."[29] The formal organization, therefore, encompasses all the relationships and channels of communication that people are expected to develop and use to meet organizational and, often, personal objectives.

In sum, one would do well to heed the advice of one former secretary of state who said that "organization or reorganization in government can often be a trap for the unwary. The relationships involved in the division of labor and responsibility are far more subtle and complex than the little boxes which the graph drawers put on paper with their perpendicular and horizontal connecting lines."[30] In an effort to avoid the organizational chart pitfall, a process for thinking through a new organizational structure will be given in skeletal form. This process should facilitate the complex task of separating those things that must be taken into account so far as structure is concerned from those that have less bearing on organizational performance.

Four Critical Questions in Organizational Design

Question #1: In What Area Is Excellence Required to Attain the Organization's Objectives?   All sorts of activities might be housed in an organizational structure, but what we are after here are what Peter F. Drucker calls "the load-bearing parts of the structure"—that is, the key activities.[31]

As noted in Case 3.1 in Chapter 3, Katrina Breakdown (pages 149–156), the Federal Emergency Management Agency (FEMA) had been created in 1979 as a completely independent agency, but in 2002 it was merged into the newly created Department of Homeland Security. Unfortunately, given the Bush administration's strong focus on terrorism, the idea that handling national disasters should also be an area in which excellence is required got short shrift. Consequently, some of FEMA's responsibilities were distributed to other governmental units. The upshot of this action was to dilute the federal government's focus on dealing with disasters. At the same time, FEMA's funding was reduced so that greater resources could be devoted to protection against terrorist attacks. Nor was FEMA headed by a highly qualified professional in dealing with natural disasters as it had been before its absorption into the new department.

Our second example of designers failing to recognize activities that should be considered "key" appears in the discussion of underplanning for the Iraq invasion (pages 228–29). On November 20, 2005, *The New York Times* reported the following: "The Pentagon's leadership, recognizing that it was caught off guard by difficulties in pacifying Iraq after the invasion, is poised to approve a sweeping directive that will elevate what it calls 'stability operations' to a core military mission comparable to full-scale combat." *Translation: Pentagon leadership now recognizes that stability operations are load-bearing parts of the structure of the Defense Department.*

Question#2: What Activities Belong Together and What Activities Belong Apart?   Before trying to answer this question, let's sort out the types of activities that can be found in an organization. According to Drucker, there are roughly four major group activities we can distinguish by their contribution.

First are *top-management activities.* These, according to Drucker, include maintaining external relations, thinking through the mission of the agency, making decisions during major crises, and building the human organization.[32] Second are *results-producing activities.* These contribute most directly to the performance of the entire enterprise. Although results-producing activities are not hard to discover in the private sector (just look for those directly producing revenue), they are less obvious in the public sector. Third are *results-contributing,* or *staff activities*—for example, advising, teaching, legal research, and training. Fourth are the *hygiene and housekeeping activities,* which range from the medical department to the people who clean the floor.

With these distinctions in mind, let's now see if we can discover some general propositions about which activities belong together and which don't.

- Results-producing activities should never be subordinate to non-results-producing activities.
- Support activities should never be mixed up with results-producing activities. Airline crashes, such as that of ValuJet 592 in 1996, led several members of Congress to call for the FAA to shed its mission of promoting aviation and focus exclusively on safety. The dual roles of cheerleading and watchdogging create a credibility gap.
- Top-management activities are incompatible with other activities. One former secretary of Housing and Urban Development argues that as presidential staff increasingly becomes involved in day-to-day decisions, it spends less and less time on broad, long-range policy issues. (The latter activity is of course termed a *top-management activity.*) Confusion is created when people at the top try to do too much: "A curious inversion occurs. Operational matters flow to the top, as central

staffs become engrossed in subduing outlying bureaucracies, and policymaking emerges at the bottom."[33]

- Advisory staffs should be few, lean, and nonoperational. Further, advisory work should not be a career; that is, it is work to which career professionals should be exposed in the course of their growth but not work that they should do for long.
- Hygiene and housekeeping activities should be kept separate from other work or else they will not get done. In a hospital, where these activities are technically under the upper levels of management, they tend to be neglected. No "respectable" manager in a hospital wants to have anything to do with them. As a result, they are left unmanaged; and that means they are done badly and expensively. But what can be done? One solution is to farm out these activities to somebody whose business is to provide such "hotel" services.

Question #3: What Decisions Are Needed to Obtain the Performance Necessary to Attain the Organization's Objectives?

Some might object that this question is unanswerable ahead of time. Not true. Although we might not be able to anticipate the exact contents of all the decisions that will confront an organization in the future, we can probably say with a high degree of certainty what their kind and subject matter will be. In most organizations, over 90 percent of the decisions managers make each year are typical and fall into a small number of categories—just as a list of frequently asked questions (FAQs) covers about 90 percent of the questions readers and customers ask.

Now, organizational designers have two choices—they can either (1) try to identify those "typical" questions in advance and assign them to particular levels and units within the organization or (2) forgo such decision analysis. If they opt for (2), then there will probably be a lot of questions that just keep bouncing around in the organization looking for a home.

To place authority and responsibility for various kinds of decisions requires that we first classify them according to kind and character. Obviously, the precise level at which a decision is made depends on the nature of the decision. According to Drucker, the more a decision is characterized by the following four factors, the higher the level will be at which it must be made:

1. *Futurity:* how long into the future the decision commits the organization
2. *Reversibility:* how fast the decision can be reversed if it proves wrong
3. *Impact:* how many other functions in an organization it affects
4. *Rarity:* how distinct the event is

The next step in decision analysis is to follow this simple principle: *A decision should be made at the lowest possible level and as close to the scene of the action as possible.* Only four things limit how much decision-making authority can be delegated within the organization, and here is where the four factors mentioned above come into play. To the extent a decision entails a long-term commitment, is not easily reversed, affects many other functions, and concerns a relatively rare phenomenon or problem, it must be made at a higher rather than a lower level.

Question #4: Where Do Specific Organizational Components Belong? To be more specific, in the final step in designing an organization, we want to determine with whom Jones, a manager in charge of activity X, will have to work, what contribution he will have to make to Smith and Lee, who are in charge of other activities, and what contribution Smith and Lee, in turn, will have to make to Jones. "The basic rule in placing an activity within the organizational structure is to impose on it the *smallest possible number of relationships*. At the same time, it should be so placed that the crucial relations, that is, the relationships on which depend its success and the effectiveness of its contribution, should be easy, accessible, and central to the unit. *The rule is to keep relationships to a minimum but make each count.*"[34] To see an extreme violation of this principle, take a peek at Figure 9.9 on page 429.

Symptoms of Effective and Ineffective Organizational Structure

An effective organization exhibits at least seven traits.[35] First is *clarity*. All managerial components and all individuals within the organization, especially the managers, need to know where they belong, where they stand, and where they have to go for whatever is needed. Second is *economy*. The minimum effort should be needed to control, to supervise, and coax people to perform. Third is the *direction of vision*. "Organization structure should direct the vision of individuals and of managerial units toward performance rather than toward efforts." Efforts, as used here, refers to things like "busy work" or "spinning one's wheels."

Fourth is *understanding one's own task and the common task*. "An organization should enable each individual, especially each manager and each professional—but also each managerial component—to understand his own task. . . . But at the same time, an organization should enable everyone to understand the common task, the task of the entire organization." An old story illustrates the point. A man comes upon a construction site and asks one worker what he's doing. "Earning a living" is the reply. A few yards away, he asks another worker the same question. "Can't you see? I'm laying bricks," this worker replies. The man decides to ask one more worker his question. The third worker puts down his trowel and with wise eyes, bright and amused, looks at the questioner. His reply: "Building a cathedral."

The fifth trait of an effective organization involves *decision making*. "An organization design . . . needs to be tested as to whether it impedes or strengthens the decision making process. A structure that forces decisions to go to the highest possible level of organization rather than be settled at the lowest possible level is clearly an impediment." In New York City, once Mayor Bloomberg hires a commissioner, he makes it clear that he (Bloomberg) is not a micromanager. One appointee recounts the brief mandate he was given: "It's your agency. Don't screw it up." The mayor gave new commissioners two pieces of advice: "Only hire people smarter than you," and "Make changes early."[36]

Sixth is *stability and adaptability*. Stability means that an organization is able to do its work even though the world around it is in turmoil. "But stability is not rigidity. On the contrary, organizational structure requires a high degree of adaptability. A totally rigid structure is not stable; it is brittle." And the seventh trait is *self-renewal*. To meet this criterion, organizations need to produce tomorrow's leaders from within. They can do this by minimizing the number of rungs of the promotion ladder. For self-renewal, it is also necessary for an organization to be accessible to new ideas.

There is no perennially effective organization. At best, organizational structure will not be a hindrance to an agency's mission. But what are the most common symptoms of serious flaws in organizational design? First is *the multiplication of management levels*—what Paul Light has called the "thickening of government." He states, "A basic rule of organization is to build the least possible number of management levels and forge the shortest possible chain of command." The reasons are not hard to see. "Every additional level makes more difficult the attainment of common direction and mutual understanding. Every additional level distorts objectives and misdirects attention."[37]

The second most common symptom of *an ineffective organization is the recurrence of organizational problems*. No sooner has a problem supposedly been "solved" than it comes bouncing back in a new form.

A third symptom of ineffective organizational structure is that *the attention of key people is on irrelevant or secondary problems.* The contrast between FEMA and the U.S. Coast Guard during the Katrina disaster in 2005 is instructive. The response of the former during the disaster was sluggish and bureaucratic. But such situations call for organizational structures that allow for improvisation; flexibility should be the true guiding principle. This is why the Coast Guard was successful. It had gotten its assets out of New Orleans before the storm and situated them in Alexandria. "We threw away the playbook," explained one Coast Guard responder. "We took all comers and didn't wait for incident management teams. We winged it. We entered the game and stayed in the game until our job was done. Too much bureaucracy can be a big, big problem in a catastrophe."[38]

A fourth symptom is *too many meetings attended by too many people.* A fifth symptom is to rely on "coordinators," "assistants," and other such people *whose job it is not to have a job."* This indicates, according to Drucker, that jobs, "rather than being designed for one defined result are expected to do a great many parts of different tasks."

The sixth symptom of an ineffective organization—namely, *constant reorganization*—especially plagues the public sector and, as such, deserves special consideration.

Reorganizing, Reinventing, and Reforming Government

The past several decades have witnessed acceleration in both the number and variety of major administrative reform statutes enacted by Congress.[39] Not all reforms are the same. First are those that seek greater efficiency through the application of scientific principles to organization and management. For example, we could cite the 1939 Reorganization Act and three post-September 11, 2001 structural reforms to address U.S. vulnerability to terrorist attacks (the Transportation Security Administration, the Department of Homeland Security, and the Office of National Intelligence Director). A second type of reform seeks improved performance through a focus on outcomes and employee engagement. An example of this type would be the Clinton administration's 1994 reinventing government package for liberation of public management through delegation of authority and team building.

(see p. 231 in Chapter 5). A third type of reform attacks tax fraud, waste, and abuse through increased auditing and investigation (for example, the Inspector General Act in 1978). The fourth type of reform seeks increased fairness through transparency in government and access to information, an example being the Freedom of Information Act in 1964.

In this section, we take a closer look at the rationale for reorganization. Then we examine some of the key concepts involved in the effort to "reinvent" referred to above. We wrap things up by considering the pitfalls in trying to improve government performance.

Rationale for Reorganization

Some (not all) attempts at reorganization are in reality efforts to escape rethinking the principles of sound management outlined previously. At the first sign of trouble, the cry goes out for reorganization. As might be expected, the times when this kind of surgery is needed are limited.

Perhaps the most obvious **rationale for reorganization** is growth. This point can be illustrated with a well-known children's story. If the giant in *Jack the Giant Killer* were in fact many times larger than a normal man, he could not have the same form as a man. In other words, if the giant had the same proportions as a normal man but was a hundred times larger in size, his bone structure would be entirely inadequate. Biological design must conform to the square-cube law, which says that if a giant were a thousand times the size of a man, his volume would increase $10 \times 10 \times 10$ and so, roughly, would his weight. But his area would increase only 10×10; hence, the cross-sectional area of his bones would increase at a far lower rate than the weight that they have to support. So, when the giant attempts to stand, his leg bone breaks. In short, the *form* of a human is inadequate for a larger being. The square-cube law explains why larger beings walk on four legs, as the elephant does, or float in the ocean, as does the whale. And the law seems to hold for organizations: Larger organizations require different forms than smaller ones.[40] For example, if an organization grows significantly, it must provide for additional reporting relationships—otherwise its managers might find themselves with more people reporting to them than they have the time and talent to properly supervise.

A second use of reorganization is to create greater efficiencies and more logical combinations of functions. For example, a state might consider consolidating several environmental agencies that had been established over the preceding two decades. The arguments for a consolidated environmental agency include that it would enhance the state's ability to deal with multimedia environmental problems. Multimedia here refers to the different media (air, land, surface water, groundwater) that constitute the "environment." Sometimes the things done to address pollution problems in one medium adversely affect pollution problems in another. A consolidated agency would presumably allow the state to solve environmental problems more comprehensively and to pool its current agency resources (for example, laboratories) for a more effective response to such problems.

A third reason for reorganization is to reflect changes in public policy. New programs often require new administrative units. This adding on of organizational units is actually one of the more common ways in which government agencies adapt. Unable to get each ambassador to accept responsibility for embassy security against terrorism, the State Department simply added a unit designed to do that.[41]

A fourth reason for reorganization is to make government more politically responsive. For instance, the consolidation of a state's environmental agencies would provide greater visibility and accountability to the public than would a fragmented regulatory structure that includes an Air Control Board, a Water Commission, and others.

A fifth reason is that the organization's environment has changed. When the environment changes, the mission usually changes; and when the mission changes, the organizational structure often needs rethinking.

The end of the Cold War meant to many both inside and outside the U.S. military establishment that the way American forces were structured needed rethinking. When you expect to fight a large ground war in Europe against Soviet armies or face the threat of nuclear annihilation from intercontinental ballistic missiles, you organize one way. When you expect different fights and face different threats, you organize defense another way. Similarly, the revolution in telecommunications, driven by the computer chip, meant to many that the organizational structure of the Federal Communications Commission—created in 1935 to regulate communication by wire and by "wireless" (that is, radio)—needed something more than an organizational tweaking. The establishment of the Department of Homeland Security is the latest and certainly one of the largest reorganizations ever undertaken in U.S. government.

Key Concepts in Reinvention

In 1993, for the eleventh time in the twentieth century, an American president proposed making government work better. The proposal, the previously mentioned *Report of the National Performance Review,* was produced and promoted heavily by Vice President Al Gore. The root problem of government, according to this report and to countless studies that preceded it, was that Washington is filled with organizations designed for an environment that no longer exists. From the 1930s through the 1960s, the federal government built large, top-down, centralized bureaucracies to do the public's business. They were patterned after the corporate structures of the age: hierarchical bureaucracies in which tasks were broken into simple parts, each the responsibility of a different layer of employees, each defined by specific rules and regulations. (See cartoon.) With their rigid preoccupation with SOP, their vertical chains of command, and their standardized services, those bureaucracies were steady—but slow and cumbersome. And in today's world of rapid change, lightning-quick information technologies, tough global competition, and demanding customers, large, top-down bureaucracies—public or private—do not work well. Moreover, many government organizations are monopolies with few incentives to innovate or improve.

Rather than focus only on the problem of modern government, the National Performance Review (NPR) searched for success—for organizations that produced results, satisfied customers, and increased productivity.   The NPR looked for efficient entrepreneurial public organizations and found them at all levels of government. Actually, the prospects for reinvention appear even

Many departments are tied up in a morass of Lilliputian do's and don'ts.

Comment: Presidents Clinton and Bush both expressed concern that administrative agencies are greatly limited in how they can use financial, human, and other resources to manage programs. Both presidents sought to give agencies more discretion to get the job done—in short, to make agencies less bureaucratic. This cartoon and caption appeared on p. 51 of *The Budget of the U.S. Government FY 2003.*

brighter at state and local levels than they do at the federal level. "National officials . . . have a harder time than sub national officials in winning electoral rewards for reform. Farther from the front lines, with less direct control over results—and less direct contact with citizens—the links between performance and politics are harder to establish."[42] The NPR also discovered that governments in other countries—Australia, New Zealand, and the United Kingdom, in particular—were reinventing themselves.

From Sydney, Australia, to Madison, Wisconsin, the NPR found many common characteristics associated with success. Because these characteristics—one might almost call them principles—have been, in effect, "baked into" this text, no lengthy exposition is required here. The following box lists these principles:

Key Concepts in Reinventing Government

entrepreneurial	market-oriented
mission-driven	decentralized
catalytic	community-oriented
results-oriented	customer-driven
competitive	

Many scholars and practitioners refer to this comprehensive reform agenda as **new public management,** a worldwide effort to transform the theory and practice of public administration. Perhaps the most fundamental concept in the reform agenda is *entrepreneurship.* The French economist J. B. Say developed the concept of the entrepreneur over 200 years ago: "The entrepreneur shifts economic resources out of an area of lower and into an area of higher productivity and greater yield." In *Reinventing Government,* the core text of the movement, David Osborne and Ted Gaebler argue that Say's definition applies equally well to the private and public sectors.[43] When they say "entrepreneurial government," they mean public institutions that habitually use their resources in new ways to heighten their productivity and effectiveness. The discussion of compliance management in Chapter 9 presents some excellent examples of entrepreneurial government.

The eight other principles in the foregoing box further define entrepreneurial government. Let's see how. Caught between rising service demands and falling revenues, entrepreneurial governments increasingly act as *catalysts*—leveraging private sector actions to solve problems. They steer more than they row, to borrow a phrase from E. S. Savas at Baruch College.

We know that monopoly in the private sector often encourages inefficiency and inhibits change. Why then, Osborne and Gaebler ask, should we embrace public monopolies so warmly? The city of Phoenix has used competition between its Department of Public Works and private companies to cut its garbage collection costs in half. And in East Harlem, Community School District 4 has used competition between public schools to prod each school to improve.

In this chapter we have seen how centralized government placed less emphasis on hierarchy and more emphasis on participation in teamwork. Osborne and Gaebler think things can be made to work better if those in public organizations—schools, public housing developments, parks, training programs—have the authority to make many of their own decisions. In Chapter 10, we will see how General Bill Creech applied the principle of *decentralization* in an organization that had a passion for centralization and standardization— the Department of Defense.

Chapter 4 explored how *customer-driven* governments use surveys and focus groups to listen to the people they serve. Chapter 5 discussed at some length the ways in which *mission-driven* governments establish clarity of purpose and simplify their administrative systems. That chapter also noted how *results-oriented* governments focus not on inputs but on outcomes when evaluating performance.

To understand what *market-oriented* government means, just think of the way some states have handled litter from bottles and cans. Rather than create elaborate and expensive recycling programs, they simply require buyers to pay a 5¢ deposit on each bottle or can—to be refunded when the bottle or can is returned. A market-oriented approach, under which fees, or "green taxes," are attached to pollution, is gaining ground among environmentalists. The idea is to force producers and consumers to pay the full social cost of their activities and to give them financial incentives to switch to packaging that does less environmental damage.

The principle of *community-owned* programs rests on a simple premise: Families and communities are more committed, more caring, more creative, and less expensive than professional service bureaucracies. Therefore, when practicable, advocates of the new public management believe that government should push control of many services out of the government agencies and into the communities—empower communities and families to solve their own problems. For example, entrepreneurial governments encourage the tenants of public housing to manage their own developments. They give parents a genuine say in how their children's schools are run. And they help welfare mothers become their children's first teachers. Chapter 9 provides other examples of such volunteerism.

Four Pitfalls of Reform

The crucial missing element from recent governmental reform is any systematic assessment of whether a given reform has worked. To some extent, that is understandable. Legislation takes time to work out. For example, the 1947 National Defense Act reorganized the Pentagon, but it was not until the Goldwater-Nichols Act of 1987 that the major flaws in the earlier "reform"—namely, a lack of coordination between the services—was corrected. (Such realities were largely ignored in the post-9/11 rush to "do something about terrorism.")

Perhaps one day some independent body will do a detailed examination of just how well past reforms have worked. But we don't really need yet another blue ribbon commission to identify some of the inherent problems in the various governmental reform efforts. Here are four of the more conspicuous pitfalls facing would-be reformers.

Monetary Illusions   A mere shifting of people and programs on an organizational chart doesn't necessarily do much to save money. For example, in California, only about out of every seven dollars that the state spends pays for the government's internal functions. The main expense for the state comes in the form of money it sends to school districts, hospitals, nursing homes, and construction companies. If the federal government laid off *every worker,* it wouldn't even balance the budget.

Further, reform isn't cheap. Letterheads have to be changed, workers have to be trained, outside consultants have to be hired to make the new system work, and so forth. Performance measures can be a powerful tool for some government agencies; for others, it's been useless and costly. Consider the case of Jane Lynch:

- Lynch, the Social Services Commissioner in Ontario County, New York, got into her field for one reason: to help people. But the longer she was on the job, Lynch says, the more helping people seemed secondary in her work. Instead her working life is driven by a relentless paper chase. "We have 33 inch-thick binders just for the financial regulations, another two binders for food stamps, another binder for child support, three for Medicaid, two for public assistance, one for the home heating assistance program. And we get 10 to 12 administrative directives every week. The last one we got was for child care; it's 150 pages long. You can't possibly read or understand it all."[44]

Cultural Conflicts   One of the main reasons why corporate mergers fail is that the cultures of the two companies clash. Why should government be immune to this phenomenon? Just because you put, say, health-care personnel and human resources personnel together in the same building doesn't mean that they will get along. They will bring with them conflicting institutional cultures; conflicts about pay, procedures, and perquisites can and often do arise.

Consider what happened when FEMA and other agencies were folded into the Department of Homeland Security. Key managers and key talent at FEMA left. Morale dropped. In fact, only 12 percent of the more than 10,000 employees at the Department of Human Services who returned a government questionnaire in 2005 said they felt strongly that they were "encouraged to come up with new and better ways of doing things." Only 3 percent said they were confident that in their department, personnel decisions were "based on merit." Fewer than 18 percent said they felt strongly that they were "held accountable for achieving results." And just 4 percent said they were sure that "creativity and innovation are rewarded." In each of these instances and many others, the responses of the Department of Human Services employees were less favorable than those of all other departments and large agencies surveyed by the Office of Personnel Management.[45]

Organizational Despecialization   Excellence in professional sports—like excellence in pin making (recall the drawing on page 300)—is achieved through specialization. An outstanding basketball player like Michael Jordan was unable to make it as a professional baseball player. Likewise, very few professional football players can play well at more than one position. In medicine, specialized clinics (for example, for treating cataracts) are cheaper and safer than even the best hospitals. Why then should not government organizations be designed for one definite result?

Government reformers have a penchant for "consolidating" functions into single organizations. The 9/11 commission in 2004 recommended establishing a National Intelligence Director with budget and personnel authority to direct counterintelligence efforts among 15 U.S. intelligence agencies. From the start, Pentagon officials objected to giving a new intelligence czar more control over Department of Defense's intelligence operations. They said, not without some justification, the step would harm the flow of intelligence to soldiers in the field where split-second decisions have to be made.

What the commission did not recommend is telling—namely, have the domestic intelligence activities of the FBI be performed by a distinctly separate new organization. The British, for example, have a special organization for domestic intelligence: MI5.

Redundancy Reduction   Since colonial times Americans have evidenced a preference for having power disbursed among separate units of government. Political philosophers might see this as a manifestation of the principle of checks and balances. But organization theorists would more likely see it as the principle of redundancy.

Engineers build redundancy into mechanical devices so that, if one part fails, the whole contraption does not crash and burn. Likewise, from an organizational standpoint, it pays to have more than a single unit perform a vital governmental function. For that reason, Richard A. Posner and others maintain that the creation of a Director of National Intelligence in 2005 made the United States *less* safe. He notes that after the 1973 Yom Kippur attack, in which Arab forces came close to overwhelming Israel, the Israelis set up a commission to determine why they were taken by surprise. They eventually concluded that the root problem was excessively centralized intelligence, and the division of Israeli spy agencies into overlapping team entities followed.[46]

Given these four pitfalls, it does not follow that government reform should never be attempted. Rather, they suggest that would-be reformers might first want to rethink a government's overall goals and then try to achieve them with the tools and organizational structure they already have in place. This could be done through interagency cooperation. It's not uncommon also to have a few people from one agency physically located in another. For example, some CIA personnel are assigned to the FBI and vice versa.

In the final analysis, if reform seems imperative, then awareness of the four pitfalls would at least suggest this: Proceed with caution.

Concepts for Review

bureaucracy	network
charismatic authority	network organization
cross-functional team	new public management
delegation of authority	organizing
division of labor	permanent team
hierarchy	public choice
informal organization	rationale for reorganization
leader–follower relationship	scalar principle
legal authority	span of control
limitations of the organizational chart	special purpose or project team
line authority	staff authority
line-staff concept	traditional authority
matrix organization	

Key Points

This chapter identified the organizational architecture that can be used by government agencies to manage and direct their operations. A central theme of the chapter was that different plans require different kinds of architecture. To succeed, an agency must match its architecture to its plans in a discriminating way. Agencies whose architecture does not fit their strategic requirements will experience performance problems. It is also necessary for the different components of the organization to be consistent with one another. The chapter made these major points:

1. Planning and decision making cannot be separated from organizing. If people are to work together effectively in managing a program, they need to know the parts they are to play in the total endeavor and how the rules relate to each other. To design and maintain the system of rules is basically the managerial function of organization.

2. Organizational design involves decisions about four elements: division of labor (specialization), hierarchy (scalar principal), span control, and line and staff.

The cornerstone of the four principles is the division of labor into specialized tasks. There are at least four ways by which the administrator can divide and place in separate departments the functions of the organization: objective, geography, process, and client.

3. Hierarchy is based on the scalar principle, which states that authority and responsibility should flow in a direct vertical line from the highest level of the organization to the lowest level. This flow is commonly referred to as the chain of command.

4. Span of control concerns the number of subordinates a superior can effectively supervise. What really matters in determining the span of control is not how many people report to the manager but how many people who have to work with each other report to a manager.

5. The line-staff concept concerns the division between those agencies and individuals engaged mainly in implementing programs and those concerned chiefly with providing advice and assistance to top management. Superior and subordinate alike must know whether they are acting in a line or staff capacity.

6. Several American economists have attempted a rigorous examination of why bureaucracies continue to grow. The scholars—who are often associated with the field of economics called public choice—start from the assumption that politicians and bureaucrats behave like consumers and business executives. According to Anthony Downs, the central problem is that government bureaucracy is not subject to the same discipline as those organizations that operate in the private sector. According to this theory, public bureaucracies are like private-sector monopolies—except that they seek bigger budgets rather than bigger profits.

7. Max Weber identified six key features of the bureaucratic structure: (1) division of labor based on functional specialization, (2) well-defined hierarchy of authority, (3) system of rules covering the rights and duties of employment, (4) system of procedures for dealing with work situations, (5) impersonality of interpersonal relations, and (6) promotion and selection based on technical competence.

8. Perhaps the greatest weakness of bureaucracy is its low capacity for innovation. Bureaucracy is not a problem-solving structure but a performance structure. It is designed to carry out standard programs, not to invent new ones. Sophisticated innovation requires a very different structural configuration–one that uses experts drawn from different disciplines into smoothly functioning ad hoc groups.

9. The matrix approach gets its name from the fact that a number of project (team) managers exert planning, scheduling, and cost control over people who have been assigned to their projects, whereas other managers exert more traditional line control (for example, technical direction, training, and compensation) over the same people. Thus, two administrators share responsibility for the same subordinate. The subordinate, in turn, must please two supervisors.

10. A team is a small number of people with complementary skills (technical, problem-solving, and interpersonal) who are committed to a common-purpose performance goal and approach (that is, how they work together) for which they hold themselves mutually accountable. Cross-functional teams consist of employees from various functional departments who meet as a team and resolve mutual problems. Permanent teams are

brought together as a formal department in an organization and report to the same supervisor.

11. In government, network organization refers to those instances in which the government chooses to create, through its power to contract and fund, a network of nongovernmental organizations to implement policy.

12. The organizational chart shows at least two things: how work is to be divided into components and who is (supposed to be) whose supervisor. But the chart does not show the degree of responsibility and authority exercised by positions on the same management level. Although the chart shows some major lines of communication, it does not show all. Nor does the chart show the informal organization—that is, "those aspects of the structure which, while not prescribed by formal authority, supplement or modify the formal structure."

13. In designing an organization, at least four questions must be addressed: (1) Should the structure be "tight," as in the traditional mechanistic organization, or "loose," as in the contemporary organic organization? (2) What should the units be? (3) What units should join together, and what units should be apart? and (4) Where do decisions belong?

14. Upon completion of the design process, one might examine the final product in terms of four design criteria: clarity, simplicity, adaptability, and coherence.

15. There are several reasons for reorganization: growth, efficiency, policy change, enhanced responsiveness, and environmental change.

16. Many scholars and practitioners around the world refer to a comprehensive reform agenda that transforms the theory and practice of public administration as new public management. Essentially, they want to see government more entrepreneurial, catalytic, competitive, decentralized, customer-driven, mission-driven, results-oriented, market-oriented, and community-oriented.

Problems and Applications

1. Not everyone is enchanted by ideas of empowerment and teamwork. For example, Richard Sennett, a sociologist at New York University, argues that because teamwork relies on "the fiction of harmony," it stresses mutual responsiveness at the expense of original thinking. Unity, he argues, requires that a team confine its members to specific tasks and superficial processes, without much reference to either the experience or perspective of individuals. In the team context, you no longer have a boss—you have a "leader." This obscures ordinary power relationships, a condition Sennett calls "power without authority." Above all, he says, the team prohibits conflict—so turning itself into a new form of domination. Do you agree or disagree? Why?

2. What are the advantages and disadvantages of using charts to illustrate organizational structure?

3. How might the following institutions look if they were restructured along the lines of a matrix organization: garbage collection service, library, drug-treatment clinic, state highway patrol, and university?

4. "In the modern world," wrote Bertrand Russell in *Authority and the Individual,* "and still more, so far as can be guessed, in the world of the near future, important achievement is and will be almost impossible to an individual if he cannot dominate some vast organization." Do you agree or disagree? Why?

5. Answer the following three questions for a university, a prison, a welfare office, and a church:

   a. Where is the excellence required to attain the agency's goals?

   b. In what areas would lack of performance endanger the results?

   c. What are the values that are truly important to the organization's members?

   Remember, first you will need to establish goals for each organization. Do you think you have made the key activities the central, load-carrying elements in your organizational structure? Have the organization's values been organizationally anchored?

6. "Governments can run into trouble when they think of their citizens as customers." Discuss.

Favorite Bookmarks

Remember, several of the Web sites noted in the Favorite Bookmarks of Chapter 1 contain valuable links to information on organizational issues in government.

www.workteams.unt.edu/mission.htm   The Center for the Study of Work Teams is at the University of North Texas and was created for the purpose of education and research in all areas of collaborative work systems.

Notes

1. J. A. Litterer, *The Analysis of Organization* (New York: Wiley, 1973), 370–71.
2. Ibid.
3. L. R. Sayles and M. K. Chandler, *Managing Large Systems: Organizations for the Future* (New York: Harper & Row, 1971), 15.
4. Robert K. Merton, "Social Structure and Anomie," *American Sociological Review,* 3 (1938): 672–82.
5. Paul C. Light, "Changing the Shape of Government," in Henry J. Aaron and Robert D. Reischuer's *Setting National Priorities: The 2000 Election and Beyond* (Washington, DC: Brookings, 1999).
6. Anthony Downs, *Inside Bureaucracy* (Boston: Little, Brown, 1967), 154.
7. C. Northcote Parkinson, *Parkinson's Law and Other Studies in Administration* (Boston: Houghton-Mifflin, 1957).
8. Ibid., 20.
9. Tamar Lewin, "Staff Jobs on Campus Outpace Enrollment," *The New York Times* (April 21, 2009).
10. Downs, op. cit.; William A. Niskanen Jr., *Bureaucracy and Representative Government* (Chicago: Aldine-Atherton, 1971); Gordon Tullock, *The Politics of Bureaucracy* (Washington, DC: Public Affairs Press, 1965), and "Public Decisions as Public Goods," *Journal of Political Economy,* 79 (July/August 1971): 913–18.
11. K. B. Lowe et al., "Effectiveness Correlates of Transformational and Transactional Leadership: A Meta-Analytic Review of the MLQ Literature," *Leadership Quarterly,* 7 (1996): 385–45.
12. Jennet Conant, *109 East Palace: Robert Oppenheimer and the Secret City of Los Alamos* (New York: Simon & Schuster, 2005), 153–54, 348.

13. From H. H. Gerth and C. W. Mills, eds., *Max Weber: Essays in Sociology* (New York: Oxford University Press, 1946).

14. Linda J. Bilmes and W. Scott Gould, *The People Factor: Strengthening America by Investing in Public Service* (Washington, DC: Brookings, 2009), 129.

15. Jon R. Katzenbach and Douglas K. Smith, *The Wisdom of Teams* (Boston: Harvard Business School Press, 1993).

16. See Walter C. Berman et al., *Handbook of Psychology, Industrial and Organizational Psychology, Volume 12* (New York: Wiley, 2004), Chapter 13.

17. Robert W. Keidel, "All the Right Corporate Moves," *Across the Board,* 23 (January 1985): 54–56.

18. Ibid., 137.

19. Peter F. Drucker, *Post Capitalist Society* (New York: Harper Business, 1993), 88.

20. R.D. Manning, "How to Fight Wildfires, *Governing* (February 1989).

21. *The Wall Street Journal* (November 7, 2005).

22. J. Richard Hackman, "Why Teams Don't Work," *Harvard Business Review* (May 2009), 101–102.

23. Elaine Ciulla Kamark, "Public Servants for the Twenty-First-Century Government," in John D. Donahue and Joseph S. Nye Jr.'s *For the People: Can We Fix Public Service?* (Washington, DC: Brookings, 2003), 141.

24. Lawrence O'Toole and Kenneth J. Meier, "Desperately Seeking Selznick: Co-Optation and the Dark Side of Public Management in Networks," *Public Administration Review* (November/December 2004): 681–693.

25. Kamark, op. cit., 142.

26. Stephen Goldsmith and William D. Eggers, *Governing by Network: The New Shape of the Public Sector* (Washington, D.C.: Brookings, 2004), 3–7, 72–73.

27. *The Washington Post* (January 13, 1997).

28. R. D. Manning, "How to Fight Wildfires," *Governing* (February, 1989).

29. B. M. Gross, *Organizations and Their Managing* (New York: Free Press, 1968), 238.

30. Dean Acheson, "Thoughts about Thoughts in High Places," *The New York Times Magazine* (October 11, 1959).

31. Peter F. Drucker, *Management: Tasks, Responsibilities, Practices* (New York: Harper & Row, 1974). We have already seen how important this question is—and the dire consequences of failing to ask it.

32. Ibid.

33. A. L. Otten, "Bureaucracy in the White House," *The Wall Street Journal* (August 23, 1973).

34. Ibid., 545.

35. The following discussion is based on Ibid., 553–56.

36. Quoted in Elizabeth Daigneau, "Elected Leaders Refocus on Results," *Governing* (January 2006).

37. Paul Light, *Thickening Government: Federal Hierarchy and the Diffusion of Accountability* (Washington, DC: Brookings, 1995), 546.

38. Douglas Brinkley, *The Great Deluge* (New York: Morrow, 2006), 578.

39. Paul C. Light, "The Tides of Reform Revisited: Patterns in Making Government Work, 1945–2002," *Public Administration Review* (January/February 2006): 6–19.

40. J. A. Litterer, op. cit.

41. James Q. Wilson, *Bureaucracy* (New York: Basic Books, 1989).

42. Donald F. Kettl, "The Three Faces of Reform," *Governing* (July 1999).

43. David Osborne and Ted Gaebler, *Reinventing Government* (Reading, MA: Addison-Wesley, 1992), xix. See also David Osborne and Peter Hutchinson, *The Price of Government* (New York: Basic Books, 2004), and *Banishing Bureaucracy* (New York: Plume, 1998).

44. *Governing* (March 2005), 30.

45. *The New York Times* (October 16, 2005). Of the 30 Cabinet departments and large independent agencies, the employees at NASA and the National Science Foundation had the highest morale.

46. Richard A. Posner, *Uncertain Shield: the U.S. Intelligence System in the Throes of Reform* (Lanham, MD: Rowman & Littlefield, 2006).

CASE 7.1
ARAVIND EYE HOSPITAL

All organizations should match their design to their missions. In the nonprofit sector, however, scale is often a problem, because many nonprofits tackle huge problems (hunger, poverty, disease) with meager resources. Fortunately, some rethink their missions, deliberately scaling back and focusing more narrowly on missions where they can expect to achieve success. Take India's Aravind Hospital, the world's largest provider of cataract surgery. Founded in India in 1976 by a retired eye surgeon, Dr. Goriudappa Venkataswamy, Aravind has achieved much by drawing the lines of organization in a way that supports its strategy.

Dr. V. (as he's known to the poor in India) started with a small, 20-bed private nonprofit hospital that performed all types of eye surgery at reasonable cost. In 1978, a 70-bed free hospital was opened to provide the poor with free eye care. Today the hospital has more than 2,500 beds in a four-hospital network performing 250,000 surgeries and treating 1.5 million patients each year. Fully 70 percent of the hospitals' patients are treated without charge. Dr. V. says his core mission is to wipe out needless blindness.

All this was the result not of luck but of designing an organization to support a strategy. Four actions, in particular, are worth noting: (1) configure patient surgery like an assembly line, (2) produce lenses in-house rather than purchasing them, (3) hold "eye camps" in rural areas to find patients, and (4) generate income to subsidize the core mission.

1. Dr. V.'s vision and methods owe a lot to Adam Smith, although he himself credits McDonald's as his inspiration. Harold L. Sirkin and his partners at Boston Consulting Group explain how Dr. V. has transformed the cataract surgery model to suit conditions in a rapidly developing economy:

   Expensive medical equipment is scheduled for round-the-clock use to drive down the cost per surgical procedure. Doctors and staff are extraordinarily efficient and productive, carrying out more than 4000 cataract surgeries per doctor per year, in comparison with an average of 400 performed by other surgeons in India. Like the cost-effective use of equipment, this task specialization is an innovation in the industry. In a traditional hospital, a surgeon admits the patient, orders tests, synthesizes the resulting information, plans the surgery, coordinates the team, and monitors postoperative care. The surgeon acts like an orchestra conductor, overseeing the entire operation and taking individual responsibility for its success. At Aravind, a surgeon moves from one operating table to the next, performing only the cataract procedure itself, while teams of nurses remain at each table and oversee the patient's care before and after the surgeon does his or her work.

2. Cataract surgery is a procedure to remove a cloudy lens from the eye and can be performed in two ways: intracapsular and extracapsular. *Intracapsular surgery* is the removal of both the lenses and the thin capsule that surrounds them. Removal of the capsule requires a large incision and doesn't allow implantation of a new lens. Thus, people who undergo intracapsular surgery have long recovery periods and have to wear glasses that look like the bottom of two Coke bottles. *Extracapsular surgery* is the removal of the lenses where the capsule is left in place and a silicone or plastic lens is implanted where the original lens was. To keep costs low, Aravind initially offered its free-care patients intracapsular surgery. But the hospital's mission was to provide the highest-quality care to poor patients, so in 1992, it decided to establish its own facility to produce lenses—Aurolab. Now, rather than spend $30 for each lens, it could provide its

poor patients with its own lenses, which cost just seven dollars each. Today Aurolab consists of five divisions: intraocular lens, suture, instruments, blades, and pharmaceutical.

3. Aravind offers a service so good that it creates its own demand. "Market driving" is a marketing term that refers to the creation of a need that didn't exist before (think of FedEx and Starbucks). As a market-driving organization, Aravind has to educate its free patients. Harriet Rubin explains:

One of the ways that the hospitals accomplish this is through community work, which their doctors and technicians almost routinely undertake. First, a representative from Aravind visits a village and meets with its leaders. Together they do the planning necessary to organize a weekend camp. Then Aravind doctors and technicians set out for the village, sometimes driving for days. Once there, they work around the clock, examining people and working to identify those who will need to be taken to Madurai for surgery.

4. About 30 percent of the hospital's patients pay—and that is important for several reasons. *Joan Magretta* writes:

The paying patients are critical to Aravind's success, making the organization self-sustaining. Those patients are drawn to Aravind by its repetition for world-class eye care. Here too, organization supports strategy. Aravind has forged research and

training collaborations with premier teaching hospitals in the United States. Aravind may be low cost overall, but it stays at the leading edge of its field, and that is its appeal to paying customers. It is also part of Aravind's appeal to its doctors. They work longer hours, for less money, in exchange for the psychic rewards that come in part from professional pride, in part from the organization's social mission. Thus, Aravind has drawn the lines of incentives in ways that reinforce its strategy.

Case Questions

1. Aravind is successful because each organizational component directly addresses the organization's mission. Discuss.
2. How would you characterize the division of labor at Aurolab?
3. How well do you think the matrix approach would work at Aravind?
4. What are the advantages for a nonprofit to be self-sustaining?

Case Sources

Harold L. Sirkin and others, *Globality: Competing with Everyone from Everywhere for Everything* (New York: Business Plus, 2008); Harriet Rubin, "The Perfect Vision of Dr. V.," *Wired* (February 2002); Joan Magretta, *What Management Is* (New York: Free Press, 2002); V. Kasturi Rangan, "Lofty Nations, Down-To-Earth Plans," *Harvard Business Review* (March 2004); www.aravind.org.

8 Leading

IT'S YOUR SHIP

Keeping good employees is tough for business, but for the U.S. Navy, it has been a major problem. Forty percent of recruits wash out before their first four-year term ends. Considering what it costs to recruit one sailor and put him or her through the nine weeks of boot camp, that is an expensive problem. In addition, only 30 percent of people who make it through their first tour reenlist for a second.

When D. Michael Abrashoff took command of the destroyer USS *Benfold,* he faced the biggest leadership challenge of his Navy career. Despite the fact that the ship was a technological marvel, most of its sailors could not wait to leave. People were so deeply unhappy and demoralized that walking around the ship felt like entering a deep well of despair. Abrashoff was shocked when the sailors literally cheered as his predecessor left the ship for the last time.

He vowed that would never happen to him. He would create an environment where sailors were so engaged with their work that they would perform at peak levels, willingly stick around for their entire tours, and maybe even gladly reenlist. But how was he to do it? Command and control leadership was the Navy's way of doing things, and the *Benfold*'s previous commander had faithfully pursued it. Abrashoff knew that he needed to be a different kind of leader to turn things around and tap into the energy, enthusiasm, and creativity of his sailors.]

What kind of leadership would you recommend Abrashoff use to get the ship back on course and inspire sailors to give their best? Do you believe a person can change his or her leadership style?

SOURCE: Based on D. Michael Abrashoff, *It's Your Ship: Management Techniques from the Best Damn Ship in the Navy* (New York: Warner Books, 2002).

For an organization to be successful in managing programs, administrators must lead and motivate their people. Individuals must relate and communicate effectively; sound decisions must be reached by individuals and groups; and decisions must be implemented in a way that appropriately involves people and obtains their active commitment to a course of action. Thus, effective public administration requires a knowledge of human motivation and behavior (one's own and that of others) and the personal skills of working with and for people. Indeed, all the other phases of program management (planning, decision making, organizing, implementing) are performed by people and affect people. The effectiveness with which these tasks are carried out depends on the administrator's skills in diagnosing human problems and taking action to solve them.

But what is **leadership**? In his eulogy to President Ronald Reagan, former Canadian Prime Minister Brian Mulroney called it "that ineffable quality." A textbook might define leadership as "the process of influencing the activities of a group in efforts toward the goal attainment in a given situation," but has that really captured the essence of leadership? Although leadership may be next to impossible to describe in words, that has not deterred thoughtful men and women from trying. The French critic Henri Peyre defined it this way:

> A broad ideal proposed by the culture of a country, instilled into the young through the schools, but also through the family, the intellectual atmosphere, the literature, the history, the ethical teaching of that country. Will power, sensitivity to the age, clear thinking rather than profound thinking, the ability to experience the emotions of a group and to voice their aspirations, joined with control over those in oneself, a sense of the dramatic . . . are among the ingredients of the power to lead men.[1]

Peyre's definition is sweeping, conjuring up visions of an indefatigable George Washington crossing the Delaware or echoes of the message that went out to the fleet in 1939 when Churchill was reappointed to his old post in charge of the Admiralty: "Winston is back."

Although the ideas Peyre discusses may sound heroic, an early management thinker, Mary Parker Follett, captured the same spirit when she described the type of leader who motivated her.

> The skillful leader, then, does not rely on personal force; he controls his group not by dominating but by expressing it. He stimulates what is best in us; he unifies and concentrates what we feel only gropingly and scatteringly, but he never gets away from the current of which we and he are both an integral part. He is a leader who gives form to the inchoate energy in every man. The person who influences me most is not he who does great deeds but he who makes me feel I can do great deeds.[2]

What makes leadership so difficult to define is that it involves—more than any other aspect of program management—invisible issues. Think of program management as an iceberg that has only a fraction of its total mass projecting above the water. See Figure 8.1.

Figure 8.1   Program Management as an Iceberg

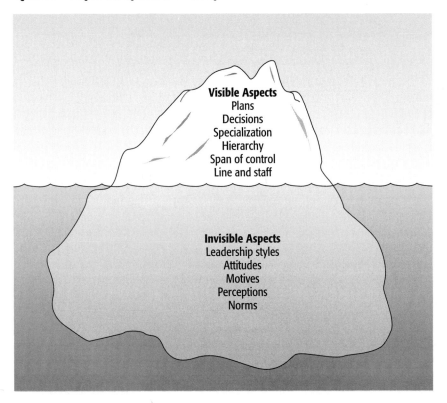

Those visible aspects are what we studied in Chapters 5, 6, and 7: plans (often written down in big, impressive three-ring notebooks), decisions (publicly announced), and organizational charts (hung on the wall to explain division of labor, chain of command, span of control, and the like). Now we need to dive below the surface of program management and carefully examine the unseen aspects that managers must master to lead successfully.

This chapter is divided into five sections, each addressing a different class of management problems encountered in organizations. Specifically, the chapter deals with the following fundamentals in managing human behavior in organizations:

1. Understanding what *leadership styles* are effective in different situations and how a manager's style fits the circumstances and resources available
2. Understanding human *motivation*—which involves employee attitude and motives— and harnessing it for group and organizational goals
3. Understanding and managing *communications*—which involves perceptions
4. Understanding what influences the patterns of behavior, or norms, that emerge over time in a *group* and how those affect the performance of a group
5. Understanding the techniques available for managing the *change* process

Research Perspectives on Leadership

Can Leadership Traits Be Identified?

In the past (especially from 1930 to 1950), the most common approach to the study of leadership focused on traits; it sought to determine what makes the successful leader from the leader's own personal characteristics. These inherent characteristics—such as intelligence, maturity, drive, friendliness—were felt to be transferable from one situation to another. The list of traits grew and grew, but no clear-cut results appeared. Finally, Eugene E. Jennings conducted a careful and extensive review of the literature on the **trait approach to leadership** and concluded: "Fifty years of study have failed to produce one personality trait or set of qualities that can be used to discriminate leaders and nonleaders."[3]

Jennings or no Jennings, the quest for traits—and *the* traits—continues. Richard E. Boyatzis and the staff of McBer and Company in Boston studied more than 2000 managers in 41 different management jobs.[4] They found ten skills relating to managerial effectiveness that stood out:

1. Concern with impact (that is, concern with symbols of power that have an impact on others)
2. Diagnostic use of concepts (that is, a way of thinking that recognizes patterns in situations through the use of concepts)
3. Efficiency orientation (that is, concern with doing something better)
4. Proactivity (that is, predisposition toward taking action to accomplish something)
5. Conceptualization (that is, ability to see and identify patterns as concepts when given an assortment of information)
6. Self-confidence (that is, decisiveness or presence)
7. Use of oral presentations (that is, effective communication)
8. Managing group process (that is, stimulating others to work together effectively in group settings)
9. Use of socialized power (that is, using forms of influence to build alliances, networks, coalitions, or teams)
10. Perceptual objectivity (that is, ability to be relatively objective; not limited by biases, prejudices, or perspectives)

This list focuses on middle-level managers. Management knowledge is not stressed because Boyatzis found that such knowledge represents threshold competency and that the successful managers selected were already well grounded.

In a more recent study, Fred I. Greenstein, a political scientist at Princeton, rates modern presidents on six qualities that bear on their effectiveness as leaders: communication, organization, political skill, vision, cognitive style, and emotional intelligence.[5] No single president scores high on all those attributes, but most successful American chief executives have possessed the right combination of the ones that matter most. Greenstein believes that the key presidential quality is emotional intelligence, which he defines as the

most important skill

president's ability to manage his emotions and turn them to constructive purposes, rather than being dominated by them and allowing them to diminish his leadership. Greenstein says that only 3 of the 12 presidents he studied stand out as fundamentally free of distracting emotional perturbations—Dwight D. Eisenhower, Gerald Ford, and George H. W. Bush—none of whom was considered a particularly strong president. Four others—Franklin D. Roosevelt, Harry Truman, John F. Kennedy, and Ronald Reagan—were marked by emotional undercurrents that did not significantly impair their leadership. Those four presidents—all great communicators except for Truman—would make most lists of the twentieth century's dominant chief executives.

Leadership Styles

The **contingency approach** has an important practical advantage over the trait approach. By emphasizing behavior and environment, encouragement is given to the possibility of training individuals. In other words, people can increase their effectiveness in leadership through training in adapting their leadership style to the situation and the followers. Needless to say, this approach does require that the administrators be good enough diagnosticians to identify clues in an environment and flexible enough to vary their behavior.

Actually, the contingency approach to leadership fits nicely the "textbook" definition given at the start of this chapter. Leadership is, to repeat that definition, the process of influencing the activities of the group in efforts toward goal attainment in a given situation. The key elements in this definition are leader, followers, and situation. Leadership, then, is a function of three variables. Symbolically,

$$L = f(l, f, s)$$

You can't get any further from the definitions of Peyre and Follett than that!

Arguably, all group objectives fall into one of two categories: (1) the achievement of some group goal or (2) the maintenance or strengthening of the group itself. The first, which we shall call **task behavior,** refers to the extent to which the leader is task oriented and directs the work of subordinates toward goal attainment. Leaders exhibiting this behavior typically give instructions, spend time planning, emphasize deadlines, and provide explicit schedules of work activities. The second dimension of leader behavior, **relationship behavior,** refers to the extent to which the leader is mindful of subordinates, respects their ideas and feelings, and establishes mutual trust. Relationship-oriented leaders are friendly, provide open communication, develop teamwork, and are oriented toward their subordinates' welfare.

Using only various combinations of these two types of behavior, we can plot an infinite number of leadership styles (see Figure 8.2). This simple taxonomy of leadership behavior has proven popular, and numerous researchers have sought to advance it. One of the more successful efforts was that of the late William Reddin, a management guru.[6] Using various

Figure 8.2 Leadership Styles

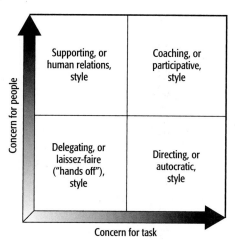

combinations of the two kinds of behavior—task and relationship—Reddin developed four **basic leadership styles:**

1. *Supporting, or human relations, style:* This manager has below average task orientation and above average relationship orientation.
2. *Coaching, or participative, style:* This manager has above average task orientation and above average relationship orientation.
3. *Delegating, or laissez-faire ("hands off"), style:* This manager has below average task orientation and below average relationship orientation.
4. *Directing, or autocratic, style:* This manager has above average task orientation and below average relationship orientation.

The crucial point about these four styles is this: *The effectiveness of managers depends on whether the style they use is appropriate for their situation.* More specifically, to know what is the appropriate style, managers must look to the culture or climate of their organizations; to the nature of the work performed (auditing, street repairs, research and development, and so on); and to the styles, expectations, and maturity of their superiors, subordinates, and coworkers. All these factors help determine which style is effective and which styles are less so.

Because effectiveness results from adopting a style appropriate to the situation in which it is used, the same basic style can be perceived as being particularly effective or particularly ineffective. Stated differently, a style that works beautifully in one situation might cause a lynch mob to form in another. What is the best management style? It all depends.

Consider the following two lists.[7] Each pair of terms could refer to identical behavior. When that behavior is exhibited in the appropriate situation, everyone nods and mutters the words on the left. But when a manager exhibits the very same pattern of behavior in a different situation, people might shake their heads and mutter the words on the right.

warm-hearted	sentimental
flexible	weak-minded
dignified	pompous
firm	rigid
businesslike	brusque
conservative	reactionary
progressive	left-wing
sensitive	soft
dynamic	overbearing

Based on your own experience, can you think of examples of how a situation has determined the appropriateness of a person's actions?

By now it should be clear that an administrator's effectiveness depends to a large degree on her ability to size up a situation. To climb outside ourselves, so to speak, and see our situation and study our actions objectively is not easy. Many mechanisms make us insensitive to our situation.

First, we tend to rationalize, or kid, ourselves. ("I didn't complete the job because other things came up." "I wasn't promoted because my boss is biased.") Second, we see in others what we do not want to see in ourselves. Freud called this tendency *projection*. So the slacker sees others as lazy; the selfish person complains that others do not share; the administrator with low concern for people complains that no one seems to take an interest in him. To maintain projection, administrators must continue to distort reality. Third, we mistake symptoms for cause (this was discussed in Chapter 6). Fourth, we are consumed by a single value—all problems are human ones, all work must be satisfying, or all bigness is bad. Fifth, we may have a high stress level. This is likely to distort our perceptions and feelings about others.[8]

Reddin's theory can be summarized very briefly. There are four basic styles that an administrator can adopt: supporting, coaching, delegating, and directing. Each of these styles can be either effective or ineffective—depending on the situation. Thus, there are really eight management styles: executive and compromiser; bureaucrat and deserter; benevolent autocrat and autocrat; and developer and missionary (see Table 8.1).

Leader as Motivator

Duke basketball coach Mike Krzyzewski writes, "I once heard a high school coach tell a kid that it was not his job to motivate players, but they should show up motivated. Well, I shook my head. I could not disagree more with a statement like that. I believe the main job of the coach is to motivate. The main job of the leader is to inspire."[9] (Coach K. is profiled on pages 360–61.)

What is meant by the output of administrators? Not the number of memos they write, phone calls they answer, meetings they attend, or deals they cut. In a fundamental sense, their output is the output of the people over whom they have influence. Management, never forget, is a *team* activity.

Table 8.1	The Less Effective and More Effective Versions of the Four Basic Management Styles	
Basic Style	When Used in the Appropriate Situation Is More Effective	When Used in the Inappropriate Situation Is Less Effective
Coaching	An *executive* is a good motivating force who sets high standards, treats everyone somewhat differently, and prefers team management.	A *compromiser* is a poor decision maker, one who is influenced too much by various pressures and who minimizes immediate problems rather than maximizing long-term production.
Delegating	A *bureaucrat* is primarily interested in rules and procedures for their own sake, wants to control the situation by their use, and is conscientious.	A *deserter* is uninvolved and passive or negative.
Directing	A *benevolent autocrat* knows what he wants and how to get it without creating resentment.	An *autocrat* has no confidence in others, is unpleasant, and is interested only in the immediate task.
Supporting	A *developer* has implicit trust in people and is primarily concerned with developing them as individuals.	A *missionary* is primarily interested in harmony.

SOURCE: Based on William Reddin, *How to Make Your Management Style More Effective* (London: Books Britain, 1987).

Administrators have two principal ways to elicit better performance from people: **motivation** (a topic for consideration here) and training (a topic for consideration in Chapter 10). In his research on motivation, eminent American psychologist and philosopher William James found that employees can maintain their jobs—that is, avoid being fired—by working at only 20 to 30 percent of their ability. But if highly motivated, employees will work at 80 to 90 percent of their ability. The simple equations that follow illustrate the difference that motivation and training can make for a hypothetical individual. Let us call him Stakhanov and give him a natural ability of 100.

First assume the employee has a supervisor who neither motivates nor trains Stakhanov:

$$\text{Performance} = \begin{array}{ccccccc} \text{Ability} & & \text{Effort} & & \text{Training} & & \text{Output} \\ 100 & \times & 0.20 & \times & 0.40 & = & 8 \end{array}$$

Now assume he has a supervisor who takes motivation and training seriously:

$$\text{Performance} = \begin{array}{ccccccc} \text{Ability} & & \text{Effort} & & \text{Training} & & \text{Output} \\ 100 & \times & 0.80 & \times & 1.5 & = & 120 \end{array}$$

Although one probably cannot measure motivation as precisely as the example suggests, we have learned a few things about it since Frederick Taylor laid the foundations for scientific management (see Chapter 1), Henri Fayol propounded principles of administration (Chapter 1), and Max Weber systematically defined bureaucracy (Chapter 7).

These three men provided us with what is known as the *classical perspective on management.* That perspective was powerful and gave managers fundamental new skills for establishing high productivity and effective treatment of employees. Indeed, the United States surged ahead of the world in management techniques, and other countries, especially Japan, borrowed heavily from American ideas. But, in the 1930s, a new, more *humanistic perspective* began to emerge. One precursor to this perspective was Mary Parker Follett, who in 1918 wrote the passage on skillful leadership quoted earlier. Another early advocate of a more humanistic perspective on management was Chester Barnard, a successful president of the New Jersey Bell Telephone Company.

In contrast to Taylor, who saw workers responding primarily to economic incentives, Barnard recognized the complexities of human motivation. He began *The Functions of the Executive* by contending that organizational studies always imply a certain view of the individual—sometimes a view that sees the individual as a product of social forces, other times a view that accepts the idea of free will.[10] Barnard does not attempt to reconcile these two positions but instead makes this tension—the tension between dependence and independence, control and freedom, reason and intuition—the cornerstone of his theory.

Another of Barnard's contributions was the concept of the informal organization. The **informal organization** occurs in all formal organizations and includes cliques and naturally occurring social groupings. Barnard argued that organizations are not machines, and informal relationships are powerful forces that can help the organization if properly managed. To see how informal relations might make teams work better, organizations have begun to look at the informal network that employees create outside their organization's formal structure. Mapping of such networks shows that most people stick together in clusters of eight to ten like-minded individuals, a group with whom they undertake the vast majority of their communications and with whom they feel "safe." Because of this informal network, senior executives might not really know what's going on in their organizations. See Figure 8.3.

In this section, we will discuss two subfields of what was identified above as the humanistic perspective: the human relations approach and the human resources approach. The human relations movement is primarily associated with the work of Fritz Roethlishberger and Elton Mayo. This work involved a famous series of experiments at the Hawthorne plant of Western Electric in Chicago. The canon of the human relations approach consists of the following two books:

- Fritz Roethlishberger et al., *Management and a Worker* (1939)
- Elton Mayo, *The Human Problems of an Industrialized Civilization* (1946)

The following trio of books constitutes the canon of the human resources approach:

- Abraham Maslow, *Motivation and Personality* (1954)
- Frederick Herzberg, *The Motivation to Work* (1959)
- Douglas McGregor, *The Human Side of Enterprise* (1960)

Figure 8.3   How the Office Really Works

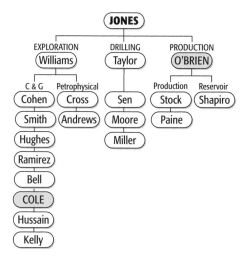

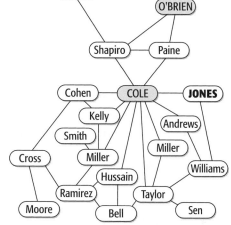

Organizational charts portray the formal structure of power and the division of labor in organizations, but they don't give the full picture. Organizations also operate through informal organizations. Rob Cross, an expert in organizational network analysis at the University of Virginia, shows us how formal hierarchies place staff by title (as shown in figure on the left) and informal organizations places staff by connections. Eugenia Levenson explains: "Imagine for a moment that you're **O'BRIEN.** You're a vice president, running a division; life looks good from your lofty perch in the hierarchy (left). But then the company surveys everyone about communication, collaboration, and backup options, and plugs the data into a network mapping program. The results are startling: The software spits out a diagram that exiles you, **O'BRIEN,** to the outer corner of a very tangled web (right). At the center, meanwhile, is an underling: **COLE.** A technical specialist with no management responsibilities, **COLE** is still one of only two people with direct access to the boss, **JONES**—and has links to seemingly everyone else.

Official job title be damned, the network analysis shows that **COLE** is an influential hub of information. Managers need to identify office **COLE**s to prevent networks from collapsing when that key person leaves. Companies facing looming boomer retirements, take note.

Sources: Rob Cross and Andrew Parker, *The Hidden Power of Social Networks* (Boston: Harvard Business School Press, 2004) and *Fortune* (June 12, 2006): 118.

These names and dates are not terribly important, but the ideas found in these books are—they changed forever the way we think about work. They are certainly worth taking a few minutes to explore.

Hawthorne Studies

In 1924, Western Electric efficiency experts designed a research program to study the effects of illumination on productivity. The assumption was that increased illumination in a factory would result in higher output. Two groups of employees were selected: a test group, which worked under varying degrees of light, and a control group, which worked under normal plant illumination. As expected, when lighting increased, the output of the test group went up. But something else happened—and it was entirely unexpected: The output of the control group also went up.

At this point Western Electric turned for help to Elton Mayo and his associates. Mayo's researchers began to implement a variety of changes, behavioral as well as physical. Rest periods were scheduled. Work hours were altered. Hot snacks were served. But no matter what was done to the workers, output continued to soar.

Baffled by the results, the researchers took a radical step: They restored the original conditions. This change was expected to have a tremendous negative psychological impact and most certainly reduce output. But output jumped to an all-time high. Why? The answer was fairly simple, but the implications were catastrophic, bringing about an almost precise reversal of the whole line of management thought and practice since the Industrial Revolution. In a nutshell, what the Harvard team found—after further investigation, including interviews with more than 20,000 employees from every department in the company—was this: The workers' productivity went up because the attention lavished on them by the experimenters made them feel that they were important to the company. No longer did they view themselves as isolated individuals. Now they were participating members of a congenial, cohesive work group.

The general lesson was patent. The significant factor affecting organizational productivity was not the physical conditions or monetary rewards derived from work but the interpersonal relationships developed on the job. Mayo found that when informal groups felt that their own goals were in opposition to those of management and their control over their job or environment was slight, productivity remained low.

Although the Hawthorne studies have received criticism for inadequacies in research design and the way in which some data were analyzed (see box: "The Hawthorne Effect Revisited"), the findings did influence many managers. If those who ran organizations were interested in increasing worker productivity, then more attention would have to be paid to the way in which relationships—especially those between supervisors and subordinates—were handled. That is the essence of the **human relations approach:** Improving relations between supervisors and subordinates leads to increased worker satisfaction (morale), which leads, in turn, to increased productivity.

In a word, the new goal for management, the golden key, seemed to be *morale*. To maintain a high level of output, the administrator had only to develop ways to satisfy the worker, to make her feel good about her work, boss, and organization. Dr. Feelgood had replaced the grim efficiency expert.

Behavioral science was making progress. The discovery of the informal group—and, in a larger sense, the humanity of the worker—was a real breakthrough in management thought. But the same cannot be said for the concept of morale. As subsequent research began to show, morale was no panacea. Given happy employees, it by no means follows with iron logic that they will feel an urge to work harder and harder. So, disillusionment set in and the scientists began to look for a new tack to improving the effectiveness of organizations.

The Human Resources Approach

The study of employee motivation really began with the work of Frederick W. Taylor on scientific management. Recall from Chapter 1 that scientific management pertains to the

The Hawthorne Effect Revisited

One of the seminal ideas in contemporary social science is the phenomenon of the "Hawthorne effect"—that is, the tendency of humans to alter their behavior when they are under study by social scientists, and thereby jeopardize the accuracy of the study. Using the statistical methods available to them at the time, the Hawthorne researchers found only a small correlation between physical and material factors and output. They concluded that unquantifiable "human relations" accounted for changes in output.

Later research by Parson as well as Franke and Kaul appeared to invalidate much of the Hawthorne study. Parson found hard evidence that the workers at Western Electric's Hawthorne plant were systematically receiving information feedback—that is, knowledge of results about their output rates. Workers also received a differential monetary award; the faster they worked, the more money they got. The combination of information feedback and differential monetary rewards—not changing environmental conditions—seemed to offer the best explanation for the gradually increasing productivity at the Hawthorne plant.

The research of Franke and Kaul is even more surprising. It virtually reverses the original findings of the Hawthorne study. Reanalyzing the raw data using more sophisticated statistical techniques and computers, Franke and Kaul found a significant correlation between output and "managerial discipline."

The firing of two workers during the course of the experiments explains most of the changes in output. "Human relations" do partially govern output—not in the sense of "humane treatment" but rather in the sense of simple discipline. Franke and Kaul also concur with Parson that the group pay incentive was of some value in raising output.

A more recent contribution to this running battle of philosophy was made by Stephen R. G. Jones, an economist at Canada's McMaster University. Jones argues that his own complex statistical manipulations of the data from the Hawthorne plant's relay assembly test room between 1927 and 1932, where five women worked, show that "interdependence" was crucial after all. "The human relations approach to industrial sociology," he maintains, "is not controverted by the original Hawthorne data from which it began."

Perhaps the main lesson to be drawn from this story is that social science researchers must avoid enthusiastically embracing a proposition that is scientifically unproven just because it is congenial with their own values.

SOURCE: R. H. Franke and J. D. Kaul, "Hawthorne Experiment—First Statistical Interpretation," *American Sociological Review* (October 1978); H. M. Parson, "What Caused the Hawthorne Effect?," *Administration & Society* (November 1978); S. R. G. Jones, "Worker Interdependence and Output: The Hawthorne Studies Reevaluated," *American Sociological Review* (April 1990).

---

systematic analysis of an employee's job for the purpose of increasing efficiency. Economic rewards go to employees for high performance. The emphasis on pay evolved into the notion of *economic man*—a person who would work harder for higher pay. But beginning with the landmark Hawthorne studies, economic man was gradually replaced by a more sociable being in the minds of managers. Economic rewards—such as friendly workgroups that met social needs—seemed more important than incentive pay systems as a motivator of work. For the first time, workers were studied as people, and the concept of *social man* was born.

The **human resources approach** carries the concepts of economic man and social man further to introduce the concept of the whole person. Human resources theory suggests that employees are complex and motivated by many factors. Proponents of the human resources approach, like Abraham Maslow, Douglas McGregor, and Frederick Herzberg—whom we are about to meet—believed that earlier approaches had tried to manipulate employees through economic and social rewards. By ensuring that employees are content and able to make major contributions, they believed managers could enhance organizational performance. The human resources approach laid the groundwork for contemporary perspectives on employee motivation.

Maslow's Hierarchy of Needs

The next chapter in the story opens with a question, much as the Hawthorne affair did. Money is presumably a great incentive to work hard, but when people are asked what is most important to them in their jobs, money often takes third, fourth, or even fifth place. Factors such as "full appreciation for work done," "a feeling of being in on things," "sympathetic understanding of personal problems," and "job security" rank higher. Why?

Speaking broadly, one might say that human motives or needs form a more complicated pattern than one is likely to suppose. In the early 1950s, U.S. psychologist Abraham Maslow did much to describe this pattern by suggesting the existence of a **hierarchy of needs.** According to Maslow, an individual's behavior at a particular moment is usually determined by his strongest need. If this is so, then it would seem useful for administrators to have some understanding of the needs that are commonly most important to people. Maslow notes five (see Figure 8.4):

Figure 8.4   Maslow's Hierarchy of Needs

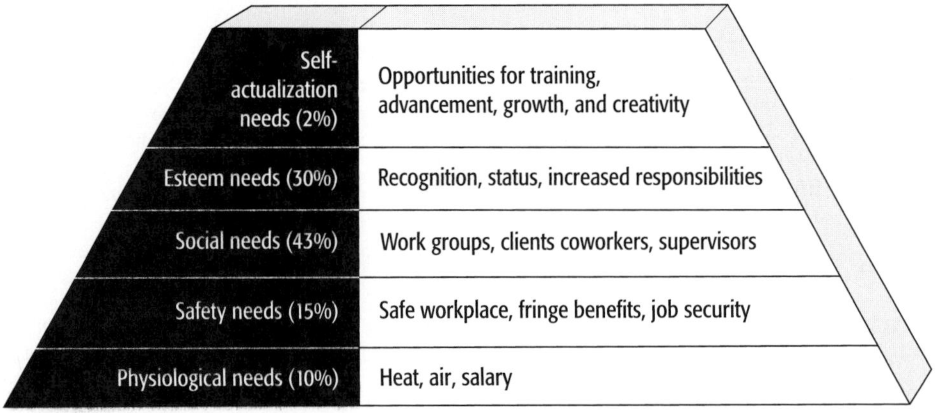

Several years ago, a group of researchers at the Stanford Research Institute asked what percentage of the U.S. population was living on each of the five levels of Maslow's hierarchy. These percentages are shown in parentheses.

1. *Physiological.* In Maslow's formulation, the physiological needs (for example, food, clothing, and shelter) are at the bottom of the hierarchy. The satisfaction of these needs is usually associated in society with money. But as these basic needs begin to be fulfilled, other levels of needs become important and motivate and dominate the behavior of the individual.

2. *Safety.* Above physiological needs, Maslow places the need for safety, or security. As with other motives, security can be a need of which the individual is aware or it can be largely subconscious and not easily identified. Do you want a job that offers a challenge to imagination and ingenuity and that penalizes failures? Or, do you find real satisfaction in the precision, order, and system of a clearly laid-out job? (Remember Sinclair Lewis's Babbitt, for whom "a sensational event was changing from his brown suit to his gray the contents of his pockets"?) How one answers these questions is a good indication of how important the security motive is. Some organizations, it has been suggested, tend to over-emphasize the security motive by providing elaborate fringe-benefit programs.[11] Although this emphasis can make employees more predictable, it cannot necessarily make them more productive. And if creativity is necessary in their jobs—which is often the case in the public sector, where a high percentage of employees are knowledge workers—overemphasis on security can actually thwart creativity.

3. *Social.* Once physiological and safety needs are fairly well satisfied, social needs become dominant. These needs reflect the desire to be accepted by one's peers and have friendships. In the organization, such needs help foster good interpersonal relations. In particular, good social relations make possible connections that can help speed the flow of work and allow people to accomplish things in ways not possible within the formal structure. But social relations can have a downside when the level of schmoozing (chatting idly, gossiping) replaces working or when the desire to be part of the group results in groupthink (as discussed in Chapter 6).

The 9/11 Commission provides an egregious example of this phenomenon. The Commission *insisted* on a unanimous report. Pressure for unanimity creates groupthink and horsetrading and requires commissioners to settle for recommendations they believe to be second, third, or fourth best. Without a chance for multiple reports and dissents, Congress and the public were led to think that there was only one solution to the intelligence failures of September 11. More fundamentally, the Commission fell into the common bureaucratic trap of addressing yesterday's problems more than tomorrow's. Due to the difficulty of anticipating threats that haven't yet occurred, the report is mostly concerned with preventing an exact replay of September 11. Such an occurrence seems remote—especially since the United States has seen such an attack, adjusted security accordingly, and now has airline passengers who are much more on guard.

This mode of thinking is regularly encountered in studies of group dynamics when concurrence seeking becomes so dominant that it tends to override realistic appraisal of alternative courses of action. And no level of decision making is immune to this strain of social conformity. An important symptom of groupthink is pressure: "Victims of group-think apply direct pressure to the individual who momentarily expresses doubts about any

Money would be among the factors motivating people at level *one* in Maslow's hierarchy of needs—which should tell us something. And it is this: Salary motivates neither the best people nor the best in people. Perhaps money can sometimes move a body or influence a mind, but it cannot move the spirit; that is reserved for belief in the organization, its people, and purpose or for the principles and values so important to self-actualizing people.

of the group's shared illusions or who questions the validity of the arguments supporting a policy alternative favored by the minority. This gambit reinforces the concurrence-seeking norm that loyal members are expected to maintain."[12]

4. *Esteem.* If one assumes then that individual social needs are met within the organization, a fourth need comes into prominence: esteem. Failure to understand this need often lies behind the administrator's complaint: "We've given our people everything—good salary, pleasant working conditions, even affection—and yet some are still dissatisfied." In other words, it is precisely because employees have had the three basic needs sufficiently satisfied that a fourth need emerges. And, like social needs, the need for esteem can cause organizational problems unless the administrator finds ways of satisfying it.

Although the need for esteem appears in a variety of forms, only one is discussed here—recognition. With each form, however, the message for the public administrator remains the same: Do things to make employees feel important. William James gave an especially gripping explanation of the importance of recognition:

> We are not only gregarious animals, liking to be in sight of our fellows, but we have an innate propensity to get ourselves noticed, and noticed favorably, by our kind. No more fiendish punishment could be devised, were such a thing physically

possible, than that one should be turned loose in society and remain absolutely unnoticed by all the members thereof. If no one turned round when we spoke, or minded what we did, but if every person we met . . . acted as if we were nonexisting things, a kind of rage and impotent despair would be a relief; for these would make us feel that, however bad might be our plight, we had not sunk to such a depth as to be unworthy of attention at all.[13]

What are the organizational implications of this remarkable passage? Simply this: People look for support from their supervisors.

5. *Self-actualization.* According to Gellerman, the need for esteem is more or less self-limiting.[14] Once people have gained the level they think they deserve, the strength of this need declines. At this point, too, one witnesses the emergence of Maslow's fifth and final need: self-actualization. What exactly is self-actualization? In *The Farther Reaches of Human Nature,* Maslow provides an answer:

Self-actualizing people are, without one single exception, involved in a cause outside their own skin, in something outside of themselves. They are devoted, working at something, something which is very precious to them—some calling or vocation in the old sense, the priestly sense. They are working at something which fate has called them to somehow and which they work at and which they love, so that the work-joy dichotomy in them disappears.[15]

An especially well-researched motive, closely related to self-actualization, is the urge to achieve. By considering this phenomenon, perhaps self-actualization can be better understood. A simple example can help distinguish the *achievement-motivated person* from the socially motivated and esteem motivated.[16] Given the task of building a boat, the achievement-motivated person would obtain gratification from the making of the boat. This intense interest in the work is, of course, quite consistent with the foregoing excerpt from Maslow. The socially motivated person would have fun playing with others and with the boat but would be less concerned about its seaworthiness. Finally, the esteem-motivated person would be concerned with the specific role he had in the project and with the rewards of success.

Achievement-motivated persons set moderately difficult but potentially surmountable goals for themselves; they prefer situations in which they can obtain tangible information about their performance; and they habitually think about how to do things better. How then should a manager handle the achievement-oriented employee? Levinson provides these guidelines: The administrator "should make demands on people, expect them to achieve reasonable goals, and even some that border on the unreasonable. He should respect their capacity to chart their own course toward those goals if they are adequately protected and supported, acknowledge what they have to contribute toward reaching collective goals, and, following Diogenes's dictum, 'Stand out of their light.' "[17]

Maslow's theory was a significant contribution to management science, for Maslow was saying—with far more precision than any of his predecessors—that different people require different treatment by management (in the vernacular: different strokes for different folks). And there is more: (a) the same person, over time, may require different treatment, and (b) management should never expect a cessation of complaints but rather should expect different ones.

Returning to our opening case, Michael Abrashoff wanted to create an organization in which people were so engaged and enthused about their work that they would willingly give their best. But he knew a leader can't order people to become cohesive, to perform better. In his time on the *Benfold*, he found that the only way to do that was one crew member at a time—an approach Maslow would undoubtedly recognize. So, when he took over command, he did something that was unusual in by-the-book command: he sat down with each man and woman, individually, in his quarters. As the ship's leader, Abrashoff wanted to get to know each of them as a person, to learn what they liked, what they hated, and what they wanted to change about the ship. Above all, he wanted to learn what motivated them. From these first-hand conversations, he learned that they wanted to excel just as much as he did. And he learned something else that was even more valuable: They had useful, smart, important ideas about how to improve the way the ship was run. Good ideas that came from the bottom up were implemented immediately.

To unleash the creativity and know-how of everyone, Abrashoff led with vision and values instead of command and control. When the crew saw that he was sincere, it responded with energy, enthusiasm, and commitment. The young captain also began handing over responsibility so that people could learn and grow. His philosophy was that, if all you do is give orders, then all you get are order takers. He wanted to develop strong leaders at all levels and help people understand that they were the ones who made the ship successful. Under his leadership, the *Benfold* set all-time records for performance and retention. In sum, Abrashoff illustrates characteristics of the coaching or participative style of leadership discussed earlier as well as the utility of Maslow's hierarchy of needs.

Douglas McGregor: Theory X and Theory Y

Douglas McGregor was heavily influenced by both the Hawthorne studies and Maslow's work.[18] His classic book *The Human Side of Enterprise* advanced the thesis that managers can benefit greatly by giving more attention to the social and self-actualizing needs of people at work. McGregor felt that managers must shift their view of human nature from a perspective he called Theory X to one called Theory Y. These are important terms in the vocabulary of management.

According to McGregor, managers of the **Theory X** model view their subordinates as by nature

- disliking work
- lacking ambition
- irresponsible
- resistant to change
- preferring to be led rather than to lead

Theory Y, by contrast, involves an alternative set of assumptions. A manager operating under a Theory Y perspective views subordinates as naturally

- willing to work
- willing to accept responsibility
- capable of self-direction and self-control
- capable of creativity

Theory Y is not just Theory X's opposite (although that is what many observers conclude). McGregor did not intend that the two sets of assumptions be forced into the hard versus soft mold. Rather, he meant Theory Y to be an integrative set of assumptions. As McGregor notes in describing the paradoxical qualities of Theory Y:

> The central principle of Theory Y is that of integration; the creation of conditions such that the members of the organization can achieve their own goals best by directing their goals toward the success of the enterprise. . . . The concept of integration and self-control (also) carries the implication that the organization will be more effective in achieving its economic objectives if adjustments are made in significant ways to the needs and goals of its members.[19]

Frederick Herzberg: Satisfiers and Dissatisfiers

In his groundbreaking *The Motivation to Work*, Frederick Herzberg reports on the results of his and his associates' empirical investigation of motivation.[20] Essentially, they found five factors that determined job satisfaction: achievement, recognition, work itself, responsibility, and advancement (see Figure 8.5). Significantly, these factors were all related to job content. In addition, they found five factors that were associated with job dissatisfaction: company policy and administration, supervision, salary, interpersonal relations, and working conditions.

These findings are most suggestive. On one hand, eliminating dissatisfiers will reduce employee dissatisfaction but will not motivate workers to high achievement levels. On the other hand, recognition, challenge, and opportunities for personal growth are powerful motivators and will promote high satisfaction and performance. The manager's role is to remove the dissatisfiers—the seven factors on the left in Figure 8.5—and then use the five motivators on the right to meet higher-level needs and propel employees toward greater achievement and satisfaction.

As we have seen in this section, quite a few scholars have tried to answer the question of what motivates employees. Although these scholars put their theories and findings in different bottles, the contents are pretty much the same. Not many of them could argue with or greatly add to the following statement by Fritz J. Roethlisberger:

> People at work are not so different from people in other aspects of life. They are not entirely creatures of logic. They have feelings. They like to feel important and to have their work recognized as important. Although they are interested in the size of their

Figure 8.5   Comparison of Satisfiers and Dissatisfiers

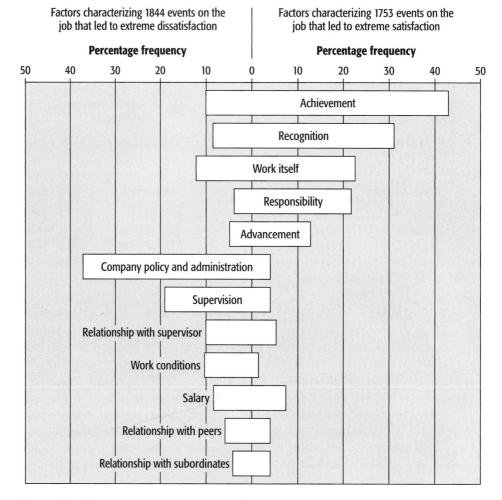

SOURCE: F. Herzberg et al., *The Motivation to Work* (New York: John Wiley & Sons, 1959).

pay envelopes, this is not the matter of their first concern. Sometimes they are more interested in having their pay reflect accurately the relative social importance to them of the different jobs they do. Sometimes even still more important to them than maintenance of socially accepted wage differentials is the way their superiors treat them.

They like to work in an atmosphere of approval. They like to be praised rather than blamed. They do not like to have to admit their mistakes—at least, not publicly. They like to know what is expected of them and where they stand in relation to their boss's expectations. They like to have some warning of the changes that may affect them.

They like to feel independent in their relations to their supervisor. They like to be able to express their feelings to them without being misunderstood. They like to be listened to and have their feelings and points of view taken into account. They like to be consulted about and participate in the actions that will personally affect them. In short, employees, like most people, want to be treated as belonging to and being an integral part of some group.[21]

Despite all the studies and all the theories, no equation can ever tell quite all leaders need to know about motivating people. Although theory can help guide us and can conveniently encapsulate complex truths, motivation remains, at least in part, a veiled art. In Chapter 10, we will consider some human resources systems for job satisfaction.

Leadership Communication

Motivation depends greatly on a leader's ability to communicate effectively. In fact, *leadership cannot happen without effective communication.* The styles of leadership we discussed earlier especially depend on powerful communication. Recall that leadership means influencing people to bring about change toward a vision, or desirable future for the organization. Leaders communicate to share the vision with others, inspire and motivate them to strive toward the vision, and build the values and trust that enable effective working relationships and goal accomplishment. Not convinced? See Working Profile—Coach Krzyzewski: Communicator on page 360.

"If the oldest complaint is nobody asked us," Winston Churchill once observed, "the next oldest is nobody ever told us." Churchill, who knew a thing or two about leadership in organizations, is suggesting here that one carefully consider communication. The sheer volume of communication that occurs in running a government program is overwhelming. According to one survey, the average U.S. office worker receives 190 messages a day. Communication permeates every management function described in this book. For example, when managers perform the planning function, they gather information; write letters, memos, and reports; and then meet with other managers to explain the plan. When managers lead, they communicate with subordinates to motivate them. When managers organize, they gather information about the state of the organization and communicate a new structure to others. Communication skills are a fundamental part of every managerial activity.

In the public sector, the problem of communication is compounded by the fact that the public is often closely involved in program planning and operations. For example, when Massachusetts's controversial "bottle bill" became law a few years ago amid turmoil created by uncertainty as to when, exactly, the law would go into effect, state agencies were deluged with calls about the law. As a result, a statewide toll-free telephone hotline was installed. The hotline quickly became not only an educational tool but also the critical link

Working Profile
Mike Krzyzewski: Communicator

Brian Bahr/ALLSPORT

In his *The Functions of the Executive,* Chester Barnard argued that one essential ingredient for a successful organization is a good, short line of communication because communication enables everyone to be tied into the organization's objectives. One leader who certainly practices what Barnard preached is Mike Krzyzewski (pronounced sha-SHEF-ski). In his more than 20 years coaching the Duke University basketball team, Krzyzewski has made the Duke program one of the most—if not the most—admired in the United States, with back-to-back national championships in 1991 and 1992 and eight Final Four appearances since 1986. In *Leading with the Heart,* he discusses how leaders use communication to move their organizations to the top.

The Duke program, he explains, employs not only an offense system and a defense system but also a communication system. People often take talking for granted—after all, we are always talking. "But leaders should not assume that people are going to talk to one another when they are performing their jobs. As a matter of fact, in business, an employee is less likely to talk to a member of his team when he's doing his job than when he's on a break." For that reason, one of the functions of a leader is to remind people to talk.

He also counsels players to talk in the huddle because they might notice things he can't see from the sidelines. During extended timeouts, he asks for the players' advice. Although that's easier to do with veteran teams than with rookie teams, he thinks it also works well with the latter. Why? "Because when the head coach asks a player for advice, it gives that player instant credibility, which, in turn, makes the entire team stronger. Communication like this permeates through the entire group."

Krzyzewski also appreciates the importance of *nonverbal communication.* Some people might wonder how a coach can get much of the message across in a 20-second timeout. Consider the following example: During a 1999 game, Duke was playing exceptionally poorly. The players had not come ready to play. So, with only a few seconds left in the first half, the coach calls a timeout. "I stepped into the huddle, looked at the players, then pulled back and sat down on the bench without saying a word. I also looked away. At that moment, I decided to coach by not coaching. And I believe they all got the message." They did; Duke won.

Off court, nonverbal communication also helps him during recruiting trips. But not the way you might think. During early meetings with the players and their parents, he watches the players when their parents speak. "I study their facial expressions and watch their reactions. The young man who rolls his eyes when his mother asks a question, I'm not sure I'm going to offer him a scholarship. I look for kids who respect parents because I believe they will have a greater chance of respecting what I say."

And Krzyzewski knows the *power of words*. Right after Duke won its first NCAA tournament, the media began talking about Duke "defending the national championship." He immediately called a team meeting, and this is what he told the players gathered in the locker room: "I don't want anybody on this team to allow the press to set our goals for us or to define our dreams for us. . . . We are not *defending* a national championship. The word 'defending' implies that we will be back on our heels protecting something. No way, guys. We cannot win another national championship on our reputation. We have to go out and earn everything we get. We are not *defending* anything. We are *pursuing* a national championship. *Pursuing!*"

SOURCE: Mike Krzyzweski, *Leading with the Heart* (New York: Warner Books, 2000), 38, 71–74, 124, and 210.

between public officials and state officials and the statewide focal point for questions and complaints about the law.

The essence of communication is not speaking and writing; rather, it is *sharing*. **Communication** thus can be defined as the process by which information and ideas travel from A to B and are then understood by B. Communication is not just sending information, for often A intends to motivate or influence the behavior of B. Once B *perceives* what A is trying to communicate—is "with" A, so to speak—A has successfully communicated with B. Managers who fail to keep these distinctions in mind, who continue to view communication simply in terms of speaking and writing, run the risk of making the following types of mistakes.

Using Gobbledygook

The first mistake is the use of language characterized by circumlocution and jargon, which is usually hard to understand. This practice is so prevalent in bureaucracy that there is even a special term for it: *gobbledygook*. (The term originated during World War II when someone fancifully reformed the word *gobble*—the throaty cry of a male turkey.)

Consider the final paragraph of a letter a manager has on her desk regarding OMB Circular A-21, a compilation of regulations governing reimbursement to universities that conduct federally financed research: "Since data is central to the issue of refined implementation guidance and legislation defers implementation, we believe it is advisable to examine the data that your organization is assembling to preclude any such unintended effects." What could this possibly mean? Never mind, the author obviously was not thinking of communication in terms of the reader's understanding. Communication for him was simply writing. Period.

There is an old axiom that should be carved on the desk of every public administrator: An order that can be misunderstood will be misunderstood. A desperate measure, defacing government property, but how else can the administrator be forced to write in a clear, straightforward manner?

Rather than struggle with that question, turn to a more answerable one: Why do administrators engage in gobbledygook? One reason is to avoid unpleasantness: We do not fire incompetent employees; we "select them out" or "nonretain them." (Note, too, the use of the collective pronoun *we.*) Nor do we ever, ever cut the budget; we make "advance downward adjustments." Unions do not strike, they engage in a "job action." Prisons are "correctional facilities."

Another reason for gobbledygook is the desire to dress up mundane thoughts and make them sound impressive.

Missing Opportunity: The Power of Words

The real tragedy of using gobbledygook is the missed opportunity. The right words can spur others to action. An impressive body of research supports the thesis that the quality of one's speech does make a difference in one's success in emerging as a leader.[22] This research suggests the following:

1. Getting a message's meaning across may require the development of innovative approaches. Not only do feelings and ideas need to be communicated, but messages have to be remembered. Memorable messages tend to be brief.
2. The timing of a statement makes a difference in a leader's influence. Those who state their opinion either early in a discussion or late in a discussion often are better able to have their opinion accepted than those who state theirs in the middle of a discussion.
3. The medium affects the message. Stationery and signatures still have more impact than electronic mail and faxes. Who would frame a computer-mailed printout?[23]
4. Style also influences the effectiveness of managers.

The last point merits emphasis. Most managers are astonished to learn just how much communication is not verbal; major parts of the shared understanding come from the nonverbal messages of facial expression, voice, manner, posture, and dress. One study found the relative weights of spoken words, voice (pitch, tone, and timbre), and facial expressions to be 7 percent, 38 percent, and 55 percent, respectively.[24] The implications of this research are obvious when a manager must decide whether to send a written or oral message. Both types of messages have their advantages and disadvantages. Written messages, for example, can be retained as permanent references from which to work and guide action during implementation. Additionally, they have the advantage of providing a legal record, although, over time, the retention of voluminous written communications can be very expensive. As a general rule, memos should be used as seldom as possible and then only to remind, clarify, or confirm.

Of paramount importance in the use of the written message are clarity and simplicity. To ensure that messages leaving his headquarters met this dual standard, Napoleon, it is said, kept on his staff a captain exceptionally lacking in intelligence. The officer's responsibility was to read all outgoing messages; if he was able to understand them, then presumably no officer in the Grande Armée would have any difficulty. Although it is unlikely that any agency head today could get such a position authorized, one can at least try to keep the reader in mind when drafting a memo.

Even then, the reader may still be uncertain as to the writer's fine meaning. Tone and nuance are not easily put into words. Accordingly, in certain instances, oral communication is preferable. The biggest advantage of oral over written communication, at least during implementation, is that it is two way. When the speaker's message creates ambiguity, the listener can ask follow-up questions (such as, "As I understand it, you mean such and such?"). At the same time, the supervisor has the opportunity to *receive* as well as impart information.

The role of the supervisor during one-on-one conversations is to facilitate the subordinate's expression of the situation or problem. One way to accomplish this is to *always ask one more question:* "When the supervisor thinks the subordinate has said all he wants to about a subject, he should ask another question. He should try to keep the flow of thoughts coming by prompting the subordinate with queries until *both* feel satisfied that they have gotten to the bottom of the problem."[25]

Finally, during face-to-face encounters, the listener must resist the tendency to evaluate communication prematurely. According to Rogers and Roethlisberger, those who would communicate should be listened to in noncommittal, unprejudiced fashion and thus be encouraged to state their full position before response is generated.[26]

Leading Groups and Teams

Work groups can be a crucial link between the individual and the larger organization—the place where the individual finds fulfillment and friendship and protection from the uncertainty and impersonality of the organization. This section is concerned with what managers need to know to participate effectively in, as well as lead, work groups. Perhaps the first thing to know is that no group "hits the ground running"; to think otherwise can lead to frustration. So, we will begin by considering the stages of group development. Then we will note some of the key characteristics of functional groups. Knowing these characteristics will help you appreciate, among other things, why "dream teams" sometimes lose to teams with "no-name" players.

Stages of Group Development

A group can be defined as two or more people who interact regularly to accomplish some goal. Typically, groups go through a period of evolution or development. Although there is no rigid pattern that all groups follow, they usually go through four stages:

1. The first stage is **forming.** As the term itself suggests, members of the group get acquainted and begin to test which behaviors are acceptable and which are unacceptable to other members of the group.
2. During the **storming** stage, members begin to disagree about what needs to be done and how best to do it. Conflict and hostility characterize this stage. Unless the group moves beyond this stage, and some do not, it will never become a high-performance team. The leader should encourage participation by each member.

3. During the **norming** stage, conflict is resolved and harmony emerges. Each member takes on certain responsibilities, and everyone develops a common vision of how the group will function. During this period, the leader should emphasize oneness within the group and help clarify group norms and values.

4. Finally, the group begins **performing**—that is, moving toward the accomplishment of its goals. Group members confront and resolve problems in the interest of task accomplishment.

At the fourth stage, the group begins to be truly productive—and maybe even begins to have some fun. But the leader should not become complacent, for without effective leadership productivity may begin to decline as the group passes through the stages of de-norming, de-storming, and de-forming. Although it is important to understand that groups start in a state of near-chaos, march through various stages, and end in a state of self-direction, we should not forget groups can go back in the other direction—sometimes just as quickly as they moved forward.

Key Characteristics of Groups: Norms, Roles, and Cohesiveness

Managers should work to establish high-performance **norms**—that is, the expectations and guidelines that are shared by group members for how members should behave. Norms serve an important function for group members in stabilizing their interactions along predictable paths. So when a manager decides that some norms are blocking group effectiveness, he or she must examine the purpose the norms serve before attempting to change them.

Managers also should recognize the potential problems associated with **roles**—that is, the characteristics and expected social behavior of individuals. Roles may develop so that, in addition to the formally appointed leader of a group, one or more *informal leaders* may arise as well. Another role is *social deviant*—a person unwilling to follow an important norm of the group. Carried further, a member who fails to follow several norms of a group where other members are less tolerant may become a *social isolate.* Roles such as these are often helpful in defining what the norms are in a group. At one end of the continuum, formal leaders are likely to adhere closely to group norms; at the other extreme, social isolates violate some and perhaps many of the group norms.

Kurt Rambis was a key player on the great Los Angeles professional basketball teams of the 1980s and is now an assistant coach with the Lakers. In a recent interview, he had this to say about the role of players:

> My first love was to shoot the basketball. But the Lakers were looking for a defender and rebounder. I settled into that role because it was stuff I enjoy doing anyway. . . . It's all part of competitiveness. *And it also fulfilled a role on a team with guys that like to score.*
>
> *Awareness of our roles was a huge part of our success.* If Magic Johnson had wanted to take 30 shots again, no one would have argued. *But he fulfilled a role in*

trying to orchestrate the team. One of the things that helped us was the unselfishness that we demonstrated. Everybody felt that his back was going to be covered. And that lends itself to guys making sacrifices.[27]

People in a group develop patterns of behavior that contribute to or detract from the functional group's ability to achieve its mission. You have probably been in a group where one person consistently cracked jokes to break the tension and reharmonize relationships, or where someone supplied technical information, or where someone kept an eye on the clock or calendar and made sure the group stuck to its agenda and made its deadline.

Finally, the manager needs to realize the importance of **group cohesiveness**—that is, the extent to which group members are attracted to the group and its mission and are motivated to remain in it. At least five factors foster group cohesiveness:

1. *Interaction:* The more people are together, the more cohesive the group will be.
2. *Shared goals:* When the group members agree on goals, the group will be more cohesive.
3. *Personal attraction:* When members have similar attitudes and values, they enjoy being together.
4. *Competition:* Competing with other groups helps cohesiveness.
5. *Success:* Winning and praise from outsiders build cohesiveness.

Once we begin to appreciate the importance of norms, roles, and group cohesiveness, we can understand how the 2004 U.S. Olympic basketball team consisting entirely of NBA stars could finish third and lose to Lithuania—and, by contrast, how the young 1980 U.S. Olympic hockey team, with no professionals, could finish first and beat the mighty Soviet Union. Dream teams lose because their leaders fail to build a culture of trust, they tolerate the competing agendas of their superstars, and they let conflicts fester.

With regard to conflicts, it should be noted that some conflict is healthy. When people in groups go along simply for the sake of harmony, problems typically result. Thus, a degree of conflict leads to better decision making because multiple viewpoints are expressed. Among top management teams, for example, low levels of conflict correlate with poor decision making. However, conflict that is too strong, or that is focused on personal rather than work issues, or that is not managed appropriately can be damaging to the team's morale and productivity. Too much conflict can be destructive, tear relationships apart, and interfere with a healthy exchange of ideas and information. Team leaders have to find the right balance—the Aristotelian golden mean—between conflict and cooperation.

Leading Change

Consider this. If it were not for **organizational change**—that is, any alteration in strategy, structure, technology, people, or culture—the manager's job would be downright easy. Planning would be simple because tomorrow would be the same as today. Decision making would be simple because the problems would remain the same and, for this set of problems, standard operating procedures could be developed. [Organizational design would be irrelevant because in a static, predictable environment, there would be no need to adapt. But that's not the way things are.] Thus, leading change is one of the most vital topics in public administration.

Examples of organizational change in the public sector are countless. Police chiefs try to change the cultures of their departments, school superintendents try to change the priorities of their districts, financial officers try to change the technologies in their offices, college athletic directors try to change their athletic programs for women to comply with new federal regulations, and on and on. Although each of these cases might be different, the key question for leaders remains the same: What should I do to increase my chances of successfully implementing change?

Two Approaches to Organizational Change

[To change their organizations, leaders cannot simply issue order like "Be more innovative," "Take risks," or "Increase the quality of services." The reason why issuing such "clear" orders doesn't work is that these orders ultimately must be executed by middle managers who are (a) concerned with preserving their power bases; (b) worried about whether they will be able to meet the demands of a new task, procedure, or technology; and (c) interested in different goals for the organization.]

[The role of the leader must be this: *Get as many people as possible initiating and working on projects that will effect the desired change.*] There are at least two ways to go about this. One is to follow an eight-stage model of planned organizational change suggested by John P. Kotter at Harvard. (Kotter's model, you might note, shares a few elements with Quinn's logical incremental planning model presented on page 215–16.) The other approach to organizational change, **organizational development (OD)**, focuses more on bringing about cultural change—which is, after all, the basis of change in strategy, structure, and technology. OD is a planned systematic process of change that uses behavioral science knowledge that can be traced back to the Hawthorne studies (discussed earlier).

Planned Organizational Change   John Kotter thinks it important for leaders to recognize that the change process goes through stages, that each stage is important, and that each may require a significant amount of time. To successfully implement change in all or selected parts of their organizations, leaders pay careful attention to the following overlapping stages:[28]

1. *Establish a sense of urgency.* Crises or threats will thaw resistance to change, but in many cases, there is no public crisis and leaders have to make others aware of the need for change. Leaders carefully scan their environment, and, after identifying potential threats or opportunities, find ways to communicate the information broadly and dramatically. For example, when William Bratton first went to New York to head the transit police in 1990, he discovered that none of the senior staff rode the subway. "They commuted to work and traveled around in cars provided

by the city. Comfortably removed from the facts of underground life . . . the senior managers had little sensitivity to riders' widespread concern about safety. In order to shatter the staff's complacency, Bratton began requiring that all transit police officials—beginning with himself—ride the subway to work, to meetings, and at night. . . . It was clear that even if few major crimes took place in the subway, the whole place reeked of fear and disorder. With that ugly reality staring them in the face, the transit force's senior managers could no longer deny the need for a change in their policing methods."[29]

2. *Form a powerful guiding coalition.* For the change process to succeed, there must be a shared commitment to the need and possibilities for organizational transformation. It is also essential that lower-level executives—especially those with a predilection for change—become involved. Often the most serious opposition to change comes from outside. In the public sector, an organization's change of strategy has an effect on other organizations—partners and competitors alike. "The change is likely to be resisted by those players if they are happy with the status quo and powerful enough to protest the changes. Bratton's strategy for dealing with such opposition is to isolate them by building a broad coalition with the other independent powers in his realm."[30]

3. *Develop a compelling vision and strategy.* Leaders are responsible for formulating and articulating a compelling vision that will guide the change effort and for developing the strategies for achieving that vision. A picture of a highly desirable future motivates people to change.

4. *Communicate the vision widely.* At this stage, the coalition of change agents should set an example by modeling the new behaviors needed for employees. They must communicate about the change at least ten times more than they think necessary. Transformation is impossible unless a majority of people in the organization is involved and willing to help, often to the point of making personal sacrifices.

5. *Empower employees to act on the vision.* This means getting rid of obstacles to change, which may require revising systems, structures, and procedures that hinder or undermine the change effort.

6. *Generate short-term wins.* Leaders plan for visible performance improvements, enable them to happen, and celebrate employees who were involved in the improvements. Major change takes time, and a transformation effort loses momentum if there are no short-term accomplishments that employees can recognize and celebrate. For example, soon after taking over at the U.S. Mint, Philip Diehl publicly set an early goal of processing 95 percent of orders within six weeks.

7. *Consolidate gains and create greater change.* Leaders change systems, structures, and technologies that do not fit the vision. They hire and promote employees who can implement their vision for change.

8. *Institutionalize change in the organizational culture.* This is the follow-through stage that makes the change stick. Old habits, values, traditions, and mind sets are permanently replaced; new values and beliefs are instilled in the culture so that

employees view the change not as something new but as a normal, integral part of how the organization operates.

Organizational Development   A more straightforward method of bringing about cultural change is OD. Although the field of OD evolved in the 1970s as a way to build more effective interpersonal working relationships, the concept has been enlarged to examine how people in groups can change to a learning organizational culture in today's turbulent environment. OD is not a step-by-step procedure to solve a specific problem but rather a process of fundamental change in the human and social systems of the organization, especially the organizational culture.[31]

The most popular OD techniques include the following:

- *Survey feedback:* a technique for assessing attitudes and perceptions, identifying discrepancies in these, and resolving the differences by using survey information in feedback groups
- *Sensitivity training:* a method of changing behavior through unstructured group interaction
- *Team building:* activities that help team members learn how each member thinks and works
- *Intergroup development:* changing the attitudes, stereotypes, and perceptions that work groups have about each other
- *Process consultation:* an outside consultant helps the manager understand how interpersonal processes are affecting the way work is being done

Actions to Reduce Resistance to Change

Whether a leader uses the somewhat messy eight-stage model or the more straightforward OD approach, some resistance from employees is virtually certain. When leaders see resistance to change as dysfunctional, what actions can they take? Well, it depends on the nature of the situation.

If some person or group will clearly lose out in a change—and they have considerable power to resist—then the leader might negotiate a formal or informal agreement before implementing the change. The downside of this action is that it can be expensive. How much do I have to give up to get this group's acquiescence? What if the agreement prompts others within the organization to ask for similar payoffs?

If the change must be done quickly, such as in a crisis, some coercion—such as the loss of a promotion or an undesirable transfer—may be necessary. The downside of coercion is that it leaves employees angry at leaders and, as a result, the change may be sabotaged.

A third action to overcome resistance is communication and education. Communication informs employees about the need for change and about the consequences of a proposed change—thereby preventing false rumors, misunderstandings, and resentment. One study found that the most commonly cited reason for failure in change efforts was that employees learned of the change from outsiders.[32]

Concluding Observations

Despite some skepticism about the reality and importance of leadership, all government programs require leaders to see that their objectives are attained. Indeed, leadership is often the single most critical factor in the success or failure of a program. For instance, research indicates that the school principal's leadership is the most important factor in determining students' success; the minister's leadership, in determining church attendance and contributions; and the soldiers' confidence in their company, battalion, and division commanders, in determining morale and cohesion. Research also indicates that governors, more than agencies, come up with innovations (55 percent to 36 percent) and that the style and performance of a U.S. president make a big difference in what happens to legislation, policy, and programs. Similarly, research in the business and industrial sector indicates that leadership is a critical factor in ensuring the survival and prosperity of a firm.[33]

Today an unprecedented array of complex problems in the public sector—toxic waste, education, AIDS, overseas competition, deregulation, illicit drugs, terrorism, fiscal stress— has greatly increased the need for governments to evolve and adapt. Accordingly, the need for unusually creative leaders in government to propel their organizations through major change has never been greater. Kotter contends, "It is not hyperbole to say that there is a leadership crisis in the United States today."[34]

But why? One explanation for the dearth of leaders might be that schools and colleges, as well as potential employers, tell young people that society needs technicians and professionals, not leaders. John W. Gardner says, "A good many of the young people who come through our graduate and professional schools are well equipped to advise leaders in a technical capacity, but they are not well equipped to lead." Only generalists, he thinks, can cope with the diversity of problems and multiple constituencies that contemporary leaders face.[35] Another popular explanation for the dearth of leaders is that public officials are frequently exposed to harsh criticism. "Who needs this?" some young people might ask. "I'd rather be an accountant, an engineer, or a consultant." A third explanation for why we do not have more leaders is simple: They shake things up. A lot of top executives do not want to cope with change. The problem can be especially severe in a large government agency, which may have an entrenched bureaucracy with no recognition of its stake in making change work.

Nevertheless, potential leaders are always present. "Leadership is," James MacGregor Burns writes, "one of the most observed . . . phenomena on earth."[36] The reason is clear. In every time and place, leaders have made a difference—they have had an impact on public affairs. The men and women who seek to lead—and not just administer—do not shrink from the problems, failures, and battles that they surely will face. As Theodore Roosevelt put it in a speech at the Sorbonne in 1910, leaders are the ones who are *willing to enter the arena:*

> It is not the critic who counts; not the man who points out how the strong man stumbles, or where the doer of deeds could have done them better. The credit

belongs to the man who is actually in the arena, whose face is marred by dust and sweat and blood; who strives valiantly; who errs, and comes short again and again; because there is not effort without error and shortcoming; but who does actually strive to do the deeds; who knows the great enthusiasms, the great devotions; who spends himself in a worthy cause, who at the best knows in the end the triumphs of high achievement and who at the worst, if he fails, at least fails while daring greatly, so that his place shall never be with those cold and timid souls who know neither victory nor defeat.

Concepts for Review

basic leadership styles	norming
committee	norms
communication	organizational change
contingency approach	organizational development (OD)
forming	performing
group cohesiveness	relationship behavior
groupthink	roles
Hawthorne effect	storming
hierarchy of needs	task behavior
human relations approach	Theory X
human resources approach	Theory Y
informal organization	trait approach to
leadership	leadership
motivation	vision

Key Points

This chapter explained how effective leaders motivate employees to perform well above expectations by using the human relations approach and the human resources approach. We also looked closely at four other issues central to leadership: style, communication, norms, and change. This chapter made these major points:

1. Like an iceberg, program management has a small visible dimension and a much larger invisible one. What we see when we look at program management are its visible aspects—plans, decisions, organizational charts, and so forth. But under the surface are other elements that managers need to understand—elements that also influence how employees work. To understand these invisible aspects is to understand something very important about leadership.

2. After conducting an extensive review of the literature on the trait approach to leadership, Eugene Jennings concluded that "fifty years of study have failed to produce one personality trait or set of qualities that can be used to discriminate leaders and nonleaders."

3. By emphasizing behavior and the environment, the contingency approach offers the possibility of training individuals to lead groups. Arguably, all group objectives fall into one of two categories: (1) the achievement of some group goal and (2) the maintenance or strengthening of the group itself. The first dimension, called task behavior, refers to the extent to which the leader is task oriented and directs the work of subordinates toward goal attainment. The second dimension of leader behavior, relationship behavior, refers to the extent to which the leader is mindful of subordinates, respects their ideas and feelings, and establishes mutual trust.

4. Using various combinations of the two dimensions of leader behavior—task and relationship—we can identify four basic leadership styles: supporting or human relations, coaching or participating, delegating or hands-off, and directing or autocratic. The effectiveness of managers depends on whether the style they use is appropriate for their situation.

5. Administrators have two principal ways to elicit better performance from people: motivation and training. William James found that employees can maintain their jobs—that is, avoid being fired—by working at only 20 to 30 percent of their ability. But, if highly motivated, employees will work at 80 to 90 percent of their ability.

6. Frederick Taylor, Henri Fayol, and Max Weber pioneered the classical perspective on management. That perspective was powerful and gave managers fundamental skills for establishing high productivity and effective treatment of employees. But in the 1930s, a new, more humanistic perspective began to emerge. Among the major subfields of the humanistic perspective are the human relations approach and the human resources approach.

7. The general lesson of the Hawthorne studies, which are closely associated with the human relations approach, was this: the significant factor affecting organizational productivity was not the physical conditions or monetary rewards derived from work but the interpersonal relationships developed on the job. When informal groups felt that their own goals were in opposition to those of management and their control over their job or environment was slight, productivity remained low.

8. The human resources approach suggests that employees are complex and motivated by many factors. Abraham Maslow's hierarchy of needs model suggests that an individual's behavior at a particular moment is usually determined by his or her strongest need—for example, physiological, safety, social, esteem, and self-actualization. Work by Douglas McGregor on Theory X and Theory Y suggests that people want to do a good job and that work is as natural and healthy as play. Work by Frederick Herzberg identified the factors that lead to job satisfaction and those that lead to dissatisfaction.

9. The essence of communication is not speaking and writing; rather, it is sharing. Communication is the process by which information and ideas travel from A to B and then are understood by B. Communication is not just sending information, for often A intends to motivate or influence the behavior of B. Once B perceives what A is trying to communicate—is "with" A—then we can say A has successfully communicated with B. Managers who ignore these distinctions risk using gobbledygook and underestimating the power of words.

10. A group is two or more people who interact regularly to accomplish some goal. Typically, groups go through a period of evolution, or development, something like the following: forming, storming, norming, and performing.

11. Task forces work on problems and projects that cannot be easily handled by a regular functional organization already in existence. They can be a powerful management tool for resolving complex and challenging problems, but they are equally effective for dealing with more mundane problems, such as overhead cost reduction.

12. Leading change is one of the most vital topics in public administration.

13. To change their organizations, leaders cannot simply issue an order. That doesn't work because the order ultimately must be executed by middle managers who are (a) concerned with preserving their power bases; (b) worried about whether they will be able to meet the demands of a new task, procedure, or technology; and (c) interested in different goals for the organization. The goal of the leader must be to get as many people as possible initiating and working on projects that will effect the desired change.

14. The organizational change process goes through stages—and each stage is important and may require a significant amount of time. Leaders pay careful attention to the following overlapping stages: establish a sense of urgency, form a powerful guiding coalition, develop a compelling vision and strategy, communicate the vision widely, empower employees to act on the vision, generate short-term wins, consolidate gains and create greater change, and institutionalize change in the organizational culture.

15. OD focuses on bringing about cultural change—which is, after all, the basis of change in strategy, structure, and technology. OD is a planned, systematic process of change that uses behavioral science knowledge, which can be traced back to the Hawthorne studies.

Problems and Applications

1. Mark Landstad, relatively new to CliffBank's investment banking division, has a veteran teammate, Nicole Collins, who appears to be a reliable ally. However, when Mark needs her help in locating vital information for his part of a presentation they will be doing together, she feigns ignorance. During the meeting, Nicole produces the data out of the blue and wows the attendees with her analysis. Knocked off balance by the sabotage, Mark clumsily seeks advice from his boss, who is a brick wall when it comes to interpersonal dynamics. How should Mark deal with his backstabbing colleague? [SOURCE: Bronwyn Fryer, "When Your Colleague is a Saboteur," *Harvard Business Review* (November 2008).]

2. Literature is an excellent vehicle to provide well-rounded, complex pictures of leaders in all walks of life—leaders whose challenges, particularly psychological and emotional ones, parallel those of senior executives. Joseph Conrad's finest short story, "The Secret Sharer," is a good example and can be read online (www.gutenberg.org/dirs/2/2/220/ 220.txt) or in *The Portable Conrad* (Penguin Books). The story concerns a young captain commanding a ship for the first time. His lurking fear receives explicit statement: "I wonder how far I should turn out faithful to that ideal conception of one's own personality every man sets up for himself secretly."

3. What skills or traits relating to leadership would you add to Boyatzis's list on page 43? Better yet, form a small group and have each member make a careful list of all the things done to them by employers that they abhor. Then have your group make another list of things done for them that they love. Discuss both lists. For a Ph.D. in leadership: Don't do the things on the first list, ever. Do those on the second, always.

4. Following are five behavior patterns that are most bothersome to managers and workplace experts. Develop an action plan to deal with each one.

   The *whiner* is always complaining and often looks for problems, imagining them if none exist.

   The *traitor* often wants to move up and is looking for ways to undermine you by making you look foolish.

   The *busybody* is a professional meddler who believes she knows everything; usually, she is wrong.

   The *slacker* talks a good game but usually does not produce.

   Dr. No is a perfectionist motivated to get every assignment right by avoiding mistakes. When things go wrong, he loses hope, lets everyone know how he feels, and often extinguishes hope and creativity in others.

5. In terms of Maslow's hierarchy, what motivates you? How would you determine what motivates employees?

6. For years the performance of a state's facilities maintenance group, which is responsible for keeping government buildings in the state capital clean and neat, was mediocre. No amount of pressure or inducement from the secretary of state, who had ultimate responsibility, seemed to do any good. What recommendations would you make?

7. You receive a rush assignment late on Friday afternoon, requiring that certain difficult engineering drawings be completed as soon as possible. The only employee you feel can do this complex task is independent, outspoken, and averse to working overtime. How do you get this employee to do something above and beyond the explicit duties of the job?

8. At 8:10 A.M. on his tenth day as Centerville's new city manager, Roland Jackson's intercom bleeped. In hushed tones, his secretary said, "Mr. Jackson, there are five garbage collectors here demanding to see you. They seem angry."

   Jackson had a crowded schedule that day and was six organizational levels removed from the sanitation workers, but he told his secretary to send them in. He believed in an open-door policy.

Sanitation workers were the lowest-paid and least-skilled workers on the city's payroll. Their occupation, as most people know, involves hard, dirty work in all kinds of weather. The five, who were all African Americans, wished to complain that their supervisor, who was white, always assigned them to the toughest routes and never allowed them to drive the truck. They wanted that changed, pronto.

Jackson was obviously in a tough position. The grievance had clear racial overtones and could escalate. Yet he did not want to undermine the authority of all those managers and supervisors who stood between him and the five angry men seated across from him. Nor could he afford to offend the union that purported to represent these workers. The workers had gone out of channels in more ways than one.

You are Jackson. It is now 8:12 A.M. How do you handle the situation? What exactly would you say?

Favorite Bookmarks

www.hbsp.harvard.edu   In a regular feature of the *Harvard Management* Update, editors recommend sites of particular value to managers seeking information on topics ranging from the new work space, managing teams, and process management to human resources management and finance to knowledge management and careers. Simply click the topics that interest you to view the site descriptions. You can also link directly to the site.

Notes

1. Quoted in *Time* (July 19, 1974).
2. Mary Parker Follett, from *The New State* (1918), as quoted in David K. Hurst, "Thoroughly Modern—Mary Parker Follett," *Business Quarterly,* 56, no. 4 (Spring 1992): 55–58.
3. E. E. Jennings, "The Anatomy of Leadership," *Management of Personnel Quarterly* (Autumn 1961).
4. R. Boyatzis, *The Competent Manager: A Model of Effective Performance* (New York: Wiley, 1982).
5. Fred I. Greenstein, *The Presidential Difference: Leadership Style from FDR to George W. Bush* (Princeton, NJ:Princeton University Press, 2004).
6. William Reddin, *How to Make Your Management Style More Effective* (Maidenhead, England: McGraw-Hill, 1987).
7. Ibid.
8. Ibid., 141–47.
9. Mike Krzyzewski, *Leading with the Heart* (New York: Warner Books, 2000), 211–12.
10. Chester I. Barnard, *The Functions of the Executive* (Cambridge, MA: Harvard University Press, 1938).
11. Saul W. Gellerman, *How People Work* (New York: Quorum Books, 1999).
12. Irving L. Janis, "Groupthink," *Psychology Today* (November 1971).
13. Williams James, *The Works of William James,* ed. Frederick H. Burkhardt (Cambridge, MA: Harvard University Press, 1988).
14. Gellerman, op. cit.
15. Abraham H. Maslow, *The Farther Reaches of Human Nature* (New York: Viking, 1971), 43.
16. David McClelland, *The Achieving Society* (Princeton, NJ: Van Nostrand Reinhold, 1961).
17. Harry Levinson, *The Exceptional Executive* (Cambridge, MA: Harvard University Press, 1968), 243.

18. Douglas McGregor, *The Human Side of Enterprise* (New York: McGraw-Hill, 1960).
19. Ibid., 49.
20. Frederick Herzberg et al., *The Motivation to Work* (New York: John Wiley & Sons, 1959).
21. Quoted in M. McNair, "What Price Human Relations?" *Harvard Business Review* (March–April 1957).
22. Barnard M. Bass, *Handbook of Leadership* (New York: Free Press, 1990).
23. J. Falvey, "Deaf, Dumb, and Blind at the Helm," *The Wall Street Journal* (April 10, 1989).
24. A. Mehrabian, *Silent Messages* (Belmont, CA: Wadsworth, 1971).
25. Andrew Grove, *High-Output Management* (New York: Random House, 1983), 76.
26. C. R. Rogers and F. J. Roethlisberger, "Barriers and Gateways to Communications," *Harvard Business Review* (July–August, 1952).
27. Quoted in *Fortune* (June 12, 2006), 122. Emphasis added.
28. The literature on organizational change is vast, often conflicting, and sometimes inconclusive. For a recent attempt to identify points of consensus among researchers, see Sergio Fernandez and Hal G. Rainey, "Managing Successful Organizational Change in the Public Sector," *Public Administration Review* (March/April 2006), 186–76. The eight stages presented in the text are from John P. Kotter, *Leading Change* (Boston: Harvard Business School Press, 1996).
29. W. Chan Kim and Renee Mauborgue, "Tipping Point Leadership," *Harvard Business Review* (April 2003), 64.
30. Ibid., 69.
31. Wendell L. French et al., *Organizational Development Transformation: Managing Effective Change* (Burr Ridge, IL: Irwin McGraw-Hill, 2000).
32. Peter Richardson and K. Keith Denton, "Communicating Change," *HRM,* 35, no. 2 (June 1996): 203–16.
33. See Bernard M. Bass, *Handbook of Leadership: Theory, Research & Managerial Applications* (New York: Free Press, 1990).
34. Philip P. Kotter, "Why Transformation Efforts Fail," *Harvard Business Review* (March–April 1995).
35. Gardner quoted in Kenneth Labich, "The Seven Keys to Business Leadership," *Fortune* (August 18, 1987).
36. James MacGregor Burns, *Leadership* (New York: Harper & Row, 1985).

CASE 8.1
DAY ONE

Jacqueline Gibson drove down Freeport Boulevard, accelerating once in a while to beat a signal. It was a crisp afternoon with just enough snap in the air to make life seem simple and sweet, if you didn't have too much on your mind. Jackie did.

She reviewed recent events. Two weeks ago the governor's office had notified her of her appointment to the position of Undersecretary of Environmental Protection, Water Resources, for the state of California. The water resources division that she would lead was responsible for ensuring that (a) rivers, lakes, estuaries, and marine waters are fishable and swimmable; and (b) groundwater is safe for drinking. In addition to these responsibilities, the water resources division was charged with (c) the engineering and construction of dams, pipeline transportation of freshwater, and the collection of all water revenues from the various cities and towns in the state; and (d) overseeing sewage disposal and marine transportation. The position involved the supervision of the division's three sections and the 990 persons who were assigned to it.

This morning, Monday, November 9, 2002, she had arrived at the state office building and went to the water resources division on the fourth floor. There she introduced herself to the greeter and was ushered into her new office, a government-green room trimmed in dark wood. The greeter told her that the secretary of environmental protection had arranged for her to meet the other undersecretaries at 9:15 A.M.

At the designated time she went to the Golden State Conference Room on the first floor where seven people were assembled around a magnificent black lacquered table. They all rose as she entered, and the secretary, a vigorous, elfin man, introduced her to the five other undersecretaries and the deputy secretary of the department, Gilberto Sanchez. All sat down and one by one the undersecretaries briefed her about what their divisions did. Jacqueline then spoke about her expectations for good working relations with them. At about 10:00 A.M., the secretary adjourned the meeting and exited, smiling warmly at her.

She then returned to her office and began looking for the files her successor had left. Surprisingly, there were none. How could that be, given the division's broad responsibilities? Later that morning, she noticed the undersecretary of the air resources division walking briskly by her open door without looking in. Around noon, she went out alone for a salad and did some errands.

She returned to her office around 1:30 p.m. and with her assistant began ordering and organizing supplies. Checking her e-mail, she found nothing of particular significance, nor were there any items requiring immediate action. At 2:45, she began meeting with her three directors individually. Each informed her deferentially that "everything was under control." No meeting lasted more than ten minutes. Around 3:45, the deputy secretary walked by her office, glanced in, and asked how things were going. "Fine, Gilberto," she said. "Won't you come in?" He stepped into her office, welcomed her once again to the department, and excused himself to get back to a meeting from which he had just stepped out.

Jacqueline returned to her desk and wondered whimsically whether she should start stacking her paper clips. Although she did not know exactly what working for state government would be like, she felt she was familiar enough with the issues. She had an undergraduate degree in marine biology plus an MPA, had done extensive volunteer work for the Natural Resources Defense Council, and had known professionally the secretary of environmental protection for several years.

As she eased her car onto the Capital City Freeway, she made a decision: This evening, if she did anything, she would develop a roadmap for becoming the leader of the state water resources division.

Case Question

1. The President of the United States gets 100 days to prove himself. It is unlikely Jacqueline will get that much time. Jacqueline needs to take charge quickly and effectively during this critical career transition period. What are some specific strategies she might follow and actions she might take?

Graham Lyth Photography

NYPD's COUNTERTERRORISM DIVISION

··

Unless objectives are converted into action, they are not objectives; they are dreams.

Peter F. Drucker

In November 2001, weeks after Al Qaeda had successfully attacked New York City for the *second* time, newly appointed police commissioner Ray Kelly decided that NYPD would fight its own war against terrorism. The federal government had provided for the city's protection in 1993 when the group later known as Al Qaeda attacked the World Trade Center, and the feds were also responsible when two planes devastated the Twin Towers. The time had come, Kelly believed, to make New York's first line of defense the NYPD rather than the U.S. military or what cops call the "three letter guys"—the CIA, DHS, FBI, CIA, and NSA.

Specifically, Kelly took three bold actions: establish a counterterrorism division; dramatically expand the intelligence division (which had been essentially an escort service for visiting dignitaries) and hire a former senior CIA official, David Cohen, to run it; and increase the number of cops working with the FBI on the Joint Terrorism Task Force. But listing these three actions does not convey the enormity of the challenge Kelly faced. According to Cohen, in the early days of the Kelly regime, everything was intense and anything seemed possible. "It was like putting tires on a speeding car," Cohen said.

Although NYPD might have 50,000 employees and a budget of nearly $4 billion, Kelly was essentially trying to transform a local police department into an organization that could compete on an international scale. If they were to make New York City safe again, Kelly and Cohen thought they needed to build something different from the federal agencies; that meant an organization with minimum bureaucracy and maximum flexibility. The result was basically a combination of crime fighting and intelligence gathering, a hybrid approach that has since become known as "intelligence-led policing." Journalist Christopher Dickey explains, "The aim should be to gather information and intelligence, identify risk, and then manage the risks by intervening selectively to protect against the threat. Sometimes that means detaining a suspect, but use of information and intimidation to disrupt potential plots may be even more effective. Sometimes, all that's required is to make a target harder to hit, or to put on a show that makes it seem so."

Plans to do this type of policing were developed in morning meetings that Kelly held with the heads of the intelligence division and counterterrorism division every day at eight o'clock sharp. Because Kelly never missed a morning, Cohen never missed a meeting. From those meetings, Cohen said, "We created the playbook."

Why would a city need its own CIA? Some would say New York City had no choice. Terrorists are obsessed with New York City, focusing on it, Dickey writes, "like a compass needle quivering toward magnetic north." Consider this. The 1998 remake of *Godzilla*, starring Matthew Broderick, was largely rejected by American audiences, but Al Qaeda sympathizers abroad loved it. The scenes of Godzilla stomping across New York City, crushing everything in its path, were mesmerizing and inspiring. One captured terrorist leader warned of an attack against "the bridge in the Godzilla movie." Interrogators had to rent the film to find out what he meant: the Brooklyn Bridge.

Moreover, organizations like the FBI and the CIA didn't always share vital information. Therefore, NYPD began to get its intelligence its own way, posting cops with their counterparts in London, Paris, Amman, Montreal, Santo Domingo, Singapore, Tel Aviv, and other foreign cities. Once the division began to gather important information on its own, it could deal with the FBI and CIA from a position of strength. "There is no such thing as information sharing," said Cohen. "There is only information trading."

Language was the key. NYPD could not run informers in immigrant communities, much less undercover cops, if it didn't have personnel who spoke the dialects. NYPD could not have the Cyber Intelligence Unit successfully patrol chat rooms if it didn't have personnel who could talk about the same street corners and schools that others in the chat room knew. A record search showed that about 2500 department employees spoke a foreign language. The department's Chinese speakers can converse in Fukienese as well as Mandarin; its Spanish linguists talk with Salvadoran, Guatemalan, Honduran, Puerto Rican, or Dominican accents. NYPD officers speak Russian, French, German, Farsi, Dari, and Pashto, too. In contrast, because of strict security clearance procedures, the CIA, the FBI, the U.S. military, and the U.S. State Department are weak in linguists.

Though language is hugely important in eliciting intelligence, the Counter Terrorism Division had other operations designed to prevent future attacks. For example:

★ OPERATION HERCULES. Every day, officers of different precincts go to a location that was chosen at random to provide a show of force to deter anyone out there who might be planning an attack. The heavily armed "Hercules team" also moves around the city at random protecting high-value targets and infrastructure and disrupting operational planning details of terrorists. The reason for this theatricality is that cops "have to make themselves seem all-powerful and all knowing."

★ OPERATION NEXUS. The NYPD also involves business in counterterrorism. A program called Operation Nexus, begun in 2002, networked police officers "with businesses that might be exploited by terrorists. Companies that sold chemicals like hydrogen peroxide or nitrate fertilizers, the stuff of homemade bombs, needed to have their consciousness raised. But so did self-storage warehouses (where components and chemicals might be hidden), exterminators (poisons and sprayers), propane gas vendors (the canisters can serve as ready-made explosives), cell phone vendors (mobiles work as timers and triggers).... some 80 different categories of businesses were deemed of interest to the police."

★ OPERATION KABOOM. Inside the windowless Counterterrorism Bureau headquarters, the Special Projects Group, or "red cell," plots terrorist attacks. The idea is to take several cops who have no particular experience with explosives and see what they can pull together from information on the Internet and from suppliers within a few hours drive of Manhattan. One model they used was the massive bomb detonated by the Irish Republican Army at Manchester, England, in June 1996. Disturbingly, the team was able to pick up 1200 pounds of ammonium nitrate—the same stuff used by the IRA—in Pennsylvania without incident.

In addition to language skills and various visible and undercover activities, the counterterrorism division has the technology to stay one step ahead of the enemy. On the ground, thousands of cops wear "personal radiation detectors" which are very effective at picking up minute traces of potentially dangerous rays. In addition to the city's 300 square miles of land, there are 165 square miles of waterways—any of which would make good entry points for weapons of mass distraction. The counterterrorism boats don't look different from other police boats on the water, but the classified technology they carry makes them unique. But the most high-tech tools are 1000 feet above the city, giving officers on the ground real-time intelligence. Dickey describes his ride one cold winter night in an unmarked NYPD helicopter:

The morning is clear in a way—in that way—that is always a little heartbreaking if you were here on September 11, 2001. There were police choppers in New York's sky then, too, but not like this one, which can see so much from so far. It is a state-of-the-art crime-fighting, terror-busting, order-keeping techno-toy, with its enormous lens that can magnify any scene on the street almost 1000 times, then double that digitally; that can watch a crime in progress from miles away, can look in windows, and sense the body heat of people on rooftops or running along sidewalks, can track beepers slipped under cars, can do so many things that the man in the helmet watching the screens and moving the images with the joystick in his lap . . . is often a little bit at loss for words. "It really is an amazing tool," he keeps saying. On the left-hand screen is a map of Manhattan. He punches in an address on the Upper East Side, my address. The camera on the belly of the machines swerves instantaneously, focuses, and there on the second screen is my building scene from more than a mile away now, but up close and personal from this surprising astral angle. The cameras and sensors are locked onto it, staying with it as the chopper turns and homes in.

Assess how well the NYPD has converted its objectives into actions. What actions besides those mentioned in the case would you recommend? What are the limitations or weaknesses in NYPD's approach? Dickey is sharply critical of "the dangerously ill-conceived, mismanaged, and highly militarized global war on terror," and sees the success of the NYPD's counterterrorism program as offering an alternative approach. Do you agree or disagree?

SOURCE: Christopher Dickey, *Securing the City: Inside America's Best Counterterrorism Force—The NYPD* (New York: Simon & Schuster, 2009).

Half the business of thinking is knowing what one is after in the first place. Before launching into this chapter, let's pause to review the structure of program management. Good program management begins with careful attention to goals and to the objectives for attaining goals. Careful attention to objectives, in turn, means considering alternative strategies for the attainment of each objective. In particular, the policy planner wants to ask what the likely effects of each alternative will be. Decision making pervades the entire process of program management. Based on the assumption that today's administrator should be acquainted with the tools and techniques of rational decision making, most of Chapter 6 was devoted to exploring this approach to decision making.

The story does not end there, however. Three vitally important, exceedingly difficult, and frequently exciting tasks remain—organizing, leading, and implementing. Once it is clear what needs to be done, the agency does not just throw everything together as did the hapless deputy in the cartoon appearing at the beginning of Chapter 7. Programs and policies, require a degree of *organization*—and, as seen in the last chapter, *leadership.*

Assume for the purposes here that **implementation** means just what the dictionary says it means: "to carry out, accomplish, fulfill, produce, complete." But what is it that is being implemented? A policy, yes—but more exactly, that part of a policy defined in Chapter 5 as a program.

The distinction between policy and program is an important one when speaking of implementation. The great difficulty in government today is not so much determining what appear to be reasonable policies on paper as it is converting objectives into specific actions. In short, there are more good solutions (that is, policies) than appropriate actions (that is, programs).

This chapter begins by offering three perspectives on implementation. The first perspective comes from Jeffrey L. Pressman and Aaron Wildavsky's slim classic *Implementation* with the chubby subtitle *How Great Expectations in Washington Are Dashed in Oakland; Or, Why It's Amazing that Federal Programs Work at All This Being a Saga of the Economic Development Administration as Told by Two Sympathetic Observers Who Seek to Build Morals on a Foundation of Ruined Hopes.* As its subtitle might suggest, this book views implementation as an exceedingly difficult process. Eugene Bardash presents us with a second perspective in another public administration classic: *The Implementation Game.* The third perspective, the one this chapter builds on, is to view implementation as a process that can be managed.

The management of implementation has two components—the strategic and the tactical. As the word has been handed down from the military, *strategy* refers to the big, important decisions. Here's a big, important question: Who will fight the war? Do we send Army ground troops into Kosovo, or do we have the Air Force bomb Serbia from 5000 feet, or do we do a little of both? Here's another: How will we wage war? Do we use economic sanctions ("economic warfare"), covert operations, conventional forces, or thermonuclear weapons ("total war")? The term *tactical,* in contrast, refers to detailed questions: what caliber of weapons to use, what color to paint the vehicles, who to put "in the loop" and who to exclude, and so on.

The problem with this strategy-tactical distinction is that sometimes, in retrospect, details can prove strategic. As Henry Mintzberg reminds us, one of the reasons Henry Ford lost his war with General Motors was that he refused to paint his cars anything but black.

Still, the distinction is useful. The second and third sections will therefore explore two strategic questions about implementation:

- *Who* will implement the program or project? For example: Which agency or agencies? Which level or levels of government? Or should the job be contracted to the private and nonprofit sectors?
- *How* will it be implemented? For example: Should efficiency or effectiveness be emphasized? Should coercive methods (for example, regulations, command-and-control) or noncoercive methods (for example, incentives, persuasion) be employed?

The final section discusses a variety of tactical considerations—some optional for implementers, others mandatory.

Three Perspectives on Implementation

The Complexity of Joint Action

Everything in the briefing room is very simple—the difficulty is on the outside, where the action is. Countless minor incidents—the kind one can seldom foresee—combine to raise the general level of complexity of a situation, so one always falls short of the desired outcome. The bureaucratic machine, as outlined in Chapter 7, is basically very simple and easy to manage. But bear in mind that few programs are of one piece. Programs generally involve many actors, every one of whom retains her potential for causing friction. In other words, program implementation involves various individuals, the least important of whom may delay things and sometimes make them go wrong.

If public administration is the realm of uncertainty and chance, it is even more the realm of differing priorities, conflicting values, confusion, exhaustion, and distrust. All these factors combine to create **complexity of joint action.** Nowhere is this phenomenon better demonstrated than in a famous study by Jeffrey L. Pressman and the late Aaron Wildavsky. Pressman and Wildavsky note among the major difficulties in implementing new social programs or program modifications two in particular: multiplicity of participants and multiplicity of perspectives.[1] These two factors converge to delay—and, in many instances, stifle—administrative efforts to secure the joint action required in program implementation. Consider their analysis of the Economic Development Administration's (EDA's) efforts in Oakland.

On the face of things, the effort to help unemployed African Americans in Oakland, California, began brilliantly. There were dedicated and powerful officials in Washington who were concerned that, if the city did not receive meaningful help quickly, it might be torn apart by riots. Officials were able to get a multimillion-dollar congressional appropriation to finance a program to provide jobs, while also enlisting Oakland businesspeople and governmental officials in the effort. And many of the usual bureaucratic barriers to action were struck down. It would be hard to think of a more propitious beginning for a government program—yet within three short years, the program was essentially a failure. Not very much money had been spent, and the number of new jobs obtained for the hard-core unemployed was ridiculously small. Why?

One answer is that government programs, even when designed to be carried out in a direct and simple manner, eventually come to involve a large number of governmental and nongovernmental organizations and individuals. In the case of the EDA's employment effort in Oakland, the authors admit to oversimplifying the situation by restricting the participants to only the EDA, the rest of the federal government, and the city of Oakland, each with its constituent elements. The EDA consisted of the initial task force, the EDA operating departments in Washington, the agency's leadership, the regional office in Seattle, and the field office in Oakland. Other federal government agencies that became involved included the General Accounting Office, the Department of Health, Education, and Welfare (HEW), the Department of Labor, and the Navy. Participants in Oakland were the mayor, city administrators, the Port of Oakland, World Airways, and several of the city's black leaders, conservative groups, and tenants of the Port of Oakland.

Some of these participants (such as the Department of Labor) became involved because they possessed jurisdictional authority over important parts of the project; others (like the Navy) entered the process when they felt their interest being impinged on; and still others (such as the African Americans in Oakland) were intentionally brought into the program by the EDA to build local support for the projects.

Each participating group had a distinctive perspective and therefore a different sense of urgency—though they all still agreed on the ends of the policy (developing jobs for unemployed minorities) and the means of achieving it (creating jobs through grants for public works). But different perspectives make or break a program. Pressman and Wildavsky give several reasons why participants can agree on the ends of a program and still oppose (or merely fail to facilitate) the means for effecting those ends:

1. Direct incompatibility with other commitments. Thus, HEW came to view one of the EDA's training proposals as competing for scarce funds with one of its own training institutions in the area.
2. No direct incompatibility but a preference for other programs. Many EDA employees viewed rural areas and small towns—not urban areas—as the proper focus of the agency.
3. Simultaneous commitments to other projects. The Port of Oakland's architect/engineer delayed his work on plans for the marine terminal because his staff was busy on other port projects.
4. Dependence on others who lack a sense of urgency.
5. Differences of opinion on leadership and the proper organizational role.
6. Legal and procedural differences. For example, regarding the quality of landfill, at every point, the Port of Oakland and the EDA had their own engineering options.[2]

Pressman and Wildavsky offer a probabilistic model that gives a wider applicability to these pessimistic conclusions about the chances of implementing programs. See Table 9.1. The calculations are based on the multiplication model of ordinary probability theory.

Table 9.1 Probability of Program Completion as a Function of Participants' Level of Agreement		
Probability of Agreement on Each Clearance Point (in percent)	Probablility of Success after 70 Clearances	Number of Agreements that Reduce Probability below 50 Percent
80	0.000000125	4
90	0.000644	7
95	0.00395	14
99	0.489	68

SOURCE: Jeffrey L. Pressman and Aaron Wildavsky, *Implementation* (Berkeley, CA: University of California Press, 1973), 107. The table assumes, of course, that each decision is independent. Do you think that assumption is warranted?

For example, if the probability of agreement is 0.8 at point *A,* 0.7 at point *B,* and 0.5 at point *C,* then the chances of obtaining agreement at all three points is

$$0.8 \times 0.7 \times 0.5 = 0.28$$

Elinor R. Bowen takes the relevance of probability theory further and offers a more optimistic view.[3] Specifically, she suggests four addenda to the Pressman and Wildavsky model. First, it should allow for *persistence.* Just because a particular participant, or clearance point, declines to agree, it does not necessarily follow that the case is closed. The implementing agency can always ask again and again. Second, it seems reasonable to assume that program elements may be collected into packages rather than decided on separately. The third addendum is the bandwagon effect: gaining additional support for a proposal simply because it seems to be winning approval. Recall the earlier illustration of the multiplicative model of ordinary probability theory. If a proposal is agreed to by *A* and *B* before it comes to *C* for agreement, *C*'s likelihood of agreement might now be a little higher than 0.5.

Finally, Bowen notes an inconsistency in the way Pressman and Wildavsky apply reductionist principles. They decompose bureaucracy into a large number of independent actors, each of whom can potentially derail the implementation process. Yet they assume a holistic posture toward policy—that is, all components of the policy must be approved for implementation to succeed. For Pressman and Wildavsky, approval of anything less than the whole initial program proposal is defeat. No partial victories are allowed in their implementation model. Is that really the way the world works?

Bowen's work suggests empirically reasonable tactics for those who would implement programs—namely, persistence, packaging, engineering bandwagons, and policy reduction.

Implementation as a System of Games

Eugene Bardach uses the **metaphor of "games"** to analyze the implementation process.[4] He argues that the game framework illuminates the process by directing attention to the players, their stakes, their strategies and tactics, their resources, the rules of play (which stipulate the conditions for winning), the rules of fair play, the nature of communication among the players, and the degree of uncertainty surrounding the outcome.

This leads to an insightful definition of implementation: a process of assembling the elements required to produce a particular programmatic outcome and the playing out of a number of loosely interrelated games whereby these elements are withheld from or delivered to the program. The following list identifies some of the more common implementation games that Bardach identifies.

- *Tokenism.* The "attempt to appear to be contributing to a program element publicly while privately conceding only a small ('token') contribution."
- *Massive resistance.* Obstructing program implementation by withholding critical program elements or by overwhelming the capacity of the administrative agency to enforce punishment for noncompliance.
- *Easy money.* A game played by parties in the private sector who wish to make off with government money in exchange for program elements of too little value. (Around Washington, consultants are called Beltway Bandits because many of them have offices along I-495, a highway that loops downtown.)
- *Up for grabs.* Often the mandate for a program will identify a lead agency and provide a modest budget but will fail to clearly prescribe what other element might be involved and for what expected purpose. "In this confused situation, the few unambiguously mandated elements are up for grabs by a number of potential clientele groups to be converted into political resources."
- *Piling on.* As onlookers see a program moving successfully in its intended direction, "some see it as a new political resource, an opportunity to throw their own goals and objectives onto the heap." The net effect of a large number of additional objectives added to the program is that the program may triple in size.
- *Tenacity.* This game can be played by anyone; all it requires is the ability and will to stymie the progress of a program until one's own terms are satisfied. Although no one player may want to kill the program, the net effect of many actors playing tenacity may be just that.
- *Territory.* All bureaucratic organizations struggle to ensure that some other organization is not given a program element that is perceived to be in "their" jurisdiction.
- *Not our problem.* Although bureaus may try to expand their territories, "this drive normally evaporates as soon as the bureau recognizes that the program will impose a heavy work load or that it will take the bureau into an area of controversy."

Implementation as a Process to Be Managed

No doubt the implementation of public policy is a complex process—certainly more complex than many policymakers imagined it to be—and no doubt the process involves a lot of game playing. But, in the final analysis, implementation is a process that can be managed. Surely, "better managed" are the two favorite words of every politician who ever kissed a baby. But, in the public sector, what do those words really mean? In the next three sections, we will try to find out.

First Strategic Question: Who Will Run the Program?

The word **privatize** did not appear in a dictionary until 1983. Broadly speaking, it symbolizes a new way of thinking about government's role in addressing a society's needs. E. S. Savas, one of the nation's leading experts on privatization, defines it as the act of reducing the role of government, or increasing the role of the private sector, in an activity or in the ownership of assets.[5] For a more precise, technical definition of privatization, consider the following continuum:

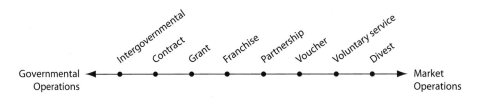

To privatize means to move from left to right, from one arrangement to another, along the continuum.

In response to increased interest in privatization, the International City County Management Association (ICMA) has been tracking the use by local governments of alternative service delivery approaches since 1982. What is interesting about the trends is how little they have changed over the years. Almost all governments responding to the ICMA's surveys use at least one form of alternative service delivery. However, despite strong political support for privatization and a reduction in opposition to it, direct public delivery is still the most common form of service delivery. Privatization involving profit-making organizations and intergovernmental contracting are the most common alternatives and their use has ranged from 15 to 20 percent of services over this period. What has risen most dramatically in recent years is the use of mixed public/private provision of services.[6]

To appreciate the degree of privatization at the federal level, we can look at data provided by fedspending.org, a Web site mandated by the Federal Funding, Accountability, and Transparency Act of 2006. Federal spending in fiscal year 2006 was $2,872 billion. Contracts accounted for almost 15 percent of that spending and grants another 17 percent. (This picture changed significantly in 2008–2009 with the passage of a massive stimulus package which will be discussed in Chapter 11.)

Now let's consider the various options shown on the continuum above. We will begin with governmental operations at the left, skip intergovernmental relations (since it was discussed at length in Chapter 3), and then consider briefly the six ways government can achieve its objectives by operating with or through third parties. Eventually, we arrive at the right end of the continuum where government opts to divest itself of responsibility for a particular objective—presumably on the assumption that it makes more sense to leave things to the market.

Governmental Operations

Roughly speaking, governments have four instruments through which they can directly influence society and the economy and achieve public purpose: (1) regulation, (2) services, (3) money, and (4) taxes.

First, unlike private actors, governments have the right to make authoritative decrees and back these decrees with the legitimate power of the state; in short, they can regulate. Even a casual look around us shows the breadth and importance of regulation by all levels of government:

- Controlling prices (electric power, local telephone service)
- Setting price floors (crops, minimum wages)
- Ensuring equal opportunity (banning discrimination in employment)
- Regularizing employment practices (over time)
- Specifying qualifications (occupational licensure)
- Providing for solvency (financial institutions, insurance, pension plans)
- Controlling the number of market participants (broadcast licenses, taxi medallions)
- Limiting ownership (media, airlines)
- Requiring premarketing approval (toxic chemicals, pharmaceuticals)
- Ensuring product safety (pharmaceuticals, toys, food)
- Mandating product characteristics and technology (automobile safety standards)
- Establishing service territories (local telephone services)
- Establishing performance standards (automobile emissions standards)
- Controlling toxic emissions and other pollutants (sulfur dioxide emissions trading)
- Specifying industry boundaries (insurance, banking, and stock brokerage boundaries)
- Allocating public resources (spectrum allocations)
- Establishing standards (telecommunications interconnections)
- Controlling unfair international trade practices (antidumping)
- Providing information (labeling)
- Rationing common pool resources (fisheries)

The second instrument of government, service, is probably what most people think of when they think of governmental operations. Services governments provide directly to citizens range from defense to education to recreation, from fire and police protection to air traffic control. This direct provision of services raises a critical question: which sector would best produce the desired results. According to Osborne and Gaebler, these are the tasks for which the *public sector* is generally perceived to be best suited:[7]

policy management
regulation
enforcement of equality
prevention of discrimination
prevention of exploitation
promotion of social cohesion

They consider these tasks particularly well-suited for the *nonprofit sector:*

social tasks
tasks that require volunteer labor
tasks that generate little profit
promotion of individual responsibility

promotion of community
promotion of commitment to welfare of others

Finally, Osborne and Gaebler would give the nod to the *private sector* for the following:

economic tasks
investment tasks
profit generation
promotion of self-sufficiency

Third, besides regulation and services, governments also provide citizens, organizations, and other governments with money. As we will see in Chapter 11, about 56 percent of all dollars collected in taxes by the federal government is recycled back to citizens as transfer payments. **Transfer payments** are payments made to individuals for which no services or goods are rendered in return. The three key money transfer payments in the U.S. system are welfare, Social Security, and unemployment insurance. Income redistribution also includes a large amount of income transfers in-kind, as opposed to money transfers. Some income transfers in-kind are food stamps, Medicare and Medicaid, government health care services, and subsidized public housing.

Fourth, governments also use tax codes to encourage and discourage certain behaviors. For example, a variety of deductions permit individuals and corporations who engage in favorite activities—such as capital investment, purchase of homes, or charitable giving—to retain funds that otherwise would be paid in taxes. Such deductions are often referred to as tax loopholes, though the more appropriate term is **tax expenditure,** since granting tax relief for an activity is the same as subsidizing that activity directly through an expenditure program. Table 9.2 shows the ten largest tax expenditures for 2006. Governments taketh as well as giveth. For example, if government wants to discourage certain activities—such as the use of carbon fuels and tobacco products—it can raise taxes on those activities.

Now let's consider the indirect ways in which governments try to achieve their objectives.

Contracting

Scope   Today all sorts of governments are contracting for all sorts of goods and services. The public sector contracts with the private and nonprofit sectors for the design, construction, and maintenance of roads and bridges; for the production of nuclear weapons; for the management of prisons and the delivery of services within prisons; for information technology; for the management of public schools; for educating, training, and placing welfare recipients and displaced workers in jobs; for child support enforcement; and for a host of other social services. Eighty percent of the largest cities in the United States contract out vehicle towing, and half contract out solid-waste collection. Over the past several decades, as society has debated government's make-or-buy decision, public agencies have shifteed more toward the *buy* alternative.[8] Consider:

Table 9.2	The Largest Tax Expenditures, 2006	
Rank	Tax expenditure	Billions ($)
1	Exclusion of employer contributioins for medical insurance premiums and medical care	125.0
2	Net exlusions of pension contributions and earnings (all)	104.6
3	Deductibility of mortgage interest on owner-occupied homes	68.3
4	Captial gains (except agriculture, timber, iron ore, and coal)	48.6
5	Deductibility of charitable contributions (all)	45.5
6	Deductibility of nonbusiness state and local taxes other than owner-occupied homes	43.1
7	Accelerated depreciation of machinery and emquipment (normal tax method)	36.5
8	Capital gains exclusion on home sales	35.3
9	Child credit[a]	30.4
10	Exclusion of net imputed rental income on owner-occupied homes	28.8

NOTES: [a] Nonrefundable portion only.
SOURCE: *Budget of the U.S. Government, Analytical Perspectives,* Fiscal 2006, Table 19.1

- Federal contractors outnumbered federal employees by more than 2 to 1. Between 1990 and 2001, federal-level contracting of services rose 24 percent in real terms.
- Today probably between 15 and 20 percent of all spending at the state level is contracted it out. Between 1996 and 2001, state contracts to private firms rose 65 percent.

Advantages and Disadvantages   The first advantage of contracting is greater efficiency. This is not always the case, but when it is the reasons are not hard to find. Marketplace competition produces goods and services efficiently, whereas nonmonopolies (like government bureaucracies) don't face the same competitive pressures to decrease costs and increase consumer value.

A second advantage is that contracting frees public administrators from routine details. As government begins to get out of the "doing," it becomes freer to concentrate its efforts on differentiating public needs from public wants; to sort out who can do what most effectively in society; to consider new approaches to long-standing problems; and to discover and disclose inconsistencies or overlapping among a program's interacting parts.

A third advantage is that contracts may increase flexibility. In some circumstances, it is easier for a contractor to start up new programs than it is for a government bureaucracy encumbered by legislative mandates and pressured by interest groups.

While seeking these advantages, public administrators must be alert to possible disadvantages to contracting. Some disadvantages are obvious. The growth of contracting makes it harder to tell where the public sector begins and ends. The traditional sorts of internal and external controls discussed in Chapter 4 diminish in importance. The challenge of realizing the ideals of administrative responsibility may become more problematic as the number of contract and subcontract workers multiplies.

A second disadvantage is that costs may actually rise. Contractors have little incentive to control expenses unless adequate safeguards are imposed. Contracting officials must therefore monitor the work of contractors—and that oversight is itself a cost. For example, an internal Energy Department report in 2002 concluded that the department's largest program, which pays contractors to clean up waste left by the nation's nuclear weapons programs, has been fundamentally mismanaged since its founding in 1989, and much of the $60 billion it has spent over that time was wasted.[9]

A third disadvantage is that contracting permits the expansion of government activities without giving the impression that government has expanded.

Collusion among bidders for contracts is a fourth disadvantage. Competition, the engine of efficiency we spoke about earlier, should not be assumed. In some areas, there is no competition. Also, contracts can be abused. For example, some contractors, who are good friends with contracting officers, gain "inside" status and are given preferential treatment. Some contractors subdivide their contract to take advantage of noncompetitive small businesses' bidding rules. In short, the opportunities for abuse extend as far as the wit of human beings—which is to say pretty far.

A fifth disadvantage is that, at a certain point, government can contract out so much technical stuff that it no longer has the human resources—or, to speak bluntly, the brainpower—to effectively monitor the contractors. To be sure, many bright people still work for NASA, an agency that once employed Werner von Braun in Huntsville, Alabama. But, over the years, the agency has contracted out so many cutting-edge activities that many in the contractor community no longer feel that they are dealing with equals—much less giants.

The sixth disadvantage of contracting is that some activities just seem inappropriate for the private sector. What is inappropriate is of course in the eye of the beholder. If someone proposes contracting out U.S.–China policy to, say, the Rand Corporation or some consortium of Berkeley political scientists, most would conclude that is not a good idea in a democracy. On the other hand, when Mayor Guiliani proposed selling 85 of the 500 gas stations owned by New York City, few would call that unreasonable or a threat to the republic.

The Process   Two laws govern contracting in the federal government—the Federal Property and Administrative Services Act of 1949 and its defense-oriented equivalent, the Armed Forces Procurement Act of 1947. These two laws have been implemented through the Federal Acquisition Regulation (FAR) in a process supervised by the Office of Federal Procurement Policy in the Executive Office of the President.

FAR establishes two basic methods of obtaining "full and open competition": sealed bidding and competitive negotiation. **Sealed bidding,** which is characterized by a rigid adherence to formal procedures, aims to provide all bidders an opportunity to compete for the contract on equal footing. Sealed bids are solicited when four conditions are met. First, time permits the solicitation, submission, and evaluation of sealed bids. Second, the award will be made on the basis of price. Third, it is not necessary to conduct discussions with the responding offerors about their bids. And fourth, there is a reasonable expectation of receiving more than one sealed bid.

The agency's contracting officer (CO) initiates a sealed bidding acquisition by issuing an Invitation for Bids (IFB) that describes the government's requirements. The agency publicizes the IFB through announcements in newspapers or trade journals; direct mailing to contractors; and, if the procurement is over $25000, publication in the federal government's *Commerce Business Daily* (CBD). In a sealed bidding acquisition, the agency must award to the responsible bidder who submits the lowest responsive bid (price).

In contrast, **competitive negotiation** is a more flexible process. If one of the four conditions just described is missing, the CO will award the contract using competitive negotiation. Unlike sealed bidding, the CO may engage in discussions with offerors and, in evaluating proposals, he or she may also consider noncost factors such as managerial experience, technical approach, and past performance. The negotiating process begins when the CO issues a Request for Proposals (RFP). The RFP must, at a minimum, state the agency's need, anticipated terms and conditions of the contract, information the contractor must include in the proposal, and factors that the agency will consider in evaluating the proposals.

In drafting the contract, certain clauses are particularly important. For example, the "changes" clause enables the government to make unilateral changes to the contract during performance, as long as those changes fall within the contract's scope. Under the standard changes clause used in fixed-price supply contracts, the CO may make changes, in writing, to the drawings, designs, or specifications; to the method of shipment or packaging; and to the place of delivery. The change doesn't necessarily work to the disadvantage of the contractor, however, because the contractor is entitled to an "equitable adjustment" to the contract if the change results in increased costs or time on the job. Another important clause in almost every government contract is "termination for convenience." This clause permits the government to terminate the contract, at any time, without cause, when in "the government's best interest."

As indicated in Figure 9.1, the final phase of the contract process concerns dispute resolution. Since government contracting began—which was before the Constitution—there has been a special process followed for disputes arising under a government contract. A contractor initiates the dispute process by presenting a claim to the CO. The "disputes" clause defines a *claim* as "a written demand or written assertion by one of the contracting parties seeking, as a matter of right, the payment of money in a sum certain, the adjustment or interpretation of contract terms, or other relief arising under the contract." If the contractor and government are unable to negotiate a resolution to the dispute, the CO must issue a written explanation of the agency's position with respect to the claim. A contractor may not commence litigation until the CO issues such an explanation. But if the CO fails to issue it, the contractor may eventually attempt to appeal the CO's denial of the claim to an administrative board of contract appeals or the U.S. Court of Federal Claims.

Figure 9.1   Public Contract Process

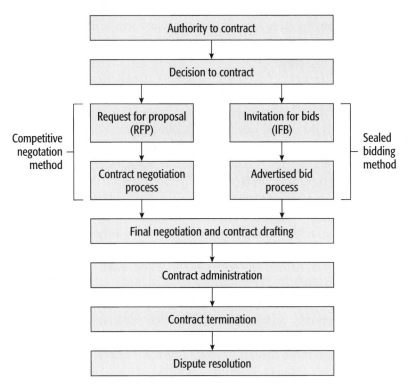

Grants

Broadly defined, a **grant** is a form of gift that entails certain obligations on the part of the grantee and expectations on the part of the grantor. Grants from a king to a composer of music or grants from a tax-exempt charity to a research scientist are clear examples. But intergovernmental transfers of funds and other assets also constitute grants. From the era of land-grant colleges to the present, a grant by the federal government has been a continuing means of providing states, localities, public and private institutions, and individuals with funds to support projects the federal government considers useful. In recent years, grants have been made to business enterprises to support public purposes, and it is these with which this section is concerned.

The grant arrangement involves the government subsidizing private firms' production, creating a profit opportunity by lowering the firms' costs of production. Two major examples of grants are wage subsidies to encourage the hiring of disadvantaged workers and capital subsidies to encourage plant locations in economically distressed areas.

Franchises

In the **franchise** arrangement, the government assures customers access to a service or product but does not pay the producer for it. Typically, the government designates a private firm as the supplier, and consumers purchase the good or service, usually with some price regulation. For example, a franchise can be used to provide toll roads (and automobile service and restaurants along them); common utilities such as electricity, gas, and water; intracity telephone service and cable television; and bus transportation.

These examples are exclusive franchises in the sense that the government does not allow for multiple utilities (each with its own power lines) within its jurisdiction. But nonexclusive or multiple franchises can be awarded in certain industries, as in the case of taxis and wrecker trucks.

Partnerships

In contrast to contracting, franchises, grants, or other arrangements between the public sector and the private sector, a **partnership** signifies that both sectors share risks and responsibilities to meet critical community needs as defined by the partners. Shared risk means that both partners could lose resources; it encourages the involvement of both the public sector and private sector in ventures that neither could successfully attempt alone. Shared responsibilities include joint decision making by representatives of the different groups that work collaboratively on the project.

Today there is growing interest in public–private collaboration on economic development projects, particularly in larger cities where there are limits to independent initiatives in responding to complex urban economic development programs. A case in point is Inner Harbor, a large commercial redevelopment project in Baltimore, which includes a world trade center, a new office building, new residential units, a marina, an aquarium, a theater, a college campus, and parkland, all financed through both private and public investment.

The New York City Department of Parks and Recreation has used partnerships in a particularly innovative way. Faced with steadily decreasing maintenance budgets as well as the impressive success of citizen-led efforts to revive some of the city's parks, the Department of Parks and Recreation embarked on a drive to increase citizen, community, and private-sector support for neighborhood parks. Using a mix of public and private resources including small grants, technical assistance, and community organizing, the partnerships engaged thousands of groups in park improvement efforts, helping to create grassroots support and neighborhood advocates for specific parks. By 2000, after only five years, the partnerships had a database of nearly 50,000 park supporters citywide, along with a list of more than 3200 organizations with an interest in parks.

If collaborative ventures are to be successful, as those in Baltimore and New York were, both sectors need new skills and new levels of flexibility and adaptability. Local administrators need to provide the expertise necessary for evaluating potential joint projects and for negotiating contractual arrangements with private-sector participants. Business participants must develop the necessary skills for negotiating with local governments, recognizing that they cannot dictate the terms of cooperation.

In today's economic and high-tech environment, partnerships are especially relevant. According to former Illinois governor Jim Edgar, partnerships are attractive because the private sector has three things government needs: resources, knowledge, and public support:

- Even with an improving economy, the public is unwilling to turn over more resources to government. If a public agency wants to do something, it may find better sources of funding in the private sector than in the city council or the legislature.
- People who work in government are quite competent, but as Edgar emphasizes, "We don't have all the expertise." By building new partnerships, public managers can tap new sources of both *wisdom* and *skills.*
- If public officials develop a program alone, they have to sell it alone. But if people from outside government are—from the beginning—partners in the design process, they become partners in the marketing process, too.[10]

By the same token, the public sector has things that the private sector needs. The California Environmental Technology Certification Program works with the private sector to develop and market new pollution prevention and cleanup products. Those proven to work receive official state certification, which gives almost instant credibility to products that might otherwise have to struggle to gain market acceptance.[11]

Vouchers

In the grant system, the government subsidizes the producer and restricts the customer's choice to the subsidized private firm, which provides the medical care, housing, mass transit, or some other good or service. In the **voucher** system, the government subsidizes customers and permits them to exercise relatively free choice in the marketplace. Rather than subsidize low-cost housing with grants, the government can simply give the customers vouchers to apply toward rent at a dwelling of their choice. Thus, part of the payment comes from government and part from the client.

In 1990, Milwaukee began a voucher system that allowed low-income parents to send their children to private schools at public expense. In one of his first moves in office, President George W. Bush announced an educational proposal that included vouchers. Advocates of the voucher approach to education argue that affluent Americans have always had the opportunity to choose their children's schools—either by sending them to private schools or by moving to neighborhoods with well-regarded systems. Vouchers, they contend, give lower-income families similar options and also improve all schools by forcing them to compete for students against other schools, both public and private. But crtics charge that vouchers siphon off much-needed funds from public schools.

Voluntary Service

Voluntary associations have been a critical part of American social dynamism since the country's founding. "Americans of all ages," wrote Alexis de Tocqueville, "are forever forming associations." By connecting people to their neighbors and to the wider world, argued de

Tocqueville, civic associations made Americans better informed, safer, richer, and better able to govern themselves and create a just and stable society.

Today voluntary associations perform a host of human services that governments are either unwilling or unable to perform. A growing number of community groups and block associations work to improve the quality of life in their neighborhoods, plugging gaps in the services of city and county bureaucracy.

Voluntary efforts are not limited to trying to lighten the burden of urban problems—drugs, homelessness, dirt, graffiti, unemployment, and loneliness among young and old. For example, after Katrina devastated the Gulf Coast in 2005, Americans did more than donate money—they offered themselves. The University of Cincinnati sent doctors and nurses to Lafayette, Louisiana. A church in Colorado shipped vans of college students to Baton Rouge. Across the country, thousands of individuals rushed to the Gulf Coast to assist the survivors of Hurricane Katrina any way they could. Volunteer organizations and charities said that an unprecedented number of people reached out to offer their services for the relief effort. The American Red Cross reported it had 26,000 volunteers in the region, whereas the Salvation Army had more than 1000 in Mississippi and Louisiana alone. VolunteerMatch, an organization that pairs volunteers with charities that need their help, saw volunteer e-mails triple to about 3000 a day.[12] According to Opinion Research Corporation, 87 percent of Americans say it is up to community volunteers to help when government programs do not do enough, and 50 percent of adults are already doing some volunteer work.[13]

Divestiture: Selling Public Assets

According to Savas, **divestment** of government assets can be carried out in five ways. First is to sell the enterprise or asset to a private buyer.

> Governments in the United States own more than $4 trillion in real estate assets, it is estimated. It is commonplace for government to sell land, buildings, equipment, and other assets that are no longer needed or to avoid future departmental expansions. The City of New York recently sold its two radio stations and its television station. At the federal level the largest privatization in the United States since the Homestead Act [of 1862] took place: the Clinton administration sold the government-owned uranium enrichment plants, helium plants, power-marketing agencies, and oil fields also went on the block.[14]

A second way to divest is by issuing and selling shares to the public, as was done with Conrail, the U.S. government-owned freight railroad in 1987. A third way is by selling the enterprise to the managers or, more broadly, to employees, as was done with the National Freight Company, the state-owned British trucking company. A fourth way is to sell the enterprise or assets to its users or its customers. For example, state-owned land may be sold to ranchers or loggers, and a rural electricity or water system may be sold to a cooperative of local users.

A fifth way to divest is by joint venture. "A joint venture can be created, whereby a private firm receives half the shares by supplying investment capital and know-how and assumes operating control; the private capital stays in the joint venture and the government receives no direct compensation for contributing its shares to the private firm. . . . A sale can also be in stages, called "tranches," whereby the government sells a portion of its holdings at a time, as Japan and Germany did with their state-owned telecommunications companies."[15]

Implications for Public Administration

Although direct government action is a relatively small portion of total government activity, it has been fairly successful. The reason is that it *eliminates transaction costs.* Let's unpack that statement. Voluntary exchanges between individuals in a market are sometimes referred to as **transaction costs,** which are broadly defined as *all* the costs associated with exchanges—including the information cost of finding out the price, quality, service record, and durability of a product, plus the cost of contracting and enforcing the contract. If you were Robinson Crusoe and lived alone on an island, you would never incur transaction costs; because you produce everything yourself, there are no exchanges on the island (at least, not until Friday arrives). Similarly, if the government stops shopping around for service providers and monitoring their performance and begins simply to provide the service itself, it no longer incurs transaction costs. The only costs it incurs are production costs. All the costs of negotiating across institutional boundaries have been internalized—and thus eliminated.

Whether government implements programs directly or indirectly, public officials need to know the different consequences of using different tools. The following consequences are especially worth exploring.[16]

- *Administrative feasibility.* How difficult will it be to set up and operate the program? Can objectives be defined with enough specificity so that the objectives of government and those of the producers are congruent? How large an organization will be required?
- *Effectiveness.* Does the program produce the intended effect in the specified time? Does it reach the intended target group? Is it responsive to government direction?
- *Efficiency.* How do the benefits compare with the costs? (Chapter 6 discusses cost-benefit analysis.) How susceptible is the program to fraud? Are there enough producers to ensure competition?
- *Equity.* Are benefits distributed equitably with respect to region, income, sex, ethnicity, age, and so forth? To what degree do those using the service pay directly for its benefits?
- *Political feasibility.* Will the program attract and maintain key actors with a stake in the program area? Indirect tools, relying on third parties such as contractors and nonprofit organizations, are usually more difficult to administer but are easier to enact than tools of direct government action. Tools that use existing structures and relationships—such as a tax structure or price system—require a minimum of administration but exhibit lower target effectiveness and have difficulty attracting political support.

Second Strategic Question: How Will the Program Operate?

There are of course many ways to run a program, but in this section, we will consider only three: case management, total quality management, and compliance management. The first two are well known in government circles; the third less so. But despite compliance management's relative obscurity—and dreary name—it may prove the most innovative.

Case Management

Much of what public-sector organizations do involves **case management:** patients in hospitals, welfare clients in a department of human resources, labor disputes in a labor relations board, apartment buildings for an office of housing code enforcement, grant proposals for a foundation, and so on. Although these organizations may be involved in very different enterprises, when the particular jargon of each organization is stripped away, one sees that their basic processing stages are similar and can be discussed in terms of the **case-processing pipeline.**[17] As shown in Figure 9.2, all cases move through several clearly delineated stages. Let us consider an application of this concept.

Acquisition   Clearly, the process by which cases enter the pipeline is vital to any case-processing program. Perhaps the most common way a case enters the system is when someone complains. For example, a neighbor or teacher might suspect child abuse. But there are other ways, besides complaints, by which cases arrive. For an authorization organization (that is, one that issues licenses or grants awards), applicants themselves bring their requests to the pipeline. A more aggressive method of case acquisition than waiting for complaints or requests to arrive is search or outreach activities. This method requires the staff to seek new cases. An example would be periodic on-site plant visits by inspectors from the Occupational Safety and Health Administration (OSHA).

The acquisition stage entails at least two other considerations. Will case identification be centralized or decentralized? Will it involve only agency staff or will it depend on other agencies for referrals?

Screening   The screening stage of case management involves determining the eligibility of potential cases. Sometimes the potential case fails to meet statutory specifications or eligibility requirements. Fortunately, not all complaints of child abuse turn out to be serious enough to warrant being logged in and referred for subsequent analysis and response.

The more precise the criteria, the more consistent the screening process. Yet the screening criteria should not be so rigid that the agency finds itself violating an important principle of administrative responsibility (discussed in Chapter 4): flexibility.

Essentially, there are two errors to avoid in the screening process. One is the acceptance of an inappropriate case. Made frequently enough, this mistake can prove quite expensive. The other is the incorrect rejection of a potential case. Made in programs such as child protection, this can be fatal.

Figure 9.2   The Case-Processing Pipeline

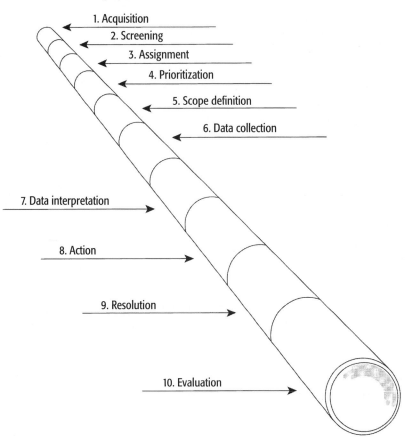
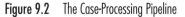

1. Acquisition
2. Screening
3. Assignment
4. Prioritization
5. Scope definition
6. Data collection
7. Data interpretation
8. Action
9. Resolution
10. Evaluation

Assignment   Once in the pipeline, the case becomes part of the active caseload. It is assigned to a processing unit where either one caseworker is designated to handle it or several caseworkers from a pool may handle parts of it. It is management's responsibility to ensure that this takes place as expeditiously as possible and that no case falls between the cracks.

Prioritization   Whatever the caseworker's title—investigator, inspector, hearing officer, social worker, attorney, adjuster, or something else—he will need to decide on the case's urgency. Because it is usually impossible for a public-sector case-processing program to promptly satisfy all the demand for its service, priorities must be set. How would you prioritize the following goals for a child protection program?

1. Close as many cases as possible, quickly.
2. Close all cases opened prior to X date.
3. Affect the lives of as many citizens as possible.

4. Make some significant response to every new case within Y days.
5. Process the more important cases quickly.
6. Process cases equitably (if slowly).
7. Process *all* cases as quickly as possible.

What negative effects could each goal entail?

Essentially, a case-processing program can be viewed as a complex queuing system. A case initially takes its place at the end of a line; a service is delivered that permits the case to move to the next queue; when that step is completed, it moves to the next queue; and so on, until the case is finally discharged. Management must determine the most efficient sequence for the separate steps or services performed.

Scope Definition   In a child protection case, a common question is whether to include the entire family or just the child who is the focus of attention. An agency might, if it chooses, define the case quite broadly and offer families far more in the way of counseling, day care, and services, such as teaching mothers budgeting skills, hygiene, and how to send their children to school on time. For example, in New York City, caseworkers are supposed to make sure that *all* the children in a household that has been reported as abusive or neglectful are doing well—but in a third of the cases, that is not done. In an enforcement case, such as OSHA might handle, the range of charges to pursue is often a matter of discretion. So, again, the scope of a case has to be defined.

Data Collection   Data collection refers to issuing subpoenas, administering tests, conducting interviews, and performing any other information-gathering activity that will help the worker decide how to handle the case.

Interpretation   Data interpretation refers to the review and analysis of these materials. In social service agencies, this process is called "assessment"; in law enforcement agencies, "determination of probable cause"; and in medical and public health agencies, "diagnosis." According to experts, some of the factors that could signal to a caseworker that a child might be in a fatal situation are the absence of a grandmother, a mother living with a boyfriend, or a history of drug abuse.

Action   In enforcement or authorization organizations, action will usually mean holding a hearing or a trial and then reaching a finding or a verdict. But in a social service agency, the action stage of case management will usually involve a service or a treatment plan designed to achieve some beneficial effect for the client. Management must ensure that the caseworkers' guidelines are clear in this vital stage of the process.

Consider this situation. Children are sent on a trial visit to their mother, who has seriously abused them. They come back with immersion burns. One might say that suggests the mother should not have her children. But that action might not be in the decision-making rules of the system. The manual might say something like this: "If you determine the child is in imminent danger, take him or her out of the household."

Resolution   Sometimes, in licensing or child protection situations, the action stage requires continual monitoring or inspection rather than a single decision. In such instances, it might be a long while before the case is closed or resolved.

Depending on the organization, resolution can take many forms—a fine, a jail sentence, a plea bargain, a consent decree, a release, an agreement, and so on. Resolution may also mean that the case has simply been passed to another agency or jurisdiction. In any event, resolution means that a case is no longer considered active.

Evaluation   Because all nine of the preceding stages must be selectively monitored, the ultimate stage of the case-processing pipeline is evaluation. Unfortunately, finding good performance measures is exceedingly difficult. When a worker might be sharing a case with other workers or, even more likely, working on several cases—of varying levels of difficulty—each day, measuring that worker's performance obviously becomes difficult. Processing time, a concern of both management and client, can be measured in at least two ways. *Throughput time* is the period from the initial acceptance of the case until its ultimate resolution. *Direct handling time* is the total time that various employees actually spend on the activities associated with handling a particular case.

Management should also try to set appropriate quality standards, which requires thinking through the final output of the program. In the context of a particular case management program, what does "adequate" mean? **Benchmarking**—that is, making comparisons to similar programs elsewhere—is of only limited help because no two programs are identical.

The basic idea of benchmarking is simple: Find the best practices that lead to superior performance in other organizations and use them for your organization. For example, the Philadelphia Office of the Department of Veterans' Affairs used the benchmarking process to improve many of its processes. It relied on information provided by an insurance-industry professional association to improve timeliness in such functions as correspondence, beneficiary changes, death claims, and others. Similarly, Defense Distribution Depot tries to mimic the distribution prowess of such private carriers as Federal Express and United Parcel Service.

Total Quality Management

Besides case management, another broad concept relevant to running a program is total quality management.

What It Is   **Total quality management (TQM)** is a management approach that strives to achieve continuous improvement of quality through organization-wide efforts based on facts and data. The methods for implementing this approach have been advanced by the teachings of such leaders as Philip B. Crosby, William E. Conway, J. M. Juran, and W. Edwards Deming (see Table 9.3). For the purposes of this chapter, quality-improvement efforts that have the same basic goals and processes as TQM but have different names, such as total quality excellence and total quality leadership, will be encompassed by the term TQM.

Early interest and efforts in TQM in the United States occurred primarily in the private sector, where firms, spurred by intense competition from Japan, began to examine Japanese

Table 9.3 Deming's 14 Points: The Shorter Version

1. Management must constantly demonstrate its commitment to the improvement of product and services—and that means spending time on it, every day.

2. Instead of inspecting for defects, improve processes.

3. *End the practice of awarding contracts on price tag alone.* Seek the best quality and work to achieve it with a single supplier.

4. Continually look for ways to reduce waste and improve quality.

5. Take training seriously.

6. Lower-level managers must believe that they can, without fear, ask questions and inform upper management about conditions that need correction—and the latter will act.

7. Get staff areas to work as a team so they can solve or foresee problems. Often staff areas are competing with each other or have goals that conflict.

8. *Eliminate slogans, exortations, numerical goals, and targets for the workforce.* These never helped anybody do a good job. Let people put up their own slogans.

9. *Eliminate work standards and quotas.* Quotas focus on quantity, not quality. They are usually a guarantee of inefficiency and high cost.

10. *Remove barriers to pride of workmanship.* People are eager to do a good job and distressed when they cannot. Too often, misguided managers, faulty equipment, and defective materials stand in the way. Management must remove these barriers.

NOTE: Deming's words, with minor modifications, are in italicized headings. The remainder of each paragraph paraphrases his discussions.
SOURCE: W. Edwards Deming, *Out of Crisis: Quality, Productivity, and Competitive Position* (Cambridge, MA: MIT, 2000).

approaches to management. In the late 1970s and early 1980s, this enhanced competition stimulated U.S. attention to the role of TQM systems in improving quality. The increased interest in Japanese management methods was soon accompanied by research that documented that U.S. firms also could reduce costs by improving quality.

Can TQM be applied in the public sector? After all, it's easy to identify quality in a four-door sedan, but how does one define the critical success factors for a government agency? One answer is to find the most important aspects of the service from the customer's point of view. A variety of methods are available:

- Informal consultation—in waiting rooms, to customer councils, or through existing user and interest groups.
- Existing data on performance and complaints.
- Customer surveys or other market research already done. The London borough of Bromley uses a "quality wheel" as a checklist so service teams won't miss any possible success factors (see Figure 9.3).
- Examinations of the critical success factors of similar organizations.
- A walk through the system as a customer, to understand it from the customer's perspective.

Figure 9.3   Bromley's Quality Wheel

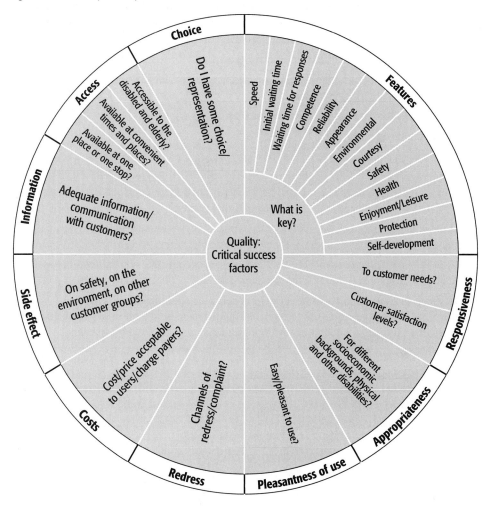

After years of experience, it is clear that TQM *can* be adapted to the public sector. Although created more for the competitive pressures that exist in the private sector, federal government managers have begun to look at TQM as an approach that can help solve governmental management problems. The number of states and localities involved in TQM is no longer in the dozens as it was a few years ago, but in the hundreds. TQM's basics have been applied in agencies and departments as disparate as mental health and motor vehicles. Cities, counties, and states nationwide now have official offices of quality, directors of quality services, and departments of excellence.

Central Theme   The theme of TQM is simply this: the burden of proof of quality rests not with inspectors but with providers of the service. In other words, employees, not managers, are responsible for achieving standards of quality. TQM means a shift from a bureaucratic mind-set to a new philosophy. Organizations traditionally have practiced the notion of achieving an "acceptable quality level." In the public sector, this notion has been captured in the disparaging expression "close enough—for government work." (Ironically, that expression once meant the opposite: workmanship was praised as being close enough to meet high government specifications.)

With the new public-management philosophy, poor workmanship and lax service have become unacceptable. Members of one department must learn about the problems in other departments, stop optimizing their own work, and work with members of other departments as a team (as seen in Chapter 7).

Targets, slogans, pictures, and posters urging employees to increase productivity must be eliminated. Such exhortations merely cause resentment because most of the necessary changes are out of their control. Although employees should not be given numerical goals (for example, ten speeding tickets issued by the end of the week), the *organization itself* must have the goal of never-ending improvement.

The TQM philosophy can give traditional executives several sleepless nights as their traditional means of control vanish and workers and their supervisors become empowered to inform upper management about conditions that need correction. Of course, because of the tremendous economic losses caused by fear on the job, people must not be afraid to ask questions, report problems, or express ideas. In short, barriers that prevent workers from doing their jobs with pride must be eliminated.

Quality circles offer one approach to implementing the TQM philosophy. A **quality circle (QC)** is a group of from 6 to 12 volunteer employees who meet regularly to discuss and solve problems affecting their common work activities. Time is set aside during the workweek for these groups to meet, raise problems, and try to find solutions. The idea is that people who do the job know the job better than anyone else and can make recommendations for improved performance. QCs also push control of decision making to a lower organizational level. Circle members are free to collect data and take surveys. In many organizations, team members are given training in team building, problem solving, and statistical quality control to enable them to confront problems and solutions more readily. The groups do not focus on personal gripes and problems. Often a facilitator is present to help guide the discussion. Quality circles use many of the teamwork concepts described in Chapter 7.

The Concept of Continuous Improvement   In North America, crash programs to patch and to spot weld here, there, and yonder and grand designs ("big wins") have been the preferred method of management improvement. Yet some would argue that continuous improvement—what the Japanese call *kaizen*—produces an even more effective result. The habit of continuous improvement has to be built into all government agencies and has to be made self-sustaining if the full promise of reinvention is to be realized. The assumption is that improving things a little bit at a time, all the time, has the highest probability of success. The goal is to implement changes smoothly and to learn how to make future changes go even more smoothly.

The approaches organizations take to implement continuous-improvement programs range from very structured programs using statistical process-control tools to simple suggestion systems relying on brainstorming and "back-of-the-envelope" analyses. This section will consider only one approach: the plan-do-check-act (PDCA) cycle.

The PDCA cycle, sometimes called the Deming Wheel, conveys the sequential and continual nature of the continuous-improvement process. The *plan* phase of the cycle is when an improvement area (sometimes called a *theme*) and a specific problem with it are identified. It is also when the analysis is done, using one or more problem-solving tools. Some of these appear elsewhere in this text, such as a process flow chart (Figure 9.1) and the nominal group technique (page 392). Three others appear in Figure 9.4. Employees

Figure 9.4   Some Basic Tools of Continuous Improvement

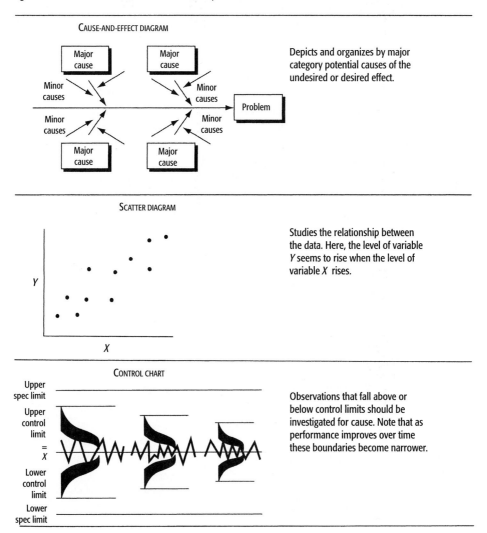

use these tools in conjunction with brainstorming approaches to arrive at an improvement. Typical of many continuous-improvement applications is the identification of countermeasures directed toward eliminating the cause of a problem or the barrier to a solution.

The *do* phase of the PDCA cycle implements the change. Experts usually recommend that the change be made on a small scale first and that any changes in the plan be documented. The *check* phase evaluates data collected during implementation. The objective is to see if there is a good fit between the original goal and the actual results. The *act* phase is when improvement is codified as the new standard procedure and replicated in similar processes throughout the organization. Then—and this is important—the cycle repeats itself: a new improvement area and specific problem are identified, a change is executed, and so on.

International Quality Standards   The global economy has been one of the main forces making total quality management in the United States increasingly significant. Many countries have endorsed a universal framework for quality assurance called **ISO 9000,** a set of international standards for quality management systems established by the International Organization for Standardization in 1987 and revised in late 2000. Hundreds of thousands of organizations in 150 countries, including the United States, have been certified to demonstrate their commitment to quality. Europe continues to lead in the total number of certifications, but the greatest number of new certifications in recent years has been in the United States.

One of the more interesting organizations to recently become ISO 9000 certified was the Phoenix, Arizona, Police Department's Records and Identification Bureau (see photo). In today's environment, where the credibility of law enforcement agencies has been called into question, the bureau wanted to make a clear statement about its commitment to quality and accuracy of information provided to law enforcement personnel and the public. The following two examples illustrate the potentially devastating consequences for police and the communities they serve if the information products and services of a unit like Records and Identification are not up to standard:[18]

- A woman leaves her vehicle in a downtown parking garage. When she returns, she finds it missing and promptly reports it stolen. Later she and her husband discover she had gone to the wrong garage. The couple calls the police to advise them of the error and ask that the vehicle be removed from "the system" as a stolen. Unfortunately, the stolen vehicle is not removed properly, and within a few months, the husband is pulled over at gunpoint by police and handcuffed in front of his 12-year-old son.
- A vehicle is carjacked by two armed suspects. The victim calls the police as soon as possible, an officer enters her report, but the vehicle is not entered into the system properly. A few hours later, another officer stops the vehicle for a minor traffic violation but receives a negative response after "running" the license plate on the mobile data terminal. Because the officer may be acting on incomplete information, his or her safety may be in jeopardy upon approaching the vehicle occupied by armed suspects.

In July 2003, the Records and Identification Bureau of the Phoenix Police Department became the first law enforcement unit in the United States to certify its quality management to ISO 9001:2000. In an "industry" where life-altering decisions are made 24 hours a day, 7 days a week, accurate, complete, and timely information is imperative.

Compliance Management

The preceding prescriptions for running a program—case management and TQM—do not account for the distinctive characteristics of regulatory responsibilities that involve the delivery of obligations rather than some service. To provide a more balanced treatment of prescriptions for how to implement, let's consider the central purpose of social regulation—the abatement, or control, of risk to society.

In *The Regulatory Craft,* Malcolm K. Sparrow at Harvard's JFK School of Government recounts the experiences of thirteen agencies that have confronted risk-control challenges directly.[19] The main objective in compliance management is to leverage limited resources through careful planning, control, and targeting. At the heart of compliance management are three core elements. First is a *clear focus on results.* This involves an explicit rejection of a principal reliance on traditional output or productivity measures as a basis for assessing effectiveness; perseverance in the search for more meaningful indicators of agency performance; and a growing reliance on measurable reductions achieved within specific, well-defined problem areas, as indicators about success.

Second is the *adoption of a problem-solving approach.* This involves the systematic identification of important hazards, risks, or patterns of noncompliance; an emphasis on risk assessment and prioritization as a rational and publicly defensible basis for resource allocation decisions; and implementing effective, creative, tailor-made solutions for each problem.

The third core element in compliance management is an *investment in collaborative partnerships.* Such partnerships with industry, unions, employees, industry associations, municipalities, and other government agencies at all levels are designed to produce a sense of shared purpose through collaborative agenda setting and prioritization.

To make these three general principles more concrete, let's consider two examples of **compliance management.**

- In the early 1990s, many children and teenagers died in Boston as victims of homicide. Extensive analysis showed that the population at risk was highly concentrated within known gangs, most of whose members were well known to the criminal justice system. Operation Cease-Fire targeted considerable enforcement capacity on any gang whose members engaged in violence and launched a carefully articulated information campaign to warn gangs of the extreme consequences that would follow an act of violence. The threat was that law enforcement, by pooling its resources and focusing on *one* gang, could invariably impose serious sanctions on that gang. This threat was far more credible than the fashionable rhetoric of "zero tolerance." The authorities twice carried out their threat, acting in concert, to put an entire gang out of business, using all available legal powers and sanctions. After the second such demonstration, gang-related violence dropped off dramatically.[20]
- The Wage and Hour Division (WHD) of the Department of Labor is responsible for enforcing labor laws in 6.5 million workplaces but has only 800 investigators to accomplish this mission. Do the math. In the garment industry, at the contractor level, noncompliance with minimum wage, occupational safety, and other labor laws is especially widespread. In an attempt to solve these systemic noncompliance problems by some 22,000 sewing contractors and to gain some leverage over the massive industry, the WHD focused its efforts on the relatively few retailers who buy the finished goods from the manufacturers. Making extensive use of existing laws, the WHD mobilized the media and public opinion against retailers and manufacturers who failed to monitor their own contractors. Concerned about their public image, retailers and manufacturers signed compliance agreements with the WHD.[21]

Now that you have a sense of how compliance works, you might want to tackle problem 2 at the end of this chapter.

Tactical Considerations

Another helpful way to understand implementation is to see it not as a set of strategic management decisions but as a collection of tools. Program administration is about conrol, and there is a toolkit for that just like anything else. Essentially, what public administrators try to do is shape the implementation process by adapting these tools, in many different contexts and combinations, to accomplish their missions. We will begin by looking at one of the most basic tools, scheduling models.

Scheduling Models

Scheduling models facilitate the coordination of activities of an enterprise and help put resources to better use. These models are useful for a wide range of activities, from a seemingly trivial task of scheduling a field office tour for a high-ranking official to a very complex job of scheduling activities in the space program. Although a wide variety of such models are in use, three in particular are examined here: **Gantt chart, critical path method (CPM), and program evaluation review technique (PERT).**

In 1917, Henry L. Gantt developed a bar chart to describe progress by comparing work done against planned objectives. Figure 9.5 shows the application of the basic Gantt charting technique to a generalized project.

The Gantt chart might be redesigned as a CPM chart. This would have several advantages. First, because bars are replaced by a network of flow plan, the network shows how events and activities are related. In CPM and PERT charts, events (for example, the point at which one would "start testing") are often shown as circles. Activities are the time-consuming elements of the program and are used to connect the various events; they are shown as arrows. Thus, the CPM chart reflects all significant program accomplishments and better approximates the complexity of the program.

Because most events depend on one or more prior events, the charts show the inter-relationship of events leading to the accomplishment of the ultimate objective. Within the project is a **critical path**—that is, the longest possible time span along the system flow plan. To determine the critical path, events are organized in sequence. The first point to be plotted along the critical path is the final event of the proposed program. From the final event, related events are plotted sequentially backwards, until the starting point is finally plotted. Next, all the expected elapsed times are summed to determine the total expected elapsed

Figure 9.5   Gantt Bar Chart

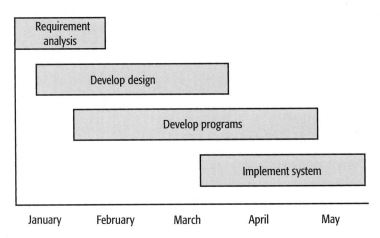

time for every path of the network. The completion date of the project is dependent on the path that takes the longest time. Because this path has the highest total elapsed time, it is called the critical path. (In Figure 9.6, the critical path is indicated by heavy arrows.)

Knowing the critical path can be very useful to the decision maker. If an activity is on the critical path, any slippage or delay for the activity will delay the completion of the entire project. Conversely, slippage in an activity *not* on the critical path will not normally affect the project deadline since the difference between the lengths of time along the critical path and the noncritical paths is slack.

Although PERT has obvious strengths—it forces careful planning, permits experimentation, encourages participation in the planning process, permits effective control, and so on—it is not without its limitations. Many capable administrators insist that one cannot wait for a problem to make itself known through such schedule-control techniques: anticipating trouble requires closer observation.

Backward Mapping

Figure 9.6 suggests a fairly typical approach to implementation: decide what goals you want to accomplish—namely, to arrive at the circle labeled 12—and then define in detail each step in the implementation process required to take you there. Richard F. Elmore calls this approach "forward mapping."[22] Unfortunately, because public executives do not control all the factors that affect the process, forward mapping often causes problems like those witnessed in Pressman and Wildavsky's Oakland study. And expected lapse times between events must be estimated—which can be tricky on unique projects.

To correct such problems, Elmore suggests **backward mapping,** a process in which public executives begin at the end, where real live administrators on the line are making

Figure 9.6   PERT Network

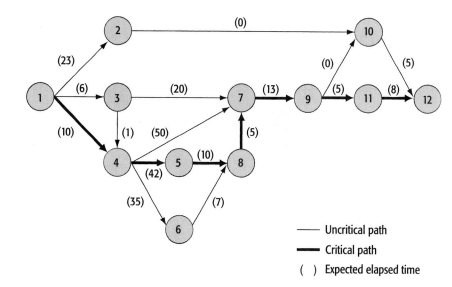

day-to-day decisions. Such a perspective forces public executives at the top to think through what will influence those decisions in a desirable direction. They then work *backward* to plan how to ensure that the system is structured best to achieve that behavior.

There is nothing new about the method of working backward. Consider the following tricky question: How can one bring up from a river exactly six quarts of water when one has only two containers, a four-quart pail and a nine-quart pail, with which to measure? Most people, when confronted with this puzzle, start with the two empty pails, try this and that, empty and fill, and when they do not succeed, they start again, trying something else. They are, of course, working forward from the given initial situation to the desired final solution. But exceptionally able people, or those who had the chance to learn in their mathematics classes something more than mere routine operations, do not spend too much time in such trials but turn around and start working backward.*

Working backward is useful in many practical situations. For example, suppose that you are writing a position paper to persuade the management of your agency to accept your idea. You might work forward by writing a paper in which you present all those details and computations that you find so fascinating and sending it to management. Or you might work backward by saying to yourself, "What I am trying to do is to convince management. If they're going to be convinced, what has to happen? I'll have to meet their objections. Now what are those objections likely to be?" By working backward—by starting with your goal—you are likely to write a convincing paper. The discipline of visualizing desired outcomes and anticipating obstacles to achieving them is effective prevention of program failure.

In *Whatever It Takes*, Paul Tough describes how Godfrey Canada used backward mapping to create the Harlem Children's Zone. During the 1990s, Canada had operated a handful of programs in upper Manhattan targeted at young people: after school drop-in centers, truancy prevention, antiviolence training for teenagers. But he became less and less sure about what his programs added up to and began to wonder what would happen if he "reversed the equation."

> Instead of coming up with a menu of well-meaning programs and then trying to figure out what they accomplished and how they fit together, *what if he started with the outcomes he wanted to achieve and then work backwards from there*, changing and tweaking and overhauling programs until they actually produce the right results? When he followed his train of thought a little further, he realized that it wasn't the outcomes of individual programs that he really cared about: what mattered was the overall impact he was able to have on children he was trying to serve. He was all too familiar with the "fade-out" phenomenon, where a group of needy kids are helped along by one program or another, only to return to the disappointing mean soon after the program ends.[23a]

---

*I hope you will actually try to solve this problem using backward mapping and discover for yourself just how quickly the solution appears. For those of little faith, here's Jack's solution. Obviously, if Jack had 1 quart in the 4-quart pail, he could simply fill the 9-quart pail and pour 3 quarts into a smaller pail, leaving 6 quarts in the larger pail. Problem solved. So how does he get 1 quart in the 4-quart pail? If he had 1 quart in the bigger pail, he could just pour it into the smaller pail. Instantly, he sees how easy getting that quart is. Just fill the 9-quart pail and pour 4 quarts into the smaller pail twice.

Wanting to break this cycle, Canada asked himself a series of questions. What was his goal for poor children? Answer: to grow into fully functioning participants in mainstream American middle-class life. What did they need to do to accomplish that? Answer: to survive adolescence, graduate from high school, get into college, and graduate from college. And what did he have to provide to help them accomplish that? Now, things got interesting.

> He believed that in troubled neighborhoods there existed a kind of tipping point. If 10 percent of the families on the block or in a housing project were engaged in one of these programs, their participation wouldn't have much influence on their neighbors, and the children who did enroll would feel at best, like special cases. . . . But if, say, 60 percent of the families were on board, then participation would seem normal, and so would the values that went with it: a sense of responsibility, a belief that there was a point to self-improvement, a hopefulness about the future. Canada's theory was that each child would do better if all children around him were doing better. So instead of waiting for residents to find out on their own about the services he was providing, his recruiters would seek out participants by going door-to-door. . . . They would create programs that were well-organized and even fun to attend. . . .

He chose as a laboratory for his grand experiment, a 24-block zone of central Harlem, an area that contained about 3000 children, more than 60 percent of whom were living below the poverty line. . . . He and his staff developed an array of new, integrated programs that followed the life of the child: a parenting class for Harlem residents with children three and under, an intensive pre kindergarten for four-year-olds, classroom aides and afterschool instruction for public school students, and a tutoring center for teenagers. Canada's objective was to create a safety net woven so tightly that children in the neighborhood couldn't slip through.[23b]

A few years into the life of the Harlem Children's Zone, Canada hit a snag (as Pressman and Wildavsky might have predicted). Specifically, school principals, a key element in the plan, were in some cases less than cooperative. However, Mayor Bloomberg's new school chancellor, Joel Klein, was cooperative. He suggested that there was a faster and easier way to move forward: open charter schools. The zone also received generous grants from philanthropists—and grew. In July 2007, Barack Obama, then a rising presidential candidate, gave a speech in Washington, DC, on urban poverty, in which he held up the Harlem Children's Zone as a model for the strategy he would follow as president. For the first time, Canada's strategy was on the table at the highest level of American politics. By the beginning of 2008, more than 7000 children were being served each year by one or another of the organization's programs.

Reengineering

TQM might be thought of as older kin to a newer managerial idea—**reengineering.** Both aim to increase productivity by rethinking processes, though reengineering, is more likely to come up with novel solutions because it starts with a more iconoclastic question.

The basic question for TQM is "How can we do this cheaper, faster, or better ?" But the basic question for reenginerring is, "Should we be doing this at all?

Reengineering, then, is the redesign of an organization's processes to achieve dramatic performance improvements. Redesign entails a complete evaluation of processes with a focus on making major reductions in the cost and the time necessary for service delivery. The following example illustrates the concept in action:

> Under Massachusetts's old system of collecting child support, a parent who failed to provide required child support went free until the care-giving spouse appealed for help. The ensuing enforcement process was custom tailored and expensive. In light of the state's budget crisis, the system was headed for disaster. The system was reengineered so that cases with similar characteristics are grouped together. The rules that determine what enforcement action to take for particular cases are loaded into a computer, which then searches various databases and enforces cases without human intervention. The state essentially took the caseworker out of the enforcement process. Now caseworkers are used for postenforcement complaints rather than preenforcement complaints. After two years, 85 percent of collections occur without caseworker involvement. The number of paying cases increased by 30 percent, and the payment compliance rate, which had been stagnant for two years, jumped from 59 percent to 76 percent.[24]

Streamlining   From successful reengineering experiences, a few design principles for government reengineering projects can be identified. One of the more important is streamlining. **Streamlining** refers to the paring down of organizations to remove nonessential layers of supervision and *reorganizing around outcomes—customers, products, and processes—not functions.*

Streamlining can also squeeze out of the dead space and time lags in work flows, as illustrated by reengineering of the travel system at the U.S. Department of Defense. Though the Pentagon can quickly move thousands of tons of humanitarian aid or hundreds of thousands of troops, sending employees on routine travel was a different story—until it reengineered the process. In the past, before Pentagon travelers could even board a bus, they had to secure numerous approvals and fill out reams of paperwork. Coming home wasn't any easier—the average traveler spent six hours preparing vouchers for reimbursement following a trip.

The Department of Defense set up a task force to reengineer the cumbersome travel system, aiming to make it cheaper, more efficient, and more customer friendly. The reengineered system reduces the steps in the pretravel process from an astounding thirteen to only four, as shown in Figure 9.7. Travel budgets and authority to approve travel requests and vouchers, which had traditionally rested in the budget channels of the various service commands, were transferred to local supervisors. Now, travelers make all their arrangements through a commercial travel office, which prepares a "should-cost" estimate for each trip. This document is all a traveler needs before, during, and after a trip. With a supervisor's signature, it becomes a travel authorization; during travel, it serves as an itinerary; after amendments to reflect variations from plans, it becomes an expense report. Other travel expenses and needed cash or traveler's checks can be charged to a

Figure 9.7   Reengineering the Travel Process at the Department of Defense

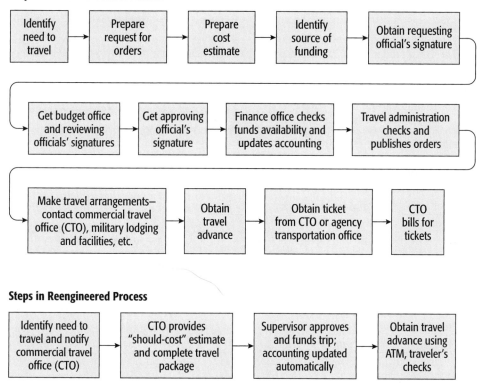

Steps in the Old Pretravel Process

| Identify need to travel | → | Prepare request for orders | → | Prepare cost estimate | → | Identify source of funding | → | Obtain requesting official's signature |

| Get budget office and reviewing officials' signatures | → | Get approving official's signature | → | Finance office checks funds availability and updates accounting | → | Travel administration checks and publishes orders |

| Make travel arrangements—contact commercial travel office (CTO), military lodging and facilities, etc. | → | Obtain travel advance | → | Obtain ticket from CTO or agency transportation office | → | CTO bills for tickets |

Steps in Reengineered Process

| Identify need to travel and notify commercial travel office (CTO) | → | CTO provides "should-cost" estimate and complete travel package | → | Supervisor approves and funds trip; accounting updated automatically | → | Obtain travel advance using ATM, traveler's checks |

SOURCE: Richard Koonce, "Reengineering the Travel Game," *Government Executive* (May 1995), pp. 28–34. Reprinted with permission from Government Executive, May 1995. Copyright 2009 by National Journal Group, Inc. All rights reserved.

government-issued travel card, with payment made directly to the travel card company through electronic funds transfers.[25]

Limits to Reengineering   The rock upon which reengineering most often founders is people. When reengineering treats people as if they were just so many lists and bytes or interchangeable parts to be reengineered, then no one wants to be "reengineered." No one likes to hear dictums like "Carry the wounded but shoot the stragglers"—language that makes workers feel like prisoners of war, not their organization's most valuable asset.

According to one major assessment of reengineering, 50 percent of 497 large companies reported that the most difficult part of reengineering is dealing with fear and anxiety in the organization. Managers worry that decades of experience will count for nothing in the new organization, and everybody worries that they will lose their job. As a result, the "soft" side of reengineering (winning over the workers) must be balanced with the "hard" side (such as installing new computers).

Thus, the blame for failure in reengineering projects lies not with technology or employees, but with management itself. Managers make two mistakes. First, they fail to spend enough time explaining what they are trying to do, preferably in a language that at least approximates "laymen's" terms. Reengineering goals should be communicated and explained consistently at all levels in the organization. This kind of communication is especially important in reducing employee skepticism and when downsizing is forcing organizations to modify their covenants with employees.

The other fatal mistake managers make is to continue to operate with obsolete thinking. So if you are going to reengineer, make sure you don't pave a cow trail. That is to say, don't streamline or improve a path or process that is illogical and inefficient to begin with. Fix it, *then* reengineer it.

Management by Objectives (MBO)

Management by objectives (MBO) is a management technique often used to develop and carry out tactical plans. At its best, MBO can provide managers within an organization a common sense of purpose and direction, and help ensure that they have challenging careers based on clear objectives.

And now the definition. George S. Odiorne at the University of Michigan gives it: "In brief, the system of management by objectives can be described as a process whereby the superior and subordinate managers of an organization jointly identify its common goals, define each individual's major areas of responsibility in terms of the results expected of them, and use these measures as guides for operating the unit and assessing the contribution of each of its members"[26]

For example, the Secretary of Health and Human Services meets with an agency director; both agree that one of the director's objectives for the coming year should be focused on the area of alcoholism.[27] But MBO goes beyond general agreements to "focus" on something. A wide-ranging dialogue between the secretary and director ensues, during the course of which the following points are ironed out:

- Treating an additional 10,000 alcoholics is "doable."
- Only alcoholic treatment centers that treat the whole problem of alcoholism—including its employment, welfare, and health aspects—will be funded.
- The objective is not just to run 10,000 more alcoholics through the program but to ensure that they are rehabilitated—that is, gainfully employed one year after treatment.
- Progress will be tracked and quarterly data provided.

As we have seen, MBO is a process in which managers and subordinates at all levels in an organization sit down together to jointly set goals, share information, and discuss strategies that could lead to goal achievement, and regularly meet to review progress toward accomplishing those goals. Thus, MBO is based on goals, participation, and feedback. On average, organizations that effectively use MBO are 44.6 percent more productive than organizations that do not. And in organizations where top management is committed to MBO—that is, where the objective setting begins at the top—the average increase in productivity is even higher: 56.5 percent. Overall, there is a 97 percent chance that organizations that use MBO will outperform those that do not use it.[28]

Still, MBO is not without disadvantages. First, MBO programs involve excessive paperwork, requiring mangers to file annual statements of plans and objectives, plus quarterly or semiannual written reviews assessing goal progress. Another disadvantage is that managers are frequently reluctant to give employees feedback about their performance. A third is that managers and employees sometimes have difficulty agreeing on goals—and when employees are forced to accept goals that they don't want, goal commitment and employee efforts suffer. Lastly, because MBO focuses on quantitative, easily measured goals, employees may neglect the important, unmeasurable parts of their jobs.

Management by Walking Around (MBWA)

In Act 4, Scene 1 of the play *Henry V,* the king strolls incognito through the English camp on the night before the battle. Wrapped in the obscurity of a commoner's cloak and further obscured by the darkness of night, the king is able to learn the feelings of the common soldiers. Most critics value this scene as proof of the greatness of Henry as a king—that is, it demonstrates his simplicity, modesty, and democratic nature. But it also contains an important lesson for implementation.

How's it going? That is sometimes all a manager wants to know. But getting a useful answer to that question from subordinates is anything but simple. How does a manager get her subordinates to tell how they are doing without seeming overly intrusive? How does a manager get people to assess their energy level honestly, to say what they are worried about, or to discuss morale in a clear and unfiltered manner? Henry V found one solution.

Five hundred and eighty-eight years after the Battle of Agincourt, the head of New York City's Human Resources Administration, Barbara Sabol, decided to voyage to the bottom of the city's welfare sea. Disguised in a sweatshirt, jeans, scarf, and wig, Sabol posed as a welfare applicant over the course of a year to experience firsthand the huge bureaucracy she administers. In her occasional journeys, she said, she suffered numerous indignities. She handed over a set of personal documents, only to have them lost. She was sent more than once to the wrong office. She waited in long and sometimes fruitless lines. She sat in seedy waiting rooms with cockroaches, broken chairs, and broken telephones. Although she had praise for most of the workers, she also described being scolded, misdirected, and made to feel, as she put it, "depersonalized."

She learned a lot. The city needed to help people search for jobs as soon as they came into welfare offices and before they got their first welfare checks, which usually takes 30 days. Employee training needed to be readjusted. Computers needed to be used more extensively. People who were getting benefits but were working should be given preference in welfare lines so they can get back to their jobs. And welfare recipients should be given more privacy as they answer questions.

In summary, approaches to assessing vital signs include regular staff meetings, weekly group leader reports (asking questions that go beyond the statistics), and management by walking around (though perhaps not in a cloak or a wig).

Other Considerations

Another implementation technique is the use of an expediter. The **expediter** is employed to ensure that others have the materials and equipment needed to accomplish their tasks and also to coordinate and accelerate the flow of information among the program's participants. Expediters can be units within a larger organization, or they can be individuals. The Program Coordination Division of the Office of Management and Budget (OMB) is an example of such a unit. If a mayor sends a trusted assistant to the city's plodding, inept, and unfocused Department of Buildings to streamline the permitting process, that would be an example of using an individual. Legislators who take a keen interest in a particular program can also serve as expediters, using their clout to remove obstacles that emerge during implementation. But whether the expediter is a single individual or an organizational unit, the position is a means by which presidents, governors, city managers, department heads, and other top executives demonstrate that things can work, that there is someone who can jump into the breach, representing their office and getting things done.

In the final analysis, however, administrators must be their own expediters, which is a way of saying that they must **follow up.** Writing a sharp note in the margin of a memo will hardly ensure that something will or will not be done. Administrators must constantly check to see if their orders are being carried out. Follow-up is hard but necessary work. As an aide to Franklin Roosevelt wrote: "Half of a president's suggestions, which theoretically carry the weight of orders, can be safely forgotten by a cabinet member. And if the president asks about a suggestion a second time, he can be told that it is being investigated. If he asks a third time a wise cabinet officer will give him at least part of what he suggests. But only occasionally, except about the most important matters, do presidents ever get around to asking three times."[29]

The administrator should also strive to build **incentives** into a program. One notorious example of ignoring the incentive question is a social welfare program in which the combined benefits to recipients make it extraordinarily unprofitable to work.

Another way of improving implementation is **participative decision making.** When faced with a policy decision, the top management in a Japanese organization refers it to a committee of "appropriate people." The decision-making process now becomes—to some Americans at least—excruciatingly slow. But finally a consensus is reached. What makes the resulting policy a good one is that the people who must participate in the implementation phase have participated in the policymaking phase; they are already presold.

Concluding Observations

A cartoon that appeared in the *Wall Street Journal* a few years ago sums up this chapter nicely. A baby bird, ready to dive from the edge of the nest, asks its mother, "Any instructions, or shall I just wing it?" What marvelous commentary on the typical

approach to teaching implementation in many public administration courses. Of course, most public administrators know that "winging it" sometimes is unavoidable, that they have to learn from their own mistakes. But, at the same time, the implementation process can be made smoother by paying attention to the strategies, tactics, and concepts outlined here.

One further point, and it concerns management fads. From vision statements in Chapter 5 to reengineering in this chapter, management theories and trends come thick and fast—apparently, faster than a lot of government employees can handle. Scenes like this one are now all too familiar:

As unproductive and stressful as many fads sometimes are, they are not without value. Competition among theories breeds useful ideas—provided managers are sophisticated and creative enough to take the new ideas and repackage them, analyze them, and modify them to fit the needs of their own organizations. The trouble with new, off-the-shelf management techniques is that they discourage critical thinking. (Will this even work for us? How should we recast it to fit our circumstances? and so on) Unfortunately, fads lead too many managers to believe that simple initiatives offer simple answers to the problems of complex, interrelated organizations. Such an unthinking attitude can and probably will have unwelcome consequences for many aspects of an agency's operation.

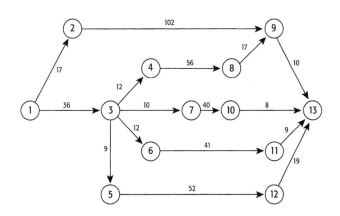

Concepts for Review

benchmarking	ISO 9000
backward mapping	management by exception
case management	management by objectives (MBO)
case-processing pipeline	metaphor of "games"
competitive negotiation	micromanagement
complexity of joint action	participative decision making
compliance management	partnership
critical path	practical drift
critical path method (CPM)	program evaluation review technique (PERT)
divestiture	quality circle (QC)
expediter	reengineering
follow-up	scheduling models
franchise	sealed bidding
Gantt chart	streamlining
grant	total quality management (TQM)
implementation	voluntary association
incentives	voucher

Key Points

This chapter explained how an exceedingly difficult task—the implementation of the program—can be made less arduous. We looked closely at three issues central to implementation: who runs the program, how it will operate, and what tactical considerations matter most. The chapter made these points:

1. Pressman and Wildavsky argue that among the major difficulties in implementing new social programs, two in particular stand out: multiplicity of participants and multiplicity of perspectives. These two factors converge to delay—and, in some instances, stifle—administrative efforts to secure the joint action required in program implementation.

2. Bardach uses the metaphor of "games" to analyze the implementation process. He argues that the game framework illuminates the process by directing attention to the players, their stakes, their strategies and tactics, their resources, the rules of play, the rules of fair play, the nature of communication among the players, and the degree of uncertainty surrounding the outcome.

3. In the final analysis, implementation is a process that can be managed.

4. Privatization symbolizes a new way of thinking about government's role in addressing a society's needs. It is the act of reducing the role of government, or increasing the role of the private sector, in an activity or in the ownership of assets. To privatize means to move from left to right—from one arrangement to another—along a continuum. Thus, the

following arrangements are possible in increasing order of market orientation: contracts, grants, franchises, partnerships, vouchers, voluntary service, and divestiture.

5. Contracting offers the following advantages: potentially increases efficiency, frees public administrators from routine details, increases flexibility, and promotes social and economic objectives. Among its disadvantages or limitations are difficulty in realizing the ideals of administrative responsibility, cost may actually increase, expansion of government activities by stealth, collusion among bidders, lack of human resources to effectively monitor the contractors, and the inappropriateness of certain activities for the private sector.

6. The Federal Acquisition Regulation (FAR) contains the uniform policies and procedures for acquisitions by all federal agencies. Sealed bidding is characterized by a rigid adherence to formal procedures. In contrast, competitive negotiation is a more flexible process that enables the agencies to conduct discussions, evaluate offers, and award the contract using price and other factors.

7. Much of what public-sector organizations do involves processing cases. Although these organizations may be involved in very different enterprises, their processing stages are similar and can be discussed in terms of the case-processing pipeline. All cases move through several clearly delineated stages: acquisition, screening, assignment, prioritization, scope definition, data collection, data interpretation, action, resolution, and evaluation.

8. Total quality management is a management approach that strives to achieve continuous improvement of quality through organization-wide efforts based on facts and data. The burden of proof rests not with inspectors but with providers of the service.

9. The PDCA cycle conveys the sequential and continual nature of the continuous-improvement process. During the *plan* phase of the cycle, an improvement area and a specific problem with it are identified. In the *do* phase, change is implemented. During the *check* phase, the data collected during implementation are evaluated. In the *act* phase, improvement is codified as the new standard procedure and replicated in similar processes throughout the organization.

10. The main objective in compliance management is to leverage a limited resource through careful planning, control, and targeting. It is characterized by a clear focus on results, the use of a problem-solving approach, and an investment in collaborative partnerships.

11. The distinction should be drawn between micromanagement and management-by-exception. In the former, CEOs bury themselves in minutiae, diverting attention from the overarching organizational goals and undermining the morale of the staff. In the latter, CEOs concentrate primarily on setting the agenda, tone, and framework; laying out principles by which the organization operates; delegating much of the process to staff; and deciding only those issues—whether large or small—that have the potential to affect the mission.

12. Scheduling models facilitate the coordination of activities of an enterprise and help put resources to better use. These models are useful for a wide range of activities, from a seemingly trivial task of scheduling a field office tour for a high-ranking official to a very complex job of scheduling activities in the space program.

13. Backward mapping suggests that public executives should begin at the end—where real, live administrators on the line are making day-to-day decisions. Such a perspective forces public executives at the top to think through what will influence those decisions in a desirable direction. They can work backward to plan how to ensure that the system is structured best to achieve that behavior.

14. Reengineering is the redesign of an organization's processes to achieve dramatic performance improvements. Redesign entails a complete evaluation of processes with a focus on making major reductions in the cost and the time necessary for service delivery.

15. Odiorne describes management by objectives as a process whereby the superior and subordinate managers of an organization jointly identify its common goals, define each individual's major areas of responsibility in terms of the results expected of them, and use these measures as guides for operating the unit and assessing the contribution of each of its members.

16. Other important tactical considerations and implementation tools include management by walking around, expediters, follow-up, incentives, and participative decision making.

Problems and Applications

1. The one bureaucracy that virtually everyone must deal with at some point is the Department of Motor Vehicles. For most, a visit to DMV is a miserable experience—waiting in line, paying money, and dealing with grumpy people behind the counter. Citizens crawl along in line, waiting to register a car or renew a license, all the while trying to quell a gnawing feeling that the transaction will unravel when they reach the clerk's window.

To be more specific, a preliminary study by the governor's office identified the following six issues:

- Customers want fast, alternate ways to receive services and information.
- Customers arrive 1+ hours before the station opens, creating a lasting backlog throughout the day.
- Many actions required of the examiners do not directly support a goal of quickly serving the customer.
- Customers are not fully educated about (a) what is required of them and (b) the services offered through self-service channels and the county clerk offices.
- Many stations exceed rated occupancy.
- A high percentage of customers fail the knowledge test on the first and second attempts, further increasing station traffic.

Using the tools and techniques presented in this chapter—along with any other ideas you have—suggest how a state might get its DMV to shed its long-standing image as the monster of government bureaucracy. What, in other words, do you recommend?

2. One particularly violent method of smuggling drugs across the U.S.-Mexican border is known as port running. Port runners would load up to 500 pounds of drugs in cars or small trucks, making little attempt to disguise or conceal it, and then drive up to the inspection booth at selected border crossing points. If the inspector asked for identification, or took too long, or asked to look in the trunk, or attempted to pull the vehicle over for secondary examination, the driver would accelerate away aggressively, smashing other vehicles out of the way if necessary and running down the inspector or anyone else foolish enough to get in the way—never mind the damage to the vehicle, the load was much more valuable. Port runners picked crossing points where, within half a mile of clearing the border, they could be lost in the backstreets of a densely populated urban area, making pursuit and arrest virtually impossible.

In January 1995, Deputy Commissioner Mike Lane formed a team to tackle the problem. The team had plenty of ideas about what to do. Enforcement agents preferred pursuit, arrest, and seizures; inspectors focused more naturally on changing inspection procedures; the intelligence group wanted to study the smuggling organizations and take them down. But most of that they had been doing already, and it was not enough. Besides, their charge was not to make arrests or break down smuggling organizations (although they were allowed to do those things if it helped); they had been charged with *eliminating the problem of port running.*

Assume that you are on Commissioner Lane's team. Before working on an action plan, the team must determine how it would assess performance. How would it know if it was making progress, if not by numbers of arrest and seizures? Obviously a decline in the number of port-running incidents would be good, but even that would be open to interpretation. What is your plan, and how will you evaluate success? What were the alternatives to your plan, and why were they rejected?

SOURCE: Malcolm K. Sparrow, *The Regulatory Craft* (Washington, DC: Brookings, 2000).

3. Do you think an agency can or should have a successful TQM program without using benchmarking?
4. Discuss the advantages and disadvantages of setting up a new agency to carry out a program.
5. Find the critical path in the following network.

Favorite Bookmarks

www.eval.org The American Evaluation Association is an international professional association of evaluators devoted to the application and exploration of program evaluation, personnel evaluation, technology, and many other forms of evaluation.

www.wmich.edu/evalctr/ess The Evaluation Support Services Web site of the Evaluation Center at Western Michigan University is intended to increase the use and improve the quality of evaluations.

Notes

1. J. L. Pressman and A. Wildavsky, *Implementation* (Berkeley: University of California Press, 1973).
2. Ibid., 99–102.
3. Elinor R. Bowen, "The Pressman-Wildavsky Paradox," *Journal of Public Policy,* 2.1 (1982).
4. Eugene E. Bardach, *The Implementation Game* (Cambridge, MA: MIT Press, 1977).
5. E. S. Savas, *Privatization and Public Private Partnerships* (New York: Chatham House, 2000).
6. *The Municipal Yearbook 2004.*
7. David Osborne and Ted Gaebler, *Reinventing Government: How the Entrepreneurial Spirit Is Transforming the Public Sector* (Reading MA: Addison-Wesley, 1992).
8. Katherine Barrett and Richard Greene, "Short on Oversight," *Governing* (May 2006): 80; Robert D. Behn and Peter A. Kant, "Strategies for Avoiding the Pitfalls of Performance Contracting," *Public Productivity & Management Review* (June 1999): 470–89.
9. Joel Brinkley, "Energy Department Contractors Due for More Scrutiny," *New York Times* (November 24, 2002), 28.
10. *Governing* (June 1995).
11. *Ford Foundation Report* (Winter 1997).
12. *Wall Street Journal* (September 8, 2005).
13. *Time* (December 27, 1999). Comparative figures for France, Germany, and Japan are 19 percent, 17 percent, and 11 percent, respectively.
14. Savas, op. cit., 130.
15. Ibid.
16. Based on Lester M. Salamon and Michael S. Lund, *Beyond Privatization: The Tools of Government Action* (Washington, DC: Urban Institute, 1989). For another useful list of attributes to consider in selecting tools, see E. S. Savas, *Privatization and Public Partnerships* (New York: Chatham House, 2000), 92–102.
17. S. R. Rosenthal and E. S. Levine, "Case Management and Policy Implementation," *Public Policy* (Fall 1980).
18. David M. Amari, "Phoenix Police Department Counts on ISO 9001:2000—24/71" *Management Systems* (May–June 2004): 33–38.
19. Malcolm K. Sparrow, *The Regulatory Craft* (Washington, DC: Brookings, 2000).
20. Ibid., 171–80.
21. Ibid., 86.
22. Richard F. Elmore, "Backward Mapping: Implementation Research and Policy Decisions," in Walter Williams, ed., *Studying Implementation* (Chatham, NJ: Chatham House, 1982).
23a. Paul Tough, Whatever It Takes: Geoffrey Canada's Quest to Change Harlem and America (Boston: Houghton Mifflin Co., 2008), p.3.
23b. Ibid p. 4–5.
24. *Governing* (February 1994).
25. Richard Koonce, "Reengineering the Travel Game," Government *Executive* (May 1995): 28–34.
26. George S. Odiorne, "MBO: A Backward Glance," *Business Horizons,* 21 (October 1978): 14.
27. R. Brady, "MBO Goes to Work in the Public Sector," *Harvard Business Review* (March–April 1973).
28. R. Rodgers and J. E. Hunter, "Impact of MBO on Organizational Productivity," *Journal of Applied Psychology,* 76 (1991): 322–26.
29. G. C. Edwards II, *Implementary Public Policy* (Washington, DC: Congressional Quarterly Press, 1980): 155.

CASE 9.1
FRIENDLY FIRE

At 11:30 A.M., on April 14, 1994, two U.S. Air Force F-15 fighters accidentally shot down two U.S. Army Black Hawk helicopters over northern Iraq, killing 26 peacekeepers on board, including 15 Americans. The helicopters had been assigned to land in a village just inside the Iraq border, pick up some personnel, and carry them deeper in the Iraq secure zone. That day's operation was part of a larger organizational undertaking, Operation Provide Comfort, that had been launched in April 1991 to relieve the suffering of hundreds of thousands of Kurdish refugees.

Implementing complex collective undertakings, such as Operation Provide Comfort, requires a high degree of both specialization and integration. For over 1000 days, coordination by standardization, plans, and mutual adjustments adequately handled the challenge of integration. On April 14, 1994, these mechanisms failed. In *Friendly Fire*, Scott A. Snook, former head of the Center for Leadership and Organization at the U.S. Military Academy and now at Harvard Business School, develops individual, group, organizational, and cross-level accounts of this accident. The following discussion is based on his rigorous analysis.

Facts of the Case

At 7:36 A.M., a U.S. Air Force Airborne Warning and Control System (AWACS) aircraft took off from Incirlik Air Base in Turkey about 400 miles from the Iraq border as the lead aircraft of 52 sorties of coalition air missions scheduled that day. Around 9:22 A.M., the two Black Hawks took off in Turkey about 150 miles from Iraq. Already airborne, the AWACS established radar and radio contact with the helicopters. The AWACS determined that at least two channels on devices known as IFF—meaning Identification Friend or Foe—were working on the helicopters.

At 11:20 A.M., the F-15 pilots—also flying out of Turkey—entered northern Iraq and notified the AWACS. Two minutes later, radar on the

lead F-15 locked onto the helicopters, then 40 miles away. They queried the helicopters using IFF equipment. But the IFF devices on the helicopters were transmitting a signal used for Turkish, not Iraqi, airspace. The F-15s told the AWACS of the radar contact and got a "clear there" response, meaning that AWACS's radar did not show anything in that location. At 11:25 A.M., however, the Black Hawks' IFF signals began appearing on the AWACS's radarscope—but no one relayed this new information to the F-15 pilots.

At 11:28 A.M., the lead F-15 pilot made a "visual pass" of the helicopters, flying 1000 feet to the left and 500 feet above them. He mistakenly identified them as Russian-made Hinds—just the type the Iraqis flew. The lead pilot asked the second F-15 pilot, his "wingman," to also make a visual identification. The wingman could not make a visual indication but called out "Talley 2," on the radio, which the lead pilot took as the required confirmation. At 11:30 A.M., the lead F-15 fired a missile. Then, moments later, the second F-15 fired. Roaring past the wreckage of the two burning helicopters, the pilot bluntly remarked on his radio: "Nobody's there. Nobody could survive that."

What Went Wrong: First Cut

Why did the F-15 pilots misidentify the U.S. helicopter? Training photos of U.S. helicopters are shot from ground level looking up, so trainees never see this overhead view. Further, the F-15 pilots had little reason to think their sightings could be anything but Hinds, since they had never been told of the presence of friendly helicopters.

In addition to the lack of proper training and a thorough briefing, a series of social interactions also may have contributed to the pilots' misidentification. The lead pilot, who was a captain, interpreted the call "Talley 2" as a positive confirmation by his wingman, who was a lieutenant colonel.

In every role except this particular combination—when the junior officer's plane leads and the senior's follows—the lieutenant colonel outranks the captain.

> This is a rare example of an inverted hierarchy in action. Since such power inversions are infrequent situations, we know little about how they actually work. . . . Perversely, the inverted pyramid may have worked double deadly duty during the actual intercept. In addition to subtly encouraging [the captain] to be more decisive than he otherwise might have been, the inversion may also have encouraged him to be less risk-averse, to take a greater chance with his call, confident that if his call was indeed wrong, surely his more experienced squadron commander would catch any mistake.

Why didn't the AWACS crew help? The two helicopters were clearly visible on the AWACS's radar four minutes before they were shot down. The technician with responsibility for surveillance in the secure zone was on his first mission, and the person who usually sat next to him had moved to another radarscope. This crew had not worked together before. The onboard commander testified that he had no idea what those radar blips meant. At the hearings, he pleaded ignorance. When questioned about his knowledge of radar, he replied, "Sir, my area of expertise doesn't lie there. I'm like a pig looking at a watch. I have no idea what those little blips mean."

This is an example of the harmful effects of diffuse responsibility. The onboard commander clearly felt that "someone else"—in this case, an apparently sharp F-15 lead pilot—bore a "greater responsibility."

Further, the ratio of leaders to followers onboard the AWACS was high: nine officers supervising six subordinates. The technicians probably assumed that if they misread the radarscope, one of these officers would intervene. This is another example of diffuse responsibility; when everyone is in charge, no one is.

The lack of integration between the Army and Air Force in Operation Provide Comfort is illustrated by the fact that the helicopters consistently used the wrong friend-or-foe electronic identification code when they were in the secure zone. For reasons that no one can quite recall, two years earlier someone had set the policy that all aircraft would use one code outside the secure zone and a different code inside. But this change had never been communicated to the helicopter operators. Why not? One reason may have been that in the Air Force, helicopters are not considered aircraft. Here is an excellent example of how communications can break down: an important word like aircraft can mean something completely different in these two different cultures.

What Went Wrong: Second Cut

Although the preceding analysis explains part of the puzzle, Snook does not think it adequately explains the shootdown in its totality. He thinks we must look across levels. "We must search for mechanisms that operate across individual, group, and organizational boundaries. We must spin a story of the shootdown that captures the dynamic, integrated nature of organizational reality—one that, while acknowledging the parts, also recognizes the whole."

In *The Fifth Discipline*, Peter Senge explains the importance of seeing the whole:

> There is something in all of us that loves to put together a puzzle, that loves to see the image of the whole emerge. The beauty of a person, or a flower, or a poem lies in seeing all of it. It is interesting that the words "whole" and "health" come from the same root (the Old English *hal*, as in "hale and hearty"). So it should come as no surprise that the unhealthiness of our world today is in direct proportion to our inability to see it as a whole.
>
> Systems thinking is a discipline for seeing wholes. It is a framework for seeing interrelationships rather than things, for seeing patterns of change rather than static "snapshots."

To study the shootdown as an organic whole, Snook constructs a causal map. This map is reproduced here in Figure 9.8 not because all the details are important to our inquiry but because it is an excellent example of systems thinking and shows why it is simplistic to say the accident was caused by "individual error". Using this map to

Figure 9.8 Accidental Shootdown of Black Hawks: A Causal Map

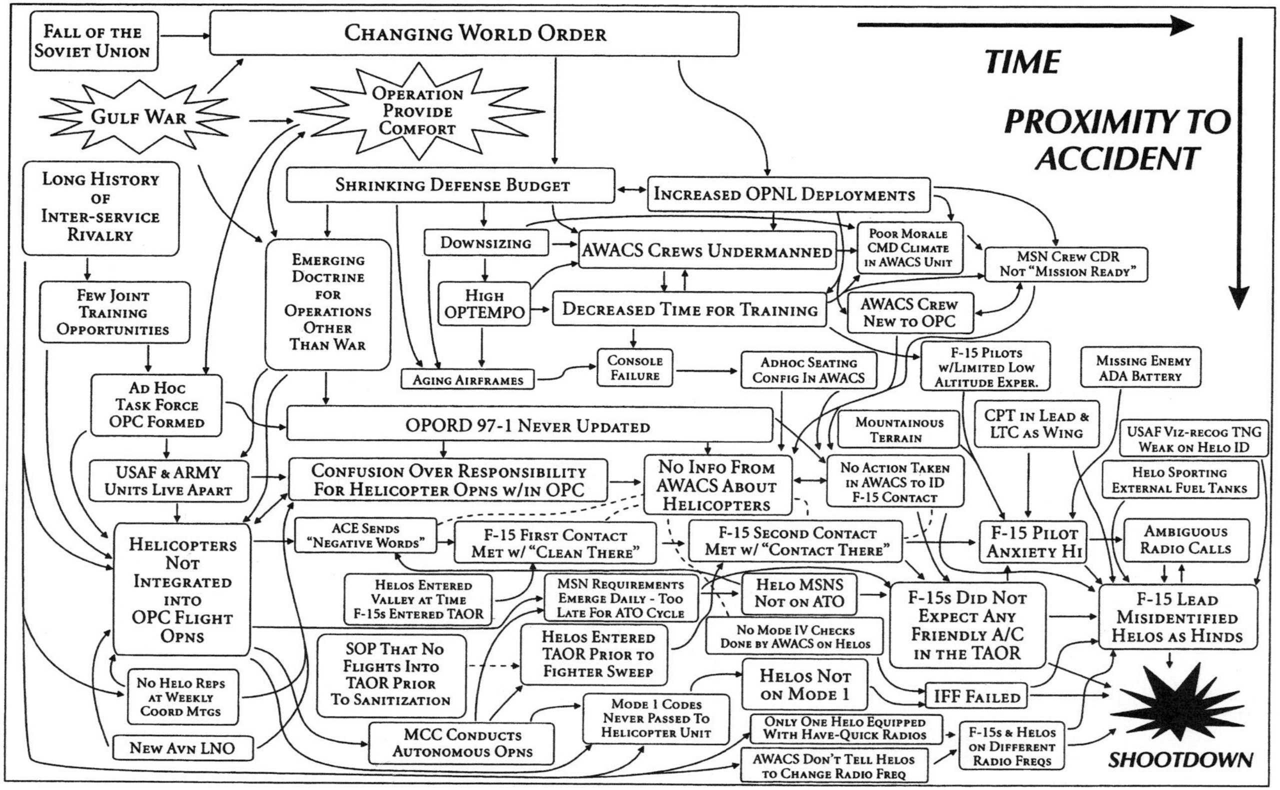

List of Abbreviations

A/C	Aircraft
ACE	Airborne Command Element
ATO	Air Traffic Control Order
AWACS	Airborne Warning And Control System
CMD	Command
CDR	Commander
CPT	Captain
IFF	Identification Friend or Foe System
LNO	Liaison Officer
LTC	Lieutenant Colonel
MCC	Military Coordination Center
OPC	Operation Provide Comfort
OPNL	Operations Plan
OPORD	Operations Order
OPTEMPO	Operational Tempo
SOP	Standard Operating Procedures
TAOR	Tactical Area of Responsibility

Source: Scott A. Snook, *Friendly Fire* (Princeton, NJ: Princeton Press, 2000), p. 21.

step back from the details and considering the shootdown as a dynamic whole, Snook is able to suggest a mechanism that operates across time and also across levels. He calls the mechanism **practical drift.**

Here's how the mechanism works. When an operational system is first designed, it is treated as a tightly coupled system. *Coupling* refers to the level of interdependence within the organizational arrangement. Loose coupling means the elements may be tied together weakly or infrequently with minimum interdependence. Tight coupling means there's no slack or buffer between two items: what happens in one directly affects what happens in the other. When tightly coupled systems are first designed, safeguards are built in to prevent worst-case scenarios.

But when these beautiful designs are implemented, they often prove unworkable in practice. So units adopt their own local variations, which get perpetuated. In the Black Hawk case, new briefers informed new crews "how we do things around here." With each generation of briefing, the entire system becomes more loosely coupled and the logic of the local task becomes more compelling. People become less and less familiar with the original, tightly coupled logic of the entire operation. What is crucial in this ongoing loosening of coordination is that each unit that is following its own unique path assumes that all other groups are behaving in accord with the original set of established rules.

As you might expect, after a disaster, the system is redesigned with even more stringent safeguards. But, ironically, the very stringency of those safeguards makes it even more likely that local units will again be forced to start making "practical" adjustments. The cycle then repeats itself.

Implications

During the implementation of any program, managers must be alert to the dangers that can result from practical drift. More specifically, Snook suggests that they should be asking questions like the following about their own operations:

1. What "friendly helicopters" have you shot down lately? What was the cause? Individual error or system design? Practical drift or some other mechanism?

   For example, in her book *The Challenger Launch Decision*, Diane Vaughn suggests a mechanism she calls the "normalization of deviance" to account for the NASA decision. According to her, technical deviations in the performance of O-rings designed to seal joints in the space shuttle's solid rocket boosters were "normalized" over time. In the years preceding the *Challenger* launch, engineers and managers together developed a definition of the situation that allowed them to carry on as if nothing were wrong when they continually faced evidence that something was wrong. This is the problem of the normalization of deviance.

2. Do you have any managers who are, like the AWACS commander, "pigs looking at watches"?

3. Do you have any important tasks for which everyone is responsible, and yet no one is?

4. Are there any situations that might make friendly "Black Hawks" look like "enemy helicopters"?

5. Do you have any long histories of "interservice rivalries" in your organization?

6. How do you learn from such tragedies? Do you learn? Is the focus on learning or on the "politics of blame"?

Case Question

Using recent news items, historical examples, and personal experiences, how many of the questions in the "Implications" section about can you illustrate?

Sources: Scott A. Snook, *Friendly Fire* (Princeton, NJ: Princeton University Press); Peter M. Senge, *The Fifth Discipline: The Art and Practice of the Learning Organization* (New York: Doubleday, 2990). 68.

PART THREE

Resources
Management

10 Human Resources Management

AP Photo/The New Haven Register, Peter Casolino

NEW HAVEN FIREFIGHTERS

In late 2003, a total of 77 firefighters in New Haven, Connecticut, took a test for promotion to the rank of lieutenant. Of the 43 whites who took the exam, 25 passed (58 percent); of the 19 blacks, six passed (24 percent); and of the 15 Hispanics, three passed (20 percent). Because there were only eight vacancies, only the top scores were eligible for promotion. None of the six black firefighters with passing scores was eligible.

Upon learning these results, and knowing that the city was nearly 60 percent black and Hispanic, city lawyers advised the city's Civil Service Board to reject the results, warning the city could be exposed to a race discrimination lawsuit by minority firefighters if it let the exam stand. The board elected not to certify the exam. Firefighters whose scores gave them a good chance at being promoted filed suit, alleging their rights had been violated under the 1964 Civil Rights Act and the Constitution's equal protection clause.

The lead plaintiff, Frank Ricci, who is dyslexic, said he prepared exhaustively for the test and paid someone to record study material so he could learn by listening.

The U.S. District Court ruled for the city, concluding that the city's efforts to avoid discrimination against minority firefighters was "race neutral" because "all the test results were discarded, no one was promoted, and firefighters of every race will have to participate in another selection process."

The firefighters appealed the district judge's ruling, and the case landed with a three-judge panel at the Second Circuit Court of Appeals in 2007. At the end of oral arguments, one appeals judge, Sonia Sotomayor, told Ricci's lawyer, "We're not suggesting that unqualified people be hired. But if your test is going to always put a certain group at the bottom of the pass rate, so they're never, ever going to be promoted, and there is a fair test that could be devised and measures knowledge in a more substantive way, then why shouldn't the city have an opportunity to look and see if it can develop that?" Ultimately, Judge Sotomayor and her colleagues upheld the district judge's decision.

In June 2009, the Supreme Court ruled 5–4 in favor of the white firefighters. Judge Antonin Scalia scoffed at the district court judge's claim that rejecting the results was racially neutral. "It's neutral because you throw it out for the losers as well as for the winners? That's neutrality?"

Some private-sector employers said the ruling might prompt them to use tests more in making hiring and promotion decisions. But the decision had others scrutinizing their existing tests to ensure they are free of bias. The impact of the decision is likely to be more muted in the private sector than in government agencies because private employers are less likely to use a test as the single or predominant criterion for a job promotion.

Ironically, civil service exams were supposed to be the fairest way for cities to hire the best firefighters and police, while opening the doors to more minorities. Exams, it was thought, provided a color-blind way to measure performance and promote minorities into leadership roles within organizations that had clearly discriminated in the past. The problem is that, for reasons not understood, minorities have not performed as well as whites on tests.

But are multiple-choice tests to measure firefighters' retention of information the optimal way to predict how someone would react at a four-alarm fire? Arguably, the most important skills of any fire department lieutenant or captain are sound judgment, steady command presence, and the ability to make life or death decisions under pressure.

In any event, New Haven city officials concluded that their written test was flawed and that there was another trusted method to select firefighting lieutenants and captains that posed less of a disadvantage to blacks and Hispanics. That method relies largely on *assessment centers* where applicants are evaluated in simulated real-life situations to see how they would handle them. Supporters of the idea say assessment centers do far better than written exams in measuring leadership and communications skills and an applicant's ability to handle emergencies. (You will learn more about assessment centers in this chapter.)

Besides the relatively narrow issue of how best to promote firefighters, this case also raises a broader issue posed to Sotomayor during her Supreme Court confirmation hearings in July 2009. Senator Herb Kohl, a Democrat from Wisconsin, asked an interesting question about 2028. By then, according to recent Supreme Court jurisprudence, some kinds of affirmative action may no longer be permissible. In *Grutter v. Bolinger* (2003), Sandra Day O'Conner upheld race-based discrimination in college admissions, but only for the current generation. Such policies "must be limited in time," she wrote, adding that "the court expects that 25 years now, the use of racial preferences will no longer be necessary to further the interest approved today." Indeed, by 2023, if current demographic trends continue, nonwhites—blacks, Hispanics, and Asians—will constitute a majority of Americans under 18. By 2042, they will constitute a national majority. In fact, in several large states today, these minorities already constitute a majority.

Is there a difference between allowing reverse discrimination in the wake of segregation and discriminating in the name of diversity indefinitely? How effective was the New Haven Fire Department's promotional system in 2003? How do the U.S. armed forces handle these issues?

SOURCES: Ed Stannard, "Firefighters Exam at Center of Supreme Court Case," *Hispanic Business News* (June 29, 2009); Ronald Dworkin, "Justice Sotomayor : The Unjust Hearings," *New York Review of Books* (September 24, 2009); Suzanne Sataline and Stephanie Simon, "Cities Yearn for Clarity on Bias in Hiring," *Wall Street Journal* (June 30, 2009); Jess Bravin and Suzanne Sataline, "Ruling Upends Race's Role in Hiring," *Wall Street Journal* (June 30, 2009); Adam Liptak, "Justices to Hear White Firefighters Bias Claims," *New York Times* (April 10, 2009); Adam Liptak, "Supreme Court Finds Bias against White Firefighters," *New York Times* (June 30, 2009); Lani Guinier and Susan Strum, "Trial by Firefighters," *New York Times* (July 11, 2009).

As you can see in Figure 10.1, the three primary goals of human resources management (HRM) are to attract an effective workforce to the organization, develop the workforce to its potential, and maintain it over the long term. Most government and nonprofit organizations employ human resource (HR) professionals to perform these three functions. HR specialists focus on one of the human resources areas, such as recruitment of employees or administration of wage or benefit programs, whereas HR generalists have responsibility in more than one area. But, in a real sense, *every public administrator needs to be an* HR generalist.

Note the box in the upper left of Figure 10.1. Organizations that are truly results oriented—whether public, nonprofit, or for-profit—consistently strive to ensure that their day-to-day HR activities support their organization's mission and move them closer to accomplishing their strategic goals. That is, they strive to ensure that their core processes support mission-related outcomes. Such organizations rely increasingly on a well-defined mission to form the foundation for what they do, and how they do it, every day. For example, many successful public and private enterprises integrate their HR management activity into their organization's mission—rather than treat it as an isolated support function. This integrated approach may include such things as tying individual performance management, career development programs, and pay and promotion standards to the organization's mission and vision.

Before looking at HRM today, we need to review its development in the United States. But this review, which is presented in the first section of the chapter, is not history for history's sake. The development of what has traditionally been called public personnel administration in the United States has not been a series of revolutions but rather a process of accumulation. This means that some of the practices begun in George Washington's administration are still followed. So, to make sense of HRM in the early part of the twenty-first century, we must begin in the late part of the eighteenth.

As indicated in Figure 10.1, part of what determines whether a particular HRM activity is effective is the environment that surrounds the activity. The environment can be segmented into its external and internal components. In the second section, as we examine both, it should become clear that the environment is one of the most important factors in determining appropriate HR practices and effective HR management—and ultimately the success or failure of an agency or a public administrator.

The remaining sections of the chapter focus on the three activities identified in Figure 10.1. The third section will cover resources planning, recruiting and testing, and classification and

Figure 10.1   General Framework of Human Resources Management (HRM)

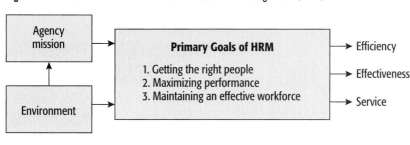

compensation; the fourth section, training and management development and advancement; and the fifth, discipline and grievances and labor relations.

The Development of Public Personnel Management in the United States

Path dependency is the view of some economists that technological change in a society depends on its own past.[1] A noted example of technological path dependency is the QWERTY keyboard, which would not be in use today except that it happened to be chosen 100 years ago. Arguably, the development of public personnel management in the United States has also been path dependent. Certainly, to comprehend the present state of affairs in public personnel management, it helps to understand something of its past. Figure 10.2 presents a historic overview of personnel management in government, focusing on the changing role of partisan loyalties and job competencies as criteria for selecting employees.[2]

The Early Years

The year 1789 found New York blossoming temporarily into a national capital. Its best houses were renovated with all possible elegance, and its streets were crowded with expectant officeholders. The wise leadership of George Washington was indispensable to the government, for the organization of the new government was no small task. In forming his administration, Washington looked for, essentially, two things: loyalty to the Constitution (still a controversial document in some quarters) and fitness of character (as measured by family background, formal education, honor, and esteem).

To help assess this "fitness of character," Washington began the tradition of senatorial courtesy, wherein a president doesn't appoint someone to a position unless the senators from the appointee's home state approve. Another precedent set in 1789 concerns the president's right to unilaterally dismiss someone whose appointment had to be confirmed by the Senate. If confirmation required Senate approval, did dismissal as well? The Congress concluded that removal is a presidential prerogative.

The election of 1828 was like an earthquake, with the Jacksonians overwhelming President John Quincy Adams and his supporters. So bitter had feelings become that, on arrival in Washington, President-elect Andrew Jackson refused to pay the usual visit of respect to President Adams. Jackson's inauguration has long been regarded as the opening of a new era in American life. The great new democratic wave that surged forward involved masses of population that American democracy had not touched. A more rapid rotation in office became the rule. Jackson, frankly announcing his belief in this, displaced many political appointees. He accepted the rule defined by William L. Marcy of New York: "To the victor go the spoils."

Patronage is the power vested in political leaders to make partisan appointments and to confer licenses, contracts, franchises, honors, and other benefits on political supporters, friends, and relatives. Although several of the early presidents had exercised unlimited patronage powers, the era of unrestrained partisanship in appointments really began with Jackson. Political opponents charged Jackson with operating a **spoils system**—that is, following the practice of awarding government jobs to one's friends and political supporters. But Jackson defended it as "rotation in office." He held that government jobs were generally so simple that any citizen of average ability could manage them and that frequent changes of personnel would tend to promote efficiency in the public service and keep employees from becoming infected with arrogance toward the public. The spoils system became entrenched, and patronage appointments reached a peak during the Civil War period.

Though the widespread use of spoils in the federal government did not come until the election of Lincoln, officials in local government began the use of patronage to build and maintain political machines. In particular, state and local officials in New York and Pennsylvania relied on bloc voting by groups of recent European immigrants and used patronage appointments as rewards for those able to deliver blocs of votes.

Reformers resented these political machines and called for a return to the pre-Jackson days when "men of character" ruled. In the late 1870s, civil service reform associations began to emerge, and in the early 1880s Senator George P. Pendleton, an Ohio Democrat, introduced legislation to end the spoils system. But the bill stood little chance of passage: powerful senators benefited too much from the spoils system.

Then a dramatic event occurred that increased support for Pendleton and strengthened the reformers' case. On July 2, 1881, a disappointed office seeker shot down President Garfield in a Washington railway station. The spoils system was now linked with evil in the minds of voters. Republican incumbents, closely identified with that system, suffered severe losses in the 1882 congressional elections. The following year, with little debate, Congress passed the Pendleton Act, which replaced the spoils system with a merit system of public personnel administration. We will take a closer look at that law later.

If the spoils system was linked with evil in the minds of voters, the concept of a merit system was linked with scientific management in the minds of many reformers. As we saw in Chapter 1, Woodrow Wilson called for a separation of politics from administration in his famous 1887 essay. Wilson considered administration to be all about technique, process, and science—in short, quite unlike politics. The merit system certainly separated politics from administration and on this foundation the scientific management movement would be built.[3]

Funded by private philanthropy, bureaus of municipal research became the agents outside government to encourage scientific management inside. The chief legacy of the scientific management era to contemporary personnel management is **position classification.** The pioneers of industrial engineering—such as Frederick Taylor (see Chapter 1) and Frank and Lillian Gilbreth (see Figure 10.2)—suggested that organizations define the duties and responsibilities of positions in accordance with what was determined to be the single most effective way of accomplishing their goals.

Figure 10.2   Development of Public Personnel Management in the United States

Government by Gentlemen:
The Guardian Period

The upper classes ruled the initial governments of the United States. George Washington appointed Thomas Jefferson, just returned from his service as minister to France, Secretary of State, and Alexander Hamilton, known for his special knowledge of finance, Secretary of Treasury.

Government by the Good:
The Reform Period

When President Garfield was shot down in the Washington railway station in July 1881 by a disappointed office seeker, voters linked the spoils system with evil. Two years later, Congress passed the Pendleton Act, thereby establishing the merit system of public personnel administration in the United States and authorizing the president to establish a civil service commission.

1789–1829   1829–1883   1883–1906

Government by the Common Man:
The Spoils Period

Andrew Jackson's inauguration in 1829 brought the "rabble" into the White House, to the distaste of established families. Party loyalty was intense, and party members were rewarded with government posts in what came to be known as the spoils system—a system that Jackson's supporters saw as a necessary "reform" of the federal personnel system.

SOURCE: Frederick C. Mosher identified the first five periods in *Democracy and the Public Service* (Cambridge: Oxford University Press, 1968), 54–55; Dennis L. Dresang, the sixth period in *Public Personnel Management and Public Policy* (New York: Addison Wesley Longman, 2003), 27.

**Government by Administration:
The Management Period**

Looking for a different approach to
public-sector administration from that
offered by Taylor, the Gilbreths, and the
bureaus of municipal research, President
Franklin Roosevelt turned to the public
administrationist Louis Brownlow to
assemble a staff and apply state-of-the-art
principles of administration to the
federal government. The Brownlow
Committee issued an influential report in
1937, stressing, among other things, the
need to enhance the management
competency of the presidential staff and
more closely integrate personnel
management with general presidential
management.

Government by Shared Power

In 1953, for the second time after
World War II, Congress called on
former President Herbert Hoover to do
a study similar to that of the Brownlow
Committee. Significantly, the report
lacked any central concern such as
fitness of character, spoils system and
reform, merit, scientific management,
and administrative principles. The
decades since the 1950s have been
characterized by the emergence of
multiple sources of power affecting the
management of public employees:
professionals, unions, minorities and
women, public managers, contractors,
and consumers.

| 1906–1937 | 1937–1955 | 1955–present |

**Government by the Efficient:
The Scientific Management Period**

In 1906, the New York Bureau of
Municipal Research was established to
encourage scientific management in
government. The fundamental idea
behind this and other such bureaus
was that there was no essential
difference between the public and
private sectors. Among the most
prominent followers of Frederick
Taylor—the father of scientific

management—were Frank and Lillian Gilbreth. Parents of twelve children, they ran their
household using scientific management principles and techniques. Two of their children
wrote a book, *Cheaper by the Dozen,* that described life with the two efficiency experts.

Whereas the private sector used position classification to increase productivity, the public sector used it chiefly to ensure equitable compensation. If people have similar job descriptions, then it follows they should be compensated equally—equal pay for equal work.

As noted in Chapter 1, the experiences of the New Deal and World War II taught members of the Roosevelt Administration that, in practice, administration and politics can seldom be separated. In seeking a new approach to public-sector administration, Roosevelt turned to the Brownlow Committee. In 1937, that committee issued an influential report recommending the following:

- The close integration of personnel management with general presidential management
- The establishment of an executive office of the president, the core of which would be the White House staff and the Bureau of the Budget
- The consolidation of all line agencies, including the independent regulatory commissions, into twelve cabinet-level departments

In their response to the New Deal and World War II, the Republican Congress formed two commissions, both headed by former President Herbert Hoover. Although the first of these (created in 1947) avoided questions of policy, the second (created in 1953) did not and made two bold recommendations that, though not adopted, were harbingers. First, by recommending a "senior civil service," the commission foreshadowed the Civil Service Reform Act of 1978 that established a Senior Executive Service (SES). Second, by pointing out government functions that compete with private enterprise, it foreshadowed the privatization efforts of the Reagan Administration in the 1980s.

Government by Shared Power

The major developments since the 1950s, according to Dennis L. Dresang, "has been the emergence of multiple centers and multiple sources of power and influence affecting the management of public employees."[4] Among those sources of power, we might note the following five: professionals ("technocrats"), unions, minorities and women, public managers, and contractors.

Professionals   Government is a major employer of professional and technical people. By the end of the 1950s, 36 percent of all professionals worked for government. Since 1960, over one-third of all government employees have been professionals or technicians. This increased professionalization of the public service has two implications. First, public executives and managers have less control over personnel selection. Let's see why. HR specialists do job analysis—that is, systematically collect information on the important work-related aspects of the job and then develop job descriptions and job specifications. A job description is a written description of the basic tasks, duties, and responsibilities required of an employee holding a particular job. Job specifications, which are often included as a separate section of a job description, are a summary of the qualifications needed to successfully perform the job. For example, job specifications for a helicopter pilot in a medium-size city might require—among many other things—a particular type of license; knowledge of certain laws and regulations, flying procedures, and navigational techniques; skill in the operation of radio equipment; ability to conduct safety inspections, maintain maintenance logs, detect aircraft malfunctions, and recognize ground conditions such as utility-line breaks; and at least 1000 hours of flight-time experience in piloting rotary-wing aircraft. It is rather unlikely that, say, a city manager is going to argue over these specifications; the manager's influence over the selection process is, accordingly, less than it would have been for a less technical appointment.

The other implication of increased professionalization is this: it has revived the political-administration debate. Often when public executives question the judgment of a professional, the tendency is for the professional to claim political interference. "A professional, almost by definition, typically seeks autonomy and a status that commands deference. The mixing in a common arena of a political official pursuing the mandates of the ballot box and a professional expecting to dominate in the policymaking process is bound to generate conflict and distrust. There are likely to be frustrations, too, because a politician and the professional need each other."[5]

Unions   Although union membership is just 7.6 percent in the private U.S. workforce, the share of government workers in unions has held steady at around 38 percent. If the Pendleton Act was the landmark legislation creating the civil service, John F. Kennedy's Executive Orders 10987 and 10988 in 1962 were the landmarks for the surge in union involvement by government employees. To be sure, the Lloyd-LaFollette Act of 1912 gave federal employees the right to organize and petition for attention to their needs, but restrictions on how they might organize and bargain seriously weakened this right. Kennedy's two orders, however, gave unions the right for the first time to bargain collectively with federal managers on a limited range of items. Moreover, they stimulated similar measures in numerous states and localities throughout the 1960s and 1970s. Today all but six states permit some form of collective bargaining.

The political influence of union members in government varies considerably by jurisdiction and profession. In urban industrial states and larger urban areas, public unions play major policymaking roles; in less industrialized regions, the involvement is less. More than 80 percent of public elementary and secondary teachers belong to the American Federation of Teachers (AFT) or the National Education Association (NEA), and more than 60 percent are covered under formal collective bargaining agreements. By the 1970s, police had become one of the most highly unionized segments of the public sector.

The scope of bargaining varies greatly, but most agreements focus on salary and fringe benefits, pay supplements, equity, union seniority, working conditions, and individual security. Police unions have successfully pushed salary levels above those prevailing in nonunion locations, and the favorable bargaining climate created in sixteen states having compulsory arbitration of unresolved disputes has increased police salaries even more. No state allows police the right to strike, but strikes do occur, usually in the form of the "blue flu" (police calling in sick on the same day). Collective bargaining is extremely decentralized, and membership in a police union is almost always limited to police department personnel of a single city or town. (Rarely do employees in different cities join together for bargaining purposes.)

Today there are three prominent and powerful public service unions and numerous lesser ones that speak for many—though certainly not all—public employees: the American Federation of State, County and Municipal Employees (AFSCME); the American Federation of Government Employees (AFGE), and the previously mentioned American Federation of Teachers (AFT).

Minorities and Women   The Civil Rights Act of 1964 opened opportunities to minorities and women tremendously. See photo. The act consisted of 11 titles, the most consequential of which was Title VII. We will have more to say about Title VII presently, but here will just note that the act prohibits discrimination on the basis of race, color, religion, gender, or national origin. Initially, the act applied only to private-sector employers, but in the 1972 amendments to the act, Congress extended coverage to include state and local governments. The federal government included its own civilian agencies under a statutory mandate for equal employment opportunities under provisions of the 1978 civil service reforms of President Jimmy Carter.

The U.S. Supreme Court upheld the constitutionality of equal employment opportunity provisions of the act in *Griggs v. Duke Power Company* (1971). A group of black employees challenged the company's requirement of either a high school diploma or a

AP Photo/Peter Cosgrove

Under public pressure to diversify its all-male, predominantly military, fighter-pilot, Apollo-era astronaut corps, NASA selected in 1978 a half-dozen medical doctors, scientists, and engineers to become the first American women astronauts. But by 1989, it had yet to select a woman with the credentials to pilot and perhaps command a spacecraft. That was the year Eileen Collins, a 32-year-old Air Force officer, applied to become an astronaut. The first woman to fly in space was the Russian cosmonaut Valentina Tereshkova in 1963. The first American woman in space was Sally Ride in 1983. But no woman, Russian or American, had ever commanded a space mission until Eileen Collins on July 19, 1999.

satisfactory intelligence test score for certain jobs previously given only to white employees. Although it was quite obvious that the company had overtly discriminated in the past, the court found that such practices had ended. The real issue was, however, that the job requirements did not seem to "bear a demonstrable relationship to successful performance of the jobs for which they were used." The Supreme Court overruled the trial court and held that the fact that both requirements disqualified more blacks than whites served to show a violation of the law. The message of *Griggs* was clear: job requirements had to be related to the performance of the job. As one justice put it, one did not need to know how to translate Virgil to shovel coal. The Civil Rights Act of 1964, as interpreted in the *Griggs* decision, put merit into the merit system.

Public Managers   By the mid-1970s, a number of state governments recognized that it was time to perform a comprehensive review of their personnel systems and make sure the various pieces fit together. A consistent theme in all these reforms was a concern for strengthening the hand of public managers. With the influence by professions, unions, and groups representing minorities and women came a fear that managers' hands were increasingly becoming tied—thus limiting the capacity of agencies to fulfill their missions.

When Jimmy Carter campaigned for the presidency in 1976, he made reform of the federal bureaucracy a major plank of his platform. The ongoing reforms by state and local government plus abuses of the Civil Service Commission during the Nixon presidency made the late 1970s a good time for reform. We will consider the major features of the 1978 reform later. Suffice for now to note that these reforms reestablished the primacy of management and public service values.

Building on Carter's reforms, the administrations of both Bill Clinton and George W. Bush further strengthened the hand of management. As part of the Clinton administration's effort to "reinvent government"—formally known as the National Performance Review (NPR)—many of the functions of personnel management were delegated to agency management, and many restrictions on managers in the form of personnel rules and regulations were eliminated.

One of the underlying themes of the Homeland Security Act, which Bush proposed and Congress approved in 2002, is to bring greater flexibility to federal personnel administration. Bargaining with labor unions over work assignments and other conditions of employment is, the Bush administration argued, incompatible with making rapid responses to ever-changing terrorist threats. Consequently, personnel in the Department of Homeland Security are exempt from collective bargaining laws and regulations.

The Homeland Security Act also included a few provisions that applied to other departments and agencies. For example, to underscore the importance of HR in strategic management, each agency now has a Chief Human Capital Officer (CHCO). Further, agency managers now have greater flexibility in hiring employees, encouraging early retirement, compensating executives, and paying for employees' higher education. Perhaps most importantly, many viewed these reforms as the shape of things to come.

Contractors   Although one of the purposes of the Second Hoover Commission was to curtail and, in some cases, abolish government activities that competed with private enterprise, it was not until the Carter administration (1977–1981) that presidents began to openly consider the advantages of relying on private enterprise to do some of the work that had been done by government. Since the administration of Reagan (1981–1989), privatization—which, as we saw in Chapter 9, included selling government enterprises and contracting with private vendors—has become an increasing trend.

What are the implications of privatization for public personnel management? The first implication is, ironically, an increased workload for agency managers. Processes have to be designed and followed for soliciting bids, negotiating agreements, and monitoring the behavior of the contractor. A specific concern here is with personnel practices. More specifically, contracts include provisions regarding how employees are to be hired and treated. Part of ensuring that vendors are meeting the needs of the jurisdiction and complying with government policies is monitoring their employment practices.

Second, when privatization means reduction in the public-sector workforce, then layoffs and job restructuring may be necessary. These necessities may be complicated if some employees are covered under collective bargaining. Understandably, unions are concerned about the negative effects of privatization on their members. And, not too surprisingly, collective bargaining in government increasingly includes provisions for union protections and union consultation when privatization is under consideration.

Third, increased privatization could contribute to a trend noted earlier: an increasingly professionalized public-sector workforce. Think about it. The jobs that are easiest to replace with contracted services tend to be the blue-collar, clerical positions that are common to many organizations, public and private. As these positions are removed from the area of responsibility for personnel managers, the workforce that remains will be more and more professional.

The Environment of Human Resources Management

As noted in the chapter introduction, an agency's environment can be segmented into its external and internal components. The *external environment* of an agency has, in turn, many possible components—economic trends, technological trends, social trends, political-legal trends, and international trends. Although each one of these components can significantly affect the success or failure of agencies and individual public administrators, we must be selective in what we examine here. Our scan of the external environment has four foci:

- Civil service reform, with a closer look at the Civil Rights Reform Act of 1978
- Other major federal laws related to HRM, with particular attention to the Civil Rights Act of 1964
- Legislation and court decisions affecting the rights of public employees, with an attempt to identify the rights of public employees with respect to political activities, freedom of speech, and privacy
- Demographic trends, with an attempt to sort out how the composition of the American population is changing with respect to race and age structure

This scan of the external environment of HRM will be followed by a look at an agency's *internal environment.* Although there are many aspects of an agency's internal environment, its overall organization culture has a profound influence on the effectiveness of HRM. Accordingly, this section concludes by considering how shared meanings within an organization determine, in large measure, how employees act.

Civil Service Reform

A classified civil service is a bureaucracy in which personnel operate in a merit system under the jurisdiction of a civil service agency. In the federal government, the classified civil service system is composed of mostly white-collar, nonprofessional, tenured personnel. Their employment is administered in keeping with traditional civil service practices.

Examinations under the civil service system are practical rather than scholarly. Each available position is described in detail, and examinations are geared to the needs of each. After passing a written test, the candidate might take an oral examination if the job warrants it. If successful with both, that person's name is placed on an eligibility list, which is set up on the basis of examination scores. Federal law requires that the agency choose from among the top three to five scores on the list, without passing over veterans. In many merit systems, there are further job requirements, such as height and weight requirements for police officers, high school or college graduation for particular occupations, and certifications or licenses for many positions (for example, attorney or physician). Such requirements, however, must be clearly job related.

Merit systems can be organized in various ways. In many jurisdictions, a nonpartisan or bipartisan commission or board is charged with general program direction and appellate functions, leaving to a personnel director (appointed by the board or the chief executive) the responsibility for day-to-day program administration. In others, a personnel director reporting to the chief executive is responsible for general program direction, with a civil service commission or board serving in a watchdog, advisory, or appellate role (or all three).

Government jobs outside the civil service system are not necessarily appointive, for many agencies have developed their own career systems. Those systems are composed of white-collar personnel, generally professionals and paraprofessionals, who are tenured in the agency and the occupation, though not in the position. Their employment is administered as a progressive, preferably planned, development. In such a system, repeated failure to attain promotion—being "passed over" too many times—can result in dismissal; hence, the expression "up or out."

The model of the career system is that of military officers. In fact, the military system has been copied or adopted by a number of other federal organizations—for example, the Foreign Service, the Public Health Service, the FBI, the CIA, and the TVA. In varying degrees, it has also been a model for state and local police systems and local fire departments. Unlike the civil service system, a career system emphasizes the individual rather than the position. As Frederick C. Mosher points out, a "nonprofessional civil servant working in the Department of the Navy is most likely to respond, 'I work for the Navy Department'; an officer, 'I am an officer (or an admiral or captain) in the Navy.'"[6]

Career systems pose several challenges to the manager. For example, members of a career personnel system, such as the naval officer, must work with other personnel in the organization who lack comparable career status. When people work together on the same project but under two distinct employment systems, the possibility of friction is great.

Critics had long argued that personnel practices made it difficult for presidents to assemble teams of highly competent officials to implement new programs. To overcome that problem, President Jimmy Carter and the head of the Civil Service Commission, Alan K. Campbell, developed a package of reform proposals. After a major struggle in Congress and Carter's expenditure of large amounts of political capital, the **Civil Service Reform Act of 1978** was passed. The most visible reform in the new law was an organizational one. The Civil Service Commission split into two units: the **Office of Personnel Management (OPM)** and the **Merit Systems Protection Board (MSPB).** Although a number of personnel functions are decentralized to line agencies, the OPM has general responsibility for recruitment, training, performance appraisal, and policy leadership in the federal government. The MSPB safeguards employees' rights to due process and equitable treatment and protects whistle-blowers against unfair reprisals.

In addition to these structural changes, the act created a separate personnel system for the highest-ranking civil service officials. The **Senior Executive Service (SES)** encompasses nearly 7000 executives. About 10 percent of SES personnel are political appointees, selected outside ordinary merit channels and loyal to the president; the remainder are, of course, career executives, committed more to federal service than to any particular president. The act makes it easier to transfer these executives from one position to another.

The act's third important accomplishment was to restate and elaborate one of the fundamental themes of public personnel administration in the United States: the **merit principle.** Simply put, staffing (recruitment), compensation, advancement, and retention should be based on merit, that is, the employee's ability, education, experience, and job performance. The merit principle rejects criteria such as patronage (political payoffs), friendship, kinship, race, and religion.

Finally, the Reform Act brought federal labor relations under one comprehensive act. It also established an independent Federal Labor Relations Authority (FLRA), giving collective bargaining for federal employees a firm legal foundation. Although scholars and practitioners may debate how much difference the establishment of the OPM, the MSPB, and the SES and the reinstatement of the merit system have made, no one can doubt the importance of this aspect of the act.

Other Major Federal Laws

Overview   The federal government has greatly expanded its influence over HRM by enacting a number of laws and regulations affecting virtually every HR activity. Table 10.1 provides a summary of these laws.[7] The basic intent of most of this legislation has been to ensure that equal opportunity is provided for both job applicants and current employees. Because the laws were intended to correct past inequalities, many organizations

Table 10.1	Federal Laws Affecting Human Resources Management	
Year	Law	Description
1963	Equal Pay Act	Prohibits pay differences based on sex (gender) for employees performing similar jobs under similar working conditions—but does not prohibit different rates of pay if they are in different jobs. The concept of comparable worth seeks to expand the principle of equal pay to situations in which men and women are performing dissimilar jobs that are, nonetheless, work of equal value to the employer. Minnesota, New York, New Mexico, Iowa, and South Dakota have instituted the principle of comparable worth. To find out how much less women earn than men in spite of this law, check out http://www.aflcio.org/issuespolitics/women/equalpay. The site also calculates how much the pay gap will cost a woman over her lifetime.
1964	Civil Rights Act, Title VII	Prohibits discrimination based on race, color, religion, national origin, or sex (gender). Makes sexual harassment in the workplace a form of discrimination, and the usual remedies apply—back pay, reinstatement, and attorney's fees.
1967	Age Discrimination in Employment Act	Prohibits age discrimination against employees between 40 and 65 years of age and restricts mandatory retirement. However, state employees cannot sue their employers for violating this law.
1990	Americans with Disabilities Act	Prohibits employers from discriminating against individuals with physical or mental disabilities or those who are chronically ill. Also requires organizations to reasonably accommodate these individuals. Again, however, state employees cannot sue their employers for violation of this law.
1993	Family and Medical Leave Act	Requires employers to provide twelve weeks of unpaid leave for family and medical emergencies. State employees can sue their employers for violation of this law. The Labor Department answers questions about FMLA at www.dol.gov/esa/whd/fmla.

have implemented **affirmative action programs** to ensure that organizational changes are made. These programs may involve such things as taking extra effort to inform minority candidates about job opportunities, providing special training programs for disadvantaged candidates, or paying special attention to the racial or gender mix of employees who are promoted.

The most important of the laws is **Title VII of the Civil Rights Act of 1964**, which prohibits organizations from discriminating on the basis of race, color, religion, sex, or national origin. (The text of Title VII is available at www.eeoc.gov/laws/vii.) Title VII prohibits discrimination in the workplace, sexual harassment, and discrimination because of pregnancy. It also permits organizations to develop affirmative action plans. Originally, "sex" was not included in the law, but two days before passage, Rep. Howard Smith of Virginia added that three-letter word. His intention was not to promote equal opportunity for women but rather to scuttle the bill. He erroneously thought no one would vote for a law that prohibited discrimination against women.

Proving Discrimination   Discrimination under Title VII means firing, refusing to hire, failing to promote, or otherwise reducing a person's employment opportunities because of race, color, religion, gender, or national origin. This protection applies to every stage of the employment process from job announcements to postemployment references and includes placement, wages, benefits, and working conditions. Plaintiffs (the complaining parties) in Title VII cases can prove discrimination two different ways: (1) disparate treatment (intentional discrimination) and (2) disparate impact (discrimination as a side effect of some rule).

1. To prove a **disparate treatment** case, the plaintiff must show that he or she was *treated* differently because of gender, race, color, religion, or national origin. There are three required steps in a disparate treatment case. First, the plaintiff presents evidence that the defendant had discriminated against him or her because of a protected trait. This is called a *prima facie* case. Prima facie ("at first sight") refers to a fact or conclusion that is presumed to be true unless someone presents evidence to disprove it. The plaintiff is not required to prove discrimination; he or she need only create a presumption that discrimination occurred. Because we are dealing with intentions here, the burden of proof on the plaintiff—or the EEOC, if it takes the case to court—is high. For example, if a correctional guard, who happens to be a black male, was reprimanded, suspended, demoted, and finally fired, can he *prove* that his race was the reason for these actions?

The next step involves the defendant presenting evidence that his or her decision was based on *legitimate, nondiscriminatory* reasons. Finally, to win, the plaintiff must prove that the employer discriminated. He or she may do so by showing that the reasons offered by the employer were simply a *pretext.*

2. **Disparate impact** becomes an issue if the employer has a rule that, *on its face,* is not discriminatory but, in practice, includes too many people in a protected group. There are also three steps in a disparate impact case. First, the plaintiff must present a prima facie case. The plaintiff is *not* required to prove discrimination; he or she need only show a disparate impact—that is, that the employment practice in question excludes a disproportionate number of people in a protected group. Next, the defendant must offer some evidence that the employment practice was a *job-related necessity.* Finally, to win, the plaintiff must prove either that the employer's reason is a pretext or that other, less discriminatory rules would achieve the same results.

This is what happened in *Griggs v. Duke Power* (1971): The power company had a steam-generating plant in Draper, North Carolina, where for many years blacks had been allowed to work only in the lowest-paying labor department. This was clearly disparate treatment, but when Title VII took effect, Duke rescinded its clearly race-based policy and opened all jobs to blacks. At the same time, it instituted a new policy that required a high school diploma to move up from the labor department to the coal handling, operations, maintenance, or laboratory departments. Alternately, blacks could take an intelligence test or a mechanical aptitude test and, if they scored at the same level as the average high school graduate, they could meet the requirement. But because blacks in the area were less educated, this requirement frustrated their ambitions. Instead of rejecting blacks for being black, the company now rejected them for lacking education. Black workers filed suit, alleging that the education and testing requirements were unrelated to, for example, the ability to shovel coal. The Supreme Court held the diploma requirement and tests were illegal unless employers could show that they were related to job performance or justified by "business necessity." They were, in short, unlawful even if no discrimination was intended.

Defending Against Charges of Discrimination

As we have just seen, an organization is permitted to establish discriminatory job requirements if they are *essential* to the position in question. Such a requirement is called a **bona fide occupational qualification (BFOQ).** For example, Catholic schools may, if they choose, refuse to hire non-Catholic teachers.

Title VII allows for two other possible defenses: seniority and merit. Suppose that an athletic director has always chosen the most senior assistant coach to take over as head coach when a vacancy occurs. (We'll assume the school is not in a very competitive league.) Because the majority of the senior assistant coaches are male, most of the head coaches are also. Such a system does not violate Title VII.

Nor are employers liable if they can show that the person whom they favor is the most qualified. Test results, education, or productivity can all be used to demonstrate merit, provided they are related to the job in question. It is easy to say that the most qualified person should be hired or promoted, but how do you measure merit? Consider the case of *Johnson v. Transportation Agency, Santa Clara County* (1987): No woman had ever held the job of radio dispatcher in this county. Although Paul Johnson scored higher on the dispatcher exam than Diane Joyce, the county hired Joyce. The case ultimately reached the U.S. Supreme Court on the issue of whether a less-qualified woman could be promoted over better-qualified man. The Court ruled that she could. Johnson's score on the dispatcher exam had been 75 out of 100; hers was 73. This two-point difference is simply not persuasive evidence that Johnson would be a better radio dispatcher than Joyce.

One of the important lessons here is this: before one concludes that a less-qualified applicant has been promoted over a better-qualified competitor, it is wise to ask about the validity of the test and the significance of the difference in scores. Indeed, employment tests are typically not very good predictors of on-the-job performance.

Affirmative Action

Title VII neither requires nor prohibits affirmative action programs. Such programs have three sources. First, courts have the power under Title VII to order affirmative action to remedy the effects of past discrimination. Second, Executive Order 11246, which President Johnson signed in 1965, prohibits discrimination by federal contractors. This order had a profound effect on the workplace because one-third of all workers are employed by companies that do business with the federal government. If an employer found that women or minorities were underrepresented in its workplace, it was required to establish goals and timetables to correct the deficiency. But these programs are permissible only if they serve a "compelling national interest" and are "narrowly tailored" so that they minimize the harm to white males. Third, an organization can voluntarily introduce an affirmative action program to remedy the effects of past practices or to achieve equitable representation of minorities.

Affirmative action is of course a sensitive issue. White males in particular protest that such programs are reverse discrimination. Two recent Supreme Court cases involving allegations of reverse discrimination are doubly interesting because they were filed by white females and, more importantly, were argued on the basis of diversity—rather than remedying past injustices.

On June 23, 2003, the Supreme Court handed down, in effect, a split decision, approving one of the University of Michigan's admissions programs and striking down another. In *Gratz v. Bollinger,* the court struck down, in a 6–3 vote, a point system used in undergraduate admissions whereby being black carried more weight than a perfect SAT score. But in *Grutter v. Bollinger,* the more significant ruling, in a 5–4 vote, the court upheld Michigan's law school program in which decisions are made by an admissions committee without a numerical scale.

Unfortunately, the court's decisions are not clear-cut enough to stop further legal cases from testing what it now means by an acceptable approach to affirmative action. In the *Gratz* decision, the court ruled that the admissions program was unconstitutional because its system of rewarding points to minority applicants made it too much like a racial quota. Quotas had been ruled out by the famous *Regents of the University of California v. Bakke* (1978) decision that, nevertheless, said that race could be taken into account as a "plus," although only as one of many other factors. Michigan thought that it had met the *Bakke* requirements. It awarded points for various nonacademic qualities, including geographic location, athletic prowess, and alumni connections, as well as race. But the court's majority opinion, written by Chief Justice William Rehnquist, said that the university's scheme was too broad, and so violated the equal protection of the laws guaranteed by the Constitution's Fourteenth Amendment—that is, it was racially discriminatory.

In the *Grutter* case (mentioned in the opening case), the court upheld the admissions program used by the university's law school, which also takes race into account but does not use a point system like the undergraduate program. Justice Sandra Day O'Connor wrote the majority opinion in this case. The law school program, she explained, is constitutional because it is a "highly individualized, holistic review of each applicant's file," rather than a rigid formula. The undergraduate points scheme, by contrast, is a "non-individualized, mechanical" system, and thus not tailored closely enough to meet the court's *strict scrutiny standard* for constitutionally acceptable racial classifications.

From a legal standpoint, the biggest advance on the *Bakke* decision is that Justice O'Connor managed to persuade a majority of the court that racial diversity—rather than a remedy for past injustice—is a public interest compelling enough to justify exceptions to the Constitution's ban on racial discrimination. "Effective participation by members of all racial and ethnic groups in the civic life of our nation is essential if the dream of one nation, indivisible, is to be realized." The court seemed particularly impressed by a brief submitted by former military leaders attesting to how important diversity is in the officer corps.

In effect, O'Connor conceded that affirmative action schemes are racially discriminatory but argued that they are necessary to ensure diversity. But such schemes have to inflict the minimum harm on those who lose out—whites and Asian Americans.

It is important to appreciate how close the ruling in *Grutter* was. If any judge in the majority were replaced with a conservative, there would likely be five votes to all but end affirmative action. But it is also important to appreciate that this would not end equal opportunity.

Sexual Harassment   Many women experience **sexual harassment** at some time in their careers. Various forms of harassment exist, and same-sex harassment is prohibited by the same laws that bar male-female harassment.

In 1980, the EEOC issued guidelines making sexual harassment a form of sexual discrimination under Title VII. The guidelines defined two situations in which harassment is illegal. One is *quid pro quo,* when submission to sexual activity is required to get or keep a job. The other is a *hostile environment,* where sexually offensive conduct is so pervasive that it becomes unreasonably difficult to work. The range of conduct that can create a hostile environment has expanded to become very broad—but is still not subject to precise definition. At first, courts often held that coarse language, innuendo, and pinups were part of work environments and that Title VII could not magically dignify the manners of male workers. Then, in a landmark case, a female welder, one of only seven women among 1000 skilled craft workers in a Florida shipyard, complained that suggestive and lewd pinups, drawings, and cartoons created a hostile working environment. A Florida court agreed with her, holding that even if men enjoy this decor, it nevertheless created an abusive climate for her.

In 1993, the Supreme Court set up a test for hostile environments. In *Harris v. Forklift Systems* (1990), the Court held that the guideline was whether sexual harassment created "an environment that a reasonable person would find hostile or abusive." There was no "mathematically precise task" for what constituted a hostile environment, but harassing conduct should be examined with respect to its "frequency" and "severity," whether it is "physically threatening or humiliating," and whether it "unreasonably interferes" with work.

Public Employees' Rights and Responsibilities

Courts as well as legislatures and chief executives have been active in defining restrictions on employee behavior. We will begin by looking at political rights, and then consider how the Supreme Court has interpreted the First Amendment with regard to free speech for public employees and the Constitution with regard to privacy.

Political Rights   The 1939 Political Activities Act, often known as the **Hatch Act,** provides the basis for restrictions on public employees throughout the United States. Public employees were never happy with these restrictions and, in 1993, finally succeeded in amending the act. Today most federal employees may now hold office in a political party, work for candidates in a partisan campaign, solicit votes, and distribute campaign literature—as long as these activities are done outside of work hours and work facilities. These reforms do not affect, however, the "little Hatch Acts" that states incorporate into their own laws.

In the 1970s, partisan decisions by officials that affected the careers of civil servants provided a couple of interesting cases. In *Abood v. Detroit,* the Supreme Court ruled that employees in unionized government jobs could not be forced to pay those portions of union service fees that were to be used to advance political causes.

In *Elrod v. Burns,* Justice William Brennan wrote that cases alleging interference with protected fundamental rights—in this instance, Republican employees who were fired by a Democratic county administration—involved three determinations. First, the Court had to decide whether there was a substantial infringement of the employees' protected freedom. In this case, there was no question that the employees were being terminated because of their political association. Second, some infringements of liberties may be justified if the government can demonstrate a sufficiently compelling reason—for example, the position involves policymaking. Third, assuming the government action did serve a "compelling interest," the Court then had to decide whether the patronage practices as used were overbroad and not sufficiently tailored to achievement of the goals without excessive interference with protected rights. Brennan concluded that the patronage system failed on the third ground. In *Elrod,* a process server and other low-level employees were fired solely because they belonged to the wrong party.[8]

Free Speech   Political activity is not confined to the pursuit of party politics such as those covered by the Hatch Act. *Pickering v. Board of Education* (1968) arose from a conflict in Illinois, when a public school teacher named Pickering was fired for writing to a local newspaper a letter criticizing the school board for placing too much emphasis on athletics. The Supreme Court ruled in Pickering's favor, stating that it is essential to maintain a *balance* between the rights of public employees as citizens and the interests of public employers in providing services. To set aside individual rights, the court argued, it is necessary for public employers to show that their ability to function properly and provide effective services is seriously threatened. This could be demonstrated in five different areas:

1. A negative effect on managerial direction and discipline
2. A negative effect on harmony among coworkers
3. A breach of the employee–employer relationship, which requires personnel loyalty and confidence
4. A negative effect on job performance
5. A destructive impact on the functions of the agency, including an undermining of public confidence

The Court was not persuaded that this case posed a threat to any of these five areas and ordered that Pickering be reinstated.

Government employees do not enjoy free-speech protection against being disciplined for exposing official misconduct at work. In an important decision that will make it more difficult for some government whistle-blowers, the U.S. Supreme Court ruled on May 30, 2006, that public workers who make allegations of misconduct in official reports and in work-related statements may be disciplined for their speech without violating First Amendment protections.

The 5 to 4 decision came in the case of *Garcetti v. Ceballos.* A supervising district attorney in Los Angeles, Ceballos, had raised questions in a memo about whether a deputy sheriff had lied to obtain a search warrant. Other prosecutors in Ceballos's office disagreed with his assessment. Ceballos was reassigned and later filed a federal lawsuit saying his supervisors demoted him in retaliation for his memo and testimony on the search warrant issue.

In his suit, Ceballos claimed his actions were protected by the First Amendment. The majority of the Supreme Court disagreed: "When public employees make statements pursuant to their official duties, they are not speaking as citizens for First Amendment purposes, and the Constitution does not insulate their communications from employer discipline." The majority justices drew a distinction between work-related speech and the speech of a concerned citizen. When an employee speaks as a citizen addressing a matter of public concern, the First Amendment requires a delicate balancing of the competing interest surrounding the speech and its consequences. When, however, the employee is simply performing his or her job duties, there is no warrant for a similar degree of scrutiny.

Privacy   Although there is no mention of privacy in the Constitution, in *Griswold v. Connecticut* (1965), the Supreme Court pulled together elements of the First, Third, Fourth, Fifth, and Fourteenth Amendments to recognize that personal privacy is one of the rights protected by the Constitution. For government employees, concerns about privacy revolve around four issues in particular: (1) drug testing, (2) searches, (3) sexual orientation, and (4) living arrangements.

1. From the employee's point of view probably the most important question concerning *drug testing* is who is going to be tested. Is everybody who works for an organization, or all those people who occupy certain types of positions, or only those about whom there is some "reasonable suspicion" going to be tested? In 1986, with Executive Order 12564, President Reagan established the federal government's drug-testing program, and the Office of Personnel Management guidelines that followed it left a great deal of discretion in the hands of agency heads regarding who will be tested. Agencies are expected to test anyone about whom they have a reasonable suspicion—that is, some information that would lead them to believe that an employee uses drugs. Further, agencies are expected to identify a set of "sensitive" job positions—personnel whose duties affect public health, national security, or just the efficient use of agency resources—and then designate some or all of them as testing-designated positions.

2. The Supreme Court dealt with *searches* in *O'Connor v. Ortega* (1987). Could a state hospital, while investigating charges of sexual harassment and malfeasance of one of its doctors, search his desk and office? The Court ruled that such a search was reasonable under the Fourth Amendment even if the hospital lacked a policy governing searches and had not given the staff any indication that it would engage in them. The Court concluded that a public employer had to be able to retrieve work-related material and investigate possible violations of workplace rules.

3. With regard to sexual orientation, the courts have been sympathetic to the position of many agencies that homosexuals are a "security risk" and can't be hired for positions in which they might handle sensitive information and be subject to blackmail. But what if the employees are openly gay? Then the threat to reveal their secret would not seem to be an effective blackmail strategy. But here's the catch: federal civilian employees operate under a system not so very different from the so-called don't ask, don't tell system created by the military in response to an executive order from President Clinton. Keep it discreet and low-key, and we will leave you alone. In contrast to the federal government, more than a dozen states and a number of major cities have provided significant protections for the privacy rights of their homosexual employees.

When Barack Obama sought the presidency, he pledged to reverse the "don't ask, don't tell" policy preventing lesbians and homosexuals from serving openly in the U.S. military. Yet on June 8, 2009, the U.S. Supreme Court rejected a homosexual soldier's challenge to the law—with the legal backing of the Obama Administration. The Obama Administration, in its brief, said a lower court acted properly in upholding the ban. "Applying the strong deference traditionally afforded to the legislative and executive branches in the area of military affairs, the Court of Appeals properly upheld the statute," argued the Solicitor General, who represents the Administration before the Supreme Court. The ban on homosexuals serving openly is "rationally related to the government's legitimate interest in military discipline and cohesion," the filing added.

But an article appearing three months later in the Pentagon's top scholarly journal disagreed with that conclusion.[9] "After a careful examination, there is no scientific evidence to support the claim that unit cohesion will be negatively affected if homosexuals serve openly," Colonel Om Prakash wrote. Instead, "it is time for the administration to examine how to implement the repeal of the ban." The article also said the law has been costly—about 12,500 homosexual men and lesbians have been discharged from the service as a result of the ban—and argued that it undermines the unit cohesion it sought to protect. However, any change in the law is up to Congress.

4. Many local governments have adopted policies concerning *living arrangements.* Specifically, they require their employees to live within the boundaries of the jurisdiction for which they work. Why? Usually to make sure that people living on salaries provided by the "taxpayers of the city" are taxpayers themselves. Often, these policies frustrate public employees, especially employees of the central city government of major metropolitan areas, who may prefer to live in suburbs or find living in the city too expensive In *McCarthy v. Philadelphia Civil Service Commission* (1976), the U.S. Supreme Court addressed the issue and found in favor of the city and its residency rule.

Demographic Trends

Besides changes in the political-legal environment, HR managers must be concerned about trends in society, especially racial diversity and the age-structure of the workforce (the ratio of older workers to youmger workers).

The U.S. Census Bureau projects that between 2005 and 2025, the white population will grow 13.2 percent; the black population, 25.7 percent; the Hispanic populations (which can include any race), 58.3 percent; and the Asian population, 61.7 percent. Such hard numbers fail to reflect the increasing rate of intermarriage. Indeed, some demographers see the United States becoming, in the long run, more beige than diverse. Others have rather unscientifically referred to this trend as the "Tiger Woods Phenomenon."

These hard numbers also fail to reflect the shifting definition of white. When Barack Obama, whose mother was white, identifies himself as black, and when New Mexico Governor Bill Richardson, whose father was white, identifies himself as Hispanic, who is white? Despite these difficulties in assigning race, the U.S. Census Bureau tells us that the United States will be majoirty minority in 2050—that is, the combined number of blacks, Asians, American Indians, and Hispanics will put whites in the minority. Texas and California are already there.

According to most demographers, racial categories as we know them are not going to continue to hold for another 50 years. Those who try to keep track of race are always going to be five or 10 years behind where society is as race becomes more about choices and less about government definitions. African Americans include descendents of African slaves, recent voluntary immigrants from Africa, and those from the Caribbean. Indeed, a Pew Research Survey released in late 2007 found that more than one-third of black respondents said that black no longer can be though of as a single race because their community is so diverse.[10]

Similarly, the single category "Hispanic" sweeps together such very different groups as Cuban Americans, Dominican Americans, Guatemalan Americans, Mexican Americans, and immigrants from Argentina—but not from Brazil. As noted, rapidly rising rates in intermarriage further blur the picture. Fifty-seven percent of third-generation Hispanic Americans and 54 percent of third-generation Asian Americans marry outside their ethnic group. Also blurring the picture is the fact that many Hispanic Americans—and Arab Americans—chose "white" or "other" when asked to pick from among the 63 categories on the 2000 Census.[11]

Then we come to Generation Y, those born between 1982 and 2002. They present a very different racial profile from previous generations. According to the Census Bureau, children under the age of 18 are twice as likely as adults to identify themselves as belonging to more than one race. (See photo on page 454.)

We will just have to wait and see how these trends play out. But for today at least, this much is clear: effective management of work-force diversity remains a growing managerial challenge. Public managers must be skilled at listening, conflict resolution, negotiations, and communications. They might need to provide support groups and mentors for employees with minority backgrounds to keep them from feeling unappreciated and wanting to leave the organization. And they certainly need to monitor the behavior of their subordinates and provide constant positive reinforcement of behaviors that foster tolerance of, and the effective use of, diversity. At the same time, managers must provide negative feedback to individuals who act otherwise. For more about government diversity programs, see Problem 5 on page 483.

Another reason why public administrators need to be concerned about demographic trends is that different generations have distinct sets of work values and styles. Today, four

Richard Perry/The New York Times/Redux Pictures

Sorting out how much weight race can be given by institutions as they engineer diversity programs is probably going to become exceedingly difficult for courts in the years ahead. In time, the court's role might seem somewhat anachronistic, and its black-and-white vocabulary quaint. Demographics, not constitutional litigation, may determine the destiny of the United States. Neil Howe, coauthor of *Millennials Rising: The Next Generation*, describes Generation Y as follows: "They can be sort of half-black, half-white, half-Asian—you don't know what they are.

generations are being asked to coexist in the workplace at once: traditionalists (those born before 1945), baby boomers, generation X, and millennials—alternatively known as gen-Y, echo boomers (because their parents were boomers), net gen, and even "generation why" (because they so often question the status quo). Born between the early 1980s and 2002, the millennial generation should be of keen interest to both public- and private-sector managers because of differences in its expectations, skills, and attitudes about work. According to those who track these things, the defining characteristics of millennials include the following:[12]

- Like structure and want organization to give them clear rules to follow
- Do not like to deal with ambiguity they will inevitably face as managers
- Tend to be opinionated and expect to be heard
- Crave feedback and praise for their accomplishments
- Want work to be relevant, have impact, and offer a diversity of experiences
- Demonstrate strong commitment to social responsibility
- Probably fit well in a team-oriented culture but may be so collaborative that they fall short on independent thinking and leadership

Two other demographic trends are worth noting: the growing number of aging baby boomers in the population and the much smaller number of young people who follow behind them. The proportion of older workers is expected to rise an average of 4 percent *per year* between 2000 and 2015. The proportion of younger workers is shrinking. No sector is feeling the effects of this demographic trend more forcefully or sooner than government. Without enough young replacements willing to fill the void, the coming retirement bubble could create huge personnel shortfalls in the 1.7 million employee federal workforce. According to David Walker, the chief of the Government Accountability Office, the retirement boom and related personnel issues are among the government's biggest "high-risk" problems. Yet little is being done to address these problems.[13]

To close the gap between future workforce supply and demand, federal, state, and local governments need a coordinated action plan that may include all phases of the employee life cycle: recruitment and selection, performance management, compensation and benefits, training and development, leadership development, career management, retention, and retirement. But before we can discuss these phases of the employee life cycle, one final aspect of the HRM environment must be explored.

Organizational Culture

Thus far we have been looking at external forces in the environment of an agency that influence its HR activities. But there is also an internal environment that exercises an influence—organizational culture.

Organizational culture can be defined as the predominant value system of an organization. When an organization's underlying values and beliefs are internalized by its members, several benefits ensue: the culture eases and economizes communications, facilitates organizational decision making and control, and may generate higher levels of cooperation and commitment. In short, organizational culture helps to overcome the centrifugal tendencies of a large bureaucracy by instilling in its members a sense of unity and common purpose.

This process can be encouraged through selection—people are hired because their personal values are already consistent with the organizational culture. It can also be encouraged through socialization—newcomers learn values and ways of behaving that are consistent with those of the organization. It can be promoted by constantly harping on watershed events in the organization's history that reaffirm the importance of its culture. And an agency can promote organizational culture through role models—exemplary individuals who convey the traits most valued by the culture.

Strong organizational cultures are rooted in strong traditions; but traditions, though important, do not by themselves *ensure* a strong organizational culture. Analysts from McKinsey & Company, a premier management consulting firm, looked at 30 companies with a reputation for having strong organizational cultures that engaged the "emotional energy" of employees. Though some companies, such as Southwest Airlines and Home Depot, excelled in this area, the analysts found that the Marine Corps outperformed them all.

While recognizing the obvious differences between the corps and a corporation, the team identified four Marine Corps managerial practices that many public and private organizations might do well to emulate. First, instead of the brief, rather perfunctory introduction to the organization's values that most firms give to employees, the marines make a huge investment by inculcating their core values (honor, courage, and commitment); assigning some of their best people to be recruiters and drill instructors; and focusing intensely on values throughout recruitment and training. Second, most organizations identify potential leaders among their frontline employees and virtually write off the rest as followers. The marines do not make that distinction; instead they train every frontline person to lead, a practice that has a powerful impact on morale. Third, most public- and private-sector managers resist devoting time and talent to the people in the bottom half of the organization, assuming that they will either function adequately or leave. The marines find the time to attend to poor and mediocre performers, even if it means personal sacrifice. Fourth, the marines encourage self-discipline as a part of building a strong organizational culture; they demand that everyone on the front line act with honor, courage, and commitment.

To summarize, an organization's culture can have an important effect on its success. By codifying and symbolizing so that everyone can see "the way we do things here," the culture can have a positive influence on employee behavior and working environments. In organizations with strong cultures, everyone knows and supports the agency's or business's objectives; in those with weak cultures—perhaps the Peace Corps can serve as an example—no clear purpose exists. Thus, organizational culture complements not only HRM but also the sense of mission, the process of strategy formulation discussed in Chapter 5.

The next logical question is, How do public managers actually change the culture? The organization's underlying value system cannot be managed in traditional ways using conventional techniques. To effect cultural change, managers must adopt a **symbolic manager** approach. Bolman and Deal explain that approach as follows:

Symbolic managers believe that the most important part of a leader's job is inspiration—giving people something they can believe in. People willgive their loyalty to an organization that has a unique identity and makes them feel that what they do is really important. Effective symbolic leaders are passionate about making their organizations the best of their kind and communicate that passion to others. They use dramatic, visible symbols that give people a sense of the organizational mission. They are visible and energetic. They create slogans, tell stories, hold rallies, give awards, appear where they are least expected, and manage by wandering around.

Symbolic leaders are sensitive to an organization's history and culture. They seek to use the best in an organization's traditions and values as a base for building a culture that provides cohesiveness and meaning. They articulate a vision that communicates the organization's unique capabilities and mission.

Organizational culture is not, of course, without liabilities. Important shared beliefs and values can interfere with the needs of the organization, the people who work in it, or the public. To the extent that the content of an organization's culture leads its people to think and act in inappropriate ways (for example, police being too aggressive), the culture will retard the attainment of positive results. Because cultures are not easily or quickly changed, that possibility should not be dismissed lightly.

Getting the Right People

Resources Planning

Human resources planning is the forecast of HR needs and the projected matching of people with expected vacancies. HR planning begins with three key questions. First, what new technologies are emerging, and how will they affect the work system? Second, what is the volume of work likely to be in the next five to ten years? And third, what is the turnover rate, and how much, if any, is avoidable? Answers to these questions help define the direction of the organization's HR strategy. Perhaps the organization will need to redefine the jobs and skills needed, begin to hire and train recruiters to look for a new set of skills, or provide new training for existing employees. By anticipating future HR needs, the organization can prepare itself to meet its objectives more effectively than if it were to react only when problems hit it in the face.

The Tennessee Valley Authority (TVA), for example, projects the skills and employee numbers (demand data) necessary to reach its goals within each of its business units. Once those numbers are in place, planners project the current employee numbers (supply data) over the "planning horizon" without new hires and taking into consideration the normal attrition of staff through death, retirement, resignation, and so forth. Comparison of the difference between supply and demand gives the "future gap" or "surplus situation." That knowledge enables planners to develop strategies and operational plans. Planners then communicate the action plan to employees and continue to evaluate and update the plan as the organization's needs change. Determining skill gaps and surplus information has helped the TVA develop a workforce plan to implement cross-organizational placement and retraining as alternatives to further employee cutbacks in the individual business units. Thus, planners provide a greater sense of stability for workers.[14]

Recruiting

Recruiting means more than just posting an examination announcement on a bulletin board. Every possible source of qualified candidates within the appropriate labor market must be reached. A program of positive recruitment includes elements such as the following:

- Writing examination announcements in clear, understandable language
- Advertising in publications that circulate to the various segments of the population, and using other media such as radio and television
- Establishing easy-to-reach job information centers
- Visiting colleges, high schools, and community organizations
- Using mobile or storefront recruiting centers
- Developing continuing contacts with minority and women's organizations

In 2001, the Office of Personnel Management made Recruitment One-Stop (ROS) one of its top e-government initiatives to attract the best and brightest candidates to the federal workforce. The ROS initiative has simplified the process of locating and applying for federal jobs. Through a series of enhancements to USAJOBS.com, the federal government's official one-stop source for jobs and employment information, ROS delivers many new job seekers features including improved job searching; clean, concise, understandable, and attractive job announcements; a "create once, use many" basic job résumé that can be used to apply to multiple vacancies, agencies, and systems; a résumé mining feature that allows fast, cost-effective candidate sourcing by federal managers and HR specialists; and online, real-time application status tracking.

If recruiting efforts have been successful, the employer has several qualified applicants. The most frequently used devices for assessing applicant qualifications are the application form, interview, and paper-and-pencil test. HR professionals may use a combination of these devices to obtain a valid prediction of employee job performance. **Test validity** refers to the relationship between one's score on a selection device and one's future job performance. A valid selection procedure will provide high scores that correspond to subsequent high job performance.

The application form is used to collect information about the applicant's education, previous job experience, and other background characteristics. Research shows that biographical information inventories can validly predict future job success. One pitfall to avoid is the inclusion of questions that are irrelevant to job success. In line with affirmative action, the application form should not ask questions that will arbitrarily adversely affect "protected groups" in their bid for employment. Background questions *must* be clearly related to the job.

The interview is used to hire persons in almost every job category in virtually every organization. The interview serves as a two-way communication channel that allows both the organization and the applicant to collect information that otherwise would be difficult to obtain. Although widely used, the interview as generally practiced is a poor predictor of later job performance. Researchers have identified many reasons for this. Interviewers frequently are unfamiliar with the job for which they are supposed to hire an employee. They tend to make decisions in the first few minutes of the interview before all relevant information has been gathered. They also may base questions on personal biases (such as against minority groups or physically unattractive persons and in favor of those similar to themselves). The interviewer may talk too much and spend time discussing matters irrelevant to the job.[15] The box insert on the next page explains how Japan and France recruit their top civil servants.

Testing

Many organizations use paper-and-pencil tests, such as intelligence tests, aptitude and ability tests, and personality inventories. A good test is not only valid but also reliable. Test reliability means that the employer can count on the test to measure the same factors in the same way each time it is given. If two people with equal skills take the test, they should receive equal scores. Some tests are very reliable but lack validity. For example, two candidates for a position could be given a test. It might fairly measure their skills, but those skills have nothing to do with the job. Other tests are valid but lack reliability. The employer must be careful that tests are both valid and reliable.

For any testing instrument to be considered useful, it must have both reliability and validity. The SAT mathematics exam for example, is viewed as reliable because a person

Global Perspective
Two Approaches to Civil Service Recruitment: A Global Perspective

Most countries have adopted one of two broad approaches to recruitment by merit. The first, called the mandarin system, is a hierarchical system with entry limited to promising candidates at the outset of their careers. "Mandarin system" traditionally referred to an elite group of civil servants in certain East Asian bureaucracies; in its more modern sense, it refers to a "corps-career" system that also includes lower and middle levels of the civil service. Recruitment is centralized and highly selective, generally on the basis of a rigorous entrance examination. Successful candidates are placed on a fast track into the best jobs in government. For the most part, these recruits, who are mostly generalists by educational background, are hired into a career stream or corps rather than for specific jobs. France and Japan best exemplify the mandarin system.

In Japan and a number of leading democracies, entering the nation's service is the most coveted choice of the best students. The reason is that in those places, career civil servants heavily influence policymaking at the highest levels. When those top students look 30 years into the future, they know they have a shot at the top.

In Japan, for example, the best students from the best department of the best university—the Tokyo University Law Department—stream into the influential ministries of Finance, Post and Telecommunications, Education, and Economy, Trade, and Industry (METI). Those who retire from the civil service at about age 55 engage in what the Japanese call *amakudari* (literally, "the descent from heaven") and take positions in big business.

Western European countries are similar to Japan in this respect. In France the very best students pass through one of the *grades écoles* (especially the École Nationale d'Administration, or ENA) and then may be into one of the five *grands corps d'état*—elite divisions of the French civil service. In Britain the dominance of Oxford and Cambridge ("Oxbridge") graduates in the senior civil service earns them the title of "mandarins," in a conscious echo of prerevolutionary China.

The second system, known as open recruitment, is a more flexible, decentralized, and increasingly market-driven approach to civil service recruitment. The Australian system, like the American, permits entry at any point in the hierarchy, without age restrictions, and complements its horizontal recruiting system with a Senior Executive Service aimed at building an elite group from within the civil service.

---

who takes a test on a Tuesday and gets a score of 650 will get a similar score if he takes the test on a Thursday. It is considered valid because scores are believed to correlate with an external reality—"scholastic aptitude"—and the test is seen as predictive of success in an academic setting. Though validity is the more important measure, it is impossible to achieve validity without reliability: if you take the SAT mathematics exam on a Tuesday and get a 650 and repeat on a Thursday and get a 400, the test is manifestly unreliable and clearly not able to gauge academic performance. Therfore, reliability is the threshold standard.

The fundamental question today is whether tests realistically measure the skills candidates must have to do their jobs effectively. Concerns over the relevance of written tests have led more and more departments and consulting firms to turn to alternative types of tests in which candidates perform tasks they would actually do if hired or promoted. For example, police candidates would be expected to handle correspondence, perform roll calls, and respond to simulated citizen complaints. Minorities tend to score much closer to whites in such performance tests, which proves that many minorities have abilities that traditional written tests do not capture.

But performance tests have their own problems. They are far more expensive and harder to administer than written tests. Because they are scored by people rather than by machines, performance tests are often seen as less objective. Most testing experts now recommend a Solomonic compromise: basing selections and promotions on a mix of written and performance tests.

Over the past 25 years, a number of researchers investigated the validity of personality measures for personnel-selection purposes. The overall conclusion from these studies was that the validity of personality as a predictor of job performance is quite low. However, at the time the studies were conducted, no well-accepted taxonomy existed for classifying personality traits. Consequently, it was not possible to determine whether there were consistent, meaningful relationships between particular personality constructs and performance criteria in different occupations.

In recent years, the views of many personality psychologists have converged regarding the structure and concepts of personality. Generally, researchers agree that five factors of personality can serve as a meaningful taxonomy for classifying personality attributes. The "big five" personality dimensions are as follows:

Extraversion	enthusiastic, spirited, extroverted, expressive, playful, gregarious, sociable, active, energetic, dominant, assertive, ambitious, courageous
Agreeableness	cooperative, helpful, amiable, cordial, friendly, empathic, understanding, considerate, courteous, generous, affectionate, easygoing, honest
Conscientiousness	organized, concise, efficient, self-disciplined, precise, cautious, punctual, deliberate, decisive, predictable, economical, logical
Neuroticism	defensive, fretful, insecure, emotionally unstable, temperamental, excitable, envious, nervous, anxious, fearful, gullible, intrusive
Openness to experience	contemplative, intellectual, insightful, complex, perceptive, bright, smart, curious, inquisitive, creative, innovative, sophisticated

Murray R. Barrick and Michael K. Mount investigated the relation of these factors to job performance for five occupational groups (professionals, police, managers, sales, and skilled).[16] Results indicated that one dimension of personality, conscientiousness, showed consistent relations with all job-performance criteria for all occupational groups. For the remaining personality dimensions, the estimated true score correlations varied by occupational group. Extraversion had the strongest influence on assessments of managerial potential. Overall, the results illustrate the benefits of using the **five-factor model of personality** in personnel selection.

In recent years, new insights into personality have been gained through research in the area of **emotional intelligence.** Emotional intelligence (EQ) includes four basic components:[17]

1. *Self-awareness:* The ability to accurately assess your own strengths and limitations and have a healthy sense of self-confidence.
2. *Self-management:* The ability to control disruptive or harmful emotions and balance one's moods so that worry, anxiety, fear, or anger do not cloud thinking and interfere with what needs to be done.
3. *Social awareness:* The ability to understand others and practice empathy.
4. *Relationship awareness:* The ability to connect to others, build positive relationships, respond to the emotions of others, and influence others.

Studies have found a positive relationship between job performance and high degrees of emotional intelligence in a variety of jobs. And, as you might recall, Fred Greenstein thought emotional intelligence the key quality of presidential leadership (see Chapter 8).

Employers love personality tests. Eighty-nine companies out of the *Fortune* 100 make use of just one of them (Myers-Briggs Type Indicator). But what do they really reveal? "Yet despite their prevalence—and the importance of the matters they are called upon to decide—personality tests have received surprisingly little scrutiny," writes Annie Murphy Paul in *The Cult of Personality.* Paul, a former editor of *Psychology Today,* argues that the virtues of tests that try to assess personality types are illusory: Research shows that a single person's scores are unstable, often changing over the course of years, weeks, even hours. (A subject may be "a good intuitive thinker in the afternoon but not in the morning," some researchers have noted.) And, worse, there is little evidence of the correlation of test scores with managerial effectiveness or team building.[18]

Selection

Once a competitive examination is completed, an employment list based on the examination results is established and the names of the highest-ranking candidates are presented to the appointing official for selection. This process is called **certification.** According to the merit concept, only a limited number of qualified candidates should be certified. To do otherwise, such as certifying a whole list of eligible candidates, for example, would change the basis for hiring from competitive merit to a "pass-fail" system.

Personnel systems usually follow the **rule of three,** which permits the appointing official to choose among the top three individuals certified, without passing over veterans. Why have a rule of three? The first reason is to overcome the objection that written tests cannot appraise personality factors adequately, that the examining process can produce individuals who may qualify intellectually but have serious personal problems. The second reason is to appease appointing officers by bringing them more into the process.

Regardless of the process by which candidates are certified, managers eventually face the decision of selecting one person to fill the vacancy. But what should the manager look for? In a word, strength. Writes Drucker:

> Whoever tries to place a man . . . in an organization to avoid weakness will end up at best with mediocrity. The idea that there are well-rounded people, people who have only strengths and no weaknesses . . . is a prescription for mediocrity . . . strong people always have strong weaknesses, too. Where there are peaks, there are valleys. And no one is strong in many areas. There is no such thing as a "good man." Good for what? is the question.[19]

Classification and Compensation

At all levels of government, the basis of the civil service is the position classification system. Simply stated, **position classification** involves identifying the duties and responsibilities of each position in an organization and then grouping the positions according to their similarities. To appreciate this important aspect of public personnel management, consider Figure 10.3 which divides all federal government white-collar jobs into 23 occupational groups. Each occupational group consists, in turn, of several specific occupations. For example, the Office of Personnel Management (OPM) divides the "investigation group" into 20 specific occupations. Note that the last named one in this list is border patrol agent. Depending on the scope and complexity of an investigator's responsibilities, which OPM spells out in excruciating detail, the position of border agent is classified as GS-5, GS-7, GS-9, or GS-11.

A good system can help the administrator make better decisions regarding the relationship of duties and responsibilities to the other concerns of personnel administration. After all, a fair compensation plan requires an understanding of the duties and responsibilities of each position ("equal pay for equal work"); effective examination and recruiting require knowledge of what the agency is examining and recruiting for; and determining the qualifications necessary for performing the job requires an understanding of what the job entails.

Although evaluating the difficulty of duties may not cause too many problems, evaluating and comparing *responsibilities* often does. How many subordinates are supervised? How much time is spent in actual supervision? Who is supervised? How much innovation is expected? To attempt to weigh these factors objectively is no easy task.

Some attack position classification as being obsolete. Although it once provided a way of treating people equitably and eliminating spoils, position classification is not always relevant to activities performed by the more sophisticated organizations discussed in Chapter 7. In such organizations, the work situation becomes too collegial, too free-form for rigid position classifications. In such an organization, position classification (or the rank-in-job approach) might be replaced with the **rank-in-person approach,** which uses the abilities and experience of the individual as the basis for making various personnel decisions (for

Figure 10.3   Federal Classification for White Collar Work: An Illustrative Example

Series	Occupational Group
0000	Miscellaneous Occupations Group
0100	Social Science, Psychology, and Welfare Group
0200	Human Resources Management Group
0300	General Administrative, Clerical, and Office Services Group
0400	Biological Sciences Group
0500	Accounting and Budget Group
0600	Medical, Hospital, Dental, and Public Health Group
0700	Veterinary Medical Science Group
0800	Engineering and Architecture Group
0900	Legal and Kindred Group
1000	Information and Arts Group
1100	Business and Industry Group
1200	Copyright, Patent, and Trademark Group
1300	Physical Sciences Group
1400	Library and Archives Group
1500	Mathematics and Statistics Group
1600	Equipment, Facilities, and Services Group
1700	Education Group
1800	Investigation Group
1900	Quality Assurance, Inspection, and Grading Group
2000	Supply Group
2100	Transportation Group
2200	Information Technology Group

Series	Occupation
1801	General Inspection, Investigation, and Compliance
1802	Compliance Inspection and Support
1810	General Investigating
1811	Criminal Investigating
1815	Air Safety Investigating
1816	Immigration Inspection
1822	Mine Safety and Health
1825	Aviation Safety
1850	Agricultural Commodity Warehouse Examining
1854	Alcohol, Tobacco, and Firearms Inspection
1862	Consumer Safety Inspection
1863	Food Inspection
1864	Public Health Quarantine Inspection
1881	Customs and Border Protection Interdiction
1884	Customs Patrol Officer
1889	Import Specialist
1890	Customs Inspection
1894	Customs Entry and Liquidating
1895	Customs and Border Protection
1896	Border Patrol Agent (BPA)*
	*See text for further breakdown.

example, setting of compensation). Examples of this kind of system include the military and college faculties. The rank-in-person concept therefore means that a person carries a rank regardless of the duties performed at a particular time.

Like position classification, **compensation** of public employees is a very important and often very controversial part of public personnel administration. Based on the discussion of motivation in Chapter 8, the importance to the employee of an adequate and equitable compensation schedule should be apparent. If the employee perceives that the plan is unfair, conflict is likely.

The Classification Act of 1949 established the general schedule in which some three-quarters of federal civil employees are found. The general schedule establishes for white-collar workers fifteen pay grades broadly defined in terms of responsibility, difficulty, and qualifications; within each grade are ten steps. Within-grade advancement occurs on a fixed schedule, though employees demonstrating "high quality performance" can receive "quality step increases."

The very top executives in the executive branch are paid under a system known as the Executive Schedule. Broadly speaking, the five Executive Schedule levels include the following job titles: level I, cabinet members; level II, deputy secretaries of major departments; level III, presidential advisers, chief administrators of major independent agencies, and undersecretaries; level IV, assistant secretaries, deputy undersecretaries, and general counsels in executive departments; and level V, deputy assistant secretaries, administrators, commissioners, and directors. The Senior Executive Service covers most managerial and policy positions in the executive branch that do not require Senate confirmation.

The federal government pays its employees at salary levels that are generally comparable to those in the private sector. However, the federal government provides fringe benefits that are 76 percent higher than those in the private sector. Why is this the case? In the 1920s, it was felt that neither civil service pay nor military pay was competitive with salaries in private business. Rather than simply raise pay, Congress decided to push costs far into the future (where current taxpayers and voters would not notice them) by setting up an exceedingly generous pension system.

Table 10.2 presents a table of General Schedule pay for 2004. General Schedule levels have ten pay steps, which allow for pay increases and differences within grades. In many state and local governments, pay is set primarily through collective bargaining (discussed at the end of the chapter).

Today the Veterans Health Administration more quickly hires nurses and pharmacists, the National Institute of Standards and Technology more easily retains top talent, and the Office of the Comptroller of the Currency more aggressively promotes continuous learning and self-improvement. These changes stem in part from the introduction of compensation systems that mirror some private-sector practices and are not bound by regular civil service law. The systems also place a premium on employee performance, especially when it comes to promotions and assignments. Newer pay systems typically give more discretion to managers in setting pay and usually deny a pay raise to employees who receive an unsatisfactory rating. They also link at least some part of annual raises to job performance. These features, which are part of planned changes at Defense and Homeland Security

Table 10.2   Salary Table 2009-GS Incorporating the 2.90% General Schedule Increase Effective January 2009

Annual Rates by Grade and Step

Grade	Step 1	Step 2	Step 3	Step 4	Step 5	Step 6	Step 7	Step 8	Step 9	Step 10
GS-1	$17,540	$18,126	$18,709	$19,290	$19,873	$20,216	$20,792	$21,373	$21,396	$21,944
2	19,721	20,190	20,842	21,396	21,635	22,271	22,907	23,543	24,179	24,815
3	21,517	22,234	22,951	23,668	24,385	25,102	25,819	26,536	27,253	27,970
4	24,156	24,961	25,766	26,571	27,376	28,181	28,986	29,791	30,596	31,401
5	27,026	27,927	28,828	29,729	30,630	31,531	32,432	33,333	34,234	35,135
6	30,125	31,129	32,133	33,137	34,141	35,145	36,149	37,153	38,157	39,161
7	33,477	34,593	35,709	36,825	37,941	39,057	40,173	41,289	42,405	43,521
8	37,075	38,311	39,547	40,783	42,019	43,255	44,491	45,727	46,963	48,199
9	40,949	41,314	43,679	45,044	46,409	47,774	49,139	50,504	51,869	53,234
10	45,095	46,598	48,101	49,604	51,107	52,610	54,113	55,616	57,119	58,622
11	49,544	51,195	52,846	54,497	56,148	57,799	59,450	61,101	62,752	64,403
12	59,383	61,362	63,341	65,320	67,299	69,728	71,257	73,236	72,215	77,194
13	70,615	72,969	75,323	77,677	80,031	82,385	84,093	87,093	89,447	91,801
14	83,445	86,227	82,009	91,791	94,573	97,355	102,919	102,919	105,701	108,483
15	98,156	101,428	104,700	107,972	111,244	114,516	121,060	121,060	124,332	127,604

departments, have caused some anxiety in those workforces. Unions, in particular, contend they could allow supervisors to play favorites.

Finally, we should note that competition for top talent in some public-sector jobs is producing a cadre of highly paid public executives. For example, Bob Kiley, who is credited with rebuilding both the Boston and New York City subway systems, was lured overseas to save the London Underground with a compensation package estimated to be worth over a half-million dollars.

Maximizing Performance

Training and Management Development

How important is training? A number of headlines help answer that question. The headline "Federal Aviation Administration's Training Courses for Inspectors Appallingly Obsolete" appeared after a Delta Air Lines crash in Texas killed fourteen. When the headline "Federal Narcotics Agents Raid the Wrong House" appeared, Justice Department officials were forced to admit that many drug enforcement agents had little enforcement experience and had been hired by agencies right after college. "Cities May Be Liable for Poor Training" appeared after the Supreme Court ruled in *City of Canton v. Harris* that cities and counties may have to pay damages if their employees are not trained properly. "Recruits in Police Academy Receive Twelve-Lesson Program on Racial Sensitivity" appeared a few months after charges of racial biases by community groups.

Proper training can, of course, do much more than reduce the footnote possibility of such indelicacies as midnight raids on the bedrooms of innocent citizens. In the first place, by providing employees with the opportunity to improve themselves, specific training and development programs help to reduce the number of dead-end jobs in an agency. Reducing the number of such jobs and providing opportunity for advancement can, in many instances, increase motivation. Further, training programs can help to remedy a situation faced by many minority groups, namely, the difficulty of attaining a government position because of skill deficiencies. Finally, training helps prepare employees for jobs that are unique to the public sector. As government continues to serve as the armature of technological progress and the champion of social progress, the number of these unique jobs will, very likely, increase.

For these reasons, then, managers should not prejudge training programs as time-consuming frills. On the contrary, they should look to their agency's employee-development branch as a key ally in their own tasks of employee motivation and program management. They should also be aware of the types of training programs available. The orientation program is perhaps the most elementary but is not unimportant. When well conceived, an orientation program can make employees more productive more quickly. **On-the-job training,** basically, is when an individual without all the needed skills or experience is hired and then learns the job from another employee.

For administrative, professional, and technical personnel, a wide variety of development programs are available, inside and outside the organization. For example, there are work-shops and institutes (such as the Federal Executive Institute at Charlottesville, Virginia), professional conferences, university and college programs, management development programs, internships, and sabbaticals. The **Intergovernmental Personnel Act of 1970** opened up federal in-service training programs to state and local employees and authorized grants to them. Similarly, the Labor Department's Public Service Careers Program and the Justice Department's Law Enforcement Assistance Administration also attempt to foster state and local training programs. Because the development of in-service training programs at these levels has lagged behind that of the federal government, these trends are to be applauded.

Nor should **job rotation**—systematically transferring employees from one job to another to provide them with variety and stimulation—be neglected as a method of providing for employee development. Herbert Kaufman furnishes an excellent example of how this type of training works.[20] Transfers in the U.S. Forest Service, he found, do not wait for vacancies; rather, they are made every three or four years to acquaint employees with the various perspectives of duties of employees at all job levels and with a variety of specialties. According to the service, such a practice seeks "the development, adjustment, and broadening of personnel." The advantages of such a program for developing a pool from which top management can be drawn are obvious. Compare it to an agency that allows its top management to progress up the ranks within one functional specialty.

Management development is training specifically targeted to improve a person's knowledge and skill in the fundamentals of management. If one is truly serious about a managerial career, management development activities should be an important part of one's personal agenda. Remember, too, the nature of one's management development needs may well vary as one progresses through different levels of responsibility. Management skills, accordingly, need continued nurturing and development.

An **assessment center** is a technique for selecting individuals with high managerial potential based on their performance on a series of simulated managerial tasks. For example, an assessment center could present a series of managerial situations to groups of applicants over, say, a two- or three-day period. One technique is the "in-basket" simulation, which requires the applicant to play the role of a manager who must decide how to respond to ten memos in his or her in-basket within a two-hour period. Panels of two or three trained judges observe the applicant's decisions and assess the extent to which they reflect interpersonal, communication, and problem-solving skills.

Assessment centers have proven to be valid predictors of managerial success, and some organizations now use them for hiring technical workers. The idea is to see whether candidates have sufficient "people skills" to fit into the work atmosphere. Assessment centers are important because they provide a more valid measure of interpersonal skills than do paper-and-pencil tests.

The first recorded use of assessment procedures was by the German army to help select officers during World War I; their first major use in the federal government was by the Internal Revenue Service in 1969. The last few years, however, have witnessed increasing application by government jurisdictions in the United States and Canada. For example, the State Department's orientation course uses simulated situations and crises, such as trying to negotiate freedom for an American tourist jailed in an unfriendly country. Diplomats in training also attend seminars at centers where, for several days, they simulate every aspect of an embassy's operation. Their instructors, all veteran Foreign Service officers, alternately praise and goad, pushing and stretching to get the maximum performance. The philosophy is simple: The more realistic the training, the fewer the surprises overseas. In general, research supports assessment centers as an effective selection method for new hires as well as for people moving up in an organization.[21]

Advancement

Most governmental jurisdictions provide that a new employee must serve a probation period for a limited time, usually six months. During this period, the manager should give the new employee special attention in matters of instruction, indoctrination, and general adjustment to the job. In theory, probation is the last phase of the testing process, for at this time the individual may be discharged without the right of appeal and reinstatement. Unfortunately, very few dismissals occur during probation. Apparently, few managers have the fortitude to judge others when careers are at stake.

A career service must provide opportunity for advancement. But that does not preclude filling positions from outside as well as from within the service to keep an organization from becoming too inbred or to obtain especially outstanding persons for positions above the entry level.

In state and local jurisdictions, a competitive promotional examination is often required of employees. In addition to examination, performance ratings can take the form of measurement of output (such as in the management-by-objectives system discussed in Chapter 9), rating characteristics, or narratives. The check-off or objective evaluation consists of rating employees on a scale concerning such qualities as writing ability, initiative, and promptness. The narrative approach allows managers to be more flexible in discussing the good and bad points of subordinates; but because such evaluations are difficult to compare and are more time consuming, they are less popular than the objective form.

The evaluation of an employee's progress measured in terms of job effectiveness is called **performance appraisal.** One criticism of performance appraisal as practiced in government is that the process is periodic rather than continuous. The manager should not wait until, say, the end of the year to tell an employee that he is not performing. Good and bad aspects of performance should be discussed *as they occur.*

Maintaining an Effective Workforce

Retaining the Best Employees

All levels of government strive to hire the new generation of the best and the brightest, sprucing up their Web sites, simplifying the application process, setting up booths at job fairs, running newspaper ads, and sending cadres of recruiters to college campuses. Unfortunately, many of these efforts are similar to turning on the faucet in your bathtub while the drain remains open. Too often the best and the brightest, once attracted to a public-sector job, don't stay. For example, the Department of Veterans Affairs has a high turnover of new claims specialists, with attrition rates reaching 49 percent at some regional offices. The training of these employees takes a minimum of 18 months, but the VA is not retaining those it trains. Similarly, the Patent and Trademark Office experiences a high turnover of skilled patent attorneys. The State Department, which continues to attract new recruits without difficulty, faces a serious problem in retaining midcareer foreign service officers.[22]

The key to retaining good workers is to provide an environment that is rewarding and flexible—both financially and personally. A National Academy of Public Administration (NAPA) study found that once reasonable pay compatibility is achieved "nonmonetary issues become more important.... [M]ost of the factors that cause people to stay or leave an organization are under the control of their immediate supervisor. People want training, career development opportunities, open communication, and flexible work arrangements. They want to be involved in decisions and in setting goals."[23]

A Gallup study of managerial behavior and organizational effectiveness came to similar conclusions. It found that responses to the following five questions were linked to employee retention:

Do I know what is expected of me at work?
Do I have the materials and equipment I need to do my work right?
Do I have the opportunity to do what I do best every day?
Does my supervisor, or someone else at work, seem to care about me as a person?
At work, do my opinions count?[24]

Research conducted over eight years at the Boston Consulting Group (BCG) has shown that some of the most successful companies are also among the most enlightened employers. Although the researchers had set out to study the characteristics of high-performing companies—not to examine human resources, but they soon discovered that all of the top performing companies had adopted unusually progressive policies toward their employees. These organizations exhibited two distinct traits. First, they paid exceptional attention to the traditional HR issues we discussed earlier—recruitment, compensation, training, performance appraisal, etc. Second, they had set up HR systems specifically for job satisfaction. The rationale for these systems is straightforward: "Satisfied employees not only perform better, but they also make better team members, coworkers, mentors, and colleagues. They are more cooperative, enthusiastic, energetic, innovative, and loyal to their employer. For all these reasons, it is in the best interest of an organization to pay attention to all the factors that determine job satisfaction and to devote resources to them."[25] In addition to compensation, these factors include the following: flexibility of work structure, staffing, and hours; personal benefits such as healthy living, child care, and elder care; and rewards and recognition for individual and team contributions.

How well has the U.S. federal government performed in these areas? According to Linda J. Bilmes, a lecturer in public policy at Harvard, and W. Scott Gould, Vice President for public sector at IBM, not as well as it could have.[26]

- **Work and Staffing Schedules**. Many countries around the world and many state governments in the United States permit greater flexibility in work and staffing schedules than the federal government. Canada allows its employees to work flexible hours and alternative work arrangements, such as telework, are commonplace. Although Utah has adopted a four-day work week, and many other states and local governments are experimenting with flexible work schedules in the federal goverment flexibility remains limited. The main permitted "alternative" is the compressed work schedule (CWS) which allows employees to work 80 hours over nine workdays, thus providing a Friday off every other week. In other compressed schedule programs, employees work ten hours a day, four days a week. Managers agreed that these programs tend to reduce absenteeism because employees have scheduled time off during regular business hours to complete necessary personal tasks. However, this flexibility is quite limited compared with that of the leading people organizations.

- **Telecommuting**. Replacing physical commuting to work with working from a remote location through a telecommunications link would appear to be an excellent idea for the government. Employees would save commuting time, not to mention the money spent on transportation, buying lunch, and related personal expenses. It is also good for the environment. But to date less than 40 percent of the federal workforce is telecommuting.

- **Job Sharing**. Leading companies use job sharing to meet various workforce circumstances. Most notably, it enables women with small children to remain employed by sharing a job with another flex-time employee, lets individuals deserving semiretirement to work part time (this may involve training the new person at the same time), and prevents redundancies when jobs are no longer needed full time. In all three cases, the federal government could use job sharing to its advantage. But supervisors need training in how to make it work and how to manage the career path of the person who is sharing a job. One agency that has begun to explore this practice is the Department of Justice which created an electronic job sharing bulletin board, where employees can express interest in or views on sharing positions.

- **Wellness**. Although federal employees have access to health insurance benefits, these can be supplemented by a variety of healthy living benefits. Such benefits are designed to strengthen the physical, mental, and emotional well-being of employees in both preventive and corrective care. For example, programs could be established to provide a range of free confidential counseling and referral services for employees whose personal problems may be affecting their health and job performance. Such programs could also address a variety of other issues: smoking cessation, promotion of exercise, weight and fitness management, vaccination, and stress reduction programs. Some programs of this nature have already been proved successful at the IRS and among civilian and uniformed personnel in the Air Force.

- **Childcare**. The leading people organizations understand that childcare is not simply a matter of providing an on-site day care center for babies and toddlers; it is about creating an atmosphere in which the company acknowledges that the parents must have the flexibility to take care of the children when necessary. "Parental responsi-bilities need to be fully recognized. A parent should not have to fabricate a dentist appointment in order to attend parent–teacher conferences during the regular work day." According to the GAO, providing federal workers with on-site or near-site childcare decreases absenteeism and allows employees to better focus on their job responsibilities.

Discipline and Grievances

Two of the more sensitive concerns of public personnel management are disciplining employees and listening to their complaints. Reprimands, suspensions, demotions, reassignments, and dismissals can obviously have an adverse effect on the career of an employee; accordingly, few managers enjoy situations that call for such forms of discipline. And yet, the public expects, quite rightly, efficient service from those paid by its taxes.

A grievance applies to a circumstance or condition that, in the opinion of those affected, constitutes a wrong and gives one just grounds for complaint. Even administrators who pride themselves on their open-door policy usually become unhappy when an employee begins to complain. A complaint seems to indicate that somehow the manager has failed, to a degree, as a manager. Whether an administrator finds discipline and grievances sensitive matters, she needs to keep several points in mind about each.

In disciplinary matters, the administrator should strive for improvement in employee performance. Such improvement is possible only if disciplinary policy and standards of performance are clearly understood by all and are impartially applied. Further, disciplinary actions should always be based on a careful assessment of the facts. Failure to do so not only is unjust but can result in considerable embarrassment for the administrator if the employee decides to refute the charges and have the disciplinary action reviewed by an impartial body.

Discipline in an organization takes many forms, oral and written reprimands being the most common. If the administrator can make it clear (1) that the objective of the reprimand is solely to correct employee action and (2) that mutual respect exists between the two, then these forms should work. Still the administrator should not turn to them too readily. Is the employee's action sufficiently important to require a reprimand? If the answer is yes, then are more indirect, less formal approaches available? A well thought-out hint or joke might suffice for the moderately perceptive employee.

If reprimands continue to prove ineffective, then more severe forms of discipline need to be considered: suspension, demotion, reassignment, and dismissal. In such cases, the administrator will probably need to turn to the personnel office for assistance.

Dismissal means being fired for cause; it does not refer to those employees who must leave government because of economic measures. Public administrators, like their counterparts in industry, avoid dismissal as long as possible. And this is for good reason: the process is unpleasant and difficult—especially when the administrator has failed to fully document the case against the employee. Even when the dismissed employee has no right of appeal for reinstatement, the administrator may suddenly face strong external pressure from legislators, influential friends, and professional groups. Internally, he might face displeasure from other employees.

Collective Bargaining: Six Critical Questions

Collective bargaining is a process whereby union and management officials attempt to resolve conflicts of interests in a manner that will sustain and possibly enrich their continuing relationship. (See Figure 10.4.) Although this process might not be a HRM tool like resource planning, testing, position classification, compensation, training and development, and performance appraisal, neither is it a "necessary evil." And the reason it is not was first articulated by one of the ablest of the Supreme Court justices, Louis V. Brandeis (1856–1941): "Don't assume that the interests of employer and employee are necessarily hostile—that what is good for one is necessarily bad for the other. The opposite is more apt to be the case. While they have different interests, they are likely to prosper or suffer together."

Labor relations is an important component of effective HRM for another reason: today public-sector unions are the fastest-growing unions in the United States. As pointed out earlier in the chapter, the unionization of public employees is substantially higher than the rate for private industry workers. Within the public sector, local government workers had the highest union membership rate, 42 percent.

Clearly, for managers in the public sector, understanding the process of collective bargaining comes with the territory. A process as important and complex as collective bargaining can

Figure 10.4   The Collective-Bargaining Process

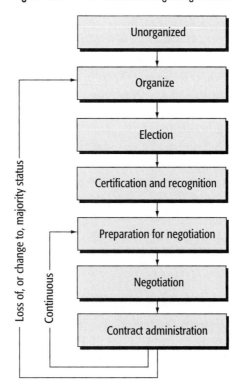

hardly be distilled into a series of questions. Nonetheless, six seem particularly important to understanding it.[27]

Who Is Going to Bargain for Management?
The bargaining structure within municipal government is very decentralized; with few exceptions, negotiations are conducted on a single-employer basis. The bargaining-unit coverage extends only as far as the municipal jurisdiction, and municipal officials are reluctant to relinquish their political autonomy and decision-making authority. How does this differ from the situation in the private sector? In the latter, you find a single employer negotiating with a single union, but you also find multi-employers bargaining. In such instances, more than one employer and the corresponding union each form one negotiating unit at the bargaining table. This type of centralized bargaining is common in the trucking, construction, and newspaper industries.

In the public sector, the chief administrative officer of the municipality will most frequently serve as chief negotiator, followed by the personnel director or an attorney retained by the city. If the negotiations activities become complex, the city is likely to employ a labor-relations professional as the chief negotiator.

In contrast to the situation in the private sector, the chief negotiator in the public sector often lacks authority to reach a final and binding agreement with the union on behalf of the public organization. The doctrine of sovereignty makes it difficult to delegate decision-making authority to specific administrative officials. Many state legislators and city council members refuse to relinquish their legislative authority to make final decisions on matters that they believe are important to effective government operations—after all, they feel directly responsible to the electorate.

The problem of determining "who is management?" can negatively affect the negotiations process in three ways. First, management can pass responsibility to other officials in the bargaining process. Union officers are often shuffled off to a variety of government officials in collective bargaining on the premise that another individual has specific authority for a particular issue or a portion of available funds.

Second, because public-sector bargaining is *multilateral*—involving various groups of community citizens, government officials, and the media as well as the formally designated negotiators—it often becomes an exercise in politics. Public-sector unions therefore often have opportunities to engage in **end-run bargaining** before, during, or after negotiations— that is, they make a direct appeal to the legislative body that will make final decisions on the agreement. Mayors can make concessions to the police association in return for its endorsement in the gubernatorial primary. Because public labor unions in many settings are politically potent, elected officials are generally more receptive to this end-run process than a corporate president would ever be.

Third, the unwillingness of some government agencies to delegate decision-making authority to a labor relations representative can result in a lack of labor relations understanding on management's side of the negotiation table. In some cases, taxpayers are affected if unions take advantage of the inexperienced management negotiators.

Who Is Going to Bargain for the Union?
Employees themselves decide by election who, if anyone, they wish to represent them in negotiations with management. But first a sufficient number

of employees (normally somewhere around 30 percent) decide whether there will be an election. They must also decide which unions will be on the ballot and which employees will be permitted to vote. A union becomes the bargaining agent for a group of employees if, and only if, it wins a majority.

It is of course impossible to have an election unless one knows who will be eligible to vote. Who will belong to the group to be represented? That decision is generally the province of a state employee relations board, though in some states the job falls to the civil service commission or to a division of the state labor department. The federal government uses the Federal Labor Relations Authority (FLRA) created by the Civil Service Reform Act (CSRA) of 1978. A group of employees permitted to bargain with their employers is known as a **bargaining unit.**

The appropriate bargaining units for exclusive recognition may be established on an agency, plant, installation, function, or some other basis to ensure a clear and identifiable community of interest among employees and to promote effective dealings with efficiency of the agency operations. The criteria used for determining a community of interest include common duties and skills, similar working conditions, and common supervision and work site. Similarly, certain positions are generally excluded from the bargaining unit, such as confidential employees, management and supervisory personnel, personnel employees, and professionals (unless they vote in favor of inclusion).

In the federal government, about 60 percent of all eligible employees are represented by various labor organizations in 2,589 bargaining units, and 87 percent are covered by labor agreements. The state of Washington, which defines its bargaining units in agency terms, has 117 separate units. Agency units have the advantage of allowing purpose or mission to play a prominent role in bargaining decisions, but this arrangement can lead to serious problems of equity for occupational groups whose members work in many different agencies. On the other hand, a single union representing a wide range of occupational groups may have trouble remaining cohesive.

What Will Management and Labor Bargain About?

Not surprisingly, public employee units would like to bargain about wages. They can, but only if the jurisdictions that employ their members agree to it. The biggest of jurisdictions, the federal government, doesn't. Less than half of the states have agreed to bargain about wages. At the local level, public employee unions have the best chance: the majority of municipalities include wages among the subjects that can be put on the bargaining table.

Two subjects are off-limits to collective bargaining in virtually every jurisdiction: the process and criteria for selecting employees and the agency mission. Why is this? Refusing to bargain about selection processes and criteria has traditionally been seen as a way of protecting the merit system. Further, some have argued that union influence over the employee selection process and criteria might undermine the policy of affirmative action. The decision not to bargain about agency mission is based on the ideal of administrative responsibility, which was discussed in Chapter 4. Elected officials—or, at least, individuals directly and clearly responsible to elected officials—are supposed to make public policy.

"When a question is put on the collective bargaining table—often behind closed doors—it tends to be one or two giant steps removed from public control."[28]

As in the private sector, the federal agency and the recognized union must meet at reasonable times and confer in good faith with respect to *mandatory* subjects of collective bargaining, such as certain personnel policies and practices and working conditions, to the extent that appropriate laws and regulations allow such negotiations. The parties are allowed to bargain over subjects that are *permissible,* but the CSRA does not require negotiation over permissible subjects. Permissible subjects include numbers, types, and grades of positions assigned to any organizational unit, work project, or tour of duty; technology of the workplace; and methods and means of performing the work.

What Happens of the Negotiators Cannot Reach an Agreement?

An **impasse** is a stalemate in negotiations between management and unions over the terms and conditions of employment. Impasses are often resolved through mediation, fact-finding, or arbitration. These impasse resolution procedures are controversial and have received considerable attention; they have been instituted in 38 states. Impasse resolution procedures may combine mediation, fact-finding, and arbitration (available in 20 states). Fact-finding is a legislatively mandated mechanism in public sector bargaining in 31 states, second only to mediation, which is required in 35.

Mediation involves a neutral third party—think of a marriage counselor—who has no binding authority but assists the parties in reaching an agreement. Of the impasse resolution procedures used in the public sector, mediation is the least intrusive and is little more than an adjunct to the negotiations process. The key ingredient for mediator effectiveness is experience, with related mediator training and knowledge. Effective mediators need tenacity—for example, not taking "no" for an answer—and they need to take an active role in the process by such actions as pressuring the parties with successive proposals for compromise, rather than simply relaying messages back and forth. Mediation tends to be more successful when the parties are unsure of themselves or have personality conflicts.

Fact-finding and arbitration both involve a neutral third party who, through a quasi-judicial hearing, assesses the bargaining positions of the union and management. If a settlement cannot be reached, the fact finder's report is published in the local media so that citizens know who is responsible for continuing the dispute. However, these recommendations are not binding. The final decisions are generally left to the elected legislative body.

Arbitration entails a binding decision by a neutral third party that settles the negotiation impasse. A variation of this technique is *final offer selection arbitration,* in which the arbitrator either selects the best package settlement presented by the union or management or resolves the impasse on an issue-by-issue basis. In either case, the arbitrator can select only one party's final offer—there is no compromise or splitting the difference.[29]

Fact-finding and arbitration can be successful in resolving impasses because these techniques provide deadlines for the parties to resolve their differences, fresh and knowledgeable perspectives, and political advantages because negotiators can blame the neutral party for the eventual settlement. Also, the mere possibility of these procedures might pressure the negotiators to resolve their differences for fear that the neutral party would not understand their position.

These techniques can also carry some disadvantages. For example, the fact-finder's recommendation and the arbitrator's decision might not resolve genuine union–management differences. Moreover, these techniques might cause the negotiators to cement their respective positions because the parties believe they can get a better deal from the third party. Instead of honestly attempting to resolve their differences in the final negotiations, the representatives focus their time and thoughts on preparing for the fact-finder or arbitrator.

Should Public Employees Be Allowed to Strike?   To repeat, the goal of the collective bargaining process is to produce a contract. When it does not work out that way and arbitration fails, labor can turn to its ultimate weapon: the strike.

The right to strike, considered by many a vital instrument for successful collective bargaining, is usually prohibited by law in the public sector. The basic argument given for prohibiting strikes is that the services provided by public organizations such as police and firefighters are essential to the general welfare and that work stoppages adversely affect the delivery of these vital services and create disorder. The words "essential services" are, however, subject to diverse interpretations. Some maintain that all public services are essential, whereas others suggest that many public employee classifications such as clerks and mechanics are not so essential. Another argument to prohibit strikes is that this weapon places too much power in the hands of the union relative to the taxpayer. Moreover, unions would unnecessarily benefit at the expense of other groups that are dependent on government revenues but do not strike.

Arguments aside, significant strikes have occurred in the public sector. The largest number of strikes occur in education, and seven states—California, Illinois, Michigan, New Jersey, New York, Ohio, and Pennsylvania—account for 90 percent of these idle days. Moreover, strikes are often prolonged until all strikers or discharged employees have been granted amnesty or reinstated to former positions.

Thus, laws have not prevented strikes. Laws have not been invoked against all employees who have participated in strikes, and when invoked, the laws have not been applied equally to all strikers. Some believe that laws prohibiting strikes may have deterred some strikes, and injunctions may have had a sobering effect on some strikers, but prohibiting strikes by passing laws has been unsuccessful. Strikes have occurred in Oregon, Ohio, and Illinois—where they are permitted—but they have also occurred where strikes are prohibited. The 60-hour strike against the New York Metropolitan Transit Authority just before Christmas 2005 was a prominent example of the latter. New York's "Taylor Law" forbids transit workers from striking. Accordingly, city and state government officials pressed the courts to impose a hefty fine. A Brooklyn judge obliged by fining the union $2.5 million, indefinitely suspending its ability to automatically collect dues, and sentencing the transit worker union local president to ten days in jail. Just three days after going on strike, transit workers returned to work without having made any progress whatsoever on the issue of wages, pensions, and health-care benefits—which was, after all, the point of their strike. (See photo on page 477.)

The New York City transport workers' contract expired on December 16, 2005. Union leaders called a strike on December 20 when talks with MTA, a state agency, deadlocked. The shutdown of the nation's largest public transit system forced millions of subway and bus riders to walk, bike, or squeeze into commuter trains in the freezing cold to get around the city at the height of the holiday shopping season. Above, thousands of New Yorkers enter lower Manhattan by foot via the Brooklyn Bridge.

Because most jurisdictions prohibit strikes, a **job action** of some kind—of which strikes are only one variety—may take another form. The "blue flu" strikes substantial numbers of police officers, and the "red rash" affects firefighters—all on the same day. Similarly, teachers can have sick-ins, and sanitation workers can engage in work slowdowns. Thus, what constitutes an actual strike against government employers may not be as easy to determine as one might think.

At the federal level, a watershed event in strike history occurred on August 3, 1981, when 13000 of the 17500 members of the Professional Air Traffic Controllers Organization (PATCO) walked off the job. Shortly thereafter, President Reagan held a press conference to announce that any air traffic controller who didn't return to work in 48 hours would be fired. He said, "Let me read the solemn oath taken by each of these employees, a sworn affidavit, when they accepted their jobs: *I am not participating in any strike against the government of the United States or any agency thereof, and I will not so participate while an employee of the Government of the United States or any agency thereof.'"*

Although Congress had made such strikes a crime in 1955, federal employees were staging strikes all the time at that point, including recent ones by postal workers and by employees at the Library of Congress and the Government Printing Office. But this time Reagan had decided to enforce the law. And not without reason: research shows that poorly enforced prohibitions and legalization of strikes increase the frequency of strikes.

Robert Poli, the PATCO president, assumed that Reagan was bluffing and would never fire the striking controllers. Reagan, of course, was not bluffing. He fired more than 11000 strikers. The government contingency plans for running the air-traffic system and replacing the fired strikers worked.

Now, fast-forward to early 2006. The federal union that Reagan fired was making new demands—a larger contract. For nearly six months, the Federal Aviation Administration (FAA) and NATCA (the union successor to PATCO) negotiated. With the airline industry under financial strain and the federal air traffic control system needing upgrades, the FAA was trying to limit growth in one of the richest contracts in government. But this time the union was in a stronger position than it was in 1981 because of 1996 legislation that gave it the right to bargain over its wages and benefits. This was a remarkable grant of power by the president and Congress; most federal unions have their pay set by the government. Not surprisingly, controller compensation through 2005 increased by 75 percent and today averages $166000. The 1996 bargaining deal included a stipulation that, if the FAA–NATCA negotiations reached a standstill, Congress could step in and make the final decision. But if Congress failed to act within 60 days – and that was a real possibility – then the FAA's offer would prevail. Not surprisingly the union preferred to continue the negotiations while operating under existing contract.

How Is a Contract Administered?   Although collective bargaining may end when the contract is ratified, labor relations do not. The provisions of the contract must be interpreted. First and most important, people besides those who negotiate a contract have to know what's in it—that means employees, frontline supervisors, midlevel administrators, union stewards, and top management. Unfortunately, that effort is not made often enough due to the underfunding of training. But failure to provide the necessary training isn't just a matter of money. "There is also the problem of finding the time, particularly the time of those who actually know what is in a contract—namely, those who negotiated it."[30]

Some jurisdictions have, however, been willing to pay for the kind of training that makes for more effective and less contentious contract administration. For example, Minnesota decided that such training would probably save money over the life of a contract and, with help from the Industrial Relations Center at the University of Minnesota, union representatives and people from the state personnel office conducted a series of workshops on each new contract renegotiated between the state and its employees.[31]

But it is not enough for everyone to know what a contract says: they have to agree on what it means. Sometimes contract language is vague—whether deliberately or accidentally—and somebody must interpret. Other times, contract language will seem precise enough on the surface, yet someone will raise a question not anticipated by the negotiators when they drafted the seemingly precise language. Again interpretations will be required. Say a state agrees to pay the tuition of state employees taking university courses related to their jobs. Which courses are "job-related"? How related should they be? Some might argue that any good university course can be considered relevant to work. After all, the British Empire was run reasonably well by men educated chiefly in Greek and Latin.

Not surprisingly, a good deal of contract interpretation comes in the context of a disagreement between employer and employee. Someone has done something the other side feels is a violation of the contract that exists between them, and the unhappy party wants it stopped. The hope is, of course, that the aggrieved party can go to the other person and convince that person to stop. It works, but not often enough to avoid the need for a formal process for handling such grievances.

The formal grievance process normally consists of four steps. First is an oral discussion, usually involving the employee, his or her first-line supervisor, and the relevant union stewards. If that discussion does not resolve the issue, next comes a written appeal to the department head. If the department head's decision does not satisfy both sides, then a further written appeal could be filed with the jurisdiction's personnel or labor relations office.

Finally, if all else fails, an arbitrator will be called on to decide if the contract has been violated. Most contracts spell out procedures for selecting arbitrators. Usually that process calls for the creation of a list of potential arbitrators with the two sides then alternating striking names from the list until only one remains. People who do this sort of arbitration—*grievance arbitration,* as opposed to interest arbitration (the type discussed on page 475)—have a great deal of discretion, but they still try to use as their primary guide the "intent" of the negotiators. Failing that, they will turn to (a) traditional practice in the organization or jurisdiction or (b) normal practice elsewhere.

A study of the attitudes of union stewards toward filing grievances in the public sector demonstrated that grievance rates tend to be reduced when management negotiators were perceived as accommodating rather than combative during hearing negotiations. Grievance rates tend to increase or decrease depending on whether union stewards perceive their union members to be combative or cooperative toward their government managers. The study also found that if an informal method of communication existed, fewer grievances were filed. Surprisingly, the clarity of a collective bargaining agreement had little effect on the number of grievances filed. If the relationship between the parties tended to be combative or cooperative, disagreements over a contract language followed that same pattern.[32]

Concluding Observations

This chapter has presented HRM as a set of activities performed by all managers rather than a set of functions locked within an HR department. An organization's human resources are its most fundamental source of effectiveness. In addition, individual managers can create effectiveness for themselves in their careers through superior management of human resources. In particular, managers who can align their management of human resources with the strategy of the organization may find themselves in a superior position relative to their peers.

Few successful managers leave activities such as recruiting, selection, training, or development of their employees entirely to the HR department. Although such departments in most governments play a formal role in all the activities covered in this chapter, successful public administrators do what they can to get the right people and maximize their performance. And for good reason. As the public sector continues to push toward being knowledge based, the effective management of people becomes increasingly important—after all, that is where critical information and knowledge reside.

Concepts for Review

affirmative action program	job rotation
arbitration	management development
assessment center	mediation
bargaining unit	merit principle
bona fide occupational qualification (BFOQ)	Merit Systems Protection Board (MSPB)
	Office of Personnel Management (OPM)
certification	on-the-job training
Civil Service Reform Act of 1978	organizational culture
collective bargaining	patronage
compensation	performance appraisal
disparate impact	position classification
disparate treatment	rank-in-person approach
emotional intelligence	rule of three
end-run bargaining	Senior Executive Service (SES)
fact-finding	sexual harassment
five-factor model of personality	spoils system
Hatch Act	symbolic management
impasse	test reliability
Intergovernmental Personnel Act of 1970	test validity
job action	Title VII, Civil Rights Act of 1964

Key Points

This chapter focused on human resources management in the government. Human resources management includes human resources planning, staffing, performance evaluation, management development, compensation, and labor relations. None of these activities is performed in a vacuum; all must be appropriate to the agency's mission and its environment. The chapter made these major points:

1. The development of public personnel management in the United States has gone through six periods: Government by Gentlemen: The Guardian Period (1789–1829);

Government by the Common Man: The Spoils Period (1829–1883); Government by the Good: The Reform Period (1883–1906); Government by the Efficient: The Scientific Management Period (1906–1937); Government by Administration: The Management Period (1937–1955); and Government by Shared Power (1955–present). The decades since the 1950s have been characterized by the emergence of multiple sources of power affecting the management of public employees: professionals, unions, minorities and women, public managers, contractors, and consumers.

2. The Civil Service Reform Act of 1978 split the Civil Service Commission into two units: the Office of Personnel Management and the Merit Systems Protection Board. In addition, the act created a separate personnel system for the highest-ranking civil service officials. The Senior Executive Service encompasses nearly 7000 executives. Thirdly, the act restated and elaborated one of the fundamental themes of public personnel administration in the United States—the merit principle. Finally, the act brought federal labor relations under one comprehensive act and established an independent Federal Labor Relations Authority.

3. Title VII of the Civil Rights Act of 1964 prohibits employers from discriminating on the basis of race, color, religion, gender, or national origin. It also prohibits sexual harassment and discrimination because of pregnancy and permits employers to develop affirmative action plans.

4. Plaintiffs in Title VII cases can prove discrimination in different ways: disparate treatment and disparate impact. Defendants have three possible defenses: bona fide occupational qualification (BFOQ), seniority, and merit.

5. Sexual harassment involves unwelcome sexual advances, request for sexual favors, and other verbal or physical conduct of a sexual nature. There are two major categories of sexual harassment—*quid pro quo* and hostile work environment.

6. Other major federal laws affecting human resources management are the Equal Pay Act of 1963, the Age Discrimination Act of 1967, Americans with Disabilities Act of 1990, and the Family and Medical Leave Act of 1993.

7. With regard to free speech, the Supreme Court has ruled that it is essential to maintain a balance between the rights of public employees as citizens and the interests of public employers in providing services. To set aside individual rights, it is necessary for public employers to show that their ability to function properly and provide effective services is seriously threatened.

8. Although there is no mention of privacy in the Constitution, in *Griswold v. Connecticut* the Supreme Court pulled together elements of the First, Third, Fourth, Fifth, and Fourteenth Amendments to recognize that personal privacy is one of the rights protected by the Constitution. For government employees, concerns about privacy revolve primarily around four issues: drug testing, searches, sexual orientation, and living arrangements.

9. In the next two decades, three important demographic trends will play out in the public-sector workforce: increasing ethnic diversity, growing number of aging baby boomers in the population, and fewer young people who follow behind them.

10. Organizational culture is the predominant value system of an organization. When an organization's underlying values and beliefs are internalized by its members,

several benefits ensue: the culture eases and economizes communications, facilitates organizational decision making and control, and may generate higher levels of cooperation and commitment. In short, organizational culture helps overcome the centrifugal tendencies of a large bureaucracy by instilling in its members a sense of unity in common purpose.

11. A symbolic manager defines and uses signals and symbols to influence culture in two basic ways: first, she articulates a vision for organizational change that generates excitement and that employees can believe in; second, she encourages the day-to-day activities that reinforce that vision. The symbolic manager makes sure that symbols, ceremonies, and slogans match the new values. Actions speak louder than words. Symbolic managers "walk their talk."

12. Human resources planning is the forecast of human resources needs and the projected matching of people with expected vacancies. Human resources planning begins with three key questions. What new technologies are emerging, and how will they affect the work system? What is the volume of work likely to be in the next five to ten years? And what is the turnover rate, and how much, if any, is avoidable?

13. Merit recruiting means more than just posting an examination announcement on a bulletin board. Every possible source of qualified candidates within the appropriate labor market must be reached.

14. Test validity refers to the relationship between one's score on a selection device and one's future job performance. A valid selection procedure will provide high scores that correspond to subsequent high job performance. Test reliability means that the employer can count on the test to measure the same factors in the same way each time it is given.

15. The big five personality dimensions are extraversion, agreeableness, conscientiousness, neuroticism, and openness to experience. One dimension of personality, conscientiousness, showed consistent relations with all job-performance criteria for all occupational groups. For the remaining personality dimensions, the estimated true score correlations varied by occupational groups.

16. Once a competitive examination is completed, an employment list based on the examination results is established and the names of the highest-ranking candidates are presented to the appointing official for selection. This process is called certification.

17. At all levels of government, the basis of the civil service is the position classification system. It involves identifying the duties and responsibilities of each position in an organization and then grouping the positions according to their similarities.

18. Management development is training specifically targeted to improve a person's knowledge and skills in the fundamentals of management. If one is truly serious about a managerial career, management development activities should be an important part of one's personal agenda.

19. The evaluation of an employee's progress measured in terms of job effectiveness is called performance appraisal. One criticism of performance appraisal, as practiced in government, is that the process is periodic rather than continuous.

20. In disciplinary matters, the administrator should strive for improvement in employee performance. Such improvement is possible only when the organization's disciplinary

policy and standards of performance are clearly understood by all and are impartially implied. Disciplinary actions should always be based on a careful assessment of the facts.

21. Collective bargaining is a process whereby union and management officials attempt to resolve conflict of interest in a manner that will sustain and possibly enrich their continuing relationship.

22. In the public sector, bargaining by management is inevitably complicated by the fact that effective government almost certainly demands the negotiating be done mostly by the executive branch, but the goal of responsible government means a place for the legislative branch, which appropriates the money, must be provided. Bargaining on the union side raises questions of bargaining unit determination—what to do with supervisors, whether employees should be grouped by agency or occupation, and so on.

23. Unions want the scope of bargaining to be broad. They certainly want to discuss wages, and they almost certainly want to discuss a great deal more. Management usually wants to keep the scope of bargaining narrow.

24. When bargaining fails, two choices appear. First is the possibility of a strike, although the federal government and most states prohibit them. Second is the process of mediation, fact-finding, and arbitration. Bringing in an outsider in any of those three roles can raise problems, but the problems are greatest in the case of arbitration. Why? Because citizens now have to face the question of the possible deleterious effect of the arbitrator on the ideal of administrative responsibility.

Problems and Applications

1. Develop a set of questions that you would ask a job candidate. (Specify the position.) With one of your classmates playing the role of candidate, conduct your interview before the class. Have the class critique your performance.

2. Select a public-sector job and then decide from among the following what the examination used to determine the fitness and ability of applicants for that job should consist of: (a) written test, (b) performance test, (c) evaluation of education and experience as shown on the application, (d) oral examination, (e) interview, (f) physical test, and (g) health examination. How would you weigh each part? Be prepared to defend your choices.

3. Do you agree with Peter Drucker's statement on the primary importance of job skill in hiring? Can you think of any other traits that might be at least equally important?

4. Identify some organization with which you are reasonably familiar. Then design a performance appraisal form for managers. (Hint: The lists of leadership traits on pages 353–356 might be a good place to start.) Would you weight the traits to determine a raw score? Why or why not?

5. Diversity means an inclusive workforce made up of people of different human qualities or who belong to various cultural groups. From the perspective of individuals, diversity means including people different from themselves along dimensions such as age,

ethnicity, gender, or race. If you were a senior manager at an organization such as the FBI, CIA, or National Security Agency, how would you address the diversity issue? More specifically, how would you answer the following three questions:

- Why have a diversity program given all the other priorities that your agency confronts?
- How is diversity defined in your organization?
- Can you give specific examples of how your diversity recruiting programs work and what kinds of things you are doing to implement your programs?

Favorite Bookmarks

www.ipma-hr.org   The Web site of the International Personnel Management Association provides links to government Web sites and other human resources Web sites.

www.fmcs.gov/aboutfmcs.htm   The Federal Mediation and Conciliation Service was created by Congress in 1947 to promote sound and stable labor management relations. The site has a reading room and offers case studies.

www.aad.english.uscb.edu   This site presents diverse opinions regarding affirmative action topics; rather than taking a singular pro or con position, it is designed to help lend many different voices to the debates surrounding the issues of affirmative action.

www.afscme.org   The American Federation of State, County, and Municipal Employees (AFSCME) is the largest union of state and local government employees.

Notes

1. See Douglas C. North, *Institutions, Institutional Change, and Economic Performance* (New York: Cambridge University Press, 1990). For a critique of the path-dependence paradigm, see Stan J. Liebowitz and Stephen E. Margolis, *Winners, Losers & Microsoft: Competition and Antitrust in High Technology* (Oakland, CA: The Independent Institute, 1999).
2. The following discussion is based on Frederick C. Mosher, *Democracy and the Public Service* (New York: Oxford, 1968) and Dennis L. Dresang, *Public Personnel Management and Public Policy* (New York: Longman, 2002).
3. Dresang, op. cit., 25.
4. Ibid., 27.
5. Ibid., 28.
6. Mosher, op. cit., 123.
7. For a more detailed look at the legal proceedings that municipal governments are subject to regarding the day-to-day human resources function, see P. Edward French, "Employment Laws and the Public Sector Employer: Lessons to be Learned from a Review of Lawsuits Filed against Local Governments," *Public Administration Review* (January/February 2009): 92–103.
8. Philip J. Cooper, *Public Law and Public Administration* (Itasca, IL: Peacock, 2000), 477.
9. Om Prakash, "The Efficacy of Don't Ask, Don't Tell," *Joint Force Quarterly* (October 2009): 88–95.
10. See June Kronholz, "Racial Identity's Gray Area," *New York Times* (June 12, 2008).
11. See Gregory Rodriguez, "Mongrel America," *Atlantic* (January/February 2003): 95–97; Ruth La Ferla, "Generation E. A.: Ethnically Ambiguous," *New York Times* (December 28, 2003); Peter H. Schuck, *Diversity in America* (Cambridge, MA: Harvard University Press, 2003).

12. Ronald Alsop, "Schools, Recruiters Try to Define Traits of Future Students," *Wall Street Journal* (February 14, 2006); Danielle Sachs, "Scenes from the Cultural Clash," *Fast Company* (January/February 2006).

13. Kelly K. Spors and John J. Fialka, "Filling a Public-Service Void," *Wall Street Journal* (September 19, 2002).

14. David E. Ripley, "How to Determine Future Work Force Needs," *Personnel Journal* (January 1995).

15. James M. Jenks and Brian L. P. Zevnik, "ABCs of Job Interviewing," *Harvard Business Review* (July–August 1989).

16. Murray R. Barrick and Michael K. Mount, "The Big Five Personality Dimensions and Job Performance: A Meta-analysis," *Personal Psychology,* 44 (1991).

17. Daniel Goleman, "Leadership That Gets Results," *Harvard Business Review* (March–April 2000), 79–90; *Daniel Goleman, Emotional Intelligence: Why It Can Matter More Than IQ* (New York: Bantam Books, 1995).

18. Annie Murphy Paul, *The Cult of Personality* (New York: Free Press, 2004). See also Malcolm Gladwell, "Personality Plus," *New Yorker* (September 20, 2004).

19. Peter F. Drucker, *The Effective Executive* (New York: Harper & Row, 1966), 72–73.

20. H. Kaufman, *The Forest Ranger: A Study of Administrative Behavior* (Baltimore, MD: Johns Hopkins University Press, 1960).

21. James Rudner, "Pre-Employment Testing and Employee Productivity," *Public Management,* 21, no. 2 (1992): 133–50.

22. Linda J. Bilmes and W.Scott Gould, *The People Factor: Strengthening America by Investing in Public Service* (Washington: Brookings, 2009), 160. See also Katherine Barrett and Richard Greene, "The Future Is Now," *Governing* (November 2007).

23. National Academy of Public Administration, Human Resources Management Panel, "A Work Experience Second to None: Impelling the Best to Serve" (Washington, 2001), page xi.

24. Marcus Buckingham and Curt Coffman, *First, Break All the Rules: What the World's Greatest Managers Do Differently* (New York: Simon & Schuster, 1999), page 33.

25. Bilmes and Gould, op. cit., page 163.

26. The following information in draws heavily on Bilmes and Gould, op. cit., pages 163–68.

27. The following discussion draws heavily on Benjamin Aaron et al., *Public Sector Bargaining* (Washington, DC: Bureau of National Affairs, 1988); Ronald D. Sylvia and C. Kenneth Meyer, *Public Personnel Administration* (Belmont, CA: Wadsworth, 2002); William H. Holley, Jr., and Kenneth M. Jennings, *The Labor Relations Process* (Fort Worth: Harcourt Brace, 1997); Dennis Riley, *Public Personnel Administration* (New York: Longman, 2002); Michael R. Carrell and Christina Heavrin, *Labor Relations and Collective Bargaining* (Upper Saddle River, NJ: Prentice Hall, 1998); Alan E. Bent and T. Zane Reeves, *Collective Bargaining in the Public Sector* (Menlo Park, CA: Benjamin Cummings, 1978).

28. Riley, op. cit., 138.

29. Actually, arbitration can take many forms. "It may be compulsory (required by law) or mandatory (required by the terms of contract). The findings of the arbitrator may be binding on both parties or only on the union—or they may be merely advisory in nature. A distinction must also be made between arbitration of issues that will go into a contract under negotiation (interest arbitration) and arbitration of disputes growing out of contract (grievance arbitration). A further distinction is between arbitration in which the arbitrator may choose to rule for one side on some issues and for the opposite on others (line-item arbitration) and arbitration that requires the arbitrator to choose between the final offers of the disputants" (Sylvia and Meyer, op. cit., 264).

30. Riley, op. cit., 148.

31. Michael Garvey and George E. O'Connell, "From Conflict to Cooperation: A Joint Labor-Management Training Program," *Public Personnel Management* (September/October 1976): 347–52.

32. Michael J. Duane, "To Grieve or Not to Grieve," *Public Personnel Management,* 20, no. 1 (April 1991): 83–90.

CASE 10.1
THE STAR AWARD

As director of the excise audit bureau in the West Dakota Department of Taxation, you have to decide who on your staff should receive a new performance bonus. The legislature created the bonus back in February, and the division of personnel has now issued all the regulations. You have the forms and instructions, and by the end of the month, you have to send your choices to the taxation commissioner, who will forward them to personnel.

Two things motivated the West Dakota legislature to create the performance bonus. First, key legislators had concluded that state employees were simply not working hard enough. Legislators constantly receive complaints about the lackadaisical attitude of state workers, and they concluded that the fixed civil service pay scale was not attracting new talent or motivating existing employees.

Second, West Dakota is running a budget surplus for the second straight year. Naturally, the legislature has cut taxes—twice. But despite those efforts, the budget continues to show a surplus. Consequently, the Speaker of the House decided to use a portion of it to reward the "stars" of state government.

The new Star Award will give the top 20 percent of employees in each unit a $5000 bonus, to be paid in 12 monthly installments during the coming fiscal year. The bonus is supposed to go to those employees who are not only "outstanding" but also genuine stars. The head of each unit must determine the criteria for choosing who the stars are. To ensure that the bonus can be included in the July payroll checks, each manager must submit a "star list" by June 20.

Your audit bureau has 15 employees with a wide range of responsibilities and job classifications—everything from clerk I to senior auditor. And, predictably, they also possess a range of talent, enthusiasm, and effectiveness. Here are the most obvious candidates for the performance bonus:

- Larry Beck, senior auditor. As a 23-year employee, Beck is clearly your most knowledgeable and effective auditor. Everyone goes to him for advice. Everyone looks up to him. But in two years, Larry will be eligible to receive his pension, and he knows it. He can still be a top performer—when he wants to. Recently, however, he has lost a little drive, although most people in the Department of Taxation still think of him as your unit's star.

- Jim Beatty, auditor III. With an advanced degree in accounting, Jim draws your unit's tough assignments. He understands the subtleties of the excise tax and thus works with both the department's legal counsel and the attorney general's office explaining the intricacies of each case and helping to formulate strategy. He can, however, be condescending toward his less knowledgeable colleagues, few of whom understand the complexity of his work.

- Rachel Gonzalez, auditor I. Straight out of law school with a verve for public service, Rachel is a real go-getter. In fact, she has struck gold several times, having gone over the books of numerous firms in such detail that she found mistakes most other auditors would have missed. Unfortunately, she also discovered some "errors" at a firm owned by the House Speaker's cousin. The firm refused to acknowledge any error, and eventually the department's legal counsel decided to settle out of court. The firm paid the taxes that Rachel claimed it owed (plus interest) but admitted no guilt for any tax violations and paid no fine. Rachel would be a gutsy choice on your part, but it might create a few problems politically when the Speaker hears about it.

- Martha Rutledge, administrative assistant II. With 35 years in the Department of Taxation, Martha knows everybody and everything. She runs your life. In fact, she really runs the day-to-day business of the audit unit, permitting you to concentrate on long-term, strategic concerns. You trust both her skills and her judgment; she really functions as your deputy director. Of course, she is still paid as an administrative assistant. It's hard to imagine Martha slacking off in her duties under any circumstances; it's also unlikely that an award would make her any more diligent. She'll be doing her same conscientious job right up until the day she leaves.

- Samantha Black, clerk I. Two years ago, straight out of high school, Samantha passed the civil service exam with flying colors. You immediately hired her, and she quickly became a real team member—both competent and cheery. Every auditor wants to give his or her clerical work to Samantha. Moreover, others in the department have heard of her talents, and she has already turned down several offers as a clerk II. You, however, don't have a clerk II position into which you can promote her.

The rest of your employees are quite proficient and professional. They're smart; to do their work, they have to be. Like any other manager in the taxation department, or in state government for that matter, you have a couple of people whom you wouldn't mind replacing. Still, you have a talented team that does its job without requiring much attention (except when you step on some politically sensitive toes). Your people are overworked and underappreciated. If the bonus is for performance, 90 percent of them deserve one. But you have only three to give.

Case Questions

1. Before turning to specifics of the case, consider the following more general question. Most would agree the six factors in the following list are important in determining whom to hire and promote:

   - Capacity
   - Experience
   - Integrity
   - Knowledge
   - Motivation
   - Understanding

   How would you rank these in relative importance? Support your answer.
2. Who in this case would you pick?

Case Reference

Robert D. Behn, "Manager's Choice," *Governing* (June 1998): 55.

11 Public Financial Management

AP Photos

FIND ME THE MONEY

During the 2008–2009 recession, the worst in 60 years, the grim news poured in from across the United States: altogether, states faced aggregate budget shortfalls of the least $230 billion from fiscal year 2009 through fiscal year 2011. (For most states, this covers the period from July 1, 2008 to June 30, 2011.) Just as important, those budgets had to be balanced. With the sole exception of Vermont, state governments, unlike the federal government, are not allowed to run deficits.

The poster child of the new hard times was California, where Governor Arnold Schwarzenegger suggested cutting virtually every state program by 10 percent. But the other obvious remedy was not on the table: Raising taxes in California remained extremely unpopular, crisis or no crisis. Moreover, since tax increases require a two-thirds majority vote in the legislature, they are easy to block. For example, when Schwarzenegger proposed closing a loophole on yachts and private airplanes that would have raised a modest $21 million (the state needed $16 billion), some legislators "reacted as though he had proposed a levy on firstborn sons" in the words of *The Economist* magazine. Cutting spending on prisons, which accounts for 10 percent of California's budget, was virtually impossible because of the power of the prison guards union. Cuts to K-12 education were opposed by powerful teachers' unions. Consequently, the main budget cuts would have to come from spending on universities and health-care programs. Not without reason, *The Economist* (February 19, 2009) ran an article on California's crisis titled "The ungovernable State" accompanied with a still from *The Terminator*.

Yet there are limits to how much a state can cut. The *San Jose Mercury News* found that if California were to lay off every one of its employees, it wouldn't solve half the problem. Furthermore, since state and local governments across the United States tried to cut spending to the bone after the 2001 recession, little fat remained, making it hard to see how states could cut their way to a balanced budget.

As suggested earlier, cutting spending is not the only remedy for a budget deficit. Governors and legislators were also considering the revenue side of the ledger. With dismay, they read the numbers: Overall, revenues from sales tax collection in 2009 were down 3.2% from the previous year, corporate income taxes were down 15.2%, and revenue from personal taxes were down 6.6%. California was hit particularly hard due to its tax code. To be more specific, one percent of earners pay nearly half of all income taxes. Since the wealthy derived much of their income from bonuses, capital gains, and stock options, the state's cash flow rises and falls with the market. Thus, when the market drops precipitously, California's fortunes fall drastically.

If the sales and income taxes are temperamental—rising and falling with peaks and valleys of the economic cycle—the property tax has always been the steady revenue source. But that changed during the 2008–2009 recession, when real estate values dropped and foreclosures rose. Given this perfect storm of declining home sales, deflated property values, mounting foreclosures, and reduced tax receipts, it was inevitable that state deficits would rise more rapidly than they did in any recession since World War II.

Even though many, if not most, economists agree with the general proposition that raising taxes in recession is bad idea, about half the states raised their taxes in 2009. Those policies run counter to the national government's effort to prime the economic pump with a $787 billion stimulus plan. Significantly, about $246 billion of these funds go to the states, presumably to offset medical costs, avoid education cuts, and help with infrastructure problems. But that money would begin to disappear in 2010 as the economy began to recover.

How then might state and local governments raise money in more creative ways? Is revenue from gambling a good idea? Winter Haven, Florida, imposes an "accident response fee" for services rendered when police and firefighters ride to the rescue. Is that a good idea? Meanwhile, Oregon was considering a mileage-based tax. Motorists would pay at the gas pump based on how much they drove, no matter how fuel-efficient their vehicle. Is that fair)? Which governmental enterprises might raise additional revenue?

Some issues go beyond the 2008–2009 recession. Are spending cuts less harmful than tax cuts? All sales and income taxes have exemptions. Would you recommend any be cut? Keep in mind that tax codes were written decades ago, when manufacturing rather than services was America's primary economic engine. Should ski tickets and cell phone ring tones be taxed today? At what point do tax codes themselves become a drag on economic growth?

Finally, to what extent were the states themselves responsible for the severity of the fiscal crisis? Clearly, some states fared better than others. For example, almost all states have a rainy day fund (RDF). Like a savings account, an RDF sets aside surplus revenues during period of economic growth for use in times of budget shortfalls. Obviously, states with RDFs were in better shape in this economic crisis than those without. Needless to say, Governor Schwarzenegger had no RDF.

Sources: Abby Goodnough, "States Are Turning to Last Resorts in Budget Crisis," *New York Times* (June 22, 2009); Neal Peirce, "Trickle down from a Downturn: State Cuts That Sting," *Houston Chronicle* (January 28, 2008); Amy Merrick, "States' Budget Woes Are Poised to Worsen," *Wall Street Journal* (June 3, 2009); *Economist* (February 19, 2009) (April 5, 2008), (November 15, 2008); and Peter A. Harkness, "Tackling Taxophobia, *Governing,* March 2009.

Public finance involves the study of how governments allocate scarce resources over time. Two features that distinguish financial decisions from many of the other decisions discussed in this book are that the costs and benefits are (1) spread out over a relatively long period of time and (2) usually not known with certainty in advance. For example, how much will a tax increase harm business efficiency? No one knows for sure.

Central to the management of government's financial resources is the budget. Administrators devote much time and energy to preparing it. Its adoption represents a critical juncture in the policy-planning process, for few major programs are conceivable without the expenditure of money.

Budgeting, however, is important for other reasons as well. Because it is the means by which public officials allocate and raise resources to achieve social objectives, budgeting answers the bedrock question of politics: Who gets how much, for what purpose, and who pays for it? In this sense, the budget provides an X-ray of the values and priorities of a free people. And because values and priorities vary from person to person, one may safely assume the budget process often involves ferocious political battles. In recent years, those battles have become, if anything, even more ferocious. The explanation for this intensification has its roots in the climb of public expenditures and taxes at all levels of government. In 1950, federal expenditures were 15.6 percent of the gross domestic product (GDP). By 1983, they reached nearly 24 percent and then began to slowly drop. In 2007, they constituted about 20 percent of the GDP. Meanwhile, state and local expenditures rose from 6.1 percent of GDP in 1951 to 13.3 percent in 2003.

Given their size and complexity, government budgets can at times seem almost beyond comprehension. But one can avoid much of that difficulty by focusing on the four basic phases of the federal budget cycle. These are shown in the following schematic.

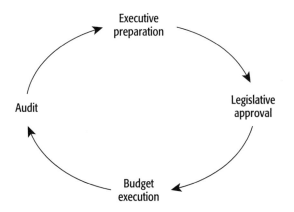

The first part of this chapter examines the four-phase process, looking chiefly at the federal budget cycle and briefly considering budgeting in state and local governments. Then, we consider the purposes of budgeting as well as the often bizarre world of budgetary politics. Following that, we turn to the dreaded "T" word—*taxation*. As the opening case suggested, it is no exaggeration to say that politicians actually fear this word. They avoid its use at all costs, and when they absolutely must use it, they use weasel words such as "revenue enhancement." (For much the same reason, they tend to refer to their favorite spending proposals as "investments.") The final section takes a look at some continuing problems in public financial management.

The Federal Budget Cycle

A strong connection exists between governmental plans (the focus of Chapter 5) and the budget. Strictly speaking, a plan is really no more than a statement of purpose—a piece of paper, a mere shadow. Not until it appears in the budget does it come to life and begin to matter. In that sense, the budget animates a plan. And there is more. Because the budget must reveal how funds are allocated among many and varied programs, it provides probably the most clear-cut way of determining national priorities.

Remember the concept of *opportunity cost* introduced in Chapter 6? Opportunity cost represents the implicit cost of the highest foregone alternative to an individual or group—in short, it is the true cost of choosing one alternative over another. Each year, the president is confronted with a multiplicity of such choices. He soon learns that spending in one area is viewed by certain groups as money not spent in their areas of special interest.

There is no universally acceptable, fair way to cut a budget. Speaking of his plan to cut all mass transit operation subsidies, a president might explain his approach with a rhetorical question: Is it fair to ask people in Omaha and Des Moines to get the people in Chicago and New York to work on time? But New Yorkers and Chicagoans would probably find that philosophy hard to buy because their taxes help the farmers of Omaha and Des Moines with water projects and agricultural subsidies.

With these ideas in mind, let's turn now to the four overlapping phases of the **federal budget cycle:** executive preparation, legislative approval, execution, and audit.

Executive Preparation

The president's transmittal of his budget proposals to Congress climaxes many months of planning and analysis throughout the executive branch. Formulation of the budget for fiscal year 2011, for example, began in the spring of 2009 (see Figure 11.1).

The **fiscal year** is a special 12-month financial period used by government for convenience in record keeping, tax collecting, spending, and general fiscal management. The fiscal year for a government can begin at any time the government chooses. In the United States, government fiscal years typically begin October 1 and end September 30; this certainly applies to the national government and a number of state governments. But many states and most local units begin their years July 1 and end them June 30. A few states and local units equate the fiscal and calendar years. The fiscal year always has a title based on the calendar year in which it ends; for example, the federal government's fiscal year 2011 begins October 1, 2010, and ends September 30, 2011.

This is the way it works: In the spring, agency programs are evaluated, policy issues are identified, and budgetary projections are made, giving attention both to important modifications and innovations in programs and to alternative long-range program plans.

Figure 11.1   Major Steps in the Budget Process

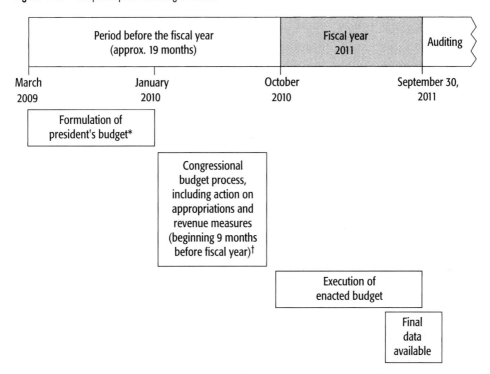

*The president's budget is transmitted to Congress on the first Monday in February.
†If appropriation action is not completed by September 30, Congress enacts temporary appropriations (that is, a continuing resolution).

In early June, preliminary plans are presented to the president for his consideration. At about the same time, the president receives projections of estimated receipts, prepared by the Treasury Department, and projections of the economic outlook, prepared jointly by the Council of Economic Advisers, the Treasury Department, and the Office of Management and Budget (OMB). As might be gathered from the title of the OMB, its director is a particularly important player in the process.

Following a review of both sets of projections—that is, of expenditures and receipts—the president establishes general budget and fiscal policy guidelines for the fiscal year that will begin about 15 months later. Tentative policy determinations and planning ceilings are then given to the agencies as guidelines for the preparation of their final budget requests during the summer. As used here, a ceiling is simply the top spending limit imposed by the president or OMB. When government expenditures exceed receipts, a budget **deficit** occurs. When receipts exceed government expenditures, you get a **surplus.** (More about the deficit later.)

Getting back to the process, agency budget requests are reviewed *in detail* by the OMB throughout the fall and are presented, along with OMB recommendations, to the president for decision. For an example of how one federal agency (*FBI*) formulates its request, see page 495.

Of all the agencies in the Executive Office of the President, perhaps most important in terms of the president's need for assistance in administering the federal government is the **Office of Management and Budget.** First called the Bureau of the Budget when it was created in 1921, it became the OMB in 1970 to reflect its broader responsibilities. Today it does considerably more than assemble and analyze the figures that each year go into the national budget that the president submits to Congress. It also studies the organization and operation of the executive branch, devises plans for reorganizing various departments and agencies, develops ways of obtaining better information about government programs, and reviews proposals that cabinet departments want included in the president's legislative program. It has a staff of more than 600, almost all career civil servants, many of high professional skill and substantial experience.

Legislative Approval

For decades, the president's budget was the only comprehensive statement of priorities and revenue and spending recommendations. But in 1974, Congress, seeking a greater role in managing the government, passed the **Congressional Budget and Impoundment Control Act,** which requires it to adopt an annual budget. The Budget Act attempted to control **impoundment**—the refusal of the executive branch to spend money appropriated by Congress—and required Congress to adopt a resolution that set a floor under revenue and a ceiling on spending. The resolution also includes categories of spending limits for 13 major federal functions, such as the military, agriculture, and transportation.

The law is intended to force Congress, after it completes work on the separate appropriations and authorizations it customarily enacts each year, to fit them into an overall framework by passing a second resolution setting final, binding targets. The Budget Act sets up a timetable for Congress to make its major fiscal decisions. All measures are to be in place by the beginning of the government's budget year, October 1, but these deadlines often are not met.

As the first step in the legislative approval phase, the president is required to submit a proposed budget to Congress by the first Monday in February. Figure 11.2 will give you some idea of the numbers involved. For the next several weeks, both House and Senate Budget Committees conduct hearings to examine the president's estimates and projections. By April 15, the budget committees are scheduled to report the first budget resolution, which sets overall goals for taxing and spending broken down among major budget categories. Congress is supposed to complete action on the first budget resolution by May 15, but that resolution often has been adopted later in the session.

On the basis of the guidelines set in the first budget resolution, Congress is supposed to approve the individual authorization and appropriation bills. The second budget resolution, due September 15, establishes firm ceilings on spending categories. But Congress has found the budget debate so contentious and time-consuming that it has been writing into the first budget resolution language that automatically readopts it as the second. On September 25,

Figure 11.2   Breakdown of the Federal Budget, Fiscal Year 2010

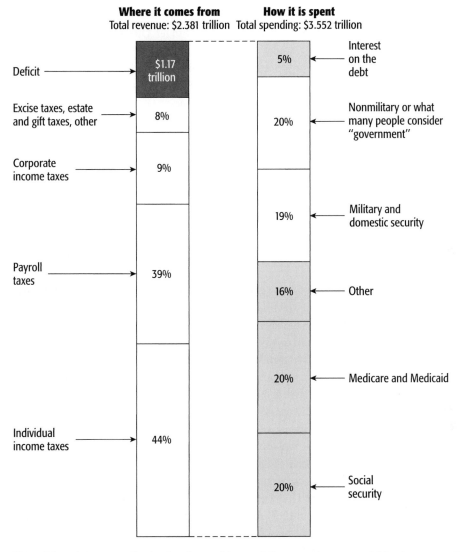

Where it comes from   **How it is spent**
Total revenue: $2.381 trillion   Total spending: $3.552 trillion

Deficit → $1.17 trillion

Interest on the debt ← 5%

Excise taxes, estate and gift taxes, other → 8%

Nonmilitary or what many people consider "government" ← 20%

Corporate income taxes → 9%

Military and domestic security ← 19%

Payroll taxes → 39%

Other ← 16%

Medicare and Medicaid ← 20%

Individual income taxes → 44%

Social security ← 20%

NOTE: Discretionary spending is what the president and Congress plan to spend. Mandatory spending is what they must spend—unless they change the law. Shaded areas of the spending bar are mandatory.

Congress is scheduled to complete action on the reconciliation bill and, by October 1, to complete action on all 13 appropriation bills.

In recent years, Congress has found it impossible to pass all the appropriation bills before the start of the fiscal year. For example, in December 2006, Congress adjourned having passed only 2 of its 11 annual spending bills, those that fund defense and homeland security. So it has resorted to a device known as a *continuing resolution,* which authorizes money for departments and agencies that have not received their regular appropriations.

More and more, the continuing resolutions have become omnibus appropriations bills, wrapping several measures into one package and in principle conforming to the spending levels set in the overall budget resolutions.

The Budget Act also created the **Congressional Budget Office (CBO).** This office advises Congress on the likely economic effect of different spending programs and provides information on the cost of proposed policies. This latter task has been more useful to Congress than the more difficult job of estimating future economic trends. The CBO prepares analyses of the president's budget and economic projections that often come to conclusions different from those of the administration, thus giving members of Congress arguments to use in budget debates.

Execution

Once approved—whether by salesmanship, analysis, or a little of both—the budget eventually is passed. The president now must either sign or veto the entire bill; he cannot choose to approve or veto only some of its provisions.

Under the law, most budget authority and other budgetary resources are made available to the executive branch through an apportionment system. Under authority delegated by the president, the director of the OMB apportions (distributes) appropriations and other budgetary resources to each agency by time periods (usually quarterly) or by activities. For an example of how an individual agency allocates these funds internally, see the Closing Case to Chapter 1 (Federal Bureau of Investigation).

Agencies may not incur obligations in excess of the amount apportioned. **Obligations** refer to the amount of orders placed, contracts awarded, services rendered, or other commitments made by an agency during a given period. Sometime during this period, payment will have to be made, probably by check. The objective of the apportionment system is to ensure the effective and orderly use of available authority and to reduce the need for requesting additional or supplemental authority.

Because expenditures can involve the purchase of resources for use both in the present and in the future, "expenditure" does not necessarily equal the current cost of providing government services. For example, part of the road salt purchased this year may be used next year. The cost of government then equals the amount of resources used during the current period—some resources coming from expenditures in that period and some from previous expenditures. *Focusing on expenditures will thus give an inaccurate view of the cost of government.* Confused? The simple flowchart in Figure 11.3 might help clear up these distinctions.

The figure shows the flow of transactions and accompanying management information requirements between the initial budget authority and final service cost. First, *budget authority* provides funding for an agency to, say, publish a bulletin. Second, an *obligation* occurs when the agency places an order for paper with, say, the Acme Printing Company. Third, *inventories* are recorded when Acme delivers the boxes of paper to the agency. Fourth, *outlay* occurs when the agency pays the bill for the paper. And fifth, *cost* occurs when the agency uses the paper to print the bulletin.

Figure 11.3   Financial Information for Management

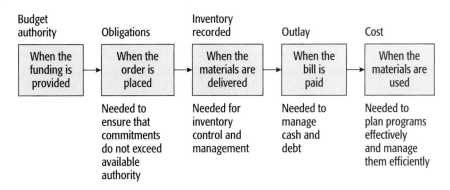

SOURCE: U.S. General Accounting Office, *Managing the Cost of Government: Building an Effective Financial Management Structure*, Vol. II, *Conceptual Framework* (Washington, DC: U.S. Government Printing Office, 1985).

It might be helpful at this point to take a look at how budget authority—provided through appropriations, borrowing authority, or contract authority—allows agencies to enter into commitments that will result in immediate or future spending. Budget authority defines the upper limit for the agency spending without obtaining additional authority. Figure 11.4 illustrates the relationship between budget authority and outlays envisioned in the 2009 federal budget. A major portion of planned outlays for the year is based on proposals in the 2009 budget, but almost 19 percent of the total is based on unspent authority enacted in prior years. Therefore, budget authority in a particular year differs from outlays for the year; outlays may result from either present or previous budget authority.

Figure 11.4   Relationship of Budget Authority to Outlays for 2009

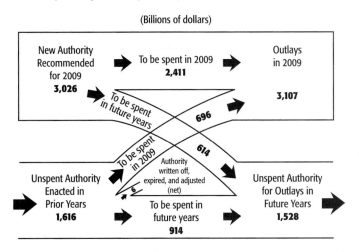

SOURCE: *Budget of the United States Government, Analytical Perspectives, Fiscal Year 2009* (Washington, DC: U.S. Government Printing Office, 2008).

Audit

The **audit** is the final phase in the budget process. Individual agencies are responsible for ensuring—through their own review and control systems—that the obligations they incur and the resulting outlays are in accordance with the provisions of the authorizing and appropriating legislation and with other laws and regulations relating to the obligation and expenditure of funds. As indicated in Figure 11.3, **outlays** are payments made (usually through the issuance of checks, disbursement of cash, or electronic transfer) to liquidate obligations. The OMB reviews program and financial reports and keeps abreast of agency programs' progress in attaining program objectives. In addition, the Government Accountability Office (GAO), as agent of Congress, regularly audits, examines, and evaluates government programs. Its findings and recommendations for corrective action are made to Congress, to the OMB, and to the agencies concerned.

Why audit? The basic reason is to make sure that the budget was executed as it was passed. Do the plans, which are reflected in the budget, match actual expenditure patterns at the close of the year—and, if they don't, have appropriate procedures been followed when making the changes? The audit also determines whether accounting controls (a) prevented fraud and waste and (b) ensured compliance with applicable laws. As the federal government has continued to grow larger and more complex, waste, fraud, and abuse have prospered. Here are some of the more popular methods that have been used to steal from government at all levels:[1]

- **Ghosting** is theft through phantom resources—that is, receiving payments for resources not actually delivered. One method, the ghost employee, involves placing on an agency payroll an individual who does not work for that agency.
- **Bid rigging** is a procurement fix that involves rigging bids on supply contracts. Suppose a section of highway is to be repaired. Potential suppliers would establish beforehand the bid winner and the winning price; other firms would submit non-competitive bids. Firms collude, knowing their turn to win will come on another project. The collusion increases the profits of the firms and increases the costs to government.
- **"Honest" graft** uses advance information to produce private profit for the individual employee. Who better to explain the concept than George Washington Plunkitt, a political boss of early twentieth-century New York City, who coined the term: "There's an honest graft, and I'm an example of how it works. I might sum up the whole thing by sayin': I seen my opportunities and I took 'em. Just let me explain by example. My party's in power in the city, and it's goin' to undertake a lot of public improvements. Well I'm tipped off, say, that they're going to lay out a new park at a certain place. . . . I go to that place and I buy up all the land I can in the neighborhood. Then the board of this or that makes its plan public, and there is a rush to get my land, which nobody cared particularly for before. Ain't it perfectly honest to charge a good price and make a profit on my investment and foresight?"[2]
- **Diversion** occurs when public assets or the service of employees are stolen for private use.

- **Shoddy material** or low-quality supplies and materials can be delivered at lower cost than can higher-quality supplies and materials. A contractor who provides lower than specified quality (shoddy material) can thus profit at public expense.
- **Kickbacks** are payments to the officials who have power to select who receives contracts, what banks receive public deposits, and who works for government agencies. The official may profit by arranging for artificially high contract awards with a portion of that payment kicked back to the government official.

Understanding the Federal Budget: A Guide for the Perplexed

As noted above, in February 2009, President Obama proposed to Congress a budget of $3.6 trillion. If that seems less than $990 billion, that is only because most people have little experience dealing in millions, billions, and trillions.

To begin to appreciate the size of this number, consider a stack of new $1000 bills. One hundred of these, or $100000, would make a stack about one-half-inch high. A stack of $1000 bills the height of the Empire State Building would be worth $6 billion. If Obama's budget were presented in $1000 bills, it would make more than 599 stacks, each the height of the Empire State Building.

Another reason the budget cannot easily be comprehended is that it consists of 190000 accounts. If one wanted to just read each of the account names (and many have long titles) to get an idea of the disposal of the taxpayers' money, how long would that take? Now imagine that the taxpayer wants to find out what is actually in the accounts and whether the money is well spent. How long would it take for just 190 of them?

Given the size and complexity of budgets, one may wonder how they ever get prepared. Part of the reason is that policymakers simplify the process in a variety of ways. For example, the system does not start from scratch each year but from a base budget that is carried over from the previous year. The starting point for each year's budget battle is a calculation of the cost of continuing existing programs without change and an adjustment of the costs merely to reflect shifts in workload (for example, increase in number of clients) and the effects of inflation. This estimate is variously called the base budget, the **current services budget,** the continuing services budget, or the recurrent budget.

Another "simplifying" device is **incrementalism.** For the most part, the budget process concentrates on marginal adjustments of the budget base. Increase 6 percent here, cut 4 percent there, and so forth.

A third factor that helps simplify the budget process is that many significant government functions are **off-budget items**—that is, they do not appear in budget totals. Included here would be public enterprises, public authorities, government corporations, and other business-type organizations that have the power to raise their own revenue. Special funds such as the Highway Trust Fund, which can be used solely for special purposes and cannot be transferred to any other program, also help simplify the process.

In the federal budget, a trust fund means only that the law requires that funds must be accounted for separately and used for specified purposes. The largest trust funds are those for civil service and military retirement, Social Security, Medicare, and unemployment insurance. These are financed largely by Social Security taxes and contributions and payments from the general fund. There are also major trust funds for transportation and bank deposit insurance, which are financed by user charges.

A final factor that helps to simplify the budget process is the cold fact that about three-fourths of the federal budget consists of so-called **uncontrollables.** Statutes mandate Medicare, Medicaid, food stamps, unemployment insurance, pensions, and farm price supports. Interest on the national debt is also uncontrollable; it must be paid this year if the government hopes to borrow next year. Given these uncontrollables, and the legislature's reluctance to tamper with the original statutes, budget negotiations begin by taking over six-tenths of the pie off the table. Trying to decide how to divide less than four-tenths of a pie is presumably less complicated than deciding on the whole thing. The uncontrollables appear in Figure 11.2 as the mandatory section of the right-hand column. Of course, simpler budgeting is not necessarily *better* budgeting, as will be argued later in the chapter.

Perhaps the most perplexing thing of all about the budget is that, strictly speaking, it is a bag rather than a document. If you are bewildered by that, then you had better not skip the photo on page 502.

The State and Local Budget Process

State, Local, and Nonprofit Budgeting: An Overview

Although the federal budget process might appear mind-boggling—with its extended cycle, series of deadlines, multiyear outlook, and intermittent congressional involvement—things do not get much better when we turn to budgeting in states, local governments, and non-profit organizations. Though the budget process still follows the general pattern outlined earlier—preparation, approval, execution, and audit—the sheer variety of systems is astonishing. But we can be brief.

Let's start with states. Most states place budgeting responsibility solely with the executive, but some establish a budget commission that has legislative representation. In one state, Arkansas, budgeting is entirely a legislative function. The federal budget cycle, you will recall, begins in October. But this is not the case with most other jurisdictions in the United States. All state governments (except Alabama, Michigan, New York, and Texas) start their fiscal years in July. The fiscal year in Alabama and Michigan coincides with the federal fiscal cycle, but New York has an April start and Texas a September start.

State budgets may be annual or biannual. At one time, state legislatures usually met only every other year, so one legislative session made appropriations for two years. States have generally moved toward annual sessions. Among the dozen most populous states, eight have annual sessions and four have biennial sessions. The eight with annual sessions are California, Florida, Georgia, Illinois, Michigan, New Jersey, New York, and Pennsylvania. The four with biennial sessions are North Carolina, Ohio, Texas, and Virginia.

For cities and towns, state law or local ordinance typically requires that certain steps be followed in the budget process and may prescribe dates by which each step must be completed. These requirements are referred to as the **budget calendar.** See Table 11.1 for a budget calendar for a small city. Virtually all local budgets are prepared by the executive, although this distinction is blurred under the commission form of municipal government. Many local governments have fiscal years beginning in January.

As previously noted, the federal government collects and then spends over $2 trillion a year. That is only slightly more than the total for state and local governments. In decreasing order of importance, here are the principal sources of funding for state and local governments: sales tax, intergovernmental revenue, property taxes, individual income taxes, and corporation income tax. The seven major areas of expenditure, in decreasing order of size, are the following: education, welfare, highways, health, interest on debt, general administration, and police. One sees different priorities for spending among various U.S. cities. Minneapolis, for example, spends significant sums on snow removal (as could be expected) and has a relatively large traditional commitment to parks (perhaps not so predictable). Meanwhile, Houston must spend considerable amounts on storm drainage.

Table 11.1 Budget Calendar for a Small City		
SAMPLE CITY		
Budget Calendar		
Year Ending September 30		
Date	Event	Requirement or Action
July 20	1st Budget Workshop	Departments'/Programs' goals due. Budget forms issued.
August 4	2nd Budget Workshop	Draft budget and documentation including revenue projections.
August 11	Regular Council Meeting/3rd Budget Workshop	Long-term GF projections, capital outlay and analysis of budget increases.
August 25	Regular Council Meeting/ 4th Budget Workshop	Budget presentations by County Health District, Chamber of Commerce, and other related organizations.
September 1	Special Council Meeting/ 5th Budget Workshop	Water/Sewer budget presentation. Call for public hearing to be held September 8.
September 3	Newspaper Publication	Publish notice of public hearing on budget to be held on September 8.
September 8	Regular Council Meeting	Public hearing on proposed budget.
September 15	Special Council Meeting	First reading of budget ordinance.
September 22	Regular Council Meeting	Second reading and vote on adoption of budget ordinance.

SOURCE: Earl R. Wilson and Susan C. Kattelus, *Accounting for Governmental and Nonprofit Entities* (Burr Ridge, IL: Irwin, 2002), 496. © 2002 The McGraw-Hill Companies. Reprinted with permission.

The budgeting issues of nonprofit organizations (NPOs) differ from those in government entities in part because NPOs rely on grants and contributions in the operation of distinct programs rather than on taxes or user charges. Grants may be received from governmental entities, other NPOs, or foundations; contributions also come from individual donors. Institutional grants and individual contributions may be given to support either specified programs or the organization as a whole. That creates problems:

> The accounting challenge is to capture total cost of each program and to match actual to budgeted costs for each grant. Difficulties arise because shared costs must be allocated across programs, grantors have different fiscal years, and terminology often differs across granting sources. For example, government grants may approve *telephone and printing cost,* but a local government grant covers *communication cost.* Further complications come when there are multiple grantors for one program and multiple programs supported by one grantor.[3]

State and Local Budgeting: The Nuts and Bolts

During the budget execution phase, just as in the federal cycle, administrators at the state and local levels try to attain program goals within monetary limitations. The steps they follow cover the entire fiscal year. Whatever the particular politics of the jurisdiction or the peculiar structural impediments, state and local finance officers have the same mission.

The Budget's Original Meaning

ANDY RAIN/epa/Corbis

Budgeting is a common practice to the extent that everybody—households, corporations, clubs, agencies, and so on—must anticipate income and expenses. Historically, the word budget (borrowed from Middle French bougette) referred to a leather bag in which England's chancellor of the exchequer carried the statement of the government's needs and resources to Parliament. In time, however, the budget came to refer to the papers within the bag rather than to the bag itself. The photo here shows a chancellor carrying the traditional budget "bag" (which is now really a red dispatch box) before speaking in the House of Commons. (Chancellor is a powerful position—as if the U.S. Treasury Secretary and Budget Director were combined.

They must plan, manage, and account for the public's money. For most finance officers (see Working Profile: The Finance Officer), that means overseeing the accounting system, managing cash flows, keeping an eye on spending decisions, and, from time to time, tapping the capital markets.

Accounting   All phases of the budget process—not just execution—require record keeping. **Accounting** is the system of recording, classifying, and reporting financial transactions in an orderly way.

The oldest type of accounting is cash accounting. Receipt transactions are recorded at the time funds are received, and disbursements are recorded when checks are issued. Other types of accounting are accrual and cost. **Accrual accounting** records expenditures when an obligation is incurred (as one records a check when it is written, not when the bank actually makes payment) and records revenues when earned (for example, when taxes are due, not when the taxpayer actually pays). **Cost accounting,** also known as **activity-based costing,** concentrates on reporting the cost of providing goods and services (for example, how much did it cost to repair one mile of city streets last year?).

Information technology is being upgraded in many places, making it easier to track all the costs associated with a single activity. But don't misunderstand. *This isn't easy.* Figuring out how much it costs to deliver a single unit of service requires a real understanding of exactly how services are delivered and who is involved. Let's say you want to know the cost of plowing one street after a heavy snowstorm. There's nobody in your city who does that job full time, so you have to figure out exactly how much of a sanitation worker's time was spent in this particular task, at what cost. How much does it cost for upkeep and storage of the snowplows? How much gas do they use? How fast are they depreciating? Then you have to figure out all the indirect costs, such as computer time, managerial overhead, and some portion (how much? that's tricky, too) of the sanitation department's space in city hall. Government budgeting makes things harder. Let's say you bought a large stock of sand and salt for the streets in 2005, but the winter was warm and a large supply was left over. So in 2006, your budget won't show any costs for sand and salt. But that doesn't mean the stuff came free.[4]

Despite the difficulties, more and more sophisticated administrators are using cost accounting data, and the reason is simple. The benefits are abundant. Utah, for example, figured out that it cost $68 a day to house inmates in state facilities, compared with $42 a day in county facilities. Knowing this, the state started trying to keep its own capital development program down and doing more contracting with counties.

Although there are many similarities between government accounting and business accounting, one difference is worth noting. In business accounting all the available resources are, in effect, in one cookie jar. But in a public-sector organization, the resources may be accounted for in several separate cookie jars, each of which is called a **fund**. Each fund has its own set of accounts, and each fund is therefore a separate entity, almost as if it were a separate business. The purpose of this device is to ensure that the organization uses the resources made available to each fund only for the purpose designated by that fund. And that is why a university president may not use the scholarship fund to expand the faculty club.

Cash Management[5]   The cash flow of state and local governments, taken as a whole, is close to a trillion dollars a year—hence, **cash management** is vitally important.

The money comes sloshing in as taxes and charges. Then, it is shifted among governments as grants and reimbursements or stored somewhere—in checking accounts, in short-term investments, or in long-term investments. Where the money is stored depends, of course, on when government needs it. Finally, it is paid out to employees, contractors, vendors, bondholders, pensioners, and grant recipients.

The distinction between short-term and long-term investments is important: the former are typically carried on as part of the daily operations of government; the latter finance trust-fund activities. Public-employee retirement systems, with assets of more than $2.1 trillion in 2002 that must be invested, are the most significant example of a trust fund for state and local governments.

Government investment policies usually require managers to maximize the safety of funds and investment returns. The problem for the manager is determining where to trade off safety for return, because the safest securities are invariably those that bring the lowest returns. In the past, government cash managers often were restricted to a short list of acceptable investments (for example, U.S. Treasury bonds). But in recent years the menu of acceptable investments has grown longer, and the manner in which investments can be made has become more varied. The upshot of these changes is that cash management has become a more sophisticated operation. As one experienced practitioner writes:

> The routine call to the local bank to pick up some U.S. notes at the next auction was replaced by the frazzled finance officer fielding inquiries from a legion of brokers, securities dealers, and bankers attempting to market the latest in repurchase agreements, government-security mutual funds, and other newfangled devices. And, of course, the current concern over the safety of funds in even the tried and true financial institutions, banks, and thrifts makes none of this easier.[6]

Purchasing   To attain their programs' objectives, state and local governments spent over $1.9 trillion in 2007. About 31 percent of that was for salaries and wages; the remainder went to purchase structures, equipment, supplies, and services of all kinds. The list of items purchased ranges from power plants to paper clips.

Essentially, public purchasing officers operate like their private-sector counterparts, seeking the greatest *quantity* of the best *quality* at the lowest *price*. But, again, difficult trade-offs must be made. Decisions must also be made about privatizing and contracting, two topics discussed in Chapter 9.

One area of steady progress in government procurement has been group buying, in which numbers of cooperating governments make their purchases together:

> Pennsylvania procurement officials like to lay out a familiar scenario: imagine you are hosting a family picnic, and you need ketchup. A lot of it. Would you drive all over town, darting into convenience stores to buy enough small packets of ketchup to feed the family? No, you'd go to the supermarket where you can buy one big bottle for a much better price.

That's common sense, but it's also a purchasing strategy that has eluded state and local governments for years. Now, some public procurement officers are realizing they can save significant amounts of money simply by monitoring state expenditures and selectively targeting vendors to get the best possible price.[7]

The concept is known as **strategic sourcing,** and many states now see it as a means of saving money through smarter purchasing. A private-sector practice for decades, strategic sourcing had been largely absent from state procurement practices until Delaware began implementing it in 2002. Today, 24 states are either practicing some form of strategic sourcing or are in the process of implementing it. Zach Patton writes:

> Shifting to a strategic sourcing approach involves some challenges. It relies on more centralized controls and much more thorough data collection. And it raises the specter of getting too cozy with a limited number of vendors. But as more states adopt the approach—and as they experience dramatic savings—they're finding ways to overcome the barriers. As a result, strategic sourcing is very quickly becoming the gold standard in state procurement.[8]

Debt Administration   Because the largest cities and counties are financial giants and even small governments are multimillion-dollar enterprises, it is fair to say that government finance is "high finance." When raising capital, state and local governments have their own market, that for tax-exempt securities. Tax exempt means that the interest income on these securities is not subject to federal (nor, frequently, to state or local) income tax. As a result, the interest rates that governments pay are the lowest in the financial markets.

Financing a large-scale project is not a daily occurrence for most government agencies, any more than buying a house or sending a child to college is for a family. Not surprisingly, many finance officers rely on advisers to assist them in the process of designing and issuing debt, or debt management. What is **debt management?** Consider: States and most local governments do not use current revenues to pay for their capital projects. And that is where debt management comes in. The objective of debt management is to raise the money necessary for the government's operations at the least cost to the taxpayer and in a manner that will minimize the effects of those operations on financial markets and the economy. Such projects—for example, the construction of universities and school buildings, prisons, or mental health facilities—are usually financed from bond revenues. Bond purchasers in effect provide states and local governments with funds necessary to finance construction. Governments, in turn, pledge to pay the bondholders the principal of the loan plus a stipulated rate of return.

States and local governments commonly offer two kinds of bonds: general obligation bonds and revenue bonds. *General obligation bonds* have the "full faith and credit" of the general treasury behind the promise that bondholders will be repaid. Not only do the issues of these bonds commit general-purpose revenues to retire their indebtedness, but they also promise that bondholders will have "first claim" to available revenues. Because of the high degree of security that this commitment affords, bond purchasers are willing to accept lower rates of return than they could get from less secure investments.

States and local governments also issue *revenue bonds* for which governments pledge specified revenues, to the extent that they are expected to be available, as the source of repayment. Unlike general obligation bonds, revenue bonds do not have resources of the general treasury behind them.

In addition to incurring long-term bonded indebtedness, governments may take on short-term debt, usually for one year or less. Financial managers typically resort to short-term borrowing to cover emergencies or temporary inability to meet payments required by law because of cash flow problems. It is considered bad practice for public administrators to need to turn regularly to short-term borrowing to balance operating budgets.

Capital Budget   What do state and local governments, foreign governments, and corporations have that the federal government does not? Answer: a capital budget. A **capital budget** separates long-term investments in buildings, bridges, roads, vehicles, computers, and the like from current operating expenses. Although the federal government separates budget items by categories (such as defense, energy, and income-security programs), it combines all capital and operating expenses; therefore, the construction of a new dam is treated the same way as, for example, a purchase of potatoes for the White House kitchen.

Cities manage their resources differently. They have an operating budget intended for day-to-day expenses (such as payment of salaries) that is financed through revenues. But they also have a capital budget intended for changes in the physical plant of the city (such as new schools and mass transit systems) that is financed through borrowing. Although important relationships exist between operating and capital budgets, capital projects have special characteristics that justify their separation from operating expenses. Two characteristics in particular contribute to the segregation.[9] First, because of their life span, capital projects have a long-range effect on the community; therefore, they need to be planned within a long-range perspective (of five or six years). Second, because many current operating decisions are subject to reversal, the ability to postpone more capital projects (usually much more easily than current services) means that, without a separate budget, important capital expenditures would often be neglected by cities.

Should the federal government have a capital budget? Some opponents are concerned that a capital budget for the federal government would serve as an excuse for more, not less, deficit spending by inviting more spending on public works projects. They fear that a capital account could make it all too easy to disguise unbudgeted operating expenses as long-term capital outlays. Other opponents are concerned about the *negative* impact a capital budget could have on social welfare programs. Because it is far easier to value such tangible assets as roads and public buildings, the argument goes, a capital budget would make it increasingly difficult to justify spending to feed the hungry or to send a young person to college on a government loan. Finally, there is a fear that trying to run the United States by business standards could blur the role the federal government plays in stabilizing the economy. The overall fiscal policy ought to be related to the needs of the economy as a whole; for example, it may sometimes be appropriate for the government to run a deficit during a recession.

But any accounting system is open to abuse, especially when, like the U.S. budget, it serves as a political document. A more businesslike budget would be neither a panacea for past ills nor a threat to the nation's fiscal priorities. The key reason for changing the way the budget is drawn should be to improve the information it offers about the country's true financial condition.

The Purposes of Budgeting

Yes, budgeting is a serious matter, but every once in a while we need to be reminded that certain administrative processes can become ends in themselves. Master satirist Charles Addams does just that by lampooning budget officials whose response to any initiative is categorical rejection.

> The budgeting process was invented by an alien race of sadistic beings who resemble large cats. The cat aliens taught budgeting to the Egyptian pharaohs, who used it as punishment during the construction of the pyramids. . . . Tragically, the cat people parked their mother ship in a warm spot of the Galaxy, curled up to take naps, and ended up getting sucked into the sun. . . . Over the years the true purpose of the budgeting process was lost. Now, due to an unfortunate misinterpretation of hiero-glyphics, budgeting is seen as a method of controlling spending.[10]

In reality, budgeting serves several valuable purposes; but ultimately and always, it must be a means to the end—the accomplishment of the organization's mission. What, more specifically, should the purpose of a budget be? Each generation has answered that question differently. As set forth in an influential article by A. Schick,[11] the generally accepted **purposes of budgeting** are control, management, and planning. *Control* he identifies as legislative concern for tight control over executive expenditures. The most prevalent means of exerting such expenditure control has been to appropriate by object of expenditure—for example, felt-tip pens, half-ton trucks, salaries, and unleaded gasoline. Financial audits then are used to ensure that money has, in fact, been spent for the items authorized for purchase. This focuses information for budgetary decision making on the things government buys, such as personnel, travel, and supplies, rather than on the accomplishments of governmental activities.

Management orientation emphasizes the efficiency with which ongoing activities are conducted. Emphasis is placed on holding administrators accountable for the efficiency of their activities through such methods as work-performance measurement (for example, how many forms typed does the agency get for X dollars spent?).

Finally, *planning* is reflected in the budget message for fiscal year 1968: "A federal budget lays out a two-part plan of action: it proposes particular programs, military and civilian, designed to promote national security, international cooperation, and domestic progress. It proposes total expenditures and revenues designed to help maintain stable economic prosperity and growth."[12] Here one sees an obvious emphasis on programs and the relationship between revenues and expenditures to accomplish the objectives of those programs.

The overall development just outlined should be viewed, however, not in terms of three separate phases but in terms of accretion. Thus, the function of the budget today is really a combination of all three purposes. Now consider how the purpose of a budget shapes its format.

Line-Item Budgeting

Say the word *budget* and the image that generally comes to mind is a list of items and their associated costs. Indeed, **line-item budgeting** for control of expenses remains at the heart of the budgeting process. The line-item budget is designed to keep spending within the limits set by the legislative body. Cost categories are established for the recording of all expenditures, and backup bookkeeping systems contain sufficient detail to ensure that all disbursements (that is, expenditures) are made in accordance with the law. The makers and keepers of line-item budgets rely on accounting skills—the ability to keep track of revenues and expenses in a systematic way. They answer the question, How was the money spent?

Unfortunately, line-item budgets can become straitjackets, requiring people to follow detailed rules when buying anything. Until only recently, budgets for military bases were drawn up three years in advance and included hundreds of specific line items. Say that a simple steam trap, which costs $100, begins to leak. Because a week's worth of lost steam costs the government $50, it makes sense to replace it quickly. But because of regulations, this process might take months—obviously losing many times the cost of a replacement trap. However, if a commander were allowed to ignore the line items and shift resources to meet this sudden need, money would be saved.

Before moving on to the next budget format, we should distinguish a line-item budget from a line-item veto. Starting January 1, 1997, the president, for the first time in history, had a line-item veto. "For years, presidents of both parties have pounded this very desk in frustration at having to sign necessary legislation that contained special interest boondoggles, tax loopholes, and pure pork," President Clinton said when signing the new law. "The line-item veto will give us a chance to change that."[13] The law would have allowed presidents to reject specific spending and tax decisions made by Congress, rather than vetoing an entire bill.

All but one governor has a similar veto power. (The governor of North Carolina has no veto authority.) But the presidential line-item veto was short-lived: The Supreme Court quickly ruled it unconstitutional on the grounds it violated the separation of powers principle.

Performance Budgeting

Oscar Wilde once defined a cynic as "a man who knows the price of everything and the value of nothing." Perhaps, then, President Franklin Roosevelt was trying to battle cynicism in government when his second administration introduced the concept of **performance budgeting.** In 1939, the Bureau of the Budget was transferred from the Treasury Department to the newly formed Executive Office of the President with the directive to "keep the president informed of the progress of activities by agencies of the government with respect to work proposed, work actually initiated, and work completed." The idea was that the work programs of several agencies could be coordinated and that monies appropriated by Congress could be expended in the most economical manner possible. The bureau would prevent overlapping and duplication of effort.

Thus began the search at the federal level for an answer to the question that, more than 40 years later, still haunts government at all levels: Is the public getting its money's worth? The end result of line-item budgeting was that government should be able to tell the public that an agency spent, say, $19,872,403.91, with so much going to salaries, wages, and fringe benefits; so much spent on various materials and supplies; and so much paid out under each of numerous contracts. But with performance budgeting, government should be able to tell the public how much public service was delivered for this $19,872,403.91. If the agency is a city sanitation department, performance measures could be given to show how many tons of trash were collected; the cost per ton and the cost per pickup; and comparative unit costs to indicate efficiency of the department against previous years, comparable departments in other cities, and comparable services provided by private sanitation companies.

Traditional performance budgeting, as already noted, attempts to budget according to the direct outputs or activities of government agencies. But government agencies exist not for outputs but for *outcomes*. Public health agencies do not exist to get high vaccination counts but to reduce infant mortality; manpower development agencies do not exist to run people through their training programs but to place those people in better jobs that they can keep; and environmental protection agencies do not exist to get high plant inspection rates but to improve environmental conditions. Performance budgeting (NPB) attempts to let real performance influence budget decisions.

The critical underpinning for building support for performance budgeting is the presence of credible performance information and measures. As previously suggested, the measures should focus not on the activities of an agency but on broader societal consequences of those activities. Budget processes tend to focus on inputs (the resources purchased by the agency) or direct outputs (the agency's activities or tasks). In contrast, the performance budget measures outcomes (the results or the extent to which agency activities have their intended effect). Table 11.2 illustrates the difference between outputs and outcomes for nine basic governmental functions.

The closer the linkage between an agency's performance goals, its budget presentation, and its net cost statement, the greater the reinforcement of performance management throughout the agency and the greater the reliability of budgetary and financial data associated with performance plans. Clearer and closer association between expected performance and budgetary requests can more explicitly inform budget discussions and focus them—both in legislatures and in agencies—on expected results rather than on inputs or transactions.

Program Budgeting

Without ever having really mastered performance budgeting, the federal government proceeded to develop an even broader view of budgeting in the early 1960s. Robert McNamara, as secretary of defense in the Kennedy administration, introduced the

Table 11.2   Outputs and Outcomes for Nine Governmental Functions

Function	Outputs (or Activities)	Outcomes (or Results)
Firefighting	Inspections performed, fire calls answered, arson investigations performed, hours of education programs offered, property value protected in service area	International Organization of Standards (ISO) fire insurance rating, dollars of fire losses, number of fire-related injuries and fatalities, number of traffic accidents during fire runs, number of reported and unreported fires
Police	Hours on patrol, responses to calls for assistance, crimes investigated by category, number of arrests	Deaths, injuries, and property losses from crime, crime clearance rate
Elementary and secondary education	Instructional days, students promoted or graduated	Test score results, parent/student satisfaction ratings, percent of graduates employed
Public health	Data on diseases collected and analyzed, sites inspected, educational programs implemented	Mortality rates, morbidity rates, cases of infectious diseases by category
Solid waste management	Waste collected and processed, residences served	Proportion of streets rated as clean, incidence of vector disease, citizen satisfaction ratings, achievement of environmental standards
Tax department	Returns processed, processing times, delinquency rates	Overall compliance rate, taxpayer compliance rates, measured uniformity of treatment of taxpayers
Environmental protection	Permits granted, inspections performed	Percentage of state residents living where air meets government ambient air quality standards, percent of groundwater that meets drinking water standards, release and generation of solid waste as percent of baseline year
Municipal sanitation	Tons of refuse collected, miles of roads cleaned, number of residential and commercial customers served	Evaluation of street cleanliness measured by periodic visual investigation, citizen satisfaction surveys, general indicators of public health
Juvenile justice	Number of children in juvenile justice system, numbers by type of placement and variety of offense, worker caseload	Juvenile justice recidivism rates, juvenile justice system clients leaving system for school or employment

planning-programming-budgeting system (PPBS) in the Defense Department. Whereas line-item budgeting is limited to *accountability* and performance budgeting extends only to the realm of *efficiency*, **program budgeting** attempts to stretch the process into issues of *allocation* among various competing agencies and programs. It was not as if funding allocation had never before taken place—legislative bodies had historically performed this function based on inputs from constituents and from affected agencies. What the proponents of program budgeting hoped to accomplish was the injection of greater rationality into the process, by first planning *goals* and *objectives,* then developing *programs* to achieve these goals, and finally budgeting for projects within each program.

Zero-Based Budgeting

Much of the decision making in the budgetary process is incremental—that is, involving minimal increases or decreases from last year's budget. Not so with **zero-based budgeting (ZBB)**—a more recent variation of PPBS. Here the basic objectives of a program are examined by taking an if-we-start-all-over-again attitude—that is, each program is challenged for its very existence each budget cycle.

ZBB involves three basic steps. First, all current and proposed programs must be described and analyzed in documents called decision packages. These documents are designed to help top management evaluate the programs in terms of purpose, consequences, measures of performance, alternatives, and costs and benefits. Next, the program packages are ranked through cost–benefit analysis (see Chapter 6). Finally, resources are allocated in accordance with this ranking.

ZBB does force top managers to pay more attention to everyday operations, because they must rank specific expenditure items. But it is probably too burdensome and detailed for normal budgeting purposes. In any event, good managers should be well acquainted with the programs in their organizations. ZBB can be useful as a resource allocation device to flag programs needing particularly close attention. The remaining activities can be budgeted for in an incremental fashion or through the use of a format similar to the following:[14]

Last year's budget	Changes caused by change in			This year's budget
	Quantity	Quality	Inflation	

Figure 11.5 summarizes the discussion thus far by showing how one government bureau might arrange the same budgetary information in four different ways: line-item, program, performance, and zero-based.

The Politics of Budgeting

This section begins with the budget battles between Republicans and Democrats—which have all the stylized drama of Kabuki, and are even more baffling.

Figure 11.5 Four Ways to Prepare a Budget (in thousands of dollars)

Agency: Bureau of Streets

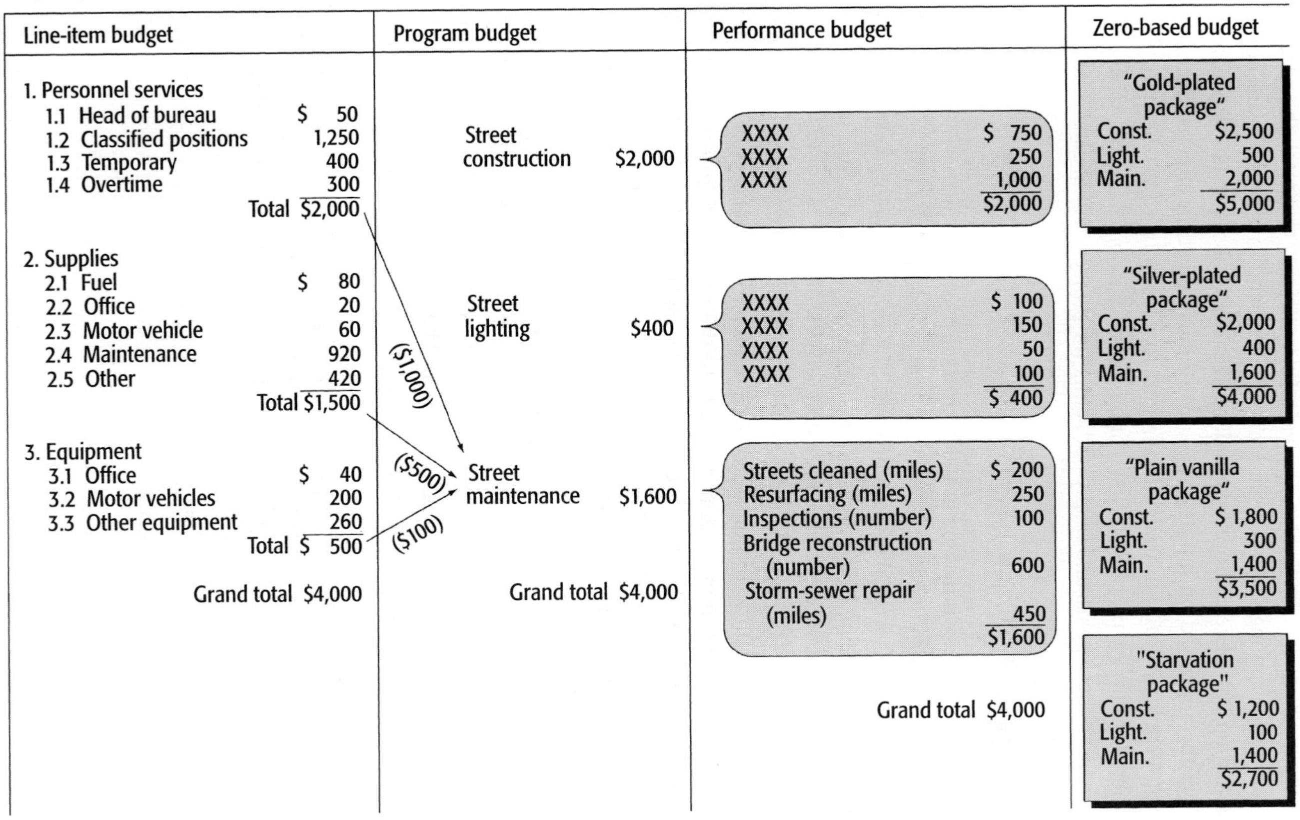

Line-item budget

1. Personnel services
   - 1.1 Head of bureau — $ 50
   - 1.2 Classified positions — 1,250
   - 1.3 Temporary — 400
   - 1.4 Overtime — 300
   - Total $2,000

2. Supplies
   - 2.1 Fuel — $ 80
   - 2.2 Office — 20
   - 2.3 Motor vehicle — 60
   - 2.4 Maintenance — 920
   - 2.5 Other — 420
   - Total $1,500

3. Equipment
   - 3.1 Office — $ 40
   - 3.2 Motor vehicles — 200
   - 3.3 Other equipment — 260
   - Total $ 500

Grand total $4,000

Program budget

- Street construction — $2,000   ($1,000)
- Street lighting — $400   ($500)
- Street maintenance — $1,600   ($100)

Grand total $4,000

Performance budget

Street construction:
XXXX	$ 750
XXXX	250
XXXX	1,000
	$2,000

Street lighting:
XXXX	$ 100
XXXX	150
XXXX	50
XXXX	100
	$ 400

Street maintenance:
Streets cleaned (miles)	$ 200
Resurfacing (miles)	250
Inspections (number)	100
Bridge reconstruction (number)	600
Storm-sewer repair (miles)	450
	$1,600

Grand total $4,000

Zero-based budget

"Gold-plated package"
Const.	$2,500
Light.	500
Main.	2,000
	$5,000

"Silver-plated package"
Const.	$2,000
Light.	400
Main.	1,600
	$4,000

"Plain vanilla package"
Const.	$ 1,800
Light.	300
Main.	1,400
	$3,500

"Starvation package"
Const.	$ 1,200
Light.	100
Main.	1,400
	$2,700

Are "Cuts" Really Cuts?

Democrats, wielding numbers rather than swords, accuse Republicans of slashing aid to hungry children and pregnant women, and Republicans, brandishing their own numbers, claim to be increasing aid to the same groups. Even more confusing, both arguments are accurate.

But neither is the whole truth. The fact is that any spending proposal can be judged only against a yardstick: what future federal spending would be if the proposal is not enacted into law. Without such a measure, it is nearly impossible to say what effect any spending change could have. Accountants call such yardsticks **baselines.**

When Congress acts on entitlement legislation, it must take account of outside factors, such as the condition of the economy and the behavior of those affected by its decisions. The cost of entitlement legislation depends on variables such as inflation and unemployment rates, demographic and income trends, and the extent to which eligible persons avail themselves of services. Future conditions can only be assumed at the time Congress acts on such legislation.

Assumptions about future expenditures are incorporated in baseline projections prepared by the CBO or OMB. The baseline incorporates assumptions about inflation as well as projected workload changes mandated by law, such as an increase in the number of persons receiving Social Security payments. Once the baseline has been projected, any executive or legislative action that would cause spending to deviate from the baseline is measured as a policy change; for example, say baseline spending would increase from $100 million in the current year to $141 million five years later. Now, say that Senator Foghorn, in an effort to "control runaway spending," suggests a policy change that would reduce projected spending below the baseline level to $125 million. This reduction results in spending higher than the current level but less than the baseline. When this occurs, politicians can portray their actions both as a spending cut *and* as a spending increase.

Budgets and Political Strategies

Aaron Wildavsky has identified group strategies within the roles pursued in the budget process on the basis of an analysis of the United States Congress. Many of these **political strategies in the budget process** are transferable to other governments. Two agency strategies are ubiquitous. The first is cultivation of an active clientele for help in dealing with both the legislature and the chief executive. The clientele may be those directly served (as with farmers in particular programs provided by the Department of Agriculture) or those selling services to the particular agency (as with highway contractors doing business with a state department of highways). Agencies unable to identify and cultivate such clientele will find budget hearings difficult because active support may be difficult to mobilize.

A second ubiquitous strategy is the development of the confidence of other government officials. Agency administrators must avoid being surprised in hearings or by requests for information. Officials must show results in the reports they make and must tailor their message's complexity to their audience. If results are not directly available, agencies may report internal process activities, such as files managed or surveys taken. Confidence is critical because in the budget process many elements of program defense must derive from the judgments of the administrators, not from hard evidence. If confidence has been developed, those judgments will be trusted; if not, those judgments will be suspect.

Another group of strategies—call them contingent strategies—depends on the budget circumstances, particularly on whether discussion concerns (1) a reduction in agency programs below the present level of expenditures (the budget base), (2) an increase in the scope of agency programs, or (3) an expansion of agency programs to new areas. Some of these contingent strategies seem strange or even preposterous. Nevertheless, they are used and should be recognized because the budget choices involved are vital parts of government action. It cannot be emphasized enough, however, that strategy and clever rhetoric alone are not sufficient; they matter not at all if the basics of the budget—its logic, justifications, mathematics, and internal consistency—are faulty.

Defending the Base

If legislators decide to reduce a program's funding from existing levels, program administrators can respond in several ways. Among the response strategies are the following:[15]

1. *A study.* Agency administrators argue that rash actions (such as cutting a program) should not be taken until all consequences have been completely considered. A study delays action.
2. *Popular program cuts.* The administrator responds to the proposed reduction by cutting or eliminating (or at least releasing to the news media plans for such action) programs with strong public support (see photo on page 515). By proposing that the school band or athletic programs be eliminated, for instance, the administrator hopes to mobilize sufficient outcry.
3. *Dire consequences.* The administrator outlines tragic events—shattered lives of those served, supplier businesses closed, the end of Western civilization as we know it—that would accompany reductions.
4. *All or nothing.* An administrator admits that any reduction would make the program impossible, so it might as well be eliminated.
5. *You pick.* The administrator responds that all agency activities are so vital that agency directors are unable to choose. Therefore, those proposing the cut should identify the targets, thereby clearly placing the political blame for the cut.
6. *We are the experts.* The agency argues that it has expertise that the budget cutter lacks.

Expanding the Base

A different group of strategies applies when the agency seeks to continue or augment operations of its existing program:

1. *Round up.* Rounding program estimates—workload, prices, costs, and so on—upward to the next-highest hundred, thousand, or million creates substantial slack.

One strategy available to administrators faced with a proposed reduction in funding is to cut or eliminate popular programs. This father and his children peer mournfully in the window of the Smithsonian's Air and Space Museum—closed on a Columbus Day weekend because of a budget crisis.

2. *"If it don't run, chrome it."* The budget presentation sparkles with data, charts, graphs, and other state-of-the-art management trappings. The quality of the show is intended to overpower its weak substance.
3. *Sprinkling.* Budget items are slightly increased, either in hard-to-detect general categories or across the board, after the basic request has been prepared. The thin layer of excess is spread so thin that it cannot be clearly identified as padding.
4. *Numbers game.* To divert attention from spending increases, agency administrators may discuss physical units—facilities operated, grants initiated, acres maintained, and so on—rather than the funds requested.
5. *Workload or backlog.* Administrators often base their request on greater client demands or a backlog of unfilled requests. *This* argument is frequently reasonable.

Proposing New Programs

Programs and agencies develop an institutional momentum. To propose a new program, one that expands the scope of agency operations, entails special challenges because the new program lacks momentum. Some strategies are characteristic of a new proposal:

1. *Old stuff.* Administrators may disguise new programs as simple extensions of existing operations, as growth and nothing new for the agency.

2. *Foot-in-the-door financing.* A project starts with a small amount of funding, possibly as a pilot or demonstration program or as a feasibility study. Modest amounts build each year until the program is operational and has developed a constituency.

3. *It pays for itself.* Supporters of a new program sometimes argue that the program will produce more revenue than it will cost. This may or may not be true.

4. *Spend to save.* Expenditure on the proposal would cause cost reduction somewhere else in the government. Whether the claimed spending reduction actually would occur is another argument.

5. *Crisis.* The proposal may be linked to a catastrophe or overwhelming problem— AIDS, economic development, homelessness, energy crisis, and so on—even though the link may be tenuous, simply because the agency perceives that such proposals are less likely to be reduced.

6. *Mislabeling.* The actual nature of a program may be hidden by mixing it with another, more politically attractive program. Examples abound: military installations may have blast-suppression areas that look strangely like golf courses; university dormitories or office buildings may have roofs that have seats convenient for viewing events on the football field; and so on.

7. *What they did makes us do it.* An action taken by another entity may place demands on the agency beyond what could be accommodated by normal management of existing programs. If school libraries are closed and teachers continue to assign reference work, local public libraries might argue for new programs to accommodate student requests for assistance.

8. *Mandates.* Some external entity (courts, a federal agency, the state, and so on) may legally require an agency action that entails greater expenditure. Rather than rearrange operations to accommodate the new requirement, an agency may seek new funds.

9. *Matching the competition.* Agencies often compare their programs with those operated by others and use the comparison as a basis for adding new programs. (Seldom does the comparison lead to a proposal that some programs be eliminated because similar agencies do not have them.)

10. *It's so small.* Program proponents may argue that a request is not large enough to require full review, that its trivial budgetary consequences do not make the review a reasonable use of time.

Taxation

The problem taxes present to the administrator and legislator, as the French finance minister J. B. Colbert once said, resembles the problem of plucking a goose: how to get the largest amount of feathers with the fewest squawks. Although government makes different choices as to how to get those feathers, a common logic and language defines tax bases and the manner in which rates are applied to the chosen base. In this section, we will examine the criteria for evaluating revenue options; the pros and cons of the various structures (income taxes, sales taxes, property and so on); and possible reforms of the federal tax system.

Criteria for Evaluating Revenue Options

In the first section of this chapter, we noted the major sources of revenue for federal, state, and local governments. In this section, we want to consider the merits of each source. To set the stage for that analysis, let us note three pragmatic concepts with which a financial manager in the public sector should be acquainted when developing a tax system: tax equity, tax efficiency, and tax overlapping.

Tax Equity   A fair tax (tax equity) would be, first, one that treats equally people in equal economic circumstances. A tax distribution that adheres to this principle provides what is technically known as **horizontal equity.**

A fair tax should also treat unequals unequally; this principle is called **vertical equity.** What is its justification? First, that taxes should be distributed among taxpayers in relation to their ability to pay. For example, those with higher incomes should pay a higher proportion of their income in taxes. If they do, then the tax is progressive. However, some American conservatives advocate a **proportional tax** on income that *takes the same proportion of taxes at each income level.* For example, everyone would pay 30 percent of their income in taxes, regardless of what the income might be; this kind of tax is called, for obvious reasons, a "flat tax." A **regressive tax** means that the ratio of tax payments to income *declines* as income rises: the more one earns, the less one pays proportionally. An excellent example of this kind of tax is a sales tax on food. Consider a family of four with an annual income of $20000. Assuming they spend $8000 on food and that the sales tax on it is 5 percent, they are paying a tax of $400 per year on food, or 2 percent of their annual income. Now contrast this hypothetical family with a professional couple (no children) making $120000 a year. They eat well, spending $8000 a year. But what percentage of their income goes to taxes on food? Obviously far less than that for our family of four. Of these three kinds of taxes, therefore the ability-to-pay principle is most closely associated with **progressive taxation.**

The second justification for the concept of tax equity is the "benefit received principle." In a sense, the principle attempts to apply a free-market approach to the distribution of taxes. Direct charges, or **user fees,** for government goods force individuals to reveal their willingness to pay for these goods. Noting that it costs $1.3 billion a year to run the U.S. Coast Guard, President Reagan in 1981 proposed that American boat and yacht owners pay a user fee for the services they receive. Although this principle faces many practical limitations at the national level (how does one apply it to a social good such as national defense?), local governments are able to apply it to many services—parking, recreation, garbage collection, libraries, utilities, and so on. Yet even at the local level there are limitations to the application of this principle. Many benefits, such as fire and police protection, accrue collectively and are difficult to measure. Or sometimes the objectives of government are in direct opposition to the principle, public assistance being a case in point.

Tax Efficiency   Another useful concept in developing a tax system is **tax efficiency.** This concept involves basically two things: economic efficiency and administrative efficiency.

Economic efficiency concerns the effect the tax has on the private sector—that is, does it disturb the relative prices of private goods, the pattern of consumption and saving, and the pattern of leisure? Ideally, all these effects would be minimal.

Administrative efficiency concerns how easy the tax is to collect. In some cities, for example, it is necessary for city agents to raid those businesses that have been remiss in paying the selected sales tax. The efforts feature unveiling photographic blowups of prominent citizens who owe taxes, publishing past-due tax rolls, and locking doors of businesses that have not paid their taxes.

The costs of compliance for the taxpayer should not be overlooked. From the standpoint of efficiency, a flat-rate national income tax—one in which everyone paid, say, 20 percent—would appear superior to a progressive tax with multitudinous loopholes and exemptions.

Tax Overlapping   The concepts of **tax overlapping** and **tax coordination** are not difficult. In a federal system such as that of the United States, two or more levels of government frequently use the same tax base. In New York City, for example, all three levels tax personal income. At the same time, in a relatively mobile society such as that of the United States, it is not uncommon for businesses and individuals to carry out economic activities that make them liable for taxes in many different taxing jurisdictions at the same level of government; for example, in different cities.

Although total elimination of these types of overlap is probably impossible, the administrator, if concerned with economic efficiency and taxpayer inequities, cannot ignore them. It is therefore necessary to try to coordinate taxing efforts at one level of government with those at the other two. Fortunately, each level tends to rely mainly on one type of tax.

Coordination between jurisdictions at the same levels can also be important. For example, different tax rates on cigarettes sometimes result in wholesale smuggling of cigarettes across state lines.

Sources of Revenue

Knowledge of these three concepts—tax equity, tax efficiency, and tax overlapping—can help an administrator and legislator appreciate the advantages and disadvantages of selecting different sources of taxes. But they must also know the characteristics of each source. Figure 11.6 summarizes the characteristics of the most popular sources of taxes.

Taxes are not the only source of revenue. Actually, nontax revenue of cities in recent years increased in relative importance, reaching close to one-half the general revenue of cities by the end of the 1960s. In general, municipal nontax revenue is composed of user charges and state and federal aid. Because the latter was discussed in Chapter 3, this discussion is limited to user charges.

The use of the price system offers significant advantages in terms of both resource allocation and equity. As William Vickrey notes, if prices are closely related to costs, there are "substantial possibilities for better utilization of resources, reduced levels of charges

Figure 11.6 Pros and Cons of Six Revenue Sources

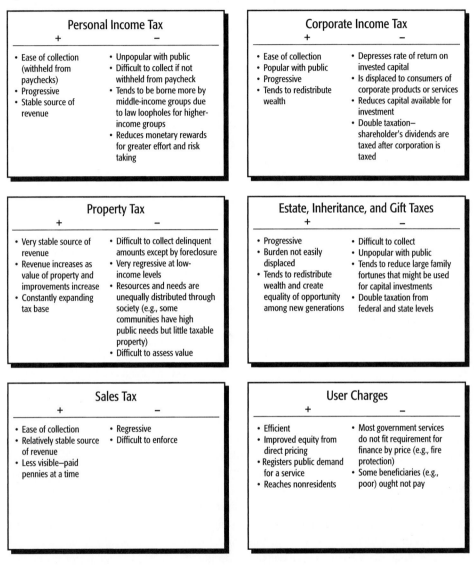

Personal Income Tax	
+	**−**
• Ease of collection (withheld from paychecks) • Progressive • Stable source of revenue	• Unpopular with public • Difficult to collect if not withheld from paycheck • Tends to be borne more by middle-income groups due to law loopholes for higher-income groups • Reduces monetary rewards for greater effort and risk taking

Corporate Income Tax	
+	**−**
• Ease of collection • Popular with public • Progressive • Tends to redistribute wealth	• Depresses rate of return on invested capital • Is displaced to consumers of corporate products or services • Reduces capital available for investment • Double taxation—shareholder's dividends are taxed after corporation is taxed

Property Tax	
+	**−**
• Very stable source of revenue • Revenue increases as value of property and improvements increase • Constantly expanding tax base	• Difficult to collect delinquent amounts except by foreclosure • Very regressive at low-income levels • Resources and needs are unequally distributed through society (e.g., some communities have high public needs but little taxable property) • Difficult to assess value

Estate, Inheritance, and Gift Taxes	
+	**−**
• Progressive • Burden not easily displaced • Tends to redistribute wealth and create equality of opportunity among new generations	• Difficult to collect • Unpopular with public • Tends to reduce large family fortunes that might be used for capital investments • Double taxation from federal and state levels

Sales Tax	
+	**−**
• Ease of collection • Relatively stable source of revenue • Less visible—paid pennies at a time	• Regressive • Difficult to enforce

User Charges	
+	**−**
• Efficient • Improved equity from direct pricing • Registers public demand for a service • Reaches nonresidents	• Most government services do not fit requirement for finance by price (e.g., fire protection) • Some beneficiaries (e.g., poor) ought not pay

on the average, and improved service, all of which are inherent in pricing policies that are imaginatively concerned in terms of economic efficiency."[16] A few examples serve to illustrate Vickrey's remark:

- Imposition of user charges can prevent excessive wasteful use of electric power or water within an urban area.
- Imposition of a price charge can ration facilities among users. A park or outdoor concert has a limited capacity; excessive demand therefore can be brought into line with supply when users must pay a fee.

- Imposition of fees and charges can help control activities that damage air and landscape or cause pollution or congestion. This is the rationale for what some think are excessive taxes on downtown parking lots. User charges also have advantages in terms of fairness.

Federal Tax Reform

Humorist Art Buchwald once said, "Tax reform is taking taxes off things that have been taxed in the past and putting taxes on things that haven't been taxed before." Nevertheless, the debate over reform rages on—in Washington, in 50 statehouses, and in thousands of city councils.

The case against the federal income tax has six arguments:

1. It is unfair; if the taxpayer is successful, she has to pay proportionately more than if she were unsuccessful.
2. It is difficult to comply with. Even the people who write the laws rely on professionals to prepare their returns. This complexity takes a toll.
3. It is intrusive. Every year countless horror stories surface about people who have had their rights infringed upon by the IRS.
4. It discourages savings and investment, thus reducing the growth of jobs and incomes.
5. It cannot reach the underground economy of drug and criminal profits; thus honest people pay more.
6. It raises the price of goods and services, thus hurting the competitiveness of U.S. products in world markets.

Basically, there are two alternatives to the current income tax system. Some advocate the previously mentioned **flat-rate income tax.** Under this scheme, everyone, regardless of income, would pay the same rate and, with few or no exceptions, probably send their returns in on a postcard. In the 1996 presidential campaign, candidate hopefuls (including the incumbent, Bill Clinton) unveiled their own flat-tax plans.

The other alternative is a general **consumption tax.** Consumption taxes are usually hailed as an efficient means of taxation. A consumption tax is less likely to distort economic behavior than income taxes. With high marginal rates of income tax, individuals may have less incentive to work hard. With a consumption tax, their extra income is not taxed until it is spent. Consumption taxes can also be levied on a wide base. In theory, people should be taxed on everything they buy; in practice, things are a little more complicated (see box: "What is a Snack").

The main argument against consumption taxes is a political one. Personal allowances and higher tax rates for higher incomes mean that income taxes are progressive. Consumption taxes are generally levied at a constant rate. This means that poor people, who consume a higher share of their current income than rich people, suffer—so consumption taxes are "unfair." This is true, though many economists argue that the most efficient response of a government should be to give poorer people benefits in cash rather than to distort the tax system.

What Is a Snack

One of the problems of the sales tax is knowing what to tax. Under California law, snacks are not really considered food and therefore are subject to sales tax. Officially speaking, the items on the left are snacks; those on the right, food. Really.

Snacks	Food
Ritz crackers	Soda crackers
Popped popcorn	Unpopped popcorn
Ding Dongs	Doughnuts
Granola bars	Granola cereal
Imitation pork rinds	Pork rinds
Chocolate bars	Chocolate chips
Thin matzo crackers	Thin matzos
Screaming Yellow Zonkers	Muffins
Slice of pie (wrapped)	Whole pie, pie slice on plate
Candy bars with nuts	Nuts

Over the past 30 years, industrial countries have gradually shifted toward general consumption taxes. Rich countries raised an average of only 3.5 percent of GDP from general consumption taxes in 1965. Three decades later, the amount has doubled to 7 percent.

The European cousin of the sales tax is the value-added tax (VAT). In principle, there is little economic difference between VAT and retail sales taxes. Both taxes should raise the same amount of money. However, the different ways in which they are collected makes VAT more efficient. Under a retail sales tax system, producers, wholesalers, and retailers do not pay tax when they buy or sell from one another. VAT, in contrast, is paid throughout the production chain; registered intermediaries (but not the final consumer) reclaim VAT by presenting a set of invoices to the tax authorities.

This makes VAT much harder to avoid. While a good is being produced, sellers have an interest in proving they have paid the tax on their inputs in order to reduce the tax liability on their sales. With a retail sales tax system, in contrast, the burden of collecting the tax lies entirely with the final seller of the good. If he fails to charge it, the tax on the whole value-added item is lost. As the tax rises, the incentive to avoid it increases. Most economists reckon that 10 percent is the highest level at which a sales tax can be set without large-scale attempts at evasion.

What Ails the Federal Budget Process?

The budget process is an intricate political drama that concerns the nation's capital for much of the year. The president's proposals, released in early February, are, despite their reams of detail, merely the opening act. They are invariably followed by months of loud partisan posturing in Congress. But it is not so much politics that ails the process—indeed, it would be hard to imagine budgeting without politics—as it is three more specific problems. They are earmarking, uncontrollable expenditures, and the deficit.

Earmarks   Although most Americans are familiar with the term pork barrel spending—the notion that a politician works to get government funds to benefit constituents often in return for their political support—"earmarking" is subtly different. It refers to the insertion of a specific funding provision for a specific named project into legislation. An earmark faces criticism because these appropriations are directly requested by individual members of Congress and are often added without scrutiny of other lawmakers. Of course, acquiring monies and projects for constituents is very much part of a legislator's role, but critics of earmarks say that earmarked projects aren't a good use of taxpayer dollars. They also worry that earmarks are another way for lobbyist dollars to put lobbyist priorities above those of others. Since earmarks are individual efforts, a lobbyist may only have to convince one legislator to move their case forward.

Consider the $636.3 billion defense spending bill passed by the House Appropriations Committee for fiscal year 2010. It included more than 1,100 earmarks, totaling more than $2.7 billion. Defenders of earmarking would say, "So what, that's less than one half of 1 percent of the bill." But defenders neglect the administrative cost of earmarking. James D. Savage has examined the extensive transaction and opportunity costs that come with the political, budgetary, and programmatic management of projects such as the 1,100 in the defense bill.

> Transaction costs include the time, energy, and resources devoted to searching for and obtaining information, the cost of bargaining and coordinating agreements among actors, and the cost of monitoring and achieving contractual compliance between principal and agent. Opportunity costs reflect the trade-offs in costs and the loss of potential gain by investing time, energy, and resources in one alternative as opposed to another, as when, for instance, government funds are allocated for one activity rather than another.

For example, say, the Office of Naval Research gets a $3 million earmark. What does that really mean? It means that $3 million cannot be spent on the Navy's identified priorities to support the activities of the U.S. Navy and Marine Corps. As Savage concludes, "Clearly, earmarking is more than an issue for the press and congressional scholars; it should also be the careful study of students of public administration and public policy.[17]

Uncontrollable Expenditures   The Budget Enforcement Act of 1990 created two legal categories of federal spending—mandatory (or "uncontrollable") and discretionary (or "controllable"). Mandatory spending includes outlays that are made according to definitions of eligibility and establishment of benefits or payment rules, rather than directly through the appropriation process. Much of the spending comes from entitlement programs such as Social Security and Medicare. Congress and presidents control the spending, but they exercise control indirectly by establishing the definitions and rules; when those conditions have been met, however, the government has a legal obligation to pay the eligible person, corporation, or other entity. Congress and the president cannot increase or decrease the outlays for a given year without changing the substantive law that created the eligibility and payment rules—which would be a Herculean task for programs like Social Security and Medicare. Because the spending is outside the annual appropriation process, Congress and the president have less capacity to exercise annual control over it.

Discretionary spending represents the rest of federal spending, the spending that flows through the annual appropriation process and through the thirteen appropriation bills. It is for federal programs and for the federal bureaucracy. Operations of agencies—the Department of Defense, the Department of Homeland Security, the Fish and Wildlife Service, the IRS, the EPA, and so on—fall in the discretionary category. This category identifies the form of the spending—not its importance to the nation. In other words, being "discretionary" does not mean that the spending is insignificant or that the nation could easily go without the program. It means that the spending goes through the traditional appropriations process and is not automatic.

Let's compare the growth rates of these two categories of spending. Between 1975 and 2005, defense spending and domestic discretionary spending rose 563 percent and 674 percent. During the same period, Social Security rose 816 percent, Medicare 2,361 percent, Medicaid 2,676 percent, and farm price supports 3,166 percent. In 1962, the president and Congress had control of nearly 70 percent of the budget; by 2007 that was down to 34 percent. See Figure 11.2.

The most mandatory of all mandatory spending is interest on the national debt. This bill must be paid if the federal government is to continue its access to national and international capital markets. But the president and Congress do have options with regard to the other forms of mandatory spending. First they could cap entitlements—essentially limiting the total amount that can be spent in a program, rather in the manner of ordinary appropriations. Second, they could make entitlement provisions less generous or, at least, constrain movements to make them more generous—for example, they could require that increases in benefits be financed by additional revenue. Third, they could make entitlements means-tested, thus ensuring that only those classified as needy according to a broader measure of affluence receive benefits.

In February 2006, President Bush signed legislation slowing the growth of mandatory spending by about $40 billion over the next five years. This is the first such legislation to reduce mandatory spending in nearly a decade. But do the math: that's less than $8 billion a year in a $2,770 + billion budget.

In sharp contrast to the explosive growth in mandatory spending, growth in total discretionary spending in fiscal year 2006 was held below the rate of inflation. The implications of these kinds of budget decisions should not be lost in the mist of numbers. Consider the following two facts:

- From the *New York Times* (June 26, 2004): "For the most part, the history of the National Park Service is a sad tale of an idealistic vision undermined by the government's neglect. . . . The parks' operating budgets have nearly always been too skimpy, and in recent years a substantial backlog of the deferred maintenance has built up. . . . Park visitors certainly notice things like bad roads and rundown buildings, which are the result of deferred maintenance. But what this summer's tourists are also going to notice is a serious reduction in staff levels. . . . It's also likely to mean inadequate law enforcement and emergency services. When people talk about smaller government, they usually don't mean fewer park rangers."

- From the *Wall Street Journal* (November 2, 2005): "The job of a prison guard, which has always been perilous, is growing harder. . . . The number of federal and state prisoners nationwide hit 1.5 million last year, up 51% compared with 1995. The number of prison officers increased 8 percent during the same period to 239000. . . . In practice, because only a fraction of guards worked any one particular shift, the shift is even more lopsided. As a result, it is not unusual for only 17 or 18 officers to be responsible for 1000 inmates."

The Budget Deficit   We have discussed the importance of the budgetary process as a mechanism for control, management, and planning. But the federal budget is also a mechanism for allocating resources between the public and private sectors of the economy. These decisions are also central to the Keynesian approach to economic management. The British economist John Maynard Keynes (1883–1946) stressed the importance of the public budget in regulating effective demand. Simply stated, if government wants to stabilize the economy—that is, increase economic growth and reduce unemployment—it should run a budget deficit. Such a deficit places in circulation more money than the government has removed from circulation, thereby generating greater demand for goods and services by citizens who have more money to spend. Conversely, if the government wants to reduce inflation in an overheated economy, it should run a budget surplus, removing more money from circulation in taxes than it puts in with public expenditures. This budget surplus leaves citizens with less money than they had before the government's actions and so would lessen total demand.

Although not all economists today are Keynesian, virtually all would agree that running deficits when the economy is sluggish, or contracting, is good. What is not so good—if not downright bad—is to run deficits when the economy is growing briskly.

Why is that? The traditional answer is that deficits could "overheat" an already expanding economy and lead to inflation. Thanks in part to globalization—what some politicians deride as "cheap foreign imports"—the inflation threat seems less real today than it once was.

Today the chief concern about running deficits in a growing economy is largely based on its adverse effect on U.S. productivity—that is, the quantity of goods and services produced for each hour of a worker's time. Let us consider how deficits and productivity are supposedly related. When the government needs to finance a budget deficit, it does so by borrowing in financial markets, much as a student might borrow to finance a college education. As the government borrows to finance its deficits, therefore, it reduces the quantity of funds available for other borrowers. The budget deficit thereby reduces investment both in human capital (students' education) and physical capital (businesses' investment in new equipment). Because lower investment today means lower productivity in the future, budget deficits are generally thought to depress growth in living standards.

Good or bad, the reality is that—except for 1998–2002—deficits have been a major feature of the U.S. economy since the early 1980s, when Ronald Reagan took office. Committed to smaller government and lower taxes to stimulate growth, Reagan found reducing government spending to be more difficult politically than reducing taxes. The result was the beginning of a period of large budget deficits that continued not only through Reagan's time in office but also through George H. W. Bush's, most of Bill Clinton's, and all of George W. Bush's.

Now we need to clarify the difference between "budget deficits" and the "federal debt." When we talk about the *deficit*, we're focusing on one year at a time. When we talk about the *debt*, we're talking about the accumulation of those deficits over time. Say, for example, that there was $4 trillion in accumulated debt. That is all the money that has been borrowed year in, year out over time. Then, with that $4 trillion in debt, in one year the government runs, say, a budget surplus of $100 billion. That surplus would be subtracted from the debt so the next year, instead of having $4 trillion in debt, we would have $3.9 trillion in debt. On the reverse side, let's say we had $4 trillion in debt, and we ran a $200 billion deficit. Then the debt would increase, and we would be up to $4.2 trillion in debt at the end of the year.

So, when you think about government and debt and borrowing, remember that the deficit is one year, and the debt is the accumulation over time. Deficits can bounce up and down in ways that don't tell us much about the long term. *Instead, look at the total debt accumulated over time as a percentage of gross domestic product.*

Figure 11.7 shows the debt of the U.S. government expressed as a percentage of GDP. From the 1950s through the 1970s, the debt-GDP ratio declined. Although the government did run budget deficits during some of these years, the deficits were small

Figure 11.7 Federal Debt as Percent of GDP, 1940–2010

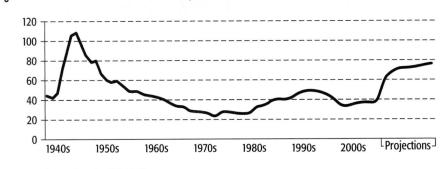

SOURCE: *The Budget for FY 2010.*

enough that the size of the government's debt grew less rapidly than the overall economy. Because GDP is a rough measure of the government's ability to raise tax revenue, the declining debt-GDP ratio indicates the economy is, in some sense, living within its means. By contrast, when the budget deficit ballooned in the early 1980s, the government debt started rising more rapidly than the overall economy. As a result, the debt-GDP ratio started to rise.

How does the U.S. debt-GDP ratio compare to that of other industrialized nations? Following are the percentages for the world's largest economies for 2008, according to the CIA:

United States	60.8
Japan	170.4
Germany	62.6
United Kingdom	47.2
France	67

Concepts for Review

accounting

accrual accounting

activity-based costing

audit

baselines

budget calendar

capital budget

cash management

ceilings

Congressional Budget and Impoundment
    Control Act of 1974

Congressional Budget Office (CBO)

consumption tax

cost accounting

current services budget
    (or base budget)

debt management

deficit

federal budget cycle

fiscal year

flat-rate income tax

fund

horizontal equity

impoundment

incrementalism

line-item budgeting

line-item veto

obligations

off-budget items

Office of Management and Budget (OMB)

outlays

performance budgeting

political strategies in the
    budget process

program budgeting

progressive tax

proportional tax

purposes of budgeting

regressive tax

strategic sourcing

surplus

tax coordination

tax efficiency

tax overlapping

uncontrollables

user fee

vertical equity

zero-based budgeting (ZBB)

Key Points

This chapter explained the workings of the public finance system in the United States and pointed out its implications for public management. The chapter made these major points:

1. Central to the management of government's financial resources is the budget. Administrators devote much time and energy to preparing it. Its adoption represents a critical juncture in the policy-planning process, for few major programs are conceivable without the expenditure of money.

2. The four basic phases of the federal budget cycle are executive preparation, legislative approval, budget execution, and audit.

3. The president's transmittal of his budget proposals to Congress on the first Monday in February climaxes many months of planning and analysis throughout the executive branch. Formulation of the budget for fiscal year 2006, for example, began in the spring of 2004.

4. In 1974, Congress, seeking a greater role in managing the government, passed the Congressional Budget and Impoundment Control Act, which requires it to adopt an annual budget. The budget act also created the Congressional Budget Office (CBO). This office advises Congress on the likely economic effects of different spending programs and provides information on the cost of proposed policies.

5. Budget authority provides funding for an agency. An obligation occurs when an order is placed by that agency for materials. Inventories are recorded when materials are delivered to the agency. Outlay occurs when the bill is paid by the agency for the materials. And cost occurs when materials are used by the agency.

6. Most states place budgeting responsibility solely with the executive, but some establish a budget commission that has legislative representation. Most states (all except Alabama, Michigan, New York, and Texas) start their fiscal years in July. State budgets may be either annual or biannual.

7. The federal government collects and spends over $2 trillion a year. That is only slightly more than the total for state and local governments. In decreasing order of importance, the principal sources of funding for state and local governments are sales tax, intergovernmental revenue, property taxes, individual income taxes, and corporate income tax. The seven major areas of expenditure in decreasing order of size are education, welfare, highways, health, interest on debt, general administration, and police.

8. Accounting is the system of recording, classifying, and reporting financial transactions in an orderly way. The oldest type of accounting is cash accounting. Receipt transactions are recorded at the time funds are received, and disbursements are recorded when checks are issued. Accrual accounting records expenditures when an obligation is incurred and records revenues when earned. Cost accounting, also known as activity-based costing, concentrates on reporting the cost of providing goods and services.

9. A capital budget separates long-term investments in buildings, bridges, roads, vehicles, computers, and the like from current operating expenses. Although the federal government separates budget items by categories such as defense, energy, and income security, it combines all capital and operating expenses.

10. The purposes of budgeting are control, management, and planning. Control is identified with the legislative concern for tight control over executive expenditures. The management orientation emphasizes the efficiency with which ongoing activities are conducted. Planning emphasizes programs and the relationship between revenues and expenditures to accomplish objectives.

11. A line-item budget used for projection and control of expenses remains at the heart of the budgeting process. The line-item budget is designed to keep spending within the limits set by the legislature.

12. Whereas the line-item budget emphasizes accountability and performance budgeting emphasizes efficiency, programmed budgeting emphasizes funding allocation among various competing agencies and programs.

13. Traditional performance budgeting attempts to budget according to the direct outputs or activities of government agencies. But government agencies exist not for output but for *outcomes*. New performance budgeting (NPB) attempts to let real performance influence budget decisions.

14. Based on an analysis of the U.S. Congress, Wildavsky identified certain groups of strategies pursued by agencies in the budget process. The first general strategy is to cultivate an active clientele for help in dealing with both the legislature and the chief executive. The second strategy is the development of the confidence of other government officials. Another group of strategies—contingent strategies—depends on the budget circumstances, and particularly on whether discussion concerns (1) a reduction in agency programs below the present level of expenditures, (2) an increase in the scope of agency programs, or (3) an expansion of agency programs to new areas.

15. Three pragmatic concepts with which a financial manager in the public sector should be acquainted when developing a tax system are tax equity, tax efficiency, and tax overlapping.

16. A proportional tax on income takes the same proportion of taxes at each income level. A progressive tax means that the ratio of tax payments to income declines as income rises. A regressive tax means that the more one earns, the less one pays proportionally.

17. The main concern over the budget deficit is its adverse effect on U.S. productivity— that is, the quantity of goods and services produced for each hour of a worker's time.

18. When we talk about a deficit, we are talking about annual deficits. When we talk about debt, we are talking about the accumulation of those deficits over time.

19. The Budget Enforcement Act of 1990 created two legal categories of federal spending— mandatory (or "uncontrollable") and discretionary (or "controllable"). Mandatory spending includes outlays that are made according to definitions of eligibility and establishment of benefits or payment rules, rather than directly through the appropriations process. Much of the spending comes from entitlement programs such as Social Security and Medicare.

20. The entire budget process—from its start in agencies to the end of the fiscal year— takes about 30 months. A lot of unforeseen events can occur during such an expanse of time. That is why budgeting sometimes involves backdoor spending, reprogramming, transfers, and supplemental appropriations.

Problems and Applications

1. The following two statements illustrate what principle discussed in this chapter?

   "The average cost of tax collection is 4 percent of the local income-tax revenue in West Dakota local governments."

   "With technological progress and economic growth, there follows a shift in emphasis to income rather than property as an index of ability to pay. Today, wealth is reflected in the person's income, not real property."

2. One response to revenue-raising limitations being placed on local government is to delete exemptions. P. S. Flores offers the following examples of welfare and charitable groups enjoying property-tax exemption: YMCA, fraternal clubs, chambers of commerce, labor unions, the American Legion, Masonic Lodges, orphanages, humane societies, hospitals, and retirement and nursing homes. Which exemptions would you delete? How would you justify it?

3. How would you interpret the following figures? Good news or bad?

   - When Ronald Reagan was elected president, the richest 1 percent of taxpayers were paying 18 percent of all income taxes. When he left office, they were paying 27 percent.
   - When Reagan was elected, the wealthiest 5 percent were paying 38 percent of all income taxes. In 1988 they were paying 46 percent.
   - The wealthier 50 percent of Americans pay 94.5 percent of all federal income taxes.

4. Two kinds of taxes not explicitly mentioned in Figure 11.6 are luxury taxes (for example, taxes on furs, jewelry, boats, and airplanes) and sin taxes (for example, taxes on alcohol, tobacco, oil, gasoline, and firearms). What impacts—secondary as well as immediate—do you think each kind of tax has?

5. Behind much of the current thinking about performance budgeting lies a commonsense theory about motivation: people should be rewarded if they do a good job and should be punished if they do not. Such rewards and punishments, goes this line of reasoning, will motivate an agency's top managers—and frontline workers as well—to do a good job. That will bring about an across-the-board improvement in agency performance. Sounds sensible, right? What are your thoughts on the subject?

Favorite Bookmarks

www.omb.gov   The Office of Management and Budget's Web site contains each year's budget as proposed by the President along with voluminous supporting information.

www.cbpp.org   The Center on Budget and Policy Priorities conducts research and analysis to help shape public debates over proposed budget and tax policies.

www.gao.gov   The Government Accountability Office Web site contains reports on budget issues, investment, government management, public services, health care, energy issues, and virtually every other major area of the federal government.

www.cbo.gov/   The Congressional Budget Office Web site contains current budget projections, current economic projections, current status of discretionary appropriations, and historical budget data. You can also find useful studies, reports, and testimony.

www.access.gpo.gov/su docs/budget/   If you ever want to know exactly how much the government spends on a particular program—clandestine operations excluded—you can find it here. The entire budget of the U.S. federal government is on the Internet.

www.virtual-u.org   Virtual U., released commercially in 2000, challenges players to test—and for those with actual ability, to hone—their management skills by plowing through ten situations that mimic the real-life world of the university president. One scenario you can play is "Balance the Budget." This means you can do such presidential things as hire and fire professors, fiddle with pay scales, raise or lower tuition, adjust departmental spending, cram more students into dorms, increase or reduce financial aid, and even dig into that sacred endowment.

Notes

1. John L. Mikesell, Fiscal Administration: Analysis and Applications for the Public Sector (Belmont, CA: Wadsworth, 2003), 156–58.
2. William L. Riordon, *Plunkitt of Tammany Hall* (New York: E. P. Dutton, 1963), 3.
3. Earl R. Wilson and Susan C. Kattelus, *Accounting for Governmental and Nonprofit Entities* (Burr Ridge, IL: Irwin, 2004), 513.
4. Katherine Barrett and Richard Greene, "The Rise of Cost Accounting," *Governing* (March 2000).
5. The following discussion of cash management, purchasing, and debt administration draws heavily from J. E. Peterson, "Managing Public Money," *Governing* (June 1991).
6. Ibid., 54.
7. Zach Patton, "Buy by Data," *Governing* (June 2006): 44.
8. Ibid., 44–45.
9. L. L. Moak and A. M. Hillhouse, *Concepts and Practices in Local Government Finance* (Chicago: MFOA, 1975).
10. Charles Adams, "Beware the Ides of April," *Policy Review* (Spring 1996): 201.
11. A. Schick, "The Road to PPB: The Stages of Budget Reform," *Public Administration Review* (December 1966).
12. Ibid., 243.
13. *Houston Chronicle* (April 10, 1996).
14. R. E. Herzlinger, "Managing the Finances of Nonprofit Organizations," *California Management Review* (Spring 1979): 67.
15. The remaining discussion of budgetary politics is based on Mikesell, op. cit., 62–67.
16. William Vickrey quoted in S. Mushkin, ed., *Public Prices for Public Products* (Washington, DC: Urban Institute, 1972).
17. James D. Savage, "The Administrative Cost of Congressional Earmarking: The Case of the Office of Naval Research," *Public Administration Review* (May/June 2009): 448–57.

CASE 11.1
DANGEROUS STRATAGEMS

AP Photo/Pioneer Press, Minneapolis Star Tribune, Brandi Jade Thomas, www.TwinCities.com

In three-fourths of the states, the treasurer or chief financial officer (CFO) is elected by citizens in statewide elections. In some states, such as New York and Texas, the comptroller is elected and performs many of the functions of the CFO. About two-thirds of local governments have an official with the title "financial officer," "financial director," or a similar title implying broad duties. Financial wizardry is not a CFO's primary calling; but when governors or mayors find their budgets unbalanced, they turn to the CFO for possible stratagems. For the past few years, politicians in far too many cities and states—not to speak of Washington, DC—have tended to rely on nine dangerous stratagems:

1. *Delay maintenance and replacement of assets—and rely on hope.* On August 1, 2007, the I-35W bridge across the Mississippi River in Minneapolis collapsed suddenly, killing 13 people. Seven months later, a federal commission said that just to maintain and upgrade surface transportation in the United States world cost $225 billion a year for the next 50 years. Ensuring safe and dependable roads, bridges and transportation systems, as well as water systems, sewage treatment plants, dams and even schools also requirers long-term planning. Unfortunately, most politicians prefer quick fixes.

2. *Sell assets.* In economic hard times, it is popular to sell land, buildings, or surplus assets.

California's real estate is one of its greatest assets and selling off state property, according to the governor's office, would raise over $1 billion. Specifically, Governor Schwarzenegger proposed the sale of seven state-owned properties to help get his budget in balance including: San Quentin State Prison, the Cow Palace, Del March Fairgrounds, Orange County Fairgrounds, Ventura County Fairgrounds, and the Los Angeles Coliseum. Schwarzenegger's proposal was rather straightforward compared to that of Governor Eliot Spitzer in New York, who wanted to securitize, or sell off, part of *future* state lottery proceeds.

3. *Lease rather than buy equipment.* Say the U.S. Air Force needs 100 Boeing 767 aircrafts to use as aerial refueling tankers. Buying them outright would cost about $20 billion and add appreciably to this year's deficit. Therefore, for political reasons, Congress and the president might prefer to lease them over a 12-year period. The budget would take far less of a hit each year, even though total cost would be higher than if the Air Force had bought the planes.

4. *Rob Peter to pay Paul.* Most budgets are made up of multiple accounts. The account that gets the most attention is called the general fund. When that general fund gets in trouble, politicians start considering **off budget funds** as resources to be tapped. New York helped balance its budget in 1992 by transferring the cost of running the Erie Canal from the general fund ("on budget") to the Thruway Authority ("off budget"). Similarly, in 2003, Massachusetts transferred management of a convention center and a parking garage (both "on budget") to the state pension fund ("off budget") to show a savings of $175 million.

5. *Nickel and dime employees.* The response to budget problems is often symbolic. David Osborne and Peter Hutchinson write: "Leaders order coffee pots unplugged, travel budgets slashed, and consultants banned. To save energy, they force workers to endure hotter offices in summer and colder offices in winter. Some even outlaw potted plants. In Missouri last year, the governor ordered that every other light bulb in government buildings be unscrewed."

6. *Make across-the-board cuts rather than targeted cuts.* In 2008, Governor Schwarzenegger proposed cutting California's budget across the board by 10 percent, meaning that every state agency from police to health to the arts would receive a 10 percent reduction in its annual budget. Less drastically, that same year, Iowa Governor Chet Culver announced a 1.5 percent across-the-board cut and said education and Medicare "won't escape unscathed." The popularity of broad-brush, across-the-board cost-cutting is easy to understand: It is a way to avoid making difficult, uncomfortable political choices.

7. *Fudge the numbers.* A budget is really just a forecast, a necessary statement of expected revenues and expenses. But every budget is based on assumptions, and CFOs can make it look better or worse simply by changing those assumptions. If they expect 1000 new students to enroll in their schools but assume (for budget purposes) only 900, they have reduced the basis for their estimate of new expenses by 10 percent. Ronald Reagan's approach in 1982 was a classic example of making the budget "work" by fudging the numbers. To justify large tax cuts, his budget director, David Stockman, forecast 5 percent growth for 1982. Theoretically, this would help create a $28 billion surplus by 1986. As it turned out, the gross national product fell by 2 percent that year—and the largest deficits since World War II soon followed. The Obama White House presented its own rosy scenario with the fiscal year 2010 budget. It expected economic growth in 2009 to decline by only 1.2 percent, whereas the non-partisan Congressional Budget Office assumed a 3 percent decline. Quite a difference.

8. *Borrow.* Even when the general fund is legally prohibited from being in debt, governments find ways to borrow. The chief way states and local governments borrow is by issuing bonds. California has proven that the politics of borrowing works for both Republicans and Democrats. In 2003, the legislature finally passed a $99 billion budget with $10.7 billion of borrowing—which was probably unconstitutional. After voter removed (recall) Democratic Governor Gray Davis from office, the new Republican governor, Schwarzenegger, immediately endorsed borrowing $15 billion more as part of his "budget balancing"

plan. Meanwhile, on the East Coast, New Jersey faced a $3.5 billion shortfall and had accumulated a $32 billion debt. Governor John Corzine therefore proposed increasing fees on toll roads and issuing up to $38 billion in bonds against future toll revenues.

Although issuing bonds is the chief way for a state to borrow, Schwarzenegger would later try another way, namely, invoking a law that lets the state demand loans of 8 percent of property tax revenue from cities, counties, and special districts. Under this law, the state must repay the municipalities with interest within three years. So, he requested $2 billion, displeasing local officials up and down the state and in effect, kicking the can down the road three years.

9. *Use accounting gimmicks.* Accounting offers many temptations to politicians who might have made a read-my-lips pledge of "no new taxes." Since we cannot consider all the gimmicks, we note here just four: manipulating the timing of expenditures and receipts, requesting funds after budget approval, making false assumptions, and making dubious promises.

Our first example involves pretending or even requiring that money you expect to receive next year will actually come in this year or pretending that expenses planned for this year will be made, technically, next year. For example, states tell school districts that are expecting a school-aid payment in May (this fiscal year) that they will get it in July (next fiscal year), thus making this year's expenses look smaller. At the same time, they tell retailers who normally submit their June sales tax receipts in July (next fiscal year) to do so in June, thus making this year's revenue look larger. In Massachusetts, Governor Deval Patrick proposed counting about $900 million in proceeds from license fees of new casinos that *the legislature had not even authorized.*

Prudent presidents and governors recognize that natural disasters happen and allow for them in their budgets. Others simply assume none will occur, lower their spending request to the legislature accordingly, and then blithely ask the legislature for supplemental funding two months later, when the flooding or whatever occurs. This works well for wars, too.

Another accounting gimmick used to make deficit projection look smaller involves the alternative minimum tax (AMT) enacted in 1969 to prevent the wealthy from using tax shelters to avoid paying any income tax. Although it was intended to hit the wealthy taxpayer, it was not indexed for inflation. That fact has meant that it could affect millions of middle-class taxpayers. If they pay it, the government would get billions of dollars more in tax revenues, which is what past budgets have falsely assumed. But it would also probably mean a taxpayer revolt. So each year the White House and Congress agree to patch the alternative tax for inflation and the extra revenues never materialize.

Finally, we come to a relatively new gimmick: PAYGO (pay-as-you-go) . Here's how it works: The president promises that "Congress can only spend a dollar if it saves a dollar elsewhere." Thus, PAYGO, provides politicians with convenient talking points and taxpayers with a false sense of security on budget reform. From 1991 through 2002, PAYGO existed as a statute and was brought back in 2007. But it never worked because Congress severely limited the amount of the budget to which it applied and, in those cases when it did apply, conveniently voted waivers.

Case Questions

1. Identify the weaknesses in each strategy. (Hint: How do you think the bond rating agencies reacted to California's 2003 budget?)
2. Which strategies are the most dangerous? Least? Why?
3. Provide a recent example of each strategy.

Case References

David A. Stockman, *The Triumph of Politics: The inside Story of the Reagan Revolution* (New York: Harper and Row, 1986); David Osborne and Peter Hutchinson, *The Price of Government* (New York: Basic Books, 2004); Jackie Calmes, "Obama Bans Gimmicks, and Deficits Will Rise," *New York Times*, February 20, 2009; Keith B. Richburg, "Governors Seek Remedies for Shortfalls," *Washington Post*, January 13, 2008; Stu Wu and Bobby White, "California Cities Irked by Borrowing Plan," *Wall Street Journal*, May 22, 2009; and http://gov.ca.gov/Fact-Sheet/12305.

12 Information Management

Silvrshootr / iStockphoto.com

MAKING IT HAPPEN

....

This case is a hybrid. The first eight paragraphs have been excerpted (with minor changes) from a special report on technology and government that appeared in *The Economist* on February 16, 2008. The final three paragraphs update events and pose questions.

The municipal administration of the District of Columbia was once a byword for bad government, with a cocaine-snorting mayor, corrupt police, and incompetent and demoralized bureaucrats. Now, under a go-ahead mayor, Adrian Fenty, it has become a model practitioner of government. The public face of this is a single Web portal, dc.gov, which allows residents to do almost anything that in the past would have involved either picking up the phone (and hanging on and on) or going to an office and waiting. The site not only lets them find out about every imaginable aspect of the city, but also provides them with a means of acting on the information. This is not just a matter of printing out

532

forms; but often of filling them in and submitting them online, too. It is possible to renew a driver's license, pay a parking fine, report broken traffic lights, request a visit from the garbage-collection service, get all manner of permits, see planning applications, and pay local taxes.

In his "war room," the size of half a tennis court, Vivek Kundra, the district's chief technology officer, points to some of the woes that the new administration inherited: hundreds of computers bought for the schools but never used (and now obsolete) because the inventory managers lost trackof them; 4.6 million unsearchable paper records of DC employees, some of them a total mess. By contrast, his display of the state of the administration as it is now seems sheer magic. The day-to-day work of the DC government is shown on simple spreadsheets with new tasks requiring action appearing on panes with a yellow background. When the tasks have been accomplished, the panes go green. If a job is not done by a set deadline, the pane goes red and the employee's supervisor is automatically notified.

Running the District in this new way is not expensive, except perhaps for the huge plasma screens on which Kundra displays his wizardry. "A litte bit of money can go a long way in terms of technology," he explains. DC owns no servers. Instead of paying $50 a month per head for commercial software, its employees use the word processor, spreadsheet, and e-mail provided free in seconds to anyone who signs up with Google. With extra storage space, security, and a different label stuck on it, that costs $50 per employee per year. Everything—including those millions of records, all now scanned and indexed—is in what Google calls the "cloud": stored somewhere on its vast farms of powerful computers rather than in the DC offices. Using off-the-shelf softare marks a big difference from traditional e-government in which security-conscious, risk-averse officials start by commissioning consultants to make an offer and go on to buy an expensive tailor-made system running on costly in-house computers.

Kundra, who has a master's degree in information technology from the University of Maryland and is a graduate of the University of Virginia's Sorensen Institute of Leadership, applies the same ruthless approach to hardware. The DC police officers are now trying iPhones in place of police radios, crackly and temperamental, that cost $6,000 apiece. By integrating the cell phone signal with the free map and satellite picture provided by Google, the control room is also able to keep track of the patrol cars. Landlines are being ditched: employees are given a budget and told to buy their own cell phones. Kundra cites Adam Smith's "invisible hand": Just as in the private sector, technological innovation works only when the market wants it. His office must "demonstrate value," he says, not simply force other agencies to use new technology by administrative fiat.

One big lesson is that e-government is not just about computers; it involves redesigning the way government works When he started the DC job, Kundra was puzzled to find that it took four weeks to take on a new employee. Once the decision to hire the candidate had been made, the paperwork trundled back and forth between finance, human resources, and other departments until everybody had signed off on it. By redesigning the process, Kundra has cut the time taken to a mere 48 hours.

Now he is putting the procurement process online. The first project is a new warehouse for the police to store evidence collected at crime scenes. The center of the procurement process is a Wikipedia-style page on which potential bidders (and the general public) can download information about the project as well as ask questions.

It is far too early to declare the DC system an all-round success. Putting a user-friendly front end on a bureaucracy is good news for citizens, as is using cheap software to monitor it more effectively, but neither solves underlying problems. Much of what Kundra has done so far involves measuring the District's problems more precisely rather than solving them.

His next task, dealing with the often appalling public-sector schools, will be tough. Using technology to get janitors and maintenance staff to deal with leaking roofs and broken toilets will help, and thousands of new computers have already arrived at the schools (bought cheaply direct from Dell, rather than through a dealer). His systems will give a far more precise picture of truancy rates, security problems, teachers' absences and incompetence, and the way all these factors interact. But they cannot make the problems disappear.

In early 2008, only a few blocks away from Kundra's "war room," Karen Evans, the Office of Management and Budget's administrator for e-government and information technology was at work. Instead of plasma screens, she used a large cardboard chart on which each of the 18 federal agencies she monitors is scored with two colored circles, one for effort, the other for achievement. Since small bureaucracies are easier to transform than large ones, Kundra's task looked small compared with the job Evans faced: scrutinizing the $71 billion that the federal government spends on technology each year; ensuring it is managed effectively; leveraging existing technologies for maximum efficiency; increasing public access to government information; improving citizen participation; helping the public sector adopt technology at least as fast as the private sector; promoting interoperability and information sharing; enhancing security; guarding privacy; and promoting technology as a tool for solving pressing problems (two wars, the economy; and health care).

Evans thinks that the United States has not done badly on "e-government 1.0," providing its citizens with information. Making the rest happen, she admits, will be a lot harder. In March 2009, Kundra got a chance to find out just how hard "making it happen" would be when President Obama appointed him Chief Information Officer (CIO) of the United States, replacing Evans, who had left OMB two months earlier.

What are the big questions Kundra will face? A number of other American cities have made efforts similar to those he made when he served under Mayor Fenty. What makes scaling up these efforts to a national level so difficult? And what challenges might a CIO at any level of government face that his or her counterpart in the private sector would not?

SOURCE: *The Economist* (February 16, 2008).

No public administrator would turn the selection and development of his or her employees over to the human resources director nor would any agency head accept without any negotiation of next year's funding allocation from the budget director. Then why should public administrators let chief information officers manage their information? *Information management concerns every manager—just as much as personnel and budgetary issues.*

Although technological trends may be making the need for the management of information more acute, the need itself is not new. That information has value is a commonplace notion in government. "Information," as anyone who deals with politicians will hear over and over, "is power." As Herbert Kaufman observed three decades ago in *Administrative Behavior of Federal Bureau Chiefs,* public managers spend most of their time accumulating and assimilating information.[1] They need information about their environment—present *and* future. They also need information about the problems that their agencies face, the available alternatives, the probable effects of those alternatives, the internal actions required for implementation, the outputs produced, and the expenditures required. Moreover, because public organizations tend to face more complex problems than do private ones, the information needs of the former are probably greater.

To appreciate how managers use information in control and decision making, data must be distinguished from information and information from knowledge. **Data** are raw, unsummarized, and unanalyzed facts. **Information** is data that are meaningful and that alter the receiver's understanding—the data that managers actually use to interpret and understand events in the organization and the environment. David Morgan, head of the City of Dallas's data-processing department, explains the distinction this way: "I can tell you at any time of the day where a squad car was. What I can't tell you is where it was needed. We've got data; we don't have information." Information, Morgan argues, is what you get when you take useful data and manipulate it in away that makes sense for program management.[2] **Knowledge** is the body of information or the comprehension and understanding that comes from having acquired and organized a great deal of information—for example, a knowledge of medicine.

With these distinctions in mind, let's take a quick look at the six sections that constitute this chapter. The first section considers how public managers acquire information. Acquiring information might seem a rather straightforward affair that has, if anything, only become easier in recent years due to tremendous advances in information technology. But before we make that assumption, we should remind ourselves that, in the final analysis, data is always what individual human beings decide to put down. Public managers should also recognize that the people around them filter information, often with good intentions— for example, to conserve their boss' precious time. Sometimes, though, subordinates filter out bad news. To be effective at information acquisition, public managers must learn how to circumvent these filters.

Processing information, the subject of the second section, is also critically important. Effective public managers become adept at searching for and identifying patterns. They know how to mine their past experience so that they can recognize problems more quickly. They know that because problems do not come to us in neat little packages, they must have an ability to "connect the dots" among disparate pieces of information.

The third section considers how government agencies ensure that data are reliably and consistently retrievable in a usable format for authorized users—but no one else. As governments can and do collect more and more information on their citizens, the process of securing information becomes more and more important. (Recall the powerful surveillance technology described in the Closing Case for Chapter 9 on NYPD's Counterterrorism Division.)

The fourth section examines how public managers access information and knowledge—within and outside their agencies. The fifth section considers strategies and techniques individuals can employ to better present information.

Don't expect these five sections to be just a tour of the latest whiz-bang information technology (IT). And why should they? To repeat, effective methods for managing information are at least as old as Plato, who presented the dialectic (the question-and-answer method used by Socrates) as a pretty good way to get at the truth—or, at least, expose what we don't know (which can be equally useful). Not only that, researchers today canot agree on how much the new technology will change public administration. G. David Garson thinks the study of information technology is caught in a struggle between *utopians* who view IT as a strong positive force that will lead to more efficient and responsive governments and *dystopians* who predict negative results such as more wasteful government spending and less privacy for both citizens and employees.[3] The sixth section will consider both the optimistic and pessimistic positions on IT's future in government.

Acquiring Information

An information revolution has swept through the public sector, and no public administrator can escape its effects. Dramatic reductions in the cost of obtaining, processing, and transmitting information are changing the theory and practice of public administration.

At the heart of this revolution are accelerating and compounding trends in computer technology and communications technology. A handy way to make the point is by reference to **Moore's Law.** Gordon Moore is one of the founders of Intel Corp., which makes 75 percent of the integrated processors used in personal computers. In 1966, Moore predicted that every 18 months, the cost of computing would drop by 50 percent as computer-processing power doubled. Moore was right. Every few years, computer power, as measured by the number of transistors per computer chip, has more than doubled. Consequently, the computer on your lap is not only smaller, but also much cheaper and more powerful than the large mainframe computers used by *Fortune* 500 companies in the early 1990s. In fact, if car manufacturers had achieved the same power increases and cost decreases attained by computer manufacturers, a fully outfitted Lexus or Mercedes sedan would cost less than $1,000.

Thanks to Moore's Law, the methods for capturing information get better and better. To get a sense of what this new technology can do today, consider these three examples:

- Virtual City System: What has 800 miles of roadway, covers 46 square miles, and fits in a PC? The answer is Boston's block-by-block video survey of the city, a visual database of municipal roads, including all property structures, property parcels, and municipal assets. To create this system, a van equipped with global-positioning-system technology and eight cameras traveled through the city shooting 30 frames per second. The Transportation Department uses the videos daily to answer inquiries from the public, issue permits, and to decide where to place trash receptacles (dumpsters). The data help resolve parking ticket appeals, when, for instance, someone argues that a parking sign reads a certain way. In short, the system brings the field into the office.
- Optical Imaging Project: In Miami-Dade County's twenty-three traffic courtrooms, the paper trail from ticket to disposition of one million cases a year was long and tortuous. Now it has been replaced by an electronic system that meshes scanning, filing, calendaring, and storage. All paper documents are scanned into the system, some 10,000 documents a day. Information is processed into the relevant form, and cases are moved along electronically.
- Smart e-mail: It is hard enough to think great thoughts—let alone to capture them for a knowledge base. That's why Tacit Knowledge Systems created applications that capture expertise as it is created. Tacit's software and server products scour e-mail, documents—anything digital—to build an ever-changing knowledge bank. How is this information used? Say you are an assistant district attorney and your case has been assigned to a judge about whom you know nothing. With Tacit, you type in the judge's name, and all the cases he or she tried immediately appear. Not only does the software provide you with a list of people who have tried cases before that judge, it also gives you details such as how often, over what span of time, and what types of cases were tried.

Please keep in mind that these three examples show what technology can do today to help us acquire information. What it will do tomorrow, we must leave to science fiction writers. In fact, rather than forage in the future, it might be more productive to go back in time and consider some decidedly low-tech efforts at information acquisition.

An Example of a Formal Reporting System: The British Civil Service in India

The British-operated civil service in India remains a useful example of a large and successful reporting system.[4] It had longevity: The British ran the Indian subcontinent from the mid-eighteenth century through World War II without making fundamental changes in organizational structure or administrative policy. It ran lean: The Indian civil service never had more than 1,000 members to administer a vast and densely populated area. It was not staffed with highly paid, highly experienced professionals: Most of the British were quite young; a 30 year old was a survivor. It was certainly not technology driven: Most officials lived alone in isolated outposts with the nearest countryman a day or two of travel away. And it was simple: The organizational structure was totally flat. Each district officer reported directly to the chief operating officer, the provincial political secretary. Each political secretary had about a hundred people reporting directly to him.

What made this information system so successful? It worked remarkably well because it was designed to ensure that each of its members had the information needed to do the job. Each month the district officer spent a whole day writing a full report to the political secretary in the provincial capital. The report looked something like this:

	Problem One	Problem Two	Problem Three	Problem Four
Expectation				
Results				
Explanation				
Outlook				
Plan				
Questions about policy: Future opportunities, threats, and needs:				

Upon receipt of this information, the political secretary wrote back a full commentary.

An Example of an Informal Network: The Eisenhower White House

Because managers' views on issues are shaped to a certain degree by the positions they hold, experienced managers correct for such bias by filtering information according to its source. In his classic work *Inside Bureaucracy,* Anthony Downs identifies a number of **antidistortion factors in the communication system.**[5] They include: (1) multiple internal information sources and overlapping responsibilities; (2) direct communication through hierarchical levels or elimination of such levels; (3) distortion-proof messages (for example, summarization of details in nontechnical language with little jargon); and (4) external sources of information.

Few presidents followed Downs's four recommendations more faithfully than Dwight D. Eisenhower. Although his aides thought that his eagerness to hear all sides before making a decision was a source of weakness and that his sensitivity to external voices led him to mediocre decisions, Eisenhower thought this trait a strength. Historian Stephen E. Ambrose writes:

> He wanted to hear every legitimate point of view, to take all possible repercussions into account, before acting. Among other things, this meant he abhorred

yes-men. During a Cabinet discussion over ways to cut spending, for example, Henry Cabot Lodge, Jr. [ambassador to the United Nations] suggested reducing grants to the states for highway programs. Eisenhower replied that "my personal opinion is that we should spend more for highways." Lodge mumbled, "I withdraw." Eisenhower wanted none of that. "It's open to discussion," he told Lodge, and reminded him that "I've given way on a number of personal opinions to this gang."

Eisenhower actively sought conflicting views. When he took office, the Canadians were threatening to build the St. Lawrence Seaway on their own if the United States would not join them in the project. Eisenhower wanted to participate, but he knew there was strong opposition, because Milton Eisenhower [his brother] and George Humphrey [his treasury secretary] were leading spokesmen for the Pennsylvania and Ohio Railroad and coal companies that opposed the project. Eisenhower thought the Pennsylvania and Ohio crowd were putting their selfish interests ahead of the obvious long-term good of the United States, but he insisted on hearing their point of view. In late April, he told Milton he realized he was "hearing only the pro side of the argument," so he invited a group of railroad presidents to the White House, and for three hours listened to their side. They claimed that the seaway would cost the United States more than $2 billion; proponents were suggesting that the cost would be less than $500 million. "In such a confused situation," Eisenhower told Milton, "you have to dig pretty deep to find out what the facts really are because each allegation is presented with a very large share of emotionalism and prejudice."[6]

In the end, Eisenhower decided to join the Canadians, and the seaway project was completed in 1959 (one of the main locks was named after him). But the point of the story is this: managers cannot afford to wait behind their desks for the formal reporting system to supply them with all the information they need. They must aggressively seek information by using internal networks (grapevines) and external networks, and they must assiduously cultivate the latter over years.

The contrast between how the Eisenhower White House managed information in the 1950s and how the Bush White House managed information in the 2000s could not be sharper. According to Bob Woodward, memos in the latter failed to circulate or arrived after they became irrelevant. Briefings conveyed only the news listeners wanted to hear. Controversial information was rarely presented to the president, who rarely asked for it. In one of many critical passages, Woodward writes, "The whole atmosphere too often resembled a royal court . . . some upbeat stories, exaggerated good news, and a good time had by all."[7]

Characteristics of Useful Information

What constitutes high-quality information? First, information is useful when it is *accurate*. Before relying on information to make decisions, you must know that the information is correct. For instance, in a hospital, the difference between 0.1 and 1.0 in a drug dosage can mean the difference between health and brain damage. Information is useful when it is *complete*. Incomplete or missing information makes it difficult to recognize problems and identify potential solutions. For example, the joint House-Senate inquiry into the 9/11 attacks found a "modest but relatively steady stream of intelligence reporting" hinting at the possibility of terrorist attacks in the United States and the use of airplanes as weapons. But the stream hinting at *a strike within the United States using airplanes as weapons* was much less steady and harder to recognize. (See Figure 12.1.)

You can have accurate, complete information, but if it doesn't pertain to the problems you are facing, then it is not *relevant* and not very useful. The CIA and National Security Agency (NSA) are still designed primarily to provide information relevant to waging a cold war against another superpower (which, of course, no longer exists). The problem is that Al-Qaeda terrorists do not attend the U.S. ambassador's parties in Budapest, where an undercover agent might hear something useful. Nor do they build large military complexes in Novaya Zemlya that can be photographed by satellite.

Information is useful when it is *timely*. To be timely, the information must be available when needed to define a problem or to begin to identify possible solutions. If you have ever thought "I wish I had known that earlier," then you understand the importance of timely information and the opportunity cost of not having it. Evaluation studies that prove conclusively a program is not working are less useful when they appear after—rather than before—another $10 billion has been spent.

Finally, information is useful when it is *economical*—that is, when its costs are less than the benefits it brings. Most of the costs of information are explicit, but some are hidden. The explicit costs consist of the following:

- *Acquisition cost* is the cost of obtaining information you don't have.
- *Processing cost* is the cost of turning raw data into usable information.
- *Securing cost* is the cost of ensuring that data is reliable and consistently retrievable in a usable format for authorized users.

Figure 12.1   Information Indicating Terrorist Activity or Terrorist Intentions from 1998

	1993	1994	1995	1996	1997	1998	1999	2000	2001
Strike in the United States	• •					• •••	• •••••	•	••• ••
Use airplanes as weapons				•	•	••••	•	•	•
Strike in the United States using airplanes as weapons			•	•			••		Sept. 11 attacks

SOURCE: Text of the report from the joint investigation by the House Permanent Select Committee on Intelligence and the Senate Select Committee on Intelligence, "Joint Inquiry into Intelligence Community Activities before and after the Terrorist Attacks of September 11, 2001" (Feb. 2002), 198–215. It is available in PDF format at http://www.gpoaccess.gov/serialset/creports/911.html and at http://www.fas.org/irp/congress/2002_rpt/911rept.pdf.

- *Accessing cost* is the cost of accessing already stored information. One of the most common misunderstandings about information is that it is easy and cheap to retrieve once the agency has it. Not so. First, you have to find the information. Then you have got to convince whoever has it to share it with you.
- *Presenting cost* is the cost of transmitting information in a readily comprehensible and persuasive form from one person (or group of people) to another person (or group).

Some costs are hidden. All the excitement about the benefits of computerization should not blind an administrator to the *indirect costs* associated with personal computers. Managers are now only beginning to quantify some of the unproductive behavior—call it "fiddling"—associated with the use of PCs. Some fiddling may eventually make a person more productive, such as learning to use a new program or reconstructing a file that was accidentally erased. But most of it is straight procrastination—the equivalent of sharpening pencils. And it costs organizations in time and salaries.

For example, there is the time people spend recovering lost data, waiting for computers to run programs or print reports, helping coworkers with their PCs, checking or formatting documents, loading and learning new programs, organizing and erasing old files, and in "other" activities (such as playing computer games). Almost all PC users can cite times when they engaged in overkill—spending hours and hours setting up statistical charts that could easily have been kept on a clipboard. This problem even has a name: the "silicon imperative." In other words, if one is *able* to do it (say, receive a fax via a PC), one *has* to do it. By offering endless options in layout and design—the promise of perfection—computers can lure users to experiment endlessly.

Finally, there is the cost of information overload. Say a senior executive has a computer program that allows employees to comment on anything they want. It is quite likely that the executive will be distracted from working on priority items while sifting through the responses to find the occasional constructive or useful employee suggestion.

E-mail presents a more pervasive problem. Mark Rosenker, vice president for public affairs for the Electronic Industries Association, probably expresses an increasingly common view when he observes, "[E-mail] is an incredibly valuable service, but when you become inundated, it gets to be just like junk mail. I wonder if we are getting E-mail trashed. It's reaching the point where I'm spending an hour a day going through junk, or using a keyboard to respond to junk, or thinking about junk, or reading junk."[8]

Before considering the processing of information, two final points about acquiring it. People tend to think that if organizations only had greater quantities of cheaper, faster, and more useful information, they could be more effective. Although in many situations better performance will result, the sad reality is that improved information sometimes has little effect on people's behavior. Who is unaware of the risks of smoking or traveling without a seat belt? Yet millions of people still act as if that information does not exist. The real problem most managers face is not inadequate information but rather the organization's unwillingness to change in the face of good information. Given the information technologies described earlier, most managers are awash in information. For that reason, now more than ever, they need to keep asking themselves four questions. What information do I really need to accomplish my organization's mission? What information am I getting that I don't really need? What information am I not getting that I could get?

And what information am I getting but ignoring? that last question should have been asked by those at the SEC Investigating Bernard L. Madoff's financial house of cards. In a scathing report, H. David Katz, SEC Inspector General, concluded that numerous "red flags— incriminating evidence in plain sight—were missed by the agency from 1992 to 2009.[9]

My second point is this: If information empowers, then its absence enfeebles. It was a lack of good information—not a lack of a powerful military establishment—that made September 11, 2001, possible. For just a few hundred thousand dollars, a handful of terrorists were able to inflict more damage on the United States than an entire Japanese aircraft carrier task force was able to inflict at Pearl Harbor on December 7, 1941. The report by Congress' Select Committee on Intelligence on the actions of the FBI and CIA before and after the attack can be read as a case study in information mismanagement:

- Sixteen boxes of plans for Islamist terror taken from Rabbi Meir Kahane's assassin in 1990 sat unopened in New York Police Department custody for years.
- The CIA and FBI failed to talk to one another; both failed to talk to the Immigration and Naturalization Service (INS) and the State Department.
- Arabic documents were mistranslated by the few overworked linguists.
- Politically correct guidelines which prohibited employing individuals with criminal records kept the CIA and FBI from recruiting terrorist informants.
- American universities vigorously protested the INS's efforts to obey the law and keep track of basic information about foreign students.
- The White House turned down offers of important information from Sudan about Al-Qaeda.
- Information about fund-raising by terrorist organizations eluded the FBI and INS for years.
- Three major national commissions that told the government to get serious about terrorism were ignored.
- Counterterrorism budgets were cut.
- Insightful FBI agents, working to delve into potential airline hijackings, were thwarted by headquarters and didn't learn of one another's efforts.
- The CIA failed to tell the State Department about two terrorists being tracked in Malaysia—eventually, they got visas and became 9/11 hijackers.

Processing Information

Processing information means transforming raw data into meaningful information that can be applied to decision making. In this section, we will consider first some of the things that can go wrong organizationally in processing information and then some of the things that can go wrong at the individual level. We will conclude with a couple of new technologies that can help managers be more effective in this phase of the information management process: data mining and data warehousing.

What Can Go Wrong Organizationally and Individually

Managers should ask themselves who needs the information, when do they need it, and how do they need it—that is, what form should it be in? What makes these questions so vital is that one of the biggest time wasters in organizations is malfunctions in processing information. Consider these two examples.

- For years, faxes from physicians asking for a bed for a patient plagued the administrator of a large community hospital. Personnel in the admissions office kept telling the doctors that no beds were available, but the administrator kept finding them. The problem was information-processing malfunction. Floor nurses were not immediately notifying admissions; however, admissions was getting notified by the front office people, who presented the bill to the discharged patient. Every morning at 5:00 A.M., the admissions office received a "bed count" report from the front office. All that was necessary to fix the situation was to ensure that when floor nurses entered into their computers the fact that a patient had left the floor, that information showed up instantaneously on the screen in the admissions office.
- In some organizations, unit A must spend hours "translating" before it can use the information it gets from unit B. The latter reports "averages"—because that is what the accounting department needs. But unit A might need ranges and extremes rather than averages. The accounting department has all the information it needs, but no one has thought to tell unit B what unit A really needs.

Whether information arrives through a formal reporting system or an informal network, a manager must be aware of certain **pitfalls in interpreting information**. You may recall at the end of Chapter 6 we discussed biases in human decision making. Well, closely related to those six biases are the follow five pitfalls in interpreting information:

1. People think that the more accurate the information is, the more informative it is. Not necessarily. Weather announcers invariably report barometric pressure to the hundredths of an inch. Who does this help?
2. People seldom think logically about very unlikely events, which explains the popularity of lotteries and the fear of being struck by lightning.
3. People are influenced by how information *looks.* Information on a computer printout might carry more credibility than the *same information* told at lunch. By emphasizing the benefits of a project over its risks, a worker can help ensure its acceptance. If the worker does not wish for the project to be adopted, she can merely emphasize the risks. In both cases, exact information is given, only with different emphases.

4. People tend to anchor their judgments on some initial point of reference—whether relevant to the task or not. This may be the initial piece of information presented in a long series, the "expertise" of the speaker, or any number of things.

5. People do not like to appear ignorant. It requires courage and self-confidence to say things like "I don't understand that. Would you please go over it again?" or "Draw me a picture" or "What does *that* mean?" Instead, we find ourselves uttering a series of "Uh-huh"s, while involuntarily nodding our heads and pretending to have knowledge we do not have.

Data Mining and Data Warehousing

One promising tool to help managers dig out from under the pile of data is data mining. **Data mining** is the process of discovering unknown patterns and relationships in large amounts of data. Data mining works by using complex algorithms to look for patterns that are already in the data but are too complex for most managers to spot on their own. (An algorithm is simply a set of rules for solving a problem in a finite number of steps.) Here is an interesting example of how data mining works in basketball:

> IBM has provided several National Basketball Association teams with data mining software called Advance Scout. The software allows basketball coaches to ask "what if?" questions like these: "What if I start a certain lineup or run certain plays?" "When should we go for more three-pointers?" and "Does this strategy lead to victory?" All coaches have ideas about why they win or lose based on player performances and statistics. This technology allows them to get quick answers to questions and automatically identify patterns that may mean the difference between winning and losing. And Advance Scout is easy to use. It asks users simple questions and makes suggestions that may help them find what they seek.[10]

Data mining typically splits a data set in half, finds patterns in one half, and then tests the validity of those patterns by trying to find them again in the second half. The data typically come from a **data warehouse** that stores, in one place, huge amounts of data that have been prepared for data mining analysis by being cleaned of errors and redundancy. Data warehousing can yield big advantages for the public administrator. Let's visit one:

Until recently, managing the criminal justice system in Iowa was something of a guessing game. For example, when the legislature considered changing the status of a misdemeanor, it was virtually impossible to predict how the change would affect the number of beds needed in county jails. Nor could the state estimate accurately how much it would spend on defense lawyers from year to year. The problem was not a lack of useful data; the data existed, but they were scattered in court computers around the state—one or more in each county. Now criminal justice information from individual computers is loaded into a single computer repository in Des Moines. Decision makers can search the warehouse quickly for data that answer nearly any question they can ask.[11]

By consolidating information and making it easily searchable, the warehouse increases that information's value. In an era of results-oriented government, access to analytical information is what state and local government managers expect. The uses of data warehousing vary from criminal justice to Medicaid, from tracking welfare-to-work programs to catching tax cheaters. Not surprisingly, today nearly every state has at least one warehousing project under way or in the planning stage.

Securing Information

Securing information is the process of ensuring that data are reliable and consistently retrievable in a usable form for authorized users—but no one else.[12] The security of information is compromised in a variety of ways: viruses, insider abuse of Internet, laptop theft, unauthorized access by insiders, system penetration, theft of proprietary information, and sabotage.

Unfortunately, some students of public administration operate under two false assumptions about information security. First, they believe, although security might be a big concern for, say, the Department of Defense, it is a relatively minor concern for most civilian agencies. Tell that to the 26.5 million U.S. veterans who came under risk after thieves stole electronic files from a VA employee's home outside of Washington on May 3, 2006. The data included Social Security numbers and birth dates, enough information to commit fraud. This event was just the latest in a series of high-profile theft cases. For example, in February 2005, Bank of America announced it lost computer files with the personal information of 1.2 million federal employees. Currently, there is little safeguard built into law to slow down this type of thing. The Privacy Act requires the Veterans Administration to take appropriate technical and administrative steps to safeguard this information, but the law is not self-enforcing. It's a right without a remedy.

More recently, computer spies broke into the Pentagon's $300 billion Joint Strike Fighter project, the Defense Department's costliest program ever. The intruders were able to copy and siphon off a huge amount of data related to design and electronic systems, potentially making it easier to defend against the aircraft. Similar incidents have also breached the U.S. Air Force's air traffic control system. Such intrusions suggest that a battle is emerging between the UnitedStates and potential adversaries over the data networks that tie the world together.

Although the security problems of the Veterans Administration, Bank of America, and the Department of Defense were well publicized, many breaches occurring in state and local government go hardly noticed. For instance, in the first three months of 2007, public administrators had to cope with security problems in agencies in seven states and three cities, one city university, and a water district in California. This does not bode well for governments that want to assure constituents that they (the governments) can protect the personal information requested from citizens.

The other misconception is that security information means that it's the hacker—the individual sitting in, say, the Ukraine who's trying to penetrate American systems—that's the real problem. In fact, technology is allowing people to pack more and more data onto smaller recording devices—whether it's a thumb drive, laptop with additional storage on it, or a computer disk—and walk out the door with it, easily concealed. This is particularly possible in a nonnational security environment where people are seldom challenged when they take things out of the office—even things that might have millions and millions of names on them. The insider threat has not received as much attention as it warrants. It's the insider who ultimately can cause catastrophic losses to organizations, whether public or private.

As information systems are increasingly distributed across organizational and geographic boundaries, the task of ensuring information security becomes more complex. In addition to the distribution of such systems, information security managers face challenges presented by the *outsourcing* of network management and operation, computer operations, and applications development. At the same time, many organizations are reluctant to increase the size of their information security organization to offset the greater demands on its services. If information security is to be maintained at levels adequate to protect the organization, information security managers must find new ways to delegate responsibility for maintaining the availability of information and information-processing resources, ensuring the integrity of information, and protecting the confidentiality of information.

Control works only if an organization clearly defines the functional responsibilities of the resource providers and users, explicitly assigns those responsibilities, and acquires the necessary skilled personnel to implement security policies to maintain an adequate level of information security required. Furthermore, in the case of outsourcing, any delegated responsibilities must be explicitly set forth in the outsourcing contract. For all information, an organization must be able to identify an "owner" to whom responsibility may be assigned and who is capable of making appropriate decisions regarding information security.

Numerous steps can be taken to secure data and data networks. Some of the most important are authentication and authorization, biometrics (identifying users by unique, measurable body features such as iris scanning), firewalls (devices that set between the computers in an internal organizational network and outside networks), antivirus software for PCs and e-mail servers, and data encryption. The National Association of State Chief Information Officers, in a research brief entitled "Keeping Citizen Trust," suggests several ways for CIOs to stay on top of the privacy issue. They range from setting security standards to "baking" privacy into IT systems—that is, designing privacy protections at a project's inception. This research brief is available at www.nascio.org.

At the federal level, President Obama outlined his cyber-security plans in a high-profile speech on May 29, 2009, announcing his intention to create a top White House cyber-security post. The official would report both to the National Security Council and the National Economic Council. Supporters said the arrangement would cement cyber security as a critical security and economic issue, but detractors said it would require the new officials to please too many masters and would accomplish little.

Accessing Information and Knowledge

Internal Access to Information

Public executives, managers, and workers inside the organization use six kinds of information technology to access and share information: executive information systems, decision-support systems, expert systems, and groupware. **Executive information systems (EISs)** are management information systems used to facilitate strategic decision making at the highest level of management. These systems are typically based on software that provide easy access to large amounts of complex data and can analyze and present the data in a timely fashion. Unlike an executive information system that speeds up and simplifies the acquisition of information, a **decision-support system (DSS)** helps managers understand problems and potential solutions by acquiring and analyzing information with sophisticated models and tools. Furthermore, unlike EISs that are broad in scope and permit managers to retrieve all kinds of information about an organization, DSS programs are usually narrow in scope and targeted toward helping managers solve specific kinds of problems. Here are a couple of examples:

- One decision-support system is for emergency room physicians. It collects data on seventeen different physiological signs such as blood pressure and respiratory rate. Then, using a database containing the medical records of hundreds of thousands of people (with 100 diseases) who receive treatment at more than 200 different emergency rooms, the DSS gives a diagnosis and rates the chances of the patient's survival using various treatments. The system helps physicians pose and answer "what if" questions by processing the latest information about the patient's health and then printing an unbiased, statistically based estimate of whether a given treatment will work.[13]
- Capital projects can be recreational parks, school buildings, irrigation facilities, communication towers—or any other undertaking that requires considerable time to plan, fund, and construct. Typically, governments authorize large bond issues to fund these projects. The timing of the sale of bonds must be such that money is available when needed. A DSS can lay out options and help managers decide on the timing of bond sales to provide and replenish cash for a set of capital projects.[14]

Expert systems are designed for problems in which sets of rules exist to solve problems. The rules are usually complex, and only a small group of experts are able to do the job well. Montgomery County, Maryland, has expert systems for helping county workers quickly determine their retirement benefits and for guiding caseworkers who take adult crisis calls. Austin, Texas, has an expert system to help property developers through the maze of local zoning and building regulations. Merced County, California, has an expert system to help welfare workers know what questions to ask applicants. The system then tells the worker what programs the applicant is eligible for and what amount of benefits the applicant is entitled to. Although it may look simple, behind the screen the computer is churning through more than 5,000 rules of eligibility. Because the government is full of experts—masters of tax auditing, building inspections, fleet maintenance, and so on—there are many potential applications of expert systems.

Among the other areas in public administration in which expert systems have been applied is law enforcement. For example, in Montgomery County, Maryland, when detectives are faced with a case they cannot solve, they turn to Residential Burglary Expert System. This sophisticated computer program applies the experience of dozens of veteran burglary detectives to the circumstances of a particular break-in and sifts through a database of thousands of solved and unsolved burglary cases.[15] The system can provide a list of other burglaries that might have been committed by the same person. It can draw a profile of the likely perpetrator; for example, "A male youth who is a drug user, lives near scene of crime in the southwest precinct, is an amateur, and had accomplices." It can then give the names of those in the database who fit that profile ranked by the probability that any of them might have committed the crime. This expert system performs in seconds what might have taken several detectives weeks to calculate.

Modern information technology systems also recognize that many organizational and managerial activities involve groups of people working together to solve problems and meet client needs. **Groupware** is software that works on a computer network or via the Internet to link people or work groups across a room—or across the globe. The software enables managers and team members to share information and work simultaneously on the same document, chart, or diagram and see changes and comments as they are made by others.

Internal Access to Knowledge

This chapter has said a great deal about information, but very little about knowledge, except to define it as "a body of information or the comprehension and understanding that comes from having acquired an organized a great deal of information." As we have seen, the importance of information has been long recognized (recall the British civil service in India), but only in recent years have managers genuinely recognized knowledge as an important organizational resource. **Knowledge management (KM)** refers to the efforts to systematically find, organize, and make available an organization's intellectual capital and to foster a culture of continuous learning and knowledge sharing so that an organization's activities build on what is already known. Thus, KM allows individuals within the organization to tap into what other people in their organization know—thereby allowing them to work smarter and more productively. KM serves as a kind of group brain; instead of solving the same problem over and over, employees help one another on challenging problems. The time employees save not having to reinvent the wheel can be devoted to attacking truly new problems. Most large multinational corporations already have formal KM programs, and there is a Web site where you can review government involvement (www.km.com).

How does KM work? Say Jane Jones is a highway engineer in the transportation department of a major metropolitan county in the northeast part of her state. She has just developed an intelligent transportation system to alleviate problems on a congested freeway system. Bob Black is working on a similar bottleneck in the southwest part of the state. If the state has a knowledge management system, then Black can log onto the state's intranet, conduct a keyboard search, and pull out a detailed report on Jones' work—complete with engineering designs, phone numbers of colleagues, and a wide range of work products that he can recycle for his own needs.[16]

The example of the two transportation engineers is fictitious, but pioneers who have been deploying these kinds of systems in private industry are seeing substantial benefits, among them faster project turnarounds, more insightful decision making based on comprehensive—not anecdotal—understanding of issues, and higher-quality solutions to problems. For at least one private-sector firm, the return on its investment has been remarkable. According to a study by International Data Corp., the return on investment for the knowledge management system at Booz Allen Hamilton consulting company was an impressive 1,400 percent.[17]

What does this mean for government? At the very least, knowledge management systems would allow government agencies to capture some of the institutional knowledge that (a) sits three doors down the hall untapped because it is unrecognized or (b) walks out the door every time an experienced employee leaves the public sector. Even bigger benefits might accrue from the productivity gains that come from simply giving one set of employees access to similar work products of others in related jobs. "People stop spending half a day chasing their tails," is the way one consultant puts it.[18]

Information technology plays an important role by enabling the storage and dissemination of data and information across the organization, but technology is only one part of a larger management system. There is no template for designing such a system, but most organizations that have knowledge management programs share certain features, such as:

- They go to great lengths to codify experiences of employees. One database might include previous reports generated and cleansed for sharing among the organizations employees. Think of it as a "know what" database. Another popular database is a directory of all the organization's experts in areas of governmental functions (police, transportation, public health, and so on) and practice (finance, human resources management, contract management, negotiating, labor relations, and so on). Think of it as a "know who" database. Users of either database can sort the data by function, time, expert, office, and a number of other criteria.

- Although knowledge management does not require the cultural sea change that the learning organization seems to, organizations with effective knowledge management systems have cultures that support—and provide incentives for—the sharing of knowledge and information. There is an ethic of response whereby if anyone—even the most junior employee—makes a call to a colleague anywhere in the organization, that call will be promptly returned.

- Some organizations suffer from the NIH (Not-Invented-Here) syndrome. It is the mindset that rejects ideas from outside the organization because "if the idea was any good, we would already be doing it ourselves." Organizations with knowledge management systems don't hesitate to search for the best ideas and the best practices from any external organization and bring them to the organization.
- "Garbage in, garbage out" is an old saying among computer programmers. One of the biggest challenges in developing meaningful knowledge management codification systems is ensuring accurate and timely data availability. During the mid-1990s, many organizations attempted to set up sophisticated knowledge management systems with databases, repositories, and expert listings. Many managers became dismayed when the systems failed to generate value for organizations because the information in the systems was inaccurate, outdated, or indecipherable to nonexperts. The cure for this is simple: have those with firsthand knowledge of the subject evaluate the input, ensure that it is in a useful form and retrievable via the relevant keywords, and periodically purge parts of the system.[19]

In the final analysis, what makes a knowledge management system work are people. Organizations with smart people who refuse to collaborate generously will benefit little from such a system. Not surprisingly, organizations using knowledge management recruit team players and richly reward people who share what they know.

External Access to Information

On December 17, 2002, President Bush signed the **E-Government Act** into law. The media paid little attention to the signing because of the drumbeat of war talk with Iraq and the absence of acrimonious partisan debate. Yet, by the simple action of signing the act, the president had taken a giant step toward launching the federal government into the information age. E-government is designed to make it easier for citizens and businesses to access government information and services by encouraging interagency information technology (IT) initiatives that, while improving customer service, also consolidate redundant systems, decrease paperwork, increase productivity, and save money. Ultimately, it is about making the federal government citizen-centric so that you can go to Web sites to get information about unemployment benefits, comment on proposed clean air rules, or apply for an import license. You save time. And the government gets more for its IT dollars.

More and more, governments see the critical importance of weaving their computing and telecommunications systems into efficient, coherent networks. Essentially, a network is *a series of channels that enables movement of information*. Four types of external networks are worth noting: agency-to-agency networks, government-to-government networks, government-to-citizen networks, and worldwide networks.

1. Illinois has used agency-to-agency networking to streamline the state's hiring process. In the past, state personnel officials mailed out lists of eligible applicants, from which agencies looking to fill positions chose individuals to be interviewed.

2. As cities, counties, and states expand exponentially the range of applications on their networks, they are also beginning to interconnect those networks to improve communication and information sharing among jurisdictions.

3. State and local governments are also relying on networks to establish electronic links between themselves and their constituents. Here are three examples of government-to-citizen networks:

  • The city is Winslow, Arizona. The day is Monday. And the temperature is 106 degrees Fahrenheit in the shade. What would it be worth to you not to wait 45 minutes in line to register your flatbed pickup? Well, the Arizona Motor Vehicle Division has given you an alternative that takes as little as three minutes: ServiceArizona electronically processes vehicle registration on the Internet or by phone. Users who connect to ServiceArizona (servicearizona.ihost.com) follow instructions on-screen and print out a receipt.

  • The weekend after Hurricane Floyd hit eastern North Carolina in September 1999, the state was online with a Web site coordinating relief efforts and providing news and links to emergency resources. State programmers used mockups created after Hurricane Fran three years earlier to post the Floyd site quickly.

  • As the Internet continues its rapid growth, many cities around the world seek to connect better with citizens. Montreal's Web site features information on the city and its government. Unlike many cities, however, Montreal's site—called Ville de Montreal—creates a real sense of community among its diverse bilingual population. It has a clean, crisp look and is well organized. The home page (found at www.ville.Montreal.qc.ca) is quick to load and frequently updated with information that is useful to users. One of the more popular links leads to La Bibliothéque de Montreal—the largest French library outside France.

Networked governments shift from bureaucratic, multilevel stovepipes to the horizontal processes of integrated government shown in Figure 12.2. Because so many government programs are interdependent, this makes good sense. For example, federal unemployment insurance and job-training programs are interrelated, and those programs are, in turn, interrelated with state programs involving social assistance. Under such circumstances, databases can be shared rather than duplicated. Information can flow much faster, paperwork bottlenecks can be unplugged, and public administrators can make decisions today—instead of tomorrow.

4. The last type of network we need to note is worldwide. Reaching across the world as well as across the hall, the Internet is a network conglomerate woven into one massive system by shared software standards. Many think the Internet is the apotheosis of the marketplace, but consider its history. It grew out of the Defense Department's Advanced Research Projects Agency Network (ARPANET), a system designed to link remote computers for purposes of weapons development, military command and control, and pure research. The government funded most of the early advances that made possible today's user-friendly home computers linked by phone lines. Where the Pentagon left off, the university and scientific community picked up.

Figure 12.2   From Bureaucratic Stovepipes to Internetworked Government

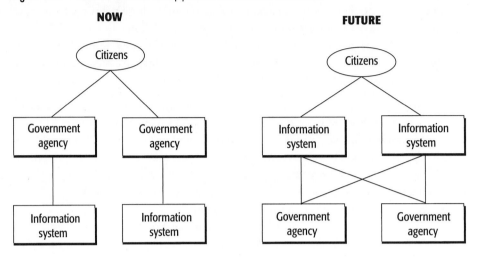

Today, the Internet provides an ideal bridge mechanism for state and local governments to use when they need to move information between and among incompatible computing systems and networks. To appreciate the effect of the Internet on government, just look at one of government's stodgier parts. Perhaps no aspect of local government is more tradition-bound or paper-intense than the municipal bond market. For example, in the past, when Montgomery County, Maryland, scheduled a bond sale, it set aside a conference room on the fifteenth floor of the county's executive office building and reserved an elevator so bidders could ride up directly. The county executive had to be in attendance. Now the county has taken such transactions into cyberspace; bidding and confirmation take minutes not hours. County officials station themselves in front of a computer screen and watch while bids come in and competition pushes underwriters to cut their prices. There is no longer a need to shuffle through the paperwork of written bids.[20]

The Art of Presenting Information

Although the communication technology we've been discussing gives public administrators powerful new ways to convey information, it does not guarantee the information will be presented effectively. Some experts believe that, in some instances, technology can actually reduce the effectiveness of communication. PowerPoint, in particular, has been the target of just such criticism. Because it is the world's most popular tool for presenting information electronically—there are 400 million copies in circulation and few government decisions take place without it—perhaps we should listen to what the critics are saying. (See box: "The Cognitive Style of PowerPoint.")

Despite the criticisms of PowerPoint, it is fair to say that in the hands of an agile expert, it can be a powerful weapon—though it is probably also true that in capable hands even a traditional pen-and-paper presentation can be powerful. For others—less agile, less

Perspectives on PowerPoint

In August 2003, the *Columbia* Accident Investigation Board at NASA released its report on why the space shuttle crashed. As expected, the report indicated ship's foam insulation was the main cause of the disaster. But the board also cited another unusual culprit: PowerPoint. NASA, the board argued, had become too reliant on presenting complex information via PowerPoint, instead of traditional pen-and-paper technical reports. When NASA engineers assessed possible wing damage during the mission, they presented the findings in a confusing PowerPoint slide—so crammed with nested bullet points that it was nearly impossible to untangle. "It is easy to understand how a senior manager might read this PowerPoint slide and not realize that it addresses a life-threatening situation," the board noted.

Edward Tufte, an emeritus professor of political science at Yale and author of *The Visual Display of Quantitative Information,* argues that PowerPoint "routinely disrupts, dominates, and trivializes content. . . . [T]he standard PowerPoint presentation elevates format over content, betraying an attitude of commercialism that turns everything into a sales pitch."

In a government or business setting, a typical PowerPoint slide shows about 40 words. With so little information per slide, many slides are needed. Audiences consequently endure a seemingly endless presentation, and many in the audience are asleep before the fifth slide. When information is presented this way, it is difficult to understand context and evaluate relationships. One wonders what the Gettysburg Address or King's "I Have a Dream" speech would look like in PowerPoint.

Still, PowerPoint has its fans. Microsoft estimates that there are 500 million users worldwide. Secretary of State Colin Powell used a PowerPoint presentation in February 2003 when he made his case to the United Nations that Iraq possessed weapons of mass destruction. Since such weapons were never found maybe Tufte is onto something.

Of course not everyone in government is a fan. In August 2005, a minority report by the latest shuttle safety task force echoed some of Tufte's concerns. Often, the group said, when it asked for data, it got PowerPoints—without supporting documents. And that brings us to what critics charge is the fundamental problem with PowerPoint: The program tends to flatten the most complex, subtle, even beautiful ideas into tedious bullet-pointed bureaucratese.

Still, it is important to rembmber that a PowerPoint presentation was never supposed to be the entire proposal, just a quick summary of something longer and better though out. Unfortunately, many managers have given up writing documents; they just write presentations, which are summaries without the detail, the backup. In the final analysis, poor slide presentations are more of the fault of the presenter than the presentation tool. Are bad books the fault of prinitng press? Are bad lectures the fault of defective blackboards or lecture notes? It is fallacious to say that ineffective, presenters are associated with X; therefore X is in effective. Ineffective people are associated with everything.

Review of Key Objectives and Critical Success Factors
• What makes nation unique -Conceived in liberty -Men are equal • Shared vision -New birth of freedom -Gov't of/by/for the people

If NASA managers didn't recognize the safety problem, perhaps it was because they were dazed from having to endure too many presentations like this.

SOURCE: Lee Gomes "PowerPoint Turns 20," *Wall Street Journal,* Gune 20, 2007; David Feith, "Speaking Truth to PowerPoint," *Wall Street Journal* July 31, 2009; Edward Tufte, "The Cognitive Style of PowerPoint" available at www.edwardtufte. com.

---

capable—a presentation can have the impact of a squirt gun. So, in the name of fighting the scourge of squirt gun presentations, let's summarize what expert presenters say about getting your points across.[21]

1. Don't read your slides. They are not note cards for the speaker. You can provide handouts after the presentation.
2. For consistency, stick with a limited number of fonts and a standard color palette. Unobtrusively placing your organization's logo in a corner of the slides reinforces your agency's identity.
3. Tell a compelling story with each slide. Start with a conflict, an obstacle, or a question, then show the audience how your approach will solve the problem. Ensure continuity.
4. Illuminate your words. Talking about pollution? Show a photo of dead birds, some smog, or even a diseased lung. Images are memorable.
5. Make brevity a virtue. Treat your bullet points as headlines and cut out needless prepositions, articles, and conjunctions. Use large type. Don't be afraid to use a little blank space.
6. The use of music clips, videos, and animation should be reserved for special emphasis or potentially convoluted explanations. Otherwise, you're just creating sensory overload.
7. Do not rush through your slide show. Leave images on the screen long enough for them to take effect.

Effective information presentation in an organization also means that managers consider carefully *how* to present it. This is not as straightforward an affair as it may seem. Experts in particular tend to get bogged down by their own knowledge and regularly miss key points when they try to convey what they know. Richard Saul Wurman puts it succinctly: "Familiarity breeds confusion."[22] Ask an expert the time, and she will tell you how to build a clock. The solution is for the expert to provide the doorknob into each thought.

The basics of effective presentations are well known and work well for those willing to thoroughly prepare: start strong, stick to a single theme, provide good examples, speak in conversational language, and end strong. But what do you do if you have to present important information to a boss who is either bored or distracted? That was the situation facing David Stockman, one of President Reagan's budget directors. Stockman explains how he met the challenge and *did* get his message across.

To convince the president it really was as bad as I was saying, I invented a multiple-choice budget quiz. The regular budget briefs weren't doing the job. I thought this might be the way.

The quiz divided the entire budget up into about fifty spending components and gave him three spending-cut choices on each, ranging from a nick to a heavy whack. Next to each choice was a description of what the impact of the cut would be (how many people would be thrown out into the snow), and of its political prospects (e.g., "previously defeated 27–2 in committee").

The exercise allowed him systematically to look at the whole $900 billion budget, to see it brick-by-brick. It also allowed him to get his hands dirty, maybe even bloody, with the practical chore of nitty-gritty cutting. Once the president went through it, he would understand that the budget was not a matter of too many bureaucrats and filing cabinets, but a politically explosive, vast, complex network of subsidies, grants, and entitlements.

The president enjoyed the quiz immensely. He sat there day after day with his pencil. He listened to his senior staff and the economic team discuss the relevant policy and political ramifications, then announced his choice and marked the appropriate box.

And rarely chose to make a whack. They were mostly nicks.[23]

Some methods of displaying and analyzing data are better than others. The difference between an excellent analysis and a faulty one can sometimes have momentous consequences. Consider the decision to launch the space shuttle *Challenger* in January 1986. The *Challenger* engineers used numbered charts that were incomplete and confusing, and seven astronauts died. (One of those charts appears in Figure 12.3.) The same *Challenger* data—the recorded effects of hot and cold temperatures on the rubber O-rings holding the rocket together—show up much more clearly in the bottom chart in Figure 12.3.

Now consider the dissemination of information *outside* the organization—from government to citizens. Informational programs in government generally take the form of a campaign on particular topics (for example, environmental consequences of product packaging or revision of the state's deer season law), steady play on a central theme for a long period of time (for example, conservation of natural resources), or the issuance of news without any specific objectives (for example, personnel change).

At the local level, information dissemination is particularly important. Consider the aggressive multimedia approach taken by Lake County, Florida, to inform and educate the public about recycling:[24]

- Public service announcements on local cable television, door hangers, and buttons were used to make a large number of people aware of the program.
- County staff members gave speeches providing detailed information about recycling.
- The county distributed a pamphlet describing businesses and nonprofit groups that accept recyclable materials. Highlights of the Florida Solid Waste Management Act were also included. Another pamphlet listed the materials that could be collected, including specific instructions for disposal.
- County staff also prepared a newsletter titled *Recycling Report*. The fall 1990 issue featured questions and answers about recycling, facts and figures about materials, and suggestions for reuse of products. The "Rappin' Recycler" character helped publicize the program.

Figure 12.3   Presenting Information Effectively: Two Views of the Same Data

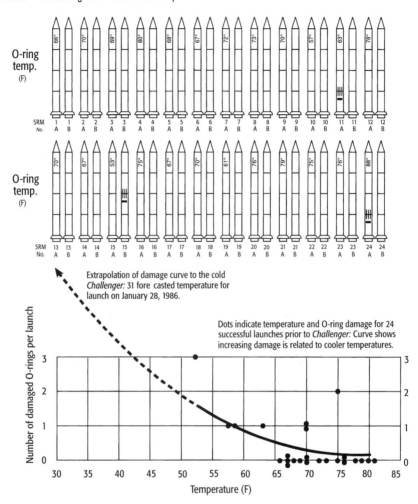

As these two diagrams demonstrate, the way in which information is presented sometimes can be a matter of life and death. Morton-Thiokol, the maker of the space shuttle's solid-fuel rocket boosters, prepared the top chart, which attempts to relate damage to the boosters to the temperature at launch time. But clutter and confusion hide the fact that might have saved the Challenger astronauts. Edward R. Tufte has redrawn the chart to make that fact crystal clear—damage had most often occurred before at low temperatures, and no launch day had been nearly as cold as the 31 degrees Fahrenheit predicted for *Challenger.*
SOURCES: *Report of the Presidential Commission on the Space Shuttle Challenger Accident* and Edward R. Tufte, *Visual Explanations* (Cheshire, CT: Graphics Print, 1990).

- The newsletter also included a telephone number for a recycling hotline. Callers could obtain information about public and private recycling activities in the county.

Chief information officers are not the only people who can help administrators manage information better. Offices of public affairs are ubiquitous in government, and they can be quite helpful in presenting information outside the agency—especially to the public and the media. That said, now comes a warning: *good public relations will not save a bad program, but bad public relations can destroy a good one.* Kelly Rossman-McKinney and R. Dee Woell write, "Good programs can be destroyed by the failure to pay attention to public relations or by inexpert handling and disclosure of core program issues. At its most basic, public relations is two-way communication with constituents. It is listening to what people are worried about and sharing with them what the agency is doing and why."[25]

How then do public administrators avoid letting bad public relations destroy their good programs? Answer: by carefully considering the eight Cs of communication. (See Table 12.1.)

Table 12.1 The Eight Cs of Communication	
Content of message	Is the message catchy? Does it mean what you think it means? Is it going to resonate with your target audience? Does it crystallize your campaign into a memorable sound bite?
Consistency and continuity	Your message has to be the same regardless of how it is delivered or by whom. Without consistency and continuity, credibility will drop.
Context of message	Is the message being delivered at a time when the audience is likely to pay attention? What is happening in your target audience's community that will make them care about the message?
Customer benefits	The target audience, the customer, always wants to know how she will benefit. Communicate the benefit to your target audience.
Channels of communication	Select those channels that are most effective for your particular audience. You would not rely too much on a Web site to educate the needy about food stamp eligibility (as did the Agriculture Department in 2003). Most people earning less than $15,000 lack Internet access.
Capability of audience	Is your message packaged properly to reach your target audience? If you want to reach a Mexican-American population with a message about organ and tissue donation, materials should be in Spanish. If you want to reach long-distance truck drivers, you will not want to spend too much money on television spots.
Credibility of messenger	Whoever delivers the message must have strong credibility with the target audience. if you want to convince kids not to drink and drive, provide an impact panel of speakers including a teenager who killed a child while driving drunk. Perhaps also include the child's mother.
Call to action	Tell people what you want them to do. The call to action can be as easy as, "Let us know what you think" and then give people a way to respond. Make sure there is a way for people to *act*.

SOURCE: Adapted from Kelly Rossman-McKinney and R. Dee Woell, "Why Public Relations Is Important Even to Public Administrators," in Peter Kobrak, *The Political Environment of Public Management* (New York: Longman, 2002), 258. © 2002 by Addison-Wesley Educational Publishers, Inc. Reprinted by permission of Pearson Education.

Looking Ahead: Whither E-Government?

Broadly defined, e-government refers to all use of digital information technology in the public sector. By the end of the first decade of the twenty-first century, information technology had become part of the public sector's infrastructure. What might the future hold?

There are reasons to believe that future change will be more incremental than dramatic. First, growth in IT spending has slowed over the years. From 1980 to 2000, worldwide IT spending grew at a compound annual growth rate of nearly 12 percent. Since 2000, however, that rate has averaged only about 3 percent. The explanation for the sharp decline, according to experts, is that the promise of IT has been largely realized; no new technological advances, they believe, would impel IT customers to replace computer technology they already have.[26]

One might reject the idea that the recent decline in growth rate signals a permanent end to rapid growth for IT because the last decade encompassed two recessions. But, even with a robust economy, there are two limits to the expansion of IT in the government. The first involves the "digital have-nots." Even where e-government works efficiently, it does not automatically bring more fairness and openness. Putting public services online is no use to those who cannot afford a computer or will have nothing to do with technology. And in most countries the heaviest consumers of public services—the old and the poor—are the least likely to use the Internet. If all services have to be provided both on- and off-line, the savings may not match the cost of new technology. Further, private-sector organizations can insist that all their customers use the Internet, but governments have to keep all channels of communication open. Even in countries with high rates of computer literacy and deep Internet penetration, a minority of people will want to go on using other means. But if only a tiny fraction of the public uses these online, how significant can e-government be?

The other limit to the expansion of e-government involves public executives themselves. Arguably, the thesis that information technology is an instrument of administrative reform is misguided because it assumes that top managers want their organizations to change and that they are willing to use IT to effect such change. Timothy L. Kraemer and John Leslie King disagree: "The empirical evidence suggests that IT has been used most often to reinforce existing organizational arrangements and power distributions rather than change them."[27] J.E. Fountain comes to similar conclusions. After researching the use of the Internet in U.S. federal agencies, she found "even the most innovative uses of IT typically work at the surface of operations and boundary spanning processes and are accepted because they leave the deep structures of political relationships intact."[28]

Transparency and Productivity

However, even the sharpest critics would have to admit that the one great benefit of e-government is that it has made getting information on any aspect of government much easier. Today, virtually all government documents intended for public consumption are online. Obviously, simply providing information does not guarantee good government, but it does make corruption more difficult. Putting laws, regulations, budget details, and legislative debates on line makes maladministration harder simply because those outside government can ask sharper questions.

Or consider how e-government sheds light on dubious or corrupt *private* marketing activities that can have disastrous consequences. In December 2008, the Securities and Exchange Commission opened easy Web access to the regulatory reports it receives from all public corporations and mutual funds. Previously, these reports had been buried in hard-to-access paper ledgers. Now companies have to report in a single format "company net profit" and "net income." It's worth noting that the WorldCom collapse in 2002, the Enron collapse in 2004, and the ongoing subprime mortgage crisis all happened in part because false and highly speculative information was hidden in complex, voluminous documents. Clearly, the Web's power to open up bureaucracy, democratize data, and reduce corruption has to be rated a big benefit.

How much has IT in government contributed to productivity? Certainly if you ask top management in the public sector why information is critical to their operations, you would probably get the same answer you would if you ask a corporate executive: it can lower operating costs and improve service. Consider the following examples:

- If a city uses handheld computers to rate the performance of its park maintenance teams, the data collection process has obviously been speeded up, allowing the park commissioner to work with fresher, more useful data.
- By investing in computers, the IRS is now better able to catch tax cheats who cost the government six times that investment.
- By using computer-based instruction to train technical personnel, the Federal Aviation Administration estimates it saves millions of dollars a year in training costs.
- The state of Florida automated accessing public assistance. Now, anyone applying for or renewing food stamps, Temporary Assistance to Needy Families, or Medicaid benefits can do so quickly and easily online, 24 hours a day, at state-run offices or in any of 2,500 "partner agencies" (churches, libraries, senior centers, homeless centers, etc.). As a result, the state has been able to reduce staff, saving $83 million annually.

Unfortunately, for every example of IT bringing cost reduction to government, critics can usually cite at least one counter example. For instance:

- Under a Texas state law that took effect in September 2005, agencies were ordered to hand over responsibility for IT infrastructure to the Department of Information Resources. By consolidating 31 datacenter operations, the state would save money. That was the theory. By January 2009, the $863 million project was in trouble. Agencies were reporting work breakdowns; thousands of documents created in the Attorney General's office were destroyed when a server crashed; other agencies were reporting lost data in multiple backup failures.
- California's Youth and Adult Correction Agency had to cancel plans for a $40 million integrated electronic inmate records system after experiencing myriad troubles early in the project.

- Illinois State Toll Highway Authority began installing electronic toll lanes in 1993. In 1995, with 40 percent of the system operating and $17.5 million already spent, the authority decided to drop the system and adopt what it thought would be a better one.
- St. Paul, Minnesota, canceled a state-of-the-art project to develop human resources software after spending $1.6 million, because it would have been too expensive to operate and maintain.

The problem with all these examples is that they provide, at best, anecdotal evidence that e-government does or does not lower cost and improve services. Actually, there have been few efforts to access the aggregate effects of e-government. Australia is one country that has, and the answers are mixed. Australia's National Office for the Information Economy in 2002 found that the majority of 38 e-government projects surveyed were likely to make things cheaper and more convenient for officials, users, or both. But for the 24 projects that were expected to result in specific cost reductions or higher revenues, each $108 invested produced a saving for the government of only $100.[29]

In the United States, the Government Accountability Office found in a survey of 24 major agencies that 226 IT projects were at high risk, totaling $6.4 billion in funding requested for fiscal year 2007. Agencies identified most projects as high risk because their delay or failure would hurt the essential business function of the agency.[30]

Why has government been unable to reap the same benefits as business, which uses IT to lower costs, please customers, and raise profits? One reason for the high failure rate is overly aggressive or unrealistic cost-reduction goals (recall the Texas consolidation project). Another reason involves the nature of the public sector: few direct rivals and smaller consequences of failure to managers. These two character- istics require little elaboration. Amazon.com must outdo other online booksellers to win readers' money. Google must beat Yahoo!. Unless each inch of such companies' Web sites offers outstanding clarity and convenience, customers go elsewhere. But if your government's tax collection online offering is slow, clunky, or just plain dull, then you have no alternative. And how about the consequences of failure in bureaucracy? These do not involve bankruptcy; they may involve writing self-justifying memos and at worst a transfer elsewhere. Bureaucrats plead that just a bit more time and money will fix the IT problem they have created. In the private sector, the relentless pressure to do more with less often sparks innovation in information technology, whereas public administrators might be tempted to go with overpriced, overpromised, and overengi- neered systems.

Yet another reason for so many private successes and public failures is simply poor project management. Although a number of factors distinguish top-performing organizations in the use of IT, the most important is that senior managers take a leadership role in a handful of key decisions. By contrast, when senior management abdicates responsibility for those decisions to IT executives, disasters often ensue. As the chief information officer for the state of Missouri put it, when left to themselves, IT managers will push for the "shiny objects."[31] Certainly, IT managers are the right people to make numerous decisions about IT management—choices of technology standards, the design of IT operations centers, and technical expertise the organization will need. *But an IT department should not be left to itself to make the strategic choices that determine the effect of IT on an organization's mission.*

Taking Responsibility

To help nontechnical managers avoid IT mistakes like those cited above, Jeanne W. Ross and Peter Weill at MIT identify six decisions for which those managers should take responsibility.[32]

1. *How much should we spend on IT?* Senior managers should define the strategic role that IT will play in the organization and then determine the level of funding needed to achieve that objective. But that's not what always happens. Worrying that they might be spending too much or too little, they ask what similar organizations are spending. If we just use that benchmark, they believe, IT issues will take care of themselves. Consequently, the organization fails to develop an IT platform that furthers its mission, despite high IT spending. Consider this example:

- FedEx is two-thirds the size of UPS, but both companies spend the same on IT. Does that mean that IT is more important to FedEx? No, it means that FedEx's mission is different from UPS's. The latter has focused on efficiency, consistency, and reliability, so it needs a centralized, standardized IT environment. In contrast, FedEx has focused on flexibility to meet the needs of its various customer segments. This decentralized approach to IT management is more expensive, but it matches the company's mission.

2. *Which programs should receive our IT dollars?* In any organization, there are numerous opportunities to use IT—some more meritorious than others. Senior management must therefore set priorities. "Leaving such decisions in the hands of the IT department means that IT executives set the priorities for what are in fact important business issues—or, just as troubling, they try to deliver on every project a business manager claims is important. Presented with a list of approved and funded projects, most IT units will do their best to carry them out. But this typically leads to a backlog of delay initiatives and an overwhelmed and demoralized IT department."[33]

3. *Which IT capabilities need to be centralized and standardized throughout the agency or government?* Senior managers need to reinforce the idea of thinking across agency boundaries instead of creating separate systems agency by agency. Every time an agency purchases technology without a view toward what other agencies are doing, or what standards are in place, silo walls are buttressed and technology efforts are likely duplicated, at extra cost to the government. Many states have safeguards in place to prevent this behavior, but it still goes on.

With a decentralized model, in which agencies handle all their own IT functions, there tends to be duplication and greater expense. For example, it costs much more to build 22 wide-area networks for 22 agencies when one would suffice. And there is no concentration of brainpower that way. You have split your expertise up around the state. That means it is difficult to handle large projects like child welfare. Only senior managers can guard against this entropy factor in government: left to its own devices, governments will always become decentralized.

Although many states and cities are looking to centralized IT operations to get rid of myriad systems and hardware that don't share data, some think the future will include new models. For example, the idea of a federated model is gaining popularity. In that model, an overarching IT department centralizes what makes sense—such as e-mail systems and other "utility" services—but agencies are left to take care of their own business applications. Where there is a monetary value from consolidating, it is logical to centralize. But if, say, health services has an application only it uses, then it would make sense to leave it in the agency.

4. *How good do our IT services really need to be?* As our earlier discussion indicated, useful information—accurate, complete, relevant, and timely—comes at a cost. It is up to senior managers to decide which of the features are needed on the basis of their costs and benefits. Otherwise, the agency may pay for service options that, given its priorities, are not worth the cost.

For some agencies, top-of-the-line services are not negotiable. The twelve Federal Reserve Banks did not debate how much data they can afford to lose if their computer system crashes; 100 percent recovery is a requirement. Similarly, the company that runs the majority of government-sponsored lotteries cannot compromise on response time. "Most of its contracts in the United States specify that customers will receive their lottery tickets within five seconds—and it takes three seconds just to print it. Nor can the company afford downtime. State governments specify penalties as high as $10,000 per minute if the system is unavailable. This is a fairly compelling justification for ensuring that computers will continue to run despite floods, tornadoes, power outages, and telecommunication break-downs, regardless of the cost."[34]

But some agencies can tolerate limited downtime for occasional slow response times. Consider the U.S. Department of Transportation's Administrative Services Center. The nature of the center's operations means that a brief downtime on its Enterprise Resource Planning (ERP) system would be an inconvenience but would not stop operations. (ERP helps organizations keep track of important activities, such as inventory control, parts ordering, and tracking orders.)

5. *What security and privacy risks will we accept?* Like reliability and responsiveness, security is a feature of IT systems that requires organizations to weigh the level of protection they want against the amount they are willing to spend. In this case, though, there is another trade-off: increasing security involves not only higher costs but also greater inconvenience. Ross and Weill illustrate with their own organization:

> Because the institution is a particularly attractive target for hackers keen to show off their skills, MIT has developed a state-of-the-art security system that success-fully repels a continuous stream of attacks. It features a firewall different from the type most organizations use to limit external access to their internal systems. But

although it provides greater protection, MIT's nonstandard approach means that the Institute cannot install most commercial software packages for applications such as course registration and student count.[35]

6. *Who do we blame if an IT initiative fails?* To avoid the kind of disasters experienced by California, Illinois, and Minnesota mentioned earlier, senior managers should assign a "sponsor" from within the organization to take responsibility for realizing the benefits of an IT initiative. "These sponsors need authority to assign resources to projects and time to oversee the creation and implementation of those projects. They should meet regularly with IT personnel, arrange training for users, and work with the IT departments to establish clear metrics for determining the initiative's success. Such sponsors can ensure that new IT systems deliver real business value."[36]

Remember: new IT systems alone have no value; value derives from new or redesigned organizational processes. That is why top management needs to assign a sponsor to work with the IT unit or consultant.

Concluding Observations

Despite all the talk about intellectual capital, few managers grasp the true nature of knowledge—let alone how to manage it. The reason: they misunderstand what knowledge is and what organizations must do to exploit it. Actually, there are two types of knowledge. Some knowledge is formal and systematic, quantifiable and explicit. This type of knowledge was of particular concern to our old friends Henri Fayol and Frederick Taylor. The other type of knowledge is tacit and often consists of highly subjective insights, intuitions, and hunches of the individual. This type of knowledge Chester Bernard discussed in his *The Functions of an Executive.* One of the keys to effective public administration is the ability to appreciate both types of knowledge—explicit knowledge and tacit knowledge.

The principles of management discussed in Chapter 1, the analytical tools discussed in Chapter 6, and the various Supreme Court decisions discussed throughout the text are all examples of explicit knowledge. They are fairly easy to express. The other kind, tacit knowledge, is not so easily expressed and highly personal. Because it is hard to formalize, it is difficult to communicate. Or, as philosopher Michael Polanyi writes, "we can know more than we can tell."[37]

Tacit knowledge is also deeply rooted in action and in an individual's commitment to a specific context—whether playing chess, making a violin, running an agency, or leading a nation. Twenty-seven years before he was first elected president of France, Charles de Gaulle wrote *The Edge of the Sword.* There he defined three crucial qualities a leader must have: *intelligence* and *instinct* to chart the right path and *authority* to persuade people to follow that path. Understandably, academics have stressed the intelligence component of leadership, but leaders themselves have always understood the crucial importance of instinct. De Gaulle wrote:

The only way in which the human mind can make direct contact with reality is by intuition, combining his instinct with his intelligence. Our intelligence can furnish us with the theoretical, general abstract knowledge of what is, but only instinct can give the practical, particular, and concrete *feel* of it. Without the cooperation of the intelligence there can be no logical reasoning, no informed judgment. But without the reinforcement of instinct there can be no profundity of perception and no creative urge. Instinct is this faculty in our make-up that brings us into closer contact with nature. Thanks to it, we can strike deeply into the order of things, and participate in whatever obscure harmony may be found there.[38]

De Gaulle thought there is a close analogy between what takes place in the mind of a leader planning an action and what happens to the artist at the moment of conception: "The latter does not renounce the use of his intelligence. He draws from it lessons, methods, and knowledge. But his power of creation can operate only if he possesses, in addition, a certain instinctive faculty which we call inspiration, for that alone can give the direct contact with nature from which the vital spark must leap."[39]

Does not our everyday language recognize the role of instinct? We say of political leaders, agency heads, diplomats, soldiers, and business executives who make good decisions that they had a "sense of reality," that they had a "gift" or "knack," or that they possess "vision" or "style."

Reason and instinct, then, do not represent rival views of leadership. Rather, they represent the creative tension at that center of leadership that both de Gaulle and Bernard wrote about in the 1930s. In this, leadership resembles the well-known picture that, looked at once, appears to show a vase, but looked at once again, turns into two people, face to face.[40] The vase resembles the well-defined and precisely structured view of knowledge—easy to understand and deeply ingrained in the tradition of Western management. The faces represent intuition—always elusive, ever changing, but full of problems and promise. The public administrator's challenge is to keep both images in view at the same time.

Concepts for Review

antidistortion factors in the communication system
authentication
authorization
biases in interpreting information
biometrics
data
data encryption
data mining
data warehouse

decision-support system (DSS)
E-Government Act
executive information systems (EISs)
expert system
firewalls
groupware
information
intranet
learning organization
knowledge

knowledge management (KM)
Moore's Law
network

processing information
virus

Key Points

This chapter focused on information and knowledge management within a government agency. We explained the strategic importance of information and surveyed the efforts underway to better manage it. The chapter made these major points:

1. Discuss the following statement by Henry Mintzberg in managing (BK Business Books, 2009): "Like conventional mail, e-mail is restricted by the poverty of words alone: there is not tone of voice to hear, no gestures to see, no presence to feel—even images can be a nuisance to create. E-mail may simply limit the user's ability to support emotional, nuanced, and complex interactions. Managing is as much about all these things as it is about the factual content of the messages... The danger od e-mail is that may give a manager the impression of being in touch while the only thing actually being touched is the keyboard."

2. An information revolution has swept through the public sector, and no public administrator can escape its effects. At the heart of this revolution are accelerating and compounding trends in computer technology and communications technology.

3. Data are raw, unsummarized, and unanalyzed facts. Information is data that are meaningful and that alter the receiver's understanding—the data that managers actually use to interpret and understand events in the organization and the environment. Knowledge is the body of information or the comprehension and understanding that comes from having acquired and organized a great deal of information—for example, a knowledge of medicine.

4. High-quality information is accurate, relevant, timely, and economical.

5. Downs identifies four antidistortion factors in a communications system: (1) multiple internal information sources and overlapping responsibility; (2) direct communication through hierarchical levels or elimination of such levels; (3) distortion-proof messages; and (4) external sources of information.

6. Processing information means transforming raw data into meaningful information that can be applied to decision making.

7. Whether information arrives through a formal reporting system or an informal network, a manager must be aware of certain biases or weaknesses in interpreting information.

8. Data mining is the process of discovering unknown patterns and relationships in large amounts of data. It typically splits a data set in half, finds patterns in one half, and then tests the validity of those patterns by trying to find them again in the second half of the data set. The data typically come from a data warehouse that stores huge amounts of data that had been prepared for data mining analysis by being cleaned of errors and redundancy.

9. Numerous steps can be taken to secure data and data networks. Some of the most important are authentication and authorization, biometrics, firewalls, antivirus software, and data encryption.

10. Public executives, managers, and workers inside the organization use six kinds of information technology to access and share information: executive information systems, decision support systems, expert systems, groupware, and knowledge management.

11. Knowledge management refers to efforts to systematically find, organize, and make available an organization's intellectual capital and to foster a culture of knowledge sharing so that the organization's activities build on what is already known.

12. Expert presenters avoid reading from their slides, stick with a limited number of fonts and standard color palette, tell compelling stories, illuminate words with pictures, make brevity a virtue, avoid sensory overload, and do not rush through their presentations.

13. Public administrators avoid letting bad public relations destroy good programs by carefully considering the eight Cs of communication: content of message, consistency and continuity, context of message, customer benefits, channels of communication, capability of audience, credibility of message, and call to action.

14. E-government, which refers to all use of digital technology in th public sector, has greatly improved transparency but has a mixed record in increasing productivity.

15. Although a number of factors distinguish top-performing organizations in the use of information technology, the most important is that senior managers take a leadership role in a handful of key decisions. Six decisions for which managers should take responsibility are: (1) How much should we spend on IT? (2) Which programs should receive our IT dollars? (3) Which IT capabilities need to be centralized or standardized throughout the agency or government? (4) How good do our IT services really need to be? (5) What security and privacy risks will we accept? (6) Who do we blame if an IT initiative fails?

16. Reason and instinct do not represent rival views of leadership; rather, they represent the creative tension at the center of leadership.

Problems and Applications

1. Discuss the following statement by Henry Mintzberg in *Managing* (BK Business Books, 2009): "Like conventional mail, e-mail is restricted by the poverty of words alone: there is no tone of voice to hear, no gestures to see, no presence to feel—even images can be a nuisance to create. E-mail may simply limit the user's ability to support emotional, nuanced, and complex interactions. Managing is as much about all these things as it is about the factual content of the messages . . . The danger of e-mail is that may give a manager the impression of being in touch while the only thing actually being touched is the keyboard."

2. Identify a government agency and outline a knowledge management program for it. Specify four features to fit the descriptions of features on pages 586–587.

3. When we design networks for the organization, are we designing them to manage important information or to manage important relationships?

4. "The new information technology makes the behavior of employees much more visible." Explain this statement and discuss its implications for employees and their bosses.

5. "The greatest threat the personal computer poses is that managers will take it seriously and come to believe that they can manage by remaining in their offices and looking at displays of digital characters." Discuss.

6. Research and then outline an information strategy for a child protection system for a large city, the war on drugs, the management of hazardous waste by the EPA, or the role of the FCC in the coming decades.

7. "Managers need more ways to convey the images and impressions they carry inside of them. This explains the renewed interest in strategic vision, in culture, and in the roles of intuition and insight in management." Explain and discuss.

8. This chapter suggested that the computer revolution tends to make decision making more democratic. Is this a good state of affairs?

Favorite Bookmarks

www.mot.cprost.ca/~iamot/index   The International Association for the Management of Technology Web site offers information about programs, including those offered by Simon Fraser University and the University of Waterloo, that aim to link engineering, science, and management disciplines to address the strategic and operational needs of organizations. Their newsletter is online.

www.intelligence.com/all.asp

www.news.com/

www.slashdot.org

www.tbtf.com/

www.techsightings.com/

So much is happening in the information revolution that it is difficult to stay current. These Web sites let someone else keep track of it all for you.

www.utexas.edu/computer/vcl/journals   Another way to stay current on the information revolution is to have links to many different computer magazines and journals. This resource will provide it.

Notes

1. Herbert Kaufman, *Administrative Behavior of Federal Bureau Chiefs* (Washington, DC: Brookings, 1981).
2. Quoted in Rob Gurwitt, "The Decision Machine," *Governing* (May 1991): 51.
3. G. David Garson, *Public Information Technology and E-Governance* (Raleigh, NC: Jones and Bartlett, 2006).
4. Peter F. Drucker, *The New Realities* (New York: Harper & Row, 1989). See also Philip Mason, *The Men Who Ruled India* (New York: Macmillan, 1987).
5. Anthony Downs, *Inside Bureaucracy* (Boston: Little, Brown, 1967).
6. S. E. Ambrose, *Eisenhower: The President* (New York: Simon & Schuster, 1984), 79–80.

7. Bob Woodward, *State of Denial* (NewYork: Simon & Schuster, 2006).

8. *Fortune* (July 11, 1994), 60.

9. David Stout, "Repeat details how Madoff's Web Ensnared SEC," *NewYork Times September 3, 2009.*

10. "Data Mining: Advanced Scout," IBM Research Web site, www.research.ibm.com/xw-scout.

11. Christopher Swope, "Info Central," *Governing* (January 2000).

12. The following discussion is primarily based on Riva Richmond, "How to Find Your Weak Spots," *Wall Street Journal* (September 29, 2003); and Ellen Perlman, "Online Privacy," *Governing* (September 2003): 29–46.

13. *Washington Post* (June 14, 2001).

14. Efraim Turban and Jay E. Aronson, *Decision Support Systems and Intelligent Systems* (Upper Saddle River, NJ: Prentice Hall, 1998).

15. John Martin, "The Computer Is an Expert," *Governing* (July 1991).

16. Marilyn J. Cohodas, "Harvesting Knowledge," *Governing* (December 2000): 66.

17. Ibid.

18. Ibid.

19. Ethan M. Rasiel and Paul N. Friga, *The McKinsey Mind* (New York: McGraw-Hill, 2002), 74–82.

20. Diane Kittower, "E-Bonding," *Governing* (July 1999).

21. The literature on professional communication is voluminous. Highly recommended are the following: Granville N. Toogood, *The Articulate Executive* (New York: McGraw-Hill, 1996) and Gene Zelazny, *Say It with Charts: The Executive's Guide to Visual Communication* (New York: McGraw-Hill, 1996).

22. R. S. Wurman, *Information Anxiety* (New York: Doubleday, 1989), 125.

23. David Stockman, *The Triumph of Politics* (New York: HarperCollins, 1986), 98.

24. *P.A. Times,* July 1, 1991.

25. Kelly Rossman-McKinney and R. Dee Woell, "Why Public Relations Is Important Even to Public Administrators," in Peter Kobreak, ed., *The Political Environment of Public Management* (New York: Longman, 2002), 257.

26. Randall Stross, "Are the Glory Days Long Gone for IT?," *New York Times* (August 9, 2009). See also Bruce Rocheleau, "Whither E-Government?," *Public Administration Review* (May/June 2007): 584–88.

27. T. L. Kraemer and J. L. King, "Information Technology and Administrative Reform: Will E-Government Be Different?," *International Journal of Electronic Government Research* (August 2005).

28. J. E. Fountain quoted in Kraemer and King, op. cit.

29. Edward Lucas, "The Electronic Bureaucrat," *Economist* (February 16, 2008).

30. Surrey data can be found at www.gao.gav/gov/cgi-bin/get rpt? GAO-o6-647

31. Quoted in *Governing* (November 2002): 27.

32. Jeanne W. Ross and Peter Weill, "Six IT Decisions Your IT People Shouldn't Make," *Harvard Business Review* (November 2002): 85–91. Copyright (c) 2002 by Harvard Business Publishing. Reproduced by permission.

33. Ibid., 87–88.

34. Ibid., 89.

35. Ibid., 90.

36. Ibid., 91.

37. Michael Polanyi, *Personal Knowledge: Toward a Post-Critical Philosophy* (Chicago: University of Chicago Press, 1962).

38. Charles de Gaulle, *The Edge of the Sword,* trans. Gerard Hopkins (New York: Criterion Books, 1960), 20–21.

39. Ibid., 21.

40. The optical illusion metaphor was adapted from John Seely Brown and Paul Duguid, "Balancing Act: How to Capture Knowledge without Killing It," *Harvard Business Review* (May–June 2000): 80.

CASE 12.1
THE U.S. ARMY

As I used to tell my kids, "You don't have to make every mistake personally. I've made plenty of them, and if you just let me tell you what they were and how you can avoid them, there's still plenty of mistakes for you to make."

Col. Orin A. Nagel, former director of Center for Army Lessons Learned

The first systematic application of management principles in the United States was not by, say, General Motors, but by the U.S. Army. From 1899 to 1904, Secretary of War Elihu Root made drastic reforms in the army's organization and efficiency, established the Army War College, and introduced the principle of the general staff (a group of officers that assist a commander by performing detailed duties of administration, planning, supply, and coordination).

The U. S. Army has also been on the cutting edge of information technology ever since 1946, when it unveiled the Electronic Numerical Integrator and Computer (ENIAC), the world's first operational, general-purpose computer. Today few institutions, if any, better exemplify the learning organization ideal than the U.S. Army; it is a premier example of a *learning organization*—in which everyone engages in problem solving.[1] This case examines four important ways in which the U.S. Army manages its information in the twenty-first century.

After-Action Reports (AARs)

Probably the best-known example of leveraging knowledge within a team is the army's use of After-Action Reports (AARs). These reviews had their beginnings in training simulations as a way for a team to engage in a mock battle to gain as much learning as possible from the training. An army brigade of three thousand or so travels to the National Training Center (NTC) in California, where it engages in simulated combat with crack units based at the center.

AARs proved so useful to team effectiveness that gradually they began to be used in nontraining situations as well. Today they have spread throughout the army, not because someone at the top has required their use but because the troops find them helpful in getting the job done. Thrust into a new kind of operation in postwar Iraq—certainly not the conventional combat for which they had been well trained—junior officers (lieutenants and captains) illustrate how AARs and the sharing of knowledge can improve a unit's next action.

Six features of AARs are worth noting. First, although they are called *After*-Action Reports, they are actually *cyclical*—part of a cycle that starts before and continues throughout each campaign or simulation. The AAR regimen includes brief huddles, extended planning and review sessions, copious note taking by everyone, and the explicit linking of lessons to future actions. The AAR cycle

---

[1]   Managers began thinking about the concept of the learning organization in 1990 after the publication of Peter Senge's *The Fifth Discipline: The Theory and Practice of Learning Organizations* (New York: Doubleday, 1990). According to Senge, other characteristics include the following:

- People and leaders have a shared commitment to learning and thinking systematically about problems. They believe they can change their environment.
- Leaders encourage open and extensive communication. In contrast, managers in a more traditional organization presume a right to financial and other information and keep it from all those without a "need to know."
- Some "slack time" is not only allowed but desired so that it can be used for learning. (Managers in a more traditional organization would find this idea inimical to the goal of efficiency.)
- People share the belief that teamwork and cooperation are critical to success.
- Leaders facilitate the creation of a shared vision for the organization's future and then keep the organization members working toward it. A learning organization's culture is one in which everyone agrees on the shared vision.

for each phase of the campaign or simulation begins when the senior commander drafts "operational orders." This document consists of four parts: the task (what actions subordinate units must take); the purpose (why the task is important); the commander's intent (what the senior leader is thinking, explained so that subordinates can pursue his goals even if events don't unfold as expected); and the end state (what the desired result is). The commander shares these orders with his subordinate commanders and then asks each for a "brief back"—a verbal description of the unit's understanding of its mission (to ensure everyone is on the same page) and its role.

The second feature is that AARs are *experimental*. As a result of the disciplined preparation described above, the action that follows becomes a learning experiment. The leaders have individually and collectively made predictions about what will occur, identified challenges that may arise, and built into their plans ways to address those challenges. So when units act, they will not only be executing a plan but also observing and testing that plan.

Third, AARs are *unemotional and egalitarian*. Colonels say where lieutenants made mistakes— and vice versa.

Fourth, they are *focused*. At the end of an AAR meeting, the senior commander identifies the two or three lessons he expects will prove most relevant to the next battle or simulation. If the units focus on more than a few lessons at a time, they risk becoming overwhelmed. If they focus on lessons unlikely to be applied until far in the future, soldiers might forget.

Fifth, they are *multilayered*. Immediately after the senior commander has identified the lessons and the meeting ends, subordinate commanders gather their units to conduct their own AARs.

Sixth, AARs are *iterative*. Those who are experienced with them know most lessons that surfaced during the first go-round are incomplete or plain wrong, representing what the unit thinks should work and not what really does work. They understand that it takes several iterations to produce dynamic solutions that will stand up under any conditions.

The Center for Army Lessons Learned (CALL)

A second example of the army's management information system is a center, based at Fort Leavenworth, Kansas, founded in 1985. Its initial role was to capture lessons from NTC. Later, as the army's mission broadened to include "operations other than war"—interventions in Somalia, Bosnia, and Haiti, plus fire fighting, flood control, and other forms of disaster relief at home—CALL was charged with learning from those experiences as well.

The model on which CALL is based involves essentially three steps. The first step is for senior leaders of the army to determine what knowledge will be needed for the future and where gaps exist in current knowledge. That is where CALL focuses.

The second step is observing and collecting knowledge. CALL observation teams are among the first troops on the ground in any army operation. They collect on-the-spot information about new practices, new techniques, problems, and trouble spots; distinguish approaches that work from those that do not; and share their findings with others. The objective here is to avoid the tragedy of having a soldier in one battalion make the same mistake (perhaps fatal) tomorrow that was made in a different battalion today.

Who are these observers that CALL sends forth? They are subject-matter experts, on loan from other parts of the army, including people with expertise in logistics, communications, linguistics, engineering, and supply. They are given training in how to be effective collectors of knowledge data. They gather multiple perspectives on each event, watching, interviewing, and taking digital photographs and video. They follow decisions that have been made to their outcomes and backward to discover the reasoning and logic that led to each decision. In so doing, they tease out tacit as well as explicit knowledge.[2] This information is then sent back to CALL, where it is analyzed by yet another group of experts who are responsible for synthesizing a large amount of disparate data from the multiple observers and then constructing

---

2   As suggested in the concluding observations of this chapter, knowledge can be either explicit or tacit. Explicit knowledge is self-conscious in that the knower is aware of the relevant state of knowledge, whereas tacit knowledge is implicit, hidden from self-consciousness. See Michael Polanyi, *Personal Knowledge* (Chicago: University of Chicago Press, 1958).

new and useful knowledge out of it. Their preliminary interpretations are put on the Internet for comment by other professionals.

The third step is creating knowledge products. Between 2002 and 2005, call catalogued 6,200 battlefield and training ground observations and produced 400 reports on them. Nancy M. Dixon writes:

> By the time the second wave of troops was sent into Haiti six months later, CALL had developed twenty-six scenarios of situations faced by the initial troops. These scenarios became a major training tool for their replacements. The scenarios included footage of actual events so that arriving troops were to some extent on familiar ground.

Empowering Soldiers to Contribute Wiki-style

The third example of army knowledge management is only a three-month pilot program but has interesting implications for many government agencies. In July 2009, the army began encouraging its personnel—from privates to generals—to go online and collectively rewrite seven of the field manuals that give instructions on all aspects of army life. The program uses the same software behind the online encyclopedia Wikipedia and could potentially lead to hundreds of army guides being "Wikified." The goal is to tap more experience and advice from battle-tested soldiers rather than relying on the specialists within the army's array of colleges and research centers who have traditionally written manuals.

Not surprisingly, top-down, centralized institutions have resisted such tools, fearing the loss of control that comes with empowering anyone among the chain of command to contribute. Yet the army seems willing to accept some loss of control. Under the experiment, the current version of each guide can be edited by anyone around the world who has been issued the ID card that allows access to the army Internet system. As is true with Wikipedia, those changes will appear immediately on the site, though there is a team assigned to each manual to review new edits. Unlike Wikipedia, however, there will be no anonymous contributors.

Advancing Knowledge About How to Lead a Company[3]

Young captains who are company commanders lead between 70 to 200 soldiers in complex, often dangerous, ever-changing environments. In spring 2000, a team of officers developed and launched www.CompanyCommand.com (CC) as a means of connecting past, present, and future company commanders in an ongoing conversation about leading soldiers and building combat-ready units. The mission of the leaders of CC was to provide cutting-edge, world-class resources for their colleagues. Use of the Web site spread rapidly. In 2002, the CC team "gifted" the Web site to the army. As a result, the Web site was placed on military servers at West Point and given the "army.mil" URL, but mission and team leaders remained the same.

CC builds on the basic principle that connections, conversations, and content can work in a mutually reinforcing manner to enable members of the professional forum to advance knowledge about commanding a company. More specifically:

- **Connecting** company commanders to each of other gives them access to the knowledge of the profession. Having a connection means more than just having contact information–it means being aware of what the other person knows. A professional community that is highly connected knows who knows what.
- Connections make **conversations** possible. It is through the back-and-forth of conversation that context and trust are established and that knowledge is both shared and created. Conversely, conversations can create connections that lead to relationships and learning.
- **Content** grows out of conversations. Content can be both the topic of conversations and an end product. For example, if five company commanders who have experience with convoy operations have a conversation, the result is valuable content that is useful to many others. To be useful, content must be current, rich

---

[3] This section draws heavily on Nancy M. Dixon and others.

in context, and relevant to the immediate needs of company commanders.

Relationships, trust, and a sense of professional community are critical factors that set the conditions for effective connections and conversations. Moreover, each positive interaction is a reinforcing process that creates stronger relationships, more trust, and a greater sense of professional community.

Here's an example of how relationships can lead to content that sparks valuable conversation. The Company Command leaders used their relationships with commanders who had served in Afghanistan to develop a booking providing valuable company-level content for company commanders going to Afghanistan for the first time. Then, they set up face-to-face conversations among past and future Afghan commanders, and those conversations were informed by the content of the book. In the course of these conversations, new relationships formed and people developed the trust necessary to bring up knowledge that could sound stupid, like, "Hey, have you ordered mousetraps? The tents in Afghanistan attract rats, and rats attract snakes, and you don't want snakes in your tent, so you need lots of mousetraps to keep the rats away."

Who would've thought that soliders in Afghanistan need mousetraps? Not the commanders who had not yet been there. That important piece of knowledge emerged only from the interplay of relationships, trust, content, conversation, and context.

Case Questions

1. What could other government agencies and nonprofit organizations learn from the army? What could individual managers learn from the After-Action Review process?
2. Although some organizations have employed AARs quite effectively, most struggle to capture the true value of such lessons-learned exercises. Why do many AAR processes fail?
3. What concepts or ideas presented in the chapter could the army use? Explain how.
4. What concepts or ideas presented in this case could other government organizations use? Be specific. What kind of federal agencies might benefit most from being "Wikified"?

5. According to some experts, the most successful knowledge management projects are not launched with a top-down, big-splash approach but rather developed bottom up. Why do you think the latter tend to be more successful?
6. Discuss the following statement by Kent Greenes, an adviser to the Company Command project:

Relationships also facilitate the most powerful kind of knowledge transfer, that which passes directly from one person's brain into another's, in a conversation where contacts can be communicated through the back-and-forth exchange. Knowledge that is codified into content—written down or put on media—before it is shared is transferred less effectively. Granted, if people have contexts and experiences very similar to those of the contributor of a piece of content, they may be able to use the content as is, but more commonly they can make use of only some of it. The unfortunate fact is, as soon as you codify content, it loses some of its meaning. *Therefore, conversation is the most powerful way to transfer knowledge.*

Case References

Noam Cohen, "Care to Write Army Doctrine?," *New York Times* (August 14, 2009); Marilyn Darling et al., "Learning in the Thick of It," *Harvard Business Review* (July–August 2005); 84–92; "Special Report American Military Tactics," *Economist* (December 17, 2005): 22–24; Nancy Dixon, *Common Knowledge* (Cambridge: Harvard Business School Press, 2000): 106–8; Nancy M. Dixon et al., *CompanyCommand: Unleashing the Power of the Army Professional* (West Point, New York: Center for the Advancement of leader Development and Organizational Learning, 2005); David A. Garvin, *Learning in Action* (Cambridge: Harvard Business School Press, 1999): 83–90; Greg Jaffe, "On Ground in Iraq, Captain Ayers Writes His Own Playbook," *Wall Street Journal* (September 22, 2004); Interview with Lieutenant General Stephen W. Boutelle, *Military Information Technology* (July 2004); Lee Smith, "New Ideas from the Army," *Fortune* (September 19, 1994).

Index